MANAGERIAL ACCOUNTING

SECOND EDITION

MANAGERIAL ACCOUNTING

JOSEPH G. LOUDERBACK III

Rensselaer Polytechnic Institute

GERALDINE F. DOMINIAK

Texas Christian University

KENT PUBLISHING COMPANY
BOSTON, MASSACHUSETTS
A Division of WADSWORTH, INC.

To the student: A Study Guide for this textbook is available through your college bookstore under the title *Study Guide for Managerial Accounting, Second Edition,* by Sanoa Hensley, Geraldine F. Dominiak and Joseph G. Louderback III. The Study Guide can help you with course material by acting as a tutorial, review, and study aid. If your bookstore doesn't have the Study Guide in stock, please ask the bookstore manager to order a copy for you.

Design and Production: Greg Hubit Bookworks

Technical Illustration: Ayxa Art

© 1978 by Wadsworth Publishing Company, Inc.

© 1975 by Wadsworth Publishing Company, Inc., Belmont, California 94002. All rights reserved. No part of this book may be reproduced, stored in a retrieval system, or transcribed, in any form or by any means, electronic, mechanical, photocopying, recording, or otherwise, without the prior written permission of the publisher.

Material from the Uniform CPA Examinations, copyright © 1958, 1959, 1961, 1966, 1969, 1970, 1971, 1973 by the American Institute of Certified Public Accountants, Inc., and is adapted with permission.

Printed in the United States of America

4 5 6 7 8 9 10—82 81 80

Library of Congress Cataloging in Publication Data

Louderback, Joseph G
  Managerial accounting.

  Includes index.
  1. Managerial accounting. I. Dominiak,
Geraldine F., joint author. II. Title.
HF5635.L886–1978   658.1′5   78-2734
ISBN 0-534-00556-X

PREFACE

This book is designed for a course in managerial accounting for students who have had one or more terms of financial accounting. It is intended primarily for undergraduate use, although like the first edition it can be used at the graduate level and in management development programs. The book is not written specifically for accounting majors but for anyone who will become a manager.

This book emphasizes the development and use of accounting information in performing managerial functions. We have identified the managerial functions as planning, controlling, decision making, and performance evaluation. The emphasis on the needs of managers is apparent even in the two chapters on product costing which appear late in the book. This part approaches product costing from the standpoint of analyzing results obtained from different product costing systems rather than concentrating on the cost accumulation procedures and problems.

We also stress the qualitative aspects of analyzing accounting data and making decisions. It is unfair to teach students that problems can be solved solely with numbers; for they will find out differently in later course work and in their careers.

The objectives of this edition are essentially the same as those of the first edition: to present in a clear and understandable fashion as much of the conceptual and practical material of managerial accounting as possible; to provide a logical and well-integrated sequence of material, building from the most elementary concepts toward more complex topics; and to show students, through discussion, illustration, and assignment material, the wide application of managerial accounting principles to business and economic problems.

Our approach to meeting these objectives is to use examples and illustrations liberally and proceed step-by-step from the principles of cost behavior and volume-cost-profit analysis, which underlie virtually all of managerial accounting and much of cost accounting, through more complex problems encountered in comprehensive budgeting, decision making, and cost accounting.

NEW FEATURES

Those familiar with the first edition will notice many changes. Besides extensive rewriting for enhanced clarity, the most important changes are:

1. Review problems with solutions in every chapter except the introduction.
2. Two new chapters on the statement of changes in financial position and financial statement analysis.
3. Splitting of the capital budgeting material into two chapters, with additional material in the second chapter.
4. Considerably more material on process costing and job order costing, including an appendix on complex problems of equivalent production.
5. An appendix discussing problems in using regression analysis.
6. Over 200 new items of assignment material, many adapted from C.P.A and C.M.A. examinations.
7. Greater use of formulas in developing concepts and examples, and a list of key formulas at the ends of chapters.
8. Additional material on not-for-profit entities.
9. A more logical arrangement of standard costing and divisional performance evaluation.

PLAN OF THE BOOK

The book consists of an introductory chapter and six parts. Part One contains four chapters, three dealing with volume-cost-profit analysis, cost behavior, and cost classification, and the fourth dealing with revenue variances and introducing problems of cost allocation. The material in Part One provides a solid foundation for the more difficult material that follows.

Because comprehensive budgeting uses many of the same tools as volume-cost-profit analysis, it is introduced in Part Two. Chapter 5 is devoted to operational budgeting and behavioral considerations. Chapter 6 treats short- and long-term financial budgeting and budgeting in not-for-profit entities.

Part Three contains three chapters on decision making. Chapter 7 builds on prior material regarding cost behavior and classification in its discussion of short-term decision making. Chapter 8 covers the basic material of capital budgeting, including income taxes. Chapter 8 deals with relatively straightforward decisions on acquiring new assets, while Chapter 9 considers more complex decisions, such as those involving tax law and replacing or disposing of assets. For students who have little or no background in present-value analysis, Appendix A discusses and illustrates how to use present-value analysis rather than how present-value factors are developed mathematically.

Part Four integrates the topics of control and performance evaluation. Chapter 10 covers responsibility accounting and organizational structure primarily from a behavioral point of view. Chapter 11 treats divisional performance evaluation. Chapter 12 uses standard variable costs and variance analysis to evaluate cost centers.

Part Five covers product costing with attention to the problems of analyzing and interpreting financial statements that use variable costing and absorption costing. Chapter 13 covers the basic techniques of variable and absorption costing, the use of predetermined overhead rates, and the concept of a standard fixed cost. Chapter 14 covers process costing, both actual and standard, and job order costing. The advantages of a standard costing system are described and illustrated. The basics of equivalent production are covered, while an appendix treats the more difficult problems associated with varying degrees of completion of cost factors. These two chapters are the most extensively changed from the first edition.

Part Six contains a chapter on quantitative methods, including linear programming, statistical decision theory, and inventory control models. Chapter 16 deals with the statement of changes in financial position, building from the techniques of cash budgeting covered in Chapter 6. Chapter 17 covers the analysis of financial statements with special attention to the interpretation (and misinterpretation) of ratios, stressing how differences in accounting methods affect the comparison of firms.

POSSIBLE COURSE SEQUENCES

The material is more than ample for a one semester course. Parts One through Five provide basic coverage of managerial accounting. If Chapters 16 and 17 are covered, Chapters 9 and 4 might be omitted without sacrificing continuity. Part Five can be omitted if product costing is not considered critical to the objectives of the particular course.

The arrangement of material provides a great deal of flexibility. It is possible to cover any chapter from 7 on after Chapter 3. Instructors who wish to introduce product costing early can go from Chapter 3 to Chapters 12, 13, and 14. Chapter 17 can be covered at any time, Chapter 16 at any time after Chapter 6. Parts of Chapter 15 can be assigned along with other chapters, especially 5, 7, 8, 9, and 12. Other suggestions for use of the book are found in the Instructor's Manual.

ASSIGNMENT MATERIAL

Material for assignment includes questions for discussion, exercises, problems, and cases. We avoid questions that require only that the student look up a specific sentence or list in the chapter. The discussion questions are meant to increase understanding of points made in the text. Exercises are generally short and to the point. They test the student on the basic points of the chapter and are listed in order of difficulty. The problems are longer than the exercises, more challenging, and frequently contain irrelevancies. Like the exercises, they are generally ordered by relative difficulty. All necessary information is given, but the student is frequently asked to provide other information before giving an answer. Cases generally contain less than all the information needed, thus alerting the student to that inconvenient characteristic of real-life situations. The cases are less straightforward than the other materials and so require more effort to identify the relevant information.

The variety of assignment material makes it possible to teach at various levels of difficulty. The later problems and cases are challenging and require the student to apply the basic principles in ways not always specifically illustrated in the text. It is impossible to provide examples of every possible situation that might be encountered in practice, and therefore it is necessary that students develop the ability to recognize that a problem exists, identify it, and apply the analytical techniques in the appropriate way.

SUPPLEMENTARY MATERIAL

The Instructor's Manual contains a test-item bank of between 10 and 15 multiple-choice questions, suggested course outlines, and notes to the instructor regarding use of assignment materials in class.

A Study Guide prepared by Sanoa F. Hensley and Lee Hensley contains key questions for students to consider when reading the text, objective questions and short problems (solutions at the end of the book), as well as outlines of chapters and comments on problems that students frequently encounter.

A list of check figures for virtually every exercise and problem is available in quantity, free, from the publisher.

ACKNOWLEDGMENTS

We wish to thank the many instructors and students whose comments and suggestions have aided us greatly in the preparation of both editions, especially the reviewers of the first edition and the following reviewers of the second: Alvin A. Arens (Michigan State University), John K. Cheever (California Polytechnic University, Pomona), Anthony DiFrancesco (San Francisco State University), S. Michael Groomer (Indiana University), Gerald D. Hamsmith (Aurora College), Maurice L. Hirsch, Jr. (Southern Illinois University, Edwardsville), Wallace Kartsen (New Hampshire College), Guy Mason (University of British Columbia), John H. McMichael (University of Pennsylvania), Paul D. Milewski (Northern Kentucky University), Roswell M. Piper (Indiana State University), and J. Hal Reneau (Arizona State University). To Al Arens and Bud Hirsch go very special thanks for their very special contributions.

We also want to express our appreciation to the American Institute of Certified Public Accountants and to the National Association of Accountants for their generous permission to use problems adapted from past C.P.A. and C.M.A. examinations, respectively.

CONTENTS

1 INTRODUCTION, 1

Management and Accounting Information, 1
Functions of Management, 1
Accountants and Managers, 2
Managerial Accounting and Functions of Management, 3
  Planning, 3   Decision making, 3   Controlling, 4   Evaluating, 5   Illustration, 5
Managerial Accounting and Financial Accounting, 7
Activities of Managerial Accountants, 9
Summary, 10
Key Terms, 10
Assignment Material, 10
  Questions for discussion, 10   Problems, 10

PART ONE   *VOLUME-COST-PROFIT ANALYSIS,* 15

2 PROFIT PLANNING, 16

Cost Behavior, 16
  *Variable costs, 17   Contribution margin, 17   Fixed costs, 18   Income
  statements—financial accounting and the contribution margin approach, 18   Total
  costs, 19   Average cost per unit, 19   Losses, 20   Summary of cost behavior and some
  misconceptions, 20   Relevant range, 21   Volume-cost-profit graph, 22*
Target Profit Determination, 25
  Contribution margin percentage, 26   Unit price determination, 27   Return on sales, 28
Summary, 30
Key Terms, 30
Key Formulas, 30
Review Problem, 31
Assignment Material, 33
  Questions for discussion, 33   Exercises, 33   Problems, 40   Case, 46

3 ANALYSIS OF COST BEHAVIOR, 48

Income Taxes and Profit Planning, 48
Problems with Variable Costs, 49
Mixed Costs, 50
  Problems with cost behavior analysis, 51   *High-low method of estimation, 51*
  Scatter-diagram method of estimation, 52   *Regression method of estimation, 53*
Step-Variable Costs, 54
Managerial Action and Fixed Costs, 55
  Discretionary costs, 55   *Committed costs, 56*
Selection of the Measure of Volume, 57
The manufacturing firm, 58   *other examples, 59*
Selling, General, and Administrative Expenses—Additional Problems, 60
Cost Structure and Managerial Attitudes, 60
  Margin of safety, 61
Summary, 63
Key Terms, 63
Key Formulas, 63
Review Problem, 64
Appendix: Regression Analysis, 65
  Simple regression, 66   *Multiple regression, 69*
Assignment Material, 71
  Questions for discussion, 71   *Exercises, 72*   *Problems, 80*   *Cases, 87*

4 ADDITIONAL ASPECTS OF VOLUME-COST-PROFIT ANALYSIS, 90

Analysis of Results, 90
Multiple Products, 92
  Weighted average contribution margin percentage, 93   *Sales mix in units, 95*
  Overall planning, 96   *Fixed costs and multiple products, 97*
Price-Volume Relations, 99
Volume-Cost-Profit Analysis in Not-for-Profit Entities, 100
  Cost analysis, 100   *Revenues and costs, 102*   *Benefits, 102*   *Fixed expenditures, 102*
Summary, 103
Key Terms, 103
Key Formulas, 104
Review Problem, 104
Assignment Material, 106
  Questions for discussion, 106   *Exercises, 106*   *Problems, 109*   *Cases, 121*

PART TWO   COMPREHENSIVE BUDGETING, 123

5 OPERATIONAL BUDGETING, 124

Comprehensive Budgets
  Budgets and planning, 125   *Budgets and control, 126*   *Organization of budgets, 126*
Developing the Comprehensive Budget, 128
  Sales, purchase, and expense budgets, 128
Sales Forecasting, 129
  Indicator methods, 129   *Historical analysis, 131*   *Judgmental methods, 131*   *Which*
  method to use, 131   *Expected values and forecasting, 132*   *Interim period forecasts, 132*

Expense Budgets, 133
Budgeting and Human Behavior, 136
   Conflicts, 136   Imposed budgets, 136   Budgets as "check-up" devices, 137   Unwise adherence to budgets, 138
Illustration, 138
   Purchases budget, 139
Purchases Budget—A Manufacturing Firm, 141
Summary, 143
Key Terms, 143
Key Formulas, 143
Review Problem, 144
Assignment Material, 145
   Questions for discussion, 145   Exercises, 146   Problems, 152   Cases, 159

6 FINANCIAL BUDGETING, 161

Illustration of Cash Budget, 161
   Cash receipts, 162   Cash disbursements, 163   Cash budget, 165   Revised financial statements, 165   Concluding comments, 167
Annual and Long-Term Budgets, 169
   Asset requirements, 169
Financing Requirements, 170
   Illustrations of annual and long-term budgets, 170   Long-term planning, 175   Illustration, 175
Budgeting in Not-for-Profit Entities, 176
   Program budgeting, 179   Zero-based budgeting, 180
Summary, 181
Key Terms, 181
Review Problem, 181
Assignment Material, 183
   Questions for discussion, 183   Exercises, 184   Problems, 187   Cases, 196

PART THREE   DECISION MAKING, 199

7 SHORT-TERM DECISION MAKING, 200

Short-Term Decisions and Accounting Information, 200
   Sunk costs, 202   Opportunity cost, 202
Segment Analysis, 203
   Allocated costs, 204
Typical Short-Term Decision-Making Problems, 206
   Dropping a segment, 206   Make-or-buy decisions, 209   Joint products, 212   Special orders, 215   Use of fixed facilities, 216
Decision Making Under Environmental Constraints, 218
Summary, 219
Key Terms, 219
Review Problem, 219
Assignment Material, 222
   Questions for discussion, 222   Exercises, 222   Problems, 225   Cases, 236

8 LONG-TERM DECISION MAKING: CAPITAL BUDGETING, Part I, 242

General Budgeting and Resource Allocation, 243
>   Cost of capital, 243

Capital Budgeting Situations, 243
>   Capital budgeting techniques, 244   Cash flow and book income, 244

The Simple Case, 245
>   Net present value method, 246   Time-adjusted rate of return, 246

Taxes and Depreciation, 248
Uneven Cash Flows, 249
>   Salvage values, 250

Decision Rules, 251
Other Methods of Capital Budgeting, 252
>   Payback period, 252   Book rate of return, 253

Summary Evaluation of Methods, 255
Investment Decisions and Financing Decisions, 255
Summary, 256
Key Terms, 256
Key Formulas, 257
Review Problem, 257
Assignment Material, 258
>   Questions for discussion, 258   Exercises, 259   Problems, 261   Cases, 268

9 CAPITAL BUDGETING, Part II, 271

Complex Investments, 271
>   Working capital investment, 272   Replacement decisions, 273   Asset disposal decisions, 276

Mutually Exclusive Alternatives, 278
>   Unequal lives, 278   Ranking investment opportunities, 280

Changes in Variables, 282
Income Taxes—Special Considerations, 284
>   Graduated (progressive) tax rates, 284   Capital gains, 285   Operating loss carryovers, 286   Investment tax credit, 287

Social Consequences of Decision Making, 288
Summary, 290
Key Terms, 290
Key Formula, 290
Review Problem—Replacement Decision, 290
Review Problem—Determining Required Volume, 294
Assignment Material, 294
>   Questions for discussion, 294   Exercises, 295   Problems, 298   Cases, 307

PART FOUR   CONTROL AND PERFORMANCE EVALUATION, 311

10 RESPONSIBILITY ACCOUNTING, 312

Goal Congruence and Motivation, 312
Responsibility Centers, 313
>   Cost centers, 314   Profit centers, 314   Investment centers, 314   Criteria for evaluation, 315

Organizational Structure, 315
    Vertical structure, 315   *Horizontal structure, 318*   *Choice of structure, 321*
Allocations and Transfer Prices, 321
    Critiques, 324   *What to do? 325*   *Effects on firm income, 326*
Summary, 327
Key Terms, 328
Review Problem, 328
Assignment Material, 329
    Questions for discussion, 329   *Exercises, 331*   *Problems, 333*   *Cases, 344*

11   DIVISIONAL PERFORMANCE MEASUREMENT, 346

Decentralization, 346
    Benefits of decentralization, 347
Performance Measures, 348
    Net income, 348   *Return on investment, 348*   *Residual income, 349*
Problems in Evaluation, 350
    Investment in assets, 351   *Liabilities, 352*   *Fixed assets, 353*   *The subject of
    evaluation—division or manager, 354*
Behavioral Problems, 355
    ROI, 355   *Transfer prices, 358*
Summary, 361
Key Terms, 362
Key Formulas, 362
Review Problem, 362
Assignment Material, 365
    Questions for discussion, 365   *Exercises, 366*   *Problems, 369*   *Cases, 378*

12   CONTROL AND EVALUATION OF COST CENTERS, 382

Performance Concepts, 382
Standards and Standard Costs, 383
Standard Costs and Budgets, 383
    Illustration of standard variable cost, 384
Variances, 385
    Alternative computation methods, 388   *Variable overhead variances, 389*   *Materials
    variances, 390*   *Interaction effects, 392*   *Interpretation of variances, 392*   *Investigation of
    variances, 393*
Setting of Standards—A Behavioral Problem, 394
    Engineering methods, 394   *Managerial estimates, 395*   *What standard–ideal, attainable,
    or historical? 395*   *Variances and future planning: revision of standards, 396*
Standard Costs and Performance Reports, 396
Control of Fixed Costs, 397
    Budget variances, 397   *Fixed costs on performance reports, 399*
A Problem Area: Fixed and Variable Costs, 399
Standard Costs for Nonmanufacturing Activities, 401
Summary, 402
Key Terms, 402
Key Formulas, 402
Review Problem, 403
Assignment Material, 405
    Questions for discussion, 405   *Exercises, 407*   *Problems, 411*   *Cases, 418*

PART FIVE   *PRODUCT COSTING,* 423

13 *VARIABLE AND ABSORPTION COSTING, AND STANDARD FIXED COSTS,* 424

Description of Methods, 425
   Inventory valuation, 426   Income determination, 427   Interpretation of results, 430
Absorption Costing and Standards, 433
   Standard fixed costs and control, 436   Predetermined overhead rates, 439
Summary of Procedures, 442
Evaluation of Costing Methods, 442
   Advantages of variable costing, 442   Disadvantages of variable costing, 443
Summary, 444
Key Terms, 445
Key Formulas, 445
Review Problem—Income Statement Preparation, 445
Review Problem—Predetermined Overhead Rate, 447
Assignment Material, 449
   Questions for discussion, 449   Exercises, 449   Problems, 453   Cases, 463

14 *PRODUCT COSTING: PROCESS, JOB ORDER, STANDARD,* 469

Cost Flows in a Manufacturing Firm, 469
Types of Cost Systems, 469
   Process costing, 470   Job order costing, 471   Standard costing, 471
Costing Method Illustrated, 472
   *Illustration of actual process costing, 473   Illustration of standard process costing, 476
   Equivalent production—beginning and ending inventories, 480   Multiple processes, 482
   Illustration of job order costing, 483*
Summary, 485
Key Terms, 485
Key Formulas, 485
Review Problem—Process Costing, 486
Review Problem—Standard Process Costing, 488
Appendix: Equivalent Production—Additional Refinements, 490
Assignment Material, 496
   Questions for discussion, 496   Exercises, 496   Problems, 501   Cases, 519

PART SIX   *SPECIAL TOPICS,* 523

15 *QUANTITATIVE METHODS AND MANAGERIAL ACCOUNTING,* 524

Quantitative Methods—An Overview, 524
Statistical Decision Theory, 525
   *Variance investigation, 526   Capital Budgeting application, 529   Payoff tables, 531
   Developing probabilities, 534*
Inventory Control Models, 534
   *The problem, 535   When to order—the reorder point, 536   Determination of safety
   stock, 537   How much to order—the economic order quantity, 538*
Linear Programming, 541
   Sensitivity analysis, 545   Shadow prices, 546

Summary, 548
Key Terms, 548
Key Formulas, 548
Review Problem—Expected Values, 548
Review Problem—Inventory Control, 549
Assignment Material, 550
    Questions for discussion, 550   Exercises, 551   Problems, 553

16 STATEMENT OF CHANGES IN FINANCIAL POSITION, 561

The Interest in Resource Flows, 561
    *Cash flows and the formal resource statement, 562   Categories of resource flows, 563
    Data for illustration, 565*
Resources as Cash, 567
    *Reconciliation of net income and cash from operations, 567   The formal statement, 569
    Working without the cash budget, 570*
Resources as Working Capital, 572
    *Reconciliation of net income and working capital from operations, 572   The formal
    statement, 573*
Operating Flows—A Special Problem, 575
Concluding Comments, 576
Summary, 577
Key Terms, 577
Key Formula, 578
Review Problem, 578
Appendix: A Worksheet Approach to Preparing Statements of Changes in Financial
    Position, 583
Preparing the Worksheet, 583
    Reconstruction of Transactions, 585
Assignment Material, 587
    Questions for discussion, 587   Exercises, 588   Problems, 592

17 ANALYZING FINANCIAL STATEMENTS, 600

The Purpose and Approach of the Analyst, 600
General Methods of Analysis, 601
    Areas of analysis, 601   Sample financial statements, 601
Liquidity, 603
    *Working capital and the current ratio, 603   Quick ratio (acid-test ratio), 604   Current asset
    activity ratios, 604   Ratios and evaluations, 607*
Profitability, 608
    *Return on assets (ROA), 608   Return on common equity (ROE), 609   The effects of
    leverage, 609   Earnings per share (EPS), 611   Price-earnings ratio (PE), 612   Dividend
    yield and payout ratio, 613   Ratios and evaluation, 613*
Solvency, 614
    Debt ratio, 614   Times interest earned, 615   Cash flow to total debt, 616
Summary, 616
Key Terms, 617
Key Formulas, 617
Review Problem, 618
Assignment Material, 621
    Questions for discussion, 621   Exercises, 622   Problems, 625

APPENDIX A   TIME VALUE OF MONEY, 632

Present Value of a Single Amount, 634
Present Value of a Stream of Equal Payments, 634
Streams of Unequal Payments, 635
Computations for Periods Other Than Years, 636
Uses and Significance of Present Values, 638
Determining Interest Rates, 638
Determining Required Receipts, 640
Summary, 640
Key Terms, 641
Key Formulas, 641
Review Problems, 641
Assignment Material, 644

TABLE A   PRESENT VALUE OF $1, 646

TABLE B   PRESENT VALUE OF $1 ANNUITY, 646

INDEX, 647

MANAGERIAL ACCOUNTING

CHAPTER 1

INTRODUCTION

Managerial accounting deals with the internal information used by economic organizations to determine their courses of action. While this book focuses most often on business firms that seek profit, much of the material applies equally to institutions that do not have this objective, such as hospitals, universities, and governmental units. We do not assume that you will either major in accounting or become an accountant. What we have to say about managerial accounting is as important to other kinds of managers as it is to accountants.

MANAGEMENT AND ACCOUNTING INFORMATION

Managerial accounting may be defined in many ways, and no reasonably concise statement can capture all its aspects. This book clarifies what is done by managerial accountants and how the information they develop is used by managers of economic enterprises.

This subject is constantly changing to adapt to a widening spectrum of needs. Managerial accounting is relatively new in curricula. It was introduced to more effectively handle changing perspectives in accounting and new approaches to the study of other functional areas of business—marketing, production, finance, and general management. Managerial accounting is a significant part of a system that provides information to managers—people whose decisions and actions spell success or failure for business enterprises.

FUNCTIONS OF MANAGEMENT

Planning and control are the most important functions of management. The **planning function** is described as the process of setting goals and developing methods for achieving them.

Planning involves an important concept of managerial method—**management by objectives**. Management by objectives means simply that managers and their subordinates will set objectives and will try to achieve these objectives. When objectives of various units within the firm conflict, the managerial accountant may gather relevant information to help resolve the conflict. For example, the sales manager may wish to increase production of a particular product to meet anticipated demand. The production manager may argue that it would be prohibitively expensive to shift production away from other products in order to meet this request. The managerial accountant may be asked to determine the effects of the changed production schedule and to recommend whether the views of the sales manager or the production manager should prevail. The accountant's analysis would not comprise the final decision, but it would heavily influence that decision.

The **control function** is described as the process of determining whether goals are being met, and if they are not, what can be done either to modify goals or to achieve existing ones. The size of most modern corporations precludes close contact among persons several levels apart in the organizational hierarchy; thus, the principle of **management by exception** was formulated. Applying this principle the manager relies on reports to keep informed on operations. If results are not in accord with plans, investigation and action may follow. Thus, accounting reports partially supplant the manager's personal supervision of activities for which he or she is responsible and has planned.

Two other functions of management sometimes viewed as subfunctions of planning and control are **decision making** and **performance evaluation**. Decision making is part of the planning function. Planning includes decisions such as what to produce, how many, what price to set. However, some specific decisions within the corporate planning process require special attention because they do not recur in the same form every year. Should a new machine be bought? Should a new product be introduced? Should we make something ourselves or buy it from someone else? These situations need special attention.

Performance evaluation could be viewed as part of the control process. Its development in managerial accounting is recent. For many years, accounting reports were regarded as substitutes for close supervision, in a way similar to the management-by-exception principle. A more modern view is that the data used for performance evaluation, and the manner of reporting, may cause managers and workers to act in certain ways. For example, if a manager is evaluated by the output of the department, he or she may not pay much attention to quality or cost of the output. Accountants and other managers are beginning to pay attention to the problems of human behavior and the role of accounting in fostering behavior that is "good" for the firm.

ACCOUNTANTS AND MANAGERS

It is common practice to distinguish between "line" and "staff" functions of managers. A line manager is one who is concerned with the primary activities of the firm—usually producing and selling a physical product. A staff manager is one who primarily serves these two line activities. For example, the financial manager is concerned with obtaining sufficient cash to keep operations running smoothly. The manager of the legal department advises other managers regarding the legal ramifications of actions (for example, whether the firm might violate a law if it sold some of its products to a customer at lower prices than are usually charged).

The managerial accountant provides information to other managers and may recommend various courses of action. This information can relate to financial statements, tax problems, dealings with governmental authorities, performance evaluation, and other matters.

Neither the managerial accountant nor any other staff managers can impose recommendations on line managers. But staff managers do have an informal authority deriving from their expertise in a particular facet of economic operations. The accountant may be consulted on matters regarding sales and production policies. All managers, line and staff, deal with policy decisions that affect how the firm responds to its environment.

MANAGERIAL ACCOUNTING AND FUNCTIONS OF MANAGEMENT

Successful managers require accounting information to plan and control adequately. Without information showing how effectively plans are being carried out, it is impossible to control the operations of the firm—to make necessary changes, to adjust plans, taking unforeseen events into consideration.

The managerial accountant is the primary, but not the only, provider of information to management. Managers also use information provided from outside the firm, such as statistics on the state of the economy, which are useful in forecasting sales; studies of population growth in particular geographical areas, which are helpful in deciding where to locate new stores, warehouses, or plants; and statistics on the state of the industry, or industries, in which the firm operates, which are useful in sales forecasting and expense analysis. (Are our profits about as good as those of other firms? Are our selling costs too high?)

Planning

Without proper planning, it is impossible to achieve goals, except by accident. Managerial accounting is closely interwoven in the planning process.

If a firm sets a target profit for a year, it must also determine how to reach that target. For example, what products are to be sold at what prices? The managerial accountant presents data that will assist managers in identifying the more profitable products, and is often required to determine the effects of alternative prices and selling efforts. (What will our profit be if we cut prices 5% and increase volume 15%? Would the spending of $250,000 on advertising be wise if it led to a 20% increase in volume? What will our net income be?)

Managerial accountants must also prepare forecasted financial statements, usually called **pro forma statements**. Among the most important of these is the cash budget, showing cash receipts and expenditures. Forecasts of cash requirements are used by the finance department to determine whether it will be necessary to borrow cash. The management of cash is crucial; more firms fail because they run out of cash due to inadequate planning than because they are unable to make a profit. Making profits and maintaining adequate cash are two different things, and success in one does not necessarily lead to success in the other.

The managerial accountant also participates in setting goals. The information provided by the managerial accountant may show that a particular goal is not achievable and he then may be asked to determine a feasible goal.

Decision Making

One of the major uses of the information provided by managerial accountants is in decision making. Some decision making is carried on continually; for example, managers must decide daily or weekly how many units of a product to buy or make, how much advertising to place in newspapers or on radio, or what prices to set for various products. Managers responsible for such decisions must receive timely reports that contain the information needed for these decisions. It is equally important that these reports not contain information irrelevant to the decision at hand. A sales manager needs, among other data, information about inventory levels, product costs, and trends in sales, and has no need for extremely detailed information about the cost to make a product. On the other hand, the production manager does need detailed information about product costs. Quite possibly, reports to the production manager would show 20 or more different categories of costs (raw materials, costs of various types of workers, etc.).

Other decisions are made at relatively infrequent intervals, such as whether to build a new factory, buy a new warehouse, introduce a new product line, enter a foreign market. These decisions usually require special analyses, and often the necessary data are not readily available in the form required. The managerial accountant will have to determine what data are needed, present those data in an understandable way, and explain the analysis to other managers.

In some ways, the managerial accountant acts as a collector of information, seeking various types of information from several other managers and putting it all together to develop the appropriate analysis for a specific decision. For example, the sales manager may provide information about the number of units of a product that are expected to be sold and the prices to be charged. The production manager will provide information about costs to manufacture the product. The accountant will assess the information received from these and other sources.

Although accounting data are used extensively by managers as they make decisions, it is important to understand that accounting data do not provide automatic answers to the questions faced by the managers. *People* make decisions, and people bring to their decisions experience, values, and knowledge which often cannot be incorporated into a quantitative analysis. Sometimes an action that seems best based on an analysis of accounting data may not be taken because of some factor not captured in the accounting data. For example, because the managers of a firm wish to maintain the firm's reputation for innovation, a new product may be launched even though it is expected to be unprofitable. The benefits of maintaining the firm's reputation are not easily determined, hence it is unlikely that a quantification of such benefits would be included in the accountant's analysis of the desirability of bringing out the new product.

Controlling

For many managers, the most common contact with managerial accounting information comes through their use of **control reports**, that is, reports detailing costs incurred by the manager and his subordinates and usually relating those costs to planned costs. Managers use such reports to determine whether some aspect of their spheres of responsibility requires special attention and perhaps corrective action. The use of control reports follows the principle of management by exception. As a rule, when planned and actual results are the same the manager assumes that operations are going according to plan and that no special investigation is needed. When significant differences between planned and actual results arise, a manager will frequently conduct an investigation to determine what is going wrong and, possibly, what subordinates need help.

Control reports do not, of course, tell managers what to do. The fact that actual results differ greatly from planned results does not tell the manager why the results differed. Control reports simply provide feedback that should help the manager to determine where attention may be required; they do not tell the manager how to correct any problems that may exist.

Control reports should be timely and relevant. Some managers may receive reports daily, some weekly, and others monthly, the frequency depending partly on the position of the manager. The closer the manager is to the actual operations, the more frequently reports will be needed. For example, factory foremen and other such supervisors may receive daily reports on production and costs; but higher level managers may desire production reports at less frequent intervals.

A most interesting topic, relatively new in managerial accounting, is the question of to what extent the format and content of various reports influence decisions made by the managers. Under some conditions, accounting reports seem to influence managers to take particular actions. If so, it is important that the managers not be influenced to take actions which are undesirable for the firm as a whole. For example, if salespeople receive reports that emphasize total dollars of sales, their attention could be directed to obtaining the highest dollar sales without regard to the profitability of the items sold. A great deal of research has been conducted on the effects of reporting on the performance of managers, and we can expect that the reports developed by managerial accountants will continue to improve as a result of such research.

Evaluating

Evaluating and control are very closely related. Managers will usually be evaluated on the basis of how well they control their operations: whether they achieve planned sales volumes, meet planned cost levels, or produce planned quantities of product.

Because in today's large business firms the top managers are far removed from the firm's day-to-day activities, these managers place great reliance on the reports by the managerial accountant of the performance of subordinate managers. The development of suitable measures of performance and the determination of information relevant to evaluating managers is an ongoing process and a matter of much interest to managerial accountants. For example, as stated in the previous section, using total sales dollars as a major point of emphasis in a control report could actually be harmful to the firm. Similarly, if a production manager is evaluated solely on whether he meets planned levels of cost, he might be tempted to cut the quality of the product, postpone preventive maintenance, reduce expenditures for worker training programs, and take other actions that might harm the firm in the long run. The problem of selecting an appropriate measure of performance is of constant concern to the managerial accountant.

ILLUSTRATION

We have diagrammed some managerial processes and related accounting activities in Figure 1-1. Usually the top level of management sets overall objectives that can be formalized into profit plans. Objectives, such as 10% growth in sales, 12% growth in profits over the next three or five years, a 20% return on total investment, and a 35% return on stockholder equity, can be put into profit plans. Other objectives, related to matters such as product

FIGURE 1-1   Management and Accounting

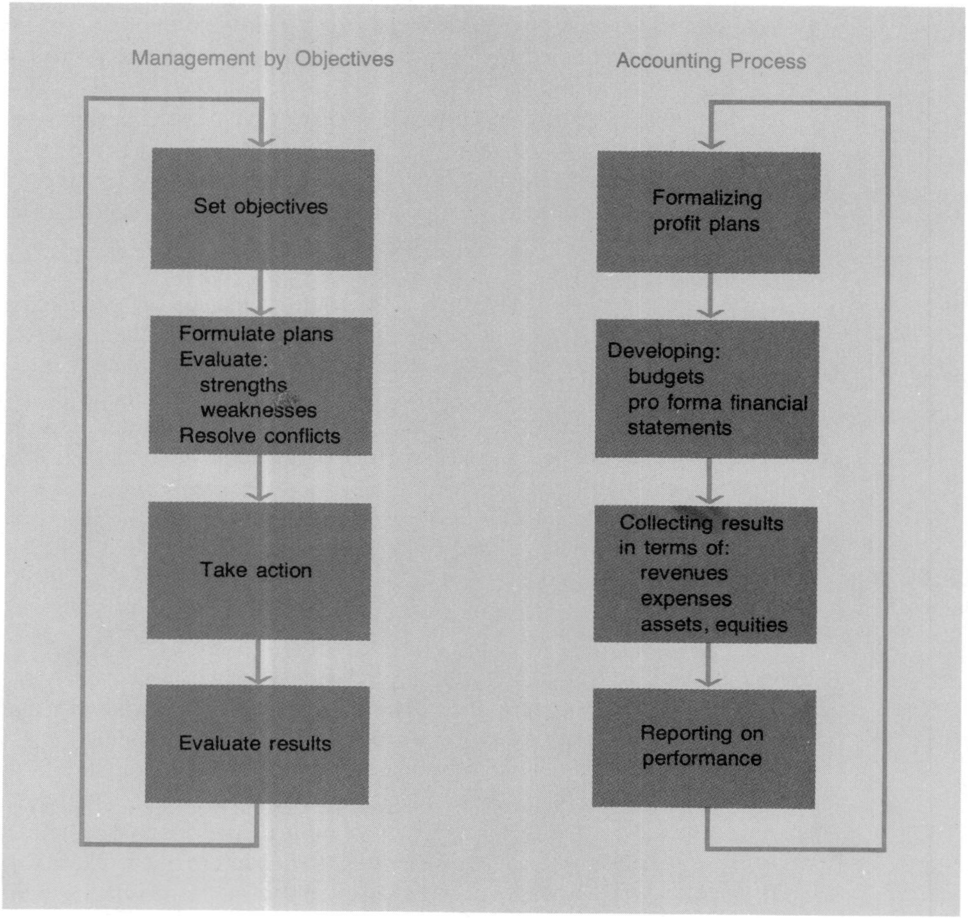

quality, pollution abatement, and employee satisfaction cannot formally be described in profit plans, but will have to be taken into account in the development of these plans. For example, top management might believe that a pollution abatement program will add 3% to costs of manufacturing their products. This increase would affect the achievement of profit goals.

Broad objectives are set, followed by detailed plans that will help realize these objectives. What new products can be introduced? What can existing products contribute to future profits and sales? Does our expertise in one area of manufacturing enable us to move into some different markets, and can some of our products be marketed more widely? Should we stress overseas operations or pay more attention to domestic business? Questions like these and others are thrashed out, and planning is then based on the strengths and weaknesses of the firm. Such plans can be expressed in budgets and pro forma financial statements.

Having established plans that are consistent with the broad objectives of the firm, managers implement these designs. Research programs on new products are undertaken, advertising and other sales efforts are directed towards customers identified in sales plans, capacity is added to the plant to meet anticipated demand, and requirements for workers, managers, and other personnel are filled. Many results of these actions will be shown within the framework of the accounting system. The results of sales efforts show up as revenues, while the efforts of the firm show up as expenses and assets. The financing aspects of the various efforts are reflected in equities—the use of long-term debt, common stock issuances, and increases in retained earnings. Constant evaluation of the varied activities occurs simultaneously with the compilation of results.

In Figure 1-1 we have shown the boxes labeled "Take action" and "Evaluate results" as independent, but there is usually continuous feedback. The most recent results are immediately evaluated so that corrective action can be taken if the results do not conform to plans. Moreover, evaluations of results often lead to reconsideration of the original objectives, the plans formulated to meet the objectives, or the actions currently being taken. Thus, it is rare that the cycle shown runs a complete course without any modifications. Plans are not static; they are subject to change.

MANAGERIAL ACCOUNTING AND FINANCIAL ACCOUNTING

There are many similarities between managerial and financial accounting. The raw materials of both are much the same—economic events. Managerial accounting, like financial accounting, deals with revenues and expenses, assets (and to a lesser degree, liabilities), and cash flows.

The major differences between financial accounting and managerial accounting are related to their basically different audiences. Financial accounting serves persons outside the firm, like creditors and equity investors. Hence, the information contained in financial accounting reports is concerned mostly with the firm as a whole. Managerial accounting information deals more with parts of a firm, with particular managers getting information related to their own responsibilities rather than to the entire firm. Although external reporting of information about segments of the business has been increasing, the basic difference in audience tends to prevail.

Because of the different audiences for financial accounting and managerial accounting information, their uses also differ. Creditors and investors use information to decide whether or not to extend credit to the firm, whether to buy, sell, or hold stock in the firm. Those inside the firm use accounting information to make decisions such as which of several products to sell, whether to borrow or sell stock, which individuals to reward for good performance, what prices to charge, etc.

The form of financial accounting reports usually differs from that presented in managerial accounting reports in that different classification schemes may be used. In financial accounting, costs are usually classified by the *object* of the expense (salaries, taxes, rent, maintenance, etc.) or by the *function* of the expense (cost of goods sold, selling expenses, administrative expenses, financing expenses). In contrast, reports for managerial accounting purposes normally follow a cost classification scheme based on the *behavior* of costs (costs that change when activity changes are shown separately from costs that do not change regardless of the level of activity). Or, managerial accounting reports may concentrate on the concept of *responsibility*, so that costs are classified according to whether or not a manager is responsible for the incurrence of the cost and can control it. These last two classification schemes (costs classified by behavior and by responsibility) underlie much of the material in this book and are critical to almost all aspects of managerial accounting.

Information incorporated in financial accounting reports may also differ in source and nature from information included in managerial accounting reports. Financial accounting reports are developed from the basic accounting system, which is designed to capture data about completed transactions, while managerial accounting reports may incorporate information not contained in the normal accounting system and related primarily to future transactions or even to alternatives to past transactions. For example, financial accounting reports (obtainable from the normal accounting system) may include the depreciation for a particular building, while a managerial accounting report could include rent from leasing out that particular building or rent that would have to be paid for the building if it weren't owned (information not obtainable from the normal accounting system).

To a great extent, managerial accounting reports are specifically designed for a particular user or a particular decision, while financial accounting reports are considered to be general purpose reports. For this reason, a particular cost may appear on one internal report and not on another; the cost may be relevant for some kinds of internal decisions and not for others. We can illustrate this point with an example from everyday life. Suppose you own a car and pay $250 insurance per year. That cost is part of the total cost of owning the car, but it is irrelevant if you are trying to determine how much it would cost to take a particular 200-mile trip. Because you pay the insurance whether you take the trip or not, you can ignore its cost in your determination of the cost of the trip. The phrase "different costs for different purposes" has often been used to describe this characteristic of managerial accounting.

Some have suggested that a major difference between financial and managerial accounting information is that the former is more related to history while the latter is more related to the future. Although there are several items in traditional financial reports that incorporate expectations about the future (estimated useful life and residual value in the computation of depreciation, for example), it is true that traditional financial accounting reports concentrate on the results of past decisions. Internal reports to managers, on the other hand, very often concentrate on what is likely to happen in the future. This particular difference between financial and managerial accounting is, however, becoming less marked, and some firms now present forecasts in their annual reports along with the historical cost financial statements. This increased emphasis on expectations (as opposed to history) stems from the realization that external users of accounting information cannot, any more than can internal managers, plan or control the past or make decisions retroactively.

Managerial accounting is bound only by the needs of managers. There are no restrictions such as generally accepted accounting principles, which must be followed in financial accounting. Financial accounting practices are directed toward providing information for general purposes, to creditors, existing stockholders and potential stockholders, suppliers, some governmental agencies, and others. In contrast, the managerial accountant, as a provider of information to other managers, is concerned with specific information requirements.

For managerial accounting purposes, market prices or replacement costs or some totally different measure will be used in a situation if one of these will help the manager make a better decision. Such alternative valuation measures are usually not allowed in financial accounting. In summary, managerial accounting is different from financial accounting in purpose, orientation, and constraints.

ACTIVITIES OF MANAGERIAL ACCOUNTANTS

How does the accountant perform his duties? A comprehensive list of activities of accountants cannot be made and is not needed, but some major activities are as follows: (1) aiding in the design of the total information system of the firm; (2) gathering data; (3) ensuring that the system is performing according to plan; (4) undertaking special analyses for management; (5) interpreting accounting data based on the particular requirements of the manager in a given situation.

The accountant "aids" in the design of the information system because the system has to serve managers other than accountants, and their needs must also be considered in system design. For example, a manager responsible for the sales of product X might need to receive sales reports for each territory each week, while his supervisor, who also supervises other managers, may need a weekly report by product line only.

Data are collected for several purposes. The actual recording of transactions in journals and ledgers is often done by clerks and by a computer. The accountant is responsible for supervising the gathering of data and monitoring the system, making sure that the results are coming out as expected. The accountant must also make sure that the output of the information system is appropriate. Suppose a particular report was designed for the sales manager to help identify sales trends by geographic area and that report has subsequently been used as the basis for computing commissions to salespeople. The report might be inappropriate for this second use because the sales data fail to reflect customer returns on which no commissions should be paid.

Special analyses are required when management is considering an unusual action. In some cases, such as the possibility of adding a new product to the firm's line, the relevant data may not be available in a form that would enable management to decide on the best course of action. The accountant will use his knowledge of the information system and data-gathering techiques to obtain this special information

Finally, the accountant may frequently be called upon to explain the results of the accounting process to other managers. Perhaps a manager is unable to understand what has happened. Or the data given to the manager may not be appropriate for the particular purpose he or she had in mind. The latter situation indicates that some change in the system may be appropriate.

The managerial accountant has gained status in recent years as his activities have become concerned more with the analysis of the operations of the firm and less with the problems of recording and computing costs of products. A program designed to provide professional certification for managerial accountants has recently been instituted by the National Association of Accountants. The Certified Management Accountant examination was first given in 1972. A brief listing of the required subject areas in the C.M.A. examination should indicate the breadth of knowledge expected of the professional managerial accountant. The examination consists of the following five parts: Economics and Business Finance; Organization and Behavior, Including Ethical Considerations; Public Reporting Standards, Auditing and Taxes; Periodic Reporting for Internal and External Purposes; and Decision Analysis, Including Modeling and Information Systems.

SUMMARY

Managerial accounting serves managers in functional areas of a business. Managers associated with sales, production, finance, and accounting, and top executives all use accounting data for planning and control, including decision making and performance evaluation.

As you study managerial accounting, you will be introduced to some of the activities carried on by managers in several areas of the business firm or other economic organization. You will be able to appreciate how the limitations of accounting affect the scope of managerial analysis. Understanding managerial accounting will be of great value to any manager.

KEY TERMS

control reports
decision making
functional area
management by exception

management by objectives
performance evaluation
planning
pro forma statement

ASSIGNMENT MATERIAL

Questions for discussion

1-1 Everyday planning and control In each of the following activities, find an analogy to the planning and control process described in the chapter. Describe the process that would be undertaken in these activities and compare with the process described in the chapter.

(a) Taking a course in college, including preparation and study, taking examinations, and evaluating test results.
(b) Taking a long trip by automobile.
(c) Decorating your own room or apartment.
(d) Being a coach of an athletic team.

1-2 Financial versus managerial accounting information The chapter illustrates that financial and managerial accounting overlap to some extent, but that managerial accounting uses information not normally used in financial accounting. For financial accounting purposes, the information needed about a particular automobile is its cost, its expected useful life, its residual value at the end of that life, and the method of depreciation to be applied. What other information about a particular business automobile might be important for managerial accounting purposes?

Problems

1-3 Review of financial statement preparation. Below is the balance sheet for Illustrative Company as of December 31, 19X4 followed by selected information relating to activities in 19X5.

Illustrative Company
Balance Sheet
as of December 31, 19X4

Assets

Current assets:
Cash	$ 10,000	
Accounts receivable	40,000	
Inventory	65,000	
Total current assets		$115,000
Property, plant, and equipment:		
Cost	250,000	
Less: Accumulated depreciation	100,000	
Net		150,000
Total assets		$265,000

Equities

Current liabilities:
Accounts payable	$ 10,000	
Taxes payable	12,000	
Total current liabilities		$ 22,000
Long-term debt:		
Bonds payable, 7%, due 19X8		100,000
Total liabilities		$122,000
Stockholders' equity:		
Common stock, no par value, 10,000 shares		
issued and outstanding	90,000	
Retained earnings	53,000	
Total stockholders' equity		143,000
Total equities		$265,000

During 19X5 the following events occurred.

(a) Sales on account were $350,000.
(b) Collections on receivables were $360,000.
(c) Cost of goods sold was $150,000.
(d) Purchases of inventory were $180,000.
(e) Payments to suppliers for inventory were $165,000.
(f) Operating expenses paid in cash were $80,000; interest on the bonds was also paid.
(g) Depreciation expense was $30,000.
(h) A dividend of $10,000 was declared and paid.
(i) Taxes payable at December 31, 19X4 were paid.
(j) Income taxes are 40% of income before taxes. No payments were made on 19X5 taxes in 19X5.
(k) Plant and equipment were bought for $70,000.

Required

1. Prepare an income statement for the Illustrative Company for 19X5.
2. Prepare a balance sheet for the Illustrative Company as of December 31, 19X5.
3. Prepare a statement of changes in financial position for 19X5 on a working capital basis.

1-4 Review of financial statement preparation Below is the balance sheet for Example Company as of December 31, 19X4, followed by selected information relating to activities in 19X5.

Example Company
Balance Sheet
as of December 31, 19X4

Assets

Current assets:		
Cash	$ 20,000	
Accounts receivable	50,000	
Inventory	120,000	
Prepaid expenses	8,000	
Total current assets		$198,000
Property, plant, and equipment:		
Cost	350,000	
Less: Accumulated depreciation	130,000	
Net		220,000
Total assets		$418,000

Equities

Current liabilities:		
Accounts payable	$ 40,000	
Taxes payable	25,000	
Accrued expenses	12,000	
Total current liabilities		$ 77,000
Long-term liabilities		
Bonds payable, 6%, due 19X7		200,000
Total liabilities		$277,000
Stockholders' equity:		
Common stock, $10 par value, 5,000		
shares issued and outstanding	50,000	
Retained earnings	91,000	
Total stockholders' equity		141,000
Total equities		$418,000

Other data relating to activities in 19X5 were as follows:

(a) Sales on account were $480,000.
(b) Cost of goods sold was $240,000.
(c) Collections on accounts receivable were $430,000.
(d) Purchases of goods for resale were $220,000.
(e) Payments of accounts payable were $210,000.
(f) Interest expense on bonds payable was paid in cash.
(g) Prepaid expenses at the beginning of the year expired and new prepayments in the amount of $6,000 were made in 19X5.
(h) Accrued taxes payable at the beginning of the year were paid.
(i) Accrued expenses payable are for wages and salaries. Total cash payments for wages and salaries during 19X5 were $95,000. At the end of 19X5, $7,000 was owed to employees.

(j) Other cash payments for expenses during 19X5 were $65,000, not including the $6,000 prepayments in (g).

(k) Common stock was sold for $40,000 (4,000 shares).

(l) **Plant and equipment were purchased for $30,000.**

(m) Depreciation expense was $40,000.

(n) The income tax rate is 40%. No payments were made in 19X5 on 19X5 income taxes.

(o) A dividend of $5,000 was declared and paid.

Required

1. Prepare an income statement for the Example Company for 19X5.
2. Prepare a balance sheet for the Example Company as of December 31, 19X5.
3. Prepare a statement of changes in financial position for 19X5 on a working capital basis.

PART ONE

VOLUME-COST-PROFIT ANALYSIS

The first part of this book discusses planning—specifically, planning for profit. The basic principle underlying each of the chapters and nearly all material in this book is that costs can generally be classified by behavior. How a cost is classified depends on whether the cost changes when the volume of activity changes. Practical considerations may complicate the identification of a specific cost behavior pattern, but such identification is essential.

The principles and techniques developed in this section are primarily discussed and illustrated in a business context. But most of these are applicable to not-for-profit economic entities, such as hospitals, universities, charitable institutions, and governmental units.

CHAPTER 2

PROFIT PLANNING

The income statements that you are most familiar with are generally based on a functional classification of costs.[1] Costs are grouped on the income statement according to the functional area of business activity with which they are associated—production (cost of goods sold), selling (selling expenses), administration (general and administrative expenses), and financing (interest expense). This kind of cost classification, though often useful, has serious drawbacks; it does not permit planning for profit because there is no direct way of telling how total costs will change if sales change. A scheme is needed that classifies costs by their behavior. To predict costs that can be expected at different levels of sales and to predict net income, **volume-cost-profit analysis** is most commonly used.

Volume-cost-profit analysis is used to answer such questions as: what profit will we earn if we sell 10,000 units? How many units must we sell to earn $40,000? What price must we charge to earn a $30,000 profit? These questions and others like them are constant concerns of managers.

COST BEHAVIOR

A cost is classified as either fixed or variable, according to whether the total amount of the cost changes as volume changes. In this chapter we shall use sales as the measure of

---

[1] In financial accounting the term "cost" denotes the initial expenditure or incurrence of a liability. "Expense" denotes expired costs—costs assigned to the income statement for a period of time. Since "cost" is the more general term, we will generally use it to refer to both expired and unexpired costs.

volume and identify costs as either fixed, or variable with sales. Not all costs fall into these categories; other measures of volume are often important, and we shall consider them in Chapter 3.

Variable Costs

Costs that change in total in direct proportion to changes in volume are called **variable costs.** To illustrate this concept, let us consider Ted's Threads, a retail store.

Ted buys shirts for $3.80 each from a wholesaler and sells them for $10 each. He also incurs a $.20 cost for wrapping materials for each shirt sold. For now, we shall assume (unrealistically) that he has no other costs. Both the cost of the shirts and the cost of wrapping materials are variable costs: they will be incurred every time a shirt is sold. For our purposes we can treat the two costs as a single variable cost of $4 per shirt, the $3.80 for the shirt and $.20 for wrapping.

Suppose that in the month of April Ted sells 500 shirts. His income statement would appear as follows:

Ted's Threads
Income Statement for April

Sales (500 units × $10)	$5,000
Variable costs (500 × $4)	2,000
Income	$3,000

Suppose that Ted sells 501 units in May. What will his income be? Instead of preparing a whole new income statement, you may find the additional income that the sale of one more shirt will bring and add it to the income for 500 units. This added income is $10 − $4 = $6. Ted's income will be $3,006. To verify this, let's prepare a new income statement:

Ted's Threads
Income Statement for May

Sales (501 units × $10)	$5,010
Variable costs (501 × $4)	2,004
Income	$3,006

Contribution Margin

The difference between sales price per unit and variable cost per unit is called the **contribution margin.** The term "contribution" is used because the amount left from a sale after variable costs are covered contributes to covering other costs and producing profit. In Ted's case, income increased by $6, his contribution margin per unit, when sales increased by one unit. If Ted sells only 499 shirts in June, his income should drop to $2,994. Sales and income generally increase or decrease in the same direction. In the absence of nonvariable costs, income is computed by multiplying contribution margin per unit by the number of units sold.

Fixed Costs

Some costs will remain the same in total whatever volume happens to be. These are called **fixed costs** and are generally incurred to provide the capacity needed to operate. Suppose that Ted pays $2,400 per month to rent a store, display counters, a cash register, and other equipment. (It was unrealistic to assume that Ted could sell his product without having a store; the store provides him with capacity—physical assets needed to conduct the business.) These costs will be the same whether he sells 300, 400, or no shirts at all. How do fixed costs affect profit planning and the prediction of income at various volumes of sales? Fixed costs reduce income, but by the same dollar amount regardless of volume. The following income statements for Ted's Threads show the effects of his fixed costs.

Ted's Threads
Income Statements at Various Sales Levels

	499 units	500 units	501 units
Sales	$4,990	$5,000	$5,010
Variable costs	1,996	2,000	2,004
Contribution margin	$2,994	$3,000	$3,006
Fixed costs	2,400	2,400	2,400
Income	$ 594	$ 600	$ 606

Notice especially that the $6 difference in contribution margin at 499, 500, and 501 units is also the difference in incomes for those levels. The presence of fixed costs does not change the significance of the contribution margin per unit. We can predict income by multiplying contribution margin per unit by unit sales, and then subtracting total fixed costs.

Thus, if we want to calculate income if 600 shirts are expected to be sold, we can take the contribution margin per unit of $6 and multiply it by 600 shirts. This gives contribution margin of $3,600, and when we subtract fixed costs of $2,400, we find income of $1,200.

An important use of volume-cost-profit analysis is highlighted by the fact that contribution margin per unit is the amount by which income of the firm will change if sales change. Thus, if Ted wonders what will happen to his profits if his sales increase by 50 shirts per month, we can tell him that his income will increase by $300, which is the 50-shirt increase multiplied by $6 per shirt. This would be true no matter what the current level of sales.

Income Statements—Financial Accounting and the Contribution Margin Approach

The approach to developing income statements in this chapter differs from the approaches used in financial accounting. In financial accounting costs are usually classified by *function* or by *object*. The income statements in Exhibit 2-1 highlight the differences between the two approaches. Notice that the sales and income figures are the same under both approaches, but the costs are different because they are classified using different criteria. The income statements are for a month in which Ted sells 500 shirts.

Exhibit 2-1
Comparison of Income Statements Using the Financial Accounting
and the Contribution Margin Approaches

Financial Accounting Approach		Contribution Margin Approach	
Sales	$5,000	Sales	$5,000
Cost of goods sold (500 × $3.80)	1,900	Variable costs:	
		Purchase cost of shirts (500 × $3.80)	1,900
Gross profit	3,100	Wrapping materials (500 × $.20)	100
			2,000
Operating expenses:			
Wrapping materials (500 × $.20)	100	Contribution margin	3,000
Rent	2,400		
	2,500	Fixed costs:	
		Rent	2,400
Income	$ 600	Income	$ 600

The major differences between the statements are in terminology and the placement of the cost of wrapping materials. If we had a great many costs, instead of only three, the advantages of the contribution margin format would be more obvious. Even with the few costs used here, you can see that using the financial accounting format requires rearranging costs in order to perform volume-cost-profit analysis.

Total Costs

A manager might want to predict total costs at a given volume of activity. He or she should compute the total variable costs at the particular level of sales and add it to the total fixed costs. Thus, if Ted wanted to determine total costs if he sold 500 shirts, he would use the following formula:

Total costs = fixed costs + (variable cost per unit × the number of units)

Total costs would be $4,400, or $2,400 fixed costs plus 500 shirts at $4 per shirt.
Why would a manager want to predict only costs, not profits? Some managers are responsible for costs but not for revenues. A manager in charge of processing purchase orders or making credit checks on customers would want to know the expected total cost, given a particular quantity of purchase orders or of credit applications. Later in this book we shall show that many measures of volume other than sales are important in analyzing managerial problems.

Average Cost per Unit

You should see that because fixed costs in total remain the same at different levels of volume, the average fixed cost per unit will change whenever volume changes. Thus, the average fixed cost per unit when Ted sells 600 units is $4 ($2,400/600) while the average when he sells 800 units is $3 ($2,400/800). The average *total* cost per unit, then, also depends upon the level of volume, **with the average total per-unit cost for Ted being $8** ($4 fixed plus $4 variable) when he sells 600 units, and $7 ($3 fixed plus $4 variable) when he sells 800 units.

Failure to recognize the dependence of average total per-unit cost on the level of volume can create problems when a manager attempts to use averages to predict future costs. **Use of the average total per-unit** cost for one level of volume will not provide a good prediction of total costs at another level of volume. For example, if we used the $8 (Ted's average total cost per unit at a volume of 600 units) to predict total costs at a volume of 800 units, we would arrive at a prediction of $6,400. But at 800 units the total cost would be $5,600 [$2,400 fixed plus ($4 × 800 units)]. Use of an average total cost per unit to predict total costs is appropriate only if all costs are variable. When there are fixed costs, such averages will not give a correct prediction at any volume level other than the one on which the average was based.

Losses

For some firms, losses are normal during parts of the year. Enterprises operating in summer resort areas may expect to suffer losses during the winter. Toy companies may expect losses during the spring after the Christmas season is over.

When should businesses continue to operate if losses are being made? They should operate if they are generating a positive contribution margin, because their losses would be greater if they stopped operating. Suppose that Ted expects to sell only 80 shirts in July. What loss will he sustain?

Ted's Threads
Income Statement for July

Sales (80 units x $10)	$ 800
Variable costs (80 x $4)	320
Contribution margin (80 x $6)	480
Fixed costs	2,400
Loss	($1,920)

If Ted does not operate at all for one month, what loss will he sustain? He will lose $2,400—his fixed costs. He will have no sales, no variable costs, no contribution margin. A loss of $1,920 is preferable to one of $2,400, so Ted will continue to operate. Each unit that Ted can sell reduces his loss by the $6 contribution margin per unit. So if he could sell 81 shirts, his loss would be $1,914. (Total contribution margin is $486 [$6 × 81] and fixed costs are still $2,400.) Thus when a business is operating at a loss, contribution margin per unit is also the amount by which losses are reduced or increased as sales increase or decrease. This is important in many decisions, as we shall be seeing later.

Summary of Cost Behavior and Some Misconceptions

Variable costs are so called because their total amounts vary with volume—expressed as **per-unit amounts they are constant.** Fixed costs are constant in total, but expressed per unit they vary inversely with volume.

These relationships may cause some confusion to persons unfamiliar with cost behavior concepts. For example, we noted above that the average total cost per unit is composed of a variable and a fixed element. Because fixed costs are the same at all volumes, fixed cost per unit will increase when volume declines and decrease when volume rises. For this reason, the average fixed cost (or the average total cost) should not be used for planning purposes. A related problem arises when a manager attempts to use, for planning purposes, an amount said to represent the profit per unit where such an amount is determined by dividing income at some level of volume by the units sold. As long as a firm has fixed costs, such a per-unit profit figure would be valid only for the level of volume on which its computation was based. To illustrate this, let us look at Ted's income statements at volumes of 600 and 800 shirts.

	600 Shirts	800 Shirts
Sales	$6,000	$8,000
Variable costs	2,400	3,200
Contribution margin	3,600	4,800
Fixed costs	2,400	2,400
Income	$1,200	$2,400
Profit per unit	$ 2	$ 3

What appears to be an additional profit per unit at the higher level of volume is, in reality, the simple result of spreading the fixed costs over a larger number of units. The nature of the company's costs has not changed at all; variable costs remain at 40% of sales and fixed costs remain at $2,400.

In the example above, notice that income as a percentage of sales varies between the two levels of volume. Perhaps the most common mistake made by individuals using accounting data is the prediction of future income by using the prevailing ratio of income to sales. At a sales level of 600 units, income is 20% of sales, while at a level of 800 units, income is 30% of sales. From the earlier discussion of the nature of fixed costs, you should see that if a company has any fixed costs, income as a percentage of sales (called **return on sales**) will increase as volume increases, and that the percentage increase in income will be greater than the percentage increase in sales. In the income statements shown above, a one-third increase in sales ($2,000/$6,000) produced a 100% increase in income.

Relevant Range

We have assumed that Ted's costs remained the same either per unit of sales (for variable costs) or in total (for fixed costs). We have also assumed that his selling price remained constant, no matter how many units he sold. These assumptions are necessary for profit planning, but are certainly unrealistic if carried to extremes. Ted could not sell one million shirts per month from a store that he is able to rent for $2,400 per month. He certainly could not sell so many shirts, even in a much larger store, by himself. A larger store and more sales help would increase his fixed costs. If he paid sales commissions based on the number of shirts a salesperson sold, his variable costs per unit would also increase. As a matter of fact, it is unlikely that any single store could sell one million shirts per month because there simply would not be that much demand for shirts in one location.

It would be quite possible, however, for a large chain of stores to sell one million shirts per month. Such a chain, Sid's Shirt City with 800 stores, would have operating characteristics quite different from Ted's single store. Nevertheless, each of the companies would have some range of volume within which its managers could plan their costs and profits. Whereas Ted's costs could be expected to remain the same, either per unit or in total in a range of from perhaps 250 to 900 shirts per month, the 800 stores of Sid's Shirt City may have a range of from 700,000 to 1,200,000 shirts per month, within which variable costs would be constant per unit and fixed costs would be the same in total.

Thus, each enterprise will have a **relevant range**—the range of volume over which the assumed relationships may be expected to hold true. If Ted expects to sell 1,200 shirts per month, he might have to hire a salesperson, thus increasing his costs. His fixed or variable costs would increase depending on how the salesperson was to be paid—straight salary (fixed) or commission of some fixed percentage on sales (variable).

One other significant aspect of range is the range of *time* over which the analysis may be valid. Volume-cost-profit analysis is a short-run device that should encompass periods of one year or less. It is likely that over longer periods of time the analysis will be less valid because of changes in prices for the firm's product, the prices the firm pays for its goods, wages, and other cost elements. When we analyze the impact that changes in volume of sales have on profits, we usually deal only with relatively short time periods; we do not expect to be able to use in our five-year profit planning the same relationships that are valid for one year.

The time period over which the analysis is valid depends to a great extent on the operating characteristics of the firm, including the nature of and demand for the product. Some firms may be able to add capacity quickly in response to increased demand for their products so that fixed costs could change rapidly.

For some firms, the prices charged and paid are relatively stable; for others, such as those dealing in some kinds of agricultural products, prices might be expected to jump around a great deal. For the latter kinds of firms, variable costs and selling prices are more volatile than for the former; they could not count on the persistence, over time, of assumed variable costs and selling prices.

Volume-Cost-Profit Graph

The complete volume-cost-profit picture for Ted's Threads is shown in Figure 2-1. First, a line is drawn to show the total fixed costs (in Ted's case, $2,400). Then, the variable costs are added to the fixed costs to give a total cost line. The difference between total costs and fixed costs at any point is the total variable cost at that point. The revenue line represents the total revenue at the various volumes of sales in units.

The point at which total revenues equal total costs is called the **break-even point** —the point at which profits are zero. **To the right of the break-even point, profits are earned** by the firm. To the left of the break-even point, the firm will incur losses. The vertical distance between the revenue line and the total cost line at any point on the graph is the amount of profit or loss (shaded areas).

The graphical approach highlights an important fact. As sales increase and contribution margin is positive (sales price is greater than variable cost per unit), it always pays to sell the product rather than quit the business. Below the break-even point, where losses are being made, the gap between revenue and total cost is constantly narrowing, thus reducing the loss. If no sales were made, the loss would be equal to the fixed costs. Any sales made will reduce this loss by contributing something to cover fixed costs.

FIGURE 2-1   Volume-Cost-Profit Chart

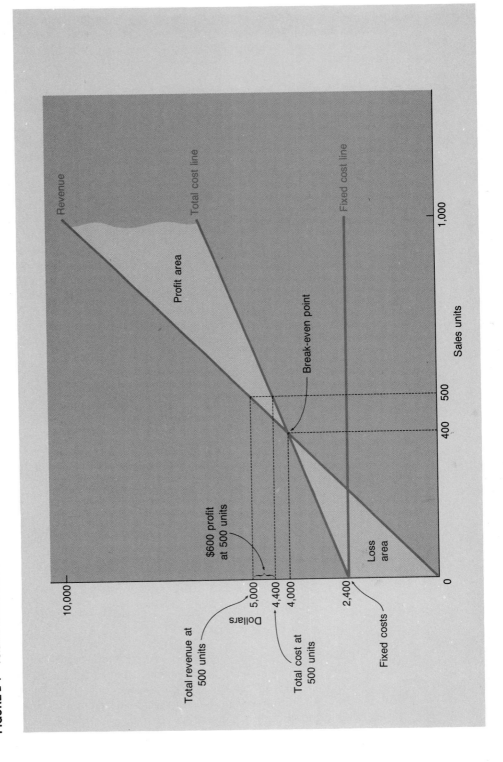

Knowledge of the break-even point can be useful for many purposes, and we can derive an equation to give us this point by using relationships we already know. For example, we know that profit is equal to total sales dollars minus total variable costs minus total fixed costs. That is,

$$\text{Profit} = \begin{array}{c} \text{total} \\ \text{sales} \\ \text{dollars} \end{array} - \begin{array}{c} \text{total} \\ \text{variable} \\ \text{costs} \end{array} - \begin{array}{c} \text{total} \\ \text{fixed} \\ \text{costs} \end{array}$$

Identifying the quantity of units sold as Q, we can restate the formula as:

$$\text{Profit} = \left(\begin{array}{c} \text{per-unit} \\ \text{selling} \\ \text{price} \end{array} \times Q \right) - \left(\begin{array}{c} \text{per-unit} \\ \text{variable} \\ \text{cost} \end{array} \times Q \right) - \begin{array}{c} \text{total} \\ \text{fixed} \\ \text{costs} \end{array}$$

Knowing that selling price per unit less variable cost per unit is contribution margin per unit, we can combine and restate the first two components of the equation to get

$$\text{Profit} = \left(\begin{array}{c} \text{contribution} \\ \text{margin} \\ \text{per unit} \end{array} \times Q \right) - \begin{array}{c} \text{total} \\ \text{fixed} \\ \text{costs} \end{array}$$

Adding fixed costs to both sides of the equation produces:

$$\text{Profit} + \begin{array}{c} \text{total} \\ \text{fixed} \\ \text{costs} \end{array} = \begin{array}{c} \text{contribution} \\ \text{margin} \\ \text{per unit} \end{array} \times Q$$

And, since we are looking for the break-even point (where profit is *zero*), the profit term drops out. Now we can solve for Q (the break-even point in units) by dividing both sides by contribution margin per unit, producing:

$$\begin{array}{c} Q \text{ (break-even} \\ \text{sales in units)} \end{array} = \frac{\text{total fixed costs}}{\text{contribution margin per unit}}$$

Applying this formula to Ted's case, we obtain a break-even point of 400 shirts, computed as follows:

$$\begin{array}{c} \text{Break-even sales} \\ \text{in units} \end{array} = \frac{\$2,400}{\$10 - \$4} = \frac{\$2,400}{\$6} = 400 \text{ shirts}$$

Although the graph in Figure 2-1 and the break-even formula derived above show sales in units, other measures of sales volume could be used just as well. One commonly-used measure is sales in dollars. The break-even point, if computed in dollars of sales, utilizes the **contribution margin percentage** (contribution margin per unit/selling price per unit) rather than the contribution margin per unit, as follows:

$$\begin{matrix} \text{Break-even} \\ \text{sales in} \\ \text{dollars} \end{matrix} = \frac{\text{total fixed costs}}{\text{contribution margin percentage}}$$

In Ted's case, the break-even sales, in dollars, is $4,000, computed as follows:

$$\begin{matrix} \text{Break-even sales in} \\ \text{dollars} \end{matrix} = \frac{\$2,400}{(\$10 - \$4)/\$10} = \frac{\$2,400}{60\%} = \$4,000$$

Note that break-even sales in dollars ($4,000) is consistent with the dollars of sales expected at the break-even point in units (400 × $10).

Other measures of volume can also be used. For example, with firms that perform services and charge on the basis of hours worked by their employees (like C.P.A. firms and law firms), a sales volume measure, for purposes of a graphic or formula presentation, could be number of charged hours—the number of hours worked by employees of the firm on the business of its clients.

Although the cost and revenue lines on the graph are extended to the vertical axis and also far to the right, we should also point out that it is probably not legitimate to extend the lines beyond the relevant range. In Ted's case, we stated that the relevant range was from 250 shirts to 900 shirts per month. Outside of this range, the facts regarding fixed and variable costs and selling price may well not apply. For example, if Ted could sell 1,000 shirts he might be able to buy them at a lower price, thus reducing his variable cost per unit. He might also have to hire additional sales help and, if they were paid salaries, his fixed costs would increase. It is also possible that to sell 1,000 shirts Ted would have to lower his sales price per unit. The volume-cost-profit graph is based on sales and cost relationships that are expected to be valid over a certain range of volume. There is no danger in planning on the basis of these relationships as long as the firm does not operate outside the relevant range. But, if such unusual levels of operations are planned, the cost and pricing structure would have to be reviewed to see if it still applied at those planned levels of volume.

TARGET PROFIT DETERMINATION

We have seen how volume-cost-profit analysis enables us to predict income when we have already predicted sales volume. Another major use of the analysis is in determining the sales volume required to earn a desired or target profit. Such a determination is simply a variation of the typical break-even situation. The break-even point tells you what sales are required to make no profit and incur no loss; by incorporating into the break-even analysis the amount or rate of profit desired, the sales volume required to achieve that profit can be readily determined.

Suppose, for example, that Ted wishes to earn a profit of $1,200 per month. What number of shirts must he sell to achieve that target? We know that total contribution margin must be equal to fixed costs of $2,400 to allow the company to break even. Hence, to achieve a profit of $1,200, total contribution margin must be $1,200 greater than fixed costs, or $3,600. To achieve a total contribution margin of $3,600 when the contribution margin per unit is $6 ($10 sales price − $4 variable cost per unit), a total of 600 units must be sold. Expressed in general terms:

$$\text{Target profit} = \left(\begin{array}{c} \text{sales, in units,} \\ \text{to achieve} \\ \text{target profit} \end{array} \times \begin{array}{c} \text{contribution} \\ \text{margin} \\ \text{per unit} \end{array} \right) - \begin{array}{c} \text{fixed} \\ \text{costs} \end{array}$$

Restating this equation to solve for the needed level of sales, we have:

$$\text{Sales, in units, to achieve target profit} = \frac{\text{fixed costs} + \text{target profit}}{\text{contribution margin per unit}}$$

Using this formula in Ted's case we have:

$$\text{Sales, in units, to achieve target profit} = \frac{\$2{,}400 + \$1{,}200}{(\$10 - \$4)} = \frac{\$3{,}600}{\$6} = 600 \text{ units}$$

Notice that the numerator of the formula is really the total contribution margin required to earn the target profit, which consists of the contribution margin required for break-even (400 units as computed earlier) plus the contribution margin required for the target profit ($1,200/$6 or an additional 200 units). In essence, when the target profit is stated in absolute terms, it becomes, in effect, a fixed cost and is treated as such in the formula.

Contribution Margin Percentage

In the computation of the break-even sales in dollars, above, the contribution margin was expressed as a percentage of sales rather than as a specific amount per unit sold. Sometimes it is helpful, or even necessary, to use a contribution margin percentage rather than a per-unit contribution margin. This would be true for Ted if he sold shirts at different prices. The analysis is the same as in the per-unit contribution method, provided that variable costs are the same percentage of sales dollars for the differently priced shirts. We will now introduce another kind of shirt that sells for $5. The cost of this shirt is $1.80 and the variable cost for wrapping materials is $.20 per shirt, making the variable cost per shirt $2.

If the percentage relationship between variable cost and sale price is to be the same for all of Ted's shirts, the relationship of variable cost to sale price for the $5 shirt must be the same as for the $10 shirt. For the $10 shirt, this is 40% ($4/$10), and the variable cost for the $5 shirt is 40% of its sale price of $2 ($5 = 40%).

If Ted's business is to break even in any month, what sales must be achieved? We can no longer use contribution margin per unit, for we have two different per-unit contribution margins. We have already computed 400 units as the break-even point if only $10 shirts are sold ($2,400/$6). If only $5 shirts are sold, the break-even point is 800 units ($2,400/$3). Thus, many break-even points can be computed, each depending upon the mix of shirts to be sold. But, since the percentage of contribution margin per sales dollar is the same regardless of the type of shirt, the break-even point in terms of sales dollars (computed earlier at $4,000) is still relevant even with this new mix of products. It does not matter how many shirts of each price Ted sells as long as total sales are $4,000. He could achieve this volume by selling 400 $10 shirts or 800 $5 shirts, or any combination that resulted in

$4,000 in sales. The use of the contribution margin percentage merely states contribution margin as an amount per $1 in sales, rather than an amount per unit sold.

If, as may often be the case, the firm chooses to set its target profit in terms of a specified return on sales, the contribution margin percentage is also useful. Consider, for example, the possibility that Ted has decided that he must earn a profit of 30% on sales. We know that his variable costs are already 40% of sales; what he is saying is that no matter what his sales are, his profit must be 30% of sales. In this context, the profit is much like any variable cost—as sales increase, the total of this item increases proportionately. Hence, we can treat his desired profit like any other variable cost, and, substituting in the formula we find:

$$\text{Sales to achieve the target profit} = \frac{\text{fixed costs}}{\text{contribution margin percentage} - \text{target profit percentage}}$$

In Ted's situation, the sales required to achieve a target profit of 30% of sales are:

$$\text{Sales to achieve the target profit} = \frac{\$2,400}{60\% - 30\%} = \frac{\$2,400}{30\%} = \$8,000$$

At a sales volume of $8,000, Ted's income statement will appear as follows:

Sales	$8,000
Variable costs (40% of sales)	3,200
Contribution margin	4,800
Fixed costs	2,400
Income (equal to 30% of sales)	$2,400

We can also find income for any level of dollar sales by using the contribution margin percentage. If Ted has sales of $8,000, what will be his total contribution margin? his income? Contribution margin in total will be $4,800 ($8,000 × 60%) and income $2,400 ($4,800 − $2,400).

Unit Price Determination

If volume of sales in units is given or can be predicted, volume-cost-profit analysis can also be used to determine what prices must be charged so as to earn the target profits. This can be done in single- or multiple-product situations, but we shall limit this analysis to the single-product firm. Assume that Ted is now selling only the shirts that have a variable cost of $4 and that his fixed costs are $2,400 per month. He wishes to earn profits of $2,000 per month and believes that he can sell 800 shirts per month. What price must he charge to achieve the desired results?

When volume, variable cost per unit, and fixed costs are known, it is easiest to build up an income statement from the bottom.

Sales	?
Variable costs (800 × $4)	$3,200
Necessary contribution margin	4,400
Fixed costs	2,400
Desired profit	$2,000

It can be seen that sales must be $7,600, the amount necessary to provide $4,400 in contribution margin when variable costs are $3,200. The unit selling price will have to be $9.50 ($7,600/800). The analysis cannot stop here; Ted must consider the prices charged by his competitors. His prices cannot be too far out of line with theirs.

Another approach is to determine the necessary contribution margin per unit by dividing the required contribution margin in total by the number of units expected to be sold. This yields $5.50 (i.e., $4,400/800). To have contribution margin of $5.50 when variable costs are $4, the selling price must be $5.50 greater than variable cost, or $9.50.

This hypothetical analysis may result in an excessive selling price. If Ted wanted to earn $4,000 per month by selling 400 shirts, he would have to price them at $20.00 (required contribution margin is $6,400/400 = $16.00 contribution margin per unit + $4 variable cost = $20.00 selling price). If similar shirts are being sold in the other stores for $10, a monthly profit goal of $4,000 on sales of 400 units is unachievable. This analysis helps show what price is required to reach a profit goal.

In both examples an expected monthly volume in units was used and our objective was to determine a required selling price. In Chapter 4 we will discuss the analysis when the set price and the expected volume are interrelated.

Return on Sales

For some businesses, industry-wide statistics on operating results are commonly available. Some retailers' associations publish percentage income statements for stores of various kinds. Such statistics help managers determine how similar their operating results are to those of other firms. One widely used measure of results is *return on sales*—the ratio of income to sales.

Although a high return on sales is desirable, it is possible that the high return has been achieved by poor decision making. A firm that prices its products too high might actually be able to earn higher profits by reducing prices and selling more units. The total profit would be higher, even though the return on sales would be lower. For example, consider a firm that sells its product at $20, has variable costs of $16 per unit, and fixed costs of $30,000 per month. If it can sell 10,000 units per month at a price of $20, its income statement would be as follows:

Sales (10,000 @ $20)	$200,000
Variable costs (10,000 @ $16)	160,000
Contribution margin	40,000
Fixed costs	30,000
Income	$ 10,000

The return on sales is 5% ($10,000/$200,000). But suppose that if the firm reduced its price to $18, then 23,000 units per month could be sold. Its income statement would be as follows:

Sales (23,000 @ $18)	$414,000
Variable costs (23,000 @ $16)	368,000
Contribution margin	46,000
Fixed costs	30,000
Income	$ 16,000

Income would increase by $6,000 (an increase of 60%) but the return on sales would have dropped to 3.9% ($16,000/$414,000). Thus, while the return on sales is one measure of profitability, it, like any other single profitability measure, should be evaluated in the light of all the circumstances.

Although a business cannot be appraised solely on the ratio of income to sales, the ratio is still a useful tool. A manager might wish to know how much must be sold, in units or dollars, to achieve a particular return on sales. Sales price is $10, variable costs are $6, fixed costs are $3,000. How many units must be sold to earn a 10% return on sales? The firm must show net income of $1 per unit of product sold ($10 × 10%) to achieve a 10% return. We can treat this $1 much as we do variable costs. Thus we subtract from the $10 selling price the $1 for profit and use $3 per unit ($9 − $6) to cover the fixed costs.

We obtain $3,000/$3 = 1,000 units. An income statement for 1,000 units is as follows:

Sales (1,000 @ $10)	$10,000	
Variable costs (1,000 @ $6)	6,000	
Contribution margin	4,000	
Fixed costs	3,000	
Income	$ 1,000	Return on sales = $1,000/ $10,000 = 10%.

The same kind of problem can be solved using contribution margin percentage. Assume the same facts except that a 15% return on sales is desired. The existing contribution margin is 40% ($4/$10) and we wish to gain 15% of sales dollars for profit. We subtract the 15% desired return on sales from the contribution margin percentage, leaving 25% to cover fixed costs. Thus, $3,000/25% = $12,000 sales required. The income statement would be as follows:

Sales	$12,000	
Variable costs (60%)	7,200	
Contribution margin (40%)	4,800	
Fixed costs	3,000	
Income	$ 1,800	Return on sales = $1,800/ $12,000 = 15%.

Return on sales changes whenever sales change because fixed costs as a percentage of sales also change. Without fixed costs, return on sales always equals contribution margin percentage, regardless of volume.

SUMMARY

Volume-cost-profit analysis is vital to planning and requires classification of costs by behavior. A cost is either fixed or variable according to whether the total amount of the cost changes as volume changes. After determining variable costs, contribution margin can be computed.

The critical points in the chapter are the recognition of the fixed/variable cost classification scheme, the analytical value of this classification, and the usefulness of contribution margin.

Volume-cost-profit analysis can be used to answer questions such as the following: What profits are earned at different levels of sales? What level of sales is needed to earn a particular profit? How will changes in cost structure affect profit? What are the effects of changes in selling prices? What price should be charged to earn a particular profit?

The validity of volume-cost-profit analysis depends on accurate estimates of assumed revenue and cost behavior within relevant ranges of volume and over short periods of time. It is unwise to view a volume-cost-profit graph as presenting a single set of conditions that is valid over wide ranges of volume. The graph should be viewed as a rough gauge of relationships over the relevant range.

Volume-cost-profit analysis is valuable in planning, selecting alternatives, analyzing results, and incorporating new information into future plans.

KEY TERMS

average total cost per unit	relevant range
break-even point	return on sales
contribution margin	target profit
contribution margin percentage	variable cost
cost behavior	volume-cost-profit analysis
fixed cost	

KEY FORMULAS

$$\text{Profit} = \begin{array}{c}\text{total}\\\text{sales}\end{array} - \begin{array}{c}\text{total}\\\text{variable}\\\text{costs}\end{array} - \begin{array}{c}\text{total}\\\text{fixed}\\\text{costs}\end{array}$$

$$\begin{array}{c}\text{Total}\\\text{costs}\end{array} = \begin{array}{c}\text{fixed}\\\text{costs}\end{array} + (\text{Variable cost per unit} \times \text{no. of units sold})$$

$$\begin{array}{c}\text{Break-even sales,}\\\text{in units}\end{array} = \frac{\text{fixed costs}}{\text{contribution margin per unit}}$$

$$\begin{array}{c}\text{Break-even sales,}\\\text{in dollars}\end{array} = \frac{\text{fixed costs}}{\text{contribution margin percentage}}$$

$$\begin{array}{c}\text{Sales, in units, to}\\\text{achieve target profit}\end{array} = \frac{\text{fixed costs} + \text{target profit}}{\text{contribution margin per unit}}$$

$$\text{Sales, in dollars, to achieve target return on sales} = \frac{\text{fixed costs}}{\text{contribution margin percentage} - \text{target return on sales}}$$

REVIEW PROBLEM

Volume-cost-profit analysis assumes that important variables (selling price, variable cost per unit, total fixed costs) do not change within the relevant range. Nevertheless, as we saw in the section on unit price determination, a manager may want to know what value for one of these variables is consistent with a particular target profit. Additionally, because prices and costs may change quickly, a manager must be alert to the effects that such changes may bring. The following problem will test your basic understanding of the principles of volume-cost-profit analysis and the extent to which changes in important variables can affect a firm's planning. You should solve the problem, one part at a time, and check your answers with those provided. Consider each question independently of the others.

The Glassman Company sells one product at $20 per unit. Its variable costs are $12 per unit and its fixed costs are $100,000 per month.

1. If the firm can sell 15,000 units in a particular month, what will its income be?
2. What is the firm's break-even point in units?
3. What is the firm's break-even point in sales dollars?
4. What sales, in units, are required for the firm to earn $40,000 for the month?
5. What sales, in dollars, are required for the firm to earn $40,000 for the month?
6. Suppose that the firm must reduce its selling price to $18 because competitors are charging that amount. What is the new break-even point (a) in units? (b) in dollars?
7. Suppose that fixed costs are expected to increase by $10,000 (to $110,000 per month). What is the new break-even point (a) in units? (b) in dollars?
8. Suppose that the firm is currently selling 10,000 units per month. The sales manager believes that if advertising expenditures were increased by $5,000, sales would also increase. How much would sales have to increase, in units, to give the firm the same income or loss that it is currently earning? Although you are told how many units are now being sold, you do not need to know this to solve the problem.
9. Suppose that the selling price is reduced to $18, but that variable costs drop to $10 at the same time. What is the new break-even point (a) in units? (b) in dollars?

Answers to Review Problem

1. The firm will earn $20,000. An income statement for sales of 15,000 units would show the following:

Sales (15,000 × $20)	$300,000
Variable costs (15,000 × $12)	180,000
Contribution margin (15,000 × $8)	120,000
Fixed costs	100,000
Income	$ 20,000

A shortcut approach is to multiply contribution margin per unit of $8 by 15,000 units, which gives $120,000 in contribution margin, then subtract fixed costs of $100,000 to get $20,000 income.

2. 12,500 units. The break-even point in units is given by the result of dividing fixed costs ($100,000) by the $8 contribution margin per unit.

3. $250,000. This amount can be determined either by multiplying the break-even point in units (from part 2) by the sales price per unit (12,500 × $20) or by applying the break-even formula that incorporated the contribution margin percentage ($100,000/40%). The contribution margin percentage is determined by dividing the sales price of $20 into the contribution margin of $8 (sales price of $20 − variable cost per unit of $12).

4. 17,500 units. The profit of $40,000 is added to the fixed costs of $100,000 and the break-even formula is then applied. Thus, the total to be obtained from sales is $40,000 plus $100,000 in fixed costs. If the company gets $8 per unit and it desires to get a total of $140,000, the total number of units it must sell is 17,500 ($140,000/$8).

5. $350,000. This amount can be determined either by multiplying the 17,500 units in part 4 by the $20 selling price per unit or by applying the break-even formula that incorporates the contribution margin percentage. To return the fixed costs of $100,000 plus a profit of $40,000, when the contribution margin percentage is 40%, requires sales of $350,000 ($140,000/40%).

6. (a) 16,667 units. If fixed costs of $100,000 must be covered when each unit carries a contribution margin of $6 ($18 sales price − variable cost of $12), a total of 16,667 units must be sold ($100,000/$6).

   (b) $300,000. This amount can be determined either by multiplying the number of units (16,667) in part (a) by the selling price of $18 or by utilizing the formula that incorporates the contribution margin percentage. Thus, 16,667 × $18 is $300,000 (rounded) or $100,000/[($18 − $12)/18] = $300,000.

7. (a) 13,750 units. With fixed costs of $110,000 and a contribution margin per unit of $8, the number of units to produce a contribution margin equal to the fixed costs is 13,750 ($110,000/$8).

   (b) $275,000. The most direct approach to this answer is simply to multiply the number of units (13,750) computed in part (a) by the sales price per unit ($20). Or, the answer could be determined by dividing the fixed costs ($110,000) by the contribution margin percentage (40%). Still another approach would be to determine what additional sales volume (beyond that required to break even with the current cost structure) would provide sufficient contribution margin to cover the additional fixed costs. It will take the contribution margin from an additional 1,250 units ($10,000/$8 per unit) to cover the added fixed costs, and the break-even point is already 12,500 units, so the total number of units required to cover the new cost structure is 13,750 (12,500 + 1,250).

8. 625 units. Current income will not be affected so long as the contribution margin from the additional units is sufficient to offset the expenditure for advertising. Hence, regardless of the level of current sales, we need only determine what additional sales will produce the contribution margin sufficient to cover the cost of the advertising. Since the contribution margin per unit is $8, the number of units needed to be sold to cover the $5,000 advertising campaign is $5,000/$8 or 625 units. You should note that the current level of sales is irrelevant to the decision of whether or not to undertake the advertising campaign. As long as the campaign will increase sales by 625 units, the company will be no better nor worse off than it would have been without the campaign.

9. (a) 12,500 units. The contribution margin per unit remains at $8 ($18 sales price − $10 variable cost) and the fixed costs remain at $100,000. Hence, the break-even point, in units, remains the same as before, or 12,500 units ($100,000/$8).

   (b) $225,000. Although the number of units to break even remains the same as before the changes in selling price and variable cost per unit, the total sales in dollars must change in order to break even. One approach is simply to multiply the break-even sales in units times the sales price per unit (12,500 × $18 = $225,000). Another approach would be to compute the new break-even point in dollars by reference to the new contribution margin percentage. Thus the fixed costs of $100,000 would be divided by the contribution margin percentage of 44.44% ($8/$18).

The emphasis in this review problem has been the possibility of changes in the structure of costs and selling prices. Managers must be alert for such possible changes and their effects on profits. Additionally, managers can analyze proposed changes to see if they will increase profits. Part 8 of this problem gave an important practical example: an increase in a fixed cost was expected to lead to some increase in volume. If the advertising manager believed that the increase in cost would generate additional sales in excess of 625 units, the plan would have been wise.

Volume-cost-profit analysis is used to answer "what if?" questions: what if we increased our prices? what if we sold more units? what if we could make the product at a lower variable cost? These questions are constantly being asked by managers.

ASSIGNMENT MATERIAL

Questions for Discussion

2-1 Significance of average cost   "If selling price is less than average cost of a unit, the firm should stop operating because it will incur losses." Is this statement true? Explain.

2-2 Break-even point   It is often said that if you lower your price, the break-even point for your business increases. Explain.

2-3 Economic profit   There is no profit unless all costs are covered. The economist's concept of cost includes a return to the owners of the capital invested in the firm. From the economist's point of view, the return to the owners should be equal to what investors would earn had they invested their capital elsewhere in the economy in an essentially similar venture. In determining a break-even point (in sales dollars) after a return to the owners of capital, how would you incorporate the economist's idea?

2-4 Cost structure   The owner of a ski shop said, "I lose my shirt for more than half the year, and make a bundle during the rest of the time. Maybe I should close up the shop during bad months and take a long vacation." Explain his comment and respond to his speculation about the long vacation.

2-5 Pricing policy   "My policy is very consistent. I set prices 20% over costs. Yet in the historically slow sales months I seem to show a greater loss than other firms in the same business." How might you analyze the problem facing this shop owner?

Exercises

2-6 Contribution margin statements   Prepare income statements for each of the following situations. Use the contribution margin format shown in the chapter.

	Unit Selling Price	Unit Variable Costs	Fixed Costs	Unit Sales
1.	$10	$ 6	$ 12,000	6,000
2.	8	3	15,000	4,000
3.	20	8	240,000	60,000
4.	25	20	100,000	30,000
5.	3	1	30,000	14,000

2-7 Contribution margin statements Prepare income statements for each of the following situations. Use the contribution margin format shown in the chapter.

Case	Sales	Variable Cost As Percentage of Sales	Fixed Costs
1.	$ 30,000	40%	$ 8,000
2.	100,000	65	32,000
3.	50,000	30	41,000
4.	700,000	50	320,000
5.	250,000	60	80,000

2-8 Contribution margin income statements and break-even points Each of the following cases is independent of the others.

Case	Selling Price per Unit	Variable Cost per Unit	Fixed Costs	Sales in Units
1.	$ 4	$3	$ 8,000	12,000
2.	8	5	33,000	18,000
3.	12	8	170,000	40,000
4.	16	8	70,000	15,000

Required

1. For each case, prepare an income statement using the contribution margin format.
2. For each case, calculate the break-even point in units and in dollars.

2-9 Contribution margin income statements and break-even points Each of the following cases is independent of the others.

Case	Sales	Contribution Margin Percentage	Fixed Costs
1.	$ 40,000	50%	$18,000
2.	120,000	60	60,000
3.	75,000	30	15,000
4.	180,000	25	48,000

Required

1. For each case, prepare an income statement using the contribution margin format.
2. For each case, calculate the break-even point.

2-10 Relationships among variables Fill in the blanks for each of the following independent situations.

| | (a) Selling Price per Unit | (b) Variable Cost Percentage | (c) Number of Units Sold | (d) Contribution Margin | (e) Fixed Costs | (f) Income (Loss) |
Case						
1.	—	90%	15,000	$30,000	$22,000	—
2.	$160	—	2,000	80,000	—	($ 2,000)
3.	40	70	—	—	60,000	12,000
4.	25	—	15,000	—	25,000	50,000
5.	4	—	26,000	52,000	—	36,000
6.	—	68	4,000	64,000	48,000	—

2-11 Relationships among variables Fill in the blanks for each of the following independent situations.

| | (a) Selling Price per Unit | (b) Variable Cost per Unit | (c) Number Sold | (d) Contribution Margin | (e) Fixed Costs | (f) Income |
Case						
1.	$ 5	$2	—	$ 3,000	$ 500	—
2.	5	—	2,000	4,000	—	$3,000
3.	—	6	4,000	12,000	4,000	—
4.	8	5	1,000	—	—	2,500
5.	10	4	—	—	600	3,000
6.	—	6	1,000	2,000	—	1,200

2-12 Volume-cost-profit graph The graph below portrays the operations of the Richmond Company.

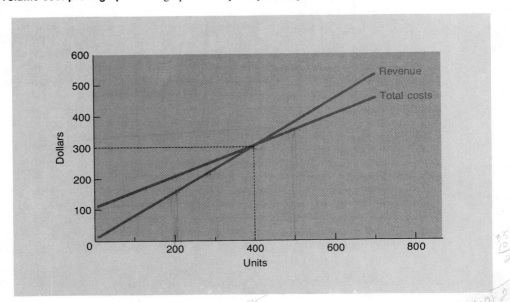

Required

Based on the graph, determine the following.
1. Sales dollars at the break-even point.
2. Fixed costs at 450 units sold.
3. Total variable costs at 400 units sold.
4. Variable cost per unit at 200 units sold.
5. Variable cost per unit at 500 units sold.
6. Selling price per unit.
7. Total contribution margin at 300 units sold.
8. Profit, or loss, at sales of 300 units.
9. Profit, or loss, at sales of 500 units.
10. Break-even sales, in units, if fixed costs were to increase by $50.

2-13 Graphs of cost behavior If one were to graph the behavior of costs in relation to volume, the following might result.

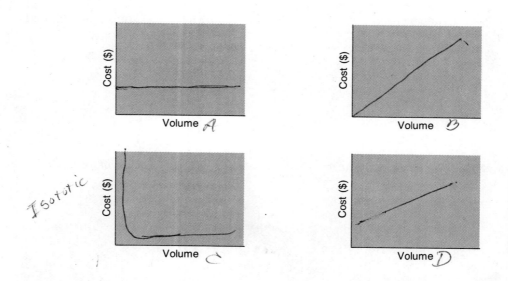

Required

Fill in the blanks using the letters of the graphs above. One letter may be the answer to more than one question.
1. Which graph shows the behavior of total variable costs?
2. Which graph shows the behavior of total fixed costs?
3. Which graph shows the behavior of variable costs per unit?
4. Which graph shows the behavior of fixed costs per unit?
5. Which graph shows the behavior of total costs?

2-14 Volume-cost-profit chart The following chart portrays the potential operations of the Weyand Company.

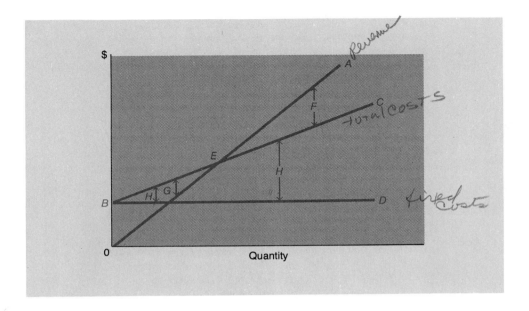

Required

Fill in the blanks with the appropriate letter(s) from the graph. You may have to indicate additions or subtractions.

1. Revenue line _____
2. Variable costs _____
3. Fixed costs _____
4. Profit area _____
5. Loss area _____
6. Total cost line _____
7. Break-even point _____
8. Contribution margin _____

2-15 Required selling price and desired return on sales   The Hedges Company sells its one product for $5, and variable costs are $3 per unit. Fixed costs are $20,000.

Required

Answer the following questions, considering each independently.

1. In order to have return on sales of 20%, how much must be sold in (a) units and (b) dollars?
2. If the firm can sell 20,000 units, at what price per unit would profits be $30,000?
3. If the firm could sell 25,000 units at $5, to what level could variable costs per unit increase and the firm show a $20,000 profit?
4. If variable costs increase to $4 per unit, and 25,000 units can be sold, at what price per unit will the firm earn a $15,000 profit?

2-16 Volume-cost-profit analysis   At the current time, the ABC Company sells its single product for $5 and has variable costs of $3. Fixed costs are $80,000 per year.

Required

Answer the following questions, considering each independently.
1. What are break-even sales in (a) units and (b) dollars?
2. If a $30,000 annual profit is to be earned, what sales are necessary in (a) units and (b) dollars?
3. If sales are 60,000 units, what will profits be?
4. If sales are $250,000 what will profits be?
5. If sales are 70,000 units
   (a) Total variable costs will be how much?
   (b) Fixed costs will be how much?
   (c) Total costs will be how much?
6. Write formulas to determine total costs at any level of sales, based on (a) dollars and (b) units.

2-17 Volume-cost-profit analysis   The McKenna Company makes a single product that sells for $20 and has variable costs of $8. Total fixed costs are $12,000 per month.

Required

Answer the following questions, considering each independently.
1. What is the monthly break-even sales in (a) dollars and (b) units?
2. If McKenna has a cumulative profit of $60,000 after 10 months, what were the sales for the 10-month period in (a) units and (b) dollars?
3. If McKenna has a cumulative loss of $30,000 after 10 months and is expected to break even for the complete year, what are the expected sales in the last two months of the year in (a) units and (b) dollars.
4. If McKenna is to earn an average profit of $3,000 per month, what are the required average sales per month in (a) units and (b) dollars?
5. Suppose that expected sales for the coming year will generate a $60,000 profit. If volume in units could be increased by 10% with a price reduction of $1.50 per unit, would the price reduction be wise?
6. Suppose that expected sales at $20 per unit will generate a $30,000 profit. An increase in volume of 15% is anticipated if the quality is improved and the price is held constant. The improvement would add an additional $1 per unit to variable costs. Would making the improvement be wise?

2-18 Profit planning   The Tinney Company, which is a wholesale shoe dealer, had the following income statement in 19X5.

Sales 40,000 pairs at $15		$600,000
Variable costs:		
Cost of goods sold	$300,000	
Variable selling costs	80,000	380,000
Contribution margin		220,000
Fixed costs:		
Selling costs	70,000	
Administrative costs	90,000	160,000
Income		$ 60,000

Mr. Tinney, the president of the firm, has asked for your assistance in planning for 19X6. He expects the selling price to remain the same, with unit volume up by 20%. He also forecasts the following changes in costs.

Variable costs:	
Cost of goods sold	up $.50 per unit
Selling costs	up $.10 per unit
Fixed costs:	
Selling costs	up $10,000
Administrative costs	up $15,000

Required

1. Determine the firm's profit for 19X6 if all forecasts are met.
2. Determine the number of units that the firm would have to sell in 19X6 to earn the same profit it did in 19X5.

2-19 Volume-cost-profit analysis   The Searfoss Company had the following income statement in February.

Sales	$100,000
Costs	110,000
Loss	($ 10,000)

The firm's contribution margin percentage at its current selling price of $20 is 40%.

Required: Consider each question independently.

1. Determine the firm's break-even point in sales dollars.
2. Determine the firm's total costs if it sells 7,000 units.
3. Determine the firm's income if it sells 6,000 units at $18 per unit.
4. Determine whether or not it would be worth the $6,000 cost of a special advertising campaign if, because of the campaign, the firm could increase its sales by 1,000 units per month at $20 per unit.
5. The firm is considering changing its selling price. The president wishes the firm to earn $10,000 per month with a sales volume of 8,000 units. What selling price will achieve this objective?

2-20 Conversion of income statement to contribution margin basis   The following income statement was prepared by the controller of the Wassenich Company. Material and labor costs are variable.

Wassenich Company
Income Statement
for 19X4

Sales (10,000 units)		$100,000
Cost of goods sold:		
Materials	$35,000	
Labor	20,000	
Factory overhead:		
Variable	6,000	
Fixed	14,000	75,000
Gross profit		25,000
Selling and administrative		
expenses:		
Variable	9,000	
Fixed	22,000	31,000
Loss		($ 6,000)

Required
1. Prepare a new income statement showing contribution margin.
2. What is the break-even point in units?
3. The president of the firm believes that sales could be increased 2,000 units if an additional $4,000 were spent on advertising. His son, the general manager, says that it would be silly to do so because the firm is losing enough already. Would it be wise to undertake the advertising campaign?

2-21   Break-even calculations   The Grager Company currently sells its product for $10 and has variable costs of $6 per unit. Fixed costs are $30,000.

Required
Answer the following questions, considering each independently.
1. What is the break-even point in (a) units and (b) dollars?
2. If fixed costs rise by 10%, what is the break-even point in (a) units and (b) dollars?
3. If variable costs decline to $4, what is the break-even point in (a) units and (b) dollars?
4. If the selling price per unit declines by 10%, what is the break-even point in (a) units and (b) dollars?
5. If the events described in 2, 3, and 4 all occur, what is the break-even point in (a) units and (b) dollars.
6. What sales dollars are required to earn $50,000 in profit?
7. If fixed costs increase by 20% and variable costs decline by $1 per unit, what sales dollars are required to earn $50,000 profit?
8. Which of the following actions would lower the break-even point in units the most:
   (a) Increasing selling price by 10%?
   (b) Decreasing variable costs by $.80?
   (c) Decreasing fixed costs by $5,000?
9. If it is expected that an advertising campaign would generate an increase of 3,000 units of sales, how much could be spent on the campaign without changing profits? (Hint: Your answer does not depend on the existing level of sales.)

Problems

2-22   Relationships   Considering each situation below independently, answer the questions. You may not be able to solve the questions in the order in which they are asked.
1. A firm had variable costs per unit of $8, a selling price of $12, fixed costs of $80,000, and a net loss of $20,000.
   (a) What were its sales in units?
   (b) What was its contribution margin in total?
   (c) What were its dollar sales?
2. A firm earned $30,000 selling 50,000 units at $5 per unit. Its fixed costs were $120,000.
   (a) What were its variable costs per unit?
   (b) What was its total contribution margin?
   (c) What would its income be if sales increased by 5,000 units?
3. A firm had return on sales of 10%, income of $30,000, selling price of $10, and a contribution margin ratio of 30%.
   (a) What were its fixed costs?
   (b) What were its variable costs per unit?
   (c) What were its sales in units?
   (d) What were its sales in dollars?
4. A firm had return on sales of 15% at sales of $300,000. Its fixed costs were $75,000 and its variable costs were $6 per unit.

(a) What were sales in units?

(b) What was its contribution margin per unit?

(c) What was its income?

5. A firm earned $50,000 selling 100,000 units. Its contribution margin in total was $110,000 and its variable costs were $3 per unit.

(a) What was its selling price?

(b) What were its fixed costs?

6. A firm sold 40,000 units with contribution margin of $5 per unit, which is 40% of selling price. Its fixed costs were $220,000.

(a) What was its income?

(b) What were its dollar sales?

7. A firm increased its income from $14,000 to $26,000 by increasing its sales $40,000. When it earned $14,000 it had sales of $90,000.

(a) What were its fixed costs?

(b) What was its contribution margin ratio?

2-23 Sensitivity of variables   The following data relate to the one product of the Cranston Company:

Planned sales in units—19X5	20,000
Selling price	$15
Variable costs	$9
Total fixed costs	$60,000

Required

Answer the following questions, considering each independently.

1. Which of the following events would reduce planned profits the most:

(a) A decrease in selling price of 10%?

(b) An increase in variable costs of 10% per unit?

(c) An increase in fixed costs of 10%?

(d) A decline in sales volume of 10%?

2. Which of the following events would increase planned profits the most:

(a) An increase in selling price of 5%?

(b) A decrease in variable costs of 10% per unit?

(c) An increase in sales volume of 10%?

(d) A decrease in fixed costs of 15%?

3. If selling prices declined by 10%, how many more units would have to be sold to achieve the planned profit?

4. If selling prices increased by 10%, by how much could variable costs per unit increase and the planned profit be achieved?

2-24 Volume-cost-profit analysis—changes in variables   During two recent months the Thompson Company had the following income statements.

	March	April
Sales	$200,000	$216,000
Variable costs	130,000	120,600
Contribution margin	70,000	95,400
Fixed costs	40,000	40,000
Income	$ 30,000	$ 55,400

You learn that the price of one product sold by the firm is generally changed each month though its purchase cost is stable at $11 per unit. The only other variable cost is a 10% commission paid on all sales.

Required

Determine the selling price, unit volume, and variable cost per unit in each of the two months.

2-25   Volume-cost-profit analysis for a hospital.   The administrator of The Caldwell Memorial Hospital is considering methods of providing X-ray treatments to patients. The hospital now refers patients to a nearby private clinic and each treatment costs the patient $25. The hospital now refers about 120 patients per month to the clinic. If the hospital decides to provide the treatment, it will have to rent a machine for $1,000 per month and hire a technician for $800 per month. Variable costs are $5 per treatment.

Required

1. The hospital administrator is considering charging the same fee as has the clinic. By how much will the hospital increase its income, or decrease its losses, if it provides the service?
2. How much would the hospital have to charge to break even on the treatments?

2-26   Assumptions of V-C-P analysis   Last year you were engaged as a consultant to the Thompson Products Company and prepared some analyses of its volume-cost-profit relationships. Among your findings was that the contribution margin percentage was 40% at the firm's planned selling price of $20. The firm expected to sell 10,000 at the $20 price, which you estimated would result in an income of $48,000. You told Mr. Thompson, the owner of the firm, that profits would change at the rate of $.40 per $1 change in sales.

Mr. Thompson has just called to tell you that the results did not come out as you had said they would. The firm earned profits of $63,200 on volume of $226,800. Although variable costs per unit were incurred as expected, the firm had higher fixed costs than expected because of a $2,000 advertising campaign during the year. The campaign was coupled with an increase in selling price and Mr. Thompson was very pleased at the results. However, Mr. Thompson asks you why profits did not increase by 40% of the added sales volume of $26,800, but rather by somewhat more.

Required

1. Reconstruct the income statement for the year, based on the actual results.
2. Determine (a) the number of units sold and (b) the selling price per unit.
3. Explain to Mr. Thompson why the results were not as you had originally forecasted.

2-27   Bus service   The Bluebird Bus Company provides service among a number of Northeastern cities. The firm's buses make 300 trips per week with an average distance of 100 miles. Fares are $.05 per mile per passenger and each bus can carry 40 passengers. The firm has the following cost structure.

Drivers' pay ($150 per week per driver)	$3,000	per week
Other salaries and wages	$5,400	per week
Other fixed costs, including depreciation and maintenance of buses	$8,000	per week
Gas, oil, and other variable costs	$.40	per bus per mile

Required

1. Determine the firm's capacity in passenger-miles. (A passenger-mile is one passenger riding one mile.)
2. Determine the firm's break-even point in passenger-miles.
3. Determine the firm's weekly income if it operates with its buses 60% full.
4. Suppose that the firm is now operating at 50% of capacity. The president of the firm believes that

if fares were reduced to $.045 per mile, the buses would run 60% full. Additional advertising and promotional costs to publicize the lower fares would be $1,500 per week. Should the firm reduce its fares?

2-28 Pricing decision—nursery school   The Board of Directors of the First Community Church of Delmar is considering opening a nursery school for four- and five-year-old children. The school would operate in a building that the church owns. The members of the board agree that the school, which would be open to all children, should break even or be within $100 either way of the break-even point.

The treasurer has prepared an analysis of the expected costs of operating the school, based on conversations with members of other churches that run similar programs. The school would be open for nine months each year, with two classes, one in the morning and one in the afternoon.

First Community Church
Expected Costs of
Nursery School Operation

Salaries, teacher and assistant	$10,600	for nine months
Utilities	$400	for nine months
Miscellaneous operating costs	$300	for nine months
Supplies, paper, paint	$2	per child per month
Snacks, cookies, juice	$4	per child per month

The best estimate of probable enrollment is 20 children in each of the two classes, which is all that the teacher and assistant can handle and still achieve the quality that the board feels is essential.

Required

1. Determine the monthly fee per child that would have to be charged in order that the school break even (round to nearest dollar) with its maximum enrollment.
2. Suppose that the monthly fee is set at $41. What is the break-even point in enrollment?

2-29 Income statement construction   The president of Conoy Industrial Products Company has asked for your assistance in preparing a planned income statement for the coming month. He gives you the following data developed by the controller who has become ill and cannot help the president.

Expected sales	20,000	units
Selling price	$25	per unit
Purchase cost	$11	per unit
Sales commissions	15%	of sales
Shipping costs	$2	per unit
Salaries	$86,000	per month
Rent	$16,000	per month
Depreciation on equipment	$120,000	per year
Advertising	$6,000	per month
Miscellaneous expenses	$4,500	per month

Required

1. Prepare an income statement for the coming month based on the planned data given.
2. Determine the break-even point for the firm, in units per month.
3. Suppose that a doubling of the advertising expense, coupled with a $2 reduction in price, would increase sales by 5,000 units over the planned volume. Would it be wise to take these actions?

2-30 Developing volume-cost-profit information   The manager of the Sans Flavour Food Store, a franchise operation, is confused by the income statements he has received from his accountant. He asks you to help him with them. He is especially concerned that his return on sales dropped much more than sales from April to May.

	Income Statements	
	April	*May*
Sales	$90,000	$75,000
Cost of sales	36,000	30,000
Gross profit	54,000	45,000
Operating expenses:		
Rent	1,200	1,200
Salaries, wages, commissions	31,500	28,500
Insurance	900	900
Supplies	1,800	1,500
Utilities	1,400	1,400
Miscellaneous expenses	4,500	4,500
Total operating expenses	41,300	38,000
Income	$12,700	$ 7,000
Return on sales	14.1%	9.3%

The manager informs you that the salaries, wages, and commissions account includes the salaries of several clerks and himself. All salespersons work on commissions of 20% of sales. Supplies are primarily wrapping paper and tape and vary directly with sales. For various reasons he had expected the $15,000 decline in sales. But he had expected income of $10,575 on those lower sales (that is, 14.1% of his expected sales).

Required

Prepare income statements using the contribution margin format for April and May, and explain to the manager the advantages of this alternative format.

2-31 Hours of operation The Quickie Food Store is now open from 8:00 A.M. to 8:00 P.M. seven days a week. The manager is considering the possibility of a 24-hour-a-day schedule. He estimates that additional sales would be $20,000 per week. Additional clerks, utilities, insurance and other items would cost $9,000 per week. Cost of goods sold, the only variable cost, is 40% of sales.

Required

1. Should the store remain open 24 hours a day? Explain.
2. What are break-even sales for the additional hours of operation?
3. Suppose that sales could be increased $12,000 per week if the store stayed open until midnight. The additional costs for clerks, etc. would be $4,000 per week. What hours should the store stay open: 8:00 A.M. to 8:00 P.M., 24 hours a day, or 8:00 A.M. to 12:00 P.M. (midnight)?

2-32 Special order The Whizzer Toy Company has just finished an analysis of its cost and sales picture for 19X6. The analysis indicates the following:

Planned selling price	$20
Variable costs per unit	$12
Total fixed costs	$320,000
Planned sales volume	50,000 units

Required

Answer the following questions, considering each independently.

1. What is the break-even point in units?
2. If sales volume were 10% higher than planned, what would be the break-even point?
3. If the company wanted to increase its profit by $20,000 over that which would be earned at planned sales volume, by how many units would sales have to increase?
4. Suppose the company could undertake a $30,000 advertising campaign in a foreign country where the company has no sales at this time. The campaign is expected to generate sales of 11,000 units if the price is set at $16. Additional shipping costs of $1 per unit will be incurred. Would the venture be profitable?
5. The preceding question indicates that this would be the first time the company tried to sell in the particular foreign country. What is the importance of the specification that the sales be made in another country?

2-33 Significance of cost-per-unit Mr. James Wilson has asked for your assistance. He is unhappy about the store he owns because it has not shown a profit for some time. He shows you the following income statement for a typical month.

Sales 10,000 units at $10	$100,000
Total costs	120,000
Net loss	($ 20,000)

He points out that his cost-per-unit is $12 ($120,000/10,000), which is greater than his selling price. "How can I make money this way?" he asks. Further investigation reveals that the store pays $6 for each unit of product it sells and also pays salaries and rent of $60,000 per month. These amounts do not change if volume changes.

Required

1. Prepare an income statement using the contribution margin format, for a month with sales of $100,000.
2. Advise Mr. Wilson as to whether he should remain in business assuming that he expects sales to be 18,000 units per month in the future.

2-34 Alternative cost behavior—a movie company Karen James, the president of Gigantic Pictures, Inc., a leading producer of movies, is trying to decide on a compensation scheme for Kirk Ruthless, the biggest box-office attraction in the country. Kirk is going to star in *The Creature That Ate the Bronx,* a science fiction thriller. For starring in a picture he normally gets $800,000 plus 10% of the receipts to the producer. (The producer normally receives 40% of the total paid admissions wherever the picture is shown.) Kirk is very optimistic about *Creature* and has offered to do the picture for $300,000 plus 20% of the receipts-to-the-producer. Costs of producing the picture other than Kirk's salary will be $2,500,000.

Required

1. What are break-even receipts to the producer under each compensation scheme proposed?
2. If total paid admissions in theaters are expected to be $14,000,000, what will income to the producer be under each compensation scheme?

2-35 Volume-cost-profit analysis for a magazine The owner of *What's Happening,* a monthly magazine with a general readership, is considering undertaking a promotion program to boost circulation. He wants to run a contest with prizes that would cost $50,000 in the year of the contest. The magazine is sold by subscription and on newsstands. Subscription price is $2.40 per year for 12 issues and the newsstand price is $.50 per copy. Variable costs per copy are $.10. Monthly fixed costs, without considering the contest prizes, are $40,000.

Required

1. If there are 300,000 subscribers, how many copies must be sold on newsstands to break even per month? Ignore the contest.
2. Suppose there are 300,000 subscribers and 30,000 issues are sold on newsstands. Ignore the contest.
   (a) What is the monthly contribution margin?
   (b) What is the income?
3. Assuming that subscriptions would not be affected by the contest, by how many issues per month must newsstand sales increase to break even on the contest?
4. The publisher expects that the contest will generate additional monthly newsstand sales of 20,000 copies, and additional subscriptions of 5,000 copies per month. In addition to the prizes, there will be increased fixed costs of $2,000 per month to operate the contest. Should the magazine sponsor the contest?
5. Assume the same facts as in 4 above. An alternative to running the contest is to offer a cut-rate subscription at $2 per year. It is anticipated that subscriptions at the special rate would be 60,000, but that newsstand sales would drop by 3,000 per month.
   (a) If the special rate were introduced, what would income for the year be?
   (b) Should the magazine run the contest or offer the special rate?

2-36 Seasonality, relevant range, and profit opportunities   The Royal Ice Cream Company currently has monthly sales from $60,000 in the winter to $170,000 in the summer. The capacity of the firm is strained in the summer, because the product must be stored in freezers. The relevant range is wide, from about $40,000 to $170,000, and the cost structure is as follows:

Variable costs	40% of sales dollars
Fixed costs	$40,000 per month

An analysis of sales by month shows the following:

November through February	$ 60,000 monthly
March through May	90,000 monthly
June through August	170,000 monthly *220,000*
September and October	80,000 monthly

Required

1. Prepare income statements for each of the groups of months given (November through February, March through May, etc.).
2. The president has been discussing the possibility of acquiring some new equipment from the Whip-itup Company, a maker of freezing equipment and storage freezers. The equipment would enable the firm to increase its production in the peak months to $220,000 per month. The president believes that all additional production could easily be sold. The equipment would be rented for $5,000 per month, but must be rented for an entire year. Sales in off-peak months would be unchanged. Variable cost percentages and existing fixed costs would not be affected. Should the new equipment be rented? Explain and support your answer.

Case

2-37 A concessionaire   Ralph Newkirk is considering entering a bid for the hot dog and soft drink concession at the new athletic stadium. He intends to bid for the concession rights at the fourteen football games that will be played during the season. There will be seven college games and seven professional games. Average attendance at college games is 20,000, at professional games 50,000. Ralph estimates that he sells one hot dog and one soft drink for each two persons attending a game.

Revenue and cost data for the products are as follows:

	Hot Dogs	Soft Drinks
Selling price	$.50	$.30
Variable costs:		
Hot dog	.080	
Roll	.040	
Mustard, onion, etc.	.005	
Soft drink and ice		.125

In addition, salespeople are paid a 15% commission on all sales, and all sales are subject to commissions. Fixed costs per game are $4,000 for rentals of heating, cooking, mixing, and cooling equipment.

The stadium management has requested that bids be made in the form of royalties on sales. The highest percentage of sales bid will win the contract.

Required

1. What percentage of sales can Ralph pay as royalty to the stadium and earn $20,000 for the season? (Round to nearest one-tenth of a percentage point.)
2. If Ralph bids 12% of sales as the royalty, what income can he expect if operations go according to plan? (Is this consistent with your answer in 1?)
3. Assuming a royalty of 12% of sales, what is Ralph's break-even point for the season, based on total attendance?
4. What kinds of information would Ralph want if he were also deciding to bid for the concession at baseball games at the same stadium?
5. Assume that Ralph has made a forecast of attendance for both kinds of games. He then learns that the star quarterback of the local professional team will retire before the coming season. What effect would the retirement be likely to have on attendance at professional games?

CHAPTER 3

ANALYSIS OF COST BEHAVIOR

As already indicated, one of the assumptions required for the use of volume-cost-profit analysis is that all costs are either fixed or variable within the relevant range. In this chapter we shall examine costs that do not fit neatly into the fixed-variable classification. We shall give some methods of dealing with these costs and show how their existence imposes limitations on volume-cost-profit analysis. In addition, we introduce some problems connected with the use of sales as the measure of volume and discuss the role of management attitudes in planning the cost structure of the firm.

INCOME TAXES AND PROFIT PLANNING

In Chapter 2 we assumed that Ted did not have to pay income taxes. Income tax law can be complex and affects planning. We concentrate here on the problem of a manager who has a target after-tax profit and wants to determine what sales are required to reach the target.

We can no longer add the desired profit to fixed costs and divide by contribution margin per unit or as a percentage because that would be computing only the profit before taxes. Assume that income taxes are 25% of profits before taxes (a simplified assumption). If Ted wanted to earn $1,200 after taxes, he could not add the $1,200 to his fixed costs of $2,400 and divide by his contribution margin percentage of 60%. If he did, he would obtain $6,000 ($3,600/60%) as his target sales. But an income statement at that level of sales would show the following:

Sales	$6,000
Variable costs (40%)	2,400
Contribution margin (60%)	3,600
Fixed costs	2,400
Profit before taxes	1,200
Taxes (25%)	300
Net income	$ 900

If Ted sells $6,000 worth of shirts, he will earn only $900.

To plan for a target after-tax profit, Ted must determine what *before-tax profit* will leave him the desired after-tax profit of $1,200. The tax rate is 25%, so only 75% of the before-tax profit will be left for Ted. The before-tax profit required for Ted to earn $1,200 after taxes is $1,600 ($1,200/75%). With this profit, the tax will be $400 ($1,600 × 25%) and the after-tax profit will be $1,200. The principle is much the same as contribution margin percentage, with before-tax income substituted for sales, and after-tax income substituted for contribution margin.

What sales are required for Ted to earn $1,200 after taxes? Adding the required before-tax profit of $1,600 to fixed costs of $2,400 gives contribution margin of $4,000. Ted's sales must be $6,667 ($4,000/60%). An income statement at that level of sales follows.

Sales	$6,667
Variable costs (40%)	2,667
Contribution margin (60%)	4,000
Fixed costs	2,400
Profit before taxes	1,600
Taxes (25%)	400
Net income	$1,200

In computing the break-even point there is no need to consider income taxes. At zero income (the break-even point), the firm pays no tax. At other levels of desired income, the tax rate does affect the determination of sales needed to earn a desired profit.

PROBLEMS WITH VARIABLE COSTS

The variable costs that we have been examining are relatively simple and easy to predict. In the example used in Chapter 2 (**pages 26 and 27**), shirts cost either $1.80 or $3.80 each, no matter how many Ted sold in a month, and each shirt sold required wrapping materials costing $.20. Suppose Ted employs a salesperson who receives a 20% commission on each shirt he or she sells. At first glance this would seem to be a straightforward variable cost, reducing contribution margin percentage from 60% to 40%. It is not that simple. The salesperson does not receive a commission on sales that Ted makes, and therefore the cost of commission will depend not on total sales dollars (as does cost of shirts), but on the dollar amount sold by the salesperson. This amount will probably change in the same direction as total sales, but unless the salesperson always sells the same percentage of total dollar sales, the cost cannot be predicted and planned for as easily as the cost of shirts.

How does Ted plan this cost? He may be able to determine an average percentage of total sales on which he has to pay the commission. He could then use this average percentage to estimate the overall effect of commissions on his variable costs and contribution margin percentage. He might find that about 50% of total sales are typically subject to commissions. His commission cost would then be 10% of total sales (20% × 50%) and his contribution margin percentage on the average would drop from 60% to 50%.

Ted would know that his planned cost of commissions would not be likely to equal his actual cost in any given month, but the differences should not be too great if the salesperson normally sells about the same percentage of the total every month.

MIXED COSTS

Some costs contain both fixed and variable elements and are called mixed costs, or semivariable costs. Figure 3-1 shows that mixed costs behave the same as total costs when there are both fixed and variable costs. Some of these costs are relatively easy to handle, some are not.

To illustrate a mixed cost we will change some of the facts related to the Ted's Threads example in Chapter 2. He still sells shirts for $5 and $10; we shall ignore the wrapping cost and assume, instead, that the shirts cost $2 and $4 respectively. Ted has decided to move his store into a new enclosed shopping mall. Instead of paying $2,400 per month rent for the store and equipment, he will be required to pay a fixed monthly amount of $1,200 plus 5% of his dollar sales. This kind of rental agreement exists in many shopping centers.

How does Ted plan his rent expense? He must break down the expense into its fixed and variable components. His variable costs are now 45% of sales (40% cost of shirts plus 5% rent), and his fixed costs are now $1,200 per month. (We are using his original situation when he was the only employee.) Ted's contribution margin percentage has fallen from 60% to 55%, but his fixed costs have been reduced from $2,400 to $1,200 per month. When the components of a mixed cost are based on contractual arrangements, such as the new rent agreement, there is no problem in separating the fixed and variable components. Notice that rent will now show in two places in Ted's income statement: as a variable and as a fixed cost. In volume-cost-profit analysis, the behavior of the cost is important; its functional classification is secondary.

FIGURE 3-1 Mixed Cost Behavior

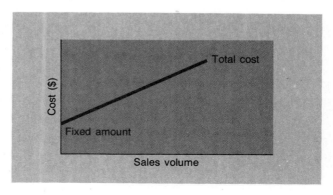

Problems with Cost Behavior Analysis

Ted's operation as described so far is relatively simple and lends itself to straightforward analysis. All of his costs are easy to predict and plan for. Unfortunately, this is not usually the case in business or in any other economic activity.

Suppose that Ted employs a person part-time to help with the store. Each month, the person works about 15 to 17 hours doing routine tasks like tagging merchandise, filling out forms for ordering merchandise and keeping the records of the business. Ted also arranges to have this person come in when Ted expects sales to be relatively heavy and he needs help to wait on customers. Suppose further that the person is paid $4 per hour.

The cost of employing the person (wages expense) is variable with the number of hours worked and not with sales. The cost will not be perfectly variable with sales; there will be a fixed component because the person works about 15 to 17 hours per month regardless of the sales level. However, there will also be some variable component, because the person works more when sales are high than when they are low. It would be useful if Ted could find some relationship between this particular cost and sales, because he will use sales as the basis for planning the amounts of cost he expects to incur. Some methods do exist for developing a cost/sales relationship for costs of this nature.

High-Low Method of Estimation

A relatively unsophisticated but widely used method of estimating the fixed and variable components of a mixed cost is the **high-low method.** The high and low points refer to the extremes of the relevant range. Volume and cost at both points are determined, and the difference in volume is divided into the difference in cost to find the variable portion of the cost. The formula for finding the variable cost factor in a mixed cost is:

$$\text{Variable cost factor in mixed cost} = \frac{\text{high cost} - \text{low cost}}{\text{high volume} - \text{low volume}}$$

Assume that Ted has found the following at the extremes of his relevant range of sales of $2,500 and $9,000:

	High	Low	Difference
Sales	$9,000	$2,500	$6,500
Wages for part-time help	408	148	260

With a sales increase of $6,500, wages increased by $260; thus the cost increased at a rate of $.04 per sales dollar ($260/$6,500). Using the high-low method we say that the variable component of this cost is $.04 per dollar of sales (or 4% of sales). Using the formula for Ted's situation:

$$\text{Variable cost factor} = \frac{\$408 - \$148}{\$9,000 - \$2,500} = \frac{\$260}{\$6,500} = \$.04 \text{ or } 4\% \text{ of sales dollars}$$

Since the total cost is a combination of the fixed and variable elements, we can compute the fixed component by subtracting the variable component from the total cost at either level of volume. In formula notation this becomes, using the high volume

$$
\begin{matrix}
\text{Fixed cost} & & \text{total cost} & & \begin{pmatrix} \text{high} & & \text{variable cost per} \\ \text{volume} & \times & \text{unit of} \\ \text{in units} & & \text{volume} \end{pmatrix}
\end{matrix}
$$

Fixed cost portion of = total cost at − (high volume in units × variable cost per unit of volume)
mixed cost — high volume

or

$$
= \text{at} \quad \text{total cost at high volume} - \begin{pmatrix} \text{high} & & \text{variable cost} \\ \text{volume} & \times & \text{percentage per} \\ \text{in dollars} & & \text{sales dollar} \end{pmatrix}
$$

At sales of \$2,500, the variable component would be \$100 (\$2,500 × \$.04) and the total is \$148, so the fixed component must be \$48 (\$148 − \$100). The same answer could be determined by subtracting the \$360 variable element at a sales level of \$9,000 (\$9,000 × \$.04) from the total cost of \$408 at that volume (\$408 − \$360 = \$48 fixed cost). The formula that Ted might use to predict his total wage cost would be: Total cost = \$48 + 4% of sales.

The rationale for the high-low method is this: because variable costs change proportionately with changes in volume, the change in total cost between two volumes must be the change in variable cost. Therefore, when you divide a change in cost by a change in volume you are finding the rate of change in cost per unit of volume. In this case, we used sales dollars as the measure of volume, but we could have used units as well.

Although the high-low method is used widely, it does have some disadvantages, which will become more clear as we discuss the next method of cost estimation.

Scatter-Diagram Method of Estimation

The **scatter-diagram method** involves determining the equation of a line that fits the various points representing costs at various levels of volume. The first step using this method is to develop a chart which plots the total amount of a particular cost at various levels of volume. Figure 3-2 is such a chart, showing the wages actually incurred by Ted at various levels of volume. The next step is to draw a line that will be as close to all the points as possible. (Note that if the cost of wages were like the cost of Ted's rent, with its fixed and variable components stated by contract, all of the points would be on a single line. Such is not the case with his wage cost; the total cost deviates at some sales level, from any line drawn.) The placement and slope of the line are judgmental. The manager "eyeballs" the data and fits the line visually.

Once a line has been drawn, the fixed and variable components of the cost are found in the following manner. The fixed component is simply that point at which the fitted line hits the vertical axis, \$66 in this case. The variable component is found by determining the cost at any point on the line, subtracting the fixed cost, and dividing the remainder by the sales volume. For example, in Figure 3-2, we show the total cost as \$241 at a volume of \$5,000 of sales. Of that cost, \$66 is the fixed component, so the variable component is \$175. Dividing the \$175 by \$5,000 gives \$.035, which is the variable cost per dollar of sales. Thus, the formula that Ted might use to predict his total wage cost would be: Total cost = \$66 + 3.5% of sales. (Notice that the \$66 fixed cost found by the scatter-diagram

FIGURE 3-2   Scatter Diagram

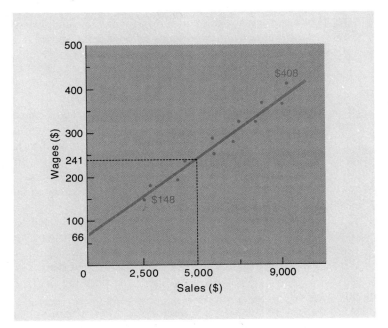

method is close to the employee's wages for the 15 to 17 hours worked on nonsales tasks.)

We now have two formulas for predicting Ted's total wage cost. Which of these formulas should Ted use? The high-low method uses only two points to estimate the cost components, while the scatter-diagram method uses many points. If either or both of the time periods used in the high-low method included some unusual event or random oddity, the calculated fixed and variable costs would reflect that event or oddity. The scatter-diagram will generally give a better picture of the cost behavior pattern than will the high-low method. Note, however, that even using the formula resulting from the scatter-diagram approach, Ted cannot expect to predict his wage costs exactly. Discrepancies can be caused, for example, by Ted's inability to predict accurately the heavy sales periods when additional help will be needed. Thus, in anticipation of a big selling day, Ted might ask the employee to work some extra hours; but if sales are less than expected, the actual wage cost would be larger than that predicted using the actual level of sales.

In short, in the real world we cannot expect to find costs behaving precisely as we predict. A major task of the managerial accountant is to try to develop improved methods and techniques for the prediction of costs.

Regression Method of Estimation

A more sophisticated method for estimating the fixed and variable components of a mixed cost is **regression analysis**. This statistical method provides an equation like the one used to describe the cost: Total cost = fixed cost + (variable cost per unit × number of units). The equation derived using this method is more precise than an equation gained from a visually fitted line; it minimizes the (squared) deviations from the line representing the equation. Knowledge of several important principles of statistics is required before you can understand and apply regression analysis, but you should be aware that advanced techniques are available for solving these kinds of problems. Those interested in a further discussion of this method are referred to the appendix at the end of this chapter.

STEP-VARIABLE COSTS

The step-variable cost also does not fit the strict classification of fixed and variable costs. It is illustrated in Figure 3-3.

The cost is fixed over small ranges of activity, then jumps abruptly to a new level and remains there until the next jump. A firm may need one shipping clerk for every $5,000 in sales. Clerks are added as sales increase, and vice versa. Related to sales, the cost of clerical salaries is not strictly variable; but it is fixed only within small ranges of sales. Other costs may be fixed over wide ranges of sales.

How can the cost for clerks be adequately planned for? Should the relevant range consist of only the very small segments over which the cost is fixed? Or should the cost be planned as if it were variable, even though this would result in predictions missing the mark? The approach to planning for such costs is to treat them as mixed or entirely variable as opposed to fixed. Figure 3-4 illustrates the planning of the cost as if it were variable or mixed.

The three dotted lines show three different philosophies of planning. The top line is conservative. Predicting the cost using this philosophy, you would regularly expect the cost to be less than planned for except at the exact points where the cost jumps. The middle line, which also treats the cost as mixed, connects the midpoints of the small ranges, which means that the predicted cost would equal the actual cost only if the planned and actual volume were both at the middle of one of the small ranges. Use of the lower line, which is the most common, would regularly show unfavorable differences between planned and actual costs except when planned and actual volume were both equal to the high point of one of the ranges.

The method to be used depends on the objectives in a particular situation. If a firm's manager desired never to be confronted with costs higher than planned for (let us call this situation an unfavorable surprise), costs would be planned for using the top line. Use of the

FIGURE 3-3 Step-Variable Cost

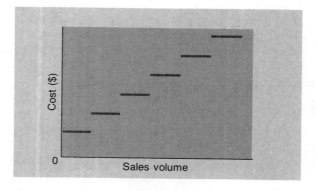

FIGURE 3-4   Planning Step-Variable Costs

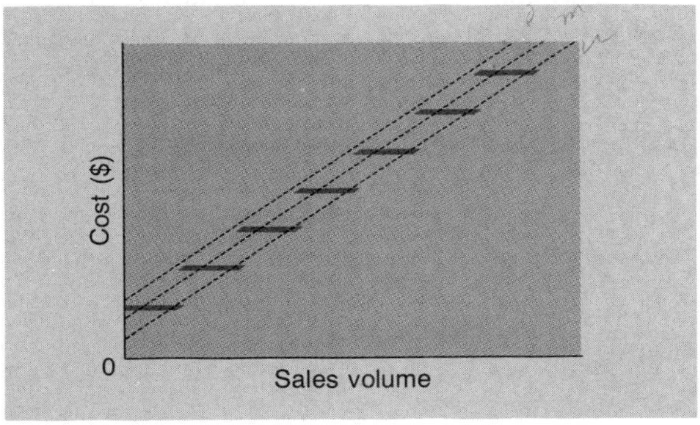

middle line for planning purposes would result in planned costs exceeding actual costs sometimes and being less than actual costs at other times. On the average, you would come the closest to predicting the actual cost. Using the third approach and planning costs based on the bottom line, a manager would expect to have actual costs exceed planned costs most of the time. In this situation, it is important that these differences not be automatically interpreted as overspending or inefficiency, for it is the planning method that ensures the consistent excess of actual over planned costs. This last approach, by producing consistent, unfavorable differences, may serve to remind the manager of the areas where changes in basic operating conditions could increase efficiency. In the example of clerical salaries, the manager would be reminded that the cost increments result directly from hiring policy.

MANAGERIAL ACTION AND FIXED COSTS

We have considered ways of dealing with costs containing both fixed and variable elements. Fixed costs can be divided into two categories: those that can be altered by managerial action and those that cannot without closing down the business. The first kind are called managed, discretionary, engineered, or programmed costs; the latter are called committed.

A constructive way of looking at fixed costs is to say that they provide the capacity to operate; they must be incurred in order that any volume be achieved. Ted, the shirt retailer, needs space to display his merchandise, giving rise to rent. He probably needs some display cases and a cash register, giving rise to depreciation, and he would probably wish to advertise.

Discretionary Costs

You may have noticed a difference between the examples of rent and depreciation and the advertising example. As long as Ted wants to operate, he has to pay rent. He may have a lease for some future period, meaning that even if he liquidates the business he must either pay the rent or find a new tenant for the duration of his lease. These costs are committed. They cannot be changed within relatively short periods of time, such as a year.

Advertising is not necessary to the running of his business, although it may be beneficial. Advertising is an example of a **discretionary fixed cost**. Ted incurs advertising costs as a result of decisions he makes each month about whether to advertise and how much cost to incur. The incurrence and amount of a discretionary cost are subject to managerial action.

Discretionary costs are fixed, once incurred. Their amounts are the result of management decisions and actions and they may be changed within fairly short time periods —yearly, monthly, perhaps even weekly. Thus, when volume-cost-profit analysis is applied, with its need to classify costs over some range, it is assumed that management policies on discretionary costs to be incurred are stable.

Because discretionary costs can be changed by managerial action, they are often the first examined when management is initiating a cost reduction program. This is sometimes unwise. Consider the long-run effects of cutting the following discretionary costs: research and product development; management training programs; programs to upgrade worker skills; advertising; maintenance; and bonuses for highly productive managers.

Research and product development is crucial to companies in such high technology fields as drugs, computers, and aircraft, and in some consumer products. Reduction of expenditures associated with personnel development may lead to reduced morale, high turnover, and lessened productivity. Deferral of routine maintenance may result in high repair expenditures when machines finally break down. Many similar examples could be given.

Discretionary costs may fool someone who is attempting to identify fixed and variable costs using past patterns of expenditures. Some discretionary costs are planned on the basis of expected volume, and may therefore seem to be variable. A firm may plan to incur advertising expense equal to 5% of sales; or research and product development may be allotted an amount equal to 2% of sales. One who is studying the pattern of cost incurrence may be led to believe that these expenses are variable. In one sense they are, but only because management has taken action that makes them so. Sales volume does not cause the advertising or research and development in the same sense that sales volume causes salespeople's commissions. It is closer to the truth to say that advertising and research and development are most probably causal factors in future sales levels. Without advertising, sales in the future may be lower than expected; without new products, the firm may lose customers to more up-to-date products of other firms.

Committed Costs

The **committed fixed cost** is the minimum cost a firm must incur to continue to exist. In many cases, committed costs arise out of decisions made many years ago. Depreciation is a committed cost. It results from past actions and cannot be changed without disposing of the assets to which it applies. Committed costs are thus those that cannot be avoided; their amounts are not subject to managerial review, decision, or action except as concerns their future levels.

The current management may commit future managements to costs by building plants, signing long-term (10-year, for example) leases for machinery or buildings, and negotiating long-term contracts at specified salaries for executives or other employees.

It is not always possible to tell whether a cost is committed or discretionary just by knowing what the cost is (rent, salary, etc.). Some costs will have both discretionary and committed elements. If part of the cost of research and product development is depreciation and property taxes on a building occupied by the research and development department, and the remainder is salaries for the staff, the only discretion management may exercise is over the salaries. The depreciation and property taxes are committed as long as the firm owns the building.

Some costs that are committed for some firms may be discretionary for others. A

20-year lease on a building entails a commitment for rent expense whereas a month-to-month lease does not. A firm that leases a machine on a month-to-month basis may cancel the lease at any time. Thus, the time period over which costs are committed may also vary.

Some costs are on the borderline between being committed and discretionary. A firm could not operate without a chief executive, but the number of lower-level managers needed is not always determinable. Some portion of management salaries is committed, some discretionary, but there would be a lot of disagreement among observers as to the precise amounts of each.

There are two major reasons for distinguishing between discretionary and committed fixed costs. One is that they are treated differently for the purpose of analyzing day-to-day operations. Because there is nothing that can be done to change committed costs over short periods of time, they are not watched as closely as are discretionary costs. Secondly, for purposes of decision making, committed costs are treated differently from discretionary costs. More will be said about this subject in Chapter 7. One example will suffice at this point. A firm operates a sales office that shows the following results, which are expected to continue indefinitely.

Sales	$100,000
Variable costs	70,000
Contribution margin	30,000
Fixed costs	50,000
Loss	($ 20,000)

Whether the sales office should be closed depends on many factors, but an extremely critical one is the nature of the fixed costs. If all the fixed costs are discretionary, the office could be closed and the firm would incur no loss because there would be no incurrence of fixed costs. If, however, the fixed costs are committed, the closing of the office would result in losses of $50,000 until the commitments expired. If the committed costs are less than $20,000, it would pay the firm to close the office, because the losses would be less than the $20,000 loss being incurred currently.

In the context of decision making, the distinction between discretionary and committed fixed costs is sometimes equivalent to and can also be expressed as a distinction between **avoidable** and **unavoidable fixed costs**. In later chapters, there will be further subdivisions of fixed costs, and it will be shown that the discretionary/committed distinction is not always equivalent to the avoidable/unavoidable distinction. However, for our present purposes, and since the committed/discretionary distinction does provide a useful starting point for analysis, you may consider the distinctions as equivalent.

In summary, fixed costs present some difficult areas of interpretation. However, the distinction between committed and discretionary costs is still useful for most managerial planning.

SELECTION OF THE MEASURE OF VOLUME

Fixed or variable costs have so far been described as they relate to changes in sales. A cost does not always vary with sales; it may vary with production, number of employees, or some other measure of operating activity. These costs, like any others, must be planned, but not by considering sales alone. Most costs will increase as sales increase, and vice versa, but the changes may not be proportional.

Suppose Ted's Threads pays 40% of its income in income taxes (a simplified assumption). The owner can plan his income tax expense after he plans his income, but he cannot plan his tax directly from sales. Here are three possible income statements for Ted's Threads.

Ted's Threads
Income Statements for Various Sales Levels

	Amount	Per Cent of Sales	Amount	Per Cent of Sales	Amount	Per Cent of Sales
Sales	$3,000	100%	$5,000	100%	$7,000	100%
Variable costs	1,200	40	2,000	40	2,800	40
Contribution margin	1,800	60	3,000	60	4,200	60
Fixed costs	600	20	600	12	600	8
Income before taxes	1,200	40	2,400	48	3,600	52
Tax (40% of income)	480	16	960	19	1,440	21
Net income	$ 720	24	$1,440	29	$2,160	31

Income tax as a percentage of sales is different at each level of sales, even though taxes change in the same direction as sales. Taxes are the same percentage of income, however, making the tax variable with income but not with sales. Also, although fixed costs as a percentage of sales decline as sales increase, income before and after taxes increases as sales increase.

For other examples, let us turn to a typical manufacturing firm.

The Manufacturing Firm

A manufacturing firm must produce its products in advance of their being sold. Thus, costs to produce the product will be incurred, and hence must be planned for, by reference to production plans. That is, although production plans may depend on expected sales, it is production plans that most directly affect the production costs to be incurred. For this reason, the behavioral classification of costs for planning in a manufacturing firm generally rests on whether the costs are fixed or variable in relation to the volume of production. (Note the importance of this difference for a firm in a seasonal industry where production must be undertaken several months before the peak selling season.)

A typical manufacturing firm will have three general types of costs: raw materials, direct labor, and manufacturing overhead. The cost of raw materials (sometimes referred to simply as materials), the goods that the firm buys and transforms into its products (steel, wood, etc.), is normally considered to be variable with the volume of production. The cost of direct labor (those employees who work directly on the company's product) is also normally considered to be variable with the volume of production. Manufacturing overhead (which consists of all production costs not included in materials and direct labor) includes costs that may be fixed, variable, or mixed. Because of the complex composition of this third element of manufacturing cost, it will be discussed in more detail.

Some items that would normally be classified as manufacturing overhead are:

Wages of materials handlers (individuals who move materials from one work area to another)
Salaries of foremen and other supervisors
Maintenance and repair costs for work performed on machinery and equipment used to make products
Wages of workers assigned responsibility for the storage and control of materials
Heat, light, and other power costs associated with the production areas
Depreciation and property taxes on factory buildings and factory machinery
Salary and office expenses of the manager (and subordinate personnel) responsible for production

From a brief review of the individual manufacturing overhead costs you should be able to see that *total* manufacturing overhead will be a mixed cost, with some variable component and some fixed component. An analysis of total manufacturing overhead into its fixed and variable components could be made using one or more of the methods discussed earlier in this chapter.

Other Examples

It is quite possible that many costs other than production costs can best be analyzed in terms of their behavior in relation to some measure of volume or activity other than sales. Consider, for example, the cost plotted in Figure 3-5, the cost of preparing invoices to customers. When the total cost of this necessary task is related to the volume of sales in dollars, there is a wide spread of values around a line drawn as a result of the scatter diagram. This wide spread of cost values means that predicting the cost is unlikely to be successful when this particular activity measure (dollars of sales) is used. Some other measure might give better results. Figure 3-6 shows this cost plotted against another activity measure, the volume of sales orders. (Ordinarily, one invoice would be prepared for each sales order received.) In searching for a measure of activity that will be a good predictor of costs, the scatter-diagram method has, as indicated above, an advantage over the high-low method. Diagrammed results such as those in Figure 3-5 warn that the particular activity measure

FIGURE 3-5 Scatter Diagram of Invoice Preparation Costs Plotted against Sales Dollars

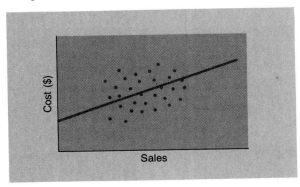

FIGURE 3-6   Scatter Diagram of Invoice Preparation Costs Plotted against Sales Orders

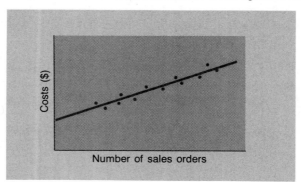

will not be a good predictor. The high-low method, because it includes only two points, would not provide this important information until after several unsuccessful attempts to predict costs.

Sometimes the activities with which costs vary may themselves vary with the volume of sales or production, although perhaps not in direct proportion. For example, consider the costs of carrying inventory. A 10% increase in sales may not lead to a 10% increase in inventory, but some increase in inventory will probably be needed to support the higher level of sales. If increases in inventory are relatively predictable, given increases in sales, it is possible to find the effects of sales increases on costs of carrying inventory, although the relationship is not direct.

SELLING, GENERAL, AND ADMINISTRATIVE EXPENSES—ADDITIONAL PROBLEMS

It is especially difficult to determine the measure of volume with which costs will vary in nonmanufacturing activities. Costs of processing sales orders, mailing invoices, keeping records of accounts receivable and payable, and other administrative activities may show little variation with changes in any single measure of volume. The cost of processing invoices may increase not with an increase in sales dollars but in the number of sales orders, because approximately the same amount of work is required to handle an invoice for $100 as one for $1,000. The number of items ordered by each customer may also affect the cost of invoice preparation because more typing is required on an invoice listing 20 items than on one listing three.

In recent years accountants have been more concerned with finding techniques for planning administrative costs, partly because such costs have increased more rapidly than manufacturing costs. One tool that has been employed with some success is multiple regression analysis—the use of two or more independent variables to predict behavior of costs. For interested readers, multiple regression is discussed briefly in the appendix to this chapter.

COST STRUCTURE AND MANAGERIAL ATTITUDES

Economic situations can usually be handled in many different ways. A firm may use a great deal of labor and little machinery or vice versa. Salespeople may be on straight salary, straight commission, or a combination of the two. Decisions in business must take into consideration the effects of different methods on the cost structure—that is, on the relative proportions of fixed and variable costs.

The income statements of two firms are presented below. Both have total costs of $80,000 at $100,000 sales, but the makeup of the costs is different between the firms. Hifixed has a higher contribution margin than Lofixed, and so income of Hifixed will increase and decrease faster than that of Lofixed if both firms experience similar changes in sales.

Income Statements

	Hifixed Amount	Hifixed Per Cent of Sales	Lofixed Amount	Lofixed Per Cent of Sales
Sales	$100,000	100%	$100,000	100%
Variable costs	20,000	20	60,000	60
Contribution margin	80,000	80	40,000	40
Fixed costs	60,000	60	20,000	20
Income	$ 20,000	20	$ 20,000	20

The graphs in Figure 3-7 show the cost behavior for the two firms.

The break-even points are different for the two firms, and the slopes of the total cost lines are different. Once Hifixed gets beyond the break-even point, its profits increase more rapidly than those of Lofixed, with the firms showing equal profits at $100,000 sales. Beyond $100,000 in sales, Hifixed earns higher profits because of its 80% contribution margin compared to 40% for Lofixed. This difference in profit potential is also reflected in the graphs; the distance between the revenue line and total cost line for Hifixed increases much more towards the right on the horizontal axis than do the distances for Lofixed.

Which cost structure is better? The answer depends on expectations about future sales levels, fluctuations in future sales, and the managers' attitudes towards risk and return. If sales are expected to be higher than $100,000, with little chance of ever being less, then Hifixed is in a better position. If sales are expected to be below $100,000 consistently, Lofixed has the advantage. If sales are expected to fluctuate from $60,000 to $130,000, analysis becomes more difficult. The profits of Hifixed would fluctuate over a much wider range than would those of Lofixed. Hifixed would suffer losses in bad years while Lofixed would not. Of course, in good years Hifixed would earn much higher profits than would Lofixed.

The cost structure depends on the attitudes of the managers of the firm. Do they prefer stable earnings or are they willing to risk losses for the chance to make high profits? The choice is like that made by investors—to buy bonds or common stocks. The former offer relatively safe, but low returns; the latter may have greater returns, but also higher risks. Much of the investment in stock may be lost in a decline of stock prices.

Margin of Safety

The differing cost structures among firms provide the basis for another measure of risk called the margin of safety (MOS). The **margin of safety** is the decline in sales that would bring

FIGURE 3-7   Volume-Cost-Profit Charts

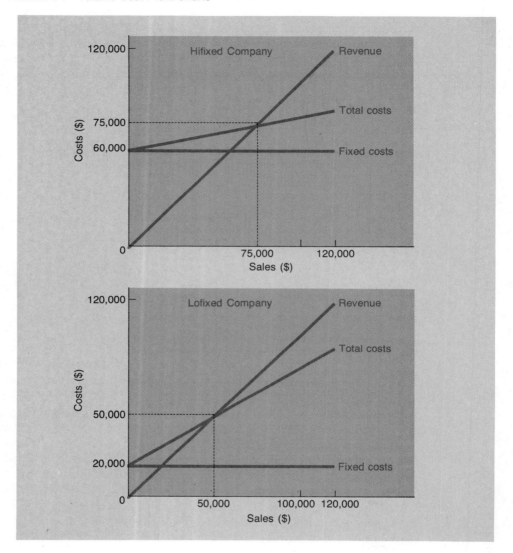

the firm or a product sold by a firm to the break-even point. This margin can be expressed either as a dollar amount or as a percentage of sales. For the Lofixed firm, above, the MOS is $50,000 ($100,000 − $50,000) or 50% ($50,000/$100,000). For the Hifixed firm it is $25,000 ($100,000 − $75,000) or 25% ($25,000/$100,000). As the term suggests, the MOS is a measure of safety, indicating the extent to which a fall in sales would bring the firm below a profitable level of operation.

The MOS can also be applied to individual products of a firm. For example, suppose that instead of being entire firms, Hifixed and Lofixed are products that a firm is considering bringing out. The fixed costs could be associated with producing the products or could be related to selling efforts like advertising and promotion. If the volumes of both products were expected to be greater than $100,000, Hifixed would be more profitable, but declines from the expected volumes would hurt Hifixed more than Lofixed because its contribution margin is higher. Again, the selection of which product to introduce would be influenced by the management's attitudes toward risk and reward.

SUMMARY

Costs do not always fit into fixed-variable classifications, and not all variable costs are variable with changes in sales. Some costs, mixed, contain both fixed and variable elements, and some, step-variable, are fixed over small ranges of activity but at different levels for different ranges. Income taxes vary with income, some manufacturing costs will vary with the number of units manufactured, some selling costs may vary with the number of orders placed by customers, and so on. It is not always easy to isolate an appropriate measure of volume to use in the planning of a given cost. But the identification of critical relationships is important to the manager for planning. Scatter diagrams, high-low estimates, and regression analysis are useful tools for analyzing cost behavior, but must be used with care. Actual costs will probably differ from planned costs, and predictions of cost behavior based on a single measure of volume may be inaccurate.

Fixed costs are generally described as either discretionary or committed. Discretionary fixed costs, while not variable with volume, are set by managers at planned levels; these levels may be changed on relatively short notice. Committed fixed costs have been set at particular levels by previous decisions that have long-term effects. In general, only future levels of committed costs may be affected by present management.

The relative proportions of fixed and variable costs in the cost structure of a firm can be greatly influenced by management. Although to some extent the proportions are dictated by the nature of the business, in many cases it is possible to do the same job in different ways. Expected sales, potential for variations from expectations, and the attitudes of managers toward risk-return relationships are some of the factors that will influence management decisions in planning a firm's cost structure.

KEY TERMS

avoidable costs
committed fixed cost
cost structure
discretionary fixed cost
high-low method
margin of safety

measure of volume
mixed cost
scatter diagram
step-variable cost
target after-tax profit
unavoidable costs

KEY FORMULAS

Margin of safety = current sales − break-even sales

Sales, in dollars to achieve target after-tax profit of $X $= \dfrac{\text{fixed costs} + [\text{after-tax profit}/(1-\text{tax rate})]}{\text{contribution margin percentage}}$

Total costs = fixed costs + (variable cost per unit of sales × number of units sold)

Total costs = fixed costs + (variable cost as % of sales × dollars of sales)

$$\frac{\text{Variable cost factor}}{\text{in mixed cost}} = \frac{\text{high cost } - \text{ low cost}}{\text{high volume } - \text{ low volume}}$$

$$\frac{\text{Fixed cost portion}}{\text{in mixed cost}} = \frac{\text{total cost at}}{\text{high volume}} - (\text{high volume} \times \text{variable cost factor})$$

REVIEW PROBLEM

The Swanboy Company had the following income statement in 19X2.

Sales (100,000 units at $6)	$600,000
Variable costs (100,000 units at $3.60)	360,000
Contribution margin (100,000 units at $2.40)	240,000
Fixed costs	180,000
Profit before taxes	60,000
Income taxes at 30%	18,000
Net income	$ 42,000

Required

1. The income tax rate is expected to rise to 40% in 19X3. Determine the dollar sales required to earn $42,000 after taxes in 19X3.
2. The firm expects sales of $660,000 (110,000 units) for the next several years. The firm currently rents machinery that can be returned to its owner at any time. If the machinery were returned the firm would save $20,000 in fixed costs per year. However, variable costs would increase to $3.80 per unit. Would it be wise to stop using the machinery?
3. The firm operates several stores in a single city. One of the stores is expected to show the following annual results for the next few years.

Sales (10,000 units)		$60,000
Variable costs		36,000
Contribution margin		24,000
Fixed costs:		
Salaries	$15,500	
Rent	6,000	
Insurance and utilities	2,000	
Miscellaneous	3,000	26,500
Loss before taxes		($ 2,500)

The firm has a 10-year lease on the space occupied by the store and the lease cannot be canceled. Determine the change that would occur in the firm's total profit before taxes if the store were closed.

Answers to Review Problem

1. $625,000. The required profit *before* taxes is $70,000, which is $42,000/60%. The required pre-tax profit of $70,000 plus fixed costs of $180,000 gives $250,000 required contribution margin,

and $250,000 divided by the contribution margin percentage of 40% ($240,000/$600,000) gives $625,000. Alternatively, because the firm needs $10,000 more pre-tax profit to get the same after-tax profit, it needs $10,000 additional contribution margin as well as $25,000 additional sales ($10,000/40% = $25,000).

2. The proposed arrangement would not benefit the firm. Comparative income statements show that profit before taxes would be $2,000 lower under the proposed arrangement.

	Current Arrangement		Proposed Arrangement	
Sales (110,000 units at $6)	$660,000		$660,000	
Variable costs	396,000	($3.60/unit)	418,000	($3.80/unit)
Contribution margin	264,000	($2.40/unit)	242,000	($2.20/unit)
Fixed costs	180,000		160,000	
Profit before taxes	$ 84,000		$ 82,000	

It is not necessary to consider income taxes here. If profit before taxes is higher under one arrangement, it will also be higher after taxes.

Another way to determine the effect would be to determine whether the decrease in contribution margin would be more than the decrease in fixed costs. At 110,000 units the firm would lose $22,000 in contribution margin (110,000 × $.20) if it stopped using the machinery. This is $2,000 more than the $20,000 saving in fixed costs.

3. The firm's total profit before taxes would drop by $3,500 per year. The $6,000 rent is a committed, unavoidable cost, and the only cost that could not be avoided if the store were closed. The loss for this store would become a loss of $6,000 if the store were closed. An income statement if the store were closed would show no revenues and one cost—the $6,000 rent.

APPENDIX: REGRESSION ANALYSIS

Regression analysis is a technique for fitting a straight line to a set of data. In contrast to the high-low method discussed in the chapter, regression analysis considers multiple observations, not just two. In contrast to the scatter-diagram method, regression analysis fits a mathematically precise line, not one that depends on the judgment of the manager drawing the line to fit the data.

The procedures for fitting a regression line, or developing a regression equation, may seem laborious to you. There are many computer programs available for doing regression analysis, and even some advanced hand calculators can be used to reduce the number of required computations.

Although regression analysis is used in many different situations, our main interest here is in predicting cost behavior—determining the fixed and variable components of a cost given a measure of volume with which the cost is thought to be associated. The first step, then, in using regression analysis is to decide what measure of volume should be used —sales dollars, production in units, number of sales invoices prepared, hours worked by direct laborers. Once a measure of volume has been selected, the procedures for developing the regression equation are relatively mechanical.

Two basic techniques, simple and multiple regression, will be presented in this appendix. Simple regression involves the development of an equation incorporating the relationship between one dependent and one independent variable. Procedures for developing the equation will be explained at some length. Multiple regression involves the development of an equation incorporating the relationship between one dependent and more than one independent variable. Because of the complexity of this approach, its use will not be required in this text and it will be only briefly discussed.

Simple Regression

Procedures.   The developing of a regression equation requires solving two equations simultaneously. These equations, which are given below, are called the *normal equations*.

$$(1) \quad \Sigma\, XY = \Sigma\, Xa + b\,\Sigma\, X^2$$
$$(2) \quad \Sigma\, Y = na + b\,\Sigma\, X$$

where X = measure of volume
Y = cost
a = fixed cost
b = variable cost per unit
n = number of observations
Σ = sum of (e.g., $\Sigma\, X^2$ = sum of the squares of the volumes)

In regression analysis, the letter Y is used to designate the *dependent variable,* the one that we are trying to predict. The letter X is used to designate the *independent variable,* the one that we believe affects the value of the dependent variable. In our applications, Y will usually be total cost, and X will be a measure of volume, like production in units, sales in units or dollars, labor hours worked, or sales invoices processed.

We shall use the following data to illustrate the procedures of regression analysis. Each piece of data—the cost in dollars at the particular volume—is called an observation. In this example, the cost is monthly factory operating cost and the volume is expressed as units of product made during the month.

Month	Units of Production	Total Factory Operating Costs
January	80	$350
February	90	390
March	85	365
April	95	405
May	100	410
June	110	425

The following schedule shows the required calculations.

Month	X	Y	X²	XY
January	80	350	6,400	28,000
February	90	390	8,100	35,100
March	85	365	7,225	31,025
April	95	405	9,025	38,475
May	100	410	10,000	41,000
June	110	425	12,100	46,750
	560	2,345	52,850	220,350

Substituting the appropriate values in the normal equations would give us:

$$(1) \quad 220{,}350 = 560a + 52{,}850b$$
$$(2) \quad\;\; 2{,}345 = \;\;6a + \;\;\;\;560b$$

We have two equations and two unknowns; to determine the values of the unknowns we must use the techniques for solving simultaneous equations. In this case, the most straightforward method is to solve for b first by eliminating a. We can eliminate a by multiplying equation (1) by 6 [the coefficient of a in equation (2)], and equation (2) by 560 [the coefficient of a is equation (1)]. Doing this gives

$$(1) \quad 1{,}322{,}100 = 3{,}360a + 317{,}100b$$
$$(2) \quad 1{,}313{,}200 = 3{,}360a + 313{,}600b$$

Subtracting equation (2) from equation (1) gives

$$8{,}900 = 3{,}500b$$
$$\text{and} \quad \$2.54 = b$$

The value of b, \$2.54, is the slope of the regression equation—the variable component of the cost.

We can now substitute the value for b in either equation and solve for a. We substitute \$2.54 for b in equation 2 and get:

$$2{,}345 = 6a + (560 \times 2.54)$$
$$2{,}345 = 6a + 1{,}422.4$$
$$922.6 = 6a$$
$$\$153.77 = a$$

The fixed component of the cost is \$153.77, the value for a. The formula for total cost is then: total cost = \$153.77 + (\$2.54 × units produced).

Problems and Pitfalls. A basic assumption in using regression analysis is that the data that have been collected are representative; that is, it is assumed that the conditions under which the observations of costs and volumes were assembled were about the same and can be expected to continue. If, in fact, one or more of the observations used in the development of the regression line are not representative of normal conditions, the regression line would not be as useful a prediction tool as desired. This point is best illustrated with an example.

Consider the scatter diagram in Figure 3-8 on page 68. The line shown in the figure represents a regression line developed as a result of all of the observations incorporated in the scatter diagram. Notice that the regression line is somewhat above nearly all of the observations save the one at the far left. The observation is clearly unusual and might best have been ignored in developing the equation. That observation might have been from a month in which the plant was shut down for a considerable period for extensive repair work. The high cost of repairs combined with the low volume of production makes the observation nonrepresentative. Great care must be taken in "throwing out" observations, but if a particular observation occurred for unusual reasons, it is best to ignore it.

FIGURE 3-8

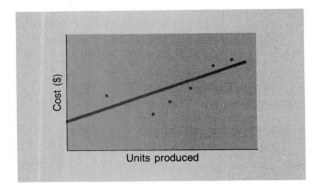

It is not sufficient, when developing data for the purpose of regression analysis, that the observations be representative of the normal conditions of the past. If the regression line is to be helpful in predicting future costs, it is equally important that the significant conditions affecting the cost in the past be the same as those that are to affect the cost in the future. An example of the failure to meet this requirement is illustrated in the scatter diagram in Figure 3-9. The x's are the observations used to develop the regression equation, which is shown in the figure. The o's are observations subsequently made. All of the subsequent observations fall above the regression line, which means that the firm would have consistently predicted its costs at levels below actual costs. One reason for this could be that some changes have taken place from the time of the x's to that of the o's. If the cost that is being predicted is electricity, it could be that an increase in rates has occurred. Thus, the predictions would generally be too low. Or if the cost being predicted is that of raw materials, perhaps material prices have increased or the product now contains more material per unit. These examples are basically the same; they involve changes in the conditions considered to be normal. If the accountant is aware of such changes in conditions as increased electricity rates, he or she could simply develop the equation by using consumption of electricity in killowatt-hours, rather than in dollars. The equation would then describe the use of electricity, not the cost. The new rates could then be applied to the predicted use in order to

FIGURE 3-9

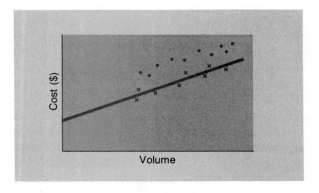

predict the cost. Or more simply, if the cost per kilowatt-hour increased by 10%, the original regression equation could be restated at a 10% higher level for both the fixed and variable components.

One final caution. As is the case with both the high-low and the scatter-diagram methods, the predictions resulting from regression analysis depend for their validity on observations over a particular range of activity, *viz,* the range over which the observations were gathered. Care must be taken in using any of these methods to predict costs for levels of activity not included within the range over which the observations were gathered. For example, if costs of power to operate machines have been analyzed in a range from 500 to 800 hours of machine time per week, there is no reason to assume that the relationships that held over that range will hold also at, say, 350 hours or 1,100 hours.

Correlation and association. Even the sophistication of regression analysis will not ensure completely accurate prediction of costs. As we saw in the chapter, some costs plotted against a particular measure of volume are scattered all over, and there seems to be no association of the cost and the measure of volume. A regression line can be fitted to any set of data no matter how widely dispersed the observations. Hence, the development of a regression equation does not tell us whether the equation will give reliable predictions. There are some statistical procedures that can be used to determine the reliability of the predictions; the results of applying these procedures are measures of the dispersion of the observations around the regression line. One widely used measure is called the correlation coefficient, which measures the extent to which two variables are associated. We will not discuss the derivation of any of these various measures, but we will describe one of them and illustrate its significance in analysis.

Standard error of the estimate. The standard error of the estimate is a number that indicates the extent to which the observations deviate from the regression line. The lower the number, the more accurate predictions are likely to be because the ''spread'' of the observations is relatively narrow. Under certain conditions having to do with statistical normality, which we shall simply assume, about 68% of the observations will fall within one standard error and about 95% within two standard errors. The significance of these relationships for cost analysis is that they provide a range of probability that the accountant can use.

For example, suppose that the regression line for total manufacturing costs is $234,000 + ($3.50 × units produced) and the standard error is $23,000. The accountant can be fairly confident that predictions of total costs will be within $23,000 68% of the time, $46,000 95% of the time. Thus, if production is 100,000 units, the predicted cost would be $584,000 ($234,000 + $350,000) and the accountant would be confident that the actual cost would be between $561,000 ($584,000 − $23,000) and $607,000 ($584,000 + $23,000) 68% of the time. He or she would also be confident that the range would be between $538,000 ($584,000 − $46,000) and $630,000 ($584,000 + $46,000) 95% of the time.

Multiple Regression

Many times there is more than one major factor that significantly influences a cost. In such cases the use of multiple regression analysis is helpful. Multiple regression analysis is essentially a technique for fitting a least-squares line when two or more independent variables are present. Multiple regression analysis would be helpful in situations like the following.

A firm operates a large factory. Its factory overhead costs are not associated with any single measure of volume such as units produced. Instead, there are a fixed component and variable components related to three different aspects of factory operations: (1) units produced; (2) direct labor hours worked; (3) machine-hours. There could be many reasons for these three measures having significant effects on overhead costs. Some costs, like packaging material, would be related to the quantity of product. When units are produced they are also packaged. Some overhead costs are related to direct labor hours, such as fringe benefits like pensions. And some costs, such as lubricants and power, would be related to machine-hours.

A multiple regression equation has the following general form:

$$Y = a + b_1X_1 + b_2X_2 + b_3X_3 \ldots b_nX_n$$

where

Y = the dependent variable to be predicted
$X_1 \ldots X_n$ = the values of the various independent variables influencing the value of Y
$b_1 \ldots b_n$ = the coefficients of the various independent variables

Suppose that a manager has performed multiple regression analysis using data from the last several months and has found the following:

Fixed component	$20,000 per month (a)
Variable components:	
Units produced (X_1)	$1.50 per unit ($b_1$)
Direct labor hours (X_2)	$6.00 per hour ($b_2$)
Machine-hours (X_3)	$ .80 per hour (b_3)

Now suppose that in July the firm has the following results:

Units produced	8,000
Direct labor hours	15,000
Machine-hours	8,000

The predicted cost would be determined using the following equation:

Cost = $20,000 + ($1.50 × 8,000) + ($6.00 × 15,000) + ($.80 × 8,000)

= $20,000	+	**$12,000**	+	$90,000	+	$6,400
fixed		**variable with units produced**		variable with direct labor hours		variable with machine-hours

= $128,400

All of the cautions associated with simple regression apply here also. In summary, it is important that observations used in development of the regression equation be representative of the conditions expected to prevail in the periods when the equation is to be used for predictive purposes.

ASSIGNMENT MATERIAL

Questions for Discussion

3-1 Cost classification   For each of the following items of cost, indicate whether it is likely to be discretionary or committed. If in doubt, describe the circumstances under which the cost would fall into one or the other category. If the cost is mixed, consider only the fixed portion.

(a) Straight-line depreciation on building.
(b) Sum-of-years-digits depreciation on a machine.
(c) Salaries of salespeople.
(d) Salaries of president and vice-presidents for production, sales, and finance.
(e) Research and product development.
(f) Advertising.
(g) Fee for annual audit.
(h) Fees for consultants on long-range planning.
(i) Utilities for factory—heating and lighting.
(j) Repairs and maintenance.
(k) Management development costs—costs of attending seminars, training programs, etc.

3-2 Changes in cost factors   In the 1972 annual report of PPG Industries, the following paragraph appears.

> Emphasis on increased productivity at all manufacturing facilities resulted in increased labor efficiency. Productivity will continue to receive attention to offset, in part, rising energy costs and increased investment in environmental control at plant locations.

What effects do you think the changes described would have on variable and fixed costs?

3-3 Types of fixed costs   Refer to Problem 2-36. Is the rental of the new freezer equipment a discretionary or a committed cost?

3-4 Cost classification   Analyze each of the following statements, explaining what is wrong with it.

(a) The controller of a firm tells you that he uses the units-of-production method for depreciation of machinery and that depreciation is therefore a variable cost for his firm, not a committed fixed cost.
(b) The same controller tells you that his firm nearly always operates at full capacity and that therefore all fixed costs are committed because they cannot be reduced.
(c) A sales manager tells you that without salespeople the firm cannot operate and that therefore salespeople's salaries are committed fixed costs.

(d) Another controller says that if committed costs are those necessarily incurred because the firm is in business, there are no such costs because the firm could reduce its costs to zero by simply closing up.

3-5 Misconceptions about cost behavior and analysis Comment on each of the following statements, pointing out the misconceptions.

(a) "All right, variable costs are the same per unit, while fixed costs change as activity changes. Therefore, variable costs are fixed and fixed costs are variable."

(b) "Advertising is a variable cost for our firm because we always spend an amount equal to 5% of sales. What could be more 'variable' than that?"

(c) "This 'high-low' method of analyzing cost behavior is no good. I found our total costs last January when we were just starting in business and this past August when we were working three shifts a day to fill some big orders. The formula I got does not help us to predict costs at other levels of activity very well at all."

(d) "Look, buddy, don't tell me about volume-cost-profit analysis. Last year it worked fine, but I know that our selling prices will be higher this year so it won't do us any good this year."

(e) "Fred, you fire that dumb controller. He just told me that we should cut our prices to sell more units. [Expletive deleted], we are already selling below our total cost per unit and reducing prices will result in even bigger losses."

3-6 Managerial Attitudes It is often said that an enterprise's behavior is to a great extent a function of its cost structure. In what way might you say that an enterprise's cost structure is a function of its behavior?

Exercises

3-7 Accuracy of predictions These scatter diagrams show costs plotted against production. Which cost would you be able to predict and plan for more easily? Explain.

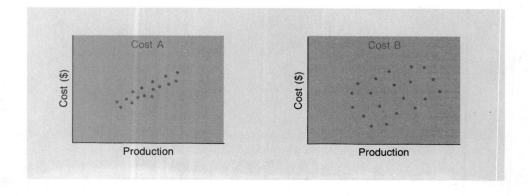

3-8 Mixed costs The president of Krackle Company has asked you to develop a behavioral classification for indirect labor cost. You have the following data available:

Direct Labor Hours	Indirect Labor Cost
8,000	$10,400
12,000	13,600

Required

Compute the fixed and variable portions of indirect labor cost based on direct labor hours.

3-9 Cost estimation A study of the office supplies used in the regional sales offices of a large manufacturer shows that the cost is semivariable. A record of sales and corresponding supply costs in one of the offices is as follows:

Monthly Sales	Cost of Supplies
$42,000	$ 862
48,000	928
36,000	826
52,000	972
38,000	828
39,000	829
45,000	895
55,000	1,035
50,000	950

Required

Determine the variable cost rate and the fixed costs using the high-low point method.

3-10 Basic relationships Fill in the blanks.

Case	Selling Price per Unit	Variable Cost per Unit	Fixed Costs	Break-even Point
1	—	$ 72	$ 24,000	8,000 units
2	$ 12	—	94,000	23,500
3	26	18	—	12,500
4	112	105	119,000	———

3-11 "I lose money on every unit, but I make it up on volume." This statement can sometimes be heard in a discussion among businessmen. Assume the following facts: In 19X5 the firm sold 10,000 units at $5 each, showing a net loss of $10,000; in 19X6 the firm sold 30,000 units at $5 each and made a profit of $30,000.

Required

1. Prepare income statements for the two years, analyzing the cost structure using the high-low method.
2. Explain the fallacy in the quotation that heads this problem.

3-12 Relationships among variables Answer the questions for each of the following situations, considering each part independently.

1. Income is $20,000, fixed costs are $40,000, and contribution margin per unit is $12.
   (a) What are sales in units?
   (b) If variable costs are $8 per unit, what is the selling price per unit?
2. Sales are $100,000, return on sales is 20%, and contribution margin is 40% of sales.
   (a) What are variable costs in total?
   (b) What are fixed costs?
   (c) If income is $2 per unit, what are variable costs per unit?
   (d) If income is $2 per unit, what is the selling price per unit?
3. Income is $50,000, fixed costs are $70,000, and sales are $300,000.
   (a) What are variable costs as a percentage of sales?
   (b) If sales increase by $40,000, by how much will contribution margin increase?
   (c) If sales increase by $40,000, by how much will income increase?
4. Income is $20,000 and contribution margin is $100,000.
   (a) By how much will income increase if sales increase by 20%?
   (b) What will income be if sales decline 10% from the current level?
   (c) What will income be if sales decline 30% from the current level?
5. Sales are $60,000, income is $10,000, and contribution margin is $20,000.
   (a) If 10,000 units were sold, what was the variable cost per unit?
   (b) If selling price decreased $1 and volume increased to 12,000 units, what would income be?

3-13 Relationships and taxes Considering each situation below independently, answer the questions. You may not be able to solve the questions in the order in which they are asked.

1. A firm earned an after-tax income of $15,000 by selling 10,000 units at $12 per unit. The company is subject to an income tax of 40%. Its total contribution margin was $90,000.
   (a) What was the variable cost per unit?
   (b) What were its fixed costs?
2. A firm had an after-tax return on sales of 7½%, net income of $21,000 after a 58% tax, a contribution margin ratio of 45%, and a selling price of $80 per unit.
   (a) How many units did the firm sell?
   (b) What is the variable cost per unit?
   (c) What were the firm's fixed costs?
   (d) What was the total contribution margin?
3. A firm experienced a 15% increase in net income when it increased its sales by 10% from 15,000 units to 16,500 units. Income taxes at 45% are deducted to arrive at net income. Net income was $63,250 at sales of 16,500 units. Variable cost per unit is $15.
   (a) What is the selling price per unit?
   (b) What were the firm's fixed costs?
   (c) What were the income taxes at sales of 15,000 units?
   (d) What was the total contribution margin at sales of 16,500 units?

3-14 Cost behavior graphs (AICPA adapted) Graphs and descriptions of cost elements are given below. For each description, select the letter of the graph that best shows the behavior of the cost. Graphs may be used more than once. The zero point for each graph is the intersection of the horizontal and vertical axes. The vertical axis represents *total* cost for the described cost and the horizontal axis represents production in units. Be prepared to discuss any assumptions you might have to make in selecting your answers.

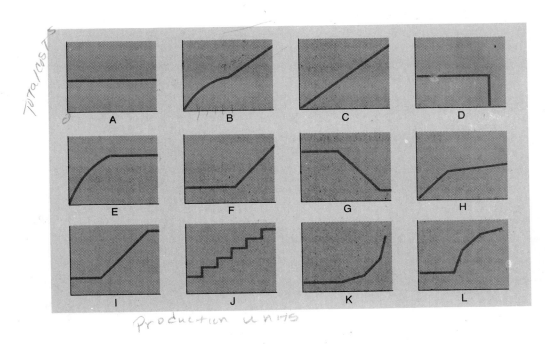

1. Depreciation of equipment, where the amount of depreciation charged is computed by the units-of-production method.
2. Electricity bill, a flat fixed charge plus a variable cost after a certain number of kilowatt-hours are used.
3. City water bill, which is computed as follows:

First 1,000,000 gallons or less	$1,000 flat fee
Next 10,000 gallons	.003 per gallon used
Next 10,000 gallons	.006 per gallon used
Next 10,000 gallons	.009 per gallon used
etc., etc., etc.	

4. Cost of lubricant for machines, where cost per unit decreases with each pound of lubricant used (for example, if one pound is used, the cost is $10.00; if two pounds are used, the cost is $19.98; if three pounds are used, the cost is $29.94; with a minimum cost per pound of $9.25).
5. Depreciation of equipment, where the amount is computed by the straight-line method.
6. Rent on a factory building donated by the city, where the agreement calls for a fixed fee payment unless 200,000 man-hours are worked, in which case no rent need be paid.
7. Salaries of repairmen, where one repairman is needed for every 1,000 hours of machine-hours or less (i.e., 0 to 1,000 hours requires one repairman, 1,001 to 2,000 hours requires two repairmen, etc.).
8. Federal unemployment compensation taxes for the year, where the labor force is constant in num-

ber throughout the year and the average annual wage is $6,000 per worker. The tax is levied only on the first $4,500 earned by each employee.

9. Rent on production machinery, where the rental charge is computed as follows:

First 10,000 hours of use	$20,000 flat fee
Next 2,000 hours of use	$1.90 per hour
Next 2,000 hours of use	$1.80 per hour
Next 2,000 hours of use	$1.70 per hour
etc., etc., etc.	

10. Rent on a factory building donated by the county, where agreement calls for rent of $100,000 less $1 for each hour laborers worked in excess of 200,000 hours, but a minimum rental payment of $20,000 is required.

3-15   Determining volume-cost-profit relationships   The Rinestone Company has a break-even point of 200,000 units and would earn $80,000 profit at 240,000 units.

Required: Fill in as many blanks as you can. Warning: Not all can be answered.
1. Selling price per unit $_____ .
2. Variable cost per unit $_____ .
3. Contribution margin per unit $_____ .
4. Fixed costs $_____ .
5. Profit at sales of 250,000 units $_____ .

3-16   Revenue and cost analysis—high-low method   The controller of your firm is attempting to develop volume-cost-profit relationships to be used for planning and control. He is not sure how this might be done and asks your assistance. He has prepared two income statements from monthly data.

	September	October
Sales	$30,000	$40,000
Cost of goods sold	18,000	24,000
Gross profit	12,000	16,000
Operating expenses:		
Selling expenses	6,000	6,600
Administrative expenses	4,000	4,700
Total expenses	10,000	11,300
Income	$ 2,000	$ 4,700

Required

1. Determine the fixed and variable components of cost of goods sold, selling expenses, and administrative expenses.
2. Prepare an income statement based on sales of $50,000.

3-17   Profit determination   Suppose that for a given company the contribution margin is $2 per unit and the firm has a target profit of $52,000 before income taxes. Fixed costs are $40,000.

Required

1. How many units must be sold to achieve the target profit?
2. Suppose that the firm pays income taxes of 40% of before-tax income. How many units must be sold to achieve an after-tax profit of $48,000?

3. If the selling price is $5 per unit, what must dollar sales be to obtain an after-tax profit of $30,000?

3-18   Cost behavior   The graph below depicts the costs experienced by Ristlimp Enterprises.

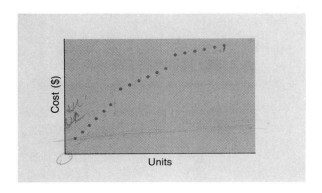

Required

1. Give some possible reasons for the observed behavior of costs.
2. How would you plan for costs that exhibited this type of behavior?

3-19   Interpretation of data   The scatter diagram shown below was used by your assistant to separate maintenance expenses into the fixed and variable components. The equation he derived is: monthly total cost = $350 + ($.80 × machine-hours), which is represented by the line drawn on the diagram.

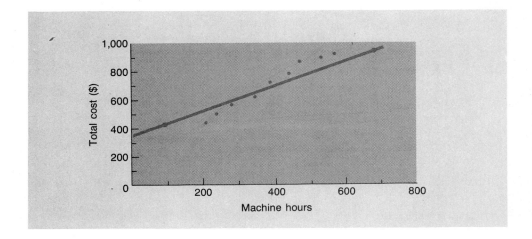

Required

Comment on the way in which your assistant fitted the line to the data and make an alternative recommendation.

3-20 Relationships among volume, costs, and profit   The Daleby Company had income of $25,000 at a volume of $150,000 and $55,000 at a volume of $200,000 in recent months.

Required

1. What are variable costs as a percentage of sales dollars?
2. How much are fixed costs?
3. What is the contribution margin percentage?
4. What volume is required for profit of $85,000?
5. If the firm pays a 40% income tax, what volume is required to earn $81,000 after taxes?
6. If contribution margin is $3 per unit, what are variable costs per unit?
7. If 60,000 units are sold, what will profits be (a) before taxes? (b) after taxes?

3-21 Cost analysis   John Grim, the president of the Grim Company, has asked for your assistance. He shows you the following income statements for two recent months.

	April	May
Sales	$150,000	$135,000
Cost of goods sold	80,000	74,000
Gross profit	70,000	61,000
Selling, general, and administrative expenses	40,000	37,000
Income before taxes	30,000	24,000
Provision for income taxes (40%)	12,000	9,600
Net income	$ 18,000	$ 14,400

Mr. Grim wonders why his profits fell by 20% from April to May when the decline in sales was only 10%. He expects sales of $180,000 in June and is concerned about the probable profit.

Required

1. Explain why profits fell by 20% when sales dropped by only 10%.
2. What profit should be expected if sales are $180,000? (You may assume that the tax rate is a constant 40%.)

3-22 Contribution margin statements, taxes

	Unit Selling Price	Unit Variable Cost	Fixed Costs	Unit Sales
1.	$10	$ 6	$ 3,000	2,000
2.	20	14	36,000	9,000
3.	12	4	220,000	31,000
4.	16	6	230,000	27,000

Required

1. Prepare income statements for each situation above, assuming a 40% income tax rate.
2. Determine the sales, in units, required to double the after-tax income that you computed for each situation.

3-23 Cost behavior—regression analysis (related to Appendix)   The following data have been collected for the purpose of determining the behavior of factory costs.

Month	Units Produced	Factory Costs
January	80	$1,300
February	110	1,640
March	70	1,120

Required

1. Determine the fixed and variable components of factory costs using the high-low method.
2. Repeat, using regression analysis.

3-24 Changes in cost structure The Manfred Company produces a single product that has variable production costs of $6 per unit. The production manager has been approached by a salesperson from a machinery maker. The salesperson offers a machine that will be rented for five years on a noncancelable lease at $24,000 per year. The production manager expects to save $.40 per unit in variable manufacturing costs if the machine is used.

Required

1. Determine the number of units that must be produced per year to make renting the machine and continuing with current operations yield the same profit to the firm.
2. Suppose that the expected volume is 80,000 units per year. Determine the change in the firm's annual profit that would occur if the machine were to be rented.
3. Would you be more likely or less likely to rent the machine if the lease were cancelable at your option rather than noncancelable for a five-year period? Explain your answer.

3-25 Fixed costs and decisions The Patterson Company operates a chain of hardware stores in a single metropolitan area. Each store has a manager, several salespersons, and a clerk or two. The vice president of the firm has been reviewing the performance of individual stores and is considering closing the Middleton store. The income statement for that store shows the following for 19X7 and future results are expected to be about the same.

Middleton Store
Income Statement for 19X8

Sales		$500,000
Cost of sales	$350,000	
Salaries	85,000	
Commissions, 10% of sales	50,000	
Rent on building	20,000	
Rent on store equipment	4,000	
Miscellaneous expenses	7,000	516,000
Net loss		($ 16,000)

If the Middleton store were closed, all personnel would be transferred to other stores. The firm is opening several new stores and would have to hire additional people even if the ones from the Middleton store are transferred. The miscellaneous expenses are fixed, but are avoidable if the store is closed.

Required

1. Assume that the rentals on building and equipment are for leases that have 12 years to run. The Patterson Company has no other use for the building and equipment and could not sublease to another firm. Determine whether the store should be closed.

2. Assume that the rentals are on month-to-month leases so that they can be canceled at any time. Determine whether the store should be closed.
3. Assume that the rentals are unavoidable, as in part 1. The Middleton store has been losing business because the firm has two newer stores relatively close by. The vice president believes that if the Middleton store were closed, the firm would find sales in its other stores increasing by $100,000 per year. The cost of sales and commissions, as percentages of sales dollars, are the same in all of the firm's stores. Fixed costs in the other stores would not be affected by the increases in sales. Determine whether the Middleton store should be closed.

Problems

3-26 Pricing and return on investment   The Backward Company has the following basic cost structure:

Fixed costs	$110,000 per year
Variable costs	$4 per unit

Over the years, the firm has been able to sell 90,000 units annually. The sales manager estimates that sales for the coming year will be the same.

The stockholders have $525,000 invested in the business and expect a profit of 8% on their investment. Income taxes are 40%.

Required

What price must the firm charge for its product if it is to realize its profit objective?

3-27 Planning step-variable costs   The Schumpet Company's purchasing department hires clerks as they are needed, and because the firm is growing there has never been a layoff of clerks. It takes one clerk to process 200 purchase orders per week. Clerks are paid $180 per week.

Required

1. Prepare three different formulae for planning clerical costs as volume changes. (You may wish to set up a chart of behavior of the cost from 200 to 2,000 orders per week.)
2. Using each of the methods in 1 above, compute the variance had 1,840 orders been processed.

3-28 High-low method, income taxes   Your assistant has prepared two income statements for your firm, McKenzie Company, at your request.

	February	*March*
Sales	$260,000	$220,000
Cost of sales	104,000	88,000
Gross profit	156,000	132,000
Operating expenses	76,000	72,000
Income before taxes	80,000	60,000
Income taxes at 40% rate	32,000	24,000
Net income	$ 48,000	$ 36,000

Required

1. Determine the fixed and variable components of each cost element, including income taxes.
2. Explain why income tax expense displays the behavior it does.

3-29 Negative fixed costs   The following costs and activity have been observed for the Kooper Company:

Month	Direct Labor Hours	Overhead Costs
1	2,200	$3,590
2	2,500	4,210
3	2,800	4,830
4	2,300	3,780
5	3,100	5,400
6	3,200	5,650

Required

1. Find the fixed and variable components of overhead costs using either a scatter diagram or regression analysis.
2. Does the pattern make sense to you? Is it possible to have negative fixed costs? Can you suggest an explanation?
3. How would you handle the negative fixed cost for planning purposes?

3-30 Cost behavior—average costs   At a dinner meeting of a local association of company accountants, the following conversation took place.

Ruth Hifixed: "My firm has enormous fixed costs, and volume is our critical problem. My cost per unit is now $6, at 100,000 units, but if I could get 200,000 units, cost per unit would drop to $4. My selling price is also too low, only $6."

Jim Lofixed: "You are lucky. My cost per unit is $5 at 200,000 units, but we cannot produce any more than 200,000. At least we are now better off than we used to be when sales were 80,000 units. At that volume we lost $.50 per unit at our selling price of $6. We were fortunate in being able to keep the same selling price at all volumes."

Required

1. Compute the profit being earned by each firm at its current level of sales.
2. Determine the fixed costs and variable cost per unit and the contribution margin per unit for each firm.
3. Compute the break-even point for each firm.
4. Which firm would earn more at 150,000 units?
5. Which firm would earn more at 100,000 units?
6. Does the way in which each controller describes his or her cost behavior help or hinder analysis of the firm?

3-31 Cost analysis   In conversation with the president of Hirsch Industries, you hear the following: "We employ 40 skilled workers and guarantee them 80 hours of work per month even if production is insufficient to keep them busy. When we crank up production beyond a 40-hour week for all of our employees, we work overtime and pay $6 per hour instead of the usual $4. Each of our workers produces two units of product per hour."

Required

1. Determine the firm's total labor cost at the following monthly volumes of production in units. Assume that a month has four weeks.
   (a) 5,000
   (b) 6,000
   (c) 7,000

(d) 10,000
(e) 14,000
(f) 16,000

2. Draw a line that represents the firm's labor costs, with clearly marked points on the horizontal axis for the volumes where the cost behavior changes.
3. What is the range, if any, over which labor cost per unit behaves like a true variable cost?

3-32 Cost per unit   The controller of the Sclaff Company tells you the following: "I am producing and selling at 60% of capacity and sales are $504,000. At this level of activity my fixed costs are $2 per unit, contribution margin is $2 per unit, and variable costs are $4 per unit."

Required: Fill in the blanks.

1. Selling price is $_____ .
2. Total fixed costs are $_____ .
3. Income at 60% of capacity is $_____ .
4. Sales at capacity are $_____ .
5. Total variable costs at capacity are $_____ .
6. Income at capacity would be $_____ .
7. Profits at 80% of capacity would be $_____ .
8. If fixed costs were reduced by 30% and variable costs increased by 20%, break-even sales would be $_____ .
9. Assuming the same facts as in 8, profits (a) at 80% of capacity would be $_____, and (b) at capacity would be $_____ .

3-33 Volume-cost-profit analysis—changes in variables   The Gemstone Company sells a single product. During a recent month it had the following income statement.

Sales (10,000 units)		$100,000
Variable costs		
Purchase price	$60,000	
Sales commissions		
(10% of sales dollars)	10,000	
Total variable costs		70,000
Contribution margin		30,000
Fixed costs		20,000
Income		$ 10,000

In the following month the firm reduced its selling price to $9 per unit and showed the following results.

Sales (12,000)		$108,000
Variable costs		
Purchase price	$72,000	
Sales commissions	10,800	
Total variable costs		82,800
Contribution margin		25,200
Fixed costs		20,000
Income		$ 5,200

The president is unhappy with the results and has some difficulty in understanding them. He asks you, "Why did contribution margin decrease by 16% when sales increased by 8%? I thought that contribution margin increased at the same percentage rate as sales."

Required: Explain why contribution margin decreased when sales increased.

3-34 Volume-cost-profit analysis for an airline Icarus Airlines flies a number of routes in the southwestern United States. The firm owns six airplanes, each of which can hold 150 passengers. All routes are about the same distance, and all fares are $55 one way. The line is obligated to provide 200 flights per month. Each flight costs $4,000 for gasoline, crew salaries, and so on. Variable costs per passenger are $5, to cover a meal and a head tax imposed for each passenger at every airport to which Icarus flies. Other costs, all fixed, are $40,000 per month.

Required

1. How many passengers must be carried on 200 flights to earn a $20,000 per month profit? What percentage of capacity does this number represent?
2. If the firm could cut its flights to 150 per month, what would be the number of passengers required to earn $20,000 per month? What percentage of capacity would this number represent (using 150 flights as capacity)?
3. Is the $4,000 per flight cost fixed or variable?
4. What is the chief problem faced by an airline or other firm with a similar cost structure?

3-35 Committed versus discretionary cost The Gladack Company makes a number of products and uses a great deal of machinery. A new product this coming year will require the acquisition of a new machine. The machine can only be leased, not purchased. There are two alternative leasing arrangements: (1) a month-to-month lease that can be canceled on 30 days' notice by either the Gladack Company or the lessor, at a monthly rental of $6,000; and (2) a five-year noncancelable lease at $5,200 per month. The new product is expected to have a life of five years, during which annual revenues will be $250,000, annual variable costs $100,000. There are no new fixed costs other than the lease payments. The president is concerned that the five-year lease removes a great deal of flexibility: if the product does not pan out as expected, the company is stuck with the machine and there are no other uses for it. He is, however, desirous of getting the machine at $5,200 per month.

Required

1. Are the rentals, under each of the alternatives, discretionary or committed fixed costs?
2. Why would the president hesitate between the choices? What could happen to make him regret choosing (a) the five-year lease? (b) the month-to-month lease?
3. Suppose that the firm takes the monthly lease option. It is now the end of the fourth year and management expects that sales of the product will be $90,000 in year five, evenly spread over the year. Should the firm use the machine for the fifth year?
4. Answer 3 again assuming that the firm had signed the five-year lease.

3-36 A concessionaire Bill has the food and drink concessions contract at a local coliseum for a one-year period, and his operation has been profitable for the first four months. He has sold peanuts, popcorn, candy, and various types of drinks. All are sold from ten stands at various locations around the building.

The Skidders Ice Frolic is scheduled for ten straight performances in April. Bill is considering adding Super Hot Dogs to his operations for these performances to determine whether they would be a good item to add to his regular line.

Bill currently pays rent each year at the rate of $100 per performance in which he operates plus 10% of his gross sales. He estimates the following costs relating to the addition of Super Hot Dogs:

(a) For each stand: rent an electric warmer—$2 per performance; extra helper to prepare the hot dogs —$10 per performance.

(b) For each hot dog: wieners, at $.10; buns, at $.05; napkins and mustard, at $.01.

The coliseum will seat 6,000 people, but a sellout is not expected for performances of Skidders Ice Frolic. Bill is concerned about setting a price and finally decides on a price of $.40 for his new product.

Required

1. What is the contribution margin per unit on his new product?
2. How many hot dogs must be sold in order to break even per performance?
3. What is the variable cost for each hot dog prepared?
4. What would be the profit on hot dogs if Bill could sell 1,000 at the first performance?

3-37 Cost structure   The managers of the Keaton Company are deciding whether to introduce a new automated process. The firm now has the following cost structure:

Variable costs	$9 per unit
Fixed costs	$60,000 per month

Volume has been averaging 20,000 units per month at a selling price of $13. However, volume varies by as much as 8,000 units from the average, both of which extremes are within the relevant range.

If the new process is introduced, variable costs will be reduced to $6 per unit, but fixed costs will increase to $110,000 per month. The relevant range will become 11,000 to 31,000 units. The sales manager is confident that a $1 per-unit price reduction will increase average sales to 25,000 units and also help reduce the wide fluctuations in sales. He thinks that sales would rarely be below 20,000 units and rarely above 30,000.

Required

1. Ignoring the suggestion to lower prices, is the introduction of the new process desirable? Explain and support your answer, describing the relevant factors.
2. Should the price be dropped if—
   (a) the current process is continued?
   (b) the new process is adopted?

3-38 Significance of unit costs   The sales manager of the Seagle Company burst into the office of the controller and exclaimed: "This will cheer you up—we just got a big order from Stanley Industries. The price is less than usual, but it should still be very profitable." The controller morosely looked up and said that he would have to see it to believe it because the sales manager was so eager to make sales that he would give the firm away if no one kept him under control.

After looking at some data the controller told the sales manager that the order was clearly not profitable. He mentioned the following points. The price per unit offered by Stanley Industries was $12, which was less than the firm's average cost per unit of $16, based on current volume of 100,000 units. Thus, even though the sales to Stanley would not affect sales at regular prices, it was obviously unprofitable.

The sales manager said that because the order was for 20,000 units, the cost per unit should be based on 120,000 units, not 100,000. He argued that there were fixed costs included in the unit cost and that these would be reduced if volume increased by 20,000 units. The controller sighed and pulled out his pencil again. He made a few calculations and then said that the cost per unit would indeed drop, but only to $14 which was still above the $12 price being offered. The sales manager shook his head and trudged out of the office. The controller wondered when people would begin to understand that selling below cost was the road to ruin.

Required: Determine the profit or loss that would have occurred had the order been accepted. Comment on the position taken by the controller.

3-39 Loss per unit A firm had a loss of $2 *per unit* when sales were 20,000 units. When sales were 25,000 units the firm had a loss of $1.10 *per unit*.

Required

1. Determine the contribution margin per unit.
2. Determine fixed costs.
3. Determine the break-even point in units.

3-40 Margin of safety The Nelson Wallet Company is considering two new wallets for introduction during the coming year. Because of a lack of production capacity, only one will be brought out. Data on the two wallets are given below.

	Model 440	Model 1200
Expected sales	$200,000	$250,000
Expected contribution margin	60,000 (30%)	150,000 (60%)
Expected fixed costs—for production, advertising, promotion, etc.	39,000	120,000
Expected annual profit	$ 21,000	$ 30,000

Required

1. Determine the margins of safety for each wallet, in dollars and as percentages of expected sales.
2. Suppose that the firm is relatively conservative; its top managers do not like to take significant risks unless the potential profits are extremely high. Which wallet would you recommend be introduced? Why?

3-41 Cost structure The Wink Company manufactures replacement parts for automobiles and sells them to distributors in the northeastern United States. The president of the firm wishes to begin selling in the Southeast, but is uncertain how to expand most profitably. Two alternatives have been selected for final consideration. Under the first, the company would use the services of independent sales representatives who would sell to distributors for a 15% commission. This plan would increase the clerical costs at the company's central office by $20,000 per year. Under the second alternative, the company would hire its own salespeople to work on straight salary. It is estimated that salaries for salespeople would be $100,000 per year; additionally, an office would be opened in the region and would cost $25,000 per year to operate.

The variable cost on parts is now 35%. The president is uncertain about demand in the Southeast and wants you to prepare analyses of profitability under both plans at various volumes. He selects $500,000, $700,000, $1,000,000, and $1,200,000 as the sales volumes to be used for comparison.

Required

1. Prepare the requested analyses.
2. Which alternative would you recommend and why? What nonquantified factors are related to the alternatives?
3. Suppose that variable costs on parts were 65%. Which alternative would you recommend and why?

3-42 Alternative revenue-cost situations The variable cost of producing a textbook is based on the number printed at a single time. Variable costs for a press run of 5,000 copies are $3.50 per copy; for a run of 10,000 are $3.20, and for a run of over 10,000 are $3. The fixed cost is $15,000 for typesetting and setup of the presses. The book will be sold for $8. Unsold copies are sold as waste paper for $.50 each.

Required

1. What will profit on the book be if—
    (a) 10,000 are printed, 6,000 sold at regular prices?
    (b) 5,000 are printed and sold?
    (c) 15,000 are printed and 6,000 sold at regular prices?
    (d) 12,000 are printed and 9,000 sold at regular prices?
2. If the firm had 10,000 printed, but could have sold 15,000, how much profit was lost because the additional 5,000 were not printed?
3. Can you determine the break-even point for the textbook? If not, explain why. What information do you need to determine a break-even point? (Hint: Make a chart showing the behavior of costs up to 15,000 books printed in a single run.)

3-43 **Pricing policy, relevant range, lost sales**   The Portland Visigoths, an expansion team in the Constellation Football League, are now playing their home games in Municipal Stadium. The stadium seats 35,000. The Visigoths play ten games, including four exhibition games, during the season at home. Tickets are priced at $10 and variable costs are $4 per ticket sold, most of which is the payment to the visiting team.

A major supermarket chain in the area has offered to buy 2,000 tickets for each game at $6. The chain will sell the tickets as part of a promotional campaign to customers who accumulate food purchases of $100. The manager of the Visigoths estimates that about half of these 2,000 tickets will be sold by the chain to the people who would attend the game anyway. This fact worries him particularly. He estimates that attendance for the coming season, without special sales, would be as follows:

Number of Games	Paid Attendance
2	35,000
4	33,000
4	30,000

Required

1. What is the total expected contribution margin without the special sale to the supermarket chain?
2. What is the expected total contribution margin if the offer from the chain is accepted?
3. What should the Visigoths do?
4. Would your answer to 3 be different if all 2,000 tickets for each game were to be sold to people who would not otherwise attend the game?

3-44 **Volume-cost-profit analysis**   The Acme Foam Rubber Company buys large pieces of foam rubber (called "loaves") and cuts them into small pieces that are used in seat cushions and other products. A loaf contains 5,000 board feet of foam rubber (a "board foot" is one foot square and one inch thick), of which 10% becomes scrap during the process of cutting up the loaf. A loaf costs $700, including freight, and the firm is currently processing 100 loaves per month.

The firm charges $.22 per board foot for its good output, $.07 per board foot for the scrap. Variable costs of cutting the loaf are $100, for labor and power to run the cutting machines. Fixed costs are $18,000 per month.

The president of the firm has asked for your assistance in developing volume-cost-profit relationships.

Required

1. Determine the firm's income when it processes 100 loaves per month.

2. Determine the firm's break-even point expressed as number of loaves processed.
3. The president tells you that your analyses in parts 1 and 2 are not what he had in mind. He says that he is accustomed to thinking in terms of board feet of good output sold. He would like to know how many board feet he would have to sell to earn $6,000 per month. Determine the firm's contribution margin per board foot of good output sold and sales required to earn $6,000 per month.

Cases

3-45 Regression analysis and managerial judgment (related to Appendix) Your firm has just hired a recent graduate of the state university. His first assignment was to prepare a regression equation to be used for predicting total factory overhead costs. The equation he developed is: total cost = $110,328 + $4.40X, where X is the number of units produced. The equation is based on the following observations.

Month	Unit Production	Total Overhead Cost
April	9,000	$146,000
May	10,000	151,000
June	12,000	164,000
July	14,000	178,000
August	3,000	130,000
September	8,000	140,000
October	11,000	156,000
November	13,000	170,000

Other data developed were as follows:

Sum of production ΣX	80,000
Sum of costs ΣY	1,235,000
Sum of squared production ΣX^2	884,000,000
Sum of cost × production ΣXY	12,720,000,000

Required

1. Plot the observations on a scatter diagram.
2. Discuss the equation computed by the new person. Would you make any changes or offer an alternative? If so, what would be your choice for an equation?

3-46 Measures of volume The controller of the Throckton Company has been to a seminar on volume-cost-profit analysis and wishes to use some of the techniques he learned. He has given you the following data and requests that you develop analyses of each cost into its fixed and variable components. He plans to use the information you develop in the profit planning of the firm. You prepare the following schedules of costs and measures of volume for the previous six months.

Sales	Labor Hours	Production Costs	Selling Expenses	Administrative Expenses
$12,000	500	$ 9,100	$3,250	$3,200
10,000	700	11,000	2,980	3,300
21,000	1,200	14,300	4,130	4,100
30,000	1,300	15,300	4,950	4,500
33,000	900	11,980	5,370	4,300
35,000	800	11,200	5,560	4,800

Required

Analyze the cost behavior patterns in accordance with the request of the controller. Indicate weaknesses and suggest possible improvement.

3-47   Volume-cost-profit analysis for a zoo   The Camp Worth Zoo has been operated by the city of Camp Worth for many years. No admission fees have ever been charged for entry to the zoo grounds, but several attractions on the grounds, such as the reptile house, do have a small admission charge. There are also rides and other amusements, food, and souvenir concessions. The income statement for the past year for the zoo is given below.

Camp Worth Zoo
Income Statement for 19X3

Revenues from special exhibits and concessions	$ 450,000
Operating costs, all fixed	1,000,000
Net loss	($ 550,000)

The Camp Worth City Council is reviewing the financial requirements for the city for the coming year, and several members are particularly disturbed by the large deficit in the operations of the zoo. One member of the council has proposed that admission charges of $1 for adults and $.50 for children be instituted in order to make the zoo self-supporting. The councilman points out that in 19X3 300,000 adults and 900,000 children toured the zoo and that if these persons had paid the proposed charges there would have been a profit for the year.

In rebuttal, a councilwoman states that attendance would fall considerably if the charges were to be levied, and that the zoo, as a public attraction and source of pride for the city, should be kept free. She points to the experience of a zoo in another city that instituted an admission charge and saw a 40% decline in attendance. She argues that the same decline in attendance could be expected in Camp Worth, and that such a decline would also result in a decrease in revenue to the city from exhibits and concessions at the zoo.

Required

1. Prepare an income statement based on instituting the admission fees and considering the argument given against the fee.
2. What do you recommend?

3-48   Unit costs   Mr. Wystop, a relatively outspoken congressman, heads a special committee investigating rising defense expenditures. He is particularly concerned by what he identifies as the gross inefficiencies and bad planning of defense contractors and their failure to develop "realistic" bids for government business. Presently being discussed are the substantial costs billed to the government on a major contract for airplanes. The history of that contract was outlined at a recent committee hearing.

In 19X3, a government agency requested bids from selected contractors for the production and delivery of 2,400 airplanes able to meet certain specifications. No aircraft heretofore developed had the capabilities incorporated in these specifications. The General Model Company prepared an analysis of the costs to develop, produce, and deliver under such a contract, and submitted a bid of $3 million per plane. After careful consideration of all the bids and the histories of the various firms in performing according to government specifications, the agency awarded the contract to the General Model Company. The contract provided for delivery of the planes over an eight-year period.

Subsequent to the awarding of the contract but before the final plans were approved for the production of the planes, the agency determined that the plane it wanted would have to accomplish several objectives different from and in addition to those stated in the initial list of specifications. Accordingly, the agency requested that the company revise its designs and produce several different variations of the first and basic plane. The agency also decided that a total of 1,000 planes would be sufficient to meet its needs, and the contract was adjusted downward in this one respect.

Still later, after some planes of the various types had been delivered, the agency determined that the number of planes it would require was approximately 600. The agency informed the company that when this number had been delivered, the contract would be terminated.

Required

1. What effect would there be on the total cost of the order when the government agency determined that several variations of the same basic plane were necessary?
2. What would be the effect on the total cost per plane as a result of the determination that several variations of the basic plane were required?
3. What would be the effect on the total cost per plane when the agency decided that the total number of planes required would be (a) 1,000 instead of 2,400, and (b) 600 instead of 1,000?
4. Suppose that a six-year period was used by the individual developing the bid for the contract. Ignoring the changes in the contract (specifications and number of planes), of what relevance to the cost per plane is the fact that the contract covered an eight-year period?

CHAPTER 4

ADDITIONAL ASPECTS OF VOLUME-COST-PROFIT ANALYSIS

We have considered the basic classifications of cost behavior and some problems entailed in planning for costs. The planned and the actual results may not coincide for several reasons. This chapter illustrates techniques for analyzing differences between planned and actual profits. It also looks at some problems in volume-cost-profit analysis, with special attention to more realistic situations than those previously considered. Finally, volume-cost-profit analysis is illustrated as a useful planning tool for not-for-profit entities.

ANALYSIS OF RESULTS

A firm's estimation of income derives from sales projections and assumptions about cost behavior. However, it is unlikely that planned and actual results will coincide exactly. Managers must effectively direct and control their operations and will be evaluated on the results; thus methods must be found to assign responsibility for differences between actual and planned results. In this chapter we concentrate on differences in income attributable to selling more or less than planned and to selling at prices different from those planned. Chapter 00 will describe in detail cost variances.

Let us consider a firm that plans to sell 20,000 units at $20 per unit. Variable costs are $12 per unit. Fixed costs are not relevant to this analysis and we shall omit them for simplicity. After the period is over, the firm finds that actual results do not coincide with planned results. More than 20,000 units were sold but the price was not $20 per unit. Total variable costs were higher than planned but were still $12 per unit, as shown in the following schedule.

	Planned	Actual	Difference
Units sold	20,000	21,000	1,000
Sales	$400,000	$399,000	$1,000
Variable costs @ $12 per unit	240,000	252,000	12,000
Contribution margin	$160,000	$147,000	$13,000

Actual contribution margin was 13,000 less than planned, but why? Our task is to determine the extent to which the difference in unit sales contributed to the difference and likewise for the difference in selling price. (Notice that total actual variable costs of $252,000 are equal to 21,000 units at $12 per unit.)

One way to analyze the differences is to prepare an income statement based on the actual sales in units but at the *planned* selling price. This statement will show what the income would have been if the only deviation from plans was the difference between expected and actual sales. Comparing this new income statement with the original plan and the actual results, we will be able to see why the total contribution margin was different from what was planned.

	Planned Results	Actual Volume at Planned Selling Price	Actual Results
Units sold	20,000	21,000	21,000
Sales	$400,000	$420,000	$399,000
Variable costs	240,000	252,000	252,000
Contribution margin	$160,000	$168,000	$147,000
Differences		$8,000	$21,000

The difference between the planned contribution margin ($160,000) and the contribution margin if the actual sales volume had been achieved at the planned selling price ($168,000) is $8,000. That difference is called **sales volume variance**. Had the firm been able to sell 21,000 units and maintain its selling price at $20 it would have earned $8,000 more than planned, which amount is the 1,000 additional units sold times the $8 planned contribution margin per unit. Thus the sales volume variance can also be computed as:

$$\text{Sales volume variance} = \text{planned contribution margin per unit} \times \left(\begin{array}{c} \text{planned sales, in units} \end{array} - \begin{array}{c} \text{actual sales, in units} \end{array} \right)$$

$$\$8,000 = \$8 \times (20,000 - 21,000)$$

If a firm sells more units than planned, this variance is favorable; if fewer units are sold than was planned, the variance is unfavorable. In the example, the variance is favorable.

The difference between the $168,000 contribution margin that would have been earned if the $20 price had been maintained and the actual contribution of $147,000 is due to the fact that the firm sold its product at less than $20 per unit. This difference is called the **sales price variance**. The variance in this case is unfavorable, because the actual selling price was less than planned. Contribution margin was $147,000 but it would have been $168,000 if the price had actually been $20. We can also calculate the sales price variance by determining the actual selling price and multiplying the difference between the actual and planned prices by the actual unit volume. The actual selling price was $19 ($399,000 actual sales/21,000 units).

$$\text{Sales price variance} = \text{units sold} \times (\text{planned price} - \text{actual price})$$

$$\$21,000 = 21,000 \times (\$20 - \$19)$$

In effect, the sales price variance is the difference between planned and actual contribution margin per unit multiplied by the actual number of units sold. Because we are trying to isolate the difference in contribution margin due to the difference in selling prices, we can say that the firm earned only $7 actual contribution margin per unit, which is $19 actual selling price minus $12 variable cost. Changes in selling price are matched by changes in contribution margin per unit, with a decrease in selling price of $1 causing a decrease in contribution margin of the same amount.

A word of caution. An unfavorable variance, either sales price or sales volume, is not necessarily a bad outcome. A firm might deliberately reduce its price in order to sell more units. The total variance in contribution margin is more important than either variance taken separately. This question of pricing policy is discussed in more detail later in the chapter.

MULTIPLE PRODUCTS

A simple situation in which two products were sold was discussed in Chapter 2. Both products had the same contribution margin percentage but different per-unit contribution margins. Most modern firms, however, sell many products with varying contribution margins, both per unit and as percentages. Does this fact destroy the usefulness of volume-cost-profit analysis for such firms? No. First, it is still possible, of course, to use volume-cost-profit analysis for each individual product, or even for groups of products where the contribution margins (either in per-unit amounts or as percentages) are equal. But firm-wide analysis is also possible, providing that the **sales mix** of the different products is generally the same (that is, providing that the various products are usually sold in about the same proportions).

There are several reasons why firms might experience the same sales mix of products. Some products are sold and used together so that the sales of the products are associated. For example, some products are normally sold together, such as tables and chairs, cups and saucers, wallpaper and paste. In other cases, though the products are not always sold together, they are used together, so that the sales of one product influence the sales of the other. Examples of such products would be cameras and film, razors and razor blades, golf clubs and golf balls. These types of products are called **complementary products**.

Even though there may be no apparent relationship among the products of a particular firm, its experience may indicate that the sales mix remains fairly constant. For example, a particular department store may consistently derive 40% of its sales from clothing, 25%

from furniture and housewares, and 35% from all its other departments. These percentages may be relatively constant over time despite the absence of obvious causes.

Where a firm's sales mix is, for whatever reason, relatively predictable, volume-cost-profit analysis is made possible by the use of the weighted average contribution margin percentage.

Weighted Average Contribution Margin Percentage

A weighted average contribution margin percentage is essentially a device for treating a multiple-product firm as if it were a single-product firm. When total sales in dollars are multiplied by the weighted average contribution margin percentage the result should be about equal to the actual contribution margin if the expected sales mix is also the actual sales mix. Let us illustrate the determination and use of a weighted average contribution margin percentage.

Consider a retail store that sells three products: shirts, shoes, and jeans. Sales dollars derived from these products are normally 30% from shirts, 20% from shoes, and 50% from jeans. Prices and variable costs for these products are given below.

	Shirts	Shoes	Jeans
Basic data:			
Selling price	$10	$20	$15
Variable cost	4	10	9
Contribution margin	$ 6	$10	$ 6
Contribution margin percentage	60%	50%	40%

Since a typical dollar of sales will be distributed among the three products in the normal sales mix, that typical dollar will be made up of $.30 from the sale of shirts, $.20 from the sale of shoes, and $.50 from the sale of jeans. Consequently, the contribution margin on a typical dollar of sales can be computed by calculating the contribution margin from the sale of each product and adding the contribution margins together. Hence, the calculation of the weighted average contribution margin would be accomplished as follows:

	Shirts	Shoes	Jeans	Total
Sales	$ .30	$ .20	$ .50	$1.00
Contribution margin percentage	60%	50%	40%	
Contribution margin	$ .18 +	$ .10 +	$ .20 =	$ .48
Weighted average contribution margin ($.48/$1.00)				48%

A more direct approach to this solution would be to deal only with percentages, as follows:

	Shirts	Shoes	Jeans	Total
Contribution margin percentage	60%	50%	40%	
Sales mix	30%	20%	50%	100%
Weighted contribution percentage	18% +	10% +	20% =	48%

If the store predicted that its sales for the coming month were going to be $30,000, it could, using its normal sales mix and sales and cost data, prepare its planned income statement as follows:

	Shirts	Shoes	Jeans	Total
Sales	$9,000	$6,000	$15,000	$30,000
Variable costs	3,600	3,000	9,000	15,600
Contribution margin	$5,400	$3,000	$ 6,000	$14,400

The individual sales figures are the sales mix percentages multiplied by the expected sales of $30,000. The variable cost and contribution margin amounts for the individual products can be derived from the basic cost data, and the total is consistent with the weighted average contribution margin computed above.

Even if a particular firm does not experience a constant sales mix in each period, the weighted average contribution margin developed from planned income statements can be useful in the analysis of actual results. Some firms, for example, may simply forecast sales for each product and build up a planned income statement, by product, for the entire firm. The above income statement could have been the result of such individual forecasts. From this income statement, a weighted average contribution margin of 48% would be determined from the totals (planned total contribution margin of $14,400/planned total sales of $30,000).

The importance of sales mix can be seen if we change the example to reverse the mix percentages of jeans and shirts. Shirts are now 50% of sales and jeans 30%. Recall that jeans have the lowest contribution margin percentage of 40% and shirts the highest at 60%. The new weighted average contribution margin percentage is calculated below.

	Shirts	Shoes	Jeans	Total
Contribution margin percentage (from previous schedule)	60%	50%	40%	
Sales mix percentage	50%	20%	30%	100%
Contribution margin per sales dollar	30% +	10% +	12% =	52%

The new weighted average contribution margin percentage is 52%, four percentage points higher than the 48% shown before. Thus, if the firm could sell relatively more shirts and relatively fewer jeans it would earn a higher contribution margin percentage.

Figure 4-1 shows the volume-cost-profit chart for the firm, assuming that the fixed costs are $10,000 per month. Note that the horizontal axis shows sales in dollars rather than, as was the case in earlier chapters, in units. We cannot use sales in units because we are dealing with three separate products and the cost and revenue lines would depend on which products made up the number of units sold. Two different total cost lines are shown in this chart, to represent two different sales mixes. The dotted line shows the variable cost percentage of 52% of sales, which holds when the weighted average contribution margin percentage is 48% (as originally computed when the sales mix was 30% shirts, 20% shoes, and 50% jeans). The solid line for total cost incorporates a variable cost percentage of 48%,

FIGURE 4-1

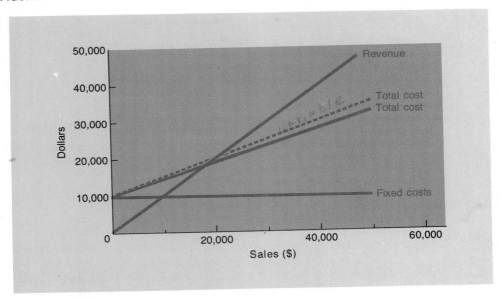

which holds when the weighted average contribution margin is 52% of sales (the second computation, when the sales mix was 50% shirts, 20% shoes, and 30% jeans).

Notice that the break-even point is lower when the contribution margin percentage is 52% than when it is 48%. Note also that at the predicted sales volume of $30,000, the profits are higher when the contribution margin is higher. Both of these results should be expected based on the principles discussed in earlier chapters.

Sales Mix in Units

Some managers may find it more convenient to use a sales mix stated in units rather than in dollars. For example, a maker of tables may find that its three kinds of tables, high-priced, medium-priced, and low-priced, sell in unit ratios of 10%, 30%, and 60%, respectively. That is, for every 10 tables sold, one will be high-priced, three medium-priced, and six low-priced. Suppose that the data relating to each table are as given below.

	High-priced	Medium-priced	Low-priced
Selling price	$300	$180	$100
Variable cost	120	110	60
Contribution margin	$180	$ 70	$ 40

When the mix is stated in units rather than in dollars the easiest way to find the weighted average contribution margin percentage is to develop an income statement for a hypothetical batch of units. In this case 10 units will be used. If the firm sells 10 tables, its income statement will appear as follows.

	High-priced	Medium-priced	Low-priced	Total
Units sold	1	3	6	10
Sales	$300	$540	$600	$1,440
Variable costs	120	330	360	810
Contribution margin	$180	$210	$240	$ 630

The weighted average contribution margin percentage is 43.75% ($630 total contribution margin divided by $1,440 total sales). Using this percentage, the firm can prepare a planned income statement based on its expected sales volume in terms of units.

Overall Planning

Because of historical trends, managers of a multiple-product firm may have some ideas about the expected sales mix and can use the weighted average contribution margin, as discussed above, for planning purposes. It is possible, however, that managers will be able to take some actions that will influence the sales mix. For example, managers may approve expenditures for special advertising campaigns or specific sales promotion plans. Managers can also encourage salespeople to concentrate on certain products, either through direct instructions or through the establishment of special commission plans. When products are complementary, as we discussed on **page 92**, the manager has an additional problem. He must not only plan for volume of one product, but also take into consideration the effects that will be felt on sales of complementary products.

Before proposing any special programs that could influence sales mix, the manager will want to know the basic sales and cost data for each product. From these data, the manager will have some idea of profitability by product and in what way the sales mix might be better. (In general, a "better" mix would be one that has more sales of the higher contribution margin products.) Often managers will study the sales and cost data for the various products and evaluate alternative strategies by assuming different mixes of sales. A technique that is used in this type of study is called **simulation**. Simulation is a computer-assisted process by which a manager provides the computer with various sets of assumptions about sales mix and other factors, and the computer calculates the level of profit or loss for each combination. Alternative assumptions could relate to but are not limited to different selling prices and different sales mixes.

In the planning of the firm's sales mix, managers should be continually evaluating the individual products or product lines. (A **product line** is a group of similar products. An example would be a "hair care" line, which could consist of shampoos, conditioners, colorings, creams, tonics, and restorers. For many types of analysis, the entire line is treated as a single product.) Quite possibly, the firm's products should be reduced or increased in number or, as indicated above, some particular products should be emphasized. When a firm has more than one product (or product line), any analysis of profitability must give special consideration to the nature of the firm's fixed costs. In the next section, we explore further the problem of fixed costs in a multiple-product firm.

Fixed Costs and Multiple Products

In Chapter 3 we introduced the concepts of discretionary and committed fixed costs and suggested that for some purposes the former might be considered as "avoidable" and the latter as "unavoidable." Further refinement and expansion of the concept of avoidability is required in planning and decision making for a multiple-product firm. For proper analysis of a product or product line in such a firm, it is necessary to know not only whether a particular cost is discretionary or committed but also whether it is **separable** or **joint**. A separable fixed cost is one that relates only to a single product or product line. A joint, or common, fixed cost, on the other hand, is one that is related to more than one product or line. (In Chapter 7, we will consider the possibility of separable and joint variable costs.)

To illustrate this new cost distinction and its significance, consider a firm that has two product lines and two factories. From Chapter 3 we are aware that the firm will have, in connection with each of its factories, some fixed costs that are committed (depreciation, etc.) and some that are discretionary (maintenance, etc.). The committed costs are likely to continue until the factory is sold, and some or most of those costs may continue even if the factory is shut down. Now consider the ways in which the factories might be used by this firm. Possibly each factory is devoted to one and only one of the firm's product lines; or, at least one of the factories may be involved in the production (and distribution, or perhaps administration) of both product lines.

If one factory is totally devoted to one of the lines, all of that factory's costs are separable with respect to that product; that is, they relate to that product alone, whether they be discretionary or committed. On the other hand, if one (or both) of the factories is used in connection with both lines, it is inevitable that some of that factory's costs will be joint costs (relating to both product lines). For example, there must be some machines and storage or work areas that are utilized in the production of both types of products, so that neither machinery nor building depreciation could be identified as relating to only one line. These costs would be joint committed fixed costs. Similarly, if there is a sales force associated with this factory, and the sales force is involved in selling both lines, the costs for sales salaries and sales travel would be joint discretionary fixed costs.

The significance of the distinction between joint and separable costs is apparent when the manager attempts to make plans for the future, including giving consideration to whether a particular product line should be dropped. In earlier, simpler examples, it was suggested that a product should be dropped if the contribution margin from it was less than the discretionary fixed costs. When analyzing the profitability of a product or product line, we modify this rule to take into consideration the fact that *some discretionary fixed costs may not be avoidable because they are joint*. If our example firm does have a sales force that markets both product lines, after dropping one line the sales force would still have to make the rounds of its customers, and sales salaries and travel costs would remain essentially the same. So, in analyzing the profitability of one of the company's product lines, these joint discretionary fixed costs are, in a sense, "committed" and as irrelevant as any other committed cost. The costs will remain after the product line is eliminated, and hence should play no part in the decision about whether or not to do away with it.

Exhibit 4-1 presents an income statement by product line suitable for use by a manager in analyzing the relative profitability of the firm's three lines. Avoidable fixed costs are subtracted from the contribution margin of each line, and the joint and committed costs are shown only in the total column. This format highlights what is often called the **product margin**, the amount by which contribution margin from the product is greater or less than the related avoidable fixed costs.

Exhibit 4-1
Davis Department Store
Product Line Income Statement
19X5
(thousands of dollars)

	Clothing	Housewares	Sundries	Total
Sales	$2,400	$1,800	$1,300	$5,500
Variable costs:				
Cost of goods sold	1,050	900	700	2,650
Commissions	240	180	130	550
Other variable costs	150	120	90	360
Total variable costs	1,440	1,200	920	3,560
Contribution margin	960	600	380	1,940
Separable-discretionary fixed costs:				
Salaries and expenses of				
department managers	80	65	40	185
Other	30	15	10	55
Total separable-discretionary fixed costs	110	80	50	240
Product margin	$ 850	$ 520	$ 330	$1,700
Committed and joint fixed costs:				
Depreciation on fixtures				155
Rent on store				300
Salaries of administrative staff				410
Utilities				140
Other				500
Total committed and joint fixed costs				1,505
Income				$ 195

Using the classification scheme shown here the manager can determine whether a product line is making a contribution to total profits for the firm. If the line's product margin is positive, then the product line contribution margin is greater than its separable-discretionary (avoidable) fixed costs and the line should be kept.

One final word. Although the above discussions have raised the issue of dropping a particular product line, no mention has been made of the firm's adding a new product line (to replace the old) or expanding its present lines to use the resources (such as factory space) that would become available if that particular product line were dropped. Regardless of what the firm decides to do with its resources, fixed costs that are joint with other products or product lines would remain after the particular line is dropped and should, therefore, be irrelevant to the decision to drop it. More specific attention will be given to the question of decision making in Chapter 7.

PRICE-VOLUME RELATIONS

In Chapter 2 you were introduced to the concept of a relevant range over which selling price was unrelated to sales volume. The concept of relevant range is of further significance in the present context because selling prices are unlikely to be constant over wide levels of sales. For example, there are about 10 million automobiles sold in the United States each year. If every carmaker doubled the price of every car sold, it is unlikely that 10 million cars would be sold. If the price of each car was halved, volume would probably increase sharply. This demonstrates the **law of demand**, which states that as prices increase, the quantity sold decreases, and vice versa. In most realistic situations, there is some price-volume interdependence even over the relevant range.

A firm sells 10,000 units of a product at $15 per unit. Variable costs are $10 per unit and fixed costs are $20,000. The sales manager states that if the price were increased to $16, volume would fall to 9,000 units. The cost structure is applicable to volumes ranging from 8,000 to 16,000 units (the relevant range). Should the price be increased? Comparative income statements can be prepared under the two sets of circumstances.

	Sell 10,000 Units at $15	Sell 9,000 Units at $16
Sales	$150,000	$144,000
Variable costs	100,000	90,000
Contribution margin	50,000	54,000
Fixed costs	20,000	20,000
Income	$ 30,000	$ 34,000

Income would be $4,000 higher at a selling price of $16. The increase in price is large enough to offset the decline in volume brought on by the price change.

The problem could also be solved by considering only contribution margin. The existing price yields $50,000 of contribution margin ($5 × 10,000) whereas the proposed price is expected to yield $54,000 ($6 × 9,000). And if the sales manager also states that volume would increase to 14,000 units if the price were reduced to $14, would price reduction be preferable to price increase? It would appear to be so. Total contribution margin would be $56,000 ($4 × 14,000), which is higher than total contribution margin at either the current price or the proposed higher price.

The possibility of an interdependence between prices and volume must be recognized and allowed for when planning profit and analyzing alternative courses of action.

VOLUME-COST-PROFIT ANALYSIS IN NOT-FOR-PROFIT ENTITIES

The term "not-for-profit entities" encompasses many different kinds of economic organizations including governmental units, universities, churches, charitable institutions like the Red Cross and American Cancer Society, and various types of clubs and fraternal organizations. The term "not-for-profit" is used in preference to "nonprofit" because it better describes the intent of such organizations. Many business firms turn out to be "nonprofit," but usually not by choice.

Income is a measure of how well a business has been run. Although maximizing profit is not the only objective of a business firm (survival, growth, product quality, good corporate citizenship being other important objectives), the earning of profits sufficient to attract capital investment is necessary to continuation of the firm. What then is the relevance of volume-cost-profit analysis to entities that do not intend to make profits?

Any economic organization is concerned with efficiency—obtaining the best possible results (output) from the resources available (input). For not-for-profit entities, results are the services provided to their constituencies. Thus a police department should be concerned with providing the best possible protection at the lowest possible cost, and a university should be concerned with providing the best possible education and other services to its students and to the community at large for the lowest cost.

Analyzing the activities of not-for-profit entities is often difficult because the services provided cannot always be expressed in dollar terms. Thus it is difficult to appraise their efficiency. Moreover, not-for-profit entities have more diverse objectives than business firms. Some charitable institutions are devoted to specific purposes, like the American Cancer Society. Others, like the Ford Foundation, engage in many kinds of activities. Some universities are heavily involved in research of various kinds; some are primarily teaching institutions.

Despite the difficulties associated with measuring the results of the activities of not-for-profit entities, some evaluations of results are always being made. Proof that some type of evaluation was undertaken is evidenced by the facts that organizations disband, governmental programs are sometimes cut back or even dropped, some charities find their donations decreasing. The creation and dissolution of not-for-profit entities are often instigated by large groups of people (the public ceases to support a particular charity), at other times by small groups (the head of a foundation decides to stop funding a particular program).

The counterpart of volume-cost-profit analysis for activities of not-for-profit entities is sometimes called **benefit-cost analysis**. Volume-cost-profit analysis can be shown to work in two kinds of situations: those that generate no revenues by themselves; and those in which there are both revenues and costs.

Cost Analysis

Several years ago, a prominent politician was criticizing the Job Corps, a federal program in which unemployable youths were given training at various camps across the country. Reacting to a progress report indicating that the cost of sending a young man through the program was $9,000, he commented that for the same money the youths could be sent to Harvard. One possible implication of his comment was that it would continue to cost $9,000 for each additional youth who underwent the training program. Yet, this may not have been the case. The $9,000 average cost may have included the cost of establishing the camps. Was there a fallacy in his reasoning? To assess the cost of continuing the program it is necessary to separate the fixed and variable components of the cost, the discretionary from the committed, so that one can determine how much more it would cost to continue the program. The important number in this analysis is the cost for each additional trainee—the variable cost.

Suppose that the following costs are incurred to house and train 100 men at a job training center for six months, the period for which a trainee is enrolled. The center was built to handle 200 men.

Food	$ 22,000
Rent of building	6,000
Salaries of instructors	68,000
Administration (salaries of head of camp, secretaries, other office workers)	30,000
Total	$126,000

The average cost per man for six months is $1,260. If 200 men were enrolled, what are the total and average costs? To find this we need to know the costs that increase with increased enrollment (variable costs and step-variable costs). There is not enough information given here to analyze all costs shown, but we can make some reasonable assumptions. The cost of food is almost certainly variable, and the cost of salaries for instructors is probably step-variable. Building rent is likely to be fixed and administration is most likely mixed.

An adequate analysis would require determining the desirable number of instructors at various levels of enrollment and the administrative expense at various levels, because these two elements are not so easily broken down by behavioral characteristics. Suppose that the total costs of operation for six months for 200 men are as follows:

Food	$ 44,000
Rent	6,000
Salaries of instructors	96,000
Administration	38,000
Total	$184,000

Average cost, $920 ($184,000/200)

Whether to expand enrollment or maintain it at existing levels depends on the variable and step-variable costs. From the standpoint of cost, whether the program should be dropped and some other substituted depends on costs beyond those committed. If the lease on the building has 50 years to run and there is no alternative use for the building, the government is committed to that cost.

Using the high-low method of analysis, it appears that the cost structure of this job training center is as follows: fixed costs $68,000, variable costs $580 per trainee. Costs for 200 men are $184,000, for 100 men are $126,000—a difference of $58,000 for 100 additional enrollees. Variable cost per trainee is $580 ($58,000/100). The variable costs of 100 enrollees is $58,000, so the remainder of the costs at that enrollment level, $68,000 ($126,000 − $58,000), is the estimate of fixed costs. Whether to increase enrollment depends on the $580 variable cost estimate, not on the $1,260 average cost for 100 trainees.

Revenues and Costs

The prior example dealt with costs alone. However, with more information, it is possible to include revenues in the analysis. Job training increases the earning power of the trainees. Further, there is a social value in providing men with job skills; presumably, their self-esteem should be greater, they are likely to be better citizens, less likely to commit crimes, etc. The measurements of these intangible benefits, of course, present serious problems. It is our intention at this time to show only the potential tangible benefits that could be expected from such a program, which benefits relate to increased earning power.

Let us say that the average trainee would earn perhaps $4,000 per year without job training, and about $7,000 with training. Each would pay about $600 per year in federal income taxes on the $4,000 income and about $1,300 on $7,000. (The actual determination of income taxes would be much more detailed and would require many estimates and assumptions. We are assuming that the numbers given are the results of such complex analysis.) This $700 difference in taxes is greater than the variable cost of providing the training ($580), but less than the average cost for the center ($920). But the benefits will continue over many years for each of the trainees. Thus, the 200 men who undergo training in one six-month period will pay back in additional income taxes $140,000 per year. The cost of their training, both fixed and variable, will be paid back to the federal government in less than a year and a half.

The federal government would be spending $184,000 in each six-month period to increase its tax receipts for several years by $140,000 per year. The expenditure appears wise based on a benefit-cost analysis and without considering the intangible but important other benefits from the program. Similar analyses can be made of other kinds of government expenditures, such as flood control projects and environmental clean-up programs.

Benefits

Some governmental activities generate little or no revenue, except in a very indirect sense. These include national defense, police and fire protection, state legislatures, and the national congress. In some of these activities, such as the provision of police protection, it is difficult to define the output, let alone assign it a dollar value to compare with input. For such cases there have been efforts to select some unit of output that is not the dollar and use this unit to measure and analyze results. The choice of the unit must be made with great care.

Consider police protection. At first it might appear that the number of arrests made would be a good indicator of the accomplishments of law enforcement activities. But the number of arrests made during a period may not be a valid measure of "good" police activity, because arrests for minor offenses count the same as those for major crimes. Moreover, citizens want crime prevented, not merely punished. Hence, good law enforcement that reduces crime will eventually also reduce the number of arrests.

Assuming that crime is prevented by having more police, there will still be a point at which the cost of adding more police would be prohibitive in relation to additional crimes prevented. The community would establish an adequate performance level for police protection by identifying some quantity of crime that would be tolerated.

Fixed Expenditures

Some not-for-profit organizations may be confronted with the problem of planning their operations in the face of a constraint on expenditures. This would be the case, for example, in situations where a decision has already been reached that a given program or service is desired at a particular level of adequacy or must be achieved with a particular level of expenditure. Thus, a community may desire the best police protection obtainable from a given level of funding. There is still opportunity for the use of volume-cost-profit analysis, because there are always alternative ways of spending funds. Police on foot can be substituted for police in cars, or sophisticated equipment can be bought, or the money can be spent on hiring more people.

A university receives a fixed amount of dollars from the state for faculty salaries. What kinds of faculty members will be hired and at what salaries? One university may emphasize the hiring of relatively young, lower-ranked persons. That university could have a larger faculty than another university that hired more senior faculty at higher salaries. Such decisions will have an impact on class size, number of courses offered, availability of faculty to students for individual study projects, and so on.

Trying to obtain the maximum benefits from a given level of funding is, of course, not peculiar to police departments and universities or even to not-for-profit entities. But there are fewer, or at least more subtle, criteria for successful performance of not-for-profit entities.

SUMMARY

A firm dealing with several products will generally need to compute a weighted average contribution margin for its volume-cost-profit analysis. This computation requires information about the sales mix, stated either in dollars or units.

The techniques of volume-cost-profit analysis are helpful in analyzing the results of operations. Differences between planned and achieved contribution margin and net income may be attributed to differences in volume, price, and mix. Managers then concentrate on those products or strategies (pricing, promotion, etc.) that can be expected to yield the best results. Managers also use contribution margin information to identify profitable products.

An important assumption in volume-cost-profit analysis is that there is no interdependency between the sales price charged and the volume of sales obtainable at that price. This assumption is often unrealistic, and managers must allow for the potential effect of a price change on volume, and vice versa.

Not-for-profit entities utilize benefit-cost analysis, a counterpart of volume-cost-profit analysis. It is difficult to define and measure benefits deriving from a particular expenditure in a not-for-profit entity. Despite these difficulties, more and more managers in not-for-profit entities are finding that adaptations of the concepts of managerial accounting can be helpful in their organizations.

KEY TERMS

benefit-cost analysis	sales mix
complementary products	sales price variance
joint cost	sales volume variance
law of demand	separable cost
product line	simulation
product margin	weighted average contribution margin

KEY FORMULAS

$$\text{Sales volume variance} = \frac{\text{planned contribution margin per unit}}{} \times \left(\text{planned sales, in units} - \text{actual sales, in units} \right)$$

$$\text{Sales price variance} = \text{units sold} \times \left(\text{planned price} - \text{actual price} \right)$$

REVIEW PROBLEM

Data on the three types of can openers sold by the McMichael Company are given below.

	Regular	Deluxe	Super
Selling price	$2.00	$3.00	$5.00
Variable costs	1.20	1.50	2.00
Contribution margin	$ .80	$1.50	$3.00
Contribution margin percentage	40%	50%	60%

Monthly fixed costs are $90,000.

Required: Consider each part independently.

1. Suppose that the sales mix in *dollars* is: Regular, 60%; Deluxe, 30%; and Super, 10%. Determine the weighted average contribution margin percentage and the monthly sales required to break even. Prepare an income statement by product line for sales of $250,000. Assume that of the $90,000 fixed costs, there are separable-discretionary costs of $10,000 for each product.
2. Suppose now that the sales mix in *units* is: Regular 50%; Deluxe, 30%; and Super, 20%. Determine the weighted average contribution margin percentage and sales required to earn $20,000 per month.
3. Suppose that in one month the firm expected to sell 40,000 Regular openers at $2 each. It actually sold 42,000, but the average selling price was $1.85. Compute the sales price variance and sales volume variance.

Answers to Review Problem

1. The weighted average contribution margin percentage is 45%, computed as follows:

	Regular	Deluxe	Super	Total
Contribution margin percentage	40%	50%	60%	
multiplied by				
sales mix percentage	60%	30%	10%	
equals, contribution margin				
per sales dollar	24% +	15% +	6% =	45%

The sales required to break even are $200,000 per month (fixed costs of $90,000/45% = $200,000).

	Regular	Deluxe	Super	Total
Sales[a]	$150,000	$75,000	$25,000	$250,000
Variable costs[b]	90,000	37,500	10,000	137,500
Contribution margin	$ 60,000	$37,500	$15,000	$112,500
Separable-discretionary fixed costs	10,000	10,000	10,000	30,000
Product margin	$ 50,000	$27,500	$ 5,000	$ 82,500
Joint fixed costs				60,000
Income				$ 22,500

[a]Based on the stated sales mix of 60%, 30%, and 10%. $250,000 × 60% = $150,000; $250,000 × 30% = $75,000; $250,000 × 10% = $25,000.

[b]These figures can be determined by using the variable cost percentages, which are 60%, 50%, and 40% (all are 1 − contribution margin percentages). Or, the number of units of each product can be determined by dividing sales for the product by selling price per unit as given in the problem. Then, the results are multiplied by variable cost per unit as given in the problem. For example, sales of the Regular model are 75,000 units ($150,000/$2). Variable costs are given as $1.20 per unit, so such costs would be $90,000 for 75,000 units ($1.20 × 75,000).

2. The weighted average contribution margin percentage is 50%, computed as follows by using a typical sales batch of 10 units distributed as stated in the problem.

	Regular	Deluxe	Super	Total
Mix	50%	30%	20%	100%
Units	5	3	2	10
Sales (no. of units × stated sales price per unit)	$10.00	$9.00	$10.00	$29.00
Contribution margin (no. of units × stated contribution margin per unit)	$ 4.00	$4.50	$ 6.00	$14.50
Weighted average contribution margin percentage ($14.50/$29.00)				50%

Sales required for $20,000 profit per month would be computed using the target profit formula from Chapter 2 and amount to $220,000 [(fixed costs of $90,000 + target profit of $20,000)/50% contribution margin percentage].

3. Because of the way in which the information is given, the easiest way to solve the problem is to deal with only the price and volume differences, as follows:

$$\begin{matrix} \text{Sales} \\ \text{price} \\ \text{variance} \end{matrix} = \begin{matrix} \text{quantity} \\ \text{sold} \end{matrix} \times \left(\begin{matrix} \text{planned} \\ \text{price} \end{matrix} - \begin{matrix} \text{actual} \\ \text{price} \end{matrix} \right)$$

$$= 42,000 \times (\$2.00 - \$1.85)$$
$$= 42,000 \times \$.15$$
$$= \$6,300 \text{ unfavorable}$$

$$\begin{matrix} \text{Sales} \\ \text{volume} \\ \text{variance} \end{matrix} = \begin{matrix} \text{planned} \\ \text{contribution} \\ \text{margin} \end{matrix} \times \left(\begin{matrix} \text{planned} \\ \text{volume} \end{matrix} - \begin{matrix} \text{actual} \\ \text{volume} \end{matrix} \right)$$

$$= \$.80 \times (40,000 - 42,000)$$
$$= \$.80 \times -2,000$$
$$= -\$1,600 \text{ favorable (favorable because actual}$$
volume was greater than planned)

Alternatively, we would prepare the following schedule, similar to the one on page 91.

	Planned Results	Actual Volume at Planned Selling Price	Actual Results
Sales	$80,000	$84,000 (42,000 × $2)	$77,700 (42,000 × $1.85)
Variable costs	48,000	50,400 (42,000 × $1.20)	50,400 (42,000 × $1.20)
Contribution margin	$32,000	$33,600 (42,000 × $.80)	$27,300 (42,000 × $.65)

$1,600
favorable sales
volume variance

$6,300
unfavorable sales
price variance

ASSIGNMENT MATERIAL

Questions for Discussion

4-1 Profit motive "The success of a governmental unit, city, state, or federal, should be judged by the amount of profit it earns, just as a business firm is evaluated." Do you agree with the statement? Explain why or why not.

4-2 Volume-cost-profit chart Explain how preparation of a volume-cost-profit graph would differ between (a) a firm that sells only one product, and (b) a firm that sells several products.

4-3 Volume-cost-profit analysis "Volume-cost-profit analysis is fine for firms that have very simple operations, but for most firms in the real world it won't work." Identify several problems involved in the use of volume-cost-profit analysis by firms with complicated operations. How can these problems be overcome?

4-4 Inventory turnover ratio You may have learned in financial accounting that one of the measures of the efficiency of a firm is the speed with which it turns over its inventory. From what you have seen in this chapter, would you put a great deal of emphasis on inventory turnover in deciding whether a firm is keeping too large or too small an inventory?

Exercises

4-5 Price-volume relationships The Watson Company makes two products, Hicost and Locost. Both products are being sold at $20 per unit and monthly volume is 3,000 units for each. Hicost has variable costs of $16 per unit and Locost has variable costs of $6 per unit. The sales manager believes that volume of either product could be increased by 20% if the price were reduced by 10%.

Required

1. Compute the effects on monthly contribution margin if the proposed price cut were implemented for each product.
2. Should either price be cut?

4-6 Product profitability and selection The following data relate to the three products sold by the Klutzy Company.

	Flibetts	Wibbets	Hobbits
Selling price	$20	$12	$10
Variable costs	8	6	3
Contribution margin	$12	$ 6	$ 7

Required

1. Which product is the most profitable (a) per unit, (b) per sales dollar?
2. Sales are currently 5,000 Flibetts, 12,000 Wibbets, and 16,000 Hobbits per year. The products can be substituted to some extent and the sales manager believes that customers can be induced to switch from Wibbets and Hobbits to Flibetts. He believes that an advertising campaign costing $60,000 would result in 3,000 buyers of Wibbets switching to Flibetts, and 8,000 buyers of Hobbits changing to Flibetts. Should the campaign be undertaken? Support your answer with calculations.

4-7 Price and volume variance   The Ripemoff Company had the following planned partial income statement for March 19X9.

Sales (12,000 units)	$120,000
Variable costs	84,000
Contribution margin	$ 36,000

Actual contribution margin was $31,000 with 10,000 units being sold. Variable costs per unit were incurred as planned.

Required

1. Compute actual sales in dollars.
2. Compute the actual selling price.
3. Compute the price and volume variances.

4-8 Volume-cost analysis in a planned economy   The Committee on Production of the socialist country of Ansgar is deciding on the kind of automobile to be produced in the coming year. The objective is to increase production to 1,000,000 cars. Two kinds of cars are now produced in Ansgar, the Phaedo and the Snope. Each is made in a separate factory, each of which could increase its production by 500,000 units over the last year.

Last year 200,000 Phaedos and 400,000 Snopes were produced. Cost data were as follows:

	Phaedos	Snopes
Variable costs	$200,000,000	$440,000,000
Fixed costs	150,000,000	180,000,000
Totals	$350,000,000	$620,000,000

One member of the Committee states that it is obvious that 400,000 more Snopes should be produced because the per-unit cost is $1,550 ($620,000,000/400,000) whereas it costs $1,750 ($350,000,000/200,000) to produce a Phaedo.

As consultant to the Committee you have been asked to recommend in which factory the additional 400,000 units should be produced. You learn that if 600,000 Phaedos were produced, the discretionary fixed costs at that factory would increase from the current $25,000,000 to $38,000,000. If 800,000 Snopes were produced, discretionary fixed costs would increase at that plant by $10,000,000. Committed fixed costs at that plant are currently $120,000,000.

Required

Which factory should produce the additional 400,000 cars?

4-9 Price and volume variances   The Klaxton Company produces a single product, the Grungy. Planned results for March were as follows:

Sales (10,000 units)	$40,000
Variable costs	16,000
Contribution margin	24,000
Fixed costs	20,000
Income	$ 4,000

Actual results were as follows:

Sales	$42,000
Variable costs	19,200
Contribution margin	22,800
Fixed costs	20,000
Income	$ 2,800

Variable costs per unit were incurred as expected.

Required

1. How many units were sold?
2. What was the selling price?
3. What was the volume variance? The price variance?

4-10 Pricing policy—public service   Speebus, the city-owned bus service of Middleville, charges $.40 for all rides on its buses. The city has a large number of citizens over the age of 65, whose incomes are generally lower than those of working citizens. One of the members of the city council has proposed that Speebus reduce its fares for persons over 65 to $.20.

At the present time, about 1,000,000 rides per month are made on Speebus buses, about 20% of which are citizens over 65. Buses are rarely crowded. The councilman estimates that the decrease in fares to older persons would increase their use of the bus service by 50%. Other users would remain the same. Even with the increase in riders expected, buses would rarely be crowded.

Required

1. How much will it cost per month for Speebus to reduce fares to riders over 65?
2. Suppose that the bus service is operating at break-even. By how much would regular fares have to be increased to get back to break-even if the reduction is granted?

4-11 Pricing to break even   The Student House of Representatives at Pedantic University sponsors a number of programs for students and faculty. Among them is a monthly movie in the school auditorium, which holds 3,200 people. The movies selected would not ordinarily be shown in the one theatre in the small town in which the university is located, and attendance at the University showings is high.

When a movie is shown only one evening, it is invariably sold out. When it is shown on two evenings, attendance at each showing averages 2,375.

Movies are rented at a cost of $2,000 for one showing, $3,000 for two showings. Other fixed costs per showing are $400 and variable costs are $.40 per person for chair rentals, tickets, and miscellaneous items. The House wishes to break even for the year on the movie program.

Required

1. Determine the prices that must be charged in order that the House break even on the movie showings for the year assuming (a) one showing of each movie, and (b) two showings of each movie.
2. Make a recommendation to the House regarding the number of times a movie should be shown, explaining the factors that influenced your decision.

4-12 Product profitability   The Wrynn Company sells three kinds of tobacco jars. The controller has prepared the following analysis of profitability of each of the jars.

	Flavorsaver	Shagholder	Burleykeeper
Selling price	$5.00	$8.00	$11.00
Variable costs	1.80	3.80	6.40
Fixed costs	3.00	3.00	3.00
Total costs	4.80	6.80	9.40
Profit	$ .20	$1.20	$ 1.60
Profit percentage to selling price	4%	15%	14.5%
Annual volume	22,000	15,000	13,000

The firm has total fixed costs of $150,000 per year. The controller obtained the fixed cost per unit figure of $3 by dividing $150,000 by 50,000 units (22,000 + 15,000 + 13,000). On the basis of his analysis, the controller suggested that the Flavorsaver model be discontinued if a substitute could be found that would be more profitable. This conclusion upset the sales manager, who had planned to undertake a $10,000 promotional campaign for Flavorsavers. He had calculated that a $10,000 expenditure would increase the volume of the product selected by 30%. Sales of the other products would be unaffected, as would existing fixed costs.

Required

Determine which product should be selected for the special promotion.

Problems

4-13 Volume-cost-profit analysis—product mix   The Happy Times Brewery produces and sells two grades of beer: regular and premium. Premium beer sells for $4 per case, regular for $3. Variable brewing costs per case are $2.50 (premium) and $2 (regular). Sales of regular beer, in cases, are double those for premium. Fixed brewing costs are $60,000 monthly, and fixed selling and administrative costs are $75,000 monthly. The only variable cost in addition to variable brewing costs is the 10% commission (based on dollar sales) paid to salespeople.

Required

1. Compute the break-even point in sales dollars per month.
2. How many cases of each kind of beer are sold at break-even?
3. The brewery is now running about $660,000 in monthly sales. The advertising manager believes that sales of premium beer could be increased by 20% if an extensive advertising campaign were undertaken. The campaign would cost $4,000 per month. However, sales of regular beer would

probably fall by about 5% because some customers now buying the regular grade would merely switch to premium. Should the campaign be undertaken?

4. If the campaign were undertaken, what is the weighted average contribution margin? Round to three decimal places.

5. What is the new break-even point in dollar sales?

4-14 Analysis of financial statements   The Gorgon Company had the following income statements in two recent months.

	January	February
Sales	$100,000	$100,000
Variable costs	40,000	47,500
Contribution margin	60,000	52,500
Fixed costs	50,000	50,000
Income	$ 10,000	$ 2,500

You learn that the firm sells two products, Squiggles and Wiggles, and that 20,000 Squiggles were sold in January, 5,000 in February. Squiggles sell for $3 and have a variable cost of $1. Sales of Wiggles in January were 40,000 units.

Required

1. What are selling price and variable costs for Wiggles?
2. Prepare income statements for January and February showing the contribution margin for each product.
3. Explain the difference between incomes in January and February.

4-15 Pricing a product   The Watson Razor Company makes razors, blades, and other shaving accessories. The firm is introducing a new razor this year, the Super-90, which has 27 comfort settings and other features that lead the management to believe that it will be a big seller. The razor has variable costs of $2 per unit. Associated fixed costs are $3,000,000 per year for production, advertising, and administration. The sales manager of Watson believes that if the razor is priced at $4 about 2,000,000 units per year will be sold. If the price is $5, about 1,500,000 units per year would be sold.

Required

1. Determine the price that would yield the higher profit to the firm.
2. Suppose that for each razor sold the firm also sells five packages of blades per year. Blades sell for $1.95 per package and the variable cost is $.75 per package. Would this information affect your analysis in part 1?

4-16 Pricing decision and costs   The sales manager for the Markham Pen Company has been trying to decide what price to charge for a new pen the firm is introducing this year. His staff has prepared a research report that indicates the following price-volume relationships.

Price	Volume
$3.00	900,000 units
2.90	1,000,000
2.80	1,100,000
2.70	1,200,000
2.60	1,260,000

The variable cost per pen is $1.20 and total annual fixed costs are estimated at $800,000. The sales manager believes that any product should be priced at 150% of total cost. He decides to use 1,000,000 units as the volume to determine the average unit cost and computes the cost at $2 per pen. He intends to set the price at $3.

Required

1. Assuming that the predictions of the staff are correct, what profit would be earned if the pen is priced at $3?
2. Again assuming the correctness of the staff's predictions, which price would yield the highest profit?
3. What is wrong with the sales manager's method of setting prices?

4-17 Price-volume relationships   The president of the Horn Company, Ms. Roberta Horn, has engaged your services as a consultant on selling prices and sales forecasts. The firm makes two products, Kappas and Gammas. You have prepared the following forecasts of sales for each product during 19X5 at various selling prices.

Kappas		Gammas	
Selling Price	Units Sold	Selling Price	Units Sold
$10	10,000	$20	7,000
9	16,000	18	9,500
8	23,000	16	12,000
7	27,000	14	16,000

Variable costs per unit are as follows: Kappas, $5; Gammas, $10. Fixed costs of production are $35,000 per year; selling, general, and administrative costs, all fixed, are $42,000 per year.

Required

Determine the selling prices that will provide the greatest profit to the company.

4-18 Product profitability   The Craven Company has hired a new assistant controller who recently graduated from the state university. Her first assignment was to prepare a break-even analysis of the firm. She gathered the following data related to operations for the latest year.

	Widgets	Blivets	Thingummies
Sales price	$4	$8	$15
Variable costs	3	4	6
Contribution margin	$1	$4	$9

Total fixed costs are $840,000. Sales are usually distributed in the following percentages of dollar sales: Widgets, 40%; Blivets, 40%; Thingummies, 20%.

Required

1. If $1 in advertising expenditures would increase sales of the one product being advertised by one unit, which product should be advertised?
2. What are break-even sales dollars for the firm?
3. By how much will the firm increase its income for each sales increase of $1?
4. What sales are necessary to achieve income of $210,000?
5. The controller has just come from a meeting with the operating managers and says that the sales

mix is likely to change to 20%, 30%, and 50%, for Widgets, Blivets, and Thingummies, respectively.

(a) Compute the new break-even point.

(b) Compute the sales volume needed to earn $210,000.

4-19   Sales interdependencies (AICPA adapted)   The Breezway Company operates a resort complex on an offshore island. The complex consists of a 100-room hotel, shops, a restaurant, and recreational facilities. Mr. W. E. Blenem, the manager of the complex, has asked for your assistance in planning the coming year's operations. He is particularly concerned about the level of profits the firm is likely to earn.

Your conversation with Mr. Blenem reveals that he expects the hotel to be 80% occupied during the 300-day season that it is open. All rooms rent for $40 per day for any number of persons. In virtually all cases, two persons occupy a room. Mr. Blenem also tells you that past experience, which he believes is an accurate guide to the future, indicates that each person staying at the hotel spends $10 per day in the shops, $20 in the restaurant. There are no charges for use of the recreational facilities. All sales in the shops and restaurant are made to guests of the hotel, which is isolated from the only large town on the island.

After talking with Mr. Blenem you discuss the firm's cost structure with its controller, who gives you the following data.

	Shops	Restaurant
Variable costs, as a percentage of sales dollars:		
Cost of goods sold	40%	30%
Supplies	10	15
Other	5	5

For the hotel, the variable costs are $6 per day per occupied room, for cleaning, laundry, and utilities. Total fixed costs for the complex are $1,200,000 per year.

Required

1. Prepare an income statement for the coming year based on the information given.
2. Mr. Blenem tells you he believes if the room rate were reduced to $35 per day, the occupancy rate would increase to 90%. What would be the effect on planned income if the rate were reduced?

4-20   Product line reporting   The Kelly Company is a wholesale firm specializing in men's clothing. The firm has three major product lines: suits, sport clothes, and accessories. The firm's most recent monthly income statement is given below.

Kelly Company
Income Statement for April 19X7

Sales		$600,000
Cost of sales		439,500
Gross profit		160,500
Operating expenses:		
Commissions	$30,000	
Salaries	75,000	
Rent	16,000	
Shipping and delivery	12,000	
Insurance	3,400	
Miscellaneous	3,900	140,300
Income before taxes		$ 20,200

The president of the firm would like a product line income statement. He gives you the following additional data.

1. The sales mix in April was 40% suits, 35% sport clothes, and 25% accessories, expressed in dollars of total sales.
2. The cost of sales percentages are 80% for suits, 75% for sport clothes, and 60% for accessories.
3. Sales commissions are 5% for all product lines.
4. Each product line is the responsibility of a separate manager and each manager has a small staff. The salaries that are directly related to each product line are $7,000 for suits, $6,400 for sport clothes, and $3,200 for accessories. All other salaries are joint to the three lines.
5. Rent is for the office and warehouse space, all of which is in a single building.
6. Shipping and delivery costs are for operating expenses and depreciation on the firm's three trucks, including drivers' salaries. Each truck serves a particular geographical area and delivers all three product lines.
7. Utilities are for heat and light in the building.
8. Insurance includes a $400 fixed amount for basic liability coverage. The rest of the insurance is for coverage of merchandise at the rate of ½ of one percent of the selling price of the average inventory on hand during the month. In April the average inventories at selling prices were equal to sales for each product line.
9. Miscellaneous expenses are all joint to the three product lines.

Required

Prepare an income statement by product, using the format of Exhibit 4-1 on page 98.

4-21   Product profitability   The Messorman Company produces three products: A, B, and C. Price and cost data are as follows:

	A	B	C
Selling price	$10	$20	$30
Variable costs	6	8	15

Monthly fixed costs are $20,000.

Required

1. Which product contributes the most per unit sold?
2. Which product contributes the most per dollar of sales?
3. Suppose the sales mix in dollars is 40% A, 20% B, and 40% C.
   (a) What is the weighted average contribution margin?
   (b) What is the monthly break-even point?
   (c) What is the sales volume necessary to earn a profit of $30,000 per month?
4. Suppose the sales mix in dollars is 30% A, 30% B, and 40% C.
   (a) What is the break-even point?
   (b) What is the sales volume necessary to earn $30,000 per month?
5. Suppose that the sales mix in units is 40% A, 20% B, and 40% C.
   (a) What is the weighted average contribution margin?
   (b) What is the break-even point in sales dollars?
   (c) How many units of each product would be sold at the break-even point computed in (b)?
   (d) What is the sales volume in units of each product necessary to earn a profit of $30,000 per month?

4-22   Product mix—evaluation of profitability   The Carver Company sells two models of Sailrite boats —regular and deluxe. Revenue and cost data for the two models are as follows:

	Regular	Deluxe
Selling price	$500	$1,000
Purchase price	. $260	$ 380
Variable cost—commissions to salespeople	10% of sales	10% of sales

Total fixed costs each month are $9,000.

Required

1. Suppose that monthly sales are currently 44 regular models and 22 deluxe models.
   (a) What would the income be with this sales mix?
   (b) What is the weighted average contribution margin ratio with this sales mix? (Round to the nearest tenth of a percent.)
2. The manager of the firm believes that the same monthly dollar sales could be achieved if the salespeople were given a 15% commission on sales of the deluxe model but that the sales mix would change to 38 regular models and 25 of the deluxe boats. Does the expected profit under this action exceed or fall short of that in 1 above?
3. Assume the same facts as in 1 above. The firm is considering offering a series of lessons in boat handling with the purchase of each boat. It is expected that all buyers would take the lessons. The firm will have to pay an instructor $20 per buyer to provide the lessons. It is also expected that 2 more of the regular models and one more of the deluxe model will be sold per month if the lessons are offered.
   (a) If the proposed action is taken, what would the monthly income be?
   (b) What would the new weighted average contribution margin ratio be?
4. Assume the same facts as in 3 above, except that only half of the buyers will take advantage of the lessons. Does your answer change? Show why or why not.

4-23 Product line income statements   The president of the Mifflan Tool Company has just received the firm's income statement for January 19X8. He is puzzled because you had told him last year, when working as a consultant to the firm, that sales of $500,000 should produce a profit of about $57,000 before income taxes.

Mifflan Tool Company
Income Statement
January 19X8

Sales		$500,000
Cost of sales		307,500
Gross profit		192,500
Operating expenses:		
Rent	$40,000	
Salaries	70,000	
Shipping and delivery	14,000	
Other expenses	30,000	154,000
Income before taxes		$ 38,500

The firm sells three products and your analysis assumed the following sales mix in dollars: hammers, 30%; screwdrivers, 20%; and chisels, 50%. The actual mix in dollars in January was 40%, 30%, 30%. The firm does not manufacture its products. Cost of sales and shipping and delivery are variable costs. All others are fixed. Data per unit for each product are given below.

	Hammers	Screwdrivers	Chisels
Selling price	$5.00	$2.00	$4.00
Cost of sales	3.00	1.50	2.00
Shipping and delivery	.20	.04	.08
Total variable costs	3.20	1.54	2.08
Contribution margin	$1.80	$ .46	$1.92

Fixed costs are not directly associated with any of the product lines. All costs were incurred as expected, per unit for variable costs, total for fixed costs. Selling prices were as expected.

Required

1. Prepare a new income statement by product, based on actual results in January. Show both gross profit and contribution margin for each product.
2. Prepare an income statement by product for January, assuming that the expected sales mix had been achieved.
3. Explain the reasons for the differences between the two statements.

4-24   Qualitative and quantitative aspects of decision making   The Speaker Committee at a large university is in charge of inviting distinguished persons to address students, faculty, and members of the public. Students and faculty are admitted free while members of the public pay $2. Students and faculty must pick up tickets in advance; any tickets left on the day of the speech are sold to the public beginning the morning of the speech. The speaker program is expected to break even for the year.

The committee is trying to decide whether to invite Marvin Gardens, a noted environmentalist, or Cayuga Waters, a famous industrialist. One student member of the committee argues that Marvin Gardens is an ideal speaker. His required fee is $800. He states that the auditorium, which holds 2,000 people, will be almost completely filled with students and faculty if Gardens speaks. He believes that only about 500 tickets would be available to members of the public and that all available tickets could be sold. One of the other members, an administrative officer of the university, says that Waters would be a better speaker. He estimates that only 500 students and faculty would show up, leaving 1,500 tickets to be bought by the public. These tickets could easily be sold to the public, he believes. Waters charges a fee of $2,000.

Required

1. Assuming that both committee members are correct in their assessments of demand for tickets, which speaker would be more profitable?
2. What other factors should be considered in reaching a decision?
3. Is there a possibility that both speakers could be invited?

4-25   Cost analysis in a university   The school of business administration at State University currently has 500 students enrolled and 25 faculty members. The school has only juniors and seniors who take all their courses in the school, an average of five courses per semester. The school offers 75 sections per semester with each faculty member teaching three sections.

Below are data for the number of sections, average number of students per section, and "student-sections," which is the total number of enrollments in all sections. Since there are 500 students taking five courses each semester, there must be 2,500 student-sections.

Number of Sections	×	Average Enrollment	=	Student-Sections
20		20		400
30		35		1,050
25		42		1,050
75				2,500

The administration of the university is considering allowing the enrollment in the school of business to increase to 1,000 students. One officer of the university objects that the cost would be prohibitive. He states that faculty salaries are now $450,000 per year and would double if enrollment were to double because twice the number of faculty now teaching would be required.

Another officer points out that it would not be necessary to double the size of the faculty because the sizes of sections could be increased, although the university policy is that no more than 45 students be enrolled in a single section.

You are assigned the task of determining the additional cost of faculty salaries required to support enrollment of 1,000 students. You determine that demand for the classes now averaging 20 students per section is such that each section would go up to 25 students if enrollment went to 1,000. All other sections would be increased to the 45 students maximum. A faculty member would be hired for each three sections per semester added, at a salary of $18,000 per year.

Required

1. How many sections would be necessary if enrollment were increased to 1,000 students? (Hint: Because 1,000 students will take five courses per semester, you must account for 5,000 individual enrollments.)
2. How much additional cost would be incurred for faculty salaries, given your answer to 1?
3. After you performed the analysis in 1 and 2, the chancellor of the university became concerned about the large class sizes. He askes you to redo the analysis of required additional faculty salaries assuming that only 40 sections would hold 45 students, 20 would still hold 25 students, and the rest would have a maximum of 36 students.

4-26 Pricing decision—effects on another product   The Rapidcal Company manufactures handheld calculators. The industry is highly competitive and pricing is critical to sales volume. Mr. Warren James, the sales manager of Rapidcal, has been trying to decide on a price for a new model that the firm will introduce shortly. The new model, the RC-89, is somewhat more sophisticated than the RC-63, which the firm has had great success with in recent years. The RC-63 now sells at retail for $20, of which 30% goes to the dealer, 70% to Rapidcal. The other variable costs for the RC-63 are $8 per unit. The variable costs for the RC-89, exclusive of dealer share, are $18 per unit.

Mr. James is especially concerned about the effects on sales of RC-63 following the introduction of the RC-89. He believes that if the RC-89 is priced at $44 retail, there would be no loss in sales of the RC-63. However, if the RC-89 were sold at $42, he thinks that some people will buy the RC-89 instead of buying the RC-63. At the $44 price, Mr. James expects sales of 150,000 RC-89s per year. For each $2 cut of the price of RC-89s, sales would increase by about 30,000 units, but about 40% of the increased sales of RC-89 would be at the expense of sales of the RC-63. At any price for the RC-89, Rapidcal would get 70%, the retailer 30%.

Mr. James also believes that a $38 retail price is rock-bottom for the RC-89. He therefore instructs you to determine the effects on the income of the firm of pricing the RC-89 at $44, $42, $40, and $38.

Required: Comply with the sales manager's request, and determine the price that should be set for the RC-89.

4-27 Line of business reporting (CMA adapted) The Riparian Company produces and sells three products. Each product is sold domestically and in foreign countries. The foreign market has been disappointing to the management because of poor operating results, as evidenced by the income statement for the first quarter of 19X8.

	Total	Domestic	Foreign
Sales	$1,300,000	$1,000,000	$300,000
Cost of goods sold	1,010,000	775,000	235,000
Gross profit	290,000	225,000	65,000
Selling expenses	105,000	60,000	45,000
Administrative expenses	52,000	40,000	12,000
	157,000	100,000	57,000
Income	$ 133,000	$ 125,000	$ 8,000

Management decided a year ago to enter the foreign markets because of excess capacity, but is now unsure whether to continue devoting time and effort to developing the foreign market. The following information has been gathered for consideration of the alternatives that management has identified.

	Products		
	A	B	C
Sales: Domestic	$400,000	$300,000	$300,000
Foreign	100,000	100,000	100,000
Variable manufacturing costs (percentage of sales)	60%	70%	60%
Variable selling expenses (percentage of sales)	3%	2%	2%

All fixed manufacturing costs are joint to the three products. All administrative expenses are fixed and joint to the three products and to the two markets. Fixed selling expenses are separable and avoidable by market, but not by product.

Management believes that if the foreign market were dropped, sales in the domestic market could be increased by $200,000. The increase would be divided 40%, 40%, 20% among products A, B, and C, respectively.

Management also believes that a new product, D, could be introduced by the end of the current year. The product would replace product C and would result in increased fixed costs of $10,000 per quarter.

Required

1. Prepare an income statement for the quarter by product, showing contribution margin for each product.
2. Prepare an income statement for the quarter by market showing contribution margin and product margin for each market.
3. Determine whether the foreign market should be dropped, assuming that management's estimates of increased domestic sales are valid.
4. Assume that the foreign market would not be dropped. Determine the minimum quarterly contribution margin that product D would have to produce in order to make its introduction desirable.

4-28 Price and volume variances (AICPA adapted) The Bay City Gas Company supplies liquified natural gas to residential customers. The results, both planned and actual, for the month of November 19X7 are given below. Although he knows that the price of gas per thousand cubic feet drops with increases in purchases by a customer, the operations manager is having difficulty in interpreting the report.

	Planned	Actual	Difference
Number of customers	26,000	28,000	2,000
Sales in thousands of cubic feet	520,000	532,000	12,000
Revenue	$1,300,000	$1,356,600	$56,600
Variable costs	$416,000	$425,600	($9,600)

Required

Compute the sales price variance and sales volume variance.

4-29 Sales strategies The Nova Company sells cosmetics through door-to-door salespeople who receive commissions of 25% of selling price. The national sales manager of Nova has been evaluating alternative selling strategies for the coming season. He is trying to decide whether any products should be discounted in price by 30%, receive increased promotional efforts, or left alone. He is now considering four products, data for which are given below.

	Mascara	Eyeliner	Lipstick	Cologne
Normal selling price	$2.50	$2.20	$2.00	$12.00
Variable cost	.90	1.00	.80	5.00
Contribution margin	$1.60	$1.20	$1.20	$ 7.00
Expected Volumes:				
Without discount or special promotion (units)	800,000	750,000	2,000,000	200,000
With 30% discount	1,650,000	1,350,000	3,200,000	380,000
With special promotion	950,000	920,000	2,150,000	240,000

If the special promotion is chosen for a particular product, its selling price and variable cost will remain the same. The additional fixed costs would be $200,000 for each product selected, primarily for advertising and incentive payments to salespeople.

If a product is selected for a price cut of 30%, variable costs will remain the same, per unit, because the firm gives its salespeople commissions based on the normal selling price during such special sales.

Required

1. For each product, determine what should be done: reduce price, engage in special promotion, or do nothing.
2. Discuss some additional factors that might influence the sales manager's decisions about each product.

4-30 Comprehensive review of Chapters 2, 3, and 4 The Tacky Company makes three products and sells them in about the same mix each month. Below are income statements for two recent months.

Tacky Company Income Statements
(In Thousands of Dollars)

	April	May
Sales	$80	$60
Costs	60	52
Income	$20	$ 8

Selling price and cost data by product are as follows:

	A	B	C
Selling price	$20	$10	$5
Variable costs	8	3	3
Contribution margin	$12	$ 7	$2
Contribution margin percentage	60%	70%	40%
Percentage of total sales dollars (mix)	40%	40%	20%

Required

1. Using the income statements for April and May, find fixed cost and variable cost as a percentage of sales dollars.
2. Determine the break-even point in sales dollars.
3. Which product is most profitable per unit sold?
4. Which product is most profitable per dollar of sales?
5. What sales dollars are needed to earn $35,000 per month and how many units of each product will be sold at that sales level if the usual mix is maintained?
6. The sales manager believes that he could increase the sales of product C by 10,000 units per month if more attention were devoted to it and less to product B. Sales of B would fall by 2,000 units per month. What would the change in income be if this action were taken?
7. In June, the sales were $100,000 with a mix of 40% A, 30% B, and 30% C. What is the income?
8. In July the firm had sales of $90,000 and an income of $22,000.
   (a) What was the contribution margin percentage?
   (b) Which product would you think was sold in a higher proportion than the usual mix?
9. Suppose the firm is currently selling 6,000 units of product C. It is felt that because this is the least profitable product it should be dropped from the mix. If C is dropped, it is expected that sales of B would remain the same and those of A would rise. By how much would sales of A have to rise to maintain the same total income?

4-31 Comprehensive problem on volume-cost-profit   You are presented with the following information about the Gammon Sales Company, based on the plans for the year 19X1:

Sales (selling price is $1 per unit)		$100,000
Variable costs:		
Cost of goods sold	$67,000	
Other operating costs	15,000	
Total		82,000
Anticipated contribution to fixed costs		18,000
Anticipated fixed costs		13,140
Planned income before taxes		$ 4,860

Required: Answer each of the following questions based on the data provided for the 19X1 plans.

1. What is the company's break-even sales volume?
2. The company's officers have analyzed the anticipated cash situation for the year and have determined that it could afford to spend $3,600 on a special advertising campaign. They are not sure, however, that the expenditure would be worthwhile. What would be the break-even point if the campaign were undertaken?
3. If, as a result of the advertising campaign, the number of units sold could be expected to increase in an amount equal to the change in the break-even point in units, would the campaign be financially advisable (that is, to the company's advantage)? Explain.

4. Assume that the company has decided not to undertake the advertising campaign and is looking for other ways to improve the financial outlook for 19X1. The purchasing agent determines that there is a supply house (other than the one with which the company now deals) that will allow the company to buy at a price 10% below the anticipated purchase price. The sales manager does not believe that the new supplier would be providing a product of equal quality, and he estimates that sales volume would decrease by about 15% if the new supplier were used. The controller has determined that the switch in suppliers will necessitate some minor changes in the administrative procedures, which changes will increase fixed costs by approximately $1,000. Would the change of suppliers be a wise decision? Explain your answer with supporting computations.

5. Are there some qualitative considerations that might influence the decision on the change in suppliers?

6. After further investigation, you determine that the Gammon Company has not one but three separate products in its line, each of which has the same selling price. The planned activity for 19X1 in more detail is as follows:

	Product			
	#1	#2	#3	Total
Sales ($1 per unit)	$50,000	$30,000	$20,000	$100,000
Variable costs:				
Cost of goods sold	30,000	21,000	16,000	67,000
Other operating costs	7,500	4,500	3,000	15,000
Total	37,500	25,500	19,000	82,000
Anticipated contribution to fixed costs	$12,500	$ 4,500	$ 1,000	18,000
Fixed costs				13,140
Planned income before taxes				$ 4,860

The company has decided not to dilute the impact of a special advertising campaign by trying to promote more than one product. Assuming there is no constraint on the total demand for any of the three products, which product would the company most probably choose to promote in the $3,600 advertising campaign? Explain.

7. The company has found an alternate supplier for each of its products. Each supplier would be willing to sell to the company at a price 10% lower than is currently being paid. In each case, however, the product from the new supplier would probably reduce the total sales of that product by 15%. However, the company can change suppliers for only one of the products at a time. Ignoring any qualitative considerations, decide for which product, if any, the company should change suppliers. Support your answer.

8. Assume that the company's directors decide to postpone the advertising campaign and continue doing business with current supply sources. At the end of 19X1, despite sales of $110,000, the company managed to show an income before taxes of only $360. Analysis of sales by product showed the following:

Sales of Product #1	$ 30,000
Sales of Product #2	20,000
Sales of Product #3	60,000
Total	$110,000

These results surprised the board of directors because operating managers assured the directors that the variable and fixed costs had behaved during the year exactly as expected; sales were in excess of the forecast. Explain the reason or reasons for the disappointing results.

Cases

4-32 Product mix, profit planning, taxes   Michael Monte, the new assistant controller of the Remley Company, has prepared a volume-cost-profit analysis for the firm based on sales of the firm's three products from 19X7. He will present the analysis to a group of managers later in the week. Data per unit are given below.

	Products		
	101	*102*	*103*
Selling price	$3.50	$4.00	$5.00
Variable costs	1.50	3.00	2.00
Contribution margin	$2.00	$1.00	$3.00

Based on the sales mix in 19X7, Michael believed that out of every 10 units sold, four would be 101s, four 102s, and two 103s. Total fixed costs were predicted to be $90,000. Total sales were expected to be 100,000 units, based on a projection of trends in recent years, and Michael had prepared the following planned income statement for the year 19X8.

	101	*102*	*103*	*Total*
Sales	$140,000	$160,000	$100,000	$400,000
Variable costs	60,000	120,000	40,000	220,000
Contribution margin	$ 80,000	$ 40,000	$ 60,000	180,000
Fixed costs				90,000
Income before tax				90,000
Income taxes (40%)				36,000
Net income				$ 54,000

At the meeting, Michael demonstrated that his analysis could be used to predict changes in profits that would be expected to follow changes in sales. As an example he said that the break-even point for the firm would be $200,000 in sales, because the contribution margin percentage is 45% and fixed costs are $90,000. He showed the other managers that target profits can also be computed, although the presence of income taxes makes it a bit more complicated than computing the break-even point. He said that if an after-tax profit figure were desired, it would be necessary to divide it by 60%, the percentage of net income after taxes to income before taxes. The resulting before-tax profit figure could be added to fixed costs and the sum divided by 45%. Thus, the sales required for profits of $90,000 would be about $533,300. [Before-tax profits would have to be $150,000, and ($90,000 + $150,000)/45% is $533,333.]

Some of the managers were becoming restless as Michael explained his analysis. Finally, the production manager said that it was all very intersting, but irrelevant. She told the group that labor costs, which are 50% of variable costs, would increase by 20% under a new union contract that she expected would be signed shortly.

The controller said that he was somewhat disappointed with Michael's presentation because he had failed to provide for a $40,000 dividend to stockholders that the president of the firm had said should be a target. The firm has a policy of not allowing dividends to be more than one-third of after-tax profits. The controller had thought that Michael would incorporate the desired dividend into his analysis to show the other managers what had to be done to meet the president's goal.

As the managers began to mumble among themselves about the irrelevance of the analysis, the sales manager announced that the assumed sales mix was no good. He said, ''I don't know how this will affect the analysis, but we expect that each product will be sold in equal amounts this coming year. The demand for 103s is increasing substantially.''

Slapping her forehead, the production manager commented that she had forgotten that the firm would have to rent some additional equipment to increase production of 103s. The rental would be $10,000 per year. She wondered what effect that news would have on Michael's figures.

As he left the meeting, Michael remonstrated with himself for not having obtained more information before going in and looking like a fool.

Required

Prepare a new analysis for the firm, incorporating the goals and changed assumptions learned at the meeting. Show the sales necessary to (a) break even, and (b) meet the profit required to pay the $40,000 dividend without violating the firm's dividend policy.

4-33 Social costs and benefits A special task force of the Department of Health, Education, and Welfare has been directed to develop ways of reducing unemployment in a particular area of the country in which there are more than 12,000 unskilled, unemployed workers. Speedy action is expected, but the group has no further guidelines except that the total funds available for the task are $4,500,000.

After some preliminary discussion at a staff meeting, two alternative programs appear to have strong support, and a committee is assigned to develop more details about each one. The first program is simply to relocate unemployed workers from the problem area to other parts of the country where jobs are available. The committee studying this program has determined that it would cost $1,400 per worker relocated and that administration of the program would cost approximately $62,000.

The second committee is investigating a program that will set up a training center. Members of this committee have determined that if the unemployed workers had certain skills currently in demand, as many as 5,000 workers could be placed in jobs now available in the area. (This maximum also seems to exist if the relocation program is adopted. That is, jobs could be found for up to 5,000 workers possessing no additional skills if the workers were relocated.)

The anticipated costs for the retraining program are $1,500 per worker, plus $150,000 for administration. The program would run for 10 weeks, and it is expected that 20% of those enrolled would not be able to acquire the necessary skills.

Most of the members of the task force interpret their congressional directive (to reduce unemployment) as meaning that the benefits of whatever program is adopted will be measured by the number of currently unemployed persons finally placed in jobs. One member believes that it would be better to measure the success by reference to the additional income taxes that workers would pay. He estimates that relocated workers would earn about $6,000 per year and pay income taxes at a 15% rate. Those who are successfully retrained would earn about $9,000 per year and pay taxes at an 18% rate.

The task force has made an effort to determine the attitudes of the unemployed workers in the area. All workers contacted expressed their willingness to take part in either type of program, though most had a preference. However, the number expressing a preference for each program was about the same.

Required

1. Given the constraint on total cost and the use of the number of workers placed in jobs as the measurement of benefits, determine how the funds should be used.
2. Given the constraint on total cost and the use of additional tax receipts as the measurement of benefits, determine how the funds should be used.
3. Do you agree with the two measures of benefit (number of workers placed in jobs and additional tax receipts)? Are there other qualitative factors to be considered?

PART TWO

COMPREHENSIVE BUDGETING

The operations of a typical enterprise require not only planning in a broad sense but also coordination of plans. A myriad of activities is carried on in an individual enterprise; the relationships among those activities are here explored.

Effective planning requires communicating enterprise objectives to the responsible parties and determining that operations are going according to plan. The comprehensive budget aids the managers of an enterprise in meeting these requirements.

Volume-cost-profit analysis and the identification of cost behavior are important in budgeting. You will also be able to apply some of the principles from financial accounting, because a comprehensive budget includes the normal financial statements associated with reports to outsiders. The budgeting process is not merely a technical or mechanical exercise. It is people who plan and people who act (according to or contrary to plans). Thus the ways in which budgets are developed and used can have an effect on the behavior of people and vice versa. Some behavioral problems entailed in the budgeting process are introduced in this Part. A more comprehensive treatment of these problems is given in Part Four.

CHAPTER 5

OPERATIONAL BUDGETING

To achieve profit goals, all functional areas of the business (marketing, production, purchasing, finance) must work in harmony. These functions are interdependent. The overall plans of the business must be so specified that the manager of each functional area knows what must be done to ensure smooth performance for other areas, and for the firm as a whole. Thus, the production department must make just enough goods so that marketing can achieve its sales objectives, but not so much that some go unsold or can be sold only at drastically reduced prices. There must be a balance between having too much inventory, which causes excessive costs for storage, insurance, taxes, interest, and obsolescence, and too little inventory, which may result in lost sales.

Similarly, the purchasing manager must ensure that enough of the right kinds of materials are available to fulfill production schedules. The finance department must make cash available for paying for material, labor, and other operating costs. Cash must be available for dividend payments, capital asset acquisitions, and repayments on borrowed funds. Cash planning is vital because many disbursements must be made in advance of collections from sales, and the plans of the various managers have implications for cash inflows and outflows. To coordinate all these activities the comprehensive budget is used.

COMPREHENSIVE BUDGETS

A **comprehensive budget** is a set of financial statements (pro forma) and other schedules showing the expected results for a future period. A comprehensive budget normally contains an income statement for the period, a balance sheet for the end of the period, a cash flow statement, production schedules, purchasing schedules, and schedules of fixed asset acquisitions. Many other components of a comprehensive budget may be prepared, depending on the needs of the firm, but the foregoing would be a minimum for a manufacturing firm. Generally, the pro forma balance sheet and cash budget are considered to be financial budgets; the others operating budgets.

A comprehensive budget is similar to a planned income statement based on volume-cost-profit analysis. A budgeted statement of cash receipts is based on a sales forecast, expected collections of accounts receivable, and planned borrowing. If the sales forecast proves accurate and customers pay their bills at the expected times, cash receipts will be as budgeted. If customers pay less quickly than expected, cash receipts will be less than budgeted and vice versa. However, comprehensive budgeting is more complex than volume-cost-profit analysis because a change in one assumption will affect results throughout the whole set of budgets, not just in one or perhaps more items in an income statement.

The degree of detail in a particular budget will vary according to the situation for which it is used. Top management will be interested in overall results and would probably not require production schedules for every product. The production manager will use schedules for each product, because it is his objective to produce as much of each product as is needed and not to overproduce one product and underproduce another. A manager in charge of production for three items will know how much of each he is to produce and how much cost he should incur in achieving the budgeted levels of output. Most managers in the firm will have budgets showing what is expected of them—what objectives they are to achieve and at what costs.

Budgets and Planning

The comprehensive budget is the most conspicuous evidence of an overall plan for a business firm. It ties together a set of diverse activities that are related to specific goals and specifies the means for their achievement. Thus the business has a formalized plan in contrast to an intuitive approach to operations.

Formalization of plans encourages managers to think about the future; they can operate the firm within the framework of the budget. A budget formalizes expectations; thus it can be a guide in judging performance in relation to those expectations. Without such a guide, the manager would only be able to assess his or her performance by the crudest rules of thumb.

The objectives of budgets must be explicitly stated, forcing careful consideration of the means available to achieve those objectives. Some of the objectives initially considered feasible may prove not so in light of the budget. Suppose the budget specifies high monthly sales in the early part of the year. When the production manager uses the sales budget as a basis for planning production, he or she may recognize that there will not be sufficient productive capacity to attain the budgeted level of sales. Or, perhaps it is only possible to provide sufficient production and inventory to meet the budgeted level of sales if the firm obtains a great deal of short-term financing. Securing necessary financing may be undesirable or even impossible. The budgets would have to be modified to accord with the lack of cash available for investment in inventory.

A budget is rarely accepted the first time around. Identifying problems before they occur, and planning ways to deal with them, are important management functions. The budget is valuable in analyzing planned operations to ensure that the formulated objectives are achievable. The budget is thus a formalized system for evaluating means and objectives.

The budgeting process makes use of the financial statements and other schedules a

FIGURE 5-1 Relationships among Financial Statements in Budgeting

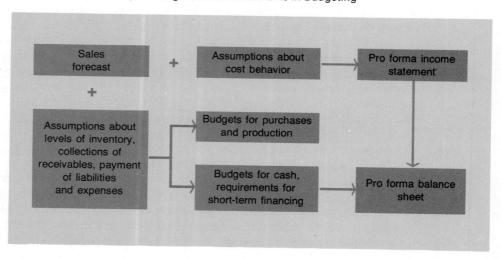

firm normally prepares, and coordinates all of these statements and schedules into a comprehensive system. Figure 5-1 illustrates how the statements are related.

Budgets and Control

A budget expresses target goals; actual results express achievements. Thus a comparison of the budget and actual results is a basis for evaluating performance, and helps control future operations. Corrective action can be taken to eliminate problems that show up in the comparisons.

The preceding statements are oversimplified, but they are nevertheless a fair statement of the role of budgets in control and performance evaluation. Actual performance is best judged by comparison with expected rather than past performance. This is true if expectations are reasonable, carefully formulated, and based on all available information. The use of past performance as a basis for judging current performance is inappropriate because it fails to consider changes in circumstances. Moreover, comparisons with past performance cannot reveal whether current performance is as good as it should have been. Although improvement over past results is desirable, it is more important to know if the improvement has been as great as it could have been. (A student who gets a 38 on an examination and follows it up with a 42 on the next examination has improved, but is still not performing adequately.)

The budgeting process incorporates all managerial functions that we have associated with managerial accounting. Planning, control, decision making, and performance evaluation are integrated in the budgeting cycle of preparation and comparison with actual results.

Organization of Budgets

Budgets are usually prepared for specific time periods, such as a year or a five-year period. Virtually all companies prepare a budget for the fiscal year, and the annual budget is normally broken down into shorter time periods—quarters, months, or even weeks. Budgets are also prepared for periods of longer than a year, usually for three, four, or five years broken down into one-year units. It is, of course, more difficult to forecast something a year or two in the future, so longer-term budgets tend to be less detailed than annual budgets.

It is also likely to be more difficult to forecast in detail for very short periods, such as a month, or a week, than for a quarter, even if the period is in the near future. This is true because many random factors may influence results for short time periods. You may be able to budget your expenditures for entertainment fairly well on a monthly basis. But breaking down that budget on a day-by-day basis is difficult. Similarly, a retailer of women's clothing may be able to predict sales for a quarter quite closely, but would have difficulty in pinning down the sales pattern week by week. A utility company providing natural gas for heating might be able to forecast the total use for the winter months, but probably could not, with accuracy, predict the volume of gas used weekly during those months.

Despite these problems, an annual budget is broken down into shorter time periods for several reasons. Progress throughout the year must be monitored and gauged against the goals set in the annual budget; this can better be done if benchmarks are available during the year. More important, the best laid plans often go astray, necessitating changes in planned operations for the remainder of the period.

Consider the following situation. The sales manager sees that actual sales for the first month of the fiscal year are higher than budgeted. She will try to decide whether the additional sales in this month will be offset by lower sales later or whether the high sales are an indication that the total expectations were too low. Suppose she concludes that sales for the rest of the first quarter, or even for the year, will be in excess of budgeted amounts. The original production budget was based on budgeted sales. If the original production plan is adhered to, inventory will be less than budgeted at the end of the first month and the first shortages may develop. The sales manager may then want to have production increased to meet the expected increases in sales. An increase in production may require the hiring of more employees, the acquisition of greater quantities of material, and other actions by various managers. Changes in plans—such as increased production—will go more smoothly and more effectively if they can be accomplished well in advance of the point at which a crisis develops.

Even if the sales manager concluded from these early results that sales for the year will not be materially greater than budgeted, the fact that there still has been an increase in the first month means that inventory will be lower than budgeted. It might then be necessary to plan a temporary increase in production sufficient to maintain the desired level of inventory. Perhaps some overtime work could be scheduled. Whether the sales in excess of expectations are a temporary or a **longer-lasting** phenomenon, there are new plans to be made, with implications for production and cash flows.

If the operations of a firm are relatively constant over the year, there is little need to break down the annual budget. But this is rarely the case. Most firms have some degree of seasonality in their sales. When business is seasonal, the firm must acquire large quantities of goods in advance of the selling season, thus creating a need for funds prior to the receipt of cash from customers.

Even if there is little seasonality in a firm's operations, there may be varying cash requirements over the year, and the cash budget is an important part of the total budget package. Many kinds of expenditures are made, each one occurring only once or twice during the year. Some taxes, insurance premiums, interest payments, dividends, and bonuses are paid in lump sums for the year. It makes a great deal of difference whether a tax payment of $100,000 must be made in January or July. The funds must be available when the payment falls due. Cash budgets prepared for the year as a whole fail to identify these irregular requirements for funds, hence they would not aid the managers in making adequate plans.

Continuous budgets. Most firms like to have plans for at least a year in advance. If budgets are prepared only for fiscal years, as the year goes by, the period for which a budget is available will shorten until the budget for the next year is prepared. To alleviate this problem some firms make use of continuous budgets. Under such a system, a budget for a month (or quarter) will be added as one of these periods goes by. Thus there would be a 12-month budget at all times. Managers are then kept aware of the needs for the next 12 months, regardless of the time of the year.

Project budgets. There are also some kinds of budgets that are not oriented to time periods, but to stages in the completion of projects. For example, a firm building a new plant is concerned with getting the plant on stream according to a time schedule (finish the exterior by March, the interior by August, begin production by December). The time periods selected, which may be of unequal length, are dependent on the project, but of no importance in themselves. The focus is on completing the various stages of the project. Of course the project budget does have implications for periodic budgeting. The project will probably require the expenditure of cash at various times, and these expenditures must be considered in preparing the cash budget.

Capital budgets. Virtually all firms prepare budgets for expenditures for fixed assets, often for many years into the future. Such budgets are called capital budgets. Like project budgets, capital budgets are required periodically because there will be expenditures associated with acquiring fixed assets.

DEVELOPING THE COMPREHENSIVE BUDGET

Sales, Purchase, and Expense Budgets

The comprehensive budget is generally developed well in advance of the period being budgeted for. This is necessary because budgets often must be extensively revised for reasons already discussed. In every case, the budget begins with a sales forecast, because expected sales will determine production requirements, labor and material needs, cash flows, and financing requirements. The way in which each of these various elements is related depends on managerial policies (how many months' supply of inventory should be kept, what credit terms are offered to customers), and operating characteristics (costs, production time).

You are already familiar with the preparation of pro forma income statements based on sales forecasts and cost behavior. The preparation of a budgeted income statement is, with minor exceptions, an extension of volume-cost-profit analysis. Other budgets, especially the pro forma balance sheet and statement of cash flow, present some technical difficulties because of the leads and lags involved. For example, revenue is generally recorded at the point of sale, though cash may not be collected for some time after the sale. The cost of goods sold is recognized at the time that revenue is recorded. But the costs to produce the inventory are incurred prior to the sale. Liabilities are recorded as incurred, but cash payments may be delayed for varying periods of time. Recognition of these leads and lags is the critical technical problem in comprehensive budgeting.

In the remainder of this chapter we shall discuss and illustrate sales forecasts, purchase budgets, and expense budgets. These budgets are usually called **operational budgets**. In Chapter 6 we will complete the process by considering **financial budgets** (pro forma balance sheet and cash budget).

SALES FORECASTING

The development of the sales forecast is critical to budgeting because virtually everything else depends on it. A number of methods have been devised to forecast sales. Not all of these methods can be used by all firms, but it is likely that most firms can use one or more of the methods described below.

Indicator Methods

The sales of many industries are closely associated with some factor in the economy. Sales of long-lasting consumer goods (cars, washing machines, furniture, etc.) generally correlate well with indicators of economic activity like the Gross National Product and personal income. Sales of baby food are associated with the number of births, general foods with population increases, and housing units with the formation of new households.

If a firm is in such an industry, it may be fairly easy to predict total sales for the industry. Then the firm tries to forecast its sales by analyzing the potential share of the market that the firm can reasonably achieve. The scatter-diagram and regression-analysis methods, discussed in Chapter 3 as they relate to cost prediction, can also be applied to sales forecasting.

The sales in many industries depend to a great extent on the sales of other industries. Textile firms watch closely the sales of clothing and take note of forecasts of sales of various kinds of clothes. Makers of cans and bottles look at forecasts for sales of beer and soft drinks. Steel companies and tire companies keep abreast of developments affecting the auto industry. In these situations, a firm tries to develop a forecast for its industry and then for itself, but the key in the former is forecasts from other industries.

The use of an indicator as a basis for sales forecasting requires, of course, that the indicator itself be predictable. Suppose you have observed over time that the sales in your industry correlate well with Gross National Product. You can use GNP to predict industry sales (and then your sales) only if you are able to predict GNP. Thus, once the relationships have been determined as well as possible (probably using regression equations) and a forecast of the indicator is available, the relationships can be used to forecast sales for the industry or firm.

On page 130 is a scatter diagram showing the number of automobiles sold plotted against per capita income (PCI). See if you can develop an equation of the form: Auto sales = Constant + (PCI × ?   ). If per capita income is forecast to be $4,800 for the coming year, what do you forecast for automobile sales? If your firm makes parts for automobiles, what could you do with your forecast of auto sales?

A line fitted to the points would hit the vertical axis at about 4 million cars. The slope would be about .5 million cars per $1,000 in per capita income. The line is at 5.5 million cars at $3,200, 7.9 million at $8,000, a difference in cars of 2.4 million for a $4,800 difference in income. Thus car sales would rise about 500 (2.4 million cars/$4,800 change in income) for each rise of $1 in per capita income. At $4,800 per capita income, sales would be forecast as follows: 4 million + (500 × $4,800) = 4 million + 2.4 million = 6.4 million cars.

FIGURE 5-2

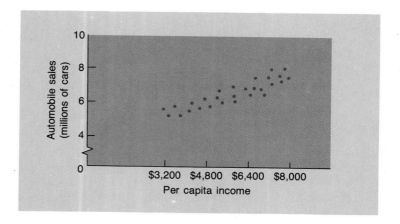

Sometimes predictions of industry sales can be directly obtained. Many trade associations publish studies that provide guidance in sales forecasting. For example, an association of appliance dealers may conduct studies to determine what kinds of appliances are likely to sell, and in what quantities. A study for the purpose of forecasting the sales of washing machines could take into account the overall economic outlook, previous sales of washing machines, the average age of machines being used (to see whether replacements will be significant), and the forecasts for new housing units. Although the study would not indicate the effects of these factors on the sales of any single dealer, each dealer should gain a more accurate picture of what is likely to happen to industry sales and thus apply it to his or her own sales forecasts.

Application of this general approach to sales forecasting is evident from the following excerpt from the 1973 annual report of Pitney Bowes Corporation.

> The retail industry in 1972 began the large-scale replacement of conventional electromechanical cash registers with electronic point-of-sale terminals. These computerized register systems can speed the checkout procedure and increase its accuracy, capture sales information and verify customer credit. They make possible better-informed and more timely decisions by store management, improved productivity, inventory control, and profitability.
>
> Industry forecasts indicate that during the next several years, when the major conversion will take place, the aggregate market for electronic point-of-sale systems and peripheral equipment will be in the order of $1 billion to $1.6 billion in the United States alone. It is estimated that the continuing market for these systems will approximate $50–$350 million annually.
>
> Pitney Bowes, by virtue of our major corporate commitment, our retail-oriented Monarch Marketing Systems and Malco Plastics subsidiaries, and our equity in Pitney-Bowes-Alpex, is in a good position to capture a significant share of this market.

Historical Analysis

The past is not always a good guide to the future, but it usually provides a starting point. Some firms analyze their sales from previous years and project the trend to arrive at a forecast. Thus, if sales have been rising at an average of 10% per year, the firm will start with a forecast based on last year's sales plus 10%. This is only a start. Are there any factors that suggest higher or lower sales? Were last year's sales abnormally high or low because of a strike, unusual weather conditions (ice cream, beer, golf balls, and many other products sell better in hot weather)? Or are there discernible changes in taste that would affect our sales? The past can be referred to for guidance on what might happen, but differences in conditions may cause what will happen to differ from what did.

A number of sophisticated statistical techniques can be used to make predictions from historical data. These techniques are beyond the scope of this book, but you will use some of them in later courses in your curriculum.

Judgmental Methods

Some firms forecast sales using intuition. The sales manager, perhaps in cooperation with other managers and the sales force, will make an educated guess about future sales. Each regional sales manager may, in consultation with sales staff, estimate the expected sales in that area, by customer or product line. Regional forecasts will be reviewed by the chief sales executive and discussed with regional managers, and a forecast for the entire company developed.

The analysis underlying these forecasts may proceed along the lines of the other methods described above, except that the procedures will be less formal. Instead of performing some regression analysis, for example, the manager may go by "feel" of the prospects for the industry and for the firm. The manager may take note of a newspaper article in which it is stated that the length of the work week is decreasing and conclude that people will have increased leisure time. If the firm makes products associated with leisure-time activities, the manager may correctly conclude that sales for the industry and for the firm will be higher than previously forecast.

Which Method to Use

The applicability of any of the methods discussed depends on the characteristics of the firm. Most firms will use a combination of methods. The use of the judgmental method alone may reflect some unwarranted optimism of the sales manager and sales force. The indicator methods may not be applicable to particular firms. Moreover, where indicators are used, there is a danger that such methods will be relied on to the exclusion of other factors. Current conditions may differ from those in force when the relationships among economic indicators and the sales of the firm or industry were first developed. Successful planning is the result of combining sound and experienced business judgment with the judicious use of the quantitative tools available.

Whatever methods are used to forecast, the sales budget for the firm as a whole is likely to have evolved from several forecasts made on a smaller scale. The original forecasts may be by individual product or product line, by geographical area, by department, or by some combination of these. A large company could have several regional sales offices, each with a manager in charge of a particular product line. The product line managers would submit forecasts to the regional sales manager, who would assemble and add them, then pass on the regional budget to company headquarters where all of the regional forecasts would be added up to obtain a budget for the firm as a whole.

Alternatively, the product managers could submit budgets directly to headquarters so that the aggregation would be by product line, rather than by region. It must be stressed that the method followed depends on the organization of the firm and should be the most effective to obtain the desired information in the form most adaptable for planning.

Expected Values and Forecasting

As just indicated, it is not unusual for several different managers to be involved in the preparation of the sales forecast. It is also possible that a firm will develop different forecasts by using different indicators or methods. When different methods are used, or different persons are preparing forecasts, the resulting forecasts are likely to differ. Indeed, even a single manager may come up with several different forecasts based on different assumptions and on his judgment about the conditions in the coming period. In such cases, the concept of expected value is sometimes used to reach a single forecast figure for use in budgeting.

The concept of **expected value** involves identifying available alternatives, assigning probabilities to each, and computing a single outcome. To illustrate, suppose that the sales vice president of a firm has been given three forecasts: one has been developed from forecasts by regional sales managers; another has been prepared by the firm's market research department; and the third originated with the firm's chief economist. The vice president will assign to each forecast a probability expressing his confidence in the accuracy of that forecast. Say that he decides to assign the probabilities 20%, 30%, and 50% to the three forecasts respectively. Below is a calculation of the expected sales using the forecast amounts and his opinions.

Source of Forecast	(1) Sales Forecast in Dollars	(2) Assigned Probability	(1) × (2) Expected Value
Regional sales managers	$6,000,000	.20	$1,200,000
Market research department	$4,500,000	.30	1,350,000
Chief economist	$5,000,000	.50	2,500,000
Expected value		1.00	$5,050,000

Notice that the probabilities assigned must add up to 1, or 100 percent. The concept of expected value has its origins in statistical decision theory and has many more sophisticated uses. In most cases, the assignment of probabilities is based on the manager's judgment and experience, sometimes refined by other statistical techniques. The probabilities are, therefore, termed subjective: different managers might assign different probabilities. As with any other managerial tool, the quality of the final information or decision rests heavily on the quality of the manager's judgment.

Interim Period Forecasts

The forecasting methods discussed apply to sales forecasting of three distinct types: (1) annual forecasts, (2) longer-term forecasts (three to five years), and (3) quarterly or monthly forecasts. Once a forecast for the year has been approved as a basis for planning, it is necessary to break it down into shorter periods.

Often the data used to forecast annual sales (economic indicators, sales for other industries) are already broken down by quarters. Where such data are available, the manager can base his quarterly forecast on the same indicator used for the annual forecast. Many firms have developed reliable criteria for breaking down annual forecasts. Their experiences may show that particular percentages of yearly sales occur in particular quarters or months (15% of annual sales are concentrated in March, 40% in the first quarter, and so on).

Sometimes firms that are in highly seasonal industries, especially those that depend on the weather, will regularly revise their forecasts based on current information about weather conditions. Such forecasts may be useful in determining when the high sales season is likely to begin, thus providing a start toward developing production and purchasing plans. A department store manager, having learned that winter weather is expected to start earlier than usual this year, can begin stocking up on winter clothing, equipment for winter sports, and cold remedies so that he will be prepared to meet the anticipated increases in sales.

EXPENSE BUDGETS

Until now, we have generally assumed that a single manager (Ted, for example) was running all aspects of the business and was therefore responsible for planning and controlling all costs. In most businesses a number of managers exercise control over costs, and higher-level managers are responsible for the costs incurred by lower-level managers.

In developing budgets, it is necessary to recognize that individual managers direct differing activities, and costs are incurred in each of these activities. Acceptable limitations on cost incurrence must be established for effective planning and control. These limitations, or allowances, set the amounts of cost that managers can incur in achieving their goals.

Two general methods are used to develop budget allowances. One approach sets the budget for a particular cost at a single amount without any reference to or consideration of the volume of activity. An allowance set this way is called a **static budget**. This approach would be used with fixed costs. The other approach sets a variable, or **flexible budget** allowance, based on volume of activity. Budgets are set in this fashion for variable costs and mixed costs. Budgets for some discretionary fixed costs could also be flexible. For example, a flexible budget allowance would be appropriate if it is the firm's policy to spend an amount equal to some percentage of sales on advertising, research and development, bonuses, and other discretionary elements of cost.

A static budget is generally set for fixed cost elements, both committed and discretionary. The budget allowance for committed costs can generally be set by reference to existing obligations because costs to be incurred have largely been set by actions already taken. Discretionary cost allowances would generally be set by managerial policy, and the manager responsible for controlling the cost would participate with higher management in determining the amount to be allowed.

A flexible budget allowance would be set using procedures similar to those employed in predicting costs. The variable cost component per unit of volume would be found by using one or more procedures outlined in Chapter 3 and the fixed component by managerial policy or reference to commitments arising out of previous decisions.

Consider two specific examples of budget allowances that would depend on measures of volume other than sales in units or in dollars. Suppose we want to establish a budget allowance for the manager of the customer billing department, and that the only costs that vary in the department are the costs of billing forms and postage. Sales in units or in dollars are not good measures of the volume of activity in that department, because the form and postage costs will be the same for each order, whether the order is for one or ten units, $30 or $500. If the cost of a billing form and postage is $.40, the budget allowance might be the monthly fixed cost plus $.40 per bill processed and matched.

The most obvious example of the need for a measure of volume other than sales is the case of a production manager. The production budget for the period must be related to production volume rather than sales. Whether units are sold or not, the cost to make them is incurred at the time of production. The production manager will incur costs before they become expenses in the income statement. Thus the budget allowance would be some fixed amount plus the variable costs of production times the number of units produced.

Suppose that, using the technique discussed in Chapter 3, the factory overhead costs to produce a particular product have been identified as given below.

Cost	Fixed Amount per Month	Variable Amount per Unit of Product
Indirect labor	$1,200	$ .50
Supplies	200	.40
Maintenance	2,400	.10
Depreciation	1,200	0
Miscellaneous	700	.05
Totals	$5,700	$1.05

Suppose further that the expected production for the coming month is 1,000 units. The original budget allowances for the month will be determined and reported as in the first column in Exhibit 5-1. Budgeted amounts for each cost element are computed by using the formula:

$$\begin{array}{c}\text{Flexible}\\\text{budget}\\\text{amount}\end{array} = \begin{array}{c}\text{fixed}\\\text{cost}\\\text{per}\\\text{month}\end{array} + \left(\begin{array}{cc}\text{production} & \text{variable}\\\text{quantity} & \times\ \text{cost per}\\ & \text{unit}\end{array}\right)$$

For example, the budget amount for indirect labor is computed as $1,200 + (1,000 × $.50) or $1,700. This exhibit is actually the beginning of a performance report which will be completed later when actual production is known.

If actual production during the month turned out to be 1,300 units, a revised budget allowance would be computed for each cost element, taking into consideration the higher production. For example, for indirect labor, the flexible budget allowance for the month would now be $1,850 [$1,200 + (1,300 units × $.50)]. In Exhibit 5-2, we have completed the performance report by inserting the flexible budget allowances for the achieved level of production, we have inserted some assumed actual costs, and we have computed a variance (difference between the revised budget and the actual costs).

Exhibit 5-1
Production Performance Report

Month _____   Product _____
Manager _____

Budget Allowances

	Budgeted Production	*Actual Production*	*Actual Costs Incurred*	*Variance*
Production, in units	1,000	═══		
Indirect labor	$1,700			
Supplies	600			
Maintenance	2,500			
Depreciation	1,200			
Miscellaneous	750			
Totals	$6,750			

Exhibit 5-2
Production Performance Report

Month _____   Product _____
Manager _____

Budget Allowances

	Budgeted Production	*Actual Production*	*Actual Costs Incurred*	*Variance Favorable (Unfavorable)*
Production, in units	1,000	1,300		
Indirect labor	$1,700	$1,850	$1,870	($20)
Supplies	600	720	705	15
Maintenance	2,500	2,530	2,470	60
Depreciation	1,200	1,200	1,200	—
Miscellaneous	750	765	780	(15)
Totals	$6,750	$7,065	$7,025	$40

When actual costs are less than the budget allowance, the variance is said to be favorable; when the reverse is true, the variance is said to be unfavorable. Hence, the variances for supplies, maintenance, and total costs were favorable. In Chapter 12 we shall discuss methods for analyzing variances.

It should be noted that in our example we assumed that the cost prediction formulas for the various cost elements applied to the actual level of production achieved. But we know from Chapter 3 that cost behavior tends to be predictable over a certain range of volume and also that a choice must be made among cost formulas when faced with step-variable costs. For this reason, some firms will prepare schedules of flexible budget allowances for several different levels of volume. These allowances will normally take into consideration the changes in cost formulas resulting from large differences in volume. Then, at the end of a period when actual volume is known, the firm will compute its flexible budget allowances based on the cost formulas relevant to that general volume range. Although the computations may be more numerous, the principles underlying the use of alternative production budgets are the same as those presented for a single budgeted production level.

BUDGETING AND HUMAN BEHAVIOR

Budgeting necessarily entails behavioral problems. These problems include the following: conflicting views, imposed budgets, budgets as check-up devices, and unwise adherence to budgets.

Conflicts

We can illustrate the problem of conflicts in budgeting by considering a matter of importance to almost any firm—its inventory level. The sales manager wants inventory to be as high as possible because it is easier to make sales if the goods are available to the customer immediately. The financial manager would like to keep inventories as low as possible because there are costs associated with having inventory: storage, insurance, taxes, interest, and so on. If a manufacturing process is involved, the production manager has a special point of view. The manager is not interested in inventory per se, but he does have an indirect interest. The production manager wants long runs of production, steady production, no rush orders, no overtime, because those conditions will minimize the costs of production. Thus three managers have different views on the desirable level of inventory. Each will be evaluated by reference to how well the individual does his or her job, so each has a lot at stake in the determination of inventory policy. The conflict is resolved with great difficulty, if at all. The managerial accountant may be called in to determine the best level of inventory for the firm. Such a determination must weigh the costs of having inventory with the cost of lost sales resulting from not having enough inventory. The task is difficult, but the objectives of the individual managers must all be considered, together with the general concern for the welfare of the firm.

Imposed Budgets

We have assumed in this chapter that cost levels, production levels, and so on were determined rather mechanically. But this is seldom the case. Managers and workers determine cost levels by how well they perform their assigned jobs. It is not uncommon for higher levels of management to set performance standards for individuals below them. When such is the case, the standards are said to be imposed, and serious behavioral problems can arise or be avoided depending on the managers' attitudes.

Some managers hold the opinion that performance standards should be set very high (costs very low)—so high that almost no one could be expected to meet the budget. This is sometimes justified on the grounds that it "keeps the managers and workers on their toes,'' and assumes that they will slacken their performances if they can easily meet a budget. Others say that budgets should be set so that they are achievable given a good, but not exceptional, performance.

Significant problems can result from the imposition of unachievable budgets. Managers tend to become discouraged and do not commit themselves to the achievement of budgeted goals. They may act in ways that seem to help achieve goals (such as scrimping on preventive maintenance to achieve lower costs in the short run). But this is likely to be harmful in the longer run (when machinery breaks down and production must be halted altogether).

The imposition of unachievable goals may also have serious financial effects. Management actions based on such a budget may be improper; that is, the budget will be useless for planning, when facilitating planning is one of its primary purposes.

Consider, for example, the implications of setting unrealistically high sales goals. Based on those goals, production plans will be made, including perhaps commitments for materials and the hiring and training of factory workers. Based on sales goals, production, and inventory policies, storage areas for inventory will be acquired. Based on sales goals, cash receipts will be planned, and the firm will estimate and perhaps negotiate certain amounts of short-term financing.[1] Now what if the sales goals are not realized? Inventory levels will be higher than expected, and additional space may have to be contracted for at unfavorable rates, or production efficiency may be interfered with to accommodate the extra inventory. Cash receipts will not materialize as planned, and additional short-term financing may have to be negotiated on terms unfavorable to the firm. If production schedules are subsequently adjusted to bring them into line with lower sales and to reduce inventory, employee relations may suffer as workers are laid off, and relations with suppliers may be harmed as delays in delivery of materials are requested.

We could say that the firm's planning based on its budget has been ineffective. At their worst, unrealistic budgets can have serious and detrimental financial effects on the firm. At the very least, unrealistic budgets will probably simply be ignored.

It is possible that imposed budgets can reflect achievable, realistic performance goals. There are, however, at least two reasons for adopting another approach, which involves participation in standard-setting by the individuals expected to meet those standards. First, although a particular manager may be generally aware of the problems associated with the tasks performed by people responsible to him, he cannot be as well informed as the persons performing the tasks. Second, a considerable body of empirical evidence suggests that allowing individuals a say as to their expected levels of performance is conducive to better performance than when those individuals are not consulted. While the manager, including the top-level managers, must take the final responsibility for establishing goals, their methods of arriving at those goals can have a significant effect on the performance of individuals affected by those goals.

Budgets As "Check-Up" Devices

Behavioral problems do not arise solely because of the procedure followed for developing budget allowances. Comparisons of budgeted and actual results and subsequent evaluation of performance also introduce difficulties. In ideal circumstances managers would use actual

---

[1]One of the advantages of the cash portion of the comprehensive budget is that it allows the firm to identify financing needs before they occur, so the managers have time to seek the best financing sources. More of this in Chapter 6.

results to evaluate their own performance, to evaluate the performance of others, and to correct elements of the operations that seem to be out of control. The budget serves as a feedback device, letting managers know the results of their actions. Having seen that something is wrong, they can take steps to correct it.

Unfortunately, budgets are often used more for checking up on managers, and the feedback function is ignored. Where this is the case, the manager is constantly looking over his shoulder and trying to think of ways to explain unfavorable results. The time spent on thinking of ways to defend the results could be more profitably used to plan and control operations. Some evaluation of performance is necessary, but the budget ought not to be perceived as a club to be held over the heads of managers. More attention will be given to behavioral problems of performance evaluation in Chapters 10, 11, and 12.

Unwise Adherence to Budgets

In our discussion of expense budgets we pointed out that the budget sets limits on cost incurrence, allowances beyond which managers are not expected to go. This can cause the manager to spend either too little or too much.

There are times when exceeding the budget may be beneficial for the firm. A sales manager may believe that a visit to several important customers or potential customers will result in greatly increased sales. However, if taking the trip would result in exceeding the travel budget, he or she will be reluctant to do so.

At the other extreme, a manager who has kept costs well under the budget might be tempted to make frivolous expenditures in order to get expenditures up to the budgeted allowance. The manager may fear that the budget for the following year will reflect the lower costs for the current year. Not wishing to be given a lower budget next year, the manager will take an undesirable action in order to protect personal interests.

ILLUSTRATION

We shall illustrate the preparation of a comprehensive budget by working with the Cross Company, a retailing firm. The illustration will be done in two parts. In this chapter we shall prepare the sales forecast, purchases budget, and tentative pro forma income statement. In Chapter 6 we shall prepare the cash budget, which requires some of the data in the budgets developed here. We shall then see how the operational and financial budgets are related, especially how the results of the cash budget may induce the managers to look again at the operating budgets and possibly make changes in them. The example uses dollar amounts that are unrealistically small because we want to avoid long and arduous computations.

The managers of the Cross Company have spent a good deal of time working up a sales forecast for the six-month period, January 1, 19X4 through June 30, 19X4. They have forecast total sales of $4,800 for the period, broken down by month as follows:

Jan.	Feb.	Mar.	Apr.	May	June
$400	$600	$800	$1,000	$1,200	$800

Sales are highly seasonal in the six-month period. May sales are three times January sales; there is a buildup in volume through May, then a drop in June.

We wish first to develop a budgeted or pro froma income statement for the six-month period. Generally, it is not necessary to do this by month, although the other budgets will be broken down by month. The managers have also decided that the following assumptions about cost behavior will provide a good basis for planning.

Cost of goods sold will be 60% of sales dollars. Other variable costs will be 15% of sales. Total fixed costs will be $240, of which $120 is depreciation expense. With this additional information we can prepare a pro forma income statement.

Cross Company
Pro Forma Income Statement
Six-Month Period Ending June 30, 19X4

Sales	$4,800
Cost of goods sold (60% of sales)	2,880
Gross profit	1,920
Other variable costs (15% of sales)	720
Contribution margin	1,200
Fixed costs (depreciation, rent, etc.)	240
Income	$ 960

In a real-life situation the preparation would be much more detailed, with several managers presenting sales forecasts and assumptions about cost behavior; their budgets would be combined and refined to obtain the budget for the firm as a whole.

Purchases Budget

Our next step is to determine what inventory level is considered desirable. In an actual situation, this can be extremely complex. We shall here assume that the interested managers have reached agreement that inventory should be kept at a level of two months' budgeted sales. That is, it has been decided that at the end of each month the firm should have on hand enough inventory to carry the sales of the following two months. This approach to setting inventory levels follows from the fact that a firm stocks inventory in anticipation of sales. Hence, if sales are expected to increase over the next period, inventory should also increase. Remember, as we move to budgeting inventory and purchases, that because inventory is carried at cost, we use costs and not sales prices to budget inventory and purchases.

From the pro forma income statement, it can be seen that the cost of goods sold ratio is 60% of sales. Hence, the required ending inventory at any month end is the sum of budgeted cost of goods sold for the following two months. We also know that at the end of December the firm had inventory of $600. With this information we can determine purchasing requirements for most of the six-month period as shown in Exhibit 5-3 on page 142. The format shown there is generally applicable for budgeting purchases. It is readily derived from the cost-of-goods sold computation used so often in financial accounting.

$$\text{Cost of goods sold} = \text{beginning inventory} + \text{purchases} - \text{ending inventory}$$

Adding ending inventory and subtracting beginning inventory from both sides, we obtain:

$$\text{Purchases} = \frac{\text{cost of}}{\text{goods sold}} + \frac{\text{ending}}{\text{inventory}} - \frac{\text{beginning}}{\text{inventory}}$$

Exhibit 5-3
Purchases Budget

	Jan.	Feb.	Mar.	Apr.	May	June	Total
Ending inventory required	$ 840	$1,080	$1,320	$1,200			
Cost of sales for month (60% of sales)	240	360 + 480	600	720 + 480			2,880
Total requirements	1,080	1,440	1,800	1,800			
Less: Beginning inventory (ending inventory of prior month)	600	840	1,080	1,320	1,200		
Purchases required	$ 480	$ 600	$ 720	$ 480			

Note that the cost of sales for each month is 60% of the budgeted sales for that month. The sum of the cost of sales for two consecutive months is thus the inventory required at the beginning of that two-month period. For example, the inventory required at the end of January ($840) is the sum of the cost of sales for February ($360) and March ($480). The circled items show the derivations of the ending inventory for January and April.

The total requirement for any one month is the amount needed to cover that month's sales plus the amount that the company has determined must be on hand at the end of that month. The total requirements can be met from two sources: goods already on hand (beginning inventory) and purchases during the month. Thus purchase requirements are total requirements less beginning inventory. You should work through the budget to be sure you understand the calculations.

Exhibit 5-3 is incomplete because we cannot determine the ending inventory required for May. To do so we need to know budgeted sales for July. Similarly, to determine the ending inventory for June it is necessary to know the budgeted sales for August. Suppose budgeted sales for July and August are $700 and $800, respectively. The complete schedule would then be as follows.

The rows for cost of sales and purchases add across to the totals, but the inventory rows and total requirements row do not. The beginning inventory in the total column is the beginning inventory for the six-month period. The ending inventory is the required ending inventory for the last month being budgeted. The total column is the result you would obtain if you were budgeting only for the six-month period as a whole.

The inventory account may be reconciled just as is done in financial accounting. The beginning balance is $600, purchases are $3,180, and cost of sales is $2,880, leaving an ending balance of $900. The ending balance, derived as part of the purchases budget, will

Exhibit 5-4
Purchases Budget

	Jan.	Feb.	Mar.	Apr.	May	June	Total
Ending inventory required	$ 840	$1,080	$1,320	$1,200	$ 900	$ 900	$ 900
Cost of sales for month	240	360 + 480		600	720	480	2,880
Total requirements	1,080	1,440	1,800	1,800	1,620	1,380	3,780
Beginning inventory	600	840	1,080	1,320	1,200	900	600
Purchases required	$ 480	$ 600	$ 720	$ 480	$ 420	$ 480	$3,180

also be used for the June 30 pro forma balance sheet. The purchases budget is also significant in the process of deriving the cash budget.

PURCHASES BUDGET—A MANUFACTURING FIRM

Just as a retailer must budget purchases to meet sales and inventory policy, so a manufacturer must budget production to meet sales and inventory policy. That is, the manufacturer must *produce* sufficient units to meet the goals, while the retailer must *purchase* those units. However, the manufacturer must purchase sufficient materials to meet production goals. Thus, both types of firms must plan purchases. And the basic idea of such planning is the same, but the development of the final budget is somewhat more complex for the manufacturer because such a firm must first develop a budget for production in units before developing a purchases budget in dollars. Units must be used first because both variable and fixed costs are associated with the production process, and the presence of the latter makes the use of dollars difficult without an intermediate budget in units.

Suppose that a manufacturer wishes to keep an inventory of the firm's product equal to the budgeted sales for the following two months (much like the retailer in the earlier example). In developing this budget for the six months beginning in January, the following data have been gathered.

Units of product on hand at December 31   200 units

Anticipated sales for the next eight months:

January	120 units	May	336 units
February	180 units	June	240 units
March	240 units	July	210 units
April	280 units	August	240 units

Variable costs of production per unit:
Materials $2.00
Labor   3.00
Manufacturing overhead:
    Fringe benefits   .40

Power	.30
Supplies	.30
Total	$ 6.00

Fixed costs of production per month:	
Rent of machinery	$ 400
Supervisory salaries	600
Insurance	100
Managerial salaries	800
Total	$1,900

The manufacturer has identified his costs as variable or fixed, as did the retailer. But, for the manufacturer, the variable production costs will vary with the number of units produced, not with the number of units sold. A production budget shows the number of units that must be produced each period to meet sales and inventory requirements. Such a determination is presented below.

Production Budget
(In Units)

	Jan.	Feb.	Mar.	Apr.	May	June	Total
Ending inventory required	420	520	616	576	450	450	450
Expected sales	120	180	240	280	336	240	1,396
Total units required	540	700	856	856	786	690	1,846
Beginning inventory	200	420	520	616	576	450	200
Required production	340	280	336	240	210	240	1,646

With this additional information it is possible to prepare a production budget in dollars.

Production Budget

	Jan.	Feb.	Mar.	Apr.	May	June	Total
Variable costs (production × $6)	$2,040	$1,680	$2,016	$1,440	$1,260	$1,440	$ 9,876
Fixed costs	1,900	1,900	1,900	1,900	1,900	1,900	11,400
Total	$3,940	$3,580	$3,916	$3,340	$3,160	$3,340	$21,276

Again, production costs for a manufacturer are similar to the costs of purchases for a non-manufacturer, the major difference being that production costs will have a fixed component whereas purchases costs will not.

The development of a complete budget for a manufacturing firm could entail one further difficulty. A production process uses some materials that may be purchased only as they are needed or purchased in advance. If materials are purchased in advance of production needs, the budgeting process must go one step further—to compute the amount of materials purchases required to meet the firm's projected production needs. This computation would be similar to those required for a purchases budget in units.

The production budget, like the purchases budget, is needed for the development of a cash budget, which will be discussed in detail in Chapter 6.

SUMMARY

Comprehensive budgeting is vital to effective planning and control. The comprehensive budget is perhaps the major planning document developed by the firm and consists of a set of financial statements and other schedules showing the expected results for a future period. The development of a comprehensive budget formalizes management objectives and helps coordinate the many activities performed within a single firm.

Sales forecasting is critical to the budgeting process; it underlies all other budgets. Several approaches are used for forecasting sales, the approach adopted depending on the reliability of available data, the nature of the product, and the experience and sophistication of the managers. The sales forecast and assumptions about cost behavior and inventory policy are used to prepare the purchases and expense budgets and a pro forma income statement. A flexible budget allowance is recommended in dealing with variable costs; it is advantageous for subsequent performance evaluation and identifying problems requiring action.

The budgeting process entails numerous behavioral problems, which can be particularly severe if managers do not participate in the development of the budget, or if budget goals are perceived as unachievable. However, used wisely, the budgeting process can help resolve conflicts among managers.

KEY TERMS

capital budget	inventory policy
comprehensive budget	operating budget
expense budget	production budget
financial budget	purchases budget
flexible budget allowance	sales forecast
imposed budget	static budget

KEY FORMULAS

$$\text{Budgeted purchases*} = \text{desired ending inventory} + \text{cost of current sales} - \text{beginning inventory}$$

$$\text{Budgeted production, in units} = \text{desired ending inventory} + \text{units needed for current sales} - \text{beginning inventory}$$

*For budgeting purchases in a manufacturing firm, "cost of current sales" becomes "cost of units of material needed for current production."

REVIEW PROBLEM

Using the following data for the Exempli Company, prepare a budgeted income statement and a purchases budget in units and dollars for January 19X4.

Budgeted sales for January	5,000 units at $20	$100,000
Budgeted sales for February	6,000 units at $20	$120,000
Cost data:		
Purchase price of product		$5 per unit
Commission to salespeople		10% of sales
Depreciation		$2,000 per month
Other operating expenses		$40,000 per month
		plus 5% of sales

Inventory policy is to maintain inventory at 150% of the coming month's sales requirements. The inventory at December 31, 19X3 is $30,000 (6,000 units at $5), which is less than budgeted.

Answers to review problem

Exempli Company
Budgeted Income Statement
for January 19X4

Sales		$100,000
Cost of sales (5,000 units at $5)		25,000
Gross profit		75,000
Variable costs:		
Commissions (10% × $100,000)	$10,000	
Variable operating expenses (5% × $100,000)	5,000	15,000
Contribution margin		60,000
Fixed costs:		
Depreciation	2,000	
Other operating expenses	40,000	42,000
Budgeted income		$ 18,000

Purchases Budget for January 19X4

	Units	Dollars
Desired ending inventory (6,000 × 150%)	9,000	$ 45,000
Cost of sales	5,000	25,000
Total requirements	14,000	$ 70,000
Beginning inventory	6,000	30,000
Purchases required for the month	8,000	$ 40,000

ASSIGNMENT MATERIAL

Questions for Discussion

5-1 **"Why bother with budgets?"**   Evaluate the following statement. "I suppose that budgets are fine for firms that can plan ahead, but I cannot. Things are too uncertain for me to make plans, and besides, I have to spend my time looking after the day-to-day operations and trying to figure out what is wrong."

5-2 **Expense budgeting**   What would be the major factors to be known in setting the budgeted amounts for the following:

    (a)   commissions to salespeople

    (b)   electricity

    (c)   taxes on land and buildings

    (d)   taxes on personal property (inventory, machinery, assets other than land and buildings)

    (e)   charitable contributions

    (f)   office salaries

5-3 **Relationships of selling expenses and sales**   The chapter suggests that there are disadvantages in budgeting such expenditures as advertising, research and development, and product promotion based on some fixed percentage of sales. What disadvantages do you see if the firm is forecasting: (1) a strong demand for its products during the coming year with a substantial increase in sales over the prior year, and (2) a relatively weak demand for its products with a decline in sales from the prior year?

5-4 **Sales forecasting—effects of external events**   For each of the following situations, indicate what effect, if any, there would be on the sales forecast that you have already prepared. Explain your reasoning.

    (a)   Your firm makes building materials. The federal government has just announced a new program designed to assist low-income families to buy their own homes.

    (b)   Your firm makes toys. The government announces that the economic outlook is better than had been thought. Personal income is likely to increase and unemployment decrease.

    (c)   One of your competitors in the furniture business has developed a process that will greatly reduce its costs. The other firm announces a cut in its prices.

    (d)   Your firm employs many highly skilled workers. A new plant is built near yours that is offering much higher wages to such workers than you are willing to pay.

    (e)   You make parts for the automobile industry. A strike against your major customer is announced by the head of the union.

    (f)   You process baby food. The number of marriages will drop sharply because of poor economic conditions.

    (g)   You make heating and air conditioning equipment. The prices of electricity, heating oil, and natural gas are expected to rise rapidly.

    (h)   You make insulation for houses and other buildings. The prices of electricity, heating oil, and natural gas are expected to rise rapidly.

    (i)   Your firm is a publisher of college textbooks. Recently released statistics show that the numbers of high school seniors and juniors have fallen off from previous years.

    (j)   Your firm makes plumbing pipe from copper. The major source of copper is Chile, which has just gone to war with one of its neighbors.

    (k)   Your firm makes golf balls, but not clubs. You read that sales of golf clubs have shot up over previously anticipated levels.

    (l)   Your firm makes recreational vehicles of the "house on wheels" variety. A new supply of oil has been discovered in the United States and the supply of oil will increase greatly.

(m) Your firm makes fertilizer. A drought in a large nation threatens to destroy its crops.

5-5   Budget requests Some organizations follow the practice of cutting back all budget requests by some set percentage, ignoring the merits of the specific requests. For example, the total budget for each department may be reduced by 5% or each line item in each department might be reduced by 5%. Explain how this practice could be considered beneficial. Is there any way in which this practice could be considered harmful?

5-6   Sales forecasting The development of a sales forecast requires estimating both (1) the number of units of products of various kinds to be sold, and (2) the prices at which those products will be sold. Moreover, while almost all sales forecasting efforts give some consideration to the general economic outlook, most firms will be concerned with more specific indicators of the outlook in their industry. For each of the firms below, identify more specifically some major factors that would be considered in forecasting sales and some of the problems that would relate to the estimates of units and prices:

(a) a maker of toys
(b) an electric utility
(c) a builder of residential housing
(d) a college textbook publisher
(e) a maker of high fashion clothing
(f) a maker of airplanes used by large, scheduled airlines

5-7   Sales forecasting—value of indicators The following conversation took place between two company presidents.

Grant: "We hired a consultant to help us with our sales forecasting and he has really done a good job. As you know, we make ballpoint pen refills and he found that our sales are very closely correlated with sales of refillable pens from four months previous. He says that four months seems to be the average life of the cartridge that most firms use in their original pens. Of course, we don't make pens, but our refills will fit the pens that nearly every firm makes."

Harrison: "We have done the same thing. Our major product is baby bottles and our consultant found that the number of bottles we sell is very closely related to the number of births about a month later. People seem to buy bottles about a month before the baby is born."

Required: Determine which firm seems to be in the better position to forecast its sales. Explain your answer.

Exercises

5-8   Purchases budget The following data refer to the operations of the Cromwill Company, a retail store.

Sales Forecast—19X9

January	$40,000
February	55,000
March	70,000
April	60,000

Other data:

1. Cost of sales is 40% of sales.
2. Inventory is maintained at one and one-half times budgeted sales for the coming month (at cost).
3. The beginning inventory is $30,000.

Required

Prepare a purchases budget for each of the first three months of 19X9, and for the quarter as a whole.

5-9 Budgeted income statement and purchases budget The following data relate to the operations of the Thomas Company, a retail store.

Sales forecast—19X4

January	$ 60,000
February	80,000
March	100,000
April	120,000

1. Cost of sales is 40% of sales. Other variable costs are 20% of sales.
2. Inventory is maintained at twice budgeted sales requirements for the following month. The beginning inventory reflects this policy.
3. Fixed costs are $20,000 per month.

Required

1. Prepare a budgeted income statement for the first quarter of 19X4.
2. Prepare a purchases budget, by month, for the first quarter.

5-10 Budgeting manpower and costs The Kramwer Company has established a policy of having a foreman for every nine workers; whenever the number of foremen divided into the number of workers is greater than nine, a foreman is hired. The firm is expanding output and has budgeted production as follows:

January	4,500 units
February	4,800 units
March	5,400 units
April	6,100 units
May	6,800 units
June	7,300 units

A production worker can produce 100 units per month. Both workers and foremen are hired at the beginning of the month in which they are to be added. Workers are paid $600 per month, foremen, $1,100.

Required

Prepare a budget of requirements for workers and for foremen, by month, in number and dollar cost.

5-11 Purchase budget The Warner Company expects the following sales by month in units for the first six months of 19X6.

	Jan.	Feb.	Mar.	Apr.	May	June
Sales	1,500	1,800	1,900	2,500	1,900	2,000

The firm has a policy of maintaining an inventory equal to budgeted sales for the following two months. The beginning inventory reflects this policy. Each unit costs $4.

Required
1. Prepare purchases budgets for as many months as you can in (a) units, and (b) dollars.
2. Explain why you had to stop where you did.

5-12 Interim period sales forecasts The Rashad Company has prepared its annual sales forecast, expecting to achieve sales of $600,000. The controller is uncertain about the pattern of sales to be expected by month and asks you to prepare a monthly budget of sales. You collect the following data from last year. The pattern of sales is representative of a normal year.

Month—Prior Year	Sales
January	$20,000
February	25,000
March	20,000
April	32,000
May	34,000
June	45,000
July	50,000
August	66,000
September	68,000
October	70,000
November	40,000
December	30,000

Required
Based on the data given, prepare a monthly sales budget for the first six months of the coming year.

5-13 Sales forecast and budgeted income statements The Weinstock Building Supply firm operates a chain of lumberyards in a large metropolitan area. The sales manager has retained a prominent economist to develop sales forecasting methods to enable the firm to plan better. The economist, for a substantial fee, has developed the following equation that he says will forecast sales quite well based on past patterns of behavior.

Monthly sales in dollars = $136,000 + ($52 × number of building permits issued in prior month)

The sales manager is confused and asks your advice. He presents you with the following data regarding actual and forecast issues of building permits. The forecasts were developed by the Association of Builders in the area and have generally been quite accurate.

March	2,300 (actual)
April	3,500 (forecast)
May	4,800 (forecast)
June	7,100 (forecast)
July	6,500 (forecast)

It is now April 3 and the sales manager would like forecasts of sales and income for as many months as you can prepare. He also states that cost of goods sold, which is all variable, is 45% of sales. Other variable costs are 8% of sales, and fixed costs are $140,000 per month.

Required: Prepare budgeted income statements for as many months as you can, given the data available.

5-14 Flexible budget and variance   The Adams Company makes a single product. Materials for a unit of the product cost $2, labor is $3, and manufacturing overhead is $20,000 per month fixed, plus $2 per unit variable (with production). In one month, production was 18,000 units and costs incurred were as follows: materials $34,900, labor $55,200, variable overhead $35,600, and fixed overhead $20,000.

Required
1. Prepare a flexible expense budget formula.
2. What should costs have been to produce 18,000 units? (Consider each element of cost separately.)
3. What were the variances between actual and budgeted costs?

5-15 Modifying a production budget   The sales and production budgets for the McPherson Company are shown below. It is now the end of January, during which actual sales were 11,000 units. The sales manager expects the sales for each of the remaining months of the year will also be 10% higher than originally budgeted. She wishes to increase production to take advantage of the higher demand. The firm has a policy of keeping inventory equal to budgeted sales for the following two months. Actual production in January was 14,000 units and the beginning inventory was 22,000 units. Below are budgeted data based on previous estimates.

	Jan.	Feb.	Mar.	Apr.	May	June
	11,000	13,200	15,400	16,500	15,400	14,300
Budgeted sales	10,000	12,000	14,000	15,000	14,000	13,000
Budgeted production	14,000	15,000	14,000	13,000	12,000	

Required
Prepare a modified sales budget and production budget through April.

5-16 Production and purchases budgets   The production manager of the Crass Company wishes to maintain an inventory of raw materials equal to budgeted production needs for the next two months. Each unit of product takes 5 lbs. of raw material which costs $2 per pound. Inventory of finished goods is usually maintained at 150% of the following month's budgeted sales. The sales budget for the first six months of the coming year, given in units, is as follows:

Month	Budgeted Sales	Month	Budgeted Sales
January	12,000	April	16,000
February	14,000	May	19,000
March	11,000	June	13,000

As of December 31, there were 170,000 lbs. of raw material on hand and 17,000 units of finished product.

Required
Prepare budgets for production and purchases of raw materials in units and pounds, respectively, for as many months as possible.

5-17 Relationships   The following data relate to the Foote Company operations for April. No change in inventories is planned.

Pro Forma Income Statement
Month of April

Sales (100 units at $40)		$4,000
Variable costs:		
Materials ($4 per unit)	$400	
Labor ($6 per unit)	600	
Overhead—manufacturing ($4 unit)	400	
Selling expenses ($2 per unit)	200	1,600
Contribution margin		2,400
Fixed costs:		
Manufacturing	600	
Selling and administrative	600	1,200
Income		$1,200

Required

Fill in the blanks.

1. Budgeted production for April is ____ units.
2. Total variable manufacturing costs for April are $____.
3. The sale of an additional 10 units would increase income by $____.
4. Total costs and expenses if 120 units were sold would be $____.
5. Break-even volume in units is ____.
6. If variable manufacturing costs increased $2 per unit, income at 100 units sold would be $____.
7. If fixed costs increased by $240, and the firm wanted income of $1,200, sales in units would have to be ____.
8. If ending inventory were to be 20 units higher than beginning inventory, manufacturing costs incurred during the period would be $____.

5-18 Budgeting production and materials purchases The Williams Company expects the following sales by month, in units, for the first eight months of 19X9.

	January	February	March	April	May	June	July	August
Budgeted Sales	1,500	1,800	1,900	2,500	1,900	2,000	2,000	1,800

The company's one product, the Tow, requires two raw materials: Tics and Tacs. Each Tow requires two Tics and three Tacs.

The firm follows the policy of having finished goods equal to 50% of budgeted sales for the following two months. Raw material inventories are maintained at 150% of budgeted production needs for the coming month. All inventories at December 31, 19X8, reflect these policies.

Required

1. Prepare a production budget for Tows for as many months as you can.
2. Prepare purchases budgets for Tics and Tacs for as many months as you can.

5-19 Relationships among sales and production budgets   Partially completed sales and production budgets for the Firmin Company are shown below. The firm maintains an inventory equal to 150% of the budgeted sales for the coming month. Fill in the blanks.

Sales Budget
(In Units)

Jan.	Feb.	Mar.	Apr.	May	June	July
3,000	3,400	4200	4600	6200	5,800	5400

Production Budget
(In Units)

	Jan.	Feb.	Mar.	Apr.	May	June
Ending inventory	5100	6,300	6900	9300	8,700	8100
Sales	3,000	3400	4200	4600	6200	5,800
Total requirements	8100	9700	11100	13,900	14900	13900
Beginning inventory	4500	5,100	6300	6,900	9300	8700
Production	3,600	4600	4800	7,000	5600	5,200

5-20 Inventory policy—conflicts   The production manager and sales manager of the Norfast Company are arguing about inventory and production policy. The sales manager wants extremely high production in the first few months of the coming year to meet anticipated high demand for the product. The production manager would like to spread production more evenly over the period in order to keep production costs low. He would prefer to keep production at or below 12,000 units each month because production in excess of 12,000 requires overtime work and hence extra pay. The extra cost is $3 per unit. The sales manager has suggested a production schedule for the first six months of the year as follows:

Month	Production in Units
1	12,000
2	15,000
3	15,000
4	9,000
5	8,000
6	7,000

The sales manager believes that any shortfall in production will result in lost sales. He estimates that one unit in sales will be lost for every five units that production falls below his request. Contribution margin is $12 at normal production cost.

The sales manager is evaluated on sales and contribution margin, based on budgets, and the production manager on his meeting or not meeting budgeted costs of production, so each manager has an important stake in the outcome of the dispute.

Required

What recommendations can you make? Support your recommendations with calculations.

Problems

5-21 Budgeted income statements—expected values   The Burke Company is preparing its comprehensive budget for 19X7. The sales manager has said that he does not wish to pin down a single estimate of sales, but would prefer to give three forecasts, along with his estimates of the probabilities he attaches to them.

Sales Forecasts	Probabilities
$ · 800,000	.3
1,000,000	.5
1,200,000	.2

Variable costs are 40% of sales and total fixed costs are budgeted as $520,000.

Required

1. Prepare budgeted income statements based on each of the three forecasts.
2. Prepare a budgeted income statement based on the expected value of sales.

5-22 Budgeting in a C.P.A. firm   Donald Ebit is a Certified Public Accountant practicing in a large city. He employs two staff accountants and two clerical workers. He pays the four employees a total of $4,800 per month. His other expenses, all fixed, for such items as rent, utilities, subscriptions, stationery, and postage are $1,200 per month.

Public accounting is, for most firms, highly seasonal, with about four months (January through April) that are extremely busy, eight months of less activity.

The most relevant measure of volume in a C.P.A. firm is charged hours—the hours worked on client business for which the clients are charged. Mr. Ebit expects his two staff accountants to work an average of 125 charged hours each month during the eight slower months, and 200 hours each per month during the January–April busy season. Clerical personnel work about 500 charged hours each per year and Mr. Ebit works about 1,400. For both the clerical personnel and Mr. Ebit, approximately 40% of their charged hours fall in the four-month busy season.

Mr. Ebit charges his clients $25 per hour for his time, $16 for the time of a staff accountant, and $9 for the time of clerical personnel.

Required

Prepare a budget of revenues and expenses for a year for Mr. Ebit's firm. Separate the budget for the period January–April and May–December.

5-23 Deficiencies of high-low method   The assistant controller of the Norgard Company has just given you the following equation for developing the monthly flexible expense budget for supplies.

Supplies expense = $1,200 + ($.10 × units produced). She also shows you the data from which she developed the equation.

Month	Units of Production	Supplies Expense
1	17,300	$2,100
2	18,500	3,050
3	12,500	2,700
4	16,200	1,900
5	9,800	2,180

Required

1. Comment on the flexible budget formula developed by the assistant controller.
2. What reasons might there be for the cost incurrence pattern for supplies?

5-24 Sales forecasting—scatter diagram and regression   The Ridley Carpet Company has engaged you as a consultant to help in its sales forecasting. After a long discussion with Robert Ridley, the president of the firm, you develop the following data:

Year	Housing Units Built (In Thousands)	Sales of Ridley Company (In Thousands)
19X1	1,300	$2,440
19X2	1,400	2,610
19X3	1,900	3,380
19X4	1,500	2,760
19X5	2,000	3,520
19X6	1,600	2,875

Required

1. Develop an equation to be used to forecast sales for the Ridley Company. Use a scatter diagram and regression analysis.
2. Mr. Ridley has learned that housing units to be built in 19X7 will be about 1.8 million. What is your forecast for Ridley's sales? Are you relatively confident about your forecast? Why or why not?

5-25 Budgeting for a hospital (AICPA adapted)   The administrator of Taylor Memorial Hospital, Dr. Gale, has asked for your assistance in preparing the budget for 19X7, which budget he must present at the next meeting of the hospital's board of trustees. The hospital obtains its revenues through two types of charges: charges for use of a hospital room and charges for use of the operating room. The use of the basic rooms depends on whether the patient undergoes surgery during the stay in the hospital. Estimated data as to the types of patients and the related room requirements for 19X7 are as follows:

Type of Patient	Total Expected	Average Stay in Days	Percentages Selecting Kinds of Rooms Private	Semiprivate	Ward
Surgical	2,400	10	15%	75%	10%
Medical only	2,100	8	10%	60%	30%

Basic room charges are $50, $40, and $30 for private, semiprivate, and ward, respectively.

Charges for use of the operating room are a function of the length of the operation and the number of persons required to be involved in the operation. The charge is $.15 per man-minute. (A "man-minute" is one person for one minute, so that if an operation requires three persons for 40 minutes, there would be a charge for 120 man-minutes at $.15 per man-minute, or $18.) Based on past experience, the following is a breakdown of the types of operations to be performed:

Type of Operation	Number of Operations	Average Number of Minutes per Operation	Average Number of Persons Required
Minor	1,200	30	4
Major—abdominal	400	90	6
Major—other	800	120	8
	2,400		

Required

1. Prepare a schedule of budgeted revenues from room charges by type of patient and type of room.
2. Prepare a schedule of budgeted revenues from operating room charges by type of operation.

5-26 Selecting an activity measure   Your firm has been having difficulty with overhead costs. Control is poor and differences between budgeted and actual costs are large. The plant manager has asked you to look at the present method of budgeting, based on direct labor hours. Your assistant prepares the following data from the past six months' operations.

Month	Direct Labor Hours	Machine Hours	Total Overhead Costs
1	8,600	12,000	$38,000
2	9,000	13,200	40,700
3	8,700	14,100	42,800
4	9,300	12,800	41,100
5	10,500	14,700	45,500
6	9,800	13,600	42,600

Required

What is your recommendation? Support with calculations or other means.

5-27 Inventory policy—carrying costs   The managers for production, sales, and finance of the Steele Company are discussing production-inventory policy. The sales manager would like the firm to increase production in order to stock more units in inventory. The production manager is willing to do so. The financial manager argues that the cost of storing, insuring, and financing the additional inventory would be prohibitive; it costs the firm $2 per month per unit to cover these costs and they are variable with the number of units on hand.

The sales manager states that if inventory were increased by 4,000 units, sales would be 1,000 units per month higher. Contribution margin per unit is $6.

Required

1. What is the value (per month) of the additional sales that would be generated by the increased inventory?
2. What are the additional monthly costs associated with carrying the additional 4,000 units in inventory?
3. What decision should be made regarding production and inventory?

5-28 Flexible and static budget   The Wilkinson Company prepares budgets for each month of its fiscal year. These budgeted amounts are shown, along with actual results, in reports that are circulated to the managers whose operations are being reported on *and* to their superiors. Excerpts from the report of the latest two months for one production department are given below.

		April			May	
	Budget	Actual	Variance	Budget	Actual	Variance
Production in units	8,000	7,000	1,000	10,000	10,500	(500)
Costs:						
Material	$16,000	$14,600	$1,400	$20,000	$20,800	($800)
Direct labor	24,000	21,600	2,400	30,000	31,300	(1,300)
Indirect labor	4,000	3,900	100	5,000	5,300	(300)
Power	7,000	6,700	300	8,000	8,400	(400)
Maintenance	5,200	4,700	500	6,000	6,200	(200)
Supplies and other	4,600	4,580	220	5,000	5,050	(50)
Total costs	$60,800	$56,080	$4,720	$74,000	$77,050	($3,050)

Required

1. Using the two sets of budgeted costs, determine the fixed and variable components of each cost.
2. Prepare new reports showing in the budget columns the amounts of cost that you would expect to be incurred given the actual production achieved. Use the same format as is shown above.
3. Comment on the desirability of the firm's method of providing information to its managers.

5-29 Preparation of flexible budget—high-low, scatter diagram, and regression analysis   The Hensley Company has used flexible budgets for some years and is now reviewing the variable overhead rate. The following data have been collected.

Month	Direct Labor Hours	Total Overhead
1	7,000	$22,000
2	8,200	24,700
3	9,100	26,700
4	8,600	25,800
5	7,800	23,800
6	7,300	23,000

Required

1. Estimate the variable overhead rate per direct labor hour using the following:
   (a) the high-low method
   (b) the scatter-diagram method
   (c) regression analysis
2. Prepare a formula for budgeting overhead costs.

5-30 Indicators for sales forecasting   The following economic indicators and other data might be useful in forecasting sales for certain kinds of firms: income per capita, population, car sales, and rate of unemployment.

      For each of the types of firms listed below, state which, if any, of the listed indicators you think would be relevant in forecasting sales. Indicate briefly why you think each indicator is relevant or irrelevant.

(a) food company
(b) maker of outboard motors
(c) home construction firm
(d) tire maker

(e) gasoline refiner
(f) textbook company
(g) jewelry maker
(h) maker of proprietary drugs (drugs sold without prescription)

5-31   Budgeting and behavior   The Rydell Company sets sales budgets for its salespeople who are evaluated by reference to whether they achieve budgeted sales. The budget is expressed in total dollars of sales and is $200,000 per salesperson for the first quarter of 19X3. The firm makes two products, for which price and cost data are given below.

	Wiffers	Trogs
Selling price	$10	$15
Variable costs	4	10
Contribution margin	$ 6	$ 5

During the first quarter of 19X3, all salespeople met the $200,000 sales budget. Wiffers are a new product that the president of the firm thinks should become a big seller, while Trogs are the standard model that has been popular for some years. The products are sold to different kinds of customers; the customers who have been buying Trogs for years are not expected to buy Wiffers. The customers for Wiffers must be sought out by the salespeople and convinced of the high quality of the product. The $200,000 budgeted sales per person is a fairly high goal, but is attainable.

Required

1. Which product should be stressed by the salespeople?
2. Under the circumstances described, which product do you think sold most?
3. If your answers to 1 and 2 conflict, what would you suggest be done in the firm's budgeting process?

5-32   Production and purchases budgets   The Drummond Company manufactures several products, including a frying pan with a wooden handle. The sales forecasts for the frying pan for the next five months are given below.

	April	May	June	July	August
Budgeted Sales	2,500	3,100	2,800	3,500	2,400

Each frying pan requires a blank sheet of iron that the firm buys from a single supplier and molds into the appropriate shape. The wooden handles are purchased in ready-to-use condition from another supplier. The firm's policy is to keep finished goods inventory at twice the coming month's budgeted sales, blank iron sheets at budgeted production requirements for the coming two months, and handles at budgeted production requirements for the coming month.

Each sheet of blank iron is made into one frying pan and costs $2. The handles cost $.40. Labor costs for shaping the iron and putting on the handle are $1.50 and variable manufacturing overhead costs are $.80. Fixed manufacturing costs are $4,500 per month.

At the end of March the firm expects to have the following inventories:

Finished pans	5,300
Blank iron sheets	5,600
Handles	4,600

Required

1. Prepare production budgets for as many months as you can, in units and dollar costs.
2. Prepare purchases budgets in units and dollars for blank iron sheets and handles for as many months as you can.

5-33 Budgeting administrative expenses   The controller of the Kaufman Company has given you the assignment to prepare a flexible budget for costs in the purchasing department. It has been determined that the typists in the department can type about 100 lines per hour and the average purchase order has 10 lines. Typists are paid $4 per hour and work a 35-hour week. When there is not enough typing to keep them busy, they file and perform other work in the office. There are order clerks who prepare purchase orders to be typed. They are paid $6 per hour for a 35-hour week and generally take 20 minutes to prepare an order for typing. They also work at other tasks when purchase orders are slack. The purchasing agent is paid $300 per week. Supplies, stationery, and so on average $.40 per purchase order.

Required

1. If normal volume in the purchasing department is 800 orders per week, how many order clerks and typists are required?
2. Based on your answer to 1 above, how much slack time will be available for clerks and typists to perform other duties?
3. If the salaries for clerks and typists, and the costs for supplies and stationery are to be budgeted as variable costs, what is the flexible budget formula?
4. What variance from the budget would you expect if 800 orders were processed during one week? (Use the data for personnel requirements developed in 1 above.)
5. What is the capacity of the purchasing department given the personnel requirement derived in 1 above?
6. What is the flexible budget formula if the personnel requirements in 1 above are treated as fixed costs?

5-34 Sales forecasting, budgeted income, and budgeted production   The Richards Company manufactures a single product that is used in automobile engines. The firm has developed a forecasting tool that has been successful in predicting sales for the firm. Written in equation form, sales = 80,000 + (.009 × automobile sales). This coming year's automobile sales are expected to be 8,000,000.

Each unit of product contains material costing $5. Direct labor is $10 per unit and variable manufacturing overhead is $12. Besides the variable manufacturing costs, there are commissions to salespeople of 10% of dollar sales. The product sells for $80 per unit. Fixed costs of manufacturing are $1,200,000 per year, fixed selling and administrative expenses are $1,800,000 per year. Both are incurred evenly over the year.

Sales are seasonal; about 60% of sales are in the first six months of the fiscal year, which begins June 1. The sales forecast by month, in percentages of annual sales, is as follows:

June	5%
July	8
August	9
September	12
October	14
November	12
December	9
January	8

The firm has a policy of keeping inventory of finished product equal to budgeted sales for the next two months. Materials are bought and delivered daily and no inventory is kept. The inventory of finished product at May 31 is expected to be 19,000 units.

Required

1. Prepare a budgeted income statement for the coming year.
2. Prepare a budgeted income statement for the first six months of the year.
3. Prepare a production budget by month for the first six months, in units.

5-35 Evaluating production policy The Wallace Company keeps an inventory of finished goods equal to twice budgeted sales for the coming month. As sales fluctuate considerably, so does production. The production manager is unhappy with the current policy because her costs increase due to fluctuating production. She states that each unit produced in excess of 10,000 per month costs an extra $5 because of overtime premium to workers and other factors. The sales manager argues that for every two units the firm is short of budgeted inventory, at the beginning of a month, one unit of sales is lost. Contribution margin per unit is $12 when production costs are normal.

Current Sales and Production Budgets for Wallace Company
(In Units)

	Jan.	Feb.	Mar.	Apr.	May	June
Sales budget (units)	4,000	9,000	12,000	10,000	14,000	12,000
Production budget (units)						
Desired ending inventory	18,000	24,000	20,000	28,000	24,000	
Sales	4,000	9,000	12,000	10,000	14,000	
Total required	22,000	33,000	32,000	38,000	38,000	
Beginning inventory	8,000	18,000	24,000	20,000	28,000	
Production	14,000	15,000	8,000	18,000	10,000	

Required

1. Compute the additional production costs that will be incurred if the firm holds to the production budget.
2. Using the table provided, prepare revised sales and production budgets assuming that production is held to a maximum of 10,000 per month, and compute the contribution margin that would be lost if the revised plan is carried out. Note that a revised sales figure is given for February (7,000 units instead of 9,000). This is required to reflect the sales manager's belief about lost sales. Sales of 2,000 units will be lost in February because the inventory at the end of January will be 4,000 units short of the original budgeted inventory of 18,000 units.

Revised Budget for Wallace Company
(In Units)

	Jan.	Feb.	Mar.	Apr.	May
Production	10,000	10,000	10,000		
Beginning inventory	8,000	14,000	17,000		
Goods available	18,000	24,000	27,000		
Less: Sales	4,000	7,000			
Ending inventory	14,000	17,000			

3. What recommendation would you make to the firm? Support your answer with appropriate calculations. What other factors might be considered?

5-36 Comprehensive budget (Adapted from a problem prepared by Professor Maurice L. Hirsch)
Banana City is a wholesaler of bananas and nuts. Mr. Bertram A. Nana, the president of the firm, has asked for your assistance in preparing budgets for fiscal year 19X7, which begins on September 1, 19X6. The following information has been gathered for your use.

1. Sales are expected to be $880,000 for the year, of which bananas are expected to be 50%, nuts 50%.
2. Sales are somewhat seasonal. Banana sales are expected to be $77,000 in November, with the rest spread evenly over the remaining eleven months. Sales of nuts are expected to be $40,000 per month except in October and November when they are expected to be $25,000 per month and in April and May when they are expected to be $35,000 per month.
3. Cost of sales, the only variable cost, is 40% for both products.
4. Inventory of bananas is generally kept equal to a one-month supply. Inventory of nuts is usually held at a two-month supply.
5. Income taxes are 40% of income before taxes.
6. Fixed expenses for the year, all incurred evenly throughout the year, are expected to be as follows.

Rent	$24,000	Depreciation	$36,000
Insurance	12,000	Interest	6,000
Wages and salaries	120,000	Other fixed expenses	156,000

7. Inventories at August 31, 19X6, are expected to be: bananas, $14,300; nuts, $27,500.
8. The firm expects to sell some land that it owns. The sale, which is expected to have a price of $6,000, will take place in October. The cost of the land on the balance sheet is $8,000.

Required

1. Prepare a budgeted income statement for the fiscal year ending August 31, 19X7.
2. Prepare a budgeted income statement for the first quarter of the fiscal year, by month, and in total.
3. Prepare a purchases budget by product for each of the months of the first quarter of the fiscal year and for the quarter as a whole.

Cases

5-37 Long-range sales budget—alternative pricing strategies The Cooper Company makes ballpoint pens and refills. A new, high-quality pen is being brought out in 19X5, and the board of directors is to be presented with a sales budget for the new pen and refills at its meeting next week, October 1, 19X4. The managers of the firm have difficulty in developing the sales budget and evaluating the two alternative prices to be charged for the pen.

One alternative is to charge $5 per pen, at which price 800,000 are expected to be sold in 19X5. The other possibility is to charge $4, at which price 1,000,000 would probably be sold in 19X5. At either price, volume is expected to increase by 5% per year for the three years after 19X5.

It has been estimated that each pen sold results in the sale of twelve refills over a four-year period, three each year including the year in which the pen is sold. The managers are especially concerned about the effects of the pricing policy on the sales of refills, which are priced at $.50 and have variable costs of $.20. Variable costs of the pens are $2 per unit.

Fixed costs directly associated with the new pen are expected to be $1,000,000 in 19X5, and to rise by 10% per year over the following three years.

Required

1. Prepare sales forecasts for the four-year period beginning with 19X5. Determine the contribution margin and net income from the sales of both pens and refills over the period, under both strategies. (Round numbers of units to the nearest thousand, with 500 units being raised to the next 1,000.)
2. Select one alternative and prepare to defend your choice to the board of directors.

5-38 Production budgeting with constraints   Firms do not commonly hire and lay off workers when moderate changes in production are contemplated. Among the reasons for this are an increased feeling of responsibility to provide regular employment; the potential decline in the available work force if skilled workers left the community permanently because they were laid off; and union contracts providing for guaranteed employment. Under these conditions stable production becomes more desirable. For these same reasons, firms that have high degrees of seasonality may try to stabilize production to keep workers busy all year.

The Robertson Company has the following sales forecast by month for the first eight months of 19X5: (in units) 3,000, 3,800, 4,200, 5,000, 5,400, 5,900, 4,800, 4,200.

The work force is now 100 men, who can produce 4,000 units per month. Overtime can be used to increase output by 10%. Since a five-man team works together, workers can be hired only in groups of five. The company's policy is to keep inventory equal to a two-month supply, and the beginning inventory is 6,800 units.

Required

Prepare a production budget for the first six months, including budgeted numbers of workers. Prepare to defend your answer.

5-39 Budgeting step-variable costs   The Corman Company manufactures several products using a great deal of machinery. Since it is critical to keep the machines running well, the firm pays a good deal of attention to maintenance. The chief engineer has determined that routine maintenance requires a complete shutdown and cleaning every 200 hours a machine has been running. This job costs $250. Excluding these major cleanings, maintenance costs for ten machines have been as follows for the past eight months. Each machine runs about the same amount of time each month as every other machine.

Month	Hours for 10 Machines	Maintenance Costs
1	2,200	$1,400
2	2,100	1,380
3	1,950	1,260
4	2,000	1,290
5	1,700	1,190
6	2,400	1,505
7	2,300	1,455
8	1,800	1,200

Required

1. Using the high-low method, prepare a flexible budget formula for maintenance costs, excluding the major cleaning at 200 hours.
2. Determine the budgeted cost levels for 1,600 hours and 100-hour intervals up to 2,500 hours, including the major cleaning costs. What can you say about the use of flexible budgets when such costs are present?

CHAPTER 6

FINANCIAL BUDGETING

In Chapter 5 we discussed and described the comprehensive budget and illustrated the development of several of its components. In this chapter we shall complete the process of preparing a comprehensive budget by developing budgets of cash flow, financing requirements, and pro forma balance sheets.

        We shall also show how financial statement data are used in the preparation of annual budgets and long-term budgets. Finally, attention is given to the special issues associated with budgeting in not-for-profit entities.

ILLUSTRATION OF CASH BUDGET

We have prepared the pro forma income statement and purchases budget for Cross Company and can now proceed to the cash budget and pro forma balance sheet. Below are the balance sheet as of December 31, 19X3 and the pro forma income statement for the six-month period after that date.

Cross Company
Balance Sheet as of December 31, 19X3

Assets

Cash	$ 60
Accounts receivable	576
Inventory	600
Plant and equipment	600
Total	$1,836

Equities

Accounts payable (merchandise)	$ 360
Accrued expenses	50
Common stock	1,000
Retained earnings	426
Total	$1,836

Cross Company
Pro Forma Income Statement
January 1, 19X4 to June 30, 19X4

Sales	$4,800
Cost of goods sold (all variable, at 60% of sales)	2,880
Gross profit	1,920
Other variable costs (15% of sales)	720
Contribution margin	1,200
Fixed costs (including $120 of depreciation)	240
Income	$ 960

The balance sheet at the beginning of the budgeted period is required because those balance sheet amounts show both resources (assets) that have already been acquired and can be used during the period and liabilities that must be paid during the period. We used the inventory figure at December 31 in preparing the purchase budget.

Cash Receipts

To develop the budgeted income statement we relied on the sales forecasts by month, as follows:

	Jan.	Feb.	Mar.	Apr.	May	June
Sales	$400	$600	$800	$1,000	$1,200	$800

To forecast cash receipts more information is needed. Does the company sell on credit or for cash only? How soon do credit customers pay their accounts? Assume that experience (adjusted for changed conditions) indicates that 20% of the sales are collected in the month of sales, 48% are collected in the month after sale, and the remainder (32%) are collected in the second month after sale. The beginning accounts receivable consists of $400 of December sales and $176 of November sales. Can you determine what the total sales were for December? for November?

Since 20% of December sales were collected in December, the $400 now in accounts receivable must be 80% of December sales. Thus, December sales were $500 ($400/80%). The $176 still uncollected from November is 32% of November sales, so November sales must have been $550 ($176/32%). The $176 will be collected in January but only $240 (48% of December sales of $500) will be collected in January on December sales. The remaining receivables from December sales, $160 ($500 × 32%), will be collected in February. The ability to recognize relationships among accounts helps understanding of the budgeting process.

We shall first determine cash inflows for the six-month period, before proceeding to cash outflows and the pro forma balance sheet. Exhibit 6-1 is a good general format for budgeting cash receipts from sales.

Exhibit 6-1
Cash Receipts

Cash *from Sales*	Jan.	Feb.	Mar.	Apr.	May	June	Total
20% of total sales for the month	$ 80	$120	$160	$200	$240	$ 160	$ 960
	+						
48% of prior month's sales	240	192	288	384	480	576	2,160
		+					
32% of second prior month's sales	176	160	128*	192	256	320	1,232
Total cash collections	$496	$472	$576	$776	$976	$1,056	$4,352

*$400 = total January sales, collected in January, February, and March ($80 + $192 + $128)

The circled items show the pattern of collection of January sales; the total is given below the schedule. Notice that cash receipts increase, but that there is a lag. Cash receipts exceed sales only in June, when sales have declined and collections are being made from the prior months in which sales were considerably higher. A firm can run out of cash because its sales are rapidly increasing, since the firm is very likely incurring cash drains to pay for the goods to be stocked in advance of sales. This will become clearer when we examine cash disbursements.

As cash receipts are related to sales, but do not coincide with sales except accidentally, so cash disbursements are related to the incurrence of costs, but do not always coincide. For example, variable costs for each month would not correspond with cash disbursements unless the costs were incurred in the same months in which payments were made.

Cash Disbursements

The major component of cash disbursements for the Cross Company is payments for purchases. To determine cash payments for purchases, the purchases budget developed in Chapter 5 (page 140) is used and the timing of payments for those purchases is assumed. If the company paid cash on delivery of goods, cash payments for purchases would equal purchases in each month. Assume, however, that Cross Company takes full advantage of the 30-day credit terms extended by its suppliers so that purchases are paid for in the month after purchase. (If Cross were granted 60-day credit, payments would be made in the second month after purchase.) To derive cash payments it is necessary only to lag payments a month behind purchases.

Exhibit 6-2
Cash Disbursements for Purchases

	Jan.	Feb.	Mar.	Apr.	May	June	Total
Budgeted purchases	$480	$600	$720	$480	$420	$480	$3,180
Payments	$360	$480	$600	$720	$480	$420	$3,060

The January payment is for December purchases as reflected in accounts payable for December 31, 19X3. The other amounts come from the purchases budget developed in Chapter 5 and summarized here. Purchases are paid for in the month after purchase, so accounts payable at the end of any month will be equal to that month's purchases. And cash disbursements for purchases will be equal to accounts payable at the beginning of the month, which is the same as accounts payable at the end of the prior month.

Two parts of the cash budget have now been developed, cash receipts from sales and cash disbursements for purchases. Other cash disbursements may be determined more easily than those for purchases. You will remember that variable expenses other than cost of sales are 15% of sales. Assume that one-third is paid in the month of incurrence, and two-thirds in the following month. The portion paid in the month after incurrence could be for commissions to salespersons, who are paid in the first week of a month for the commissions they earned in the previous month. Thus in each month, cash disbursements related to variable costs will be 5% of that month's sales, plus 10% of the sales of the previous month.

Exhibit 6-3
Cash Disbursements—Variable Costs

	Jan.	Feb.	Mar.	Apr.	May	June	Total
5% current month's sales	$20	$30	$ 40	$ 50	$ 60	$ 40	$240
10% previous month's sales	50*	40	60	80	100	120	450
Total	$70	$70	$100	$130	$160	$160	$690

*December accrued expenses

The total cash disbursements for variable costs ($690) do not correspond with variable costs on the income statement ($720) because of the timing of the payments for variable costs. This difference is explained by examining the Accrued Expenses. The disbursement made in January ($50) was accrued in December (10% × $500 sales in December). This payment is not an expense in 19X4. At June 30, 19X4, $80 is owed for commissions on June sales of $800. The cash disbursement for June commissions is made in July. Total disbursements of $690 include $50 expenses in 19X3, and do not include $80 of June expense that will be paid in July ($690 − $50 + $80 = $720).

The cash component of fixed costs is assumed to be paid evenly over the six-month period. Depreciation, a noncash expense, is $120 out of the $240 fixed costs, so the cash portion is $120 ($240 − $120), or $20 per month. The complete cash disbursements budget is as follows:

Exhibit 6-4
Cash Disbursements—All Costs

	Jan.	Feb.	Mar.	Apr.	May	June	Total
For purchases (Exhibit 6-2)	$360	$480	$600	$720	$480	$420	$3,060
Variable costs (Exhibit 6-3)	70	70	100	130	160	160	690
Fixed costs	20	20	20	20	20	20	120
Total	$450	$570	$720	$870	$660	$600	$3,870

Cash Budget

We are now ready to prepare the cash budget.

Cash Budget

	Jan.	Feb.	Mar.	Apr.	May	June	Total
Beginning balance	$ 60*	$106	$ 8	($136)	($230)	$ 86	$ 60
Collections (Exhibit 6-1)	496	472	576	776	976	1,056	4,352
Total available	556	578	584	640	746	1,142	4,412
Disbursements (Exhibit 6-4)	450	570	720	870	660	600	3,870
Ending Balance	$106	$ 8	($136)	($230)	$ 86	$ 542	$ 542

*From 12/31/X3 balance sheet, page 161

The total column covers the six-month period so that the beginning balance is the balance at December 31, 19X3 from the balance sheet. Although the firm will complete the six months with a good deal more cash than it had at the start of the period, it has budgeted cash deficits in March and April, and a balance of only $8 at the end of February. Budgets should therefore be broken down into relatively short time periods. If the firm had prepared a budget only for the entire six-month period, the managers would not have become aware of the deficits, and plans would not have been made for dealing with the problem.

What could the firm do now? It could consider borrowing cash to tide it over the period during which the deficits appear. The firm could also reconsider its inventory policy, reduce its purchases, and consequently reduce its needs for cash. But this action might adversely affect sales.

Assume that the firm can borrow cash at 6% interest. If the firm decides to borrow to offset the expected cash deficits, the cash budget must be revised. Any borrowings must take place at the beginning of the month in which they are needed. Assume that repayments are made at the earliest possible time, which is at the end of a month in which a surplus of cash is budgeted. Under these circumstances, a loan must be outstanding for at least two months. Suppose that borrowings must be in multiples of $10, and that interest is paid at the time of repayment. Assume that the firm has a policy of maintaining a minimum cash balance of $50 at all times. (Many companies maintain a minimum cash balance as a matter of policy. A minimum cash balance is usually established to make room for variations from planned cash flows and unexpected cash requirements.) A revised cash budget appears in Exhibit 6-5 on page 166.

Now that the cash budget has been revised, so must the original budgeted income statement be revised. The firm now must incur $4 in interest expense in order to meet its sales objectives, given its expectations about cash collections and its inventory policy.

Revised Financial Statements

We shall now prepare a "revised" pro forma income statement for the six-month period and a pro forma balance sheet for June 30. The income statement is modified to include the interest expense necessary to finance the budgeted operations. In addition, a pro forma income statement for January 1 to March 31 is prepared and a pro forma balance sheet for March 31.

Exhibit 6-5
Revised Cash Budget

	Jan.	Feb.	Mar.	Apr.	May	June	Total
Beginning balance	$ 60	$106	$ 58	$ 54	$ 50	$ 82	$ 60
Collections	496	472	576	776	976	1,056	4,352
Total available	556	578	634	830	1,026	1,138	4,412
Disbursements	450	570	720	870	660	600	3,870
(1) Indicated balance	106	8	(86)	(40)	366	538	542
(2) Minimum required cash	50	50	50	50	50	50	50
1 − 2 = (3) Excess (deficit)	56	(42)	(136)	(90)	316	488	492
(4) Borrowings		50	140	90			280
(5) Repayments					(280)		(280)
Interest					(4)*		(4)
4 + 1 − 5 = (6) Ending balance	$106	58	54	50	82	538	$ 538
Cumulative borrowings		$ 50	$190	$280	$—0—	$—0—	

*6% × 4/12 (four months) × $ 50 = $1.00
6% × 3/12 (three months) × $140 = 2.10
6% × 2/12 (two months) × $ 90 =   .90
                                 $4.00

Pro forma statements are prepared for the shorter period to check your understanding by reviewing the pro forma results, and because a firm would ordinarily prepare pro forma statements more frequently than once every six months. In this instance, one important reason for the latter is that this firm has to obtain a short-term loan. A potential lender would

Cross Company
Pro Forma Income Statements

	Three Months Ending March 31, 19X4	Six Months Ending June 30, 19X4
Sales	$1,800	$4,800
Cost of goods sold (60% of sales)	1,080	2,880
Gross profit	720	1,920
Other variable costs (15% of sales)	270	720
Contribution margin	450	1,200
Fixed operating costs	120	240
Operating income	330	960
Interest expense	1.20*	4
Income	$ 328.80	$ 956

*At March 31, loans were outstanding for $190. Accrued interest was:
$ 50 ×2/12 × 6% = $0.50
$140 × 1/12 × 6% = 0.70
                  $1.20 Total accrued interest and interest expense

want to see monthly cash budgets and pro forma statements at least each quarter, if not each month. The lender will want information to help him decide whether the firm can repay the loan and will also be interested in whether the management makes good use of budgets. The manager can compare the balance sheets at March 31 and June 30 with the pro forma as a check on whether operations are proceeding as planned. For example, if the sales forecast proves accurate, but accounts receivable are higher than budgeted, cash inflows from collections would be lower than budgeted. This could be a danger signal; credit might have been extended to slow **payers** in order to increase sales.

Cross Company
Pro Forma Balance Sheets

Assets	As at *March 31, 19X4*	As at *June 30, 19X4*
Cash (from cash budget, Exhibit 6-5)	$ 54	$ 538
Accounts receivable (credit sales for month plus 32% of prior month's credit sales	832	1,024
Inventory (from purchases budget, Exhibit 5-4)	1,320	900
Plant and equipment (beginning balance less depreciation for 3 and 6 months)	540	480
Total assets	$2,746	$2,942

Equities		
Accounts payable (from purchases budget, Exhibit 5-4)	$ 720	$ 480
Accrued expenses (10% of the month's sales)	80	80
Short-term loan (from cash budget, Exhibit 6-5)	190	0
Accrued interest on loan	1.20	0
Common stock (beginning balance sheet)	1,000	1,000
Retained earnings (beginning balance plus income for period)	754.80	1,382
Total equities	$2,746	$2,942

Concluding Comments

All statements and schedules that make up the comprehensive budget have been prepared; thus, it is now possible to point out other advantages that accrue from the budgeting process.

The cash budget and pro forma balance sheets are a basis for asset management. The managers can see that a large amount of cash will be available at the end of June and can begin to look for profitable uses for this cash. At the very least, the firm can buy marketable securities like government bonds and earn safe, though low, returns. Idle cash earns no return and should be put to some use in the business, or paid to stockholders as dividends.

Knowing well in advance that further cash will be needed, the firm is more likely to find financing to carry over the months in which deficits are budgeted. It will be able to explain to potential lenders why the money is needed and give reassurance on how the loan will be repaid. If the firm waits until its cash balance is precariously low to seek a loan, it may have to pay a higher interest rate or may not get a loan on any terms.

The budgets are interrelated; the cash budget, which is prepared next to last, just before the pro forma balance sheet, shows that the previously prepared pro forma income statement must be modified to include interest expense. The original profit goal of $960 cannot be achieved. The firm must either seek short-term financing, attempt to get along with less inventory, or take some other action to ensure that it does not run out of cash, injure its credit rating, or go bankrupt.

Our example is much simpler than would be the case in practice. If the company's experience indicates that some portion of its credit sales will not be collected, the cash receipts budget would reflect collections of less than the expected sales. There could be a number of special receipts and disbursements, such as interest or dividend revenue, payments for taxes, dividends, or fixed assets, and repayments of long-term debt.

The firm in the basic illustration does no manufacturing. Chapter 5 shows that development of a budget for a manufacturer is more complex than for a nonmanufacturer, but the principles are virtually the same. Would the cash budget for a manufacturer differ from that of a nonmanufacturer?

As we showed in Chapter 5, the production budget for a manufacturer is similar to the purchases budget for a retailer. If we know when the costs of production are paid, we can easily compute cash requirements for production. We shall continue the example started in Chapter 5, page 142. The production budget showed the following:

Month	No. of Units Produced
January	340
February	280
March	336
April	240
May	210
June	240

The breakdown of production costs was as follows: materials at $2 per unit; other variable costs at $4 per unit; and fixed costs of $1,900.

Materials are bought as needed (no inventory of materials is maintained) and are paid for in the month after purchase. All other production costs requiring cash are paid in the month incurred. Assume that production in December was 300 units. (Why must we make some assumption about December production?) The budget for cash disbursements for manufacturing costs would be as follows:

	Jan.	Feb.	Mar.	Apr.	May	June
Units produced	340	280	336	240	210	240
Cash disbursements:						
Materials ($2 × prior month's production)	$ 600	$ 680	$ 560	$ 672	$ 480	$ 420
Other variable costs ($4 × current production)	1,360	1,120	1,344	960	840	960
Fixed costs	1,900	1,900	1,900	1,900	1,900	1,900
Totals	$3,860	$3,700	$3,804	$3,532	$3,220	$3,280

The totals would be included in the computation of total disbursements, as on page **164,** in place of the disbursements for purchases. The remainder of the budget package would be completed accordingly.

In principle there is little difference between the budgets for the retailer and the manufacturer. In practice, the manufacturer's budget is likely to be more complicated. For example, some production costs may not require cash outlay (depreciation). Also the materials used for production may be purchased in advance of production needs. In such a situation the cash disbursements for materials will be determined by a separate materials-purchases budget.

ANNUAL AND LONG-TERM BUDGETS

The techniques of financial statement analysis can be used to assist managers in budgeting for longer periods of time and in assessing long-term asset requirements and financing requirements—long-term debt and stockholder equity. "Long term" usually means a period of one or more years.

Asset Requirements

We have shown how operational and financial budgets relate to each other in the short term. Using budgeted sales and known relationships of current assets to sales, it was possible to develop budgets of purchases and pro forma balance sheets showing budgeted amounts of cash, accounts receivable, and inventory. What was shown on the asset side of pro forma balance sheets earlier in the chapter was essentially a statement of asset requirements—the amounts of various assets required to enable the firm to meet its goals of sales and income. The firm might have to reconsider its sales and profit goals if it could not obtain the financing needed to carry its planned levels of assets.

In the **long term, similar analyses must be made.** If the firm plans for increasing sales, it must also plan for the assets that will support the planned sales. Managers cannot expect to increase sales without having to stock more inventory, provide greater capacity, and allow receivables to increase. In addition, the desired cash balance can be expected to increase with higher sales volume.

Usually, in the long term, the planned levels of sales dictate the necessary levels of assets. Thus, we shall be using ratios of various assets to sales to determine required amounts of assets. The analysis is less precise in long-term budgeting; there is less certainty in the long-term plan. The manager must make allowances for changes in prices and price levels, but such changes are extremely hard to predict over relatively long periods of time. Predictions are more general, seeing in broad terms what needs will be. As time passes, the budgets of asset needs can be refined.

FINANCING REQUIREMENTS

A firm requires financing, in the form of liabilities or stockholder equity, because it has assets that are used to generate sales. The need for assets creates the need for financing—the items listed on the equity side of the balance sheet. The elements on the equity side of the balance sheet are often referred to as the *sources* of the elements on the asset side. As the need for assets increases because of increased sales, so does the need for sources to finance the required assets. A few sources of financing are available almost automatically. For example, most firms do not pay cash on delivery of merchandise; they incur a liability for accounts payable. When a vendor does not demand immediate payment for the goods he has sold to the firm, he is providing a source of financing. The firm does not pay cash on receipt of goods, so it has, in effect, obtained a short-term loan—a source of financing. Similarly, if the firm earns income and does not distribute assets in an amount equal to net income, retained earnings will increase. Increases in retained earnings are sources of financing.

Most firms cannot meet all financing needs through funds provided by operations and trade creditors. The Cross Company used short-term credit. However firms cannot use short-term loans too liberally. If working capital (current assets − current liabilities) and the current ratio (current assets/current liabilities) get too low, creditors will be reluctant to lend to the firm. Thus, more permanent financing will be sought.

For more permanent financing, long-term debt is used or additional common stock is issued. A growing firm generally requires higher and higher levels of assets to support its increased sales and therefore needs more sources of financing than a firm that is not growing. Sometimes the goals and objectives expressed in a budget cannot be met because the means are not available; such means include productive capacity, personnel, and availability of materials, as well as financing. A firm might not be able to obtain the loan necessary to support its short-term requirements and would therefore have to scale down its purchases of goods; this could, in turn, reduce sales and profits. The same situation occurs in long-term budgeting. The firm might not be able to obtain the long-term financing to support the asset levels believed necessary to reach the levels of sales projected.

In some cases, the firm sees that advance planning is needed to obtain financing. For example, potential long-term lenders might demand that the firm maintain some ratio of equity capital to long-term debt. Thus, the firm might have to seek new common-stock financing before it is able to secure additional long-term debt.

Illustrations of Annual and Long-Term Budgets

Two types of procedures are used in budgeting for longer periods: those that are used for a one-year period and those that are more appropriate for three- to five-year periods broken down into annual periods. Differences between the two types are primarily matters of detail; for a one-year budget the composition of assets and equities is more detailed than for longer periods.

Following is a set of financial statements for the Style Shop, a retailer of men's and women's clothing. The balance sheet shows percentages that each asset and two of the

Style Shop
Income Statement
for Year Ending December 31, 19X3

Sales	$400,000
Cost of goods sold (60% of sales)	240,000
Gross profit	160,000
Other variable costs (20% of sales)	80,000
Contribution margin (20% of sales)	80,000
Fixed costs	30,000
Income before income taxes	50,000
Income taxes (40% rate)	20,000
Net income	$ 30,000

Style Shop
Balance Sheet
as of December 31, 19X3

Assets			Item as Percentage of Sales in 19X3
Current assets:			
Cash	$ 25,000		6.25%
Accounts receivable	60,000		15.0
Inventory	80,000		20.0
Total current assets		$165,000	41.25%
Fixed assets:			
Building and equipment	120,000		30.0
Less: Accumulated depreciation	60,000		15.0
Net fixed assets		60,000	15.0
Total assets		$225,000	56.25%

Equities			
Current liabilities:			
Accounts payable	$ 40,000		10.0%
Accrued expenses	10,000		2.5
Accrued income taxes	15,000		
Short-term loan	30,000		
Total current liabilities		$ 95,000	
Long-term bank loan (6%)		30,000	
Total liabilities		125,000	
Stockholders' equity:			
Common stock	60,000		
Retained earnings	40,000		
Total stockholders' equity		100,000	
Total equities		$225,000	

current liability items bear to sales. These percentages are used to develop the pro forma balance sheet as of the end of the coming year.

We are assuming that the relationships in 19X3 will hold for 19X4. If available information suggested that this were not the case, appropriate adjustments could easily be made. For instance, if variable costs as a percentage of sales were expected to increase or decrease, the new percentage would be used in the preparation of the pro forma income statement.

First, we prepare a pro forma income statement for 19X4 based on a sales forecast of $440,000, a 10% increase in sales over 19X3.

Style Shop
Pro Forma Income Statement
Year Ending December 31, 19X4

Sales	$440,000
Cost of goods sold (60% of sales)	264,000
Gross profit	176,000
Other variable costs (20% of sales)	88,000
Contribution margin (20% of sales)	88,000
Fixed costs	30,000
Income before income taxes	58,000
Income taxes (40% rate)	23,200
Net income	$ 34,800

Assume for the present that the firm will not pay a dividend in 19X4; thus, it is possible to determine the retained earnings on the pro forma balance sheet as $74,800 ($40,000 beginning balance plus $34,800 net income).

All the items in the asset section of the pro forma balance sheet at the end of 19X4 can be computed by taking their percentages of sales for 19X3 and multiplying these percentages by 19X4 sales of $440,000.

Style Shop
Partial Pro Forma Balance Sheet
as of December 31, 19X4

Assets			*Percentage of 19X4 Sales*
Current assets:			
Cash	$ 27,500		6.25%
Accounts receivable	66,000		15.0
Inventory	88,000		20.0
Total current assets		$181,500	41.25%
Fixed assets:			
Building and equipment	132,000		30.0
Accumulated depreciation	66,000		15.0
Net fixed assets		66,000	15.0
Total assets		$247,500	56.25%

We have now established asset requirements based on the 19X3 relationships of assets to sales. How much financing is available for these assets? We assume that current liabilities for accounts payable and accrued expenses will also bear their historical relationships to sales. This assumption is a bit weak for accounts payable, because one might expect payables to vary with purchases and not sales; however, because inventory is increasing in the same percentage as sales, we can legitimately expect that accounts payable will do likewise. If inventory is expected to increase by 10%, purchases will also be 10% higher in 19X4 than they were in 19X3. We have no information about 19X3 purchases and will assume, for simplicity, that 19X4 purchases are 10% more than those of 19X3.

Such a simplifying assumption about accrued income taxes would not be reasonable. This liability will depend on the net income of the firm and the amounts that are paid to the government during the year. (Firms pay estimated taxes throughout the year, much as individuals have taxes withheld from their paychecks.) A reasonable assumption would be that accrued income taxes at December 31, 19X4 will bear the same relationship to net income as they did at December 31, 19X3. Accrued income taxes at the end of 19X3 were 50% of 19X3 income ($15,000/$30,000), so they would be $17,400 at the end of 19X4 (50% × $34,800). The short-term loan was paid during 19X4.

Assuming that long-term debt and common stock remain the same, we can now fill in the available sources of financing on the equity side of the pro forma balance sheet as below. At this point, the balance sheet amounts are only tentative because the firm requires additional sources of financing if it is to have the asset amounts already derived. The equity side of the balance sheet would, at this stage, equal the asset side only by chance.

Style Shop
Pro Forma Statement of
Available Equities as of December 31, 19X4

Current liabilities:		
Accounts payable	$44,000	
Accrued expenses	11,000	
Accrued income taxes	17,400	
Total current liabilities		$ 72,400
Long-term bank loan		30,000
Total liabilities		102,400
Stockholders' equity:		
Common stock	60,000	
Retained earnings	74,800	
Total stockholders' equity		134,800
Total available equities		237,200
Total assets required		247,500
Difference—financing required		$ 10,300

Testing the firm's tentative plans has revealed that assets are greater than available equities, given the cash balance desired and the assumptions regarding other balance-sheet items. What now? There are several options. The deficiency in equities could be offset by reducing the desired cash balance from $27,500 to $17,200. Total assets would be reduced to $237,200, matching total available equities. (This is what would occur if no other action were taken.) Or, management might decide that other assets could be reduced (inventory, for example) or fixed asset purchases could be postponed. Or, additional financing could be obtained, possibly long term, either debt or equity, to bring total equities up to $247,500.

The first two suggestions could prove unwise. A cash balance of $17,200 could be too low for safety, and attempts to reduce other asset requirements could adversely affect sales in 19X4 or later. Seeking additional long-term financing may prove desirable, or it may not, but the manager now knows that if the assumptions are borne out by experience, he or she must take some action to prevent the cash balance from becoming too low. There is no provision for dividends. A dividend payment would reduce cash and retained earnings in equal amounts, creating an even greater strain on cash requirements.

This balance sheet is not being prepared completely on expected transactions. The objective was to determine what additional financing must be secured in order to have $247,500 in total assets at December 31, 19X4. The procedures used are similar to those used in developing the month-by-month cash budget, where a tentative budget is prepared and revision is required because of deficits. The initial cash budget allowed us to determine how much short-term financing was needed to operate as we wished. The same holds true when budgeting for longer periods using the broader approach of the Style Shop.

It is a matter of choice whether you budget a particular amount of cash and then determine whether you require additional financing, or leave cash until last and then determine whether the budgeted balance is enough. Using the latter approach, the available equities could exceed required assets. If that is the case, the difference is an increase in cash over the amount budgeted. The excess could be used to reduce debt, pay dividends, or make investments in marketable securities that will earn interest.

Budgeting that uses the relationships of balance sheet items to income statement items is sometimes criticized for the oversimplified assumptions made about certain balance sheet amounts varying directly with sales. Areas in which this assumption is weakest are fixed assets and accounts payable. Fixed asset acquisitions are generally budgeted carefully and known far in advance. They can therefore be determined directly by reference to the separate budget for capital expenditures (the capital budget). However, fixed assets are much more likely to vary with sales over longer periods of time than, say, one year. Fixed assets take longer to come into operation after it is decided that they are required. For example, if a new building is required, a site must be found, specifications must be written, bids must be collected from several contractors, and construction must be completed. Most capital acquisition programs provide capacity to meet demand that is foreseen several years, not months, in the future.

Accounts payable are generally related to purchases. A firm makes its payments on an average of 30, 60, or some other number of days after purchase. For a more precise budgeting process, purchases for the year could be determined in order to find accounts payable. However, if purchases increase (or decrease) from year to year in about the same proportion as sales, there is no harm in budgeting accounts payable by reference to sales, rather than to purchases.

In an actual situation, the managers of a firm would probably have developed other relationships for use in budgeting, sometimes much more sophisticated than those shown here. The material presented here should be viewed as introductory.

Long-Term Planning

In the previous section the firm had options for financing anticipated requirements for assets. If long-term financing were sought there were two major alternatives—debt and equity. The choice can be critical. A poor decision is difficult to correct because the issuance of a long-term debt or equity cannot be undertaken frequently.

The choice between debt and equity financing is similar to that between fixed and variable costs. Debt financing requires periodic interest payments and, probably, periodic repayment of principal. These periodic payments are a drain on cash and cause bankruptcy if the firm does not generate sufficient cash inflows to service the debt. Equity financing relates to variable costs in that the payments for equity capital (dividends) can be expected to vary to some extent with income; investors generally expect to receive dividends. However, equity financing does not require periodic payments. If sufficient cash is not **available**, no dividend has to be paid. Consequently, equity financing is less risky to the firm than debt financing.

Judicious use of debt can increase the return earned by stockholders. You will remember from the discussion of cost structures that if revenues are rising, a firm with a preponderance of fixed costs will show a faster increase in profits than a firm with a large proportion of variable costs. The question, then, is usually not whether to use debt, but how much. Finding the answer to this question is the province of managerial finance. The point here is to understand how the budgeting process can be used in developing and assessing the financial strategy of the firm. The proportion of debt that can be carried by a firm depends largely on the same factors that govern the desirable proportions of fixed and variable costs —namely, expected levels of revenues, stability of revenues, and managerial attitudes toward risks (see Chapter 3).

One way in which a firm might develop long-range financing plans is to predict asset requirements, determine available financing from current liabilities and existing stockholder equity, find an acceptable amount of long-term debt, and finally determine whether sufficient equities are available from these sources. If not, there is a "financing gap," a difference between asset requirements and available equities. This gap must be filled with additional equity, or debt and equity, in a mix considered desirable.

In the illustration that follows, expenditures for fixed assets are also incorporated in the budget.

Illustration

The process of long-term financial planning is shown on the following pages with data, assumptions, and policies of the Klep Company. These data are the bases of a table to determine

Sales forecast in 19X4	$ 800,000
19X5	$1,000,000
19X6	$1,300,000
19X7	$1,700,000
19X8	$2,100,000
Stockholder equity	
12-31-X3	$ 412,000
Net fixed assets 12-31-X3	$ 600,000

Net income is expected to be 10% of sales over the period of the forecast.

Dividends of 40% of net income will be paid each year.

Current asset requirements are expected to be 30% of sales budgeted for the following year.

Net fixed assets are expected to be 75% of sales budgeted for the following year.

Depreciation is 10% of beginning of year net fixed assets.

Desired current ratio of 3 to 1, so that current liabilities cannot exceed one-third of current assets.

Desired ratio of long-term debt to equity of .5 to 1 (long term cannot exceed 50% of stockholder equity).

year-by-year financing requirements and required expenditures for fixed assets. Exhibit 6-6 shows the analysis for 19X4 and 19X5 and how the numbers were derived. See if you can fill in the rest of the table. Answers appear on page 178. A schedule such as Exhibit 6-6 gives the manager an idea of future financing needs, as well as future asset requirements. A plan can now be devised for seeking additional debt and equity financing to satisfy line (13), "additional requirements." It is generally expensive and undesirable to obtain equity financing frequently; therefore the firm might obtain funds from a large issue of common stock in 19X4, an issue that would enable it to finance without additional debt until 19X8 or so. Funds received in excess of the amounts currently needed might be invested or used to retire debt. As needs become more pressing, additional debt could be issued up to the limit prescribed by the .5 to 1 debt/equity ratio.

BUDGETING IN NOT-FOR-PROFIT ENTITIES

Not-for-profit entities, especially governmental units, make extensive use of budgeting, but the budgeting process is not usually of the type described earlier. First, such entities are likely to budget on the basis of cash flows (expenditures and receipts) as opposed to revenues and expenses. Second, the process is more likely to begin with the expenditures as opposed to the receipts. That is, in most cases, the problem will be to determine what receipts are required to support the budgeted level of expenditures, as opposed to what costs will be incurred as a result of the budgeted level of revenues.

Budgets for expenditures are not usually as geared to activity levels as are budgets for businesses. Nevertheless, some kinds of activity analysis might be used in determining budget allowances for a particular category. For example, a university might budget faculty positions by applying some formula based on student enrollment. Thus, an academic department might be given one position for each 300 credit hours expected to be taught. If the department is expected to teach 2,800 credit hours during the coming year, it would be authorized nine and one-third positions (2,800/300). The one-third position would probably be filled by part-time instructors.

Exhibit 6-6
Financing Requirements for Klep Company
(In Thousands of Dollars)

		19X4	19X5	19X6	19X7
	(1) Sales	$800	$1,000	$1,300	$1,700
(1) × 10%	(2) Net income	80	100		
(2) × 40%	(3) Dividends	32	40		
(2) − (3)	(4) Add to stockholder equity	$ 48	$ 60		
(1) for next year × 30%	(5) Current assets required	$300	390		
(5)/3	(6) Permissible current liabilities	100	130		
(5) − (6)	(7) Working capital to be financed from long-term sources	200	260		
(1) for next year × 75%	(8) Net fixed assets required	750	975		
(7) + (8)	(9) Total long-term financing required	950	1,235		
	(10) Stockholder equity [prior year plus (4)]	460	520		
(10) × 50%	(11) Permissible long-term debt	230	260		
(10) + (11)	(12) Total available long-term financing	690	780		
(9) − (12)	(13) Additional requirements	$260	$ 455		
(8) + year's depreciation − beginning-of-year fixed assets	(14) Expenditures for fixed assets	$210	$ 300*		

*$975 + ($750 × 10%) − $750 = $300

On the revenue, or receipt, side, budgeting by governmental and other not-for-profit entities could be relatively simple or quite complex. School districts and some municipalities like towns and cities rely chiefly on property taxes for their revenues. Property taxes are levied based on the assessed valuation of real property (land and buildings) in the area. Once the total assessed valuation has been determined, the tax rate can be set by dividing the required revenues by the assessed valuation. If the Montmar School District requires $4,580,000 in revenues and the assessed valuation of property in the district is $54,000,000, the rate would be .08482 ($4,580,000/$54,000,000), which is $84.82 per $1,000 of assessed value. You should note that the required revenue is determined on the basis of the budgeted expenditures, which at least partially explains the need for careful planning and monitoring of budgeted expenditures.

For governmental units that depend heavily on income and sales taxes, as do most states, the determination of required tax rates would be more complex. Estimates of total incomes subject to the income tax and of transactions subject to the sales tax would be required. Forecasting methods such as those described in Chapter 5 may be used, and very sophisticated forecasting models may be developed and used by individual states.

Answers to Exhibit 6-6
Financing Requirements for Klep Company
(In Thousands of Dollars)

		19X4	19X5	19X6	19X7
	(1) Sales	$800	$1,000	$1,300	$1,700
(1)× 10%	(2) Net income	80	100	130	170
(2) × 40%	(3) Dividends	32	40	52	68
(2) − (3)	(4) Add to stockholder equity	$ 48	$ 60	$ 78	$ 102
(1) for next year × 30%	(5) Current assets required	$300	$ 390	$ 510	$ 630
(5)/3	(6) Permissible current liabilities	100	130	170	210
(5) − (6)	(7) Working capital to be financed from long-term sources	200	260	340	420
(1) for next year × 75%	(8) Net fixed assets required	750	975	1,275	1,575
(7) + (8)	(9) Total long-term financing required	950	1,235	1,615	1,995
	(10) Stockholder equity [prior year plus (4)]	460	520	598	700
(10) × 50%	(11) Permissible long-term debt	230	260	299	350
(10) + (11)	(12) Total available long-term financing	690	780	897	1,050
(9) − (12)	(13) Additional requirements	$260	$ 455	$ 718	$ 945
(8) + year's depreciation − beginning-of-year fixed assets	(14) Expenditures for fixed assets	$210	$ 300	$397.5*	$427.5†

*$1,275 + ($975 × 10%) − $975 = $397.5
†$1,575 + ($1,275 × 10%) − $1,275 =$427.5

Development of the receipts budget for nongovernmental not-for-profit entities is probably more related to the problems of business entities. The variety of such entities rivals the variety of business entities, and the need for forecasts of revenue-related factors is no less. For example, tuition charges in a private school must be set by utilizing forecasts of enrollments and contributions. The various service charges of a hospital must be established by forecasting expected utilization. All the forecasting methods discussed in Chapter 5 are used in making such forecasts.

Governmental units like towns, states, school districts, and the federal government usually require voter or legislative approval of their budgets. Once adopted, the budget must be strictly adhered to; overspending is often illegal. In addition, budget authorizations tend to be on a line-by-line basis. That is, specific amounts are authorized for specific categories of expenditures, such as salaries, equipment, supplies, travel, postage, etc. (The detail in such budgets can be overwhelming, with specified amounts for categories such as Grade II Typists and Grade IV Carpenters.) The budgeting process used in most governmental units tends to have two major disadvantages in practice. The first relates to the line-by-line approval procedure, and the second relates to the ways of arriving at the amounts for each line.

Because of the line-by-line approval procedure, individual managers within a governmental unit may be allowed to exercise little or no discretion in how they use the budgeted funds to achieve the expected objectives. The managers are usually not allowed to increase spending on one item even if they can make equivalent decreases in other items. This inflexibility can lead to actions inconsistent with the objectives of the entity. For example, suppose that an accounting instructor in a public university is invited to a worthwhile seminar on a contemporary accounting topic; the dean and faculty are in favor of the trip but the travel budget is exhausted. Even if funds remain in the budget allowances for supplies, or telephone, or secretarial help, the trip cannot be authorized. This could be true even if the receipts budget had been devised to cover the total budgeted expenditures. The problem lies in concentration on individual items and type of cost rather than on the objectives to be accomplished.

A further problem that can result from the line-by-line approval procedure is that it has tended to encourage the establishment of current budget allowances based on prior year's (or an average of prior years') budget allowances or actual expenditures for each item. Thus, each department might be given a 5% increase or decrease in some or most of its line items. In a broader approach, each department might be given a 5% increase or decrease and allowed to spread the total increase or decrease over whatever items are available. Either approach ignores the question of objectives or assumes that the increased or decreased benefits of changes in one segment are equal to the increased or decreased benefits of any other. Further, when the current allowance is based on prior expenditures, there is a tendency to spend right up to the allowance in order to avoid cuts in the next period's budget.

Two alternative budgeting approaches, discussed below, have been developed to at least partially eliminate these problems.

Program Budgeting

Because of the need to concentrate on objectives, another type of budgeting is coming into more widespread use in not-for-profit organizations. This type of budgeting is called program budgeting (or PPBS, which stands for planning, programming, budgeting systems). The emphasis is on the desired results of the unit's efforts, and managers are relatively free to shift expenditures from one category to another, if such a shift will increase the unit's likelihood of achieving those results. With its emphasis on results, program budgeting is closely related to management by objectives. To highlight the differences between traditional budgeting and program budgeting, consider the following two ways in which a city or county might classify its expenditures.

Traditional Budgeting by object	*Program Budgeting*
Salaries and wages	Law enforcement and judiciary
Outside services	Transportation
Equipment	Parks and recreation
Supplies and maintenance	Health and hospitals
Insurance	Housing
Travel	Education
Miscellaneous (detailed)	General support and administration

The use of program-based categories does not automatically solve the area's problems; however, it does provide a start in analyzing the effectiveness of the municipal government, and in making changes that will advance the desires and goals of the residents.

Zero-Based Budgeting

Zero-based budgeting is another approach to developing an expenditures budget. Under this approach, the base for determining the current year's budget for any expenditure is zero. Past expenditure levels are irrelevant. Every proposed expenditure for the current year must be justified under the current environment and with current goals in mind regardless of how much (or how little) was spent for the item in the past.

Two factors prompted the development of this approach to budgeting. First, as stated above, there is a tendency, under the line-by-line budget-approval process, to use the prior year's budget allowances as a starting point for establishing the current year's budget. Second, and perhaps more importantly, it is entirely possible that the intended results of past expenditures have been achieved, so that either no additional expenditures are required or a different level of expenditures is required to maintain that level of achievement.

For example, suppose the federal government perceived a serious deficiency in the quality and quantity of housing for a group of its citizens. It might authorize expenditures for identifying and rehabilitating existing substandard housing and for the construction of additional housing units of acceptable quality. Because a serious deficiency in existing housing prompted the program in the first place, it is likely that the problem of identifying and then rehabilitating existing substandard housing units will require considerable attention and cost. When the initial, serious deficiency is corrected, expenditures relating to housing can be reduced to the level necessary to *maintain* the desired level of housing of acceptable quality. New housing units may continue to be needed, and rehabilitation will be required as additional housing units drop below the standard. But the backlog, so to speak, should disappear. A budget allowance based on expenditures required to correct accumulated past deficiencies would not be appropriate in such a situation. Moreover, should current information suggest that adequate housing of acceptable quality is available for the particular group of citizens, continuation of *any* budget allowance related to achieving that objective should be questioned.

Zero-based budgeting may not be applied every year. It can be very costly to make complete cost justifications on an annual basis. The fact that such justification will be required periodically should be sufficient to prompt careful evaluation of expenditures during the interim periods.

It is implicit in program budgeting that a program must be justified in order to be kept. A program might need several years to get to the point where its objectives are being accomplished, and it is also costly to make a complete reevaluation of every program every year. However, there should be frequent reviews of progress to determine whether particular programs are doing their intended jobs.

SUMMARY

Financial budgets, like operational budgets, use forecasts and assumptions about the behavior of the various factors incorporated in them. Financial budgeting develops detailed budgets of cash receipts and cash disbursements, and a pro forma balance sheet. Effective financial budgeting depends on good operational budgeting. The detailed cash budgets utilize data from the purchases and expense budgets and from the pro forma income statement.

Having completed the preliminary cash budget, it may become apparent that additional financing is needed; managers can plan in advance to meet this need. Financial budgets are often prepared for relatively long time periods. Such budgets assist managers in assessing long-term asset and financing requirements.

The presentation of the budgeting process is now complete. Comprehensive budgeting brings together many strands of management. A comprehensive budget is the most conspicuous process of communication within a firm and facilitates the coordination of major functional areas—production, sales, and finance.

Budgeting takes place in not-for-profit entities as well as businesses. Although many of the same principles apply, there are some identifiable differences in the budgeting process of not-for-profit entities, the most significant difference being that receipts are normally budgeted based on budgeted expenditures. Two additional budgeting approaches, program and zero-based budgeting, have been introduced for governmental units, to help offset the tendency in not-for-profit budgeting to concentrate on detailed expenditures rather than objectives.

KEY TERMS

cash budget	minimum cash balance
financial budgeting	pro forma financial statements
financing gap	program budgets
long-term budget	zero-based budgets

REVIEW PROBLEM

This problem is a continuation of the Review Problem from Chapter 5. Using the following additional data, prepare a cash budget for January 19X4 and a pro forma balance sheet for January 31, 19X4. Prepare supporting budgets for cash receipts and cash disbursements.

Exempli Company Balance Sheet
December 31, 19X3

Assets		*Equities*	
Cash	$ 20,000	Accounts payable	
Accounts receivable	30,000	(merchandise)	$ 12,000
Inventory (6,000 units)	30,000	Common stock	200,000
Building and equipment (net)	200,000	Retained earnings	68,000
Totals	$280,000		$280,000

1. Sales are collected 40% in month of sale, 60% in the following month.
2. Purchases are paid 40% in month of purchase, 60% in the following month.
3. All other expenses requiring cash are paid in the month incurred.
4. The firm will declare a $3,000 dividend on January 10 and pay it on January 25.
5. The budgeted income statement and purchases budget from the solution in Chapter 5 (page 144) are given below for convenience.

Exempli Company Budgeted Income Statement
for January 19X4

Sales		$100,000
Cost of sales		25,000
Gross profit		$ 75,000
Variable costs:		
Commissions	$10,000	
Other variable expenses	5,000	15,000
Contribution margin		$ 60,000
Fixed costs:		
Depreciation	$ 2,000	
Other operating expenses	40,000	42,000
Budgeted income		$ 18,000

Purchases Budget for January 19X4

Desired ending inventory	$45,000
Cost of sales	25,000
Total requirements	$70,000
Beginning inventory	30,000
Budgeted purchases	$40,000

Answers to review problem

Cash Budget

Beginning balance	$20,000
Receipts, see below	70,000
Cash available	$90,000
Disbursements, see next page	86,000
Ending balance	$ 4,000

Cash Receipts Budget

Collection from December sales	$30,000
Collection from January sales	
($100,000 × 40%)	40,000
Total	$70,000

December sales will all be collected by the end of January. Because sales are collected by the end of the month following sale, all accounts receivable at the end of a month are expected to be collected in the coming month.

Cash Disbursements Budget

Merchandise ($40,000 × 40%) + $12,000	$28,000
Commissions	10,000
Various operating expenses	45,000
Dividend	3,000
Total	$86,000

Exempli Company Pro Forma Balance Sheet
January 31, 19X4

Assets		*Equities*	
Cash (cash budget)	$ 4,000	Accounts payable‡	·$ 24,000
Accounts receivable*	60,000	Common stock	200,000
Inventory (purchases budget)	45,000	Retained earnings§	83,000
Building and equipment†	198,000		
Totals	$307,000		$307,000

*60% of January sales of $100,000 (40% was collected in January).
†$200,000 beginning balance less $2,000 depreciation expense.
‡60% of January purchases of $40,000 (40% was paid in January).
§Beginning balance of $68,000 plus budgeted income of $18,000 minus dividend of $3,000.

Notice that cash declined by $16,000 (from $20,000 to $4,000) even though income was $18,000. The budgeted cash balance of $4,000 might be too low in management's judgment, and the firm might wish to seek a short-term bank loan.

ASSIGNMENT MATERIAL

Questions for Discussion

6-1 Cash budgeting—effects of external events   You are controller of a large manufacturing company and have recently completed your cash budget for the coming year. You now learn of each of the following events, which you are to consider independently. For each event, indicate (1) whether you would expect it to influence your cash receipts or disbursements, and (2) in which direction. Explain your answer and state any assumption you make.

1. The sales manager informs you that customers are not paying their bills as quickly as usual because of high interest rates in the economy.
2. The production manager has found a way to keep production at a desired level with less labor than had been used in the past.
3. The sales manager informs you that, due to a strike at the plant of a competitor, your firm's sales should be higher than budgeted.
4. Your banker has just told you that the interest rate on a loan you have negotiated will be lower than originally planned.
5. Production workers are granted a 5% pay increase, to begin immediately.
6. Your suppliers, whom you have been paying 45 days after purchases were made, are now requiring payment in 30 days.
7. Inventory policy is being changed from the carrying of the next two months' requirements to 150% of the next month's requirements.
8. A special advertising campaign is to be undertaken. Sales are expected to increase substantially.

6-2 Publication of budgets   In financial accounting you studied the composition of the various financial statements usually distributed to persons, or groups of persons, outside the economic enterprise. Included among these statements were the balance sheet, income statement, and funds statement. In this chapter it is suggested that a comprehensive budgeting program involves the preparation of the same statements using budgeted data. Budgeted financial statements are not normally made available to persons outside the organization. Do you see any advantages to publishing these budgeted statements as part of the annual reports? Do you see any disadvantages?

Exercises

6-3 Cash receipts budget   The Nisson Company expects the following sales for the first six months of 19X2. Figures are given in thousands of dollars.

	Jan.	Feb.	Mar.	Apr.	May	June
Budgeted Sales	$900	$1,200	$1,100	$1,600	$2,200	$2,500

Cash collections are made as follows: 2% of sales become bad debts, 30% of sales are collected in the month of sale, 40% in the first month after sale, and 28% in the second month after sale. Sales in November 19X1 were $1,200, in December $800.

Required

Prepare a schedule of budgeted cash receipts for the six-month period ending June 30, 19X2, by month.

6-4 Production and cash disbursements budgets   The following data relate to the Griffon Company and its single product, the Totam.

(a) Sales forecast, January through June, 19X9 (in units): 1,200; 1,400; 1,700; 2,000; 2,400; and 2,100.
(b) Inventory policy: inventory is maintained at 150% of budgeted sales for the coming month.
(c) Cost data: materials $4 per unit; direct labor $5 per unit; and variable overhead $4 per unit.
(d) Materials are purchased daily and are paid for in the following month; all other costs requiring cash disbursements are paid as incurred.
(e) The beginning inventory for January is 1,800 units.

Required

1. Prepare a budget of production for each month of the period for which you have data (in units).
2. Prepare a budget of cash disbursements for each month for which you have data. Production in December 19X8 was 1,200 units.

6-5 Cash receipts and cash budget   Refer to the data in the preceding exercise. The Totam sells for $20 per unit. All sales are on account with 30% collected in the month of sale, 70% in the month after sale. Sales in December 19X8 were 1,000 units.

The firm maintains a minimum cash balance of $5,000, the amount on hand at January 1, 19X9. Borrowings are made in multiples of $1,000 at the beginning of a month, and are repaid at the end of the first month in which sufficient cash is available. Interest at 9% per year is repaid when loans are repaid.

Required

1. Prepare a schedule of budgeted cash receipts for each of the months for which you have data.
2. Prepare a cash budget for each month for which you have data.

6-6   Cash budget—quarters The Walton Company expects the following results by quarters in 19X4 in thousands of dollars.

	1	2	3	4
Sales	$1,500	$2,100	$3,300	$2,400
Cash disbursements:				
Production costs	1,400	2,000	1,600	1,700
Selling and general	200	400	580	320
Purchases of fixed assets	0	200	400	400
Dividends	20	20	20	20

Accounts receivable at the end of a quarter are one-third of sales for the quarter. The beginning balance in accounts receivable is $600,000. Cash on hand at the beginning of the year is $130,000, and the desired minimum balance is $100,000. Any borrowings are made at the beginnings of quarters in which the need will occur, in $10,000 multiples, and are repaid at the ends of quarters. Ignore interest.

Required

1. Prepare a cash budget by quarters for the year.
2. What is the loan outstanding at the end of the year?
3. Can the firm be operating profitably in view of the heavy borrowing required?

6-7   Comprehensive budget The following data apply to the Micro Company, a retail store that is preparing its budgets for 19X7.

Forecasted Sales		Balance Sheet Data December 31, 19X6	
January	$60,000	Cash	$ 8,000
February	60,000	Accounts receivable:	
March	70,000	November sales	16,000
April	90,000	December sales	50,000
		Inventory	54,000
		Accounts payable (merchandise)	27,000

Other data are as follows:

(a) Sales are on credit with 60% of sales collected in the month after sale, 40% in the second month after sale.
(b) Cost of sales is 60% of sales.
(c) Other variable costs are 10% of sales, paid in the month incurred.
(d) Inventories are to be 150% of next month's budgeted sales requirements.
(e) Purchases are paid for in the month after purchase.
(f) Fixed expenses are $3,000 per month; all require cash.

Required

1. Prepare budgets of purchases for each of the first three months of 19X7.
2. Prepare separate budgets of cash receipts and disbursements and a cash budget for each of the first four months of 19X7.
3. Prepare a budgeted income statement for the four-month period ending April 30, 19X7.

6-8 Cash budgeting—account analysis Using the following information, prepare cash budgets and supporting schedules for all months that you can. The beginning cash balance is $12,000.

	January	February	March	April
Sales	$88,000	$105,000	$90,000	$110,000
Accounts receivable, end of month	$26,000	$ 31,000	$22,000	$ 29,000
Purchases	$64,000	$ 51,000	$70,000	$ 56,000
Accounts payable, end of month	$31,000	$ 25,000	$32,000	$ 28,000

At the beginning of January, receivables were $28,000 and accounts payable were $18,000.

6-9 Comprehensive budget The following data pertain to the Dipsy Company, a retail store.

Sales Forecasts—19X8

January	$ 80,000
February	90,000
March	110,000
April	120,000
May	100,000

Balance Sheet
December 31, 19X7

Cash	$ 15,000	Accounts payable	$ 28,000
Accounts receivable	60,000	Accrued sales commissions	7,000
Inventory	102,000	Common stock	160,000
Net fixed assets	200,000	Retained earnings	182,000
Totals	$377,000		$377,000

Other data are as follows:

(a) All sales are on credit with 40% collected in the month of sale, 60% in the month after sale.
(b) Cost of sales is 60% of sales.
(c) The only other variable cost is a 7% commission to salespeople that is paid in the month after it is earned. All sales are subject to the commission.
(d) Inventory is kept equal to sales requirements for the next two months' budgeted sales.
(e) Purchases are paid for in the month after purchase.
(f) Fixed costs are $10,000 per month, including $4,000 depreciation.

Required

1. Prepare a budgeted income statement for the three-month period ending March 31, 19X8.
2. Prepare a cash budget for each of the first three months of 19X8 and all necessary supporting budgets.
3. Prepare a pro forma balance sheet as of March 31, 19X8.

Problems

6-10 Municipal budgeting—revenues The City of Wentworth is preparing its budget for 19X9. Total required revenues are $32,000,000. The city has two major sources of revenue, sales taxes and property taxes. The sales tax is 1% of taxable retail sales, which includes virtually all sales except for food and medicine. The assessed valuation of taxable property is $340,000,000.

An economist hired by the city has forecast total taxable retail sales at $752,000,000 for 19X9.

Required
1. Determine the property tax rate that is needed to meet the city's revenue objective, assuming that the estimate of retail sales is correct.
2. The city council is considering a proposal to reduce property taxes on homes owned by people over 65 years of age. It is proposed that the rate on such homes be set at $30 per $1,000 assessed valuation. The total assessed valuation of homes owned by people over 65 is $36,000,000. Determine the rate that would have to set on the remaining taxable property in order to meet the revenue objective if the proposal is adopted.

6-11 Cash budget—one month The Stony Acres Department Store makes about 20% of its sales for cash. Credit sales are collected 20%, 30%, 45% in the month of sale, month after, and second month after sale, respectively. The remaining 5% become bad debts. The store tries to purchase enough goods each month to maintain its inventory at two and one-half times the following month's budgeted sales. All of its purchases are subject to a 2% discount if paid within 10 days and the store takes all discounts. Accounts payable are then equal to one-third of that month's net purchases. Cost of goods sold, without considering the 2% discount, is 60% of selling prices. The firm records inventory net of the discount.

The general manager of the store has asked you to prepare a cash budget for August and you have gathered the following data.

Sales:	
May (actual)	$240,000
June (actual)	220,000
July (actual)	320,000
August (budgeted)	330,000
September (budgeted)	290,000
Inventory at July 31	455,700
Cash at July 31	65,000
Purchases in July (gross)	210,000
Selling, general, and administrative expenses budgeted for August	91,000 (includes $18,000 depreciation)

The firm pays all of its other expenses in the month incurred.

Required
Prepare a cash budget for August.

6-12 Cash budget—six months The Jackson Company makes a single product that sells for $20. Cost data are as follows:

(a) Variable manufacturing costs (all require cash) are $8 per unit.
(b) Fixed manufacturing costs are $5,000 per month (including $3,000 in depreciation).
(c) Selling and administrative expenses are $7,000 per month fixed and $2 per unit variable. All require cash.

Other data are as follows:

(d) A two-month supply of finished goods is maintained. Beginning inventory is 1,700 units.

(e) Raw materials are bought as needed. There is no inventory, and payment is made at the time of purchase. The **per-unit** cost is included in the variable manufacturing cost of $8.

(f) All sales are on credit with 40% collected in the month after sale, 60% in the following month.

(g) The $2 per unit selling and administrative expense is paid in the month after sale.

(h) Bank loans can be obtained at 8% interest in $1,000 multiples. A loan is taken out at the beginning of the month and repaid at the end, if sufficient cash exists. (Partial repayments can be made.) Interest is paid when loans are repaid.

(i) The minimum desired cash balance is $30,000. The balance at January 1, 19X6 is $35,000.

(j) Accounts receivable at January 1, 19X6 are $15,000 from November sales and $20,000 from December sales.

(k) The sales budget for the first ten months of 19X6 is as follows (in units): 800; 900; 1,200; 1,500; 1,800; 2,100; 2,300; 1,800; 1,900; and 1,400.

Required

1. Prepare a cash budget for the first six months of 19X6, by month and in total. Provide all necessary supporting schedules and budgets.

2. Is the firm profitable? **Explain.**

6-13 Cash budget—changes in assumptions   Using the data in the previous problem, prepare new budgets assuming that sales for the last four months of the eight-month period are forecast to be 200 units lower per month. What lessons can be learned by comparing the results of this problem with those of the previous one?

6-14 Cash budget—modification of problem 6-12   Refer to problem 6-12. Solve it assuming the following:

(a) Of the $8 variable manufacturing cost, $3 is for materials that cost $1 per pound. Three pounds of material are used to make a unit of finished product.

(b) Materials inventory is kept equal to the requirements for budgeted production for the following two months.

(c) Materials are paid for in the month after purchase.

(d) The beginning inventory of materials is 8,100 lbs., $8,100.

(e) Purchases of materials in December were 2,000 lbs.

6-15 Long-range financial budget   The Millard Company has retained you to develop a financing plan for the next few years. You collect the following information about the firm's expectations, goals, and policies.

Sales Forecasts

19X4	$1,200
19X5	1,500
19X6	1,600
19X7	1,700

The firm expects a return on sales of 10%. The directors of the firm would like to maintain the policy of distributing dividends in an amount equal to 60% of net income each year. The directors would also like to have a current ratio of at least 2 to 1 and do not want long-term debt to exceed 60% of stockholder equity.

Current asset requirements are 30% of expected sales in the coming year, net fixed assets are 80% of budgeted sales for the coming year. At the end of 19X3, net fixed assets are $960, stockholders' equity is $750, and working capital is $190.

Required

Prepare a schedule showing financing requirements for 19X4, 19X5, and 19X6 and propose a plan for meeting the requirements.

6-16   Budgeting equations (CMA adapted)   Your firm has just acquired a new computer, and one of the first things that the president wants it to be used for is the preparation of the firm's comprehensive budget. He assigns you the task of formulating a set of equations that can be used to write a program to perform the computations required for the budgets. You consult with the chief programmer, and the two of you decide that the following notation should be used, which will make it easy for the programmer to prepare the necessary programs.

S_0 = sales in current month (units)
S_1 = sales in coming month (units)
S_{-1} = sales in prior month (units)
S_{-2} = sales in second prior month (units)
P = selling price per unit
CGS = cost of goods sold per unit (purchase price)
OVC = other variable costs per unit
FC = total fixed costs per month
FCC = fixed costs per month requiring cash disbursements
PUR = purchases in current month (units)
PUR_{-1} = purchases in prior month (units)

You examine the records of the firm and decide that the firm's policies or experienced relationships are as follows:

1. Collections on sales are 30% in the month of sale, 50% in the month after sale, and 20% in the second month after sale.
2. Inventory is maintained at twice the coming month's budgeted sales volume.
3. Purchases are paid for 60% in the month after purchase and 40% in the month of purchase.
4. All other costs are paid as incurred.

Required: Prepare equations that can be used to budget for the following:

1. Net income for the current month.
2. Cash receipts in current month.
3. Purchases in current month in units.
4. Purchases in current month in dollars.
5. Cash disbursements in current month.

6-17   Comprehensive budget—continuation of problem 5-36 (Adapted from a problem prepared by Professor Maurice L. Hirsch)   The following information about Banana City is available, in addition to that given in problem 5-36.

1. Sales of bananas are for cash only. Sales of nuts are on credit and are collected two months after sale.
2. Banana City's suppliers give terms of 30 days for payment of accounts payable. Banana City takes full advantage of the 30-day payments. (Assume that all months have 30 days.)
3. The firm must take quarterly payments on its income taxes. The payment for the first quarter of fiscal year 19X7 is due on January 15, 19X7. The liability for taxes payable shown on the balance sheet below is to be paid on October 15.
4. The fixed expenses of the firm that require cash disbursement are paid as incurred with the following exceptions: **(a) insurance premiums are all paid on November 1 in advance for the next 12 months;**

and (b) interest payments are all made on January 1. The $156,000 "other fixed expenses" shown in part 8 of problem 5-36 all require cash disbursements evenly over the year.

5. The balance sheet for August 31, 19X6 is given below.

Assets		Equities	
Cash	$ 15,000	Accounts payable (merchandise)	$ 26,000
Accounts receivable	75,000	Taxes payable	31,000
Inventories	41,800	Accrued interest	4,000
Prepaid insurance	2,000	Long term debt, 6%	100,000
Land	8,000	Common stock	150,000
Equipment (net)	210,000	Retained earnings	40,800
Totals	$351,800		$351,800

6. Sales in the last part of fiscal year 19X6 are given below.

	June	July	August
Bananas	$31,000	$34,000	$32,500
Nuts	37,000	41,000	34,000

7. The firm expects to pay a dividend of $12,000 in October.

Required

1. Prepare budgets of cash receipts and disbursements for each of the first three months of fiscal year 19X7 and for the quarter as a whole.
2. Prepare a cash budget for the quarter, by month and in total.
3. Prepare a pro forma balance sheet for November 30, 19X6.

6-18 Pro forma balance sheet and financing requirements Using the following data for the Caldwell Company, prepare a statement of asset requirements and available equities as of December 31, 19X6. Balance the two either by adding to cash or to long-term debt, depending on whether assets are less than equities or vice versa.

Caldwell Company
Budgeted Income Statement
for 19X6

Sales	$100,000
Cost of goods sold	70,000
Gross profit	30,000
Selling, general, and administrative expenses*	18,000
Income before taxes	12,000
Income taxes (40% rate)	4,800
Net income	$ 7,200

*Includes $8,000 depreciation expense

Balance Sheet Data, December 31, 19X5

Plant and equipment	$100,000
Accumulated depreciation	50,000
Common stock	60,000
Retained earnings	30,000
Asset requirements:	
Cash—minimum desired balance	$ 10,000
Accounts receivable	30% of sales
Inventory	40% of cost of sales
Plant and equipment—net	60% of sales
Equities available:	
Accounts payable	50% of inventory
Income taxes payable	50% of income tax expense

A dividend of $4,000 will be paid in cash during 19X6.

6-19 Sales discounts and cash collections The Riddell Company has sales of $90,000 per month. Collections are slow; all payments are made in the second month after sale, a 60-day collection period. The credit manager has proposed that a 2% discount be offered to customers who pay within 10 days. He believes that all customers would take advantage of the discount.

    The firm now has average accounts receivable of $180,000 (two **months' sales)** and maintains a loan at the local bank in the amount of $200,000 for financing its current asset requirements. The controller states that he could reduce the loan dollar for dollar with a decline in accounts receivable. The loan bears interest at ¾% per month (9% annual rate).

Required

1. Determine the amount by which monthly income would be reduced because of the 2% discount.
2. Determine the savings in interest, per month, that the firm can obtain by reducing its accounts receivable.
3. Should the discount be offered?
4. Answer 1 and 2 above, assuming that only half of the customers would take the discount, with the others continuing to pay in the second month after sale. (Hint: Accounts receivable will not be $90,000.)

6-20 Comprehensive budget Below is the balance sheet of your firm, Flybynite Industries, at December 31, 19X5. Also shown is a projected income statement for the first three months of 19X6, prepared by your chief accountant, Robert Cratchit. You are happy with the projection and gloat about it to your banker, Gettin Hirates. Mr. Hirates, always anxious to lend money, has asked if you will need any cash to get through the first quarter. "Of course not" is your reply. Later, back at your office, Cratchit informs you of the following:

1. Sales are all on credit and are collected 50% in the month of sale, 50% in the month after sale.
2. It is company policy to build up inventory so that inventory is always equal to the next two months' sales in units. However, at December 31, 19X5 your inventory is depleted because of the dock strike.
3. You pay for purchases 50% in the month of purchases, 50% in the following month.
4. You are committed to paying the recorded cash dividend of $2,000 in March.
5. All cash expenses are paid in the month incurred, except for purchases.
6. The accounts receivable at December 31, 19X5 will be collected in January; the accounts payable at December 31, 19X5 will be paid in January.

7. The monthly breakdown of projected sales is as follows: January, $20,000; February, $30,000; and March, $50,000. In addition, April sales are expected to be $20,000, and May sales $20,000.
8. Cash should not go below $5,000.

Flybynite Industries
Balance Sheet
December 31, 19X5

Cash	$ 5,000		Accounts payable	$16,000	
Accounts receivable	10,000		Dividend payable	2,000	$18,000
Inventory	24,000	$39,000	Owner's equity		61,000
Plant and equipment net of					
accumulated depreciation		40,000			
Total assets		$79,000			$79,000

Projected Income Statement
Three Months Ending March 31, 19X6

Sales (10,000 units @ $10)		$100,000
Cost of sales (10,000 units @ $6)		60,000
Gross profit		40,000
Operating expenses:		
Wages and salaries	$9,000	
Rent	3,000	
Depreciation	3,000	
Other expenses	1,500	16,500
Income		$ 23,500

Required

Do you regret your reply to Mr. Hirates? Explain by preparing the appropriate schedules. (If borrowings are necessary, assume that they are in $1,000 multiples at the beginning of the month and that repayments are at the ends of months with 6% annual interest on the amount repaid.)

6-21 Cash budget—continuation of problem 5-34 The Richards Company (see page 157) collects its sales 30% in the month of sale, 30% in the next month, and 40% in the second month after sale.

Fixed production costs not requiring cash are $40,000 per month. All selling, general, and administrative expenses require cash and are paid in the month incurred, except for sales commissions, which are paid in the month after incurrence.

All production costs requiring cash are paid 80% in the month of production, 20% in the month after production. This includes payments for materials, of which no inventory is kept since they are delivered daily.

Selected balance sheet data at May 30 are as follows:

Cash	$120,000	(equals the desired minimum balance)
Accounts receivable:		
from May sales	336,000	
from April sales	120,000	
Liabilities:		
Sales commissions	48,000	
Production costs	66,000	

Required

Prepare a cash budget for the Richards Company for the first six months of the fiscal year, by month. If the need arises, show borrowings required to maintain the desired minimum balance of cash, in multiples of $10,000. Repayments are made at the ends of months and interest at 1% per month is paid when a repayment is made.

6-22 Analysis of budgets   Below are shown various budgets for the Simpson Company for the first three months of 19X6. Answer the following questions about the assumptions and policies used in formulating them.

1. What are variable manufacturing costs per unit?
2. What are monthly fixed manufacturing costs requiring cash disbursements?
3. What are the firm's expectations about cash collections from receivables? (All sales are on account.)
4. What were sales in December 19X5?
5. What are accounts receivable at March 31, 19X6?
6. What proportion of variable selling and administrative expenses is paid in the month incurred and what proportion is paid the following month?
7. What are accrued expenses payable for selling and administrative expenses at March 31, 19X6?
8. How much cash does the firm expect to have at March 31, 19X6? (The beginning balance is $200.)
9. If the firm could sell 2,000 additional units in the three-month period, what would income be? be? (Ignore interest expense.)
10. Look at the production budget. From comparisons of inventories, sales, and so on, determine the firm's inventory policy.
11. Does the beginning inventory for January reflect this policy? Show why or why not.
12. What are budgeted sales for April?

Simpson Company Budgeted Income Statement
for Three Months Ending March 31, 19X6

Sales (10,000 units)		$10,000
Variable costs:		
Production	$3,000	
Selling and administrative	1,000	4,000
Contribution margin		6,000
Fixed costs:		
Production	1,800	
Selling and administrative	2,400	4,200
Income		$ 1,800

Sales by month: January 2,000 units, February 3,000 units, March 5,000 units.

Production Budget (in units)

	January	February	March
Desired ending inventory	4,500	7,500	6,000
Units sold	2,000	3,000	5,000
Total requirements	6,500	10,500	11,000
Beginning inventory	2,500	4,500	7,500
Production	4,000	6,000	3,500

Cash Receipts Budget

	January	February	March
Collections:			
December sales	$ 600		
January sales	500	$ 1,500	
February sales		750	$ 2,250
March sales			1,250
Total collections	$1,100	$ 2,250	$ 3,500

Cash Disbursements Budget

	January	February	March
Production costs:			
Variable	$1,200	$ 1,800	$ 1,050
Fixed	400	400	400
Selling and administrative:			
Variable—current month	120	180	300
—prior month	32	80	120
Fixed	800	800	800
Totals	$2,552	$ 3,260	$ 2,670

6-23 Cash budget—variable minimum balance The chief financial officer of the Bland Company has asked for your help in preparing a cash budget. He plans to maintain a minimum balance based on the budgeted disbursements for the coming month and is unsure how to proceed. He tells you the following about his policy. "If the coming month's budgeted receipts are greater than budgeted disbursements, I want to hold a balance equal to 10% of budgeted disbursements and invest any excess cash in short-term government notes. If budgeted disbursements are greater than budgeted receipts, I want to have enough cash to make up the budgeted deficit and have 20% of budgeted disbursements on hand to begin the month. We will borrow if the indicated balance is less than required."

The budgets for sales and purchases in the coming months are as follows.

	Sales	Purchases
April	$500,000	$470,000
May	$780,000	$550,000
June	$900,000	$560,000
July	$600,000	$480,000
August	$650,000	$600,000

Sales are collected 30% in the month of sale, 70% in the following month. Purchases are paid for 50% in the month of purchase, 50% in the following month. Sales in March were $450,000 and accounts payable for merchandise at March 31 were $185,000. Cash at March 31 was $140,000. Fixed expenses requiring cash disbursements are $110,000 per month.

Required

1. Prepare a schedule by month for the April–July period indicating the amounts that would have to be borrowed, or would be available for investment, in each month. Borrowings would be repaid as soon as possible and are not included in the determination of disbursements for the purpose of

setting the desired balance. Borrowings would be repaid before investments were made and investments would be sold before borrowings are made. Ignore interest.

2. Discuss the policy. What advantages or disadvantages does it have in comparison to a policy of having a set number of dollars as the desired minimum balance?

6-24 Pro forma balance sheet and cash budget   The president of the Stern Department Store has requested your assistance. He will be seeking a large bank loan in a couple of months for the purpose of opening a new store and has been told by his banker that the March 31, 19X8 balance sheet should look good if the loan is to be granted. The banker said specifically that working capital (current assets minus current liabilities) should be at least $500,000 and that the current ratio (current assets divided by current liabilities) should be at least 2 to 1.

It is now approaching the end of January and the president is becoming anxious. He asks you to prepare a cash budget for February and March and a pro forma balance sheet as of March 31. The balance sheet at the end of January is expected to be about as follows, in thousands of dollars.

Assets		Equities	
Cash	$ 140	Accounts payable (merchandise)	$ 410
Accounts receivable	240	Short-term loan (due in August)	150
Inventory	680	Taxes payable	40
Building and equipment (net)	1,800	Common stock	2,000
		Retained earnings	260
Totals	$2,860		$2,860

The sales forecast for the months of February, March, April, and May are, respectively: $780,000; $650,000; $600,000; and $820,000. Cost of sales averages 60% of sales. Receivables are collected 70% in the month of sale, 30% in the following month. Inventory is normally maintained at budgeted sales requirements for the following two months. Purchases are paid for in 30 days.

The taxes payable shown in the balance sheet are due on March 15. Although the firm normally keeps a minimum cash balance of $80,000, the president asks you to disregard this for purposes of the budgets. He also informs you that monthly fixed costs of operation are $265,000, of which $30,000 is depreciation. All fixed costs requiring cash are paid as incurred.

Required

1. Prepare the cash budget and pro forma balance sheet that the president wants.
2. Determine whether the firm will be likely to meet the criteria set by the bank.

6-25 Cash budgeting—a lender's viewpoint   You are the chief assistant to Mr. Barnes, the loan officer of the Metropolitan National Bank. In December 19X4 Mr. Barnes discussed a loan with Mr. Johnson, manager-owner of a local dry goods store. Mr. Johnson has requested a loan of $250,000 to be repaid at June 30, 19X5. The store is being expanded and additional inventory is needed. From the proceeds of the loan, $200,000 will be spent on remodeling and new fixtures. The rest will be spent for additional inventory. At Mr. Barnes' request, Mr. Johnson submitted a budgeted income statement for the six months ending June 30, 19X5.

Sales	$900,000
Cost of goods sold	360,000
Gross profit	540,000
Selling, general, and administrative expenses	300,000
Income (before interest)	$240,000

Mr. Johnson said that since $50,000 in depreciation was included in selling, general, and administrative expenses, the firm would generate $290,000 in cash flow, more than enough to repay the loan with $10,000 in interest (8% annual rate). Mr. Barnes asks you to check out the forecast; you obtain the following information:

1. Sales are expected to be $100,000 in January, $140,000 in February, and $165,000 in each of the rest of the months of the entire year.
2. Merchandise is held equal to two months' budgeted sales.
3. Accounts payable are paid in 30 days.
4. About half of sales are for cash. The rest are collected in the second month after sale (60 days).
5. Cost of goods sold is variable, and 15% of sales is the variable portion of selling, general, and administrative expenses. All selling, general and administrative expenses, except depreciation, are paid in the month incurred.
6. At December 31, 19X4 the following balance sheet is expected:

Johnson Store, Inc.
Pro Forma Balance Sheet
December 31, 19X4

Cash (desired minimum)	$ 20,000	Accounts payable	$ 30,000
Accounts receivable	40.000	Common stock	200,000
Inventory	60,000	Retained earnings	115,000
Building and equipment	375,000		
Accumulated depreciation	(150,000)		
Totals	$345,000		$345,000

Required

Determine whether the firm can repay the loan with interest at the end of the first six months of 19X5. If not, explain why in terms that will make Mr. Johnson understand where he made his mistakes.

Cases

6-26 Comprehensive budget—annual period   The Larsen Company makes fertilizer in a midwestern state. The firm has nearly completed a new plant that will produce twice as much as the old plant, which is being scrapped. Swen Larsen, the owner, has consulted you about his financing requirements for the coming year. He knows that he will require additional financing because of the doubling of production and he intends to obtain a loan as soon as possible. He is on good terms with local bankers and anticipates no difficulty in obtaining the loan, but is anxious that it not be too large or too small.

The production process in the new plant is highly automated and can be carried out with a work force of the same size as that used last year in the old plant . The income statement for last year and the year-end balance sheet are shown below.

Larsen Company
Income Statement
for 19X4

Sales	$600,000
Cost of goods sold	420,000
Gross profit	180,000
Selling, general, and administrative expenses	120,000
Income	$ 60,000

Larsen Company
Balance Sheet
December 31, 19X4

Assets		Liabilities and Owner Equity	
Cash	$ 22,000	Accounts payable	$ 10,000
Accounts receivable	40,000	Common stock	400,000
Inventory	140,000	Retained earnings	122,000
Plant and equipment—old plant	-0-		
—new plant	330,000		
Totals	$532,000		$532,000

You learn that depreciation expense on the old plant was $10,000 per year, all of which was included in cost of goods sold. The new plant will be depreciated at $30,000 per year. Wages paid last year to production workers were $100,000. Material purchases were $200,000, which is also the amount of material cost included in cost of goods sold (the beginning and ending inventories of materials were the same). Factory overhead, other than depreciation, was $110,000 last year. It is expected that factory overhead, other than depreciation, will be $140,000 in the coming year.

Selling, general, and administrative expenses are expected to be $130,000 during the coming year. Sales will be only 120% of last year's sales because it will take some time to reach the full output of the new plant. Mr. Larsen expects to spend $90,000 buying new equipment to complete the plant. This expenditure will be made as soon as he obtains the new loan. The factory will be operating at full capacity the last few months of the year, so ending requirements for current assets should be double the beginning amounts. Accounts payable are closely related to the amount of inventory carried.

Required

Prepare a pro forma income statement for 19X5, and a pro forma balance sheet (as far as possible) for December 31, 19X5. State any assumptions you have to make and indicate how much Mr. Larsen must borrow from the bank.

6-27 Budgeting and industry data   Ralph Robertson is considering opening a menswear store in a new shopping center. He has had a great deal of experience working in men's stores and is convinced that he can make a success of his own store. He has asked you to develop a financing plan that he can take to a bank to obtain a loan. He knows that a bank manager will be more receptive to an applicant who has made careful plans of his needs. He gives you the following data obtained from a trade association's study of stores of the kind and size he plans to open (1,200 square feet of selling space).

Average sales per square foot	$70 per year
Average rent	$500 per month plus 5% of sales
Average gross profit	45% of sales
Average annual operating expenses (excluding rent and depreciation):	
at $60,000 sales annually	$19,200
at $90,000 sales annually	$26,700
Inventory requirements	four-month supply
Investment in fixtures and equipment (useful life of five years)	$22,000

Ralph plans to sell for cash only. He will have to pay cash for his first purchase of inventory, then he can get 30 days' credit from suppliers. His other operating expenses, including rent, will be paid in the month incurred.

Ralph expects to have a steady growth in sales for the first four months of operation (January through April 19X8) and to reach the monthly average for the industry in May. His projections for the first four months are as follows: $4,000; $4,500; $5,200; and $6,100.

Required

1. Prepare a budgeted income statement for the year 19X8.
2. Prepare a schedule showing his total financing requirements through April. Ralph will invest $10,000 of his own money.

PART THREE

DECISION MAKING

Part Three illustrates the basic principles of short- and long-run decision making. The concepts described in Part One that relate to cost behavior are critical to analyses in short- and long-run decisions. The distinction between fixed and variable costs, and the identification of fixed costs as discretionary or committed are especially important. As has been seen in Part One, decision making is largely a part of the planning process. Alternative courses of action are detailed and evaluated, and resources and constraints are appraised.

A basic difference between short- and long-run decisions is that the major analytical techniques of the latter require recognition of the time value of money and the use of present values. For a review of the basic concepts of present-value determination consult Appendix A.

CHAPTER 7

SHORT-TERM DECISION MAKING

Managers are constantly taking actions that affect the firm. New products are introduced, old products dropped. Prices are raised and lowered. Component parts previously made internally are subcontracted, or vice versa. These actions, and others, are taken as the result of a decision—a determination that one course of action will be followed and others not. A manager can never be sure that his decision was the best possible one because the outcome of any other course of action will never be known. But the manager can get a fair degree of confidence if the decision was based on the best available information and he or she understood the significance of the information.

Short-term decision making usually involves periods of less than a year and is not normally concerned with matters such as purchasing additional machinery or providing more physical capacity. The general question in short-term decision making is usually "what is the best use of our existing resources?" In Chapter 8 we shall examine long-term decision making, where existing facilities are not a constraint, and the question becomes "what resources should we have?"

SHORT-TERM DECISIONS AND ACCOUNTING INFORMATION

Accounting data are an important, but not the only, source of information needed for short-term decision making. In many cases, the accountant will come up with an analysis that shows a particular course of action to be better than others. Yet other managers may decide that another course will be taken because the savings do not offset possible unfavorable consequences that cannot be measured. (Would you accept a job that paid more than any other job you could get if it involved living in an uncomfortable climate or had no challenge or chance for advancement?)

Most information that is quantifiable can ultimately be expressed in terms of dollars and therefore is at least potentially accounting data. Still other information cannot be expressed quantitatively, or can be expressed only as gross estimates or broad ranges. If, for example, a firm considers selling some of its product to a discount chain at a price less than that charged to its regular customers, some ill will (lost sales) may result if the existing customers learn of the price break. This is a serious problem, but monetary estimates of the effects of such customer ill will are not often easily obtained.

It is always possible that qualitative factors could, in some circumstances, override a decision indicated by an analysis using purely quantitative factors, but the starting point in considering alternatives is the analysis of quantifiable factors. At this level of analysis there is only one basic rule to consider—the alternative that promises the highest net income for the firm is best. The rule is not easy to apply, and two subrules may be helpful:

1. The only revenues and costs that matter in decision making are expected future revenues and costs that are different for the alternative courses of action. Such revenues and costs are called **differential** revenues and costs.
2. Revenues and costs that have already been realized or incurred are relevant only to the extent that they may aid in predicting future revenues and costs.

In applying these rules in all but the most simple of situations, two additional important concepts come into play: the concepts of sunk costs and of opportunity costs. We will first illustrate application of the basic rules, and then introduce the two new concepts.

Basic Example. Your firm needs a particular type of machine for a series of special jobs that will produce $800,000 of contribution margin over the next eight months. Two versions of this type of machine are available: the Fast and the Slow. The Slow costs $60,000 and will last for one year; the Fast costs $80,000 and will also last for only one year. Neither machine will have any value at the end of the year, and there is no market for used machines of this type. For the operation of either machine, the firm will have to hire a specially trained worker, at a wage of $15,000 for the period. The other operating costs, all fixed, for these machines are $220,000 and $100,000, for the Slow and the Fast machines, respectively. Under these circumstances, and so long as the two machines will both do the intended job, which machine should be **acquired**?

Applying the basic rules, an appropriate analysis of this relatively simple decision might proceed as follows:

Decision

	Acquire Slow Machine	Acquire Fast Machine
Acquisition cost	$ 60,000	$ 80,000
Other operating costs	220,000	100,000
Total relevant costs	$280,000	$180,000

The Fast machine is the best choice because use of this machine will involve the least total cost to the firm.

The above analysis reflects two important parts of the decision rules given. First, note that the only costs included in the analysis were *future* costs, the costs of acquiring and operating the individual machines. Note also, however, that only *differential* costs are included. The $15,000 wage cost for the machine operator is not included because it would be the same under either alternative. It would be possible, of course, to include the $15,000 in the analysis. But if so, it would have to be included under both alternatives and, hence, the conclusion would be the same (*viz.*, to buy the Fast machine rather than the Slow machine). Similarly, because revenues and variable costs (i.e., contribution margin) were the same regardless of which machine was selected, they are also irrelevant.

Sunk Costs

To say that only differential future revenues and costs are relevant to decision making means that amounts expended in the past are irrelevant. Amounts paid for assets in the past are called **sunk costs** and should be ignored for decision making. This conclusion applies not only to the purchase cost of existing assets but also to their book values (cost less accumulated depreciation). An application of the concept of sunk cost can be illustrated by changing the previous example slightly.

Suppose that it was today that you learned of the Fast machine and that only yesterday the firm purchased a Slow machine. In discussing the problem, the president of your firm states that buying the Fast machine now would be unwise because the firm would take a loss of $60,000 (ignoring taxes) if it junked the Slow machine that it has already purchased. Is he correct?

No. It would still be wise to purchase the Fast machine even if it does mean junking the machine purchased yesterday. The reason is, once again, that the firm's future costs will still be lower if that course of action is followed. Even if the future cost of the machine operator's wages is included in the analysis (which does no harm, but accomplishes nothing), the future operating costs of the already-owned Slow machine ($220,000 + $15,000 = $235,000) are greater than the future costs to both buy and operate the Fast machine ($80,000 + $100,000 + $15,000 = $195,000). Like the machine operator's wages, the sunk cost of acquiring the Slow machine is irrelevant. It would be the same under both alternatives, and it could be included under both, but the difference in favor of acquiring the Fast machine would remain $40,000. Indeed, this would be true whether the Slow machine had been acquired at $1, $1,000, or $1,000,000.

Opportunity Cost

Though it is true that the acquisition cost and book value of existing assets are not relevant in decision making, there may be some relevant costs related to existing assets. These costs are called **opportunity costs**. An opportunity cost is the benefit foregone by taking one course of action and thus precluding another. The opportunity cost of using an asset for purpose A is the benefit that could have been derived from using that asset for purpose B. If several alternatives are available, the cost of using the asset for purpose A is the benefit that could be derived from using it for the most profitable alternative purpose. The concept of opportunity cost can apply to resources other than existing fixed assets. For example, in determining the cost of going to college, you must include the cost of the resource, time; its cost is the salary that could be earned if you were not enrolled in school.

We can incorporate the concept of opportunity cost into the previous illustration by slightly changing the facts about the Fast and Slow machines. Continue the assumption that the Slow machine was recently purchased but, still ignoring taxes, let us assume that the machine could be sold immediately for $50,000. Would it still be wise to acquire the Fast machine? Definitely. The total relevant cost associated with the decision to keep and operate the Slow machine is now $270,000 ($220,000 + $50,000 cost to forego the opportunity to sell the machine).

In this case, the decision would not change. But in many cases, the proper consideration of the opportunity costs is critical to making the right decision, and omission of such costs can lead to unwise decisions. For example, suppose that the other operating cost for the Fast machine were expected to be $170,000 rather than the previously stated $100,000. The proper analysis would look something like this:

	Decision	
	Keep the Slow Machine	*Buy the Fast Machine*
Acquisition cost		$ 80,000
Operating costs	$220,000	170,000
Cost of retaining the Slow machine (resale price foregone)	50,000	
Total costs	$270,000	$250,000

The correct decision would be to sell the Slow machine and purchase the Fast one. But note that omission of the opportunity cost would have led to the unwise decision of keeping the Slow machine. (That is, total costs would *appear* to be lower, at $220,000 versus $250,000.) Remember, then, that while the original purchase price of the Slow machine is still irrelevant, its resale value is quite relevant to the decision about whether it ought to be kept or sold.

In summary, then, the major relevant quantifiable factors in decision making are the differential (sometimes called **incremental**) revenues and costs, and opportunity costs. Sunk costs are not relevant for decision making.

SEGMENT ANALYSIS

The activities of a firm are often broken down to examine the relative profitability of the segments—the areas of activity into which the firm can be divided. In Chapter 4 we considered the case of a firm with multiple products, but other criteria can be used for partitioning or segmenting a firm's activities. For example, a maker of office equipment might produce and sell typewriters, bookkeeping machines, desk calculators, and computers. The firm might sell to businesses, governmental units, hospitals, and other types of organizations. The firm may have divided its sales area into 22 regions in the United States and 45 regions in various foreign countries. Hence, in this company, segment analysis could be done by product line, type of customer, and region.

As a matter of fact, a firm might go about partitioning its activities so that several segments were added together to make larger segments. For example, if the office equipment firm above carried several models of electric and manual typewriters, each model could be viewed as a segment, a group of models could be viewed as a segment, and all electric models and all manual models could be viewed as segments composed of groups of models.

One basic use of segment analysis is to evaluate segments and to decide whether a particular segment of the firm's activities should be continued or dropped. The technique applied to such a decision is to determine what would happen to the income of the entire firm if that particular segment were dropped. This approach builds on important concepts introduced in Chapters 3 and 4, avoidability and separability of costs, and relates those concepts to the terms *differential* or *incremental costs* as used in this chapter.

The same general rule applies as in the analysis of the multiple-product firm: the costs critical for decisions about the segment are the avoidable costs. In the terminology of this chapter, avoidable costs would be considered incremental because they can be changed (in the sense that if the segment is dropped the costs will disappear). Similarly, as noted in Chapter 4, some costs are joint to several products or product lines, and some costs are separable to particular products or lines. This same possibility exists when a firm is segmented using other criteria, such as geographic area. Joint costs identified through segment analysis remain unavoidable and therefore should not be considered as incremental.

Whether particular costs are joint or separable depends on how the firm is being segmented. For example, if each salesperson handles all of a firm's product lines, but calls on only one type of customer (say, hospitals) in his or her assigned region, the salaries and travel expenses of the sales force would be joint with respect to product lines, but separable with respect to regions and types of customers. On the other hand, if each salesperson sold only one product line, but called on all types of customers in a region, salaries and travel expenses would be joint with respect to types of customers and separable with respect to product lines and regions.

A rather significant analytical advantage can be obtained from being able to identify relatively small segments within a firm. The smaller the segments become, the more costs tend to be joint, and hence unavoidable, and, as a result, irrelevant to most short-term decisions. For our office equipment firm, if one model typewriter is dropped from the line it is unlikely that any machinery or workers would be eliminated or any salaries and travel expenses reduced. But if typewriters were dropped altogether, some costs that appear to be joint could probably be avoided. Even if the firm's salespeople sold all of the firm's products it is possible that they would stop calling on customers whose purchases were limited to typewriters, and they would probably spend less time with most of their customers. Hence, it might be possible to reduce the size of the sales force and widen the territories covered by some of the salespeople.

In any situation involving a decision to drop a segment, the facts of the particular case are important. The use of general rules may be helpful, but the individual costs must be examined to determine whether any saving would result. Identification of separable costs is often complicated because the accounting records of the firm may show allocations of particular costs among various segments. This common problem deserves special consideration.

Allocated Costs

One of the chief difficulties in analyzing segments of a firm is that many firms show allocated costs as expenses in the reports for a particular segment. For example, if a rented machine is used in the manufacture of several products, the income statement for each product would probably show a portion of the rent on the machine. If the rent is $10,000 per year and a total of 20,000 units of all products are made, each unit of product could be charged with $.50 ($10,000/20,000). Suppose that one product that is currently accounting for 4,000 of the 20,000 units is dropped. The $2,000 (4,000 units × $.50) expense currently appearing on the income statement for that product will not be avoided. On the contrary, the remaining 16,000 units of other products will simply be charged with $.625 per unit ($10,000/16,000). As a result, the *apparent* profitability of the remaining products would be reduced when, in fact, the reduction is due to the decision to drop one of the products.

Allocated costs are joint costs. Indeed, if they were separable there would be no need to find ways to allocate them. They relate to several segments. And, when a segment is dropped, there is usually no reduction in the total of the costs being allocated. For this reason, allocated costs are irrelevant to a decision about whether a particular segment should be dropped.

Several reasons have been given for including various cost allocations in segment reports. Some managers argue that because joint costs contribute to the operations of the firm, they must "benefit" individual segments and, therefore, each segment should be charged a "fair share" of the costs. There is also an unfortunate carryover, from our earlier training in mathematics, that the whole must equal the sum of its parts. Thus, some argue that the net income for a set of products, or parts of the firm, must add up to the net income for the firm as a whole. Note, however, that it is always possible to *make* this happen simply by allocating the joint costs. The manager must remember that the additivity of the parts is contrived, not natural.

One further reason has been given for employing allocations in segment reports. Some firms are said to follow the policy of "full-cost pricing." Under such a policy, the firm will try to price its various products so that it can cover all costs and provide a margin of profit. To accomplish this, allocations are made among the products; the total cost for a product is divided by the number of units of that product to arrive at a cost per unit; then, a price will be set that will show each type of product to be "profitable" in the sense that an income statement for each product will show a positive net income after all allocations have been made. It is true that a firm must cover all its costs, separable and joint, before it can make a profit; but allocation procedures, no matter how sophisticated, cannot change the nature of a cost from joint to separable. And, if a cost is joint to a segment and, hence, unlikely to change with a decision to discontinue that segment, it is important that the information managers use to make that decision not indicate action different from that indicated by ignoring the joint cost.

The fact that allocated costs often appear on segment income statements does raise an important point about providing information within a firm. A firm's information system must serve several purposes. It must provide data for the preparation of financial statements, for completion of income tax and other governmental forms, as well as for managerial decision making. Most often, the system will be designed around the needs of financial accounting and taxation, where specific, regular information requirements are known with some certainty, and adjustments will then be made to meet the needs of internal decision makers. One of the major areas where cost allocations are needed is for the determination of unit costs of inventories. This particular topic will be examined more fully in Chapters 13 and 14. Because the firm's information system and resulting segment reports may be designed for several purposes, a manager should study such reports carefully to ensure that only relevant costs are included in his analysis for a particular decision. Further discussion of the problems of allocated costs appears in Chapters 10 and 11, which deal with the evaluation of performance of segment managers.

TYPICAL SHORT-TERM
DECISION-MAKING PROBLEMS

Dropping a Segment

The most recent income statement (by product line) and other information for a grocery store are given below. Future income statements are expected to show about the same results.

	Produce	Meats	Canned Goods	Total
Sales	$10,000	$20,000	$20,000	$50,000
Variable cost	6,000	8,000	12,000	26,000
Contribution margin	4,000	12,000	8,000	24,000
Fixed costs:				
Separable, discretionary	3,500*	6,000*	2,000*	11,500*
Joint, allocated on the basis of				
sales dollars	2,000*	4,000*	4,000*	10,000*
Income (loss)	($ 1,500)	$ 2,000	$ 2,000	$ 2,500

*Deduction

A manager looking at this report by segments might immediately say that the produce line should be dropped because it is showing a loss. Would this be wise? If sales of meats and canned goods would not be affected by the dropping of produce, the only revenue lost would be the $10,000 from produce. On the other hand, there would be savings by avoiding variable and separable discretionary fixed costs. But, by definition, there would be no reduction in the joint fixed costs if produce were not being sold.

The correct answer can be obtained either by analyzing the differences or by preparing a new income statement based on selling only meats and canned goods. Consider first the differential approach.

	If Produce Dropped
Gains:	
Variable costs avoided	$ 6,000
Separable fixed costs avoided	3,500
	9,500
Lost revenue	10,000
Increase (decrease) in income	($ 500)

The firm will be $500 worse off if the decision is made to drop produce. The reduction in income is often called *incremental loss* and can be computed directly from the product line income statement by subtracting separable fixed costs from contribution margin.

We could also approach the analysis by showing an income statement for the firm, assuming the produce line is dropped.

	Meats	Canned Goods	Total
Sales	$20,000	$20,000	$40,000
Variable costs	8,000	12,000	20,000
Contribution margin	12,000	8,000	20,000
Fixed costs:			
Separable, discretionary	6,000*	2,000*	8,000*
Joint	5,000*	5,000*	10,000*
Income	$ 1,000	$ 1,000	$ 2,000

*Deduction

The total income is $500 less than before, as was indicated in the earlier analysis. The joint fixed costs have simply been reallocated, thus reducing the incomes of the remaining product lines.

Based on the information available, the produce line should be retained. Its revenues cover both variable costs and separable fixed costs, thereby helping cover joint costs and providing income. However, the analysis is not complete; there may be alternative uses for the space currently used to store and display produce. Suppose that this space could be rented to another firm. How much rent would have to be received to make it profitable for the firm to discontinue selling produce and rent the space? To drop the sale of produce would result in $500 less income; it would therefore take at least $500 in rental income to offset the loss resulting from the discontinuance. Using a term introduced in this chapter, the rental income foregone if the firm continues to sell produce is the opportunity cost of selling produce. The decision can be reached by comparing incremental profit of the current course of action with the opportunity cost. *If opportunity cost exceeds incremental profit, the opportunity should be taken; if not, the firm should continue on its present course of action.*

Let us see how this analysis works in a more complex situation. Assume that hardware could be substituted for produce in the product mix. Expected revenues from this new product are $15,000, variable costs are expected to be $9,000, and separable fixed costs will be $3,000. A pro forma income statement for this product mix would be as follows:

	Meats	Canned Goods	Hard-ware	Total
Sales	$20,000	$20,000	$15,000	$55,000
Variable costs	8,000	12,000	9,000	29,000
Contribution margin	12,000	8,000	6,000	26,000
Separable fixed costs	6,000	2,000	3,000	11,000
Incremental profit	6,000	6,000	3,000	15,000
Joint fixed costs—allocated on the basis of sales dollars	3,636	3,636	2,728	10,000
Income	$ 2,364	$ 2,364	$ 272	$ 5,000

Notice that incremental profit is computed in this income statement. This statement shows that selling hardware would increase income by $3,000 over what it would be if only meats and canned goods were sold ($5,000 income if hardware is added versus only $2,000 if it is not). Sales of produce yielded incremental profit of only $500. The $3,000 incremental profit from selling hardware would be the opportunity cost of continuing to sell produce. If the firm were currently selling hardware, and the only alternative available was the sale of produce, the opportunity cost of selling hardware would be $500—the incremental profit foregone by not selling produce. Following the principle stated earlier, since the incremental profit selling hardware is greater than the opportunity cost, the firm should continue to sell hardware.

A convenient alternative format for the statement above is shown below.

	Meats	Canned Goods	Hard-ware	Total
Sales	$20,000	$20,000	$15,000	$55,000
Variable costs	8,000	12,000	9,000	29,000
Contribution margin	12,000	8,000	6,000	26,000
Separable fixed costs	6,000	2,000	3,000	11,000
Incremental profit	$ 6,000	$ 6,000	$ 3,000	15,000
Joint costs—unallocated				10,000
Income				$ 5,000

The major difference between the alternative formats is that the second format does not allocate joint costs, but rather subtracts them in the Total column. This way the joint costs are not shown under each segment, thus helping to avoid confusion for those people who may look only at the "bottom line" of an income statement.

Complementary Effects and Loss Leaders. In the decision to continue or drop a segment, it was assumed that no matter what was done with the space first devoted to produce, the sales of the other segments would remain the same. In many instances, however, there will be **complementary effects;** that is, the sales of some products will be affected by the sales of the other products being carried. The approach used in the previous analysis, emphasizing the effects of a decision on *total* profits, is particularly important when complementary effects exist. Emphasizing total profits may lead managers to sell one or more products at a loss if such a sale will bring a sufficient increase in the sales of other products.

Consider the manager of a local pizza parlor who has been disturbed by the lack of business at lunchtime. He attributes this to the "specials" of competing restaurants at lunchtime and is anxious to change the situation. He has prepared the following income statement, based on a normal week, for the 11:00 A.M. to 2:00 P.M. period. The costs shown are all incremental.

	Pizza	Beverages	Total
Sales (200 pizzas @ $1.80)	$360	$100	$460
Variable costs	120	40	160
Contribution margin	$240	$ 60	300
Waitress salaries			80
Income			$220

He is interested in developing his own luncheon special, and is considering offering all the free beverages a customer can drink with each pizza. He believes that such an offer could double his pizza sales. Based on his past experience and an educated guess, he anticipates that beverage consumption would increase to two and one-half times the present level. To take care of the additional business, he believes he will have to hire additional part-time waitresses for $40 per week for the three-hour period during which the special will be run. There will be no revenue from beverages, but there will be costs, so he will obviously lose money on beverages. Can he gain enough on the sales of pizza to make it up? Using his estimates of the effects of the special (which are the best information available), he can prepare a budgeted income statement.

	Pizza	Beverages	Total
Sales	$720	$ 0	$720
Variable costs	240*	100†	340
Contribution margin	$480	($100)	380
Waitress salaries			120
Income			$260

*Variable costs computed at the same rate as before, one-third or 33⅓% of selling price.
†Variable costs computed two and one-half times the costs experienced previously.

Though one of his products shows a *negative* contribution margin, the manager can increase his total profits by $40 per week ($260 − $220) if his expectations are realized. A loss leader of this sort can be helpful because the products are complementary.

The potential for complementary effects is more obvious in some cases than in others. For example, one can readily see the relationship between sales of golf clubs and golf balls, or lawn spreaders and fertilizer, or gasoline and motor oil. But the loss-leader rationale is responsible also for many "specials" that involve products only vaguely complementary. What prompts supermarket offers of incredibly inexpensive name-brand items in return for a newspaper coupon? The sale of well-known products for a few pennies to any customer purchasing a specific dollar amount of other merchandise also has an obvious objective.

Emphasis on the total profit picture is also constructive for product evaluation. A product that is selling at a loss (that is, an incremental loss) may be so essential to the sales of other products being carried that it should not be dropped. Whenever a firm is contemplating the elimination of a specific product, the effect of such action on sales of other products must be considered.

Make-or-Buy Decisions

Many manufactured products are the result of assembling several component parts into a unit of final product. Most components can be either bought from an outside supplier or made by the assembling firm using its own facilities. Several qualitative factors must be considered when deciding whether to purchase or make a component. Will the quality of the component sold by the supplier be consistently equal to what can be achieved in the firm's plant? Will the supplier be reliable in meeting delivery commitments? Is it possible that the supplier who quotes a specific price now will raise prices once he feels you are a captive customer?

The quantitative factors to be considered are the incremental costs to make or to buy and any existing opportunity costs. Suppose that the XYX Company now makes a major component for its final product. Annual requirements for this component are estimated at 20,000 units and costs at that level of production are as follows:

Materials	$ 10,000
Direct labor	40,000
Manufacturing overhead:	
Variable	80,000
Fixed, not separable	60,000
Total costs	$190,000

An outside supplier has offered, for $160,000, to produce and sell to the firm sufficient units of the component to meet the annual requirements. Let us first assume that the firm has no alternative uses for the space now used to make the component. A comparison of incremental costs would show the following:

	Decision	
	Buy	*Make*
Purchase price	$160,000	$ 0
Materials		10,000
Direct labor		40,000
Variable overhead		80,000
Total costs	$160,000	$130,000

The total outlays of the firm will be lower by $30,000 if the firm manufactures the component rather than purchasing it from an outside supplier. The fixed manufacturing overhead is irrelevant because it will continue to be incurred whether the component is bought or made. The analysis could also be based on total costs, as below.

	Total Costs	
	Buy	*Make*
Purchase	$160,000	$ 0
Materials		10,000
Direct labor		40,000
Variable overhead		80,000
Fixed overhead	60,000	60,000
Total	$220,000	$190,000

The schedule is the same as the previous one except that fixed overhead is included under both alternatives because it exists whether the component is made or bought. The difference in total costs is $30,000, as it was when only incremental costs were included. A short-cut method in problems like this is to add the fixed overhead to the purchase price and compare that result with total cost to make. If total cost to make is less than the sum of the purchase price and fixed overhead, the component should be made; if not, it should be purchased.

Assume that instead of having no alternative uses for the space occupied in making the component, the managers believe that it could be rented to another firm for $20,000 annually. What is the correct decision?

	Decision	
	Buy	*Make*
Purchase price	$160,000	$ 0
Incremental cost to make (from previous analysis)		130,000
Opportunity cost—rent		20,000
Total	$160,000	$150,000

The decision is still to make the component. The opportunity cost could either be added to the cost to make, as above, or subtracted from the cost to buy. The total costs would be different, but the difference between them would still be $10,000.

In some instances a firm may not know how much rent could be obtained by leasing the space. The managers might then ask how much rent they would have to get to *equalize* the costs of buying and making. The advantage in favor of making is $30,000, without any rental opportunity; therefore the monetary advantage would disappear if rent of more than $30,000 could be obtained on the space.

A make-or-buy decision is often complicated by special machinery that is used in the production of the component. If the equipment cannot be used for any other purpose and cannot be sold, the previous analysis is still appropriate. Both the cost and the present book value of the equipment are sunk costs and hence irrelevant. If the equipment could be rented, such rent would be the opportunity cost of using the equipment and would be added to the opportunity cost indicated above. If the equipment could be used elsewhere in the plant or could be sold, the problem becomes more complex. The net proceeds from the sale would reduce the cost of buying from an outside supplier. However, the firm must recognize that sale of the equipment would eliminate the ability to return to in-house production if the supplier should prove unreliable or change prices. Thus, the sale of the machinery would turn this short-term decision into a long-term one; and it is extremely important that management be aware of this shift.

The opportunity to use the equipment in another area of production might eliminate the need to purchase new machinery. Again, the situation has longer-term effects. Prospects for renewal of the supplier's contract, estimated remaining useful life of the equipment, and alternative uses of the equipment must all be considered when making the decision. Problems related to long-term decisions will be covered more fully in Chapters 8 and 9.

Joint Products

When a manufacturing process invariably produces two or more separate products, the outputs are called **joint products**. The process that results in the joint products is called a **joint process**. The refining of crude petroleum results in a number of distinct products, such as gasoline, various grades of oil, and kerosene. The processing of cattle results in hides, hoofs, various cuts of meat, and other items (fat, organs, lips). Some of these joint products are quite valuable; some have little or no value. Some may be sold just as they emerge from the joint process or processed further. A meat packer may sell hides to a tanner. If he has the expertise and the facilities, he may tan the hides and make shoes, gloves, and other products from the hides.

Manufacturers who produce joint products regularly face the decision of whether to sell them at the split-off point—the point at which they emerge from the joint process—or to process them further. The decision cannot be based on the total costs of the individual final products, or even on the total variable costs. To produce any of the joint products, the firm must undertake the joint process, incurring all the costs to perform that process. Hence, the costs incurred prior to split-off are irrelevant in determining whether the joint products, once produced, should be sold then or processed further. The costs of the joint process (or processes) are relevant only in determining whether that process should be carried on at all. A refiner may incur variable costs for material, labor, and overhead of $18 per barrel of crude oil refined. But this cost does not relate to any one of the outputs, such as gasoline, fuel oil, and motor oil. If it decided to refine at all, these costs will be incurred in proportion to the total quantity of crude oil refined, and independent of whether any of the individual products are desired. Thus, in an analysis to determine whether to sell a product at split-off point or process it further, all costs—fixed and variable—prior to the split-off must be considered sunk costs. If the joint process is undertaken, both variable and fixed costs must be incurred.

Consider the following example. A chemical company makes two products, Alpha and Omega, in a single joint process. Each 1,000 lbs. of raw material put into the joint process yields 600 lbs. of Alpha and 400 lbs. of Omega. Both Alpha and Omega can be sold at the split-off point or can be processed further. Selling price and cost data per batch (1,000 lbs. of raw material) are given below.

	Alpha	*Omega*
Selling price at split-off	$1,200 ($2 per lb.)	$1,600 ($4 per lb.)
Selling price after additional processing	$3,600 ($6 per lb.)	$2,000 ($5 per lb.)
Costs of additional processing, all variable	$900 ($1.50 per lb.)	$500 ($1.25 per lb.)

Assuming that a batch of each product has already been produced in the joint process, what should be done with each product? We can analyze the results of both alternatives for each product. Alpha is analyzed as follows:

Decision on Alpha

	Sell at Split-off	Process Further
Sales	$1,200	$3,600
Incremental cost		900
Incremental profit	$1,200	$2,700

Alpha should be processed further because the firm's profit will be $1,500 higher ($2,700 − $1,200) if this course is followed. We can reach the same conclusion by examining just the changes in revenues and costs involved in processing Alpha further.

Change in revenue ($3,600 − $1,200)	$2,400
Change in costs	900
Change in profit	$1,500

Similar analysis reveals that Omega should be sold at split-off rather than being processed further.

Decision on Omega

	Sell at Split-off	Process Further
Sales	$1,600	$2,000
Incremental costs	0	500
Incremental profit	$1,600	$1,500

The firm would be $100 worse off ($1,600 − $1,500) if it processed Omega further. Doing so would increase revenues by $400 ($2,000 − $1,600) but would also increase costs by $500, which is greater than the increase in revenues.

The above analytical approaches are appropriate when the only incremental processing costs are variable costs. However, when the additional processing involves some fixed costs, a slightly different approach is necessary. The unit for analysis (in the previous example, one batch of raw material) must be chosen carefully to correlate with the nature of the fixed costs. To see why this is necessary and how it works, let us assume that the further processing of Alpha involves incremental, avoidable fixed costs of $10,000 per month. Note that such costs are *joint* to all units produced during the month and hence cannot be identified with a single batch unless the firm is able to process only one batch per month. Let us assume that 10 batches per month are processed; the output of Alpha would be 6,000 lbs. (10 × 600 lbs. per batch). The analysis shown below indicates that the firm should still process Alpha beyond the split-off point.

Decision on Alpha

	Sell at Split-off	Process Further
Sales: 10 × $1,200 per batch	$12,000	
10 × $3,600 per batch		$36,000
Incremental costs:		
Variable 10 × $900 per batch		9,000*
Fixed and avoidable		10,000*
Incremental profit	$12,000	$17,000

*Deduction

The additional revenue from processing further ($36,000 − $12,000) is still greater than the additional costs incurred by undertaking the extra processing ($19,000).

The general rules for determining whether products should be sold at the split-off point or processed further are as follows: if the additional revenue gained by processing further is greater than the additional cost of further processing, the product should be processed further; if the additional revenue from further processing is less than the additional cost of further processing, the product should be sold at split-off.

The decisions resulting from application of the above rules are important, for they are needed for the analysis in support of an even more basic decision: whether to undertake the joint process itself, from which the joint products emerge. In deciding whether to operate a joint process, the question is whether the *best* incremental profit that can be earned from the individual products is greater than the incremental cost to operate the joint process.

From the earlier analyses we know that Alpha should be processed further and that Omega should be sold at split-off. These courses of action are wise only if it is profitable to make the products at all. To make that decision, we now need to consider the costs of the joint process itself. Let us assume that these costs are $1,000 per batch of raw material; $8,000 in incremental, avoidable fixed costs per month; and **$20,000** in monthly unavoidable fixed costs. With this additional information *and* the results of the earlier decisions about the best use of the individual products, we can construct an analysis showing the incremental profit from operating the joint process.

	Alpha	Omega	Total
Sales (10 batches):			
Alpha, after extra processing	$36,000		$36,000
Omega, sold at split-off		$16,000	16,000
			52,000
Incremental costs of additional processing of Alpha	19,000	0	19,000
Incremental profit on products	$17,000	$16,000	33,000
Incremental costs of joint process:			
Variable ($1,000 per batch)			10,000
Fixed and avoidable			8,000
Total			18,000
Incremental profit from operating joint process			$15,000

The key figure in the above analysis is the incremental profit from operating the joint process. If it is negative, the joint process should not be operated even though the individual joint products may have positive incremental profits considering only their individual revenues and incremental costs (the line "incremental profit on products"). The unavoidable fixed costs of the joint process are irrelevant. Even if the unavoidable fixed costs of the joint process ($20,000) exceed the incremental profit ($15,000), the joint process should be operated. Why? Because without operating the joint process, the firm would still incur the unavoidable fixed costs. Any incremental profit reduces the net cost to the firm.

One final word of caution. As indicated in the discussion of analyzing segments of the business, many segment reports include allocated costs. This is particularly common when reports are prepared for joint products; the costs of the joint process are often allocated among the various joint products. The most common allocation schemes used are to assign the joint costs in proportion to either the quantities produced or the relative sales values of the products. Such allocated costs are, as stated earlier, irrelevant to decision making on the individual segments, and should accordingly be ignored in analyses relating to the joint products.

Special Orders

Retail chain stores that sell merchandise under their own names affect the operating decisions of firms that manufacture the products. Many manufacturing firms make both products to be sold under their own brand names and nearly identical products that are sold at lower prices under the brand name of a chain store (called *house brands*). The manufacturer sells to chains at lower prices than to dealers who sell the products under the manufacturer's brand name. This also occurs when manufacturers accept special, one-time orders for their products at lower prices than usual. Why would a firm take such orders? Because, as we shall see, such orders can improve the firm's profits.

The following budgeted income statement is for a manufacturer who has just been approached with an opportunity to sell 20,000 units of a product at $10 per unit to a discount store. Sales of 60,000 units are planned, although the plant has the capacity to produce 100,000 units. As the controller of the firm, you are asked to evaluate the offer.

ABC Company Budgeted Income Statement

	Per Unit		
Sales (60,000 units)	$15		$900,000
Manufacturing costs:			
Materials	4	$240,000	
Direct labor	3	180,000	
Overhead (one-third variable)	6	360,000	
Total	13		780,000
Gross margin			120,000
Selling, general, and administrative expenses			80,000
Operating income			$ 40,000

The variable portion of selling, general, and administrative expenses is $12,000 for sales commissions. Commissions would not have to be paid for the 20,000 unit special order. The president has some misgiving about accepting the order, even though sufficient capacity should be available. **He sees that manufacturing costs are $13 per unit ($780,000/60,000) and that a $10 per-unit price will be below this average cost.**

Only the incremental elements should be considered in making a decision.

	Per Unit		Incremental Analysis of Special Order
Revenues (20,000 units)	$10		$200,000
Manufacturing costs:			
Materials	4	$80,000	
Direct labor	3	60,000	
Variable overhead	2	40,000	180,000
Incremental profit			$ 20,000

Accepting the special order would increase income by $20,000 and, therefore, the order should be accepted.

In this example, the only incremental costs were variable manufacturing costs. In another example there might be some variable selling, general, and administrative expenses connected with any kind of sales, and those variable costs would be included in the analysis. It is more likely that where the special order requires a large increase in production, some additional fixed costs will have to be incurred, and those costs will have to be incorporated in the incremental analysis.

Both quantifiable and nonquantifiable factors generally exist when trying to decide about a special order. If the firm is already planning to operate at full capacity, the order will be rejected because acceptance would require the firm to sacrifice sales at regular (higher) prices, thus reducing profits. If operation at full capacity is not planned, there may still not be sufficient capacity to fulfill the order when it is due. Possibly so large an order as the above could not be filled if delivery were required within one month. Only if one month's production plus present inventory were sufficient to fill orders of regular customers at regular prices and also fill the special order would the special order be accepted. Much would depend on the seasonal pattern, if any, of regular sales. More important still is whether selling some **output at reduced prices will affect planned future sales at regular prices. Prospective customers may take advantage of the reduced price, if any, that is offered by the special-order customer, or existing customers may be irritated and not buy the products any more.**

Use of Fixed Facilities

So far we have recognized limitations of capacity in terms of units that can be produced, but we have not considered capacity limitations when two or more products could be produced and sold in various combinations. A manufacturer may be able to produce and sell any combination of two products so long as the total unit sales do not exceed 500 units. It becomes more complicated if a firm has available a specified quantity of some fixed input factor—machine-hours, space, labor of a specialized variety—and could produce different quantities of different products within the limits of the available factor. Suppose a firm can make and sell two products and has a machine which is used in the production of these products. Revenue and cost data for A and B are as follows:

	A	B
Sales price	$10	$6
Variable costs	6	4
Contribution margin	$ 4	$2

Regardless of which product or combination of products is produced, fixed costs will be the same—costs for use of the machine and productive space.

If the machine time required to produce a unit of A is the same as that required for a unit of B, all available time would be used to produce A. It is more profitable to make A, because its contribution margin is twice that of B. However, suppose that a unit of A requires 5 hours machine time, a unit of B needs 2 hours, and only 500 machine-hours are available. There are two ways to solve the problem. One is to determine what total contribution margin would be obtained by making only As or only Bs. This would yield the following:

	A	B
Maximum production in units	100 (500 hours/5)	250 (500 hours/2)
Contribution margin per unit	$ 4	$ 2
Total contribution margin	$400	$500

This method determines the total contribution margin that can be obtained by giving all the scarce factor (machine time) to the making of each product in turn. The one with the highest total contribution margin should be made.

The second method **determines which product has the highest contribution margin** *per unit of the fixed factor*. In the example, the contribution margin per machine-hour that can be earned by making only one or the other product is computed. One must determine how many units, or fractions of units, can be made per hour and multiply this by contribution margin per unit of product.

	A	B
Hours required to make	5	2
Number made in one hour	1/5	1/2
Contribution margin per unit	$4	$2
Contribution margin per hour	$.80	$1

Product B has a higher contribution margin per machine-hour and should thus be made over product A. Both methods indicate the same choice. Specific results of the two methods can be confirmed by multiplying the contribution margins per hour by the number of available hours. Thus 500 hours × $.80 = $400, total contribution margin if only product A is made. And 500 × $1 = $500, total contribution margin if only product B is made.

An assumption critical to the example was that the firm could sell as many of either product as could be produced. Suppose that only 200 units of product B can be sold, even though 250 can be made. (This is more realistic because it is not common that a firm will be able to sell all of a product that can be produced.) Even taking this into consideration, product B is still more profitable than product A. However, since only 200 units of B can be sold, only 200 units should be produced. Using 400 hours to produce Bs leaves 100 hours to make units of A. In that time, 20 units of A can be produced (100 hours/5 hours per unit). From the sale of all produced units of both products, the contribution margin will be as follows:

	A	B	Total
Sales	$200	$1,200	$1,400
Variable costs	120	800	920
Contribution margin	$ 80	$ 400	$ 480

Contribution margin is $20 less than it would be if 250 units of B could be sold. In some cases there may be several constraints imposed on the firm. A detailed discussion of this problem is reserved for Chapter 15.

DECISION MAKING UNDER ENVIRONMENTAL CONSTRAINTS

The cost structure of a firm is always a major factor in decisions. There are many other constraints imposed upon the firm that must be considered in decision making, such as total sales potential for its products, product interdependencies, and types of customers. Still other constraints are part of the legal environment of the firm.

The United States has a number of laws that managers must recognize when deciding among various courses of action. Anti-trust laws forbid actions that may reduce competition substantially. Various aspects of environmental protection laws restrict actions that may have detrimental effects on wildlife, increase pollution, etc. At various times economic controls, such as wage and price controls, have prevented price increases except as costs justified them. Profit margins have been controlled and firms were not permitted to increase these margins by raising prices. The Robinson-Patman Act forbids the charging of different prices to customers unless there are intrinsic cost differences in serving the different customers. We shall limit our discussion to the major law dealing with pricing practices.

Robinson-Patman Act. This act forbids discriminatory pricing. The Federal Trade Commission is the regulatory agency responsible for enforcing the Act. The Act does not, of course, forbid the charging of different prices for different goods. Hence, to ensure compliance with the law, manufacturers who engage in private brand sales usually make some modifications to the items offered for private branding. The passing of the Act was partially stimulated by the practice of selling to large customers (say, grocery chains) at lower prices than to corner grocery stores, enabling the large customers to charge their customers lower prices and endangering the existence of smaller firms.

Manufacturing costs are not of particular significance when differences for like products are justified by referring to their cost differences. The Federal Trade Commission will not permit a firm to justify lower prices to some customers on the grounds that the incremental cost of production is less than the average cost including fixed costs. Because fixed costs are distributed over all products of a firm, the manufacturing cost of all units of the same product comes out the same. Differences in distribution costs can be a valid defense against charges of unlawful discrimination. The example we showed of a special order on page 215 included the fact that sales commissions did not have to be paid on the special order. This fact could be used as a partial defense against a suit for discrimination.

If a suit alleging price discrimination is filed, the managerial accountant will sometimes help prepare the evidence for the defense. It could be shown, for example, that distribution costs are lower for some customers than for others. Or perhaps the accountant can show that larger orders require fewer deliveries and hence result in lower costs.

SUMMARY

Managerial accountants are frequently asked for information to be used in short-term decision making. The essential quantitative factors that influence such decisions are differential revenues and costs, including opportunity costs. Costs and revenues that are the same whatever action is taken can be ignored. Thus, separable discretionary costs will be relevant while joint costs and separable committed costs will not be.

Typical examples of short-term decisions are: whether to drop a product or product line; whether to produce a component internally or purchase it from an outside supplier; whether to further process one or more joint products; whether to accept a special order; and how to utilize the services available from critical fixed facilities.

As a general rule, the action that is expected to result in the highest income for the firm as a whole should be pursued. This decision rule considers only the quantifiable factors in a given situation. In most decisions, there will be some factors that can be identified as having monetary effects but for which no reliable estimates can be made. Still other factors, such as a company policy against certain types of products, may not lend themselves to quantification at all. These unquantified factors should not be ignored.

KEY TERMS

allocated cost	joint process
complementary effects	joint products
differential cost and revenue	make-or-buy decision
incremental cost and revenue	opportunity cost
incremental profit	segment analysis
joint cost	sunk cost

REVIEW PROBLEM

The Andrews Company makes three products. Revenue and cost data for a typical month are as follows.

	Product			
	X	Y	Z	Total
Sales	$300	$500	$800	$1,600
Variable costs	100	200	400	700
Contribution margin	200	300	400	900
Fixed costs:				
Separable and avoidable	80	100	120	300
Joint, allocated on sales dollar basis	60	100	160	320
Total fixed costs	140	200	280	620
Profit	$ 60	$100	$120	$ 280

Required: Answer each of the following questions independently.

1. If product X were dropped, what would the profit of the firm be?
2. The firm is considering the introduction of a new product, P, to take the place of X. Product P would sell for $7 per unit, have variable costs of $5 per unit, and separable-avoidable fixed costs of $120. How many units of product P would have to be sold to maintain the existing income of $280?
3. The firm charges $10 per unit for product Z. One customer has offered to buy 40 units of Z per month at $8 per unit. Fixed costs in total and variable costs per unit would not be affected by the sale. Andrews Company has the capacity to produce 110 units of Z per month. If the offer is accepted, what will the firm's monthly income be?
4. Closer analysis reveals that X, Y, and Z are joint products of a single raw material that goes through a single process. The cost of the joint process, including raw material, is the $320 joint allocated fixed cost, and all other costs are incurred to process the three products beyond the split-off point. If the sales values of X, Y, and Z are $110, $220, and $230, respectively, at split-off, could the firm increase its profits by selling one or more products at split-off? If so, which product or products should be sold at split-off and what would the increase in total profit for the firm be?
5. At the current dollar levels of sales of X and Z, unit sales are 100 and 200, respectively. Both products are made on a single machine that has a limited capacity. The machine can make five units of X per hour, or eight units of Z.
   (a) Assuming that all units made of either product can be sold at existing prices, should the firm continue to make both products? If not, which product should it make?
   (b) Assuming that the machine is being operated at its capacity of 45 hours per month, what would happen to the firm's monthly profits if it concentrated on the more profitable product as determined in part (a)? Give the dollar increase in profits that would occur. (Hint: Remember that if only one product is made, the firm will save the avoidable fixed costs on the product that is dropped.)

Answers to review problem

1. $160. The firm would lose the contribution margin from the sale of X but would save $80 by not having to pay separable-avoidable fixed costs. Net reduction in profit is $120 ($200 − $80), which should be subtracted from current profit of $280 to arrive at $160. The $120 is the incremental profit on X.
2. 120 units. To achieve the same profit, the new product must provide the same incremental profit as would be lost by discontinuing the sale of X. Incremental profit from X is $120 (see part 1). The sale of P must provide contribution margin sufficient to cover both the new separable-avoidable fixed costs and the $120 profit. Since the new fixed costs would be $120, the contribution margin

needed is $240 ($120 fixed costs plus the desired profit). P carries a contribution margin of $2 per unit ($7 − $5), so a total of 120 units ($240/$2) would have to be sold.

3. $350. It is important to see here that if this special order is accepted, the company will have to curtail its regular sales at the regular price. [The firm's capacity is 110 units and planned sales are 80 units ($800/$10 selling price). If 40 units are sold to the new customer, regular sales will be cut by 10 units.] The analysis might proceed as follows:

Gain from contribution margin on special order ($8 – $5*) × 40 units	$120
Lost contribution margin because of loss of sales of 10 units at regular price	
($10 – $5*) × 10 units	50
Gain on special order	70
Planned profit	280
New monthly income	$350

*Variable cost per unit ($400/80 units = $5 per unit)

4. The firm could increase its profits by $20 per month by selling product Y at split-off, as shown by the following analysis.

	X	Y	Z
Sales with further processing	$300	$500	$800
Additional processing costs:			
Variable costs	100	200	400
Avoidable fixed costs	80	100	120
Total additional processing costs	180	300	520
Profit if further processed	120	200	280
Split-off values	110	220	230
Advantage (disadvantage) of further processing	$ 10	($ 20)	$ 50

5. (a) The firm should concentrate on product Z rather than product X. This can be shown even without knowing the number of hours available; the contribution margin per hour of machine time spent on product Z is the largest.

	X	Z
Contribution margin per unit	$2 ($200/100)	$2 ($400/200)
Units that can be made in one hour	5	8
Contribution margin per hour	$10	$16

As long as the company can sell all the units it makes of either product, total contribution margin will be greater by concentrating solely on product Z.

(b) Profit would increase by $200. The analysis involves both contribution margin and incremental profit. If the firm used its capacity of 45 hours to produce only Z, it could make 360 units of Z (45 × 8), which would bring total contribution margin of $720 (360 × $2 per unit). This is an increase of $320 ($720 − $400 contribution margin already anticipated). However, the firm would lose the current *incremental profit* from product X, which is $120 (see part 1). Thus, if the firm concentrated on product Z it would gain $200 ($320 additional contribution margin from Z − $120 incremental profit lost from not producing X).

ASSIGNMENT MATERIAL

Questions for Discussion

7-1 Price determination—postal service What do you think would be the major problem in developing an analysis to determine prices to be charged for the various classes of mail handled by the postal service?

7-2 Incremental costs One of your classmates, who believes that he thoroughly understands the principle of incremental costs, places an advertisement in the school paper that reads as follows:

Wanted—Ride to Linville

I will pay all of the incremental costs involved in taking me to Linville. Call Bob at 555-9999.

Linville is 1,200 miles from the university. Did your classmate make a mistake in wording the advertisement the way he did?

7-3 Cost analysis. While standing in line waiting to use a telephone, you hear the following part of a conversation. "No dear, I'm going to play golf today." (Pause) "Look, sweetie, I know it costs $6 for a caddy and $3 for drinks after the round, but it really does get cheaper the more I play, really. Look, the club dues are $1,000 per year, so if I play 50 times it costs, ah, let's see, $29 per round. But if I play 100 times it only costs, um, just a second, yeah, about $19 per round." (Pause) "I knew you'd understand, see you at dinner, bye." How did the golfer figure the cost per round? Comment on her analysis.

7-4 The generous management. Several years ago, a leading newspaper ran an advertisement for itself. The advertisement stated that the paper, which cost the customer $.40, cost the publisher $.53 for paper, $.09 for printers' labor, $.05 for ink, $.15 for salaries of editorial employees (reporters, editors, etc.), and $.18 for other operating expenses such as executives' salaries, rent, depreciation, and taxes. Thus, the opportunity to buy a paper for $.40 that had a cost of $1.00 was presented as a great bargain. Is the firm actually charging the buyer less than cost? What assumptions did you make to arrive at your answer? How can the management be so generous to its readers?

Exercises

7-5 Product selection—capacity constraint The Winston Company makes three products, all of which require the use of a special machine. There are only 200 hours of machine time available per month. Data for the three products are as follows.

	Gadgets	Supergadgets	Colossalgadgets
Selling price	$12	$16	$21
Variable cost	7	8	10
Contribution margin	$5	$8	$11
Machine time required in minutes	6	10	15

The firm can sell as much of any product as it can produce.

Required

1. Determine which product should be made and the total monthly contribution that would be earned.
2. How much would the selling price of the next most profitable (per machine-hour) product have to rise to be as profitable, per machine-hour, as the product you selected in part 1?

7-6   Special order   The Devio Company produces high-quality golf balls. A chain of sporting goods stores would like to buy 20,000 dozen balls at $7 per dozen. The balls would be sold at retail for $12, $3 less than usually charged. The chain would obliterate the Devio name so that customers would not be able to tell who had made them. Devio Company can produce 200,000 dozen balls per year. Budgeted results for the coming year, without considering the order from the chain, are given below.

Sales (150,000 dozen at $10 per dozen)	$1,500,000
Cost of goods sold	800,000
Gross profit	700,000
Selling and administrative expenses—all fixed	540,000
Income	$ 160,000

Cost of goods sold contains variable costs of $3.50 per dozen balls. The rest of the cost is fixed.

Required

1. Determine whether the order should be accepted.
2. Might your answer to part 1 change if the Devio name were to appear on the balls sold in the chain stores?

7-7   Special order   The Woolen Products Company makes a heavy outdoor shirt in one factory. Revenue and cost data relating to the coming year's operations are budgeted as follows.

Sales (230,000 shirts)	$2,300,000
Cost of sales	1,380,000
Gross profit	920,000
Selling and administrative expenses	575,000
Income	$ 345,000

The factory has capacity to make 250,000 shirts per year. The fixed costs included in cost of goods sold are $460,000. The only variable selling, general, and administrative expenses are a 10% sales commission and a $.50 per shirt licensing fee paid to the designer.

A chain store manager has approached the sales manager of Woolen Products offering to buy 10,000 shirts at $7. The sales manager believes that accepting the offer would result in a loss because the average cost of a shirt is $8.50. He feels that even though sales commissions would not be paid on the order, a loss would still result.

Required

1. Determine the income that would result if the order were accepted.
2. Suppose that the order was for 40,000 shirts instead of 10,000. What would be the income if the order were accepted?
3. Assuming the same facts as in 1 above, what is the lowest price per shirt that the firm could accept and still earn $345,000?

7-8　Joint products　TAB Company produces four joint products at a joint cost of $60,000. The products are currently processed further and sold as follows:

Products	Sales	Additional Processing Costs
M	$180,000	$101,000
N	132,000	80,000
O	52,000	40,000
P	12,000	15,000

The products could be sold at split-off for the following: M $80,000; N $36,000; O $10,000; and P Zero.

Required

Which product(s) should be sold at split-off?

7-9　Dropping a product—complementary effects　The Kaiser Face Care Company makes three products in the same factory. Revenue and cost data for a typical month are given below, in thousands.

	Product			
	Razors	Blades	Shaving Cream	Total
Sales	$300	$500	$400	$1,200
Variable costs	200	150	120	470
Contribution margin	100	350	280	730
Fixed costs				
Separable and discretionary	120	130	90	340
Joint, allocated on basis of				
relative sales dollars	60	100	80	240
Total fixed costs	180	230	170	580
Income (loss)	($80)	$120	$110	$ 150

Required

1. Determine income for the firm if razors were dropped from the product line.
2. Suppose that if razors were dropped, the sales of blades would decline by 10% and those of shaving cream by 20%. Determine the income for the firm if razors were dropped.

7-10　Make or Buy　The Weaver Company has a machine that is used to make a component for its products. An outside supplier has offered to sell the component to the Weaver Company for $9 each. Current use of the component is 30,000 units per year, which is well within the capacity of the machine. Other data are as follows:

Direct labor	$ 90,000
Materials	60,000
Overhead	180,000
Total cost for 30,000 units	$330,000

Overhead is about 50% fixed, 50% variable.

Required

1. Should the component be bought or made?
2. Suppose that the machine could be rented to another firm for $50,000 per year. Would your answer change?

7-11 Joint products   The Grevel Company slaughters cattle, processing the meat, hides, and bones. The hides are tanned and sold to leather manufacturers. The bones are made into buttons and other sundries. In a typical month, about 3,000 cattle are processed. A segmented income statement for such a month follows:

Income Statement
(In Thousands of Dollars)

	Totals	Meat	Hides	Bones
Sales	$500	$300	$120	$80
Cost of cattle*	300	180	72	48
Gross profit	200	120	48	32
Additional processing costs, avoidable	80†	40†	20†	20†
Allocated costs‡	60†	30†	15†	15†
Income (loss)	$ 60	$ 50	$ 13	($ 3)

*Allocated on the basis of relative sales value (60% of sales).
†Deduction.
‡Allocated on the basis of additional processing costs, all unavoidable.

Required

1. Is the firm losing money by processing the bones into buttons and sundry items? Explain.
2. A tanner has offered to buy the hides as they come off the cattle for $7 each. He has seen the income statement and contends that income from the hides segment would be $21,000 if hides were sold directly to him (3,000 hides × $7). Should his offer be accepted?
3. If the bones could be sold without further processing, how much would have to be received per month to keep total profits the same as they are now?

Problems

7-12 Salesperson's time as scarce resource   The Lombard Company sells to both wholesalers and retailers. The firm has 20 salespeople and cannot easily increase the size of the sales force. An analysis has shown that a salesperson's call on a wholesale customer yields an average order of $90, on a retailer $50. However, prices to wholesalers are 20% less than to retailers. Cost of goods sold (all variable) is 60% of prices charged to retailers. A salesperson can call on 7 wholesalers or 12 retailers per day. (The greater number of retailers reduces travel time between calls.)

Required

1. Should salespeople concentrate on wholesalers or retailers? Provide an analysis based on one salesperson for one week showing the difference.
2. What other factors require consideration?

7-13 Product pricing—off-peak hours   Marie Angelo, the owner of Gino's Pizzeria, is considering the possibility of introducing a "luncheon special" to increase business during the slow time from 11:00 A.M. to 1:00 P.M. on weekdays. For $1.50 on any weekday, she will give a customer all the pizza he or she can eat. Marie has prepared the following data for current business during those hours for a one-week period.

	Pizza	Beverages	Total
Sales (average pizza price, $2)	$300	$84	$384
Variable costs	100	21	121
Contribution margin	$200	$63	263
Discretionary costs—salaries of students hired			180
Current incremental profit, lunch period			$ 83

She estimates that if she offers the special price, she will be serving about 300 pizzas per week to about 250 customers. (Some customers are expected to eat more than one pizza, given the lower price.) She also anticipates that variable costs per unit will be about 20% higher than they are now because people will want more toppings than they now order (pepperoni, sausage, hamburger, etc.). Beverage sales will bear the same relationship to the number of customers that they do now when each customer eats one pizza. The increase in the number of customers would entail an increase in personnel during the hours of the special, increasing discretionary costs by 50%.

Required

1. Evaluate the monetary effects of the proposed "luncheon special."
2. Are there any other critical factors that should be taken into account? If so, what are they?

7-14 Special order—capacity limitation   The Weston Tire Company has been approached by a large chain store that offers to buy 50,000 tires at $16. Delivery must be made within 30 days. The productive capacity of Weston is 320,000 tires per month and there is an inventory of 10,000 tires on hand. Expected sales at regular prices for the coming month are 300,000 tires. The sales manager believes that about 40% of sales lost during the month would be made up in later months.

Price and cost data are as follows:

Selling price		$22
Variable costs:		
Production	$11	
Selling	3	14
Contribution margin		$ 8

The variable selling costs on the special order would be $1.50.

Required

1. Determine whether the special order should be accepted.
2. Determine the lowest price that Weston could charge on the special order and not reduce its income.
3. Suppose now that the chain offers to buy 40,000 tires per month at $16. The offer would be for an entire year. Expected sales are 300,000 tires per month without considering the special order. Assume also that there is no beginning inventory and that any sales lost during the year would *not* be made up in the following year. Determine whether the offer should be accepted and determine the lowest price that Weston could accept.

7-15 Special orders and qualitative factors   The Robinson Radio Company has had a reputation for high-quality products for many years. The firm is owned by descendants of its founder, Allan Robinson, and continues the policy of producing and selling only high-quality, high-priced radio and stereo components.

Recently James Giselle, the president of a chain of discount stores, proposed that the Robinson Company make and sell him a cheaper line of components than it currently produces. Giselle knows that Robinson has excess capacity and that many other firms produce lower-quality lines for sale in discount stores. Giselle believes that, even though the Robinson name will not appear on the components, buyers will become aware that Robinson does in fact make the components. Giselle tries to convince the management that its only potential for growth lies in the private-brand field, because Robinson now sells only to devoted aficionados who would not settle for less than Robinson components.

Giselle proposes that Robinson sell to the chain at 70% of its current selling price to other outlets. Variable costs are now about 60% of normal selling price, but would be reduced by 20% per unit if the cheaper components were made. The first-year order is to be $1,050,000, for which Robinson has enough excess capacity.

Required

1. Evaluate the monetary effects of the proposed deal.
2. How would you evaluate qualitative factors such as the attitudes of the managements and the family owners and the reputation of the firm? Do they outweigh the quantifiable factors, in your judgment?

7-16 Product profitability The president of the Hardway Company asked the sales manager to examine the sales program and determine if a different emphasis on products would improve profitability. Accordingly, the sales manager prepared the following revenue and cost data on the company's product.

		Hard		Way
Selling price per unit		$30		$28
Costs per unit:				
Fixed,* manufacturing	$6		$6	
Selling	3		3	
Variable, manufacturing	5		7	
Selling	3	17	4	20
Income per unit		$13		$ 8

*All unavoidable

To complete the above analysis, the sales manager assigned the fixed costs to the products according to a formula related to their present sales volumes. Sales of Hard were currently 8,000 units and sales of Way were 4,000 units; therefore two-thirds of total fixed costs were assigned to Hard and the remainder to Way. The sales manager knew from a discussion with the plant superintendent that the company's productive capacity could be used to produce the two products in any combination so long as the total did not exceed 15,000 units. Nevertheless, the described method was used to assign fixed costs to the two products because there did not seem to be a better method.

Required

Consider each situation independently.

1. Suppose that a given outlay for advertising will increase the demand for Hard by 100 units or for Way by 100 units. Other things being equal, on which product should the advertising be concentrated?
2. What is the maximum amount that the company would be willing to spend to increase sales of Hard by 1,000 units?
3. The sales manager has been discussing advertising campaigns with an advertising agency. He has received two proposals. (a) For $38,000 the agency will conduct a campaign that can be expected to increase the demand for Hard by 2,800 units. (b) For $14,000 the agency will conduct a campaign that can be expected to increase the demand for Way by 1,700 units. The advertising agency also reported that, if desired, it could do both campaigns for $48,000. What would the additional income be under each alternative?

7-17 Opportunity costs Martha Crain and her husband Jim own a leather goods store in a large city. Their most recent year's income statement showed the following results.

Sales		$102,000
Cost of sales		60,000
Gross profit		42,000
Other expenses		
Rent (monthly lease)	$3,000	
Utilities	1,200	
Advertising	800	
Supplies	700	
Insurance	400	
Licenses and fees	180	
Miscellaneous	420	
		6,700
Income		$ 35,300

Martha and Jim were discussing the results and were both pleased. Martha said that it was nice to own your own business and not have to work for someone else and Jim agreed. He commented that he had been earning $17,000 per year before the store had been opened and that she had been earning $18,000. She replied that it was true, but that their hours were much longer working in the store than when they were employed. "Of course," she went one, "we have $50,000 invested in the business, which is a lot, but we also don't have to fight the traffic to get there."

Required: Assume that the Crains could sell the business for $50,000, invest the proceeds at 8% interest, and go back to their former jobs. Should they do so?

7-18 Pricing policy and excess capacity The electric utility industry faces several problems in achieving optimal use of its facilities. First, electricity cannot economically be stored; thus the firms must be able to generate enough electricity to meet demand at all times. Second, the use of electricity is seasonal, especially in warmer climates where air conditioning requires high-peak requirements in the summer months.

The executives of the Southern Electric Company are evaluating a proposal by the sales manager. The proposal calls for the firm to offer discounts on electrical service to those customers who will use electrical heating equipment. The controller has amassed some data at the request of the sales manager. These data appear below.

Current generating capacity—monthly	20 million kilowatt-hours (Kwh)
Kwh sold—typical winter month	7 million
Kwh sold—typical summer month	18 million
Price per 1,000 Kwh	$35
Variable cost per 1,000 Kwh	$19

The proposal is to reduce the price of electricity to $29 per 1,000 Kwh if the customer uses electrical heating equipment. It is anticipated that about 5 million additional Kwh per month could be sold in the winter, a total of about 22 million additional hours per year. The total annual sales in Kwh are now 120 million. The users expected to convert to electrical heating now consume a total of about 30 million Kwh per year. Sales to customers currently using electrical heating equipment, who would also qualify for the discount, are about 10 million Kwh per year.

Required

Evaluate the monetary effects of the proposed decision.

7-19 Use of facilities   The Chapman Company needs a new machine that it can either acquire from another firm for $85,000 or build itself. If the machine is built by the firm, it will require materials costing $20,000 and 2,000 hours of labor time at $5 per hour. The firm incurs other variable costs at the rate of $6 per labor hour. One of your assistants has developed the following analysis showing the relative costs of the methods of acquisition.

	Make	Buy
Purchase price		$85,000
Materials	$20,000	
Labor ($5 × 2,000 hrs.)	10,000	
Variable overhead ($6 × 2,000 hrs.)	12,000	
Fixed overhead	40,000	
Totals	$82,000	$85,000

Your assistant explains that he included the fixed costs because the firm would lose sales of 4,000 units by making the machine. The number of workers, and of hours worked, cannot be increased; and, since each worker makes two units per hour, using workers for 2,000 hours on the machine reduces units available for sale. Because 4,000 units is 2% of budgeted sales for the year, he allocated 2% of fixed manufacturing costs to the making of the machine.

Each unit of product sells for $22 and has total variable costs of $8.

Required: Determine whether the machine should be bought or made.

7-20 Sales premiums   Mrs. Nelson Coffee Company has been experiencing difficulties in achieving sales goals because of increased competition in the areas it serves. The sales manager has proposed the following to stimulate sales. The firm will place a coupon in each one-pound can of coffee. A customer who returns 10 coupons will receive merchandise that costs the firm $1. In addition, mailing and handling costs will add 20% to the cost of the merchandise. The sales manager expects an increase in sales of about 50,000 one-pound cans per month and further predicts that only about 70% of the coupons will be redeemed. The firm currently sells 250,000 one-pound cans per month at $.70, with variable costs being $.55.

Required: Should the plan be adopted based on the sales manager's estimates?

7-21 Opportunity costs   The Valley Corporation makes all its products in batches. It costs $42,000 to set up the production facilities to make a batch, which can run from 10,000 to 60,000 units. The size of a batch depends on the expected demand for the product in the coming year because only one batch of each product is made during a year. Any units not sold during the year in which they are made become worthless.

The variable cost of nudniks, one of the firm's products, is $4 per unit. Sales last year were 40,000 units at $7 per unit. It has been decided to make 45,000 units this year.

Required

1. If 30,000 nudniks are sold, what is the incremental profit?
2. Assume that all 45,000 units made were sold, but 60,000 units could have been sold. What was the opportunity cost of not making the additional 15,000?
3. What are break-even sales when 35,000 nudniks are produced?
4. Suppose that normal demand is 30,000 units and that a new customer might be persuaded to buy 10,000 units. Thus, sales will be either 30,000 or 40,000 units. Production must be completed before it is known whether the new customer will buy. How may units would you make and why? Support your answer with calculations.

7-22 **Joint products—changes in mix** The Brewer Company produces three products from a single raw material. The production process is now set up to yield the following quantities of each product from 10 lbs. of raw material: Nyron, 3 lbs; Xylon, 3 lbs.; and Krylon, 4 lbs. Each product can be further processed; price and cost data are given below.

	Nyron	Xylon	Krylon
Selling price at split-off (per pound)	$2	$4	$ 6
Additional processing costs (per pound)	1	3	8
Selling price after additional processing (per pound)	7	6	12

Required

1. Which product(s) should be sold at split-off?
2. Suppose that by changing the joint production process the firm could get 6 lbs. of Nyron, and 2 lbs. of Xylon and Krylon from 10 lbs. of raw material. Additional costs to process the raw material would be $10,000 per month. The firm processes 100,000 lbs. of raw material per month. Should the production process be changed? Show calculations.

7-23 **Make or buy** The Christensen Appliance Company is bringing out a new washing machine. The machine requires a type of electric motor that the firm does not use in its current line of products. The purchasing manager has gotten a bid of $30 per motor from the Wright Motor Company for any number the firm would need. Delivery is guaranteed within two weeks after order.

  The production manager of Christensen Company believes that the firm could make the motor by extensively converting an existing model. Additional space and machinery would be required if the firm were to make the motors. The firm now leases, for $28,000 per year, space that could be used to make the motors. However, the space is now used to store vital materials, so the firm would have to lease additional space in an adjacent building to store the materials. That space could be rented for $42,000 per year. It is suitable for storage, but not for converting the motors. The equipment needed to convert the motors could be rented for $35,000 per year.

  The treasurer of the firm has developed the following unit costs based on the expected demand of 14,000 units per year.

Materials	$12.20
Direct labor	10.00
Rent for space	2.00
Machinery rental	2.50
Other overhead	7.00
Total cost	$33.70

  The "other overhead" figure includes $4 in fixed overhead that would be allocated to conversion of the motors.

Required

1. Determine whether the motors should be bought or made.
2. Determine the volume of motors at which Christensen Company would show the same total income whether it bought or made the motors.
3. Suppose that the firm had decided to make the motors, however wisely or unwisely according to your analysis in part 1. One-year contracts have been signed for the additional space and for the equipment. These contracts cannot be canceled. Determine the price that Wright Motor would have to offer Christensen to induce it to buy the motors.

7-24 Special order and relevant range The president of Ipswick Company has just received an offer to purchase 10,000 of the tables made by his firm. The offer is to be filled any time during the coming year and the offer price per table is $60. The budgeted income statement for the year without this order is as follows:

Sales (45,000 tables @ $90)		$4,050,000
Cost of goods sold:		
Materials	$ 675,000	
Direct labor	900,000	
Overhead	1,475,000	
Total cost of goods		3,050,000
Gross profit		1,000,000
Selling, general, and		
administrative expenses		640,000
Income		$ 360,000

The president believes that the order should be rejected because the price is below average total cost of $82 per table. He asks you to check the matter further because he knows that some costs are fixed and would not be affected by the special order.

In your analysis you find that $800,000 in overhead is fixed, and that a 10% commission on sales is the only variable selling, general, and administrative expense.

Required

Answer the following questions, considering each situation separately.

1. Assuming that the relevant range for the firm is between 30,000 and 60,000 tables, that existing sales would not be affected, and that the 10% sales commission would not have to be paid, what effect would there be on income if the order were accepted? Should it be accepted?
2. The relevant range is the same as in 1 and existing sales would be unaffected, but the 10% sales commission would have to be paid. What is your decision? Support with calculations.
3. The relevant range is now 30,000 to 50,000 tables. If the special order is accepted, sales at regular prices would fall to 40,000 units. The 10% sales commission would not be paid on the speical order. Should the order be accepted?
4. The relevant range is the same as in 3, but production could be increased to meet the special order as well as regular budgeted sales. For all units produced above 50,000, labor cost per unit and per unit variable overhead would be 20% higher than budgeted. Fixed production overhead would increase by $38,000. No sales commission would be paid, and other selling, general, and administrative expenses would remain the same as budgeted. Should the order be accepted?

7-25 Value of new products—effects on sales of other products The Jackman Grocery Store is a medium-sized operation in a suburb of a large city. Joe Jackman, the owner, is contemplating the addition of the department to sell either hardware or beer and wine. He has talked to several other owners of similar stores and has reached the following conclusions:

1. A hardware department would generate sales of $40,000 per year with a gross profit of 60%. No other variable costs would be added. Fixed costs added would be $12,000. There would be an increase of 5% in sales of groceries because of increased traffic through the store.
2. A beer and wine department would generate sales of $60,000 per year with gross profit of 40%. No other variable costs would be added, and fixed costs added would be $18,000. Sales of groceries would increase by 8%.

The income statement for a typical year for grocery sales alone is as follows:

Sales	$600,000
Cost of goods sold (variable)	240,000
Gross profit	360,000
Other variable costs	120,000
Contribution margin	240,000
Fixed costs	140,000
Income	$100,000

Required

1. Ignore the effects on sales of groceries for the moment. Compute the change in income that would result from adding (a) the hardware department, and (b) the beer and wine department.
2. Recompute the effects on income of adding each department, considering the effects on sales of groceries. Which department should be added and why?
3. What can be learned from the problem?

7-26 Special orders—effects on existing sales   The Huntinpeck Company makes high-quality typewriters that are sold only by department stores and office equipment dealers. A large discount chain has offered to buy 30,000 typewriters this year at an average price of $35. The budgeted income statement for the coming year shows the following without considering the special order.

Sales (80,000 units at average price of $50)	$4,000,000
Variable production costs (average of $20)	1,600,000
Contribution margin	2,400,000
Fixed costs (production and selling, general, and administrative)	1,600,000
Income	$ 800,000

The 30,000 units to be bought by the chain would be in the same mix as the firm currently sells. The firm has the capacity to produce 140,000 units per year.

Required

1. Should the order be accepted if there would be no effect on sales at regular prices? Support your answer with calculations.
2. Suppose that accepting the order from the chain would result in a 10% decline in sales at regular prices because some current customers would recognize the chain store's product and make their purchases at the lower price. The sales mix would remain unchanged. Should the special order be accepted?
3. By how much could sales at regular prices decline before it became unprofitable to accept the order?
4. Assuming the same facts as in 2, what other factors should be considered before the order is accepted?

7-27 Reduced prices   *Elephants Today* is a successful monthly magazine. The subscription price is $12 per year. Advertising rates for the magazine are determined by the total circulation of the magazine; the more the circulation, the higher the rate. Following is the budgeted income statement for the coming year and some additional information.

	Total	Subscription	Advertising
Revenue	$9,600,000	$8,400,000	$1,200,000
Variable costs	3,200,000	2,800,000	400,000
Contribution margin	6,400,000	5,600,000	800,000
Fixed costs ($1,700,000 are not assignable to either activity)	4,000,000	2,000,000	300,000
Income	$2,400,000	$3,600,000	$ 500,000

A total of 1,200 pages of advertising is budgeted at a rate of $1,000 per page. That rate prevails for 700,000 circulation. The per-page rate increases to $1,200 at 900,000 circulation, and to $1,400 at 1,000,000 circulation.

The managers of the magazine are considering a promotion proposal made by the circulation director (sales manager). He feels that a direct mail campaign costing $180,000 could result in 350,000 new subscriptions being immediately obtained if they were priced at $4 for the first year on a special introductory offer. If the new subscriptions were received, certain fixed costs would increase because the firm would be operating at a level beyond its current relevant range. Costs of processing and updating subscription lists would increase by $40,000, and fixed advertising costs would increase by $60,000. Variable advertising costs vary with the number of pages of advertising and will therefore not change in total if the campaign is undertaken.

Required

1. Should the campaign be undertaken based solely on the quantifiable factors?
2. What other factors should be considered by the managers?

7-28 Services of an athlete—jumping leagues   The Fort Bluff Titans of the Cross Continental Football League have been approached by Flinger Johnson, the star quarterback of the Snidely Whips, a team in the other major football league—the Nationwide Football League. Johnson is unhappy with his current salary and would like to jump leagues if a satisfactory arrangement can be made. His contract has run out, so he is free to negotiate with the opposing league.

The owner of the Titans believes that acquiring Johnson would be a boon to attendance, estimating that he would be worth 10,000 additional admissions in every game he played. No team in the Cross Continental League comes close to filling its stadium, and even with Johnson there would be no sellouts. There are six teams in the league, each playing each of the others twice, for a total of ten games. Each team plays every opponent once at home and once away. Tickets sell for $8 per game and variable costs are about $2 per ticket. The home team collects $6 per admission, the visiting team $2. The home team pays the variable costs.

Required

1. What is the additional annual income to the Titans that would be attributable to acquiring Johnson?
2. What is the additional annual income to all of the teams in the Cross Continental League?
3. Why is it necessary to state that there would be no sellouts even if Johnson were playing? If there were, how would it affect your analysis?
4. Suppose that Johnson demands $400,000. Should the Titans meet his demand?
5. Suppose that the other teams in the league agree to pay part of Johnson's salary. How much could each team pay without reducing its profits below the current level? (Include the Titans and each of the other five teams.)
6. Johnson is now being paid $200,000 per year. Suppose that the teams in the Nationwide League decide to try to keep Johnson. The member teams estimate that if Johnson jumps, 8,000 admissions will be lost for each game in which he would have played. Ticket prices are $11, with $2 variable costs, and each team plays 12 games.
   (a) How much would the total profits of the teams in the league fall if Johnson did jump leagues?
   (b) How much of a raise could be given to Johnson to yield the same total profit that would be earned if he jumped leagues?
   (c) Assume the same facts except that each team has 50% of its games sold out. There are usually 3,000 more requests for tickets than seats available for the sellouts. If Johnson were to jump, the total number of requests for tickets per game in which his old team plays would drop by 8,000. How would this additional information affect your analysis?

7-29 Product processing   The Taylor Plywood Company makes high-quality wall paneling used in homes and offices. The firm buys walnut logs and processes them into thin sheets of veneer that are glued to sheets of plywood to make the paneling. The firm also makes the plywood from various kinds of wood. The firm has enough capacity to make 1,000,000 square feet of veneer per month and 1,200,000 square feet of plywood. Capacity in the gluing operation is 1,300,000 square feet per month.

At the present time the firm can sell its paneling for $178 per 1,000 square feet. Veneer and plywood can be sold separately for $74 and $81, respectively, per 1,000 square feet. Cost data developed by the firm's accountant are given below, per 1,000 square feet.

	Plywood	Veneer	Paneling
Materials	$18	$16	$ 34
Direct labor	25	20	55
Overhead	32	29	93
Totals	$75	$65	$182

The figures shown for paneling are cumulative. They are the sums of the costs of veneer and plywood plus the additional costs associated with the gluing operation. Thus, no new materials are added in the gluing operation because the paneling cost for materials is equal to the sum of the veneer and plywood costs for materials. Direct labor in the gluing operation is $10 per 1,000 square feet, $55 total minus $25 for plywood operation and $20 for veneer operation.

The accountant who prepared the data above stated that the firm should stop making paneling because it is unprofitable, and instead make and sell the veneer and plywood.

You learn that the overhead figures given above contain both fixed and variable overhead. The variable portion of overhead is 80% of direct labor cost. All fixed overhead is unavoidable.

Required

1. Determine what the firm should do. How much of each product should be produced and sold?
2. Determine what the firm should do if the price of paneling dropped to $164 per 1,000 square feet.
3. Assume that paneling can be sold for $178 and veneer for $74, as in part 1. At what price for plywood would the firm earn the same profit selling all of its plywood and veneer separately as it would combining them into paneling?
4. Assume the same prices as in part 1. Suppose that the firm could increase its capacity in any of the three operations by renting additional equipment on a month-to-month lease. Determine the maximum monthly cost that the firm could incur to increase capacity by 100,000 square feet in each of the three operations, considered independently.

7-30 Comprehensive joint products problem   The Steger Chemical Company buys a single raw material for $.10 per pound. The material is put through a process from which three products emerge. The processing is done in batches of 1,000 pounds of material and requires 10 labor hours per batch. The joint process has associated fixed costs of $2,200 per month, of which $1,200 is avoidable. The output of a 1,000-pound batch is as follows:

Product	Quantity in Pounds	Selling Price per Pound
Algex	300	$ .90
Gamex	200	1.80
Deltex	400	.75
Waste	100	0

Each of the three usable products can be put through further processing. Algex can be made into two new products, Nonex and Querex. The variable cost to process a 100-pound batch of Algex is $40 for labor and overhead. Fixed costs associated with the process are $12,000 per month, of which $4,800 is avoidable. The output per 100 pounds of Algex is:

Product	Quantity in Pounds	Selling Price per Pound
Nonex	45	$3.00
Querex	40	2.00
Waste	15	0

Gamex can be processed further and sold for $1.90 per pound. The additional processing requires one labor hour per 100 pounds.

Deltex can be refined and sold for $1.20 per pound. The additional refining requires three-fourths of a labor hour per 100 pounds put into the refining process. Evaporation during the process takes 10% of the quantity put into the process. The refining process also has incremental, avoidable fixed costs of $2,200 per month.

For all processes, the cost per hour of labor time is $20, which includes labor and variable overhead. The firm can process 10 tons of raw material per month and can sell all of any product it makes. Selling and administrative expenses are $1,600 per month.

Required: Answer each question independently of the others, unless otherewise stated.

1. Determine the firm's best production plan. Which products should be sold at split-off, and which processed further?
2. Prepare an income statement for a month, based on your answer to part 1.
3. The selling prices of some of the products might change in the next few months. The president of the firm is concerned about the possibilities and the potential effects on the firm's operations. Specifically, he asks you the following questions.
   (a) **At what price per pound for Querex** would the firm earn the same profit processing Algex into Nonex and Querex as it would selling Algex at split-off?
   (b) At what price per pound for Gamex, after further processing, would the firm earn the same profit processing it further as it would selling it at split-off?
4. The firm has the opportunity to rent equipment for $2,000 per month. Using the equipment would enable the firm to increase its capacity to 12 tons of raw material per month. No other costs would be affected. All additional output of any product could be sold at the prices given. Determine the effect on the firm's monthly profit if the equipment is rented.
5. The president of the firm has learned of a new process. The process could be used to make a new product called Postex. Each 100-pound batch of Postex requires 50 pounds of Nonex and 50 pounds of Gamex (as it emerges from the joint process). Postex could be sold for $4 per pound. The combining process would require two labor hours per 100-pound batch. Additional fixed costs of $800 per month would also have to be incurred. Determine the effect on monthly profit of making Postex.
6. Another new process is also available. In this process the firm would combine Algex and Gamex (after Gamex has been further processed) into Zentex. A 100-pound batch of Zentex requires 50 pounds of each of the other products and three labor hours. Additional fixed costs would be $1,500 per month. Zentex can be sold for $2.50 per pound. Determine the effect on the firm's monthly profit of making Zentex.

7-31 Processing decision Most beef bought in stores comes from cattle that have been fattened on feed-lots. A feedlot is an area consisting mainly of pens and barns in which cattle are kept tightly packed and fed on diets designed to increase their weights rapidly. The cattle are bought from ranchers when they weigh about 500 pounds, at a cost of $260, including freight. After the cattle are fattened, their selling price is $.50 per pound and the buyer pays the freight.

The average animal gains weight in the following pattern.

First month	140 lbs.
Second month	130
Third month	120
Fourth month	<u>100</u>
Total potential gain	490 lbs.

For each month that an animal is on the feedlot, it eats $52 worth of feed. The lot can hold 5,000 head of cattle at a time.

Required

1. Assume that there is a shortage of animals available for fattening. The lot is only able to buy 600 head per month. Determine the number of months that each animal should be kept on the lot before being sold.
2. Suppose that the supply of animals is very high so that the lot is operating at full capacity. Determine the number of months each animal should be kept.

Cases

7-32 Peanuts for peanuts*

The Time:	Hopefully never, but then everybody knows the outcome of wishful thinking.
The Scene:	A small neighborhood diner in a small New Jersey town about twenty-five miles from New York City. The operator-owner, Mr. Joseph Madison, is preparing to open for the day. He has just placed a shiny new rack holding brightly colored bags of peanuts on the far end of the counter. As he stands back to admire his new peanut rack, his brother-in-law, Harry, a self-styled efficiency expert, enters from the back door.

Harry. Morning Joe. What're you looking so pleased about?

Joe. I jus' put up my new peanut rack—the one I tole you about the other night.

Harry. Joe, you told me that you were going to put in these peanuts because some people asked for them. But I've been thinking about it and I wonder if you realize what this rack of peanuts is costing you.

Joe. It ain't gonna cost. Gonna be a profit. Sure, I hadda pay $25 for a fancy rack to hol' the bags, but the peanuts cost 6¢ a bag and I sell 'em for 10¢. I figger I can sell 50 bags a week to start. It'll take twelve and a haf' weeks to cover the cost of the rack and after that I make a clear profit of 4¢ a bag. The more I sell, the more I make.

Harry (shaking his finger at Joe). That is an antiquated and completely unrealistic approach. Fortunately, modern accounting procedures permit a more accurate picture which reveals the complexities involved.

Joe. Huh?

Harry. To be precise, those peanuts must be integrated into your entire operation and be allocated their appropriate share of business overhead. They must share a proportionate part of your expenditures for rent, heat, light, equipment depreciation, decorating, salaries for waitresses, cook. . .

Joe. The cook? What's he gotta do wit' the peanuts? He don' even know I got 'em yet.

*Used with the permission of Rex H. Anderson, Senior Vice-President. INA Reinsurance Company.

Harry. Look, Joe. The cook is in the kitchen; the kitchen prepares the food; the food is what brings people in; and while they're in, they ask to buy peanuts. That's why you must charge a portion of the cook's wages, as well as a part of your own salary to peanut sales. Since you talked to me I've worked it all out. This sheet contains a carefully calculated cost analysis which clearly indicates that the peanut operation should pay exactly $1,278 per year toward these general overhead costs.

Joe (unbelieving). The peanuts? $1,278 a year for overhead? That's Nuts!

Harry. It's really a little more than that. You also spend money each week to have the windows washed, to have the place swept out in the mornings, to keep soap in the washroom and provide free cokes to the police. That raises the actual total to $1,313 per year.

Joe (thoughtfully). But the peanut salesman said I'd make money—put 'em on the end of the counter, he said—and get 4¢ a bag profit.

Harry (with a sniff). He's not an accountant; and remember, he wanted to sell you something. Do you actually know what the portion of the counter occupied by the peanut rack is worth to you?

Joe. Sure. It ain't worth nuttin'. No stool there—just a dead spot at the end.

Harry. The modern cost picture permits no dead spots. Your counter contains 60 square feet and your counter business grosses $15,000 a year. Consequently, the square foot of space occupied by the peanut rack is worth $250 per year. Since you have taken that area away from general counter use, you must charge the value of the space to the occupant. That's called opportunity cost.

Joe. You mean I gotta add $250 a year more to the peanuts?

Harry. Right. That raises their share of the general operating costs to $1,563 per year. Now then, if you sell 50 bags of peanuts per week, these allocated costs will amount to 60¢ per bag.

Joe (incredulously). What?

Harry. Obviously, to that must be added your purchase price of 6¢ a bag, which brings the total to 66¢. So you see, by selling peanuts at 10¢ per bag, you are losing 56¢ on every sale.

Joe. Something's crazy!!

Harry. Not at all. Here are the figures. They prove your peanut operation just can't stand on its own feet.

Joe (brightening). Suppose I sell lotsa peanuts—thousand bags a week, mebbe, 'stead of fifty?

Harry (tolerantly). No, Joe, you just don't understand the problem. If the volume of peanut sales increased, your operating costs will go up—you'll have to handle more bags, with more time, more general overhead, more everything. The basic principle of accounting is firm on that subject: "The bigger the operation the more general overhead costs must be allocated." No, increasing the volume of sales won't help.

Joe. Okay. You so smart, you tell me what I gotta do.

Harry (condescendingly now). Well—you could first reduce operating expenses.

Joe. Yeah? How?

Harry. You might take smaller space in an older building with cheaper rent. Maybe cut salaries. Wash the windows biweekly. Have the floor swept only on Thursdays. Remove the soap from the washrooms. Cut out the cokes for the cops. This will help you decrease the square-foot value of the counter. For example, if you can cut your expenses 50%, that will reduce the amount allocated to peanuts from $1,653 down to $781.50 per year, reducing the cost to 36¢ per bag.

Joe. That's better?

Harry. Much, much better. Of course, even then you'd lost 26¢ per bag if you charged only 10¢. Therefore, you must also raise your selling price. If you want a net profit of 4¢ per bag, you would have to charge 40¢.

(Harry is looking very confident, now, but Joe appears flabbergasted.)

Joe. You mean even after I cut operating costs 50%, I still gotta charge 40¢ for a 10¢ bag of peanuts? Nobody's that nuts about nuts! Who'd buy 'em?
Harry. That's a secondary consideration. The point is, at 40¢, you'd be selling at a price based upon a true and proper evaluation of your then reduced costs.

(Joe does not look convinced; then, he brightens.)

Joe. Look! I gotta better idea. Why don't I jus' throw the nuts out—so I lost $25 on the rack. I'm outa this nutsy business and no more grief.

(Harry is shaking his head vigorously.)

Harry. Joe, it just isn't that simple. You are in the peanut business! The minute you throw those peanuts out, you are adding $1,563 of annual overhead to the rest of your operation. Joe—be realistic—can you afford to do that?
Joe (by now completely crushed). It's unbelievable! Last week I wuz makin' money. Now I'm in trouble—jus' becuz I think peanuts onna counter is gonna bring me some extra profit. Jus' becuz I believe 50 bags of peanuts a week is easy.
Harry (by now smiling and satisfied that his brother-in-law will not be so quick to argue with him in the future). That is the reason for modern cost studies, Joe—to dispel those false illusions.

Curtain falls.

Required

1. Who's nuts?
2. Identify and evaluate the position(s) expounded by Harry.

7-33 Dropping a segment Tom Johnson, the owner of Johnson's Drug Store, is opposed to smoking and would like to drop the tobacco counter from the store. He has determined from industry statistics and opinions of other drug store managers that the tobacco counter creates a good deal of other business for the store because many people who come in just for cigarettes, cigars, and pipe tobacco buy other articles. Moreover, some people will go elsewhere for drugs and sundries if they know that tobacco is not being sold.

The manager estimates that sales of drugs would drop by 5%, and sundries by 10% if the tobacco counter were removed. The space now occupied by the tobacco counter would be devoted to greeting cards, which are not now sold in the store. Estimated annual sales for greeting cards are $8,000, with an associated cost of goods solds of $3,000.

If the tobacco counter is dropped, one full-time clerk could be dropped. But a pharmacist would have to handle the greeting card sales which would result in a further drop in drug sales of 2% (from the current level).

Carrying costs of the inventory of greeting cards are expected to be about $300 less per year than those associated with tobacco.

You have been asked by the manager to advise him in this decision. He has provided you with a budgeted income statement for the coming year assuming that tobacco products are retained.

Johnson's Drug Store
Budgeted Income Statement
for Coming Year

	Tobacco	Drugs	Sundries	Total
Sales	$27,000	$120,000	$33,000	$180,000
Cost of goods sold	9,000	50,000	11,000	70,000
Gross profit	18,000	70,000	22,000	110,000
Operating expenses:				
Salaries	6,700	36,000	7,300	50,000
Occupancy costs (rent, utilities,				
maintenance, etc.)	3,000	7,000	4,000	14,000
Miscellaneous	1,500	6,700	1,800	10,000
Total operating expenses	11,200	49,700	13,100	74,000
Income before taxes	$ 6,800	$ 20,300	$ 8,900	$ 36,000

You learn that occupancy costs are allocated to each product group based on percentages of space occupied for display of those products. These costs will not change in total if greeting cards are substituted for tobacco. The salary of the manager, $18,000, is allocated to departments based on relative sales and is included in the salaries amount in the income statement. Miscellaneous expenses are allocated based on relative sales volume and would be unaffected by the change except for the cost of carrying inventory.

Required

How much will it cost Mr. Johnson to exercise his convictions about smoking?

7-34 Alternative uses of space Several years ago the Star Department Store began leasing some of its space to Clothes Horse, Inc., a chain of boutiques specializing in high-priced women's clothing and accessories. The boutiques are usually separate stores in shopping centers, but the management of Clothes Horse wished to experiment with an operation in a department store and Star was willing, as the space was then not needed for its own operations.

Clothes Horse pays Star a monthly rental of $3,000 plus 5% of its gross sales, and the arrangement has been profitable for both parties. Star pays all electricity, gas, and other costs of occupancy, which are negligible when considered incrementally because the space would have to be lighted and heated anyway. The lease is about to expire and Clothes Horse is eager to renew it for another year on the same terms. However, some of the department heads of Star have indicated a desire to take over the operation of the boutique, and others have requested the use of the space to expand their selling areas.

After reviewing all the requests, Ron Stein and Bill Rausch, Star's executive vice president and general manager, respectively, have narrowed the range of choices to the following: (1) renew the lease with Clothes Horse; (2) keep the boutique, but place it under the women's wear department head, Margot Miller; (3) use the space to expand the shoe department, which is located next to the boutique.

The boutique had total sales of $400,000 in the first ten months of the current year, and the monthly rate is expected to double for the last two months, which come at the height of the Christmas season. Stein and Rausch expect a 10% increase in sales in the coming year if Clothes Horse continues to operate the boutique. Ms. Miller has presented the following budgeted income statement for the coming year, which she believes she could achieve if she took over the operation of the boutique.

Sales		$380,000
Cost of sales		171,000
Gross profit		209,000
Salaries	$75,000	
Advertising and promotion	14,000	
Supplies	7,000	
Miscellaneous	8,000	
		104,000
Profit		$105,000

Stein commented that Ms. Miller is generally too optimistic and that her estimate of sales volume was probably about 10% too high. He noted that she had provided for fewer salespeople than were employed by Clothes Horse and that the somewhat reduced level of service would not help business. He felt that expenses other than cost of sales would probably be about as she had estimated, even at the lower volume which he thought would be achieved.

The manager of the shoe department believed that if the space were used to expand his department his sales would increase by about $200,000 with a gross profit ratio of 45%. He would only need to add one salesperson, who would work on a 10% commission, like the other employees in that department. Virtually all other store employees worked on salary, not commission.

Rausch brought up the subject of traffic through the store and both men agreed that it had increased since Clothes Horse opened the boutique. They were uncertain about the effects of the increased traffic on sales in the store's own departments, and so Rausch told Stein that he would investigate the matter.

Rausch instructed several of his assistants to interview people in the store, particularly in the boutique, regarding their shopping habits. Several days later the results were in and he went to Stein's office to discuss them. The following major conclusions were contained in the reports Rausch had received.

1. About 40% of the dollar sales made in the boutique are to people who come especially to shop there. These people have to walk through parts of the store to get to the boutique and spend about 20% as much in the store as they do in the boutique.
2. The remaining 60% of the boutique's dollar sales is made to people who come for other reasons. Many seem to drop in on their way in or out of the store, some plan to shop in the store's other departments as well as in the boutique. These people spend about twice as much in the store's own departments as they do in the boutique.

After a discussion lasting nearly an hour, Stein and Rausch decided that the people who came in especially to shop in the boutique would not patronize the store at all if Clothes Horse did not operate it. The executives believed that only the popularity of the Clothes Horse name induced these people to come in.

Of the other group, they believed that about 10% of the patronage would be lost if Clothes Horse did not operate the boutique. This loss of sales would be spread fairly evenly throughout the store. The average gross profit ratio in the store is 45% and other variable costs are an additional 8% of sales.

Required: Determine the best course of action for the store.

7-35 Volume-cost-profit analysis—a restaurant For several years you have eaten at least once a week at Château Ecole, a restaurant owned and operated by Mr. Henri Laval. You and Mr. Laval have become friendly, and so you are not surprised when he asks you for advice after your supper one evening. "I have been approached by a salesman from the Chargall Credit Card Company," he says. "He wants me to affiliate with them and accept their credit card. I do not now accept any credit cards, but perhaps I should consider it. They charge 7% of the amount charged on their cards, including the tip. This seems very high to me, but the salesman said that more people would come in if I accepted their card.

"I have asked several of my regular customers if they would like me to accept the credit card and they say yes. But I am afraid of getting the 'expense account crowd' in here. Those people like places that accept credit cards because they get written records of their purchases automatically when they get their bills, which is easier than getting receipts from me. My friend Jacques Desjarden, who owns the Cafe Epicure, says that his business increased by 20% when he started to accept the cards. I think that would happen to my business too.

"I would have to hire a couple more waiters and extra kitchen help if business went up by 20%. At least three more waiters at $80 per week, four more kitchen helpers at $150 per week. I don't know if it is worth it. I will give you my income statement for last year and you will tell me what will happen to my income, OK? I will give you supper for a month for helping me out."

The income statement for the previous year and some other data are given below.

Sales		$640,000
Expenses:		
Food and beverages	$224,000	
Salaries:		
Waiters	62,400	
Other, including chefs, kitchen help	215,000	
Rent	24,000	
Utilities	30,000	
Supplies and maintenance	18,000	
Depreciation on equipment	30,000	
Miscellaneous	16,000	
		619,400
Income		$ 20,600

Mr. Laval tells you that tips to waiters average 18% of sales. He also says that utilities would increase by about 10% if business went up by 20% and that miscellaneous expenses would increase about $3,000 if credit cards were accepted because of billing, filling out forms, and other activities. Finally, he tells you that he expects that his sales will be about half cash, half on credit card if he accepts the Chargall Card because many of his regular customers will use the credit card instead of paying cash.

Required: Make a recommendation to Mr. Laval, based on the information available.

CHAPTER 8

LONG-TERM DECISION MAKING CAPITAL BUDGETING, Part I

In the short term, managers use existing resources to obtain the highest possible returns. These actions do not involve new commitments of cash to investment in machinery, buildings, land, and other long-lived assets. However, opportunities to obtain returns over long periods of time are constantly being considered. These usually require additional investment in buildings, machinery, and equipment. When a decision entails returns lasting longer than one year and the commitment of large amounts of cash, it is called a **capital budgeting** decision.[1]

Capital budgeting decisions are generally more risky than short-term decisions; the investment will be recouped over a long period of time, making it difficult for the firm to reverse its decision without incurring substantial losses. For example, suppose a firm raises its prices expecting to improve its profits, and sales fall so much that profits fall. Usually the firm can simply lower its prices again. Although the firm may suffer a decline in profits for a short period, it can recover fairly quickly once the managers see their error. But suppose a firm builds a plant especially to make a particular product. The plant may have little value in any other use (a low opportunity cost). If the product is unsuccessful, the firm will have made a nearly worthless large investment. A poor capital budgeting decision is sometimes reflected in annual reports as a "write-off." You may have seen some of these described as "Loss on Disposal of Facilities" or some other descriptive title.

[1]The one-year cutoff is arbitrary, but is in general use.

GENERAL BUDGETING AND
RESOURCE ALLOCATION

In short-term decision making, considering only quantifiable factors, action is desirable if the incremental revenues exceed the incremental costs. In the long term, the firm must find the best uses for its capital. In capital budgeting decisions, an action is desirable if the expected rate of return is greater than the rate that must be paid to the suppliers of capital (cost of capital).

The study of cost of capital is the province of managerial finance. Only a brief introduction to the concept will be given here in order to provide you with a more complete understanding of the capital budgeting process.

Cost of Capital

Cost of capital is the cost, expressed as a percentage, of obtaining the capital resources to operate the firm. Capital is obtained from two sources, creditors and owners, corresponding to the divisions of liabilities and owners' equity on the balance sheet. The cost of capital supplied by creditors is the effective interest rate. For example, if the firm would have to make annual interest payments of $80,000 in order to obtain $1,000,000 from a sale of bonds with that face value, the effective interest rate is 8% ($80,000/$1,000,000).[2]

The cost of equity capital is more difficult to determine, for it is based on how much investors expect the firm to earn. In a simple situation this cost may be approximated by finding the expected earnings and dividing this by the market value of the stock. Thus, if a firm is expected to earn $3 per share and the market price of the stock is $30 per share, the cost of equity capital is 10% **($3/$30).**

Determining the cost of capital for a firm is usually a complex task. We are interested in cost of capital primarily because it is the *minimum rate of return on investment that should be acceptable for a new project.* This rate serves as a **cutoff rate of return.** Any project not expected to yield this rate should be rejected; projects expected to yield higher rates should be accepted.

The practical difficulties of determining cost of capital may cause a firm to adopt a specified minimum acceptable rate without any real analysis. A rate so set is often called a **target rate of return**, and the firm will use this rate in deciding which projects to accept. In this chapter we will assume that cost of capital has been estimated and is to be used in the decision to accept or reject a project.

Before you go any further, be sure that you understand the material in Appendix A at the back of the book. You must understand what is being accomplished by discounting, but for specific answers you can refer to available tables.

CAPITAL BUDGETING SITUATIONS

Investments are usually made either to increase revenues or to reduce costs. Investment opportunities that can increase revenues, such as outlays to increase productive capacity or bring out a new product, do not have to be taken. A firm could continue to operate as it

---

[2]You may recall the determination of bond prices and effective interest rates from financial accounting. There are complications if bonds are issued at prices other than face value, but these problems are not important for our purposes.

has in the past. Investments made to reduce costs differ from those where additional revenues are expected in that the decision to reduce costs assumes that management has decided to continue to operate in its present business and is trying to determine the least expensive way to do so.

There are two basic types of cost reduction situations. First, in some situations where there is the opportunity for cost reduction, there is no choice whether the operations will be performed if the firm is to remain in business. An automobile maker must assemble its cars; it cannot simply produce the parts and sell them to consumers. This follows from a *decision* that the firm will be an automobile maker. Given this decision, the manufacturer must find the least expensive method of performing an essential function: whether to use large amounts of labor or large amounts of machinery; or whether to use existing machinery or replace it with more efficient equipment.

The second type of cost minimization situation covers projects not related to essential operations. There may be a top-level management decision to provide a cafeteria or a parking lot for employees. The firm will be seeking the least-cost method of providing the service. Although the firm may gain benefits from a cafeteria (through improved employee morale), future costs will be increased rather than decreased. Nonessential investments do not fit neatly into the ordinary justification of investment (to increase cash available to the firm), but they are, nonetheless, important.

Capital Budgeting Techniques

In a typical investment situation, a manager authorizes an investment with the intention of receiving returns sufficient to both recoup the original investment and adequately reward the company for the risk taken. But the returns are to come in the future, often over a period of many years. That is, he must wait for them, both the return *of* the investment and the return *on* it. Hence, when making an investment decision, the manager tries to determine, considering the time value of money, whether the rate of return associated with a particular investment is greater or less than the minimum acceptable rate—cost of capital. There are two ways to do this: (1) find the rate of return associated with the project and compare that rate with the cost of capital, or (2) using the cost of capital, find the present value of the future returns and compare it with the cost of the investment.

The second method is usually easier to apply. Present value of future returns is compared with the cost of obtaining them—the investment required. If the cost to obtain returns is less than the present value of the returns, the investment is desirable. This method is called the *net present value* method, or *excess present value* method. Later in the chapter, two other commonly used techniques are considered.

In three of the four methods of capital budgeting to be discussed, returns are defined as *cash flows*. In light of the emphasis given to income in prior chapters, and probably in your first course in accounting, some time should be taken to explain why cash flow is to be used.

Cash Flow and Book Income

In Chapter 7, related to short-term decisions, the emphasis in each short-term decision problem was on the change in total income for the coming year as a result of the decision to be made. Changes in revenues, in variable costs, and in avoidable fixed costs were considered. These changes share one important thing: *they affect the current cash flows of the enterprise.*

With minor exceptions resulting from the leads and lags associated with the accrual versus the cash bases of accounting, the incremental profits determined were, as a matter of fact, incremental cash inflows. That is, changes in income because of the particular decision *were* changes in cash flows because of that decision. None of the decisions considered involves changes that would affect income but not cash flows, or vice versa.

The long-term decisions discussed in this chapter differ in one important respect from those covered in Chapter 7. If the investments required by the long-term decisions involve the acquisition of depreciable assets, the changes in incomes resulting from those decisions invariably are *not* also changes in cash flows. This is because of the accounting treatment of depreciation. Future incomes *will* be affected by the acquisition of depreciable assets, but the change in future incomes will *not* be equivalent to the changes in future cash flows. For, as you know from financial accounting, depreciation expense reduces income but does not require a cash outlay in the year in which it affects income.

When a depreciable asset is acquired, a cash outlay occurs in the year of acquisition. Though the cost of that asset may be allocated over the years in which the asset is used, there is no associated outlay of cash in those years even though the incomes of those years are reduced by the depreciation expense. Hence, the change in incomes of year 19X5 or 19X6 as a result of a particular long-term investment decision in 19X1, will not be the same as the change in cash flows of years 19X5 and 19X6 as a result of that same decision. The change in income will be smaller than the change in cash flow because income has been reduced by depreciation expense which required no cash flow. For this reason, when the decisions being considered involve depreciable assets and future incomes, we must be more specific in our analyses. We cannot use income as a substitute for cash flows (as we did in Chapter 7), because income will not be a good measure of cash flows.

Depreciation is, of course, a legitimate deduction in arriving at reportable net income. Were it not for tax laws, we could readily derive the cash flows associated with a particular investment decision by simply adding the reported depreciation expense back to the net income and arrive at the operating cash flow for the year. Or, we could simply determine the cash flows, and ignore the net income amount because it would be influenced by depreciation. However, depreciation is also a legitimate deduction for income tax purposes. Hence, the income taxes to be paid in a given year, which *are* a cash outflow in that year, are affected by the depreciation expense assigned to that year. So to determine the cash flows for a year, we must know what the depreciation expense will be for that year for tax purposes. We will explain specifically, later in this chapter, how to deal with the special problems resulting from the relationship between depreciation and income taxes.

There is one final and important point that you should bear in mind as we proceed. As with all management decisions that deal with the future, the numbers that will be used (for cash flows, useful lives, etc.) are *estimates*. They are almost never known with certainty. In Chapter 9 we illustrate several techniques that are used because of this uncertainty in dealing with the future.

THE SIMPLE CASE

A firm with a cost of capital of 12% is considering the purchase of a machine. The machine would be used for making a proposed new product that will sell for $10 per unit, and variable costs are expected to be $1 per unit. There will be incremental fixed costs requiring cash disbursements of $5,000 per year. Sales volume is expected to be 3,000 units per year. The machine will have a life of five years, after which it will have no value. The company expects to be able to sell the product for about five years. The machine costs $60,000. An analysis of the annual cash flows is given below.

Annual Cash Flows
Years 1–5

Revenues ($10 × 3,000)		$30,000
Variable costs ($1 × 3,000)	$3,000	
Incremental fixed costs requiring cash	5,000	
Total costs requiring cash		8,000
Expected net cash inflow		$22,000

Using this information, the proposed investment will be analyzed using two basic methods.

Net Present Value Method

When using the **net present value method** the question to be answered is whether it is wise to invest $60,000 today in order to receive $22,000 per year for five years. The investment will be worthwhile if the present value of the $22,000 to be received per year for five years is greater than the $60,000 outlay required today (which, obviously, has a present value of $60,000). The present value of the future cash flows of $22,000 minus the $60,000 required investment is called the **net present value** or the **excess present value**. If it is positive (present value of the future cash flows is greater than the required investment), the investment is desirable. If it is negative, the investment is undesirable.

To determine the net present value we must first find the present value of $22,000 per year for five years at 12%. Looking at an appropriate present value table (Table B, page 646), the multiplying factor for a series of payments of $1 for five years at 12% is 3.605. Multiplying this factor by $22,000 we obtain $79,310 as the present value of the future cash flows ($22,000 × 3.605). This means that if you put $79,310 in a bank that paid 12% interest, it would grow sufficiently to allow five annual withdrawals of $22,000. Put still another way, if a 12% return is desired, and payments of $22,000 annually for five years are expected, you would be willing to pay up to $79,310 for this investment. Therefore, you would be more than happy to pay only $60,000, and the investment is desirable. The net present value is $19,310 ($79,310 − $60,000). In general terms, an investment is worthwhile if the net present value is positive. Below is a summary of the analysis.

Present value of future cash flows ($22,000 × 3.605)	$79,310
Investment required	60,000
Net (excess) present value	$19,310

Time-Adjusted Rate of Return

Another approach to analyzing investment opportunity is to find the expected **time-adjusted rate of return**. This method poses the question "What return are we earning if we invest $60,000 now and receive $22,000 annually for five years?" The investment is desirable if the rate of return is higher than the cost of capital. The time-adjusted rate of return is also called the **internal rate of return**, the **discount rate**, and the **true rate of return**.

Where net cash flows are equal in each year, the internal rate of return is not difficult to find. The rate equates the present value of the future cash flows with the amount to be invested now. Consider that the computation of the present value of the future flows is as follows:

$$\text{Present value of future flows} = \text{annual cash returns (flows)} \times \text{the factor related to the interest rate and the number of periods of returns}$$

In computing the time-adjusted rate of return, we assume that the present value, above, is the cost of the investment and try to determine what interest rate is associated with the factor that, when multiplied by the known annual returns, equals the cost of the investment.

The first step is to find the factor related to both interest rate and number of periods of returns. From the equation above, we know that:

$$\frac{\text{Present value of future flows}}{\text{annual cash returns}} = \text{factor related to the interest rate and number of periods}$$

In our example:

$$\frac{\$60,000}{\$22,000} = 2.727$$

We know that this factor, 2.727, relates to some interest rate; we also know that the number of periods involved is 5. Hence, the interest rate can be found by looking at the factors listed in the 5-period row in Table B. In the 5-period row under the 24% column, the factor is 2.745; in that row, under the 25% column, the factor is 2.689. Hence, the rate of return on this project is between 24% and 25%. (You should have been able to tell that the rate of return on this project was greater than 12% because the net present value, as computed in the previous section, is positive.)

Although we could interpolate to find a more exact rate, the true rate, it is obvious that it falls between 24% and 25%, and is higher than the cost of capital, thus showing that the investment is desirable. We are dealing with estimates of future cash flows; it is therefore unnecessary to be too precise in finding rates of return.

Please notice that this investment would be analyzed the same way if it involved reducing costs rather than increasing both revenues and costs. For example, suppose the machine were a labor-saving device that could be used in the manufacture of a product already being sold. Suppose that the machine would allow the firm to save $5 per unit in variable costs and that operation of the machine will involve incremental cash operating costs of $3,000 per year. The company expects to sell 5,000 units of the product each year. The cash flows would then be calculated as follows:

Cash savings (5,000 units × $5)	$25,000
Less: incremental cash fixed costs	3,000
Net cash flow (savings) per year	$22,000

It is the net cash flow that is important, not whether that flow results from increased revenues or reduced cash costs. Once the net cash flows have been determined, it is irrelevant how they will be gained.

TAXES AND DEPRECIATION

The introduction of income taxes necessitates that we perform further calculations to obtain cash flows. Continuing with the example of the new product, assume a 60% income tax rate and straight-line depreciation for income tax calculations. The initial outlay of $60,000 remains the same, but now the annual cash flows are different because the added income from the project is reduced by income taxes. The net cash flow for each of the five years is computed below.

Net Cash Flow for Each Year

	Tax Computation	Cash Flow
Revenues	$30,000	$30,000
Cash expenses	8,000	8,000
Cash flow before taxes	22,000	22,000
Depreciation on tax return	12,000	
Taxable income	$10,000	
Tax at 60%	$ 6,000	6,000
Net cash flow per year		$16,000

Depreciation on the asset reduces taxes. The $12,000 in depreciation expense saves $7,200 in taxes (60% × $12,000). This saving is called the **tax shield or tax effect of depreciation**.

Notice that net income is not computed in the schedule. All that is required is the determination of pre-tax cash flows and taxes, the only other cash flow involved. You might find it easier to compute cash flow after taxes by preparing an income statement and adding depreciation back to net income, much as you might have done in financial accounting to determine cash or working capital flows. This approach is shown below.

Revenues	$30,000
Cash expenses	8,000
Cash flow before taxes	22,000
Depreciation	12,000
Income before taxes	10,000
Tax at 60%	6,000
Net income	4,000
Add back depreciation	12,000
Net cash flow per year	$16,000
Present value factor for 5 years at 12%	3.605
Present value of future cash flows	$57,680
Investment required	60,000
Net present value	($ 2,320)

Using either approach, the cash flows are now $16,000 per year (rather than $22,000) which, when discounted at 12%, have a present value of $57,680. The net present value is minus $2,320; the investment is not desirable. To compute the time-adjusted rate of return, we find the present value factor which, when multiplied by $16,000, equals $60,000. The factor being sought is 3.75 ($60,000/$16,000). The factor closest to this in the 5-year row in Table B is 3.791, the factor for 10%. The rate of return is therefore a little over 10%.

UNEVEN CASH FLOWS

We have assumed that all cash inflows were received equally each year. But revenues or cash expenses, or both, may vary among the years. If depreciation is not taken on a straight-line basis for tax purposes, the tax paid each year will vary. Or the revenues may grow in the early years and decline in the later years of the investment. Or perhaps the investment has a salvage value that would increase the cash flow in the last year.

We shall change the example by using sum-of-the-years'-digits depreciation, but continue the assumption of a 60% tax rate. We no longer have a constant stream of payments because the different amounts of depreciation each year result in different amounts of taxes in each year.

		Year 1	Year 2	Year 3	Year 4	Year 5	Total
	(1) Cash flow before taxes	$22,000	$22,000	$22,000	$22,000	$22,000	$110,000
	(2) Depreciation	20,000	16,000	12,000	8,000	4,000	60,000
(1) − (2)	(3) Taxable income	2,000	6,000	10,000	14,000	18,000	50,000
(3) × 60%	(4) Taxes	1,200	3,600	6,000	8,400	10,800	30,000
(1) − (4)	(5) Net cash flow— operations	$20,800	$18,400	$16,000	$13,600	$11,200	$ 80,000

It is necessary to discount each cash flow separately because the stream of payments is not uniform. This is done below.

Year	Cash Flow	Present Value Factor for 12% Table A (page 646)	Present Value
1	$20,800	.893	$18,574
2	18,400	.797	14,665
3	16,000	.712	11,392
4	13,600	.636	8,650
5	11,200	.567	6,350
Totals	$80,000		$59,631

The investment is still undesirable because the present value of expected returns is less than the investment cost of $60,000. But notice that the use of sum-of-the-years'-digits (SYD) depreciation increased the present value by $1,951 ($59,631 − $57,680). The total cash flows from a given project will be the same regardless of the method of depreciation. Using the straight-line method, the flow was $16,000 per year for five years or $80,000. But using the accelerated method (SYD), the flows will come in faster and this is desirable. SYD depreciation is valuable because it reduces taxes in the early years (below what they would be if straight-line depreciation were used) while increasing them in later years.

The rate of return on the investment can also be found, but is more difficult to determine when cash flows vary among the years. Essentially, the determination is a matter of trial and error. Many computer systems that incorporate a time-sharing capability have computer library programs that can be used for this purpose.

In our illustrations and in most of the problems at the end of this and the next chapter, we shall use straight-line depreciation for tax purposes because it is simpler to work with than SYD. You will be able to use the annuity table instead of having to discount each flow separately. However, you should see that it benefits the firm to use SYD, or another accelerated depreciation method like double-declining balance, for tax purposes because it increases the present value of the future cash flows. Therefore, most firms will use accelerated depreciation for tax purposes. The only exception to the value of accelerated depreciation is when the tax rate is expected to increase. If the rate will be higher in later years than in early years, it *might* be advantageous to use straight-line depreciation.

Salvage Values

The cash flows could be uneven for most projects involving the acquisition of fixed assets because of the salvage values at the ends of the useful lives of those assets. To incorporate this factor into the analysis, it is necessary only to find the cash flow from the salvage value and discount it separately. Assume that the new asset analyzed earlier will be sold at the end of its useful life for $5,000, and that the salvage value will be considered in the computation of depreciation; for simplicity the straight-line method will be used. There will be no tax on the salvage value when it is received because the book value of the asset will be equal to its selling price at the end of the five years.

The new cash flow schedule and the present value of the project would be as follows.

Cash Flows Years 1–5

	Tax Computation	Cash Flow
Revenues	$30,000	$30,000
Cash expenses	8,000	8,000
Cash flow before taxes	22,000	22,000
Depreciation ($55,000/5)	11,000	
Taxable income	$11,000	
Tax	$ 6,600	6,600
Net cash flow per year		$15,400

Summary of Present Value of Investment

Operating cash flows	$15,400 × 3.605 = $55,517
Salvage value	5,000 × 0.567 = 2,835
Total present value	$58,352
Investment required	60,000
Net present value	($ 1,648)

If the firm had chosen to ignore the salvage value of the asset in its computation of depreciation for tax purposes (this is permitted where salvage value is 10% or less of cost), the final sale of the asset would have resulted in a taxable gain. (The book value would have been zero and the full proceeds of the salvage value would have been taxable.) A taxable gain could also result if the proceeds from final sale exceed the estimated salvage value. If a taxable gain is expected (as in the case where salvage value is ignored for depreciation purposes), the expected cash flow from the salvage value in year five would have to be reduced by the expected applicable income tax.

DECISION RULES

The decision rules associated with the two methods of analysis we have described are simple. Using the net present value method (discounting at cost of capital or cutoff rate of return), any project having a positive net present value should be accepted; others should be rejected. Using the time-adjusted rate of return method, a project having a rate of return greater than the firm's cost of capital (or its cutoff rate) should be accepted. The relationship of the two criteria is as follows:

1. If the internal rate of return is less than the cost of capital (or cutoff rate), the net present value will be negative.
2. If the net present value is greater than zero, the internal rate of return is greater than the cost of capital (or cutoff rate).

When analyzing any single project for acceptance or rejection, both methods will lead to the same decision. The problem of multiple investment opportunities will be discussed in Chapter 9.

As in other decision areas, there may be qualitative factors that override a capital budgeting decision that seems best solely on quantifiable data. A project may show a positive net present value and still be rejected by the firm. For example, a firm committed to producing high-quality, high-priced products may reject a project if the proposed product is relatively cheap. Or a firm that manufactures toys might not make toy guns because of the personal convictions of the president. On the other hand, a firm might undertake an investment that showed a negative net present value if the project would bring the firm considerable prestige or perhaps enhance its image as an innovator. Where qualitative reasons support the undertaking of a project, analysis of the quantitative factors should not be ignored, because it will give managers a better idea of the cost of the project to the firm.

OTHER METHODS OF CAPITAL BUDGETING

The net present value and internal rate of return methods are theoretically sound. It is some-times argued that their use is not practical because of the many estimates involved (cost of capital, cash flows, useful lives, etc.). Critics of these methods advocate other methods, which we shall now cover. However, each of these methods requires many of the same estimates as do the net present value and internal rate of return methods.

Payback Period

One of the most commonly used methods of capital budgeting is the **payback period** tech-nique. The manager estimates future net cash inflows from an investment and determines how long it will take for the investment to be recovered. If a project requires an outlay of $10,000 and will generate annual net cash inflows of $4,000, it has a payback period of 2.5 years ($10,000/$4,000). Thus,

$$\frac{\text{Payback}}{\text{period}} = \frac{\text{investment required}}{\text{annual cash returns}}$$

The payback computation does not exclude the possibility of a payback period longer than the life of the project. Payback thus evaluates the rapidity with which an investment will be recovered. Obviously, a project would not be acceptable if the computed payback period exceeded the life of the project. The method may be useful in situations in which maintaining liquidity is a critical factor for the firm.

Decision rules when using the payback technique may be stated in several ways. A firm may set a limit on the payback period beyond which an investment will not be made. A firm might also use payback to decide among available investments so that the investment with the shortest payback period would be selected.

The payback method has a very serious fault. It does not indicate the profitability of the investment. It emphasizes the return *of* the investment but does not investigate the return *on* investment. The life of the project after the payback period is ignored altogether. Consider the two investment possibilities described below.

	A	B
Cost	$10,000	$10,000
Useful life in years	5	10
Annual cash flows over the useful lives	$ 2,500	$ 2,000

Under the payback criterion, investment A would be better than investment B because its payback period is shorter. Investment A has a payback period of four years ($10,000/$2,500), and B one of five years ($10,000/$2,000). Yet it should be obvious that investment B is superior; the returns from A will cease one year after the payback period, while B will continue to return cash for five more years.

The payback method has another serious fault in that it ignores the timing of the expected future cash flows. This fault, like the method's failure to consider years after the payback period, can also be an impediment to good decision making. Consider two in-vestments, X and Y, as described below.

	X	Y
Cost	$10,000	$10,000
Cash flows by year:		
1	$ 2,000	$ 6,000
2	6,000	3,000
3	2,000	1,000
4–8	3,000	3,000

Both X and Y have payback periods of three years, with equal returns over years four through eight. But the investment in Y will be recovered much more quickly than that in X, which is desirable. If two investments promise equal total returns, the one that generates the returns more quickly is the more desirable. The rate of return on investment X is approximately 29%, whereas that on investment Y is about 31%.

Despite its faults, payback does have some uses. It can be a rough screening device for investment proposals because a relatively long payback period will usually mean a low rate of return. As a practical matter, the payback period is automatically computed in the process of calculating the time-adjusted rate of return on an investment with equal annual cash flows. For example, suppose you have an investment opportunity with a cost of $100,000, a life of fifteen years, and a promised annual cash flow of $25,000. To compute the internal rate of return on this project, you would begin by dividing the cost by the annual returns and you would get the factor 4.0 ($100,000/$25,000). This factor is the payback period, four years. You would then proceed to look up, in Table B, the interest rate associated with 15 periods such that the factor in the table was approximately 4.0. The factor for 24% and 15 periods is 4.001. Thus, this project promises a 24% rate of return and a payback period of four years.

Book Rate of Return

Another commonly used capital budgeting method that does not take account of the time value of money is the **book-rate-of-return** technique. Under this method, the book income for each year of the useful life of a project is computed, and the annual book income is divided by the average book investment in the project. That is,

$$\text{Average book rate of return} = \frac{\text{annual future book income}}{\text{average book investment}}$$

To illustrate, assume a $20,000 investment offering an opportunity for pre-tax cash flows of $5,000 per year for eight years, and assume a tax rate of 40%. The book income for each of the eight years, assuming straight-line depreciation is used, would be as follows:

Pre-tax cash flows	$5,000
Depreciation ($20,000/8 yrs.)	2,500
Pre-tax income	2,500
Income taxes	1,000
Net income	$1,500

The average book investment in this project will be $10,000 ($20,000/2). (Note that the book investment in the project declines each year because of the annual depreciation charge.) With an annual net income of $1,500, and an average book investment of $10,000, the average book rate of return is 15% ($1,500/$10,000)[3] This return is an *average* rate of return because we have used the average book investment. In each year, the rate of return computed using book amounts will be different because the book investment in the project will change with each year's depreciation. **By using book investment at the beginning of the year,** in year one the rate of return will be 7.5% ($1,500/$20,000); in the last year, the rate of return will be 60% ($1,500/$2,500).

Let us compare these results with those obtained using the time-adjusted rate of return method. The net cash flows for the project would be $4,000 (net income of $1,500 plus depreciation of $2,500). Dividing the cost by the annual cash flows yields a factor of 5 ($20,000/$4,000). The factor closest to 5 in the 8-period row of Table B is 4.968, which is associated with 12%. Hence, the internal rate of return on this project is approximately 12%.

The example below illustrates the deficiencies of the book-rate-of-return method. Investments A and B require identical investments ($10,000), produce identical total net incomes, and therefore identical average net incomes, and identical average rates of return of 26.7%. However, investment A is clearly superior to investment B; the flows come in faster for A.

	A	B
Pre-tax cash flows by year:		
1	$10,000	$ 2,000
2	5,000	5,000
3	1,666	9,666
Totals	16,666	16,666
Depreciation	10,000	10,000
Income before taxes	6,666	6,666
Income taxes (40%)	2,666	2,666
Total net income	$ 4,000	$ 4,000
Average net income	$ 1,333	$ 1,333
Average book rate of return ($1,333/$5,000)	26.7%	26.7%

Assuming straight-line depreciation, the time-adjusted rate of return on investment A is about 23%, whereas that on investment B is only about 15%. Many firms use one method to compute depreciation for their income statements and another (usually faster method) to compute depreciation for their tax returns. In those cases, the book rate of return will differ even more markedly from the time-adjusted rate.

The book-rate-of-return method not only usually misstates the true rate of return if cash flows and net incomes are uniform, but also fails to consider the timing of the cash flows. Either flaw is serious enough to render it an unsatisfactory method of capital budgeting.

[3]Others may prefer to use the original investment in the denominator.

SUMMARY EVALUATION OF METHODS

The critical difference between the net present value and internal rate of return methods and the payback and book-rate-of-return methods is the attention given to the timing of the expected cash flows. The first two methods (called **discounted cash flow techniques**) consider the timing of the cash flows; the last two methods do not. Because they recognize the time value of money, the discounted cash flow techniques are conceptually superior. Nevertheless, both payback and book rate of return are in wide use.[4]

It is sometimes argued that the discounted cash flow techniques are too complex, or that they require too many estimates to make them useful in practice. There is, we believe, little merit in these charges. All of the four methods require about the same estimates. The discounted cash flow methods require estimates of future cash flows and the timing of those flows. The book-rate-of-return method requires estimates of net income in each future year, which necessitates making the same estimates as those required to estimate cash flows. It also requires decisions about both the tax and the book methods of depreciation to be used; the discounted cash flow methods need to use only the tax method of depreciation. The payback method requires the estimation of cash flows but not of useful life. One point in favor of the payback method is that it emphasizes near-term cash flows. Near-term cash flows are usually easier to predict than flows in later years. However, as we pointed out, unless consideration is given to useful life, the payback method could lead to very poor decisions.

The net present value method does require an estimate of the cost of capital or a decision as to a minimum acceptable rate of return; this is true also of the internal rate of return method. But the book-rate-of-return method requires such a decision also. And the payback method requires a decision regarding the minimum acceptable payback period. In short, the discounted cash flow techniques do not seem to be any more unrealistic or impractical than the other two approaches, and the conceptual superiority of the former argues strongly for their use.

INVESTMENT DECISIONS AND FINANCING DECISIONS

The following statement is a red herring that is often thrown into capital budgeting problems: the investment will be financed with debt capital obtained at a particular rate of interest, say 7%. It is tempting to use the interest rate instead of the cost of capital as the discount rate. It is also tempting to subtract the interest payments to be made on the debt in the determination of cash flow.

The firm cannot accept projects that will return less than the cost of capital because it must earn a satisfactory return for *all* of its suppliers of capital, both creditors and owners. Both are concerned with the safety of their investments, as is often measured by some form of solvency ratio such as the debt/equity ratio. If investors see that the ratio of debt to equity (or of debt to total assets) is increasing as more debt is accumulating, they will become concerned about the solvency of the firm. What will happen then? Both creditors and stock-

---

[4]Klammer found that 57% of firms responding to a survey used discounted cash flow techniques in 1970, which was up from 19% in 1959. Thomas Klammer, "Empirical Evidence of the Adoption of Sophisticated Capital Budgeting Techniques," *Journal of Business,* October 1972, pp. 387–397.

holders will demand higher returns because of the increased risk of insolvency (or worse, they will refuse to supply capital). If the firm makes too liberal use of debt because it has investment opportunities the returns on which exceed the *interest rate* but not cost of capital, it will find itself unable to raise capital except at exorbitant rates. In addition, in situations where the use of equity capital to finance a project is contemplated, mixing the financing decision with the investment analysis might lead to an unwise decision. This could occur if the cost of equity capital was higher than the firm's cost of capital and the project was expected to earn less than the former but more than the latter.

The second temptation is understandable because there are interest payments that have to be met if debt is issued. If common stock is issued, it is likely that dividends will also be paid. Cost of capital includes the cost of obtaining debt and equity capital. The fallacy of subtracting interest payments in the determination of cash flows is this: the use of cost of capital as the discount rate automatically provides for not only the recovery of the investment, but also a return at least equal to cost of capital. Therefore, if interest payments are subtracted, you are providing for the cost of debt twice—once by subtracting interest payments, once by using a discount rate that includes the cost of obtaining both debt and equity capital.

SUMMARY

Decisions on the commitment of resources for time periods longer than a year are called capital budgeting decisions. To evaluate such decisions, the investment required must be identified together with its resulting cash flows. Future cash flows may occur because of additional revenues, additional costs, or cost savings. Critical to capital budgeting is the fact that most, if not all, of the numbers used in the analyses are estimates. Also critical is recognition of the cash-flow effects of the accounting treatment of depreciation.

Effective evaluation of capital budgeting decisions uses present value analysis. The two approaches recommended are the net present value and the internal rate-of-return methods. Other methods often used are conceptually inferior because they fail to consider the time value of money. But such methods may be useful as rough screening devices for investment opportunities.

Discounted cash flow methods are used to decide on undertaking an investment. The solution is based on the firm's cost of capital. The interest rate that must be paid on borrowings for making the particular investment is not relevant to the analysis.

KEY TERMS

book rate of return
cash flows
cost of capital
cutoff rate of return
discounted cash flow techniques
discount rate
excess present value
internal rate of return

minimum rate of return
net present value
payback period
present value
target rate of return
tax shield from depreciation
time-adjusted rate of return
time value of money

KEY FORMULAS

Present value of future flows = annual cash returns × present value factor

Net present value = present value of future flows − required current investment

$$\text{Payback period} = \frac{\text{investment required}}{\text{annual cash returns}}$$

$$\text{Average book rate of return} = \frac{\text{annual future book income}}{\text{average book investment}}$$

REVIEW PROBLEM

The Dwyer Company has the opportunity to market a new product. The sales manager believes that the firm could sell 5,000 units per year at $14 per unit for five years. The production manager has determined that machinery costing $60,000 and having a five-year life and no salvage value would be required. The machinery would have fixed operating costs requiring cash disbursements of $4,000 annually. Variable costs per unit would be $8. Straight-line depreciation would be used for both book and tax purposes. The tax rate is 40% and the firm's cost of capital is 14%.

Required
1. Determine the increase in annual net income and in annual cash flows expected from the investment.
2. Determine the payback period.
3. Determine the book rate of return on the average investment.
4. Determine the net present value of the investment.
5. Determine the internal rate of return of the investment.
6. Suppose that the machinery has salvage value of $5,000 at the end of its useful life. The firm does not consider the salvage value in determining depreciation expense. (Annual depreciation is the same as before.) The tax rate on the gain at the end of the asset's life is 40%. What would your answer be to part 4, above?

Answers to review problem

1.

	Tax Computation	Cash Flow
Sales (5,000 × $14)	$70,000	$70,000
Variable cost (5,000 × $8)	40,000	40,000
Contribution margin (5,000 × $6)	30,000	30,000
Fixed cash operating costs	4,000	4,000
Cash flow before taxes	26,000	26,000
Depreciation ($60,000/5)	12,000	
Increase in taxable income	14,000	
Income tax at 40% rate	5,600	5,600
Increase in net income	8,400	
Add depreciation	12,000	
Net cash flow per year	$20,400	$20,400

2. Payback period, about 2.941 years, which is $60,000 divided by $20,400.

3. The book rate of return on the average investment is 28%, which is annual net income of $8,400 divided by the average investment of $30,000 ($60,000/2).

4. $10,033, calculated as follows:

Net cash flow per year	$20,400
Present value factor, 5-year annuity at 14% (Table B)	3,433
Present value of future net cash flows	$70,033
Less investment	60,000
Net present value	$10,033

5. The internal rate of return is a little over 20%. The factor being sought is 2.941, which is the payback period calculated in part 2, above. The closest factor in the 5-year row of Table B is 2.991, which is the 20% factor. Because 2.941 is less than 2.991, the rate is more than 20%. (Notice that the higher the rate, the lower the factor.)

6. The only change required is the determination of the present value of the salvage value less tax on the gain.

Salvage value	$5,000
Tax at 40%	2,000
Net cash flow, end of year 5	$3,000
Present value factor for single payment, 5 years at 14% (Table A)	.519
Present value of salvage value	$1,557
Net present value from part 4	10,033
Net present value	$11,590

Please notice that we did not have to recompute annual net cash flows. The firm still used $12,000 for depreciation expense. Therefore, at the end of five years the machinery would have a book value of zero and the gain on disposal would equal the salvage value.

ASSIGNMENT MATERIAL

Questions for discussion

8-1 Rental payments and installment purchase Is there any difference between the cost of (a) renting a car for $60 per month and (b) buying a car for $3,600 which is expected to have no value at the end of five years and for which you are permitted to make payments of $60 per month for five years?

8-2 Interest rates and economic activity The federal government is concerned with regulating the level of economic activity—especially with encouraging production and investment to maintain high employment while not allowing excessive inflation. The government is able to do this by changing interest rates through the Federal Reserve Board. How can this ability to influence interest rates be used to stimulate or discourage investment?

8-3 Expenses and expenditures In financial accounting a distinction is drawn between an expenditure and an expense. Is this distinction relevant in the analysis of capital expenditures?

Exercises

8-4 Discounting

1. Find the approximate internal rates of return for each of the following investments.
   - (a) Investment of $22,000 with annual cash flows of $5,000 for seven years.
   - (b) $20,000 investment with annual cash flows of $4,650 for 15 years.
   - (c) An investment of $80,000 with a single return of $125,000 at the end of three years.
2. Find the net present values of the following investments using discount rates of 8%, 10%, and 16%.
   - (a) Annual flows of $10,000 for 10 years are produced by an investment of $60,000.
   - (b) An investment of $120,000 with annual cash flows of $20,000 for 12 years.
   - (c) An investment of $30,000 with annual flows of $8,000 for four years and a single return of $7,200 at the end of the fifth year.
3. Repeat 2 above using a discount rate of 10% and a 40% income tax rate. Assume straight-line depreciation on the amount of the investment over the entire life of the cash flows.

8-5 Comparison of net present value and rate-of-return methods   The Jones Company is thinking of buying some new equipment that promises to save $4,000 in cash operating costs per year. The equipment will cost $22,000. Its estimated useful life is 10 years, and it will have zero disposal value.

Required

1. Compute the net present value if the minimum desired rate of return is 10%.
2. Compute the time-adjusted rate of return.

8-6 Discounting   Solve each of the following independent problems.

1. Harry Smith will be starting college in one year. His father wishes to set up an investment for Harry to use for the $3,500 he will need each year for four years. Harry will make withdrawals at the beginnings of the school years. If Mr. Smith can invest at 9%, how much must he invest today to provide for Harry's college expenses?
2. Brute McGurk is a senior in high school who weighs 450 pounds and runs the 100-yard dash in 8.7 seconds. He has been offered $300,000 per year to play professional football, but would like to go to college. He believes that if he does go to college he will be able to earn $400,000 per year playing football after he graduates. In either case, his playing career will be over at 30, which gives him 12 years if he turns professional immediately. Assuming that going to college would cost him nothing and that his football salary would be paid at the ends of years, what should he do if the interest rate is 10%?
3. Henry Jackson is about to retire from his job. His pension benefits have accumulated to the point where he could receive a lump-sum payment of $120,000 or $20,000 per year for ten years, paid at the ends of years. Jackson has no dependents and fully expects to live ten years after he retires. If he can invest at 10%, which option should he take?

8-7 Time value of money   Answer the following questions.

1. A person received a single payment of $3,220 as a result of having invested some money five years ago at an interest rate of 10%. How much did the person invest?
2. An investment opportunity requiring $5,000 is available. It will return a single payment at the end of ten years. The interest rate is 14%. How much will be received at the end of ten years?
3. An investment of $1,000 returned a single payment of $3,700. The interest rate earned was 14%. How many years elapsed between the investment and the return?
4. A person received seven annual payments of $1,000 from an investment made seven years ago. The interest rate was 12%. What was the amount of the investment?
5. An investment of $1,000 returned $343 annually for some years. The rate of interest earned was 14%. How many payments were received?

6. A $10,000 investment made today will provide a 10% return. The returns will be paid in equal annual amounts over eight years. What is the amount of the annual payment?

8-8 Effects of depreciation methods   The controller of the Eustace Company has been attending a seminar on taxation. She has learned that sum-of-the-years'-digits depreciation offers a faster write-off for tax purposes than straight-line depreciation, which the firm now uses. The president of the firm is unimpressed, saying that it hardly matters how assets are depreciated because the total tax deduction for tax depreciation over the life of the asset is the same no matter what method is used.

Required

Prepare a response to the president's position, using as an example a $100,000 asset with no salvage value, a four-year life, and a 40% tax rate. The asset produces cash flows before taxes of $45,000 per year and cost of capital is 18%.

8-9 Comparison of methods   The Ringding Company has three investment opportunities; these are summarized below.

	A	B	C
Cost	$10,000	$10,000	$10,000
Cash inflows by year (after tax):			
Year 1	5,000	8,000	1,000
Year 2	5,000	1,000	2,000
Year 3	—0—	1,000	3,000
Year 4	1,000	11,000	16,000
Totals	$11,000	$21,000	$22,000

Required

1. Rank the investment opportunities in order of desirability using (a) payback period, (b) average book rate of return (use average net book value of the investment as the denominator), and (c) net present value using a 10% discount rate.
2. Comment on the results.

8-10 Yesterday's decisions   Mark Quinton, president of Ajax Industries, is talking with Dan Weber, a salesman for a machinery company, about a new model of a machine currently used by Ajax. Quinton is staring, unbelieving, at Weber and saying, "But it was just yesterday that I spent $50,000 for what you now call your 'old model.' I sure am not interested in buying another machine to do the same job. The machine I just bought will last for one year and cost me $25,000 to operate for that year. Agreed, it has no resale value. But after putting out $50,000 I am not about to buy your $10,000 model even though it will do the same job as mine will for $12,000 for the year. Next year, when I have to replace the one I just bought, I'll be glad to talk to you; but I would lose $50,000 if I bought what you're trying to sell me now."

Required

As Dan Weber, respond to Mr. Quinton's remarks and support your reply with calculations.

8-11 Comparison of methods   Below are data relating to three possible investments.

	X	Y	Z
Cost	$40,000	$10,000	$20,000
Useful life—years	10	4	20
Annual cash savings	$ 7,675	$ 3,720	$ 3,375

Required

Rank the investments according to their desirability using the following: (a) payback period, (b) internal rate of return, and (c) net present value using a discount rate of 10%. (Ignore taxes and depreciation.)

8-12 Relationships Fill in the blanks for each of the following independent cases. In all cases the investment has a useful life of ten years and no salvage value. Ignore income taxes.

	(a) Annual Cash Inflow	(b) Investment	(c) Cost of Capital	(d) Internal Rate of Return	(e) Net Present Value
1.	$ 50,000	$241,650	14%		$
2.	$ 80,000	$	12%	18%	$
3.	$	$300,000		16%	$ 81,440
4.	$	$400,000	14%		$121,600
5.	$100,000	$		10%	($131,200)

8-13 Cost savings The Wisconsin Valve Company has been considering the purchase of some new machinery. The firm makes a number of different types of industrial valves, one of which is the model A-404. At present, the A-404 sells about 40,000 units per year, but the sales manager believes that 45,000 per year could be sold if production could be increased beyond the current capacity of 40,000 units. The bottleneck in production is caused by the grinding operation, which is now done manually. An automatic grinder could be purchased for $300,000. It would have a four-year useful life and salvage value of $20,000. The firm would use sum-of-the-years'-digits depreciation with no provision for salvage value in determining the depreciation charges.

The A-404 sells for $80 and has variable costs of $44, of which about $3 is incurred in the grinding process. Using the automatic grinder would reduce the variable cost to $2.50 per unit. Using the grinder would increase fixed costs requiring cash by about $60,000 per year. The tax rate is 40%, including the expected rate on the salvage value, and the firm has a target rate of return of 16%.

Required: Determine whether the new automatic grinder should be purchased.

Problems

8-14 Installing a sprinkler system The Walton Company operates several factories, one of which was built some thirty years ago and is not in good condition. That factory has a fire insurance policy covering machinery, inventory, and the building itself. The premiums on the policy are $18,000 per year.

Recently, an inspector from the fire insurance company has recommended that the premium be increased to $35,000 per year because the factory's fire protection has been diminished. The reason is that its existing sprinkler system has stopped functioning and cannot be repaired at a reasonable cost. The plant manager was told by the inspector that a new system, costing $90,000 and with a ten-year life and no salvage value, would be needed to continue the existing premium of $18,000 per year.

The system would be depreciated on straight-line basis. The tax rate is 40% and Walton's cost of capital is 10%.

Required: Determine whether the sprinkler system should be bought.

8-15 Expanding a product line The Kiernan Company makes office equipment of various sorts, like tables, desks, chairs, and lamps. The sales manager is trying to decide whether to introduce a new model desk. The desk will sell for $450 and have variable costs of $240. Volume is expected to be 4,000 units per year for five years. To make the desks the firm will have to buy additional machinery that will cost $1,500,000, have a five-year life, and no salvage value. Straight-line depreciation will be used. Fixed cash operating costs will be $250,000 per year.

The firm is in the 40% tax bracket and its cost of capital is 10%.

Required

1. Determine, using the net present value method, whether the new desk should be brought out.
2. Compute the payback period.
3. Determine the approximate internal rate of return that the firm expects to earn on the investment.

8-16 New product—a textbook   After reviewing selected chapters and detailed outlines, the Raven Publishing Company is considering bringing out a new textbook on managerial accounting. (The firm has no other textbook on this subject.) Raven expects volume over the three-year life of the first edition to be 25,000, 18,000, and 13,000 books, respectively. The book will sell for $12 at retail, of which Raven gets 75%. (College bookstores will keep 25% of the retail price.) Variable costs associated with each book are as follows:

Paper and cover	$1.50
Royalties to author	1.40
Other (printing, etc.)	1.10
Total	$4.00

Fixed costs directly associated with the book will be $20,000 per year. In addition, it costs about $75,000 to set up and print a new book. Moreover, special advertising and promotion costs of $25,000 will be incurred almost immediately upon signing a contract for the book, and approximately $12,000 will be spent at the end of the first and the second years to advertise and promote the book ($12,000 for each campaign).

The company's tax rate is 40%, and setup and promotion costs are deductible in the year such costs are incurred. The company's cost of capital is 16%.

The author desires a $9,000 initial payment, which amount is deductible for tax purposes equally over the three years.

Required

1. Determine whether the book should be published.
2. A survey suggests that sales would be 10% higher if the book were more expensively produced (more artwork and use of color). Variable costs would increase to $4.50 per book, fixed costs would remain the same and setup costs would be $85,000. Should the more expensively produced book be published?

8-17 Capital budgeting and reported earnings   The president of Calco Industries has been disturbed by reports that the firm's stock is not considered a good buy. Calco has been a rapidly growing company in a field that stresses swift technological advances. Calco has an extensive research program and an ambitious building schedule, with $10 million plant and equipment expenditures planned for next year. The firm's stock is currently selling at $125, about 25 times earnings per share of $5 last year. Increased growth in earnings per share is viewed as necessary to sustain the price of the stock.

The firm has a cutoff rate of return of 20% after taxes, using discounted cash flow techniques. The president wonders whether to institute another capital spending constraint: by the second year of operations a project must be expected to increase earnings per share by at least $1 for each $1,000,000 invested. He feels that such a requirement would help to keep the price of the stock from falling due to disenchantment of stockholders and financial analysts whose recommendations are often acted on.

He shows you the following proposal.

Investment	$2,000,000
Cash inflows by year (before taxes):	
1	$ 600,000
2	800,000
3	1,050,000
4	1,110,000
5	1,500,000

The tax rate is 40%. There are 200,000 shares of common stock outstanding. Straight-line depreciation is used for both tax and book purposes.

Required

1. Determine whether the investment meets the 20% rate of return criterion.
2. Determine the effects of the investment on earnings per share.
3. What suggestions can you make to resolve the conflict?

8-18 When-to-sell decisions   The Smooth Scotch Company has a large quantity of Scotch whisky that is approaching its sixth anniversary. When it reaches age six it can be sold for $700 per barrel. If it is held until it is ten years old it can be sold for $1,100 per barrel.

Required

1. Determine the internal rate of return that would be earned if the Scotch were held until it was ten years old.
2. Suppose that the firm has cost of capital of 16%, that the price of six-year-old Scotch is $700 per barrel, but that the price of ten-year-old Scotch in four years is in doubt. What is the minimum price per barrel that the firm would have to receive four years from now to justify keeping the Scotch until it is ten years old?
3. Suppose now that the following schedule of prices is expected. Determine the point at which the Scotch should be sold using the criterion of highest internal rate of return. (Assume that the cutoff rate of return is low enough that all of the rates you compute would be acceptable. That is, the best decision is not to sell now.)

Years of Age	Expected Price
6	$ 700
7	800
8	940
9	1,200
10	1,350

4. Redo part 3 assuming that cost of capital is 10% and the net present value criterion is to be used to make the decision.

8-19 Funding a pension plan   The Edwardian Company has reached an agreement with the labor union that represents its workers. The agreement calls for the firm to pay $100,000 per year for the next ten years into a pension fund for the benefit of employees. The payments would begin one year from now.

The firm has excessive cash on hand from the sale of some of its assets, so the treasurer approaches the head of the union and asks if it would be all right to make a single, lump-sum payment to discharge the ten-year obligation. Before the head of the union gives a reply, the treasurer decides to determine the maximum amount that the firm could pay right now. The firm is in the 40% tax bracket and has cost of capital of 12%. The annual payments would be deductible for tax purposes in the years in which they were made and the single payment would be deductible in the current year.

Required

Determine the maximum amount that the firm could pay in a lump-sum settlement of the obligation.

8-20   Bond refunding   The Expost Company has outstanding a $1,000,000 (par value) issue of bonds bearing a 10% interest rate. The bonds mature in 10 years. Current interest rates are lower than they were when this issue was sold and the firm can now raise cash on a 10-year bond at 8%. The directors of the firm are considering retiring the outstanding issue and replacing the old bonds with 8%, 10-year bonds. The firm would have to pay a premium of 5% over par value to buy back the currently outstanding issue. It would also have to spend $60,000 in legal fees and other costs to market the new issue. The premium is tax deductible in the year of refunding, but the costs of issuing the new bonds must be amortized evenly over 10 years. The tax rate is 25%, and the company's cost of capital is 12%.

Required

Should the old issue be replaced?

8-21   Capital budgeting by a municipality   The City Council of Dullsville is considering the construction of a convention center in the downtown area. The city has been losing employment to surrounding suburbs, and tax revenues have been falling. The proposed center would cost $22,000,000 to build, and the city would incur annual cash operating costs of $300,000. The city controller has prepared the following estimate of receipts from the center over its estimated useful life of 30 years.

Rentals of space for trade shows, conventions, etc.	$1,400,000

The controller states that the estimated revenues were based on total annual convention attendance of 200,000 persons.

He reports that at 6% interest, the rate the city would have to pay on bonds to build the center, it would be a losing proposition. The present value of $1,100,000 ($1,400,000 − $300,000) annually for 30 years at 6% is $15,141,500, well below the cost of the center. (Assume this computation is correct.)

One member of the council comments that the rentals are not the only source of revenues to the city. To support this position she offers studies showing that the average person attending a trade show or convention spends $300 in the city in which the event is being held. Because of the various taxes in effect, the city receives, on the average, about 1% of all of the money spent in it.

Required

1. Prepare a new analysis, incorporating the additional tax receipts expected if the center is built.
2. Why is 6% used as the discount rate when it is the interest rate, not cost of capital? (Is the interest rate the same as the cost of capital to a city?)

8-22   Choosing a depreciation method—rising tax rates   The Burke Company has the opportunity to invest $60,000 in machinery that will save $30,000 per year in cash operating costs. The useful life of the machinery is four years and no salvage value is expected. The controller has suggested that

SYD depreciation be used, but the financial vice president thinks that straight-line depreciation would be better because the tax rate is expected to increase substantially over the next few years. In the first year of the life of the investment the tax rate is expected to be 30%, in the second year 40%, and 50% thereafter. The firm's cost of capital is 10%.

Required

1. Compute the net present value of the investment using straight-line depreciation.
2. Repeat 1 using SYD depreciation.

8-23 **Buying company cars** The Girven Company is a large distributor of household products. The firm employs salespeople who drive their own automobiles on company business and are paid $.15 per mile by the firm. Each salesperson drives about 20,000 miles per year on company business.

The controller of the firm has been looking into the possibility of buying cars for the salespeople. After checking on prices and operating costs, he developed the following information.

	Year			
	1	2	3	4
Operating costs per car:				
(based on 20,000 miles per year)				
Gas and oil	$950	$950	$950	$950
Insurance and taxes	200	200	200	200
Replacement parts and				
maintenance	80	130	460	180
Depreciation	1,000	1,000	1,000	1,000
Totals	$2,230	$2,280	$2,610	$2,330

The depreciation expense is based on a $6,000 original cost per car, with provision for $2,000 expected resale value at the end of four years. The controller added the total operating costs for each year, getting $9,450, and divided by the 80,000 total expected miles to get a per-mile cost of about $.12. He concluded that the cars should be bought because the average cost per mile was less than what was currently being paid to salespeople for using their own cars.

The firm is in the 40% tax bracket and its cost of capital is 14%.

Required

Determine whether the firm should purchase cars or continue paying salespeople for using their own cars.

8-24 **Capital budgeting for a computer service firm** Many firms are in the business of selling computer time to others. Customers include other business firms, universities, hospitals, and so on. One such computer service firm, Compuservice, Inc., currently has a Whizbang 85, a high-speed machine that it rents from the manufacturer for $22,000 per month. The firm is considering the purchase of a Zoom 125, which is the fastest machine of its type available. The Whizbang 85 would be kept even if the Zoom were bought. Cal Kulate, the president of Compuservice, believes that a number of new customers would be attracted if the firm acquired the Zoom 125. He estimates additional revenues of $30,000 per month. Additional costs requiring cash would be $2,000 per month for maintenance and salaries for added operators. The Zoom sells for $1,000,000 and has a useful physical life of about 15 years. However, computer experts have estimated that the Zoom will probably be technologically obsolete in six years.

The firm would use straight-line depreciation of $125,000 per year in order to depreciate the computer to its estimated salvage value of $250,000 at the end of six years. The firm's tax rate is 40% and its cost of capital is 16%.

Required

Evaluate the proposed purchase.

8-25 Reevaluating an investment Ten years ago the Kramer Company, of which you are the controller, bought some machinery at a cost of $200,000. The purchase was made at the insistence of the production manager. The machinery is now worthless and the production manager believes that it should be replaced. He gives you the following analysis, which he says verifies the correctness of the decision to buy the machinery ten years ago. He bases his statement on the 24.6% return he calculated, which is higher than the firm's cutoff rate of return of 20%.

Annual cost savings:	
Labor	$21,000
Overhead	40,000
Total	61,000
Less straight-line depreciation ($200,000/10)	20,000
Increase in pre-tax income	41,000
Income taxes at 40%	16,400
Increase in net income	$24,600
Average investment ($200,000/2)	$100,000
Return on investment	24.6%

Required

Do you agree that the investment was wise? Why or why not?

8-26 Purchase commitment The Ralston Company buys copper from a number of suppliers, including the Boa Copper Company. The president of Boa has offered to sell Ralston up to 1,000,000 pounds of copper per year for five years at $.40 per pound if Ralston will lend Boa $2,000,000 at 6% interest. The loan would be repaid at the end of five years with the interest being paid annually.

Ralston uses at least 1,800,000 pounds of copper per year and expects the price to be $.54 per pound over the next five years. The tax rate is 40% and Ralston's management considers the relevant discount rate to be 10%.

Required

1. Determine whether the offer should be accepted by the Ralston Company.
2. Determine the price at which copper would have to sell, per pound, over the next five years to make accepting the offer worthwhile.

8-27 New product—complementary effects The Elmendorf Company makes a variety of cleaning products. The firm's research and development department has recently come up with a new glass cleaner that is superior to all of the products on the market, including the one that Elmendorf currently makes. The new cleaner would be priced at $6 per case and would have variable costs of $2 per case. The firm would have to buy additional machinery costing $10,000,000 to make the new cleaner. The machinery would have a ten-year life. Volume of the new cleaner is expected to be 800,000 cases per year for ten years. In addition to the variable costs, there would be increased fixed costs of $200,000 per year requiring cash disbursements.

The machinery would be depreciated using the straight-line method with no provision for salvage value. There is about $100,000 expected salvage value at the end of ten years. The tax rate is 40% and cost of capital is 14%.

One problem with making the investment is that sales of the firm's existing cleaner would be affected. Volume of the existing cleaner is expected to fall by 300,000 cases per year. A case of the existing cleaner sells for $5 and has variable costs of $3.

Required

Determine the net present value of the proposed investment.

8-28 Uses of space (AICPA Adapted)   The Lansdown Company manages large office buildings in the downtown area of a major city. One of the buildings it manages has a large unused lobby area. A manager of the firm believes that a newsstand should be placed in the lobby. He has talked to managers of several other office buildings and has projected the following annual operating results if the company establishes a newsstand.

Sales	$49,000
Cost of sales	40,000
Salaries of clerks	7,000
Licenses and payroll taxes	200
Share of heat and light bills on the building	500
Share of building depreciation	1,000
Advertising for the newsstand	100
Share of Lansdown's administrative expense	400

The investment required would be $2,000, all for equipment that would be worthless in ten years. Before presenting the plan to his superiors, the manager learned that the space could be leased to an outside firm that would operate the same kind of newsstand. The other firm would pay $750 rent per year for each of the ten years. Because the lobby is heated and lighted anyway, Lansdown would supply heat and light at no additional cost. Lansdown's cost of capital is 12%. (Ignore taxes.)

Required

1. Determine the best course of action for Lansdown.
2. Determine how much annual rent Lansdown would have to receive to equalize the attractiveness of the alternatives.

8-29 New product (CMA adapted)   The Crampton Company makes toys and other products that have relatively short lives.

The firm's management is considering the introduction of a promotional gift for office equipment dealers. Sales personnel have reported a great deal of interest in such an item and the firm has received commitments for the product for a three-year period, at the end of which there will no longer be a demand for the product.

To produce the required quantities Crampton will have to buy some machinery and rent some additional space. Space requirements will be about 25,000 square feet; the firm has 12,500 square feet of unused space now that it is leasing for $3 per square foot. The lease has ten years to run. Another 12,500 square feet adjoining the Crampton plant could be rented at $4 per square foot per year for three years.

The cost of equipment required would be $900,000. Additional costs would be $30,000 for modification, $60,000 for installation, and $90,000 for testing. These activities would be carried out by an independent engineering firm. All of the above costs would be capitalized and depreciated over three years using the SYD method, including provision for $180,000 in salvage value.

The following estimates of revenues and expenses for the three-year period have been developed.

	19X6	19X7	19X8
Sales	$1,000,000	$1,600,000	$800,000
Materials, labor, and other variable costs	400,000	750,000	350,000
Allocated general overhead	40,000	75,000	35,000
Rent	87,500	87,500	87,500
Depreciation	450,000	300,000	150,000
Total costs	977,500	1,212,500	622,500
Profit before taxes	22,500	387,500	177,500
Income taxes at 40% rate	9,000	155,000	71,000
Net income	$13,500	$232,500	$106,500

The firm has a cutoff rate of return of 20%.

Required

Determine whether the project should be accepted.

8-30 Long-term special order The Nova Company makes indoor television antennae that sell for $8 and have variable costs of $3. The firm has been selling 200,000 units per year and expects to continue at that rate unless it accepts a special order from the ACR Television Company. ACR has offered to buy 40,000 units per year at $5, provided that Nova agrees to make the sales for a five-year period. ACR will not take fewer than 40,000 units.

Nova's current capacity is 230,000 units per year. Capacity could be increased to 260,000 units per year if new equipment costing $100,000 were purchased. The equipment would have a useful life of five years, no salvage value, and would add $18,000 in fixed cash operating costs. Variable costs per unit would be unchanged.

Nova would use straight-line depreciation for tax purposes. The tax rate is 40% and cost of capital is 14%.

Required

Determine the best course of action for Nova Company. Be sure to consider all of the available alternatives.

Cases

8-31 Capital budgeting in a not-for-profit entity Dr. Bennett, director of the McPherson Institute, is reviewing the status reports of current research projects. The McPherson Institute performs basic research in physics, and is supported entirely by donations and the earnings on endowment funds. Endowment funds are contributions to provide permanent funding. (The earnings from investment of such contributions are available for operations, but the amount contributed cannot be used.)

Current research reports show that one of the institute's major projects is reaching a stage where a series of crucial experiments must be undertaken. The experiments can be carried out in either of two ways. One way requires the use of many highly educated scientists and technicians; the other requires the purchase of a very expensive machine, the cylipotron.

The cylipotron costs $800,000 and will last for 10 years. It will cost $20,000 per year to operate in order to perform the desired experiments. The machine may subsequently be used for other experiments, but reports on the current project indicate that experiments will cover the coming 10-year period. If the other approach is taken, the institute will have to spend about $150,000 per year on additional salaries and other costs. This estimate represents, in the view of the project director, a reasonable amount for the work involved without the advantage of the use of a cylipotron.

The institute is a not-for-profit organization, and is therefore not subject to federal or state income tax.

Required

1. What is the rate of return earned by the cylipotron in preference to the available alternative?
2. Suppose that Dr. Bennett has been in contact with a wealthy woman who has expressed an interest in the current project and is considering making donations to pay for its continuation through the experiment stage. If the woman can earn a 14% return on her personal investment, would it be better for her to buy the cylipotron and make annual donations of $20,000 for 10 years, or make annual donations of $150,000 for 10 years?

8-32 Introduction of new product   Jerry Dollink, the controller of Radsiville Industries, Inc., tells you about a meeting of several top managers of the firm. The topic discussed was the introduction of a new product that had been undergoing extensive research and development. Jerry had thought that the product would be brought out in the coming year, but the managers decided to give it further study.

The product is expected to have a market life of 10 years. Sales are expected to be 40,000 units annually at $90. The following annual costs were presented by James Barker, the manager of the division that would produce and sell the product.

Materials	$18 per unit
Direct labor	12
Overhead (manufacturing)	22
Selling and administrative expenses	12
Total costs	$64 per unit

Barker went on to point out that equipment costing $2,000,000 and having an expected salvage value of $100,000 at the end of 10 years would have to be purchased. In addition, receivables would be expected to increase by 25% of annual sales revenues ($900,000) because the firm generally collects its receivables in 90 days. Inventory could be expected to increase by $1,000,000. Adding the $900,000 that had already been spent on research and development brought the total outlay related to the new product to $4,800,000.

Depreciation of $190,000 per year would reduce taxes by $76,000 (40% rate). The $26 per-unit profit margin would produce $1,040,000 before taxes, $624,000 after taxes. The net return would then be $700,000 annually, which is a rate of return of less than 8%, far below the firm's cost of capital at 14%. Barker concluded that the product should not be brought out.

Jerry tells you that Barker is a strong believer in "having every product pay its way." The calculation of the manufacturing overhead cost per unit includes existing fixed costs of $300,000 allocated to the new product. Selling and administrative expenses were also allocated to the product on the basis of relative sales revenue. Commissions of $4 per unit will be the only incremental selling, general, and administrative expenses.

Required

1. Prepare a new analysis. The increases in receivables and inventory should be treated as part of the initial investment. They will be recovered in full at the end of the life of the product.
2. Explain the fallacies in Barker's analysis. Comment on why you might treat items differently from the way he did.

CHAPTER 9

CAPITAL BUDGETING, Part II

In Chapter 8 we examined some of the basic principles of capital budgeting, concentrating on decisions in which the firm was considering the purchase of new productive assets. In this chapter we consider some other kinds of capital budgeting decisions, ones that do not fit the pattern of those we discussed in Chapter 8. The basic principles remain the same; in all cases the new features to be discussed require somewhat different methods of computing the net cash flows to be derived from the investment or of computing the amount of investment required. Because of the importance of the many estimates in any capital budgeting decision, we will introduce an analytical technique to help identify the most critical estimates.

Special consideration is given to certain aspects of income tax law that affect capital budgeting decisions. Finally, we conclude this chapter and this Part with a discussion of the social consequences of decision making and a brief look at the special problem of decision making in the public sector.

COMPLEX INVESTMENTS

For many investment opportunities, the required investment is not simply a single cash outflow for the acquisition of some new depreciable asset. The determination of the required investment may be complicated by the fact that the opportunity requires an additional investment in working capital or involves the replacement of already existing assets. Or it is possible that the decision involves no investment at all, but rather a disinvestment. These three special cases will be considered here.

Working Capital Investment

An investment proposal usually requires not only an increase in noncurrent assets such as equipment and plant, but also an increase in working capital elements such as accounts receivable and inventory. For example, unless all sales are for cash, the anticipated increases in sales due to the introduction of a new product will also probably increase receivables. A larger inventory will probably have to be carried to support the higher sales levels. These increases are also investments, and investments in working capital are just as important as investments in plant and equipment. In evaluating investment opportunities, the minimum desired rate of return must be earned on current assets as well as on noncurrent assets. There is, however, a difference between investments in working capital and in noncurrent assets. At the end of the useful life of a physical asset there is often salvage value to be recovered through sale of the asset. Working capital investments are typically recovered in full because the larger receivables and inventory will be turned into cash during the final operating cycle in the life of the project.

It is not particularly difficult to deal with projects that require investment in current assets. There are no tax effects associated with either the initial increase in working capital or its recovery at the end of the useful life of the project.

Consider an investment for a new product that is expected to have a useful life of five years. Additional revenues from the product are estimated to be $20,000 annually, with additional annual cash costs of $6,000. The investment required is $30,000 in equipment and $35,000 in receivables and inventory. Straight-line depreciation is to be used, the equipment has no salvage value, the firm's cost of capital is 12%, and the tax rate is 40%. The cash flows and present value of the project are computed below.

Cash Flows Years 1–5

	Tax Computation	Cash Flow
Revenues	$20,000	$20,000
Cash expenses	6,000	6,000
Pre-tax cash flow	14,000	14,000
Depreciation ($30,000/5)	6,000	
Taxable income	$ 8,000	
Tax at 40%	$ 3,200	3,200
Net cash flow per year		$10,800

End of Year 5

Recovery of working capital investment	$35,000

Summary of Present Value of Investment

Operating cash flows $10,800 × 3.605	$38,934
Recovery of working capital investment $35,000 × 0.567	19,845
Total present value	58,779
Investment required ($30,000 + $35,000)	65,000
Net present value	($ 6,221)

The investment is undesirable. If only the noncurrent asset investment were considered, the investment would appear to be desirable. The present value would be $38,934 and the investment $30,000, thus providing a positive, fairly high net present value. But failure to consider the working capital requirements would lead to a bad decision. Consideration of working capital requirements shows how both long- and short-term planning techniques must be employed in particular situations.

When an investment opportunity requires an additional commitment to elements of working capital, we see that the major change in the analysis involved the computation of cash flows in the first and final years of the project. The second case to be considered, the replacement decision, is special because it involves unusual complications of the cash flows not only in the first year but also in the years of the project's life.

Replacement Decisions

Many capital projects involve investing in assets of a type not previously used by the firm. Businesses also frequently face the problem of whether to invest in assets much like those already owned. The latter situation entails a **replacement decision**. Such decisions are made when economic or technological factors make it possible to perform tasks at lower cost. Faster and more efficient machines and labor-saving devices enable the firm to earn higher returns by replacing existing assets. Replacement decisions typically involve essential operations. The focus is on how to perform those operations.

The analysis of cash flows is more complex in replacement decisions than in decisions on whether to purchase new assets: annual cash flows are usually after-tax savings in cash expenses instead of increased revenues; there are tax differences if depreciation on the replacement is different from that on the existing asset; and the determination of the net cost to purchase the replacement can be complicated if the existing asset can be sold. We shall illustrate two methods for evaluating replacement decisions: the incremental approach and the "total project" approach.

Your firm now owns a machine for which it paid $100,000 five years ago. Plant engineers believe the machine has a remaining useful life of five years. The machine is being depreciated at $10,000 per year. Salvage value five years hence is expected to be $10,000, which is being ignored for depreciation purposes; hence, the $10,000, when received, will be taxed at the prevailing tax rate, which is expected to be 40%. The machine has cash operating costs before taxes of $30,000 per year. A new machine has come on the market that sells for $60,000, has a five-year life with no salvage value, and costs only $15,000 per year to operate. It would be depreciated over five years using straight-line depreciation. The existing machine could be sold now for only $20,000. The book value of the old machine is now $50,000 ($100,000 less five years' depreciation at $10,000 per year); sale at this time would produce a loss for tax purposes of $30,000 ($50,000 book value − $20,000 sale price). Cost of capital for this firm is 16%. As with any capital project, there are two considerations: initial investment and future cash flows. In a replacement decision, the computation of each of these is different from the computations we have made thus far. First we shall determine the initial investment. The calculation is on page 274.

The book value or cost of an existing asset is sunk and irrelevant to decisions. However, book value does affect taxes if the asset is sold and so must be considered in determining those taxes. A net outlay of $28,000 is required to buy the new asset. The sale of the old asset reduces the outlay for the new one by $32,000 because the firm will receive $20,000 from the sale of the old asset and save $12,000 in income taxes. Lest it appear that

	Tax Computation	Cash Outlay
Book value of old machine	$50,000	
Sale price, which is a cash inflow	20,000	($20,000)
Loss for taxes, which can be offset against regular income	$30,000	
Tax saved (40%)	$12,000	(12,000)
Total cash benefit from sale		(32,000)
Purchase price of new asset		60,000
Net outlay for new asset		$28,000

sales at a loss are always desirable because they reduce taxes, consider that if the old asset could be sold for $60,000, creating a taxable gain of $10,000 and additional taxes of $4,000, the sale would bring in $56,000, substantially more than the $32,000 shown above.

Below is the computation of future cash flows, using the incremental approach.

Annual Cash Savings Years 1–5

		Tax Computations	Cash Flows
Pre-tax cash savings:			
Cash cost of using old asset		$30,000	
Cash cost of using new asset		15,000	
Difference in favor of replacement	(1)	15,000	$15,000
Additional depreciation:			
Depreciation on old asset		10,000	
Depreciation on new asset ($60,000/5)		12,000	
Additional tax deduction for depreciation	(2)	(2,000)	
Total increase in taxable income (1) + (2) =	(3)	$13,000	
Additional tax ($13,000 × 40%)	(4)	$ 5,200	5,200
Additional cash flow (1) − (4)			$ 9,800

Salvage Values—End of Year 5

	Tax Computation	Cash Flows
Old asset	$10,000	
New asset		
Difference in favor of old asset	$10,000	($10,000)
Less: tax on difference	$ 4,000	4,000
Difference in favor of not replacing		($ 6,000)

The $9,800 per year for five years is then discounted at 16%, yielding a present value of $32,085 ($9,800 × 3.274). The $6,000 difference in cash flows from salvage values is discounted at 16%, yielding $2,856 ($6,000 × 0.476), which is subtracted from the present value of the $9,800 annual flows.

Summary of Present Values of Investment

Present value of savings from using new machine	$32,085
Less: present value of difference in salvage values	
(in favor of old machine)	(2,856)
Present value of future net savings	$29,229
Required investment	28,000
Net present value	$ 1,229

The present value of the future net savings ($29,229) is greater than the net outlay required ($28,000), and so the replacement is desirable. If the new asset had had some salvage value, the present value of future cash flows would have been greater and the investment would be even more desirable. If the salvage value of the new asset was expected to be even greater than that of the old, the difference in favor of the new asset would have been added to the $32,085.

A replacement decision can also be analyzed using a total project approach (instead of making comparisons of the incremental cash flows). In the total project approach we calculate individually the present value of the future outflows using the existing assets and the proposed asset. The decision depends on which alternative has the lower present value of future outflows (minimizes costs).

For the example just given, the present value of the future outflows if the existing machine is used is calculated as follows.

Decision—Operate Existing Machine

	Tax Computation	Cash Flow
Annual operating costs	$30,000	$30,000
Depreciation	10,000	
Total tax deductible expenses	40,000	
Tax savings expected (40%)	16,000	16,000
Net cash outflow expected per year		$14,000
Present value factor for 5 yrs. at 16%		3.274
Present value of future operating flows		$45,836
Less: present value of salvage value ($6,000 × .476)		2,856
Present value of future cash outflows on existing machine		$42,980

Consider, now, the present value of the future cash flows if the new machine is purchased.

Decision—Sell Existing Machine, Buy New Machine

	Tax Computation	Cash Flow
Annual operating costs	$15,000	$15,000
Depreciation	12,000	
Total tax-deductible expenses	27,000	
Tax savings expected (40%)	10,800	10,800
Net cash outflow expected per year		$ 4,200
Present value factor for 5 yrs. at 16%		3.274
Present value of future operating flows		$13,751
Net outlay required for the new machine		28,000
Total present value of buying new machine		$41,751

Comparing the two alternatives, we find:

Total present value of buying new machine	$41,751
Total present value of using existing machine, computed above	42,980
Difference (in favor of replacing)	($ 1,229)

The present value of the various outlays associated with using the existing machine is greater than that of the outlays associated with acquiring and using the new machine. Note that the $1,229 difference is equal to the net present value we computed using the incremental approach ($29,229 − $28,000 = $1,229). The two approaches should give the same results, and the choice between them is a matter of convenience.

In the replacement decision considered above, it was possible to continue use of a currently owned asset. However, the same two analytical approaches could be used if one of the firm's essential assets has reached the end of its useful life and alternatives exist as possible replacements. For example, suppose that a firm needs a new fork-lift truck because one of its existing trucks is about to be scrapped, Perhaps two different models are available as replacements, each with a different acquisition cost and associated annual operating costs. Because the firm has committed itself to replacing the old truck, the decision becomes one of how to minimize the future costs. Either the incremental or the total project approach could be used in the analysis.

Asset Disposal Decisions

Throughout this and the preceding chapter we dealt with decisions that required a current outlay of cash to achieve some favorable change in future cash flows. Often, a new machine was considered for its ability to reduce labor and labor-related costs. But the opposite situation could also exist: a firm might consider whether it would be better to use a currently operating machine, or dispose of it and utilize other means to accomplish the same end. In such a case, no current investment is required; indeed, a disinvestment is contemplated. Here the analysis is much the same as with acquisition decisions, but the point of view is shifted.

Consider a firm that owns a machine with a book value of $30,000 and a remaining useful life of only three years. Depreciation expense is $10,000 per year, no salvage value is expected. If the machine were sold, cash operating costs would increase by $5,000 per year. Suppose further that the firm has received an offer of $16,000 for the machine. The firm's tax rate is 40% and the cost of capital is 12%. What should the firm do?

Here, the firm must compare the savings derived from the machine's use with the opportunity cost of using it. Selling of the asset will result in an immediate $16,000 inflow *plus* the tax saving that could be obtained from the book loss, calculated as follows.

	Tax	Cash Flow
Selling price	$16,000	$16,000
Book value	30,000	
Loss for tax purposes	$14,000	
Tax saving at 40%	$ 5,600	5,600
Total inflow and present value of sale		$21,600

Thus, the inflow to be gained from disposing of the asset now is $21,600.

What does the firm gain from retaining this asset for the remainder of its useful life? The analysis below shows the cash flows associated with keeping the machine.

	Tax	Cash Flow
Annual cash savings	$ 5,000	$ 5,000
Less: depreciation	10,000	
Reduction in taxable income	$ 5,000	
Tax saving at 40%	$ 2,000	2,000
Net cash flow per year		7,000
Present value factor (3 year annuity @ 12%)		2.402
Present value of future flows		$16,814

The present value of the cash savings, because of the machine's use, coupled with the present value of the tax shield provided by depreciation, total only $16,814. This should be compared with the amount that could be gained from the disposal of the asset $21,600, whose present value is, of course, $21,600. Clearly, the asset should be disposed of now, despite the expected increases in cash operating costs.

In the analysis of this particular decision, the tax savings related to the available depreciation deductions could be considered either a cost of disposing of the asset now, or a savings resulting from the use of the asset. Either treatment of the depreciation is acceptable; the important thing is to consider the depreciation (and associated tax saving) only once.

You might wonder if a firm would be confronted with the type of decision described above. Why, for example, is the firm not contemplating replacing the soon-to-be scrapped machine? How could the sales value of the used machine exceed its future value to the firm? You should remember, first, that the usefulness of the machine to the firm depends on the market for the product in whose manufacture it is used. If the product for which the machine is used in this firm is not expected to be marketable after the end of the machine's life, the firm would have no desire to replace the machine. If such is the case, revenues derived from the sales of the product for the next few years would be the same whether or not the existing machine is used (remember that the machine simply saves cash operating costs), and hence, the revenue side of the picture is irrelevant. The attractive current sales value for this machine may derive from its potential for use in the production of an entirely different product which is not, for any number of reasons, included in the firm's marketing plans.

MUTUALLY EXCLUSIVE ALTERNATIVES

If we recognize the fact that the resources available (internally and externally) to any given firm are not limitless, we must admit that all of its investment opportunities are, in a sense, competing with each other for the firm's available resources. Investments which are wise under the decision rules given in Chapter 8 (have positive net present value or internal rates of return in excess of minimum acceptable rates) remain so regardless of the available funds. However, in some cases, the competition among alternative opportunities is more specific, as when the firm has two or more ways of accomplishing a given goal, the selection of any one of which precludes the selection of the others. When this particular situation exists, we call the competing proposals **mutually exclusive alternatives.**

Some of the decisions already considered would fit this definition—the replacement decision, for example. If the firm keeps its present equipment it does not buy the newer model or models, or vice versa. Mutual exclusivity can also arise as a matter of policy. For example, a firm may have a policy of introducing no more than one new product in a particular year.

Whether the exclusivity is inherent in the proposals or the result of management policy, it is not unusual when the competing alternatives have unequal lives. It has also been suggested that still another evaluation technique, the profitability index, can be particularly useful in ranking and deciding among alternatives. These two special topics are discussed in the next sections.

Unequal Lives

In cases where alternative investment opportunities have different useful lives, the standard analytical techniques can be used, but the analysis must go further. We shall illustrate one of the several ways to deal with this special problem.

Assume the following facts about two mutually exclusive investment opportunities, different versions of a machine that is required for a particular job essential to the firm's operation.

	Model G-40	Model G-70
Purchase price	$40,000	$70,000
Annual cash operating costs	8,000	6,000
Expected useful life	4 years	8 years

Neither machine has any expected salvage value at the end of its useful life. The firm's cost of capital is 14% and its tax rate is 40%. It plans to use straight-line depreciation for tax purposes on either machine.

What we want to do is make the two projects comparable; the method we shall illustrate, in effect, equalizes the useful lives of the two opportunities by assuming that we replace the one with a shorter life at the end of its useful life. In this case, we can equate the useful lives by assuming the purchase of one G-40 now and another one at the end of the four years. Forecasting the purchase of a machine in the future, we must also forecast the expected future cost of that machine. Let us assume that a G-40 will cost $44,000 at the end of the four years, but would have the same operating costs and useful life as the one to be bought today.

The calculation of the present value of the future flows associated with acquiring the longer-lived model is shown below.

G-70

	Tax Computation	Cash Flow	Present Value
Annual operating costs	$ 6,000	$ 6,000	
Depreciation ($70,000/8 years)	8,750		
Total tax deductible expenses	14,750		
Tax savings at 40%	5,900	5,900	
Net cash operating outflows		$ 100	
Present value factor for 8-year annuity at 14%		4.639	
Present value of future operating flows			$ 463
Purchase price			70,000
Total present value of future outflows			$70,463

The calculation of the present value of the future flows associated with the shorter-lived model is somewhat more complicated because the cash flows in the first four years of the time period are not the same as those in the last four years. This is true because of the higher cost of the replacement model and the resulting difference in the tax shield from depreciation. The situation is not unrealistic, however, and the cash flows would be computed as shown on page 280.

The flows associated with years five through eight are, as you can see, discounted separately; that is, the flow for each year is discounted to its present value by using the present value factor from Table A. There are some shortcut methods available that your instructor may wish to illustrate.

Notice in the analysis that the present value of the replacement G-40 is substantially less than its actual cost. This is to be expected because replacement will not be needed for four years.

Comparing the present values of the future outflows for each alternative, it would appear that the least expensive alternative is to buy two G-40s, one now and one at the end of the four years. However, the two present values are not significantly different ($69,069 versus $70,463), and the firm will wish to consider other factors. For example, how confident is the firm in its forecast of the replacement cost of the G-40 in four years? What is the likelihood of a significant change in technology? These and other factors will influence the final decision.

G-40

	Tax Computation	Cash Flow	Present Value
Annual operating costs, years 1–4	$ 8,000	$ 8,000	
Depreciation, years 1–4 ($40,000/4)	10,000		
Total tax deductible expenses	18,000		
Tax savings at 40%	7,200	7,200	
Net cash operating outflows per year, years 1–4		$ 800	
Present value factor, 4-year annuity at 14%		2.914	
Present value of operating outflows, years 1–4			$ 2,331
Present value of replacement at end of year 4 ($44,000 × .592 single payment factor, 4 years)			26,048
Operating flows, years 5–8			
Annual operating costs	$ 8,000	$ 8,000	
Depreciation ($44,000/4 years)	11,000		
Total tax deductible expenses	19,000		
Tax savings at 40%	7,600	7,600	
Net operating cash outflows per year, years 5–8		$ 400	
Present values of operating flows, years 5–8:			
Year 5 $400 × .519			$ 208
Year 6 $400 × .456			182
Year 7 $400 × .400			160
Year 8 $400 × .351			140
Purchase price of G-40 at present time			40,000
Total present value of future outflows			$69,069

Ranking Investment Opportunities

In Chapter 8, the two discounted cash flow techniques (net present value and internal rate of return methods) were said to be conceptually superior to other methods discussed. It is possible, however, that if two or more proposals are *ranked* using each of the two methods, the rankings will not be the same. That is, the proposals that rank first and second using the net present value method might rank second and first using the internal rate of return method. If the proposals are mutually exclusive, there is now a conflict; using net present value as the criterion, we would pick the one with the higher present value; using internal rate of return as the criterion, we would pick the one with the higher rate of return.

   To deal with such a situation, some accountants have expressed a preference for a third criterion, the profitability index, to evaluate mutually exclusive alternatives. The **profitability index** (sometimes called the **benefit-cost ratio**) is the ratio of the present value of the future cash flows to the investment required. Thus, an investment with present value of future cash flows of $118,000 and a required investment of $100,000 would have a profitability index of 1.18.

$$\text{Profitability index} = \frac{\text{present value of future flows}}{\text{investment required}} = \frac{\$118,000}{\$100,000} = 1.18$$

This third approach is also sound because its use of present values gives explicit recognition to the problem of the timing of the cash flows. However, the net present value approach is to be preferred over either the profitability index or the internal rate-of-return approaches except under special circumstances. Let us see how the three criteria would perform in an example. Below are data for two mutually exclusive investment opportunities confronting a firm that has a cost of capital of 10%.

	Investment Opportunities	
	X	Y
Investment required	$50,000	$10,000
Life of investment	1 year	1 year
Cash flows, end of year 1	55,991	11,403
Present value of cash flows at 10% cost of capital (.909 × cash flow)	50,896	10,365
Net present value of project	$ 896	$ 365
Internal rate of return:		
Interest rate associated with factor .893 ($50,000/$55,991)	12%	
Interest rate associated with factor .877 ($10,000/$11,403)		14%
Profitability index:		
$50,896/$50,000	1.018	
$10,365/$10,000		1.037

Project Y has both a higher internal rate of return and a higher profitability index number than does Project X, which is higher using only the net present value criterion. *Provided that the 10% cost of capital is the rate at which alternative investments could be made,* Project X should be selected. The simplest way to show this is as follows.

Consider that Project Y is accepted (outlay of $10,000), and that another, hypothetical project is available for the investment of the additional $40,000 that would have been required for Project X. This second project will be accepted because its return is 10%, which is not less than the cost of capital. What cash would the firm have at the end of the year? The firm's cash position is summarized below.

Cash provided by investment in Project Y		$11,403
Cash provided by investment in second project:		
Investment returned	$40,000	
Earnings on the investment (10%)	4,000	44,000
Total cash available to firm at end of year		$55,403

Note, however, that had the firm invested the entire $50,000 in Project X, it would have had $55,991 at the end of the year. This is more than can be obtained by accepting Project Y and using the excess investment funds for another project.

The only time that the project with the higher profitability index or higher internal rate of return should be chosen in preference to the one with the higher net present value is when investing in the former will enable the firm to invest additional cash at a rate *greater* than the cost of capital *and* that opportunity is not available if the firm chooses the higher net present value project. Thus, in our example situation, we would choose Project Y only if there were additional available investments with returns in excess of 10%, which investments would have to be foregone if the extra $40,000 were invested in Project X. In selecting its evaluation criterion, each firm will have to consider its particular circumstances.

CHANGES IN VARIABLES

In each analysis of an investment opportunity we have tried to determine whether the project could be expected to earn an acceptable rate. In each case, the determination required estimates of useful life and expected cash flows for the project, and these estimates were critical to the decisions. It is sometimes valuable to approach the evaluation of a project from a different direction, determining instead what cash flows or useful life the project must have in order to produce the desired rate of return.

Suppose that a project is expected to generate net cash flows after taxes of $3,000 per year, but the life of the flows is questionable. The investment required is $12,000 and the cost of capital is 12%. The life is expected to be 10 years, but the manager is concerned that it might be shorter. How long must the useful life be to make the investment desirable? The payback period is four years ($12,000/$3,000), so the present value factor is four. What is the number of years for which four is closest to the present value factor of an annuity at 12%? Referring to Table B (page 646), under the 12% column you find 3.605 for five years and 4.111 for six years. Thus the useful life must be nearly six years to make the investment desirable. The manager can then compare this required useful life with his expectations and reservations to decide whether to go ahead.

Now consider that although the manager is confident of his estimate of the project's useful life, he is uncertain about the estimate of cash flows. What cash flow is required to make it advisable to invest $12,000 if cost of capital is 12%? Here we are trying to find the cash flow to be multiplied by a known present value factor—the factor for 10 years and 12%, which is 5.65. Dividing $12,000 by 5.65, we obtain $2,124 (rounded). This amount is the lowest annual cash flow that will yield a 12% return on a $12,000 investment if the flows last for 10 years. The manager can now see how far cash flows could fall before the investment becomes undesirable. With the original estimate of cash flow of $3,000, the project is clearly desirable; but if the flows were to fall by $876 annually, it would be a borderline case.

Such an analysis that tests decisions to observe to what extent they are affected by changes in one or more relevant factors is called **sensitivity analysis**. In this case, the investment is not too sensitive to changes in either useful life or cash flow; the life estimate would have to be in error by four years or the cash flow in error by about 30%. In some other cases, sensitivity analysis may lead managers to reject a project that would be profitable only if the estimates are very close to being accurate. In illustrating this point, we shall also show how to make the computations when income taxes are considered.

Assume that a firm with a cost of capital of 14% and in the 40% tax bracket can bring out a new product to sell at $22. Variable costs are $4, fixed costs requiring cash outlays are $100,000 annually, and the estimated annual volume is 10,000 units. The investment required is $200,000, all for depreciable assets with a five-year life and no salvage value. For simplicity, we use straight-line depreciation.

The present value of the cash flows from this project are computed below.

		Tax	Cash
Expected contribution margin (10,000 × $18)		$180,000	$180,000
Fixed costs:			
Cash	$100,000		(100,000)
Depreciation	40,000		
		140,000	
Taxable income		$ 40,000	
Tax, at 40%		16,000	(16,000)
Income after taxes		24,000	
Add back depreciation		40,000	
Cash flow per year		$ 64,000	64,000
Present value factor, 5-year annuity at 14%			3.433
Present value of cash flows			$219,712
Investment required			200,000
Net present value			$ 19,712

Based on the available estimates, the project has a positive net present value and should be accepted. But how far can volume fall before the investment becomes only marginally desirable?

First, for the project to achieve a present value equal to the investment, the required after-tax cash flow would have to be $58,258 ($200,000/3.433). Because depreciation can be added back to net income to get cash flow, we can, instead, subtract depreciation from the *required* cash flow to obtain required after-tax income. We then divide the after-tax income by (1 − tax rate) to get the required pre-tax income, just as we did in Chapter 3. From then on, ordinary volume-cost-profit analysis is used to determine the required volume. The full computation is shown below.

Required after tax cash flow	$ 58,258
Less: depreciation	40,000
Equals: required after-tax income	18,258
Divided by 60%, which is (1 − 40% tax rate) gives required profit	
before taxes	30,430
Add fixed costs including depreciation	140,000
Required contribution margin	$170,430
Divided by $18 contribution margin per unit gives required	
sales volume of	9,468 units

In this calculation we have essentially prepared a cash flow schedule and tax computation schedule from the bottom up, a technique used in very early chapters. Please notice that 9,468 units is only 532 units less than the estimated volume, or 5.32% below the estimate. The margin of safety here is not very large and a relatively small decline in volume would render the investment undesirable even though it had a fairly high net present value when the 10,000 units estimate was used.

Sensitivity analysis thus gives management an idea of the extent to which unfavorable occurrences like lower volumes, shorter useful lives, or higher costs are likely to affect the profitability of a project. It is used because of the uncertainty that prevails in almost any real-life situation. Additionally, there are other ways to deal with uncertainty, some of which will be introduced in Chapter 15.

INCOME TAXES—SPECIAL CONSIDERATIONS

Some special features of the income tax laws can significantly affect the firm in its decision making and must be recognized when preparing analyses to assist decision makers. Through all previous chapters, the income taxes paid by the firm were treated very generally. A tax was said to exist, and a flat tax rate was assumed to apply to all the firm's revenues and expenses. It was also assumed that the firm's taxes were affected only by revenues and expenses. Neither of these assumptions is strictly in accord with reality.

The first assumption, a flat tax rate on all revenues and expenses, is not valid because of the existence of progressive tax rates and of special rates for the taxing of so-called capital gains. The second assumption becomes invalid when the government provides for the carryover of the operating losses from one entity (and year) to another, and allows a reduction in taxes to entities that acquire certain types of assets. These special features of the income tax law are the subject of the next several sections.

Graduated (Progressive) Tax Rates

In recent years the tax rates for corporations have been 22% on the first $25,000 in taxable income, 48% on all income *over* $25,000. For corporations that expect to earn more than $25,000 without considering new investments, the 48% rate is applicable to all of the income expected from an investment. But if the firm expects income to be less than $25,000, the tax computation on a new investment would be changed. For the amount of additional taxable income needed to bring the total taxable income up to $25,000, the firm should use the 22% rate. Any income over $25,000 should be reduced by the 48% rate. (We have used a 40% rate most of the time because it makes the calculations easier than would a 48% rate.)

The problems of dealing with progressive income tax rates are most important for unincorporated businesses (partnerships and sole proprietorships) because the profits of such firms are taxed using the rates applicable to the individuals. If a person owns a business, his tax rate could vary from 14% to 50%, or even higher.

For example, according to the tax rate schedule in a recent year for a single taxpayer, the tax on a taxable income of $26,000 would be $7,590. The tax on the next $6,000 of income (that is, income over $26,000 and up to $32,000) would be computed at 45%. The 45% is called the **incremental tax rate**. For the *next* $6,000 of income (over $32,000 and up to $38,000), the incremental tax rate would be 50%. The taxes associated with these three levels of income are summarized below.

Taxable Income	Total Tax	Computational Notes
$26,000	$ 7,590	
$32,000	10,290	$7,590 + 45% of the $6,000 excess over $26,000
$38,000	13,290	$10,290 + 50% of the $6,000 excess over $32,000

Notice that the *average* tax rate (total tax/taxable income) is lower than the incremental tax rate. Thus, the average tax rate on income of $26,000 is about 29% ($7,590/ $26,000), on income of $32,000 is about 32%, and on income of $38,000 is about 35%. This occurs because the rates are lower for the various income increments prior to $26,000, beginning at 14% for the first $500 in taxable income.

Because income taxes are an element of a firm's cash flow and incremental cash flows are critical to capital budgeting, it is important that the progressive tax rates be recognized in the development of those cash flows. Suppose that a person owning an unincorporated business has a chance to invest $80,000 to receive cash flows, before taxes, of $25,000 per year. Before the analysis can proceed, we must know what the person expects to earn this year *without* this particular investment. Let us say that he expects to have a taxable income of $26,000, and that the investment, all in depreciable assets, will have a useful life of five years. What will the incremental cash flows from this investment be if the tax rates are as given above?

		Tax	Cash
Cash flow before taxes		$25,000	$25,000
Depreciation ($80,000/5)		16,000	
Increase in taxable income		9,000	
Increase in income taxes:			
Tax on first $6,000 at 45%	$2,700		
Tax on next $3,000 at 50%	1,500		
Total increase in taxes		4,200	4,200
Net cash flow per year			$20,800

Once the incremental cash flow has been computed, the remainder of the analysis for this decision can be completed in the normal manner.

Capital Gains

A **capital gain** is the profit made on selling an asset that is not normally held for resale; that is, assets other than inventory. To qualify for the capital gains tax rate, which for corporations has been 30% in recent years, the asset must be owned for at least one year. The sale of an asset (and hence the related cash effect on taxes) may be relevant to capital budgeting proposals in at least two places. First, the cash flow expected from the sale of an existing asset affects the calculation of the investment required in the new asset. Second, the sale of the proposed asset at the end of its useful life will be included in the determination of future cash flows.

We shall provide here only some general rules regarding application of the capital gains tax. They would not automatically apply to the sale of any particular asset. The rules for determing how much of a gain qualifies for the special capital gains tax rate and how much of the gain will be taxed at the regular income rates are very complex.

If the asset being sold at a gain is land or some other nondepreciable asset, the entire gain is likely to qualify for the capital gains rate. If the asset is a building, and straight-line depreciation has been used, the entire gain is also likely to qualify for the capital gains tax rate. However, if the asset has been depreciated using an accelerated method, the difference between the actual depreciation taken and the amount that would have been taken using straight-line depreciation is subject to the ordinary income tax rate.

For example, if a building with a book value of $20,000 using sum-of-the-years'-digits method depreciation is sold for $30,000, the gain ($30,000 − $20,000 = $10,000) would be taxed partially at the capital gain rate and partially at the ordinary tax rate. To compute the tax effect of the gain, we need to know what the book value of the building would have been if straight-line depreciation had been used. Let us assume that the book value would have been $26,000. The tax computation would proceed as follows:

Selling price	$30,000	
Book value using straight-line depreciation	26,000	
Gain taxed at capital gain rate		$ 4,000
Book value using straight-line depreciation	26,000	
Book value using accelerated depreciation	20,000	
Gain taxed at ordinary income tax rate		6,000
Total gain		$10,000

The appropriate tax rates for this particular enterprise can be determined and applied to these two segments of the total recorded gain. The final cash flow attributable to the sale of this asset will be the $30,000 selling price less whatever the total tax is that has been computed using the two rates.

Finally, for machinery and equipment, the only part of a gain subject to the capital gains rate is the excess of the selling price over the original cost of the asset. That is, in order to get the special capital gains treatment for a gain from selling a machine, it would have to be sold for more than was paid for it. Any gain that does not meet this test is taxed at ordinary tax rates.

Once again, the rules in the tax laws relating to capital gains are very complex. In a practical situation, the firm's internal or external tax counselor should be consulted about the applicability of the capital gains tax.

Operating Loss Carryovers

The tax law provides that, within limits, a corporation experiencing a loss in one year may offset such losses against profits earned in other years, so that the tax paid on those profits will not be what would otherwise be expected. This offsetting opportunity is called the

operating loss carryover. The law also provides that, under certain circumstances, the operating loss carryover of one entity can be used to offset the profits earned by another entity that purchased the first. This provision of the law is what prompts people to say that a firm was purchased because it had a "tax loss."

The law allows a firm to "carryback" or "carryforward" an operating loss, applying the loss to years in which the firm has earned profits. The limits are specific: the loss can be carried back for three years and forward five years. An example will make this clear. Suppose that BN Company has the following history of taxable incomes and taxes.

Year	Taxable Income	Tax at 40% Rate
1	$20,000	$ 8,000
2	40,000	16,000
3	50,000	20,000
4	(150,000)	?

The loss of $150,000 in year four is "carried back" for the previous three years. This means that the firm can get a refund from the government of all of the taxes paid in the three previous years because the loss in year four was greater than the taxable incomes earned in the previous three years. Moreover, even after carrying back the loss the firm still shows a $40,000 loss for the entire four-year period ($20,000 + $40,000 + $50,000 = $110,000, which is $40,000 less than the year four loss). This $40,000 loss can be carried forward for five years. This means that until the firm earns a total of $40,000 in the next five years, it pays no tax. After the firm earns $40,000, the loss carryforward is exhausted and the firm pays taxes at the rates in effect at the time.

The existence of the loss carryover provision must be considered in the firm's capital budgeting and other decisions. In effect, the tax rates applicable to different years may be different, and the analysis used in the example of progressive tax rates would be appropriate.

Suppose now that BN Company is expected to earn no taxable income in the future, and to provide no cash flows. Is the firm worthless? Not entirely; its loss carryforward might be an attractive investment for another firm that anticipates having taxable income. If the Jones Company expects to earn more than $40,000 in taxable income and has a cost of capital of 14% and a tax rate of 40%, a purchase of BN Company may be in order. At a tax rate of 40%, the Jones Company could save $16,000 in taxes ($40,000 × 40%) if it could use the BN operating loss to offset its own operating profits. We could even compute the maximum that Jones Company might be willing to pay to acquire BN. To gain the cash tax saving of $16,000 one year hence, Jones might be willing to pay up to $14,032 ($16,000 × .877, factor for 14% for one year), the present value of the saving.

Here again, we have provided only the general rules relating to a special feature of the income tax laws. Applicability of the rules in a particular situation depends on the specific circumstances. The carryover of losses by the same firm is not severely restricted, but the transfer of losses through acquisition is subject to several constraints.

Investment Tax Credit

At various times since 1962, Congress has provided businesses with an opportunity to reduce their taxes as a result of decisions to acquire certain types of assets. This tax benefit is called the **investment tax credit.** The types of qualifying investments and the size of the credit have varied, but the mechanics of the credit have remained essentially unchanged. If a firm acquires, in 19X6, an asset that qualifies for a credit, the firm may deduct, directly from its tax payment for that year, an amount equal to some specified percentage of the acquisition cost of that asset. At this writing, the credit is 10% for assets with useful lives of at least seven years, somewhat less for shorter-lived assets.

Suppose that a firm purchased a qualifying asset for $100,000. On its tax return for that year, after making all the appropriate normal computations to arrive at taxable income and related income taxes, the firm could reduce its tax payment by $10,000 (10% of the cost of the asset). There are, of course, limits on the total amount of the credit for any one year, and provisions for dealing with credits in excess of those limits. But the general implication of the credit is clear; the acquisition of an asset can affect the firm's cash flow for income taxes in a way other than through the tax shield of depreciation. Hence, the availability of the tax credit must be incorporated in the analysis developed to evaluate the investment opportunity.

For analysis purposes, the expected credit is subtracted from the acquisition cost of the new asset. The credit is considered as part of the required investment.

Because the availability of the investment credit could, in effect, promise a return of 10% of the cost of a project within one year, qualification for the credit should be determined for each investment opportunity, and the appropriate credit incorporated in each analysis.

SOCIAL CONSEQUENCES OF DECISION MAKING

Throughout this book, and particularly in this and the two preceding chapters, we have, for the most part, assumed that the consequences of an action were limited to the entity taking that action. Such an assumption is not always warranted. The action of a single entity may have many effects, desirable or detrimental, for other entities or persons not associated with the deciding entity.

For example, a firm might find that the use of a particular machine that saves labor time is justified on economic grounds. But the decision to use the machinery may put people out of work. The workers who lose their jobs will suffer if they cannot find other jobs within fairly short periods of time. If they do not find work, they will receive unemployment compensation or some other type of payment that is borne by the taxpayers of the state. If they move away from the area to find work, they must incur moving costs; and there may be problems in uprooting their families. The reduced payroll of the plant may adversely affect the community because of declines in economic activity like retail sales. Other jobs may be lost as a result of the factory's layoffs. Although some of these implications have been specifically referred to in previous discussions of "qualitative considerations" of decision making, they were not specifically incorporated into the analyses.

Costs that are not borne directly by the entity making a decision and taking an action are called **social costs** or externalities. **Social benefits** (also called externalities) are benefits not accruing directly to the entity making a decision. A firm that decides to hire additional workers who are currently unemployed (as opposed to hiring them away from other firms) will provide benefits to the workers in the form of income and increased self-esteem, to the community in the form of increased economic activity and higher taxes to the government, and to the taxpayers in the form of reduced expenditures for unemployment compensation.

The firm will not benefit directly from these other benefits, even though its action caused them. Although it may not be possible for business managers to give direct and monetary recognition to externalities, it should be possible to at least try to recognize their existence as individual decisions are studied.

The question of social benefits and costs is critical in decisions made by governmental units like municipalities, states, and the federal government. Decision making for these and for other not-for-profit entities should be based on estimates of discounted benefits and costs, just like those of business firms. The major differences between the techniques used by business firms and governmental units are of several types. One difference is that governmental units do not pay income taxes, which makes their decision making somewhat simpler than that of business firms. But other factors in the governmental decision-making process make decisions much more difficult.

These special factors fall into three general categories: (1) measurement problems; (2) problems in determining whether a particular effect is a benefit or a cost; and (3) problems in the distribution of benefits and costs.

Measurement problems arise in the decisions of governmental units because, as we mentioned in Chapter 4, the benefits and costs are not just monetary. If an unemployed person obtains a job, there are monetary benefits in the form of the person's increased income. The government will benefit from additional taxes paid by the employed worker. But other benefits like increased self-esteem of the worker are not readily measurable, nor expressible in dollar terms. Cleaner air is economically beneficial to the people because of fewer deaths from respiratory ailments, less sickness, and reduced cleaning bills for clothing and buildings. But the monetary value of the increased pleasantness that would accompany cleaner air is not readily measurable.

The second factor, determining whether an effect is beneficial or costly, may well depend on one's point of view. The government has sanctioned actions that have reduced the populations of wolves and coyotes in sheep and cattle-raising states. These programs have been favorably received by ranchers, deplored by conservationists. Programs that result in growth in population of a particular area may also receive mixed reviews. Some states and towns have actively sought industrial development, while others have discouraged it.

The problem of the distribution of benefits and costs has been a difficult social question since the beginning of government. A city or town might be considering the construction of a municipal golf course. Analyses may show that the fees received will be insufficient to earn the minimum desired rate of return, which would mean that the taxpayers would be subsidizing those who use the golf course. The town government might still decide to build the golf course because it feels that the people who would use it deserve some recreation even if the general taxpayers must pay some of the costs. Similar reasoning could apply to municipally owned bus services, zoos, libraries, and parks.

The criterion that is most generally advocated for decision making by governmental units is the maximizing of "social welfare." Because of the many problems in identifying and quantifying social benefits and costs, the application of this decision rule has generally meant the maximizing of economic benefits—those subject to monetary estimates. To the extent that this can be done, the same general analytical approaches proposed for business decision making can be used in the public sector. And, like the business manager, the decision maker in the public sector must make an effort to at least identify and consider the unquantified but relevant factors before reaching a final decision.

SUMMARY

A proper analysis of investment requirements and future cash flows is critical if the manager is to make good decisions about investing available funds. Required investment should include consideration of any required increases in the firm's working capital. Where the decision involves disposal of already-owned assets (replacement decisions or simple disposals), the analysis may be particularly complex.

Mutually exclusive investment alternatives may bring certain analytical problems. A third discounted cash flow technique, the profitability index, has been suggested to assist in decision making. This technique can be useful, but the firm's special circumstances in terms of available funds and investment opportunities should be considered before selecting a single capital budgeting technique for general use.

Whatever technique is used, many firms have found it helpful to perform sensitivity analysis in connection with investment opportunities. The use of sensitivity analysis is prompted partially by the number of estimates involved in a typical capital budgeting situation.

Computation of the cash flows for any investment opportunity requires current knowledge of many special features of the income tax laws, including the investment credit, capital gains taxes, and progressive tax rates. These factors influence both the amounts and timing of cash flows and hence the present values of those flows.

Qualitative issues are associated with almost every investment opportunity. This is true in both the private and the public sectors. Decision makers in both sectors should make every effort to identify and quantify as many factors as possible, and give full consideration to those factors that remain unquantified.

KEY TERMS

benefit-cost ratio
capital gain
incremental tax rate
investment tax credit
mutually exclusive alternatives
operating loss carryover
profitability index

progressive tax rate
replacement decision
sensitivity analysis
social benefit
social cost
total project approach
working capital investment

KEY FORMULA

$$\text{Profitability index} = \frac{\text{present value of future flows}}{\text{required investment}}$$

REVIEW PROBLEM—Replacement Decision

The Eamon Company owns a machine with the following characteristics.

Book value	$55,000
Current market value	40,000
Expected salvage value at end of 5-year remaining useful life	0
Annual depreciation expense, straight-line method	11,000
Annual cash operating costs	18,000

The firm's cost of capital is 14% and the tax rate is 40%.

Required

1. The firm is considering selling the machine. If it does so, total cash operating costs to perform the work now done by the machine will increase by $16,000 per year, to a total of $34,000. Determine whether the machine should be sold.
2. Suppose now that the firm is considering replacing the machine with one that has the following characteristics.

Purchase price	$80,000
Useful life	5 years
Expected salvage value	$5,000
Annual cash operating costs	$3,000

Straight-line depreciation at $15,000 per year would be taken on the new machine. Additionally, because the new machine is more efficient, the firm could reduce its investment in working capital by $15,000. Determine whether the new machine should be bought.

Answers to review problem

1. The machine should not be sold.

Present Value of Sale

	Tax	Cash Flow
Selling price	$40,000	$40,000
Book value	55,000	
Loss for tax purposes	15,000	
Tax saving at 40%	6,000	6,000
Total inflow and present value		$46,000

Present Value of Keeping Machine

	Tax	Cash Flow
Annual cash operating costs saved ($34,000 − $18,000)	$16,000	$16,000
Less depreciation expense	11,000	
Increase in taxable income	5,000	
Increased tax at 40%	2,000	2,000
Net annual cash flows		14,000
Present value factor for 5-year annuity at 14%		3.433
Present value of keeping machine		$48,062
Present value of sale		46,000
Difference favoring keeping machine		$ 2,062

Please notice that here, unlike the example on page 277, the firm has greater taxable income if it keeps the machine than if it sells it. This is because tax deductible expenses are higher if the machine is sold, $34,000 to $29,000. (The $29,000 is $18,000 operating costs plus $11,000 depreciation.)

2. The new machine should be bought and the existing one sold. The incremental investment of $19,000 is less than the present value of the future cash flows of $31,200.

Investment Required

	Tax	Cash Flow (Inflow)
Selling price of existing machine	$40,000	($40,000)
Book value	55,000	
Loss for tax purposes	15,000	
Tax saving at 40%		(6,000)
Reduction of working capital requirements		(15,000)
Net inflows		(61,000)
Less: purchase price of new machine		80,000
Net required investment		$19,000

Notice that the reduction in working capital requirements is treated as a reduction of the required investment. At the *end* of the five years we would have an increase in working capital. The example in the text showed additional working capital requirements at the beginning and recovery at the end. This reverses the example.

We shall calculate the annual cash flows and present values using both the total project and incremental approaches.

Incremental Approach—Annual Cash Flows

	Tax	Cash Flow
Savings in cash operating costs ($18,000 − $3,000)	$15,000	$15,000
Additional depreciation ($15,000 − $11,000)	4,000	
Increase in taxable income	11,000	
Increased tax at 40%	4,400	4,400
Net annual cash flow		$10,600
Present value factor for 5-year annuity at 14%		3.433
Present value of annual cash flows		36,390
Add, present value of recovery of salvage value [$5,000 × .519 (factor from Table A)]		2,595
Subtotal		$38,985
Less: increase in working capital at end of 5 years ($15,000 × .519)		(7,785)
Present value of future cash flows		$31,200
Required investment		19,000
Net present value		$12,200

Because depreciation expense taken over the five years is $75,000 (5 years × $15,000), the new asset would have a book value of $5,000 at the end of its life, which is equal to its expected salvage value. There is no tax effect because there is no expected gain or loss.

Total Project Approach

Keep Existing Machine

	Tax	Cash Flow
Cash operating costs	$18,000	$18,000
Depreciation	11,000	
Total expenses	29,000	
Tax savings at 40%	11,600	11,600
Net cash outflow		6,400
Present value factor for 5-year annuity at 14%		3.433
Present value of annual operating flows		$21,971

Buy New Machine

	Tax	Cash Flow
Cash operating costs	$ 3,000	$ 3,000
Depreciation	15,000	
Total expense	18,000	
Tax saving at 40%	7,200	7,200
Net cash *inflow*		4,200
Present value factor for 5-year annuity at 14%		3.433
Present value of annual inflows		14,419
Add: present value of salvage value (above)		2,595
Subtotal		$17,014
Less: present value of increase in working capital at end of 5 years (computed above)		7,785
Net present value of future inflows		$ 9,229

The existing machine has a present value of *outflows* of $21,971, while the new machine has a present value of *inflows* of $9,229. The advantage to replacing is $31,200 ($9,229 + $21,971), which is what we calculated earlier as the present value of replacing using the incremental approach. The net present value is again $12,200.

Present value of inflows—replace	$ 9,229
Present value of outflows—keep existing machine	21,971
Total present value	31,200
Required investment	19,000
Net present value of replacing	$12,200

We should mention a point about the fact that using the new machine would result in net annual cash inflows rather than outflows. This happens because depreciation is so high that the tax saving is greater than the annual cash operating costs. You should not conclude that if a replacement asset would yield a positive cash flow it is automatically a wise investment. In the example used here, if we changed the working capital investment from a negative $15,000 to a positive $15,000 the replacement would not be wise.

REVIEW PROBLEM—Determining Required Volume

The Chapman Products Company is considering a new product. It would sell for $10 and variable costs would be $6. New equipment costing $150,000 and having a five-year useful life and no salvage value would be needed, and would be depreciated using the straight-line method. The machine would have cash operating costs of $20,000 per year. The firm is in the 40% tax bracket and has cost of capital of 12%.

Required: Determine how many units per year the firm would have to sell in order that the investment earn 12%. Round calculations of required after-tax cash flow and required pre-tax profits to the nearest $100.

Answer to review problem

Annual sales would have to be about 17,325 units. The first step is to calculate the after-tax cash flow per year that would be required to meet the firm's minimum rate of return of 12%. The required flow is $41,600 ($150,000 investment/3.605, the factor for an annuity of five years at 12%). From this amount we proceed to total required contribution margin and the required volume, as follows:

Required after-tax cash flow per year	$41,600 (rounded)
Less, yearly depreciation ($150,000/5) which would reduce income but did not affect cash flow	30,000
After-tax profit required	11,600
Divided by 1 − 40% tax rate	.60
Pre-tax profit required	$19,300 (rounded)
Fixed costs ($20,000 + $30,000)	50,000
Contribution margin required	$69,300
Contribution margin per unit ($10 − $6)	$4
Number of units of sales necessary to obtain required contribution margin ($69,300/$4)	17,325

ASSIGNMENT MATERIAL

Questions for Discussion

9-1 Stock prices and interest rates   The prices of stocks traded on various exchanges will sometimes move rapidly in a direction opposite that of the changes in interest rates. Why does this happen?

9-2 Returns and income   If all the forecasts for a specific capital project turn out as estimated, will the reported annual net income for the project be equal to the returns used in the analysis of the project?

9-3 Factors in capital budgeting   The government frequently takes action that alters the economic climate. For each of the events listed below, indicate whether firms would be more inclined, less inclined, or the same regarding their capital spending plans. Comment on what particular kinds of firms would be affected and how. Consider each independently.

1. Assets that are now depreciated over ten years for income tax purposes can be depreciated over five years if the assets are used to produce energy.
2. Gasoline engines are outlawed for automobiles; electric cars only are approved for production.
3. For some years the price of cotton has been kept artificially high by government price supports. These supports are to be removed.
4. A high tariff on foreign automobiles is removed.
5. Corporate income taxes are raised from 52% to 56%.
6. All nations of the world sign a treaty to outlaw war, and they mean it.
7. Persons with low incomes are given cash grants for attending college.

9-4 Capital budgeting—effects of events   A particular capital expenditure proposal for a new machine has been analyzed, based on currently available information. In what way(s) would each of the following events (not anticipated at the time the analysis was done) affect the analysis? Consider each event independently.

1. The interest rate on long-term debt increases.
2. The company signs a new contract with its union. The contract includes a negotiated wage rate for all categories of workers that is higher than the prevailing rate.
3. The company raises the selling prices for its products.
4. A proposal to increase taxes on real property (land and buildings) is approved by the voters of the city in which the firm has its manufacturing plant.
5. Congress passes a law that provides for a credit against corporate income taxes; the credit is to be computed as a specified percentage of the cash invested in new long-lived assets.
6. Congress approves the use of a depreciation rate that provides much faster recognition of depreciation expense than was heretofore available.
7. The *Wall Street Journal* carries a report of a new product that is likely to be a good substitute for the product made by the machine being considered.

Exercises

9-5 Comparison of alternatives   The Stanley Company must make a choice between two machines that will perform an essential function. Machine A costs $40,000, has a 10-year life, no salvage value, and costs $12,000 per year to operate (cash costs). Machine B costs $80,000, has a 10-year life with $10,000 salvage value, and costs $3,000 per year to operate. The tax rate is 40% and cost of capital is 10%. Straight-line depreciation will be used for either machine.

Required
Which machine should be bought? Explain.

9-6 Retirement options   Mr. Ralph Mathews will retire in a few months, on reaching his 65th birthday. His firm provides a pension plan that offers two options: (1) a lump-sum payment of $120,000 on the day of retirement; and (2) annual payments of $15,000 per year beginning on the date of retirement and ending at death. Mr. Mathews is not sure which option he should select and asks for your assistance. He tells you that he has no savings now, that he could earn a 14% return if he invested part of the lump-sum payment, and that he would like to spend $20,000 per year during his retirement. He has no relatives or other heirs and is not concerned about leaving an estate. He tells you that he could live on $15,000 per year, but would much prefer to spend $20,000 and be more comfortable.

If he chose the lump-sum payment, he would take out $20,000 to live on during the first year of retirement and invest the remainder. He would then withdraw $20,000 at the beginning of every year hence until the money ran out.

Required
Advise Mr. Mathews on how long he could afford to keep up a $20,000 per year standard of living.

9-7 Nonessential investment   The Glassman Company is building a factory several miles from the nearest town. The factory will be landscaped to make it more attractive, but the selection of trees and shrubbery is in doubt. Two plans have received wide support among the managers. One is to plant ordinary varieties of shrubs and trees that would cost $120,000 initially, with annual costs of $18,000 for fertilizer, water, and other maintenance. The other plan involves planting some varieties of hybrids that require less maintenance than those considered in the first plan. Annual maintenance costs of the hybrids would be only $4,000 per year, but their initial cost would be $230,000.

The managers have decided that a 20-year life is appropriate for both types. Cost of capital is 10%. (Ignore taxes.)

Required: Determine which shrubs and trees, the ordinary or the hybrid, should be planted based on the least-cost criterion.

9-8 Tax planning   Frank Mint owns 1,000 shares of stock for which he paid $10,000 several years ago. The stock is now worth $35,000 and Mint wishes to sell it. It is now late in 19X4 and Mr. Mint wonders whether to sell the stock late in December 19X4, or early in January 19X5. Either way, the gain on the sale would be taxed at 25%. If the sale were made in December 19X4 the tax would be paid March 31, 19X5. If the sale were made in January 19X5, the tax would be paid on March 31, 19X6.

Mr. Mint believes that 12% is his relevant discount rate, which is 1% per month. Present value factors for single payments at an interest rate of 1% per month are given below.

Months until Payment	Present Value Factor
3	.971
15	.861

For simplicity, assume that whenever the sale is made Mr. Mint will get the $35,000 on January 1, 19X5.

Required

1. Determine whether Mr. Mint should sell the stock in late December or early January.
2. Assume the same facts as given except that the tax rate will be 30% on gains recognized in 19X5. Determine whether Mint should sell the stock in December or January.

9-9 Relationships   The Miller Company invested $100,000 in depreciable assets and earned a 10% internal rate of return. The life of the investment, which had no salvage value, was five years.

Required

1. Determine the net cash flow that Miller earned in each year, assuming that each year's was equal.
2. Assume now that the tax rate is 40% and that Miller used straight-line depreciation for the investment. Determine the annual pre-tax cash flow that would have been earned to provide a 10% after-tax return.
3. The investment related to a new product that had a selling price of $10, variable costs of $4, and cash fixed costs of $20,000 per year. Assuming a 40% tax rate and straight-line depreciation, determine how many units would have to be sold to earn a 14% internal rate of return.

9-10 New asset decision   Fleckman Company makes a full line of office furniture and related products. The sales manager wants to bring out a new chair that will sell for $200. Variable costs per unit are expected to be $110, volume to be 4,000 chairs per year, and additional fixed costs to require cash disbursements of $200,000 per year. The chair would have to be made on a special machine that costs

$500,000 and has a useful life of five years. The machine would have no salvage value. The firm requires a return on investment of 14%. Ignore income taxes.

Required

1. Compute the present value of the future cash flows associated with the introduction of the chair. Should the investment be made?
2. Compute the payback period.
3. Determine the approximate return on investment that the firm will earn.
4. What number of chairs must be sold per year in order that the firm earn just 14%?
5. Suppose that 3,000 chairs per year can be sold. What price would have to be charged to make the investment yield just 14%? (Round to next highest dollar.)

9-11 Progressive tax rates   John Bowersox owns and operates a small firm that makes a variety of metal products. The firm is not incorporated and so Bowersox pays income taxes at the rates for individuals. He is considering the purchase of some new machinery that would enable his firm to increase sales by $110,000 per year. Contribution margin averages 40% of sales. The machinery would cost $40,000, have a useful life of five years with no salvage value expected, and would add $20,000 annually to fixed cash operating costs.

Straight-line depreciation would be used for tax purposes. Bowersox estimates his cost of capital to be 14%, and expects to earn $20,000 per year in taxable income for the next five years if he does not acquire the new machinery. Tax rate schedules for individuals are given below. No changes are expected in the rates over the coming five years.

Tax Schedule

Taxable Income		Tax
Over	But Not Over	
$20,000	$22,000	$5,230 plus 38% of the amount over $20,000
$22,000	$26,000	$5,990 plus 40% of the amount over $22,000
$26,000	$32,000	$7,590 plus 45% of the amount over $26,000
$32,000	$38,000	$10,290 plus 50% of the amount over $32,000

Required: Using the net present value method, determine whether Bowersox should acquire the machinery.

9-12 Mutually exclusive investments   The Vineland Manufacturing Company needs additional productive capacity to meet greater demand for its products. Two alternatives are available. The firm can choose either one, but not both.

	A	B
Required investment in depreciable assets	$1,000,000	$2,000,000
Annual cash operating costs	$ 320,000	$ 100,000
Useful life	10 years	10 years

Under either alternative the firm expects additional revenues of $600,000. Additional variable costs are included in the cash costs given above. Straight-line depreciation will be used for either investment and neither is expected to have any salvage value.

The tax rate is 40% and cost of capital is 10%.

Required

1. For each alternative, compute:
   (a) net present value
   (b) approximate internal rate of return
   (c) profitability index
2. Make a recommendation on which alternative should be chosen.

9-13 Buying a warehouse—capital gains tax The Stout Company is a distributor of electrical supplies. The controller of the firm believes that if the firm had a warehouse in the Boston area, it could save $380,000 per year in shipping and delivery costs. A suitable building is available at a cost of $1,500,000. Of that amount, $600,000 is attributable to land, which cannot be depreciated for tax purposes. Straight-line depreciation with a 10-year life would be used for the building, an annual amount of $90,000.

At the end of 10 years the firm expects to sell the land and building for $900,000. The tax rate on ordinary income is 40% and the capital gains rate is 30%. Cost of capital is 16%.

Required

Determine whether the Stout Company should buy the warehouse.

Problems

9-14 Pollution control and capital budgeting The Stailair Paper Company operates a plant that produces a great deal of air pollution. The local government has ordered that the polluting be stopped or the plant will have to be closed. The firm does not wish to close the plant and so has sought to find satisfactory ways to remove the pollutants. Two alternatives have been found, both of which reduce the outflow of pollutants to levels satisfactory to the government. One, called the Entrol, costs $1,000,000, has a 10-year life with no salvage value, and has cash operating costs of $150,000 annually. The other, the Polltrol, costs $2,000,000, has a 10-year life with no salvage value, and has cash operating costs of $240,000 annually. However, the Polltrol compresses the particles it removes into solid blocks of material that can be sold to chemical companies. Annual receipts from selling the material are estimated at $280,000.

Either device would be depreciated on a straight-line basis. Cost of capital is 16% and the tax rate is 40%.

Required: Determine which device the firm should buy.

9-15 Replacement decision and sensitivity analysis The Richmond Company owns a machine that cost $50,000 five years ago, has a book value of $25,000, and a current market value of $14,000. The machine costs $20,000 per year to operate and will have no market value at the end of five more years.

The firm has an opportunity to buy a new machine that costs $60,000, will last five years, have no salvage value, and costs $5,000 per year to operate. It will perform the same functions as the machine currently owned.

The firm has a cost of capital of 12%. Ignore income taxes.

Required

1. Determine whether the new machine should be purchased.
2. Determine the approximate rate of return that the firm would earn on the investment.
3. Suppose that the production manager knows that the new machine is more efficient than the old, but not how much more. What annual cash savings would be necessary for the firm to earn 12%?
4. Suppose that the estimate of annual cash flows is considered reliable, but that the useful life of the new machine is in question. About how long must the new machine last in order that the firm earn 12%?

9-16 Determination of required cost savings   The Grunch Company has an opportunity to buy a machine that will reduce variable production costs. The machine costs $50,000, has no salvage value, a useful life of five years, and costs $12,000 per year to operate. Cost of capital is 14%.

Required

1. Ignoring taxes, what reduction in variable costs per year would be necessary to make the investment desirable?
2. Answer 1 above assuming a tax rate of 40% and straight-line depreciation.

9-17 Benefit/cost analysis   The Department of Health has made studies regarding treatments for two diseases, a type of kidney disease and a type of heart disease. The following data have been assembled.

	Kidney Disease	Heart Disease
Cost to save one life	$100,000	$150,000
Average age of victim at death	40 years	50 years
Average annual income of victims	$ 15,000	$ 25,000

The heart disease appears to be caused partly by stresses that affect higher-income people, which accounts in part for the difference in incomes between the two types of victims.

The department believes that a discount rate of 10% is appropriate. It also assumes that a person will work until age 70 (30 additional years for persons cured of kidney disease, 20 for those cured of heart disease).

Required

1. Compute the net present value of saving a single life from each disease. The cost to save the life is incurred immediately and the annual incomes are assumed to be received at the ends of years.
2. Suppose that a lack of trained personnel makes it impossible to pursue treatment for both diseases. Whichever disease is selected for treatment, the same amount will be spent. Which disease would you prefer to see treated and why?

9-18 Selling an asset   The Franklyn Printing Company does several types of printing using several different presses. One press that has a book value of $60,000 and is being depreciated at $10,000 per year is used for special jobs the demand for which has been declining. The press is expected to be operated for 500 hours per year for its remaining useful life of six years. It will have no salvage value at that time.

Franklyn charges $40 per hour to use the press. Customers supply their own paper, ink, and plates, so that the hourly cost of $14 to operate the press is for power and operators' wages. Because of heavy demand in its other lines of business, and the shortage of skilled operators, the press is run by regular operators when time permits.

Franklyn has received an offer of $40,000 for the press, but the president is reluctant to sell it because the sale would result in a $20,000 loss. There are no alternative uses for the space currently occupied by the press.

Franklyn has cost of capital of 14% and the tax rate is 40%.

Required

Determine whether the press should be sold.

9-19 Increased sales and working capital   The Thomas Company now makes several products in a labor-intensive fashion. The products, which are made in about equal quantities, average $5 in variable costs of which labor is $2.50. Fixed costs are $300,000 annually. The firm has had difficulty in expanding production to meet increased demand and is considering purchasing a large machine that will enable a production increase of 25% with the same size work force. Sales are currently 100,000 units at $9 average selling price. The firm expects to sell all its production at $8 per unit if the machine is bought.

Variable costs per unit other than labor will remain the same and fixed costs will increase by the amount of depreciation on the new machine. The machine costs $100,000 and has a useful life of 10 years. There will be increased working capital requirements of $60,000. Straight-line depreciation will be used for tax purposes, the tax rate is 40%, and cost of capital is 12%.

Required

Should the machine be bought?

9-20 Backing a play   Ronald Clark, a famous playwright, proposes that your firm back his forthcoming play, *The Sour Fruit*. He has prepared the following analysis.

Investment:	
Sets and other depreciable assets (straight-line basis)	$200,000
Working capital	100,000
Total investment	$300,000
Annual gross receipts expected:	
4 years	$600,000
Annual salaries of actors and other personnel	$200,000
Rent, $20,000 fixed, plus 5% of gross receipts	
Royalty to Clark, 10% of gross receipts	
Other cash expenses	$140,000

Your firm has cost of capital of 14% and the tax rate is 40%.

Required

1. Should you back the play on the basis of the information given?
2. By how much could annual gross receipts increase or decline before you would change your decision?

9-21 Capital budgeting—required revenues   The 1972 annual report of General Telephone and Electronics discusses the company's application to the Federal Communications Commission for permission to establish a domestic satellite communications system. The following paragraphs are taken from the annual report.

The system's five earth stations would be interconnected through 10 transponders leased in a 12-channel satellite proposed by Hughes Aircraft with "back up" channels on a second 12-channel Hughes satellite. The 10 leased channels would provide the system with a total capacity of either 12,000 one-way voice-grade circuits, 10 television circuits, or various combinations of the two circuit types.

In its applications, GTE Satellite Corporation said the satellite system would be operational 24 months after receipt of FCC approval. The total gross investment for the system is estimated at more than $52 million, and the annual operating costs would amount to approximately $27 million.

Required

1. Assume that GTE has evaluated the rate of technological development in satellite communications and has estimated that innovation would make systems currently being developed obsolete in about 20 years. If GTE requires a rate of return of 8% on its investments, what must be the annual revenues from the new system to justify the investment? Ignore taxes.

2. Suppose that the projected revenues from the new system did not meet the requirements in 1 above. What other factors might influence GTE to undertake the investment?

3. Suppose that the company was willing to simply recover its investment and operating costs on the planned satellite system. Assuming the life in 1 above, what would the annual revenues from the system have to be to justify the investment?

9-22 Replacement decision   The management of Bettel Metals Inc. is considering acquiring a new production machine. The new machine would be more efficient than the one currently in use and would save the firm $6,000 annually because of its greater operating speed. To keep the old machine operating at the present level of efficiency, some repairs costing $5,000 would have to be made now. The repair cost is tax deductible this year. The annual depreciation charge on the old machine, which is expected to last 10 years, is $1,800. No scrap value is expected at that time.

The cost of the new machine is $37,300, including freight and installation charges. The old machine now has a book value of $18,000 and a market value of $12,000. The new machine has an expected useful life of 10 years and no expected scrap value. Straight-line depreciation would be used on the new machine.

The firm is in the 40% tax bracket.

Required

1. Compute the net cash outlay if the new machine is purchased.
2. Evaluate the proposal, assuming a minimum required rate of return of 10%.

9-23 Determining required volume and selling price   The Barkum Company is considering investment in a new product. Variable costs will be $4 per unit and selling price $6. Fixed costs requiring cash will be $10,000 per year. The required investment is $80,000 with no salvage value, and cost of capital is 10%. The product has an expected life of eight years.

Required

1. Ignoring taxes, how many units must be sold per year to make the investment desirable? (Round the required cash flow to the nearest $100.)
2. Assume the same data except that 10,000 units can be sold per year and the selling price is in question. What selling price is necessary to make the investment desirable?
3. Answer 1 above, assuming a 40% tax rate and straight-line depreciation of the $80,000 investment.

9-24 Lease/purchase and obsolescence   In some industries certain kinds of equipment are leased rather than purchased. One reason has been that leasing makes it easier for the user to acquire newer equipment if technological progress is rapid. The user may not be committed for as long a period of time in some leases as he would be if the equipment were purchased. One type of equipment that has been leased a great deal is computer hardware—a central processing unit and various peripheral devices.

The controller of the Stockton Company has been analyzing the firm's policy regarding computers, which are now being leased on a one-year basis. He is convinced that the firm is acting unwisely and should buy the equipment. Selected data related to currently leased equipment are as follows:

Cost of equipment	$1,500,000
Annual lease payment	$ 400,000
Physical life of computer	10 years
Tax rate	40%

Based upon these data, the controller calculates a net present value of purchasing the equipment at $64,800, using straight-line depreciation for tax purposes and a 14% discount rate. (The lease payments are fully deductible for tax purposes.)

The director of the computer center argues that the controller has not considered that the firm has had to upgrade its equipment every three or four years, leasing newer, faster computers because of the growth in the use of the computer throughout the firm. Anticipating that the growth in use will continue, the director suggests that a four-year economic life be used, rather than the ten-year physical life. He believes that if the equipment were purchased, it could be sold at the end of four years for 20% of its purchase price.

Required

1. Verify the controller's computation of the net present value of purchasing the computer.
2. Prepare a new analysis based on the director's comments. Equipment should be depreciated down to salvage value over four years (no gain or loss on disposal).

9-25 Attracting industry Minerla is a small town with little industry and high unemployment. The mayor and members of the town council have been trying to interest businesses in locating factories in Minerla. Newman Industries has agreed to the following proposal of the town government. The town will build a $4,000,000 plant to Newman's specifications and rent it to Newman for its estimated useful life of 20 years at $100,000 per year provided that Newman employs at least 600 currently unemployed citizens of Minerla.

An economist from the state university has projected the following annual results if the plant is built.

Increases in retail sales in Minerla	$6,000,000
Increase in property tax base	4,400,000

The mayor expects some increases in the cost of town government to result from the additional employees that Newman would transfer to the new factory.

Additional fire and police protection	$30,000
Additional school costs	40,000
Additional general governmental costs	15,000
Total annual additional costs	$95,000

The town levies a 1% tax on all retail sales and taxes property at a rate of $80 per $1,000. The relevant discount rate is 9%.

The mayor has been told that the state spends about $2,000 per year for each unemployed person in the form of direct support. He also has been told by the economist from the university that total unemployment is likely to fall by about 1,500 persons because the presence of the factory would help to create other jobs in the town.

The council feels that the factory should be built provided that the benefits to the town government do not exceed the costs.

Required

1. Determine whether the additional receipts to the town, less the additional costs, justify the building of the factory.
2. Assuming that your answer to part 1 is no, list and discuss other factors that might be considered and other actions that might be taken.

9-26 Return on investment The production manager of the Hammand Company recently approached the controller with the following commentary. "You have been telling me that we shouldn't invest in new equipment unless we'll earn a 16% rate of return, right? So that should also hold for *keeping* equipment, shouldn't it? We have a machine that has a book value of $80,000 and a remaining life of four years. We can't sell it now because it was built especially for our requirements. Now, the work that the machine does could be done as well with more workers. Look at these data."

Annual pre-tax cash cost to hire additional workers if machine scrapped	$60,000
Annual pre-tax cash operating costs of machine	55,000
Difference	$ 5,000

"See," he went on, "we save $5,000 in cash by keeping the machine, plus we get an $8,000 tax saving on depreciation because we are in the 40% bracket and we are depreciating $20,000 per year. But the critical thing is that the investment is not the $80,000 book value, but zero, because we cannot get anything for the machine. So we should keep the machine, right?"

Required: Determine whether the machine should be scrapped. Show calculations to support your answer.

9-27   Modification of equipment   The Rice Company has a number of machines that have been used to make a product that the firm has phased out of its operations. The equipment has a total book value of $600,000 and remaining useful life of four years. Depreciation is being taken using the straight-line method at $150,000 per year. No salvage value is expected at the end of the useful life.

The firm can sell the equipment for $320,000 now. The equipment can also be modified to produce another product at a cost of $400,000. The modifications would not affect the useful lives or salvage value and would be depreciated using the straight-line method. If the firm does not modify the existing equipment it will have to buy new equipment at a cost of $800,000. The new equipment would also have a useful life of four years, no salvage value, and would be depreciated using the straight-line method. The product that would be made with the new equipment or modified existing equipment is essential to the firm's product line.

The cash operating costs of new equipment would be $50,000 per year less than with the existing equipment. Cost of Capital is 16% and the tax rate is 40%.

Required: Determine whether the new equipment should be bought or the old equipment modified.

9-28   Dropping a product   The Stracke Company makes a number of products in several factories throughout the country. The managers of the firm have been unhappy with the results shown by Quickclean, a spray cleaner for household use. Quickclean is made in only one factory. A typical income statement for Quickclean shows the following annual results.

Sales	$4,400,000
Variable costs	3,700,000
Contribution margin	700,000
Fixed costs	975,000
Net loss	($ 275,000)

The production manager tells the sales manager that about $620,000 of the fixed costs shown above require cash disbursements. These are all avoidable. The remaining $355,000 in fixed costs is $100,000 in depreciation on equipment used only to make Quickclean, and $255,000 in allocated costs. The equipment used to make Quickclean has a useful life of five more years and no salvage value is expected at the end of five years. The book value is $500,000 and straight-line depreciation is being used.

Stracke Company has a cost of capital of 14% and the tax rate is 40%.

Required

1. Assume that the machinery used to make Quickclean has no resale value. If the product is dropped the machinery will be scrapped. The loss is immediately tax deductible. Determine whether Quickclean should be dropped.

2. Assume that the machinery could be sold for $200,000. Determine whether Quickclean should be dropped.

9-29 New product—complementary effects   Ralph Berger, the general manager of the McKeown Division of Standard Enterprises, Inc., is considering the introduction of a new product. It will sell for $20 per unit and have variable costs of $9. Volume at that selling price is estimated at 120,000 units per year. Fixed costs requiring cash disbursements would increase by $300,000 annually as a result of adding the product, mainly in connection with operating some machinery that would be purchased for $2,000,000. The machinery would have a useful life of ten years, no salvage value, and would be depreciated using the straight-line method.

The new product would be made in a section of the factory that is physically separate from the rest of the factory and is now being leased to another firm for $120,000 per year. The other firm has expressed an interest in renewing the lease, which expires this month, for an additional ten years.

Berger expects inventories to increase by $500,000 if the new product is brought out. He also expects customers to pay for their purchases two months after purchase, but is uncertain how or whether to consider these factors.

The cost of capital is 20% and the tax rate is 40%.

Required:

1. Determine whether the new product should be introduced.
2. Suppose that if the new product were brought out the sales of an existing product would increase by 30,000 units per year. The existing product sells for $10 and has variable costs of $6. The increase in sales of this product would lead to increases in inventories and receivables of $60,000. Determine whether the new product should be brought out.

9-30 Trade-or-sell decision   Current federal tax law requires that when an asset is traded in on another similar asset, no gain or loss is recognized for tax purposes. The book value of the asset traded in is added to the cash paid and that total amount is the "tax basis" of the new asset. The tax basis is the amount to be depreciated over the new asset's useful life. This rule does not apply if an asset is sold and a new asset bought from someone else. This provision of the tax law can affect replacement decisions when the firm can either sell the old asset or trade it in on a new asset.

The Morton Company has a machine with the following characteristics:

Annual cash operating costs	$65,000
Book value	$200,000
Resale price—currently	$110,000
Annual depreciation, remainder of 10-year life	$20,000
Expected resale price—end of 10 years	0

A new machine is available that sells for $250,000, has a 10-year useful life with no expected resale value, and costs $30,000 annually to operate (cash operating costs).

The production manager of Morton Company has been approached by a dealer who will sell the machine to the firm for $130,000 and the existing machine. He believes that this deal would be better than selling it for $110,000 and buying the new machine for $250,000.

The controller asks you to prepare an analysis of the alternatives. He points out that if the trade-in option is used, there would be no immediate tax effect and that the tax basis would be $330,000 ($200,000 book value of existing machine plus $130,000 cash payment), so that annual depreciation expense would be $33,000.

The tax rate is 40% and cost of capital is 14%.

Required

1. Determine the net present value of selling the existing machine and buying the proposed machine.
2. Determine the net present value of trading in the existing machine on the new machine.

9-31 Sensitivity analysis—competing products. The Brokjaw Company makes and sells candy in large lots for other firms that package and sell the candy under various brand names. Brokjaw does not sell directly to the retail outlets that handle its products.

The sales manager has concluded that the firm could maintain its existing sales and obtain additional annual sales of 800,000 pounds directly to retailers by packaging the candy itself. To do so the firm would have to hire additional salespeople for $80,000 annually and also acquire packaging machinery at a cost of $200,000. The machinery being considered would last for 10 years with no salvage value and would be depreciated on a straight-line basis for tax purposes.

Other data are as follows:

(a) Variable costs are $.10 per pound.
(b) Current sales in pounds and dollars are 12,000,000 pounds and $3,600,000.
(c) Selling price on retail business is $.40 per pound.
(d) Annual cash costs of operating the new machinery are $40,000.
(e) Tax rate is 40%.
(f) Cost of capital is 16%.

Required

1. On the basis of the information provided, is the investment desirable?
2. What sales in pounds would have to be achieved to make the investment yield 16% (the break-even point)?
3. Suppose that the firm would lose some of its regular sales if it began selling directly to retailers. What decline in regular sales, in pounds, would reduce the anticipated additional earnings to the point where just the 16% return would be earned?

9-32 Sensitivity analysis. The Carter Pen Company makes several models of ballpoint and soft-tip pens. A model of soft-tip pen currently being made is the Scribbler, which has been moderately successful. The machinery used to make the Scribbler now requires replacement and the firm is trying to decide whether to continue its manufacture.

The alternative to continuing to produce the Scribbler is to bring out a more expensive soft-tip pen, the Brush. It is believed that if both pens were produced, they would take sales from each other and so only one should be produced. Data on the two investments are given below.

	Scribbler	Brush
Selling price	$.80	$2.20
Variable costs	.40	.90
Additional annual cash fixed costs	$300,000	$800,000
Required investment, all depreciable assets	$800,000	$1,500,000
Expected annual volume of sales, in units	2,000,000	1,250,000

Neither investment would have salvage value at the end of the useful life, which is four years for both investments. Straight-line depreciation would be used for tax purposes. The tax rate is 40% and cost of capital is 16%.

Required

1. Using the net present value criterion, determine which product should be made.

2. The president is concerned about the effects on profitability of declines in volume from the expected figures. Determine the unit volume for each product that would give the firm a 16% return on each. (Round the required after-tax cash flows and pre-tax incomes to the nearest thousand dollars.) Determine the percentage decline from the original estimates that each volume represents. Would the new information have any effect on your decision in part 1? ·

9-33 Closing a plant—externalities The Fisher Manufacturing Company operates a plant in Vesalia, a small city on the Platte River. The firm has been notified that it must install pollution control equipment at the plant, at a cost of $4,000,000, or else close the plant. The plant employs 400 people, virtually all of whom would lose their jobs if the plant were to close. The firm would make a lump-sum payment totaling $800,000 to the people put out of jobs if the plant were closed.

A buyer would be willing to purchase the plant for $400,000, which equals its book value. Fisher could shift production to the Montclair plant if it closed the Vesalia plant, with no increase in total cash production costs. (That is, the increase in Montclair's cash production costs would equal the cash operating costs of the Vesalia plant.) However, shipping costs would increase by $900,000 annually because the Montclair plant is much further away from customers than the Vesalia plant.

If the equipment were purchased, it would have a 10-year useful life with no salvage value. Straight-line depreciation would be used for tax purposes.

The tax rate is 40% and cost of capital is 14%.

Required

1. Considering only monetary factors, determine whether the firm should install the pollution control equipment or close the plant.
2. What other factors might be considered?

9-34 Product modification (CMA adapted) The Williams Company manufactures office equipment and sells it through wholesalers. All sales are for cash.

The general manager of the firm recently learned that a patent on a semiautomatic paper collator could be bought for $60,000. The collator is much faster than a manually operated model that Williams now sells. If the patent were bought, Williams would have to spend $40,000 modifying existing production equipment to make the semiautomatic model and would no longer be able to make the manual model. The modifications would not change the remaining useful life of the equipment (four years), nor would they change the salvage value which is expected to be negligible.

Variable costs to produce the semiautomatic model would be $1 more than for the manual model, but fixed costs other than depreciation on the modifications and amortization of the patent would be unchanged.

The firm currently sells 100,000 units of the manual model at $4 each, with variable costs of $1.80 and total fixed costs of $120,000 per year. The fixed costs include $20,000 in depreciation expense on the existing equipment. The firm has a tax rate of 40% and cost of capital of 20%.

Market research analysts employed by the firm have come up with three important findings relating to the firm's decision: (1) the patent will be worthless in four years because of expected technological advances; (2) if Williams does not buy the patent, a competitor will, with the result that sales of the manual model would decline to 70,000 units per year; and (3) at a $4 price, sales of the semiautomatic model would be 190,000 units per year for four years.

The engineering department has concluded that inventory requirements would be $12,000 more if the semiautomatic model were produced than if the firm were to keep making the manual model.

The firm will use SYD depreciation on the modifications to production equipment, straight-line amortization for the patent.

Required: Determine the course the firm should take.

9-35 Evaluating an investment proposal Your new assistant has just brought you the following analysis of an investment opportunity the firm is considering. The investment relates to a new manufacturing process that would be used to make one of the firm's major products.

Required Investment

New machinery (10-year life, no salvage value)	$350,000
Research and development	60,000
Administrative time	10,000
Total investment	$420,000

Annual Cash Flows (10 Years)

Savings in cost over old process:	
Labor	$ 75,000
Materials	80,000
Variable overhead	40,000
Depreciation	(35,000)
Total operating savings	160,000
Less: interest on debt to finance investment	28,000
Net savings before taxes	132,000
Less: income taxes at 40% rate	52,800
Net cash flow after taxes	$ 79,200

Your assistant tells you that the new machinery would replace old machinery that has a 10-year remaining useful life with no salvage value. The existing machinery would be scrapped if the new machinery is bought, and the salvage value would be equal to the cost of having it removed. The existing machinery has a book value of $110,000. Straight-line depreciation is used for the existing machinery and would also be used for the new machinery.

Your assistant also tells you that the listed costs for research and development and for administrative time relate solely to this project and contain no allocations. The costs have been incurred already, so their amounts are certain.

The item in the analysis for interest on debt is for $350,000 at 8%, which would be borrowed if the new machinery is acquired.

Based on his analysis and the firm's cost of capital of 16%, he recommends that the project be rejected.

Required: Determine whether the investment should be made, supporting your answer with appropriate calculations.

Cases

9-36 Alternative uses of assets (AICPA adapted) The Miller Manufacturing Company has been producing both toasters and blenders in its Syracuse plant for several years. The Syracuse factory building is rented, with the lease requiring $80,000 rent per year. When the lease expires at the end of four years, the company intends to cease all operations at that location and scrap the equipment.

Blender production is approximately 50,000 per year and the company expects to continue production at that level. However, because of intense competition and price erosion, the company has decided to stop making toasters.

Two areas of the Syracuse plant, encompassing about 30% of the total plant floor space, have been devoted to the production of toasters. The equipment used to make toasters has a current book value of $140,000 and is being depreciated at $35,000 per year. The company has received a firm offer of $20,000 for all the equipment now used in toaster production, and the buyer is not interested in anything less than all the equipment. If the equipment were sold, the space now used for toaster production could be subleased for $12,000 per year.

Because the production of blenders is to be continued, the production manager was asked if he had need of the space and/or equipment now devoted to toaster production. He said that though he had no need for additional productive capacity for tasks currently being undertaken at the plant, he would be interested in the possibility of using the space and equipment for the manufacture of a blender part now being purchased from an outside firm. The part is a blade assembly that the firm purchases for $5 per unit. The contract with the outside vendor runs for four more years and requires that Miller buy at least 5,000 assemblies per year.

Either of the two areas now used for toaster production could be converted to facilitate the production of the blade assemblies. The production manager estimates that the variable cost to produce an assembly would be $3.60 and no additional fixed costs requiring cash would be incurred. However, the equipment now used would have to be converted. He estimates that it would cost about $40,000 to convert enough of the equipment to make 35,000 assemblies per year and $80,000 to convert enough equipment to make 60,000 assemblies. Because the prospective buyer of the equipment wants all or none of it, conversion of any of it means the company must forego the sale.

The company's tax rate is 40% and its cost of capital is 14%. Straight-line depreciation would be used on costs of converting equipment.

Required: Determine the best course of action for the company.

9-37   Mutually exclusive investments   The Seagle Company requires some machinery for an essential task that will be carried out for the next ten years. Two machines that meet the firm's needs are available. Data on them are given below.

	Rapidgo 350	Rapidgo 600
Purchase Cost	$50,000	$90,000
Annual operating expenses, exclusive of depreciation	12,000	15,000
Salvage value at end of useful life	5,000	10,000
Useful life	5 yrs.	10 yrs.

Either machine would be depreciated using the straight-line method and provision would be made for salvage value. The firm expects to have to pay $60,000 to replace the Rapidgo 350 at the end of five years, if that machine is selected. The other data applicable to the Rapidgo 350 given above would be applicable to the replacement model as well.

Cost of capital is 16% and the tax rate is 40%.

Required: Determine the course of action the firm should take.

9-38   Expanding a factory   The Fisher Company requires additional factory space and machinery to increase its production. The production manager and president have been trying to decide which of two alternative plans to accept. Data on the two plans are as follows.

	Plan A	Plan B
Investment required	$4,000,000	$5,500,000
Additional fixed cash operating costs per year	600,000	800,000
Additional capacity in machine-hours per year	200,000	280,000

Both investments would be depreciated using the straight-line method with no provision for salvage value. There is no salvage value expected for either investment at the end of their ten-year useful lives.

The production manager believes that Plan B should be accepted because the cost-per-machine-hour and investment-per-machine-hour figures are lower than for Plan A. The president is unsure about this and asks the sales manager whether the capacity would be fully utilized. The sales manager provided the following data.

	101-X	201-X	305-X
Potential increased sales, in units	30,000	40,000	30,000
Contribution margin per unit	$18	$24	$40
Machine-hours required per unit	2	4	5

The firm pays income taxes at a 40% rate and has cost of capital of 12%.

Required

Determine which, if either, expansion plan should be accepted and how the increased capacity should be used. (That is, how much of each product should be made.)

9-39   Challenging determination of cash flows   The Klonman Company makes a single product that sells for $20 per unit. The firm is currently operating at full capacity with three shifts seven days per week for the firm's 40 workers, 10 of whom work each shift. The critical factor in production is a machine that performs several operations on each unit at a rate of 10 units per hour. The machine cost $364,000 two years ago, has a remaining useful life of five years, and is being depreciated using the sum-of-the-years'-digits (SYD). Depreciation charges were determined giving no consideration to salvage value, even though the machine will be worth $20,000 as scrap at the end of its useful life. It is now worth $200,000. Any gain or loss on disposal of the machine is taxable or deductible at 40%.

A new machine has just been developed that will produce 12 units per hour. The machine costs $450,000 and has a useful life of five years, with no salvage value, and would be depreciated using the SYD method. In addition to its greater speed, the machine would save 10% of material cost because of reduced scrap. Material cost is $6 per unit, variable overhead $2 per direct labor hour. All other costs are fixed.

The sales manager estimates that sales could be increased by 20% if the price were dropped to $18, and that a 5% increase in volume could be achieved at the prevailing price of $20. Workers are paid $4 per hour plus a $2 premium for hours worked on Saturdays and Sundays. The firm's cost of capital is 16% and the tax rate is 40%. The schedules of workers can be adjusted to achieve any output. The firm provides, as a matter of policy, 40 hours of work for each worker.

Required

1. What are the alternatives?
2. What should be done? (Round all calculations to even dollars.)

CONTROL AND PERFORMANCE EVALUATION

Part Four discusses in depth the management functions of control and performance evaluation. Both functions are more effectively carried out through the principles and techniques incorporated into a responsibility accounting system. An essential step in the development of such a system is the identifying of costs as fixed or variable and fixing responsibility for each cost. Fixing responsibility for cost elements is also important if the fullest advantage is to be derived from comprehensive budgeting. In this part, the emphasis shifts from planning to control, the evaluating of actual results in relation to planned or budgeted results.

Human behavior and the ways in which accounting methods can elicit particular kinds of behavior are treated extensively in the three chapters in this Part. The major thrust of responsibility accounting is behavioral; the critical factor in its success is the extent to which the system encourages or discourages behavior consistent with the best interests of the firm.

CHAPTER 10

RESPONSIBILITY ACCOUNTING

Earlier chapters developed the basic concepts of managerial accounting and illustrated some of their uses. We are now ready to look more closely at the control process, particularly the area of performance evaluation. **Responsibility accounting** is the name given to that aspect of the managerial process dealing with the reporting of information to facilitate control of operations and evaluation of performance.

GOAL CONGRUENCE AND MOTIVATION

The responsibility accounting system is part of an overall management system; it is the most formal communication device in the management system. A major objective of any management system is to ensure that managers are working in harmony toward the objectives and goals of the firm, to ensure that there is **goal congruence**. Therefore, the responsibility accounting system should also assist in achieving this condition.

Motivation is obviously important in achieving goal congruence. The relationship of performance evaluation to motivation and the achievement of desired goals is illustrated by a familiar situation. Every individual undertaking a task has a desire to look good. When a person is going to be judged by a particular criterion or set of criteria, it is likely that the person will act in a way that will raise his or her standing relative to those criteria. For example, knowing examination grades to be the *sole* factor in the determination of the grade in a particular course, a student might be expected to direct all efforts to achieving high examination grades. If class quizzes don't count at all, the student may study only when an examination is imminent. The criteria for performance evaluation have encouraged the individual to act in a certain way. Sometimes that action may be unwise because the result is not consistent with the goals and intentions of the evaluator. The student may cheat on the exams, sleep through class, or not attend at all.

Careful selection of evaluation criteria is equally important in economic organizations. For example, it has been reported that at one time the Soviet government was interested in increasing production of nails in several factories. The managers of those factories were evaluated on the basis of the weight of nails they produced. The factories began to limit their production to large, heavy nails, ignoring the smaller sizes, because a given weight could be produced much more quickly if production was concentrated on larger sizes. Once it became clear that the measure of performance was not producing the desired effects, the government changed the criterion for evaluation to the number of nails produced. The country was inundated with small brads and tacks.

One of the major difficulties in performance measurement systems is a tendency to rely on a single criterion for evaluation. Too often, the use of a single criterion encourages managers to focus their efforts on that single measure to the exclusion of other important aspects of their jobs.

In addition to the selection of performance criteria, implementation of a responsibility accounting system requires reports on performance. The person being evaluated must be kept informed of his progress in meeting the criteria upon which he is being judged. For example, the student expects examination papers to be graded and returned. Moreover, he has a right to expect that the grade will not appear to be influenced by any factor he could not control, such as the weather on examination day or the instructor's mood while grading. Similarly, reports to managers must recognize managers' needs for feedback on their own efforts and should not allow factors beyond their control to reflect on their reported performance. Thus, noncontrollable costs should be excluded from performance reports. Otherwise a manager may believe his or her performance is unfairly depicted, and this may lead to a lack of commitment in meeting goals that are within the manager's control.

It is difficult to determine exactly what a manager can be held responsible for. In almost any firm the performance of a particular manager will depend to some extent on the performance of other managers. The sales manager cannot sell goods that have been shoddily made. Although it is impossible to eliminate the effects of interdependencies, the factors that a given manager controls should be defined as clearly as possible.

There are thus three guidelines for judging a responsibility accounting system:

1. Criteria for evaluating performance must have an influence on behavior that will simultaneously bring out the best interests of both manager and firm.

2. The manager must know how well he is doing in relation to those criteria so that he can adjust his actions accordingly.

3. The reports to the manager should include only those factors that he can control.

Any good system will follow these guidelines to some extent; no system can entirely achieve these ideals.

A basic step in the implementation of responsibility accounting is the establishment of responsibility centers within the firm.

RESPONSIBILITY CENTERS

In order that managers can be held accountable for their performances, it is essential that they have clearly defined areas of responsibility—activities over which they exercise control. A manager might be in charge of a production department within a large plant, or of the entire plant. A manager could be responsible for a specific product, a full product line, or a geographical area.

In Chapter 7, we discussed the many possible ways of segmenting an entity's activities. When segments of an entity are identified on the basis of the managers responsible for them, the segments are called **responsibility centers**. In general, three kinds of responsibility centers are used: cost centers, profit centers, and investment centers. The type of responsibility center reflects the breadth of control on the part of the manager.

Cost Centers

Cost centers are segments in which the managers are responsible for costs incurred but have no revenue responsibilities. A cost center can be relatively small, like a single department with a few people who perform one or several operations on a product. A cost center can also be quite large, like the administrative area for a very large firm. A factory could be a cost center if its manager is responsible for controlling costs and has no responsibility for sales. Some cost centers are composed of a number of smaller cost centers; for example, a factory may be segmented into many departments, each of which is a cost center.

Profit Centers

Profit centers are entity segments in which the managers are responsible for controlling both costs and revenues. In such a center it is possible to compute a residual figure, like net income, contribution margin, or incremental profit, for evaluation performance.

A profit center can be either natural or artificial. A **natural profit center** sells its output outside the firm. It operates in external markets and therefore earns revenues much the same as does an entire firm. (A single firm may have one or more subunits that operate independently in all important respects.) An **artificial profit center** sells its output primarily within the firm. The selling price in such cases is called a **transfer price**. A firm that mines iron ore, makes it into steel, fabricates the steel, makes products out of the fabricated steel, and sells the products to outsiders could establish profit centers at various stages. The mining operation can "sell" the ore to the steel-making division, which can in turn "sell" the steel to the fabrication division, and so on. The output of a profit center need not be a physical product; a firm's computer center could charge operating units for computing services, and the maintenance department could charge operating departments for repair work performed. Because there are advantages to operating an area as a profit center, artificial profit centers are becoming more common.

Investment Centers

An **investment center** is an entity segment in which the manager can control not only revenues and costs but also investment. Thus, for an investment center it is possible to compute a residual figure, such as income, *and* a return on investment.

The concept of an investment center is popular because the manager is treated much as if he or she were the chief executive of an autonomous firm. The manager of an investment center has much wider responsibility than does the manager of a particular functional area within a firm and it is often possible to evaluate performance with a higher degree of reliability. The setup of responsibility centers is unique to each firm. Such factors as size, industry, operating characteristics, and managerial philosophy influence the organizational structure of the firm.

Criteria for Evaluation

Many criteria could be used to evaluate performance. Performance could be considered "good" if it is better than in the previous year. One common criterion is the extent to which actual performance meets budgeted performance. Managers of cost centers that are production departments would be evaluated on whether they produced the required quantities of product at budgeted costs. Managers of nonmanufacturing departments, like a computer center, or market research department, would usually be evaluated on whether budgeted costs were met.

The manager of a profit center would normally be evaluated on a comparison of actual profit and budgeted profit. Alternatively, he or she could be evaluated on whether the center earned more or less profit than the year before, or more or less than other profit centers within the same firm.

Any evaluation approaches used for profit centers can also be applied to investment centers because a profit figure is identified in both types of segments. An additional evaluation criterion, return on investment, is available for investment centers. The special problems of evaluating investment centers are taken up in the next chapter, but most of the comments on profit centers in this chapter are applicable to investment centers also.

In general, it seems that the most useful basis for evaluating managers is a comparison of budgeted and actual performances. There are, of course, some problems with using budgets for performance evaluations. For example, with expense budgets, the amounts used as comparisons with actual figures must be based on actual outputs. That is, budget allowances must be flexible and not static. Problems of budget comparisons will be discussed in this and the next chapter.

ORGANIZATIONAL STRUCTURE

Most firms are organized into hierarchies of managers. The structure of the hierarchy greatly influences how individual managers will function and be evaluated, and how the responsibility accounting system will be structured. There are two basic approaches to the structuring of responsibilities within a firm. The first is the **vertical structure**, in which much responsibility is assigned to the highest levels of management, and the responsibilities of lower levels are relatively narrow. In organizations structured in this manner, responsibility is said to be **centralized**. The second approach to structuring responsibilities is the so-called **horizontal structure,** in which many types of responsibility are assigned to managers at the lower levels. In organizations structured in this manner, responsibility is said to be **decentralized**.

In this chapter, we will examine responsibility accounting systems with differing structures in two firms.

Vertical Structure

A simplified organizational chart for a vertical structure is presented in Figure 10-1. There are no profit centers because only the president has control over both revenues and costs. Each manager is charged with the operations of a functional area.

Costs would be accumulated for each cost center at the lowest level. The costs of several of these centers would be accumulated at a higher level and some other costs, not associated with the lowest level centers, would be added. This process would continue until the highest level cost centers were reached. Then the president would be charged with all costs, revenues, and investment of the firm.

For the operation of a single plant, there might be three levels of cost centers: work areas, departments, and the plant as a whole. The work areas are run by managers who are charged with the costs directly attributable to their own operations. Such costs could include wages, materials, and some overhead items. At the department level, the costs of several work areas are combined and costs directly traceable to the department, but not to particular work areas, would be added. These added costs are joint costs, like the salary of the department manager and depreciation on assets used in all work areas (such as fork-lift trucks that carry semifinished products from one work area to another).

The departmental costs would then be accumulated for reporting to the plant manager. Again, the total costs at this higher level would be greater than the sum of the departmental costs. Added to the departmental costs would be the salary of the plant manager, the costs of payroll, accounting, and the personnel office, depreciation on the factory building, and so on.

Much the same process would take place in determining the total of all manufacturing costs for the firm. The vice president for manufacturing would be charged with the total costs of each plant, plus other costs that are not controllable at the plant level. The vice president for manufacturing has a salary; his staff members have salaries. There may be several costs that are under the vice president's control, but not the control of plant managers.

FIGURE 10-1 Vertical Organizational Structure

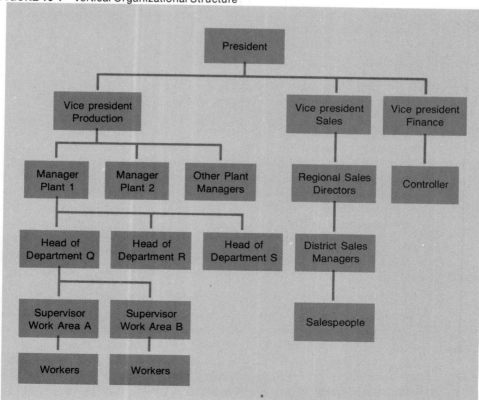

A set of reports might appear like those in Exhibit 10-1. The amount of detail drops as the reports go to a progressively higher-level manager. This occurs for several reasons.

1. Excessive detail cannot be assimilated and is irrelevant to the decisions that the president makes. To give the president a report showing individually the costs incurred by hundreds of work areas in scores of departments would be ridiculous.

2. A manager is usually concerned with the performance of those who report directly to him. Thus, there is no need to draw attention to the specific performances of the subordinates of the manager's subordinates.

3. The principle of management by exception implies that a manager should be concerned with problem areas—segments in which operations are not going according to plan. A manager is normally in a position to judge operations only one level down.

Exhibit 10-1
Sample Reports (Vertical Organization)

Supervisor of Work Area A	Budget	Actual	Variance (Unfavorable)
Direct labor	$ 1,500	$ 1,600	($ 100)
Materials	1,000	900	100
Overhead (itemized)	1,500	1,800	(300)
Totals	$ 4,000	$ 4,300	($ 300)

Department Head—Department Q	Budget	Actual	Variance (Unfavorable)
Work Area A	$ 4,000	$ 4,300	($ 300)
Work Area B	3,800	4,000	(200)
Others (itemized)	8,000	7,800	200
Total work area costs	15,800	16,100	(300)
Departmental costs—salaries, etc.	1,000	950	50
Totals	$ 16,800	$ 17,050	($ 250)

Plant Manager—Plant I	Budget	Actual	Variance (Unfavorable)
Department Q	$ 16,800	$ 17,050	($ 250)
Department R	18,500	18,700	(200)
Department S	21,000	20,800	200
Total departmental costs	56,300	56,550	(250)
Plant manager's costs:			
Plant manager's office	8,000	8,000	—
Personnel office	4,000	4,100	(100)
Accounting department	2,000	2,200	(200)
Other (itemized)	5,600	5,100	500
Totals	$ 75,900	$ 75,950	($ 50)

Vice-President—Manufacturing	Budget	Actual	Variance (Unfavorable)
Plant 1	$ 75,900	$ 75,950	($ 50)
Plant 2	87,000	89,500	(2,500)
Plant 3	106,500	108,200	(1,700)
Plant 4	83,000	82,100	900
Plant 5	137,600	143,250	(5,650)
Total plants	490,000	499,000	(9,000)
Vice president's office costs (itemized)	30,000	32,000	(2,000)
Totals	$ 520,000	$531,000	($11,000)

President	Budget	Actual	Variance (Unfavorable)
Sales	$1,000,000	$970,000	($30,000)
Functional area costs:			
V-P manufacturing	520,000	531,000	(11,000)
V-P sales	125,000	128,000	(3,000)
V-P finance	70,000	72,000	(2,000)
Totals	715,000	731,000	(16,000)
Costs not controlled by vice-presidents:			
Headquarters expense	60,000	64,000	(4,000)
Other	35,000	33,000	2,000
Total costs	810,000	828,000	(18,000)
Net income	$ 190,000	$142,000	($48,000)

The marketing activities of the firm are similarly arranged. Each city in which a plant is located could have a district sales office, with regional sales offices to direct activities in a large geographical area. The headquarters of the firm would house the office of the sales vice president, who would direct the regional managers. The cost accumulation process would be the same as for manufacturing, except that costs would be for sales salaries and commissions, regional and district advertising, travel, entertainment, and so on. Some costs would be attributable to regional offices, not to district offices within the region. Other costs would be associated only with the vice president's office.

The marketing department must meet sales budgets and will incur costs. The department would not, however, be treated as a profit center in this kind of organization. To do so would be inconsistent and create a false picture of profitability because manufacturing costs would not be included in the computation of profit. The marketing department can be made into an artificial profit center by using transfer prices.

Horizontal Structure

In a firm organized horizontally, many individuals at relatively low managerial levels within the organization will have broad responsibilities. A manager might be in charge of both production and sales for a given product line or geographical region. A horizontally organized firm will probably have a number of profit centers, and perhaps several investment centers. The chart in Figure 10-2 depicts a firm that is organized horizontally. Because organizational differences influence the responsibility accounting system, the reporting system for the entity shown in Figure 10-2 would differ considerably from the system associated with the firm described earlier.

FIGURE 10-2   Horizontal Organizational Structure

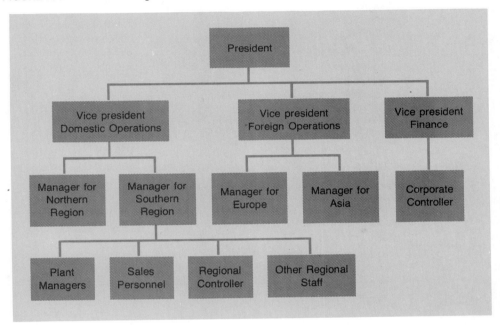

The firm in Figure 10-2 has two major profit or investment centers, domestic and foreign operations. Within each of these major divisions there are separate profit centers for geographical regions. Sample reports might look like those in Exhibit 10-2 on page 320. For reasons of space, we have omitted budgeted figures and variances from the reports shown in Exhibit 10-2. In practice, of course, budgeted figures and variances would be shown.

The principles of segment analysis discussed in Chapters 4 and 7 are generally applicable to performance reporting. One major exception is that many firms will include committed, but separable or traceable, costs in performance reports for segments. Committed costs are not relevant for making decisions about whether to drop a segment in the short run. Such costs are not controllable in the short run either, and so there is an argument for not showing them in performance reports. However, they are relevant for long-run decisions because they will not be committed forever; they are renewed periodically as machinery and buildings are replaced and top managers rehired. We show such committed, traceable costs separately in Exhibit 10-2 to highlight them. In practice, they might be shown together with discretionary costs because of the difficulty of separating committed and discretionary costs for some items. For example, as we mentioned in Chapter 3, a firm or segment could not get along without *some* managers; but the minimum committed cost associated with having managers may not be easy to determine.

Exhibit 10-2
Sample Reports, Horizontally Organized Firm

Domestic Operations	Total	Northern Region	Southern Region
Sales	$800,000	$300,000	$500,000
Variable costs:			
Production	300,000	80,000	220,000
Selling and administrative	90,000	20,000	70,000
Total variable costs	390,000	100,000	290,000
Contribution margin	410,000	200,000	210,000
Traceable fixed costs:			
Discretionary (production and selling and administrative)	110,000	40,000	70,000
Committed (production and selling and administrative)	120,000	60,000	60,000
Total traceable fixed costs	230,000	100,000	130,000
Regional profit	180,000	$100,000	$ 80,000
Costs joint to regions, traceable to domestic operations:			
Production	30,000		
Selling and administrative	80,000		
Total joint costs	110,000		
Profit from domestic operations	$ 70,000		

Report for Firm	Total	Domestic Operations	Foreign Operations
Sales	$1,800,000	$800,000	$1,000,000
Variable costs:			
Production	700,000	300,000	400,000
Selling and administrative	210,000	90,000	120,000
Total variable costs	910,000	390,000	520,000
Contribution margin	890,000	410,000	480,000
Traceable fixed costs:			
Discretionary (production and selling and administrative)	210,000	110,000	100,000
Committed, including costs joint to regions	480,000	230,000*	250,000
Total costs traceable to segments	690,000	340,000	350,000
Profit for domestic and foreign operations	200,000	$ 70,000	$ 130,000
Costs joint to domestic and foreign operations:			
Production	70,000		
Selling and administrative	50,000		
Total joint costs	120,000		
Income	$ 80,000		

*Consists of the $120,000 traceable discretionary fixed costs from the domestic report plus the $110,000 costs joint to the northern and southern regions.

Choice of Structure

Is the vertical or horizontal structure better? It depends on the attitudes and philosophies of the top management and on the firm's basic operations. Some company presidents feel uncomfortable if subordinates make many important decisions and therefore would prefer a vertical structure. Others prefer to give subordinates a good deal of discretion and would opt for the horizontal structure.

A firm must be fairly large to use a horizontal structure. If a single plant made all of a firm's products for both domestic and foreign markets, there would be so many joint costs that the use of profit or investment centers would introduce a great deal of artificiality. In the performance reports in Exhibit 10-2, we show some joint production costs, both joint to regions (on the report on domestic operations) and joint to domestic and foreign operations (on the report for the entire firm). The presence of these joint costs indicates that (1) some plants in the United States make products that are sold in both the northern and southern regions; and (2) some plants, either in the United States or abroad, make products that are sold both domestically and overseas.

Even if a firm decides that a horizontal structure would be better than a vertical structure, there remains the question of how the individual segments should be identified. Should the segmentation be based on product line? on geographical area? type of customer (retail, wholesale)? The choice depends to some extent on how well the chosen segments can be evaluated; and that depends to some extent on the amount of joint costs that would be present if a particular structure were chosen. If specific factories serve a single region, then a geographical structure might be best. But if individual factories are involved in only one product line that is sold throughout the nation, or the world, an organization based on product lines might be better.

The choice of structure is therefore not a simple process, subject to a few rules, but a critical decision requiring much thought and investigation.

ALLOCATIONS AND TRANSFER PRICES

We have been recommending that the firm's accounting system operate in a particular way: that managers be held responsible for only those costs over which they can exercise control. Such is not always the case in practice. Since an objective of cost accounting, as opposed to managerial accounting, is to allocate as much cost as possible to units of product, and to the lowest level of cost centers, there is a tendency to allocate costs controllable at one level to all the cost centers at a lower level. Moreover, there is a tendency to allocate costs of **service departments** to the operating departments. The personnel office, accounting department, maintenance department, and computer center are examples of service departments. The sample reports in Exhibit 10-1 showed that the sum of the costs charged to work areas is less than the total cost of departments, and that the sum of departmental costs is less than the total factory cost. It would be possible to allocate some of the costs down to lower levels and across to operating areas. The cost of the cafeteria is basically a factory cost, but some basis could be used to allocate it among departments. The number of workers in each department could be so used, and while it might be expected that the number of employees would have some effect on the costs of the cafeteria, those costs cannot be controlled by the managers of operating departments. Similarly, depreciation on the building could be allocated to departments based on square or cubic feet of the factory used, machine-hours, or some other basis. But again, the allocation would not reflect a controllable cost at the department level.

The argument generally used to support allocations, particularly of service departments, is that the managers of operating departments receive benefits from the service departments and should be charged for those benefits. Such allocated charges can be viewed as transfer prices whether or not the service units are viewed as profit centers. The term "transfer price" is usually employed when a department is charged a preset amount for the use of another department's personnel or equipment. Thus if the computer center of a firm charges $30 per hour for use of the computer, we would call the charge a transfer price. If the users of the computer are charged based on the relative amount of use they make of it, we would call the resulting charge an allocation.

The argument that managers who receive benefits should be charged for them is appealing. However, there is usually no way in which *all* such costs can be allocated without introducing arbitrariness. And the significance of the introduction of arbitrariness is that the bias inherent in the particular allocation method can have serious behavioral consequences, sometimes favorable for the firm, but sometimes not.

Examine the following common methods of charging operating departments for the services of a maintenance department and try to decide if any or some methods invite abuses. Do this before looking at the discussion that follows the descriptions. Assume that the firm has two operating departments, fabrication and assembly; the maintenance cost that would be assigned to each of these operating departments under the various methods will be calculated. The following data relate to the activities of the operating and maintenance departments for a given year.

Operating Departments	Hours of Maintenance Service Used
Fabrication	20,000
Assembly	10,000
Total hours	30,000

Costs of the Maintenance Department for the Year

	Budgeted	Actual
Fixed	$ 75,000	$ 90,000
Variable:		
$5 per hour	150,000	
$5.50 per hour		165,000
Total costs	$225,000	$255,000

Assume further that the cost of obtaining similar service from an outside maintenance firm is $8 per hour.

Method 1.   Allocate all maintenance costs to operating departments pro rata based on the number of hours of maintenance work performed in each department. Using this method, the per-hour cost to be allocated for the year would be $8.50 ($255,000 actual cost divided by 30,000 hours of maintenance service), and the total cost would be assigned as follows:

Fabrication	(20,000 × $8.50)	$170,000
Assembly	(10,000 × $8.50)	85,000
Total maintenance cost allocated		$255,000

Method 2.   Allocate to each operating department a fixed amount, regardless of use of maintenance. The total cost incurred by the maintenance department could, under this method, be allocated to the two departments in any amounts so that the combination added up to $255,000.

Method 3.   Charge each operating department a per-hour rate for maintenance based on what it would cost the department to obtain the services from outside the firm. This would make the maintenance department an artificial profit center. Using this approach, the charge to each department for maintenance service would be as follows:

Fabrication	(20,000 × $8)	$160,000
Assembly	(10,000 × $8)	80,000
Total maintenance cost allocated		$240,000

Using this method, the maintenance department would show revenues of $240,000, costs of $255,000, and therefore a loss of $15,000. This transfer price does not change the actual cost incurred but simply spreads that cost around differently. The total cost of $255,000 has been incurred; but $240,000 would be charged to the operating departments and the maintenance department would show the remainder as a $15,000 loss.

Method 4.   Charge each department a per-hour rate based on budgeted variable costs[1] predetermined for maintenance costs. Charge the fixed cost budgeted for maintenance to other departments in amounts based on some criterion like the expected long-run use of maintenance service. Because fixed costs usually reflect the building up of capacity or ability to serve, this method seems to have found a good deal of favor. If we assume that the expected long-run use of maintenance is 40% for assembly and about 60% for fabrication, we would have the cost allocations shown below.

	Fixed		*Variable*	*Total*
Fabrication	(60% × $75,000)	$45,000	$100,000	$145,000
Assembly	(40% × $75,000)	30,000	50,000	80,000
Total		$75,000	$150,000	$225,000

[1]The term *standard* is often employed to describe budgeted variable costs.

Note that only the $225,000 budgeted costs are allocated. Variable costs are being charged at the rate of $5 per hour, the budgeted cost per maintenance hour.

Critiques

The first method has serious drawbacks. When actual rather than budgeted costs are allocated, the inefficiencies of the maintenance department will be passed on to the operating departments. The maintenance department spent $30,000 more than budgeted, and the entire cost was allocated to the operating departments. When actual costs are allocated, the maintenance department manager knows that the costs, however high, will be spread over the operating departments, and may not be evaluated separately. He is not motivated to fulfill his responsibility efficiently.

The system also may induce undesirable behavior from the managers of operating departments using maintenance service. Under method one the allocation of maintenance costs to the two departments was as shown on page 323. Suppose that in the next year the fabrication department uses 20,000 hours again, but that assembly uses only 5,000 hours. The costs incurred by the maintenance department in the second year are $90,000 fixed (the same as the prior year) and $5.50 per hour variable (also the same as in the prior year). Total variable costs incurred are $137,500 ($25,000 × $5.50) and total costs are $227,500 ($90,000 + $137,500). For the second year, the charge for maintenance service would be $9.10 per hour ($227,500 total maintenance cost divided by 25,000 hours) and the costs would be allocated as follows:

Fabrication	(20,000 × $9.10)	$182,000
Assembly	(5,000 × $9.10)	45,000
Total maintenance cost allocated		$227,500

The fabrication department has had more costs allocated to it even though it used the same number of hours of maintenance service as in the prior year. *Fixed costs per hour* were higher in the second year because the total hours of maintenance service used was lower. The manager of the fabrication department is allocated more cost even though he used the same amount of service, because the manager of the assembly department used fewer hours. Such an allocation method could lead a manager to postpone desirable maintenance. Each operating manager knows that the less the service is used, the less the charge, and that the use fellow managers make of the service also affects the amount he is charged. Under this allocation method, there is a tendency to underuse the service.

Method two produces a tendency to overuse the service. Since each manager knows that his charge will not vary with use, he will try to get as much work performed as is possible. While having the work done may be good for the firm, the situation can also lead to conflicts and to strains on the maintenance department. This method does encourage the use of services, which might be an objective of the firm.

For example, a firm may have installed a new computer system that is believed to be beneficial for planning and control purposes. Managers might not wish to use the computer until they can be sure the benefits outweigh the costs. One way to encourage their using it is to charge little or nothing. Another is to charge a flat amount with no charge for use. Either way, the manager will be more inclined to use the computer than if there were some charge based on the amount of use he orders.

Method three treats the maintenance department as a profit center. It also treats the operating managers as if their departments were separate firms in the sense that their charges are based on what they would have to pay to obtain the services if there were no internal maintenance department. A problem with this method is that the outside cost might not be easy to determine. The outside cost, used as a transfer price, might also be so high that it would discourage the use of the service.

If reliable outside market prices are available, there is a significant potential advantage of treating a department as a profit center. If the department consistently shows losses, the manager is alerted to the possibility that the firm could benefit from shutting down the department and buying outside. Such a decision would have to take into consideration the structure of fixed costs (avoidable and unavoidable) and would be made along the lines described in Chapter 7 in connection with make or buy decisions.

Method four is perhaps the best under most circumstances. The operating managers are being charged at budgeted rates, with an additional lump sum based on budgeted fixed costs; therefore any current inefficiencies of the maintenance department are not passed on to the operating managers. The budgeted variable cost might be low enough to encourage necessary use of the service; but because there is a charge based on use, overuse may be discouraged.

There is really no answer to the question of which transfer price/allocation approach is best. No single method will serve all decision-making and performance evaluation needs.

What to Do?

Ideally, a manager should be charged with the incremental cost associated with carrying out his or her function. Thus, if some amount of cost of a service department, or portion of cost of a joint activity is attributable to the manager of a particular department, it should thus be charged.

If allocations are to be made, amounts allocated should reflect budgeted costs, not actual costs. This prevents managers from being charged for inefficiencies in the departments, the costs of which are being allocated. There should be charges for the quantity of the service received based on standard variable costs of providing the services, if it is feasible to isolate variable costs. Budgeted fixed costs could be allocated in lump sum amounts, not based on use of services, but on some idea of the long-run percentages of the service capacity required by each operating department. Thus, the budgeted fixed costs of the personnel department could be allocated based on expected numbers of employees in the operating departments, the costs of the accounting departments by the expected volume of transactions originating in the operating departments, and the costs of maintenance by the average expected number of machine-hours run in each department.

It is important that the allocation to a particular department should not be affected by what other departments do. If the amount allocated to a particular department increases or decreases, while the total cost being allocated remains about the same, the change should be because the manager used more or less of the service than previously.

Compromises are possible. The performance report could show controllable and uncontrollable (allocated) costs separately. If the higher-level managers, the ones evaluating the performance reports, recognize the distinction, there is less likelihood of misunderstanding and complaining from the lower-level managers.

There are similarities between the principles described here and those given in Chapters 7, 8, and 9. You will recall that joint costs were ignored in decisions involving a segment to which they were allocated. These costs are ignored because they would not change as a result of future action. The rationale for focusing on controllable costs is the same; the manager cannot do anything about costs that are arbitrarily allocated; and to include them in performance reports as if they were under the manager's control obscures analysis and does not facilitate controlling of operations.

The use of allocations or transfer prices gives opportunities to apply the responsibility principle. Consider a situation where the sales manager has control over the credit terms offered to customers and the level of inventory.

The sales manager would like to have a high inventory. In addition, if liberal credit terms are offered to the customers of the firm, there are likely to be higher sales. It would be reasonable to assign to him a charge (at the cost of capital) on the investment in receivables and inventory. He would be less likely to allow receivables and inventory to increase excessively if he were charged with the cost of carrying these assets. However, the major objective of a new, growing company might be to establish a strong demand for its products by getting as much market penetration as early as possible. Under these circumstances, it might be wise to allow receivables and inventory to increase more than would be tolerable in an older, more established firm.

Effects on Firm Income

One final point bears remembering. Allocations and transfer prices are managerial accounting devices, and changes in them cannot, by themselves, change the total income of the firm. Changes in the firm's income *may* come about because a change in an allocation or transfer price induces managers to change their operations in some way. But so long as the managers of the individual segments continue to operate as they have been, the firm's total income will not be affected. We can illustrate this with an example.

Suppose a firm is organized into two segments, manufacturing and selling, and each segment is a profit center. The manufacturing segment "sells" to the selling segment which, in turn, sells to outsiders. Data for the two segments are as follows:

	Manufacturing	Selling
Selling price	$20	$30
Variable costs:		
Manufacturing costs	$12	
Selling costs		$3
Fixed costs	$100,000	$50,000

If the firm produces and sells 200,000 units, an income statement by segment would show the following. The variable costs for the selling division are the $3 selling costs plus the $20 the segment is charged by the manufacturing division.

	Manufacturing	Selling
Sales 200,000 × $20	$400,000	
200,000 × $30		$600,000
Variable costs at $12 per unit	240,000	
$23 per unit		460,000
Contribution margin	160,000	140,000
Fixed costs	100,000	50,000
Income	$ 60,000	$ 90,000

Total income is $150,000 ($60,000 + $90,000). Suppose now that the transfer price is lowered to $15 per unit. This will reduce the revenues of the manufacturing segment and the costs of the selling segment, but will not affect income. An income statement for 200,000 units with the $15 transfer price is given below.

	Manufacturing	Selling
Sales 200,000 × $15	$300,000	
200,000 × $30		$600,000
Variable costs at $12 per unit	240,000	
at $18 per unit		
($15 + $3)		360,000
Contribution margin	60,000	240,000
Fixed costs	100,000	50,000
Income (loss)	($ 40,000)	$190,000

The income for the firm is still $150,000 ($190,000 − $40,000), even though the incomes for the segments have been changed. Notice that the reduction in revenues to the manufacturing division of $100,000 ($400,000 − $300,000) is exactly offset by the reduction in variable costs of the selling division ($460,000 − $360,000 = $100,000). Because a transfer price is revenue to one segment and a cost to the other segment, the price does not affect total income for the firm unless a change in the transfer price induces the manager of some segment to make some change in the operations of that segment.

SUMMARY

Managers must have accounting information to control their operations; and they must be evaluated on bases that are consistent with the goals of the firm. Responsibility accounting should assist in achieving goal congruence and in motivating managers. No one responsibility accounting system is appropriate for all firms, or for the same firm over its entire lifetime. The responsibility accounting system must parallel the organization structure of the firm. The structure of the firm itself depends on the nature of the firm's operations and on the attitudes and management styles of top managers.

The reporting segments of a responsibility accounting system may be cost centers, profit centers (either natural or artificial), or investment centers. In most firms, all three types of responsibility centers are found. Whatever the plan for segmenting the firm for reporting purposes, the individual managers can be made responsible for only that which they can control.

Cost allocations may be a troublesome aspect in responsibility accounting as they have been shown to be in previous discussions of decision making. Conflicting objectives of cost allocation are charging managers for benefits they receive, and reporting on the controllable aspects of the manager's operations in order to increase their motivation. Transfer prices, the selling prices established for artificial profit centers, can produce problems similar to those associated with cost allocations. The pervasive behavioral considerations in responsibility accounting make it difficult to draw general conclusions about the best or most useful approaches to follow.

KEY TERMS

artificial profit center
cost center
goal congruence
horizontal (decentralized)
   organization structure
investment center
natural profit center

performance report
profit center
responsibility center
service department
transfer price
vertical (centralized)
   organization structure

REVIEW PROBLEM

The Wolfert Company makes and sells air conditioners and operates in three regions: the Northeast, Southeast, and Southwest. Data for 19X5 are given below, in thousands of dollars.

	Northeast	Southeast	Southwest
Sales	$2,400	$5,600	$3,800
Variable cost of sales	1,220	2,200	1,700
Variable selling costs	170	330	240
Traceable fixed costs:			
Selling	240	400	280
Administrative	320	440	380

Joint fixed costs for administration were $450 and for selling were $110 (both in thousands of dollars). The firm operates four plants. Data regarding those plants are given below, again in thousands of dollars.

	New Orleans	Houston	Atlanta	Philadelphia
Fixed production costs for 19X5	$780	$340	$310	$210
Region(s) in which product sold	Southwest and Southeast	Southwest	Southeast	Northeast

Required

Prepare a performance report by region, showing contribution margin and regional profit. Show allocated costs as lump-sum deductions in the total column.

Answers to review problem

	Northeast	Southeast	Southwest	Total
	(In Thousands of Dollars)			
Sales	$2,400	$5,600	$3,800	$11,800
Variable costs:				
Production	1,220	2,200	1,700	5,120
Selling	170	330	240	740
Total variable costs	1,390	2,530	1,940	5,860
Contribution margin	1,010	3,070	1,860	5,940
Traceable fixed costs:				
Production	210	310	340	860
Selling	240	400	280	920
Administrative	320	440	380	1,140
Total traceable fixed costs	770	1,150	1,000	2,920
Regional profit	$ 240	$1,920	$ 860	3,020
Joint fixed costs:				
Production				780
Selling				110
Administration				450
Total joint costs				1,340
Income				$ 1,680

Notice that the fixed production costs of the New Orleans factory are shown as joint to the regions. They are actually joint to the Southeast and Southwest, which makes them joint if one is looking at either region, rather than the two regions together.

ASSIGNMENT MATERIAL

Questions for Discussion

10-1 Responsibility accounting and decision-making data   What similarities do you find between the material in this chapter and that in Chapters 7 and 8 on the data used in short-term and long-term decision making?

10-2 Cost classification   The president of Your Company has just returned from a seminar for executives where cost classification was extensively discussed. He has asked that you prepare a report showing all costs of the company classified in the following ways: (a) variable vs. fixed, (b) controllable vs. uncontrollable, and (c) relevant vs. irrelevant. Could you respond to his request?

10-3 Relationships with previous material

1. What similarities do you see between the suggestions made in this chapter and those made in Chapter 7 on evaluating segments of a business?
2. In Chapters 2, 3, and 4 the focus was on cost behavior. Does the material presented in this chapter follow that same emphasis? Explain.

10-4 Responsibility centers—universities   What problems would there be in establishing and evaluating responsibility centers in the following: (a) universities, (b) colleges or schools within universities, and (c) departments within colleges?

10-5 Responsibility reporting   A recent annual report of a major manufacturer carried the following paragraph (paraphrased).

> Specialization also continues within each marketing force as we increase the number of personnel. We are experiencing a steady rise in the number of customers as well as in the variety and complexity of products and equipment. As a result, an increasing proportion of our salespeople are now concentrating on just one or a few industries —or on certain product categories.

Suppose that in the past the salespeople sold all products made by the firm to all kinds of customers in different industries. What effects would the new method of directing the efforts of the individual salespeople have on the responsibility reporting system?

10-6 Organizational structure   In the letter from the chief executive officer in the 1973 annual report of Genesco Inc. are found the following paragraphs and chart.

> NEW ORGANIZATION STRUCTURE
>
> In many ways the most significant internal change has been Genesco's new management organization structure. At the Board meeting at the end of February, the Directors designated me the chief executive officer of the corporation. I then designed and implemented a new management structure. As shown in the chart above, the chief operating officers and the chief administrative officer report directly to me. Each officer is responsible for a major area of Genesco's operations.
>
> Reporting to the chief operating officers are the group presidents, each of whom is responsible for a number of related operating companies. Reporting to the group presidents are the presidents of the operating companies.
>
> In this chain of command, each executive knows his responsibilities, has the authority to take the action necessary to produce results, and knows that he is accountable for those results. This organization permits the rapid, decentralized decision making necessary in the apparel industry.

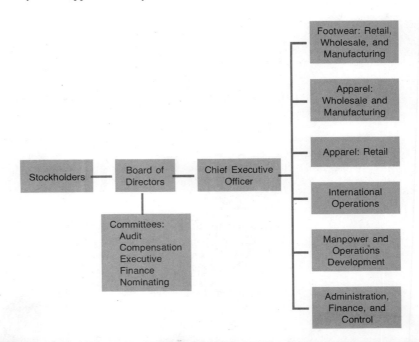

Which of the group presidents is likely to be designated as responsible for an investment center? a profit center? a cost center?

Exercises

10-7 An artificial profit center   The president of your firm has been to a seminar at which the profit center concept was urged on the participants as a means of "correctly evaluating departments." Accordingly, the president states that he is going to establish as many profit centers as possible, beginning with the legal department. From now on, he says, departments using the services of the legal department will be charged at $30 per hour, about twice the average cost of lawyer's salaries. Costs of the legal department are not now being allocated. What problems do you foresee with the president's intentions?

10-8 Cost allocation methods   The following data refer to the three departments of the ABC Company.

	A	B	C
Sales	$300,000	$200,000	$500,000
Square feet of space occupied	8,000	6,000	6,000
Number of employees	60	90	150

Total joint costs for the year are $100,000.

Required ~

Allocate the joint costs to departments on the bases of (a) sales dollars, (b) square feet of space occupied, and (c) number of employees.

10-9 Cost allocations   The Bremen Company allocates costs among its three products on the basis of relative sales dollars. Data from 19X6 are as follows:

	W	X	Y	Total
	80,000	160,000	360,000	
Sales	$100,000	$200,000	$300,000	$600,000
Joint costs	20,000	40,000	60,000	120,000

In 19X7, joint costs were again $120,000. However, sales of product Y increased to $360,000, while those of W and X declined to $80,000 and $160,000, respectively. The changes were in volume only; prices were the same in both years.

Required

Allocate the joint costs for 19X7 using relative sales dollars and comment on the usefulness of this basis for allocation.

10-10 Cost allocations   The Cooper Company allocates maintenance costs based on relative use of the service. Last month its three operating departments had the following activity and allocation of cost:

	Finishing	Fabricating	Assembly	Total
Maintenance hours	2,000	3,000	3,000	8,000
Cost allocated	$20,000	$30,000	$30,000	$80,000

Data for the current month are as follows:

	Finishing	Fabricating	Assembly	Total
Maintenance hours	2,000	2,000	2,000	6,000
Costs	?	?	?	$72,000

You learn that maintenance expense is a mixed cost, with a fixed component of $48,000 per month and a variable component of $4 per hour.

Required

1. Allocate the maintenance cost for the current month using the method followed by the firm.
2. Criticize the method used, citing the results in 1 above and those for the prior month as examples.

10-11 Effects of allocations The Grungi Company has two service departments: building services and administration. The firm has three operating departments. Some data associated with the operating departments are presented below.

	Operating Departments		
	A	B	C
Total separable departmental costs	$360,000	$ 440,000	$1,200,000
Square feet of space occupied	6,000	9,000	15,000
Machine-hours worked	42,000	70,000	88,000
Sales value of production	$900,000	$1,000,000	$2,100,000

Costs for the service departments are as follows: building services $160,000; administration $300,000.

Required

1. Allocate service department costs on three different bases.
2. Comment on the results in 1 above.

10-12 Transfer prices and goal congruence The controller of the Calvert Company has set a number of transfer prices to be used by service departments within the firm, all of which are cost centers. One is for stenographic services. The charge is $10 per hour, which is based on total budgeted hours of available service and total budgeted costs for the stenographic pool. The manager of one of the operating departments, a profit center, has obtained a price of $8 per hour for stenographers' time from an outside agency. The task will take about 50 hours. The manager informs the controller and the manager of the stenographic pool of the outside price and is told to take it if he so wishes; the price set internally will not be lowered.

Required

Comment on the position taken by the controller and the manager of the stenographic pool. (Budgeted costs for the pool are about 90% fixed.) Make a recommendation.

10-13 Profit centers and behavior The Blue Giant Detergent Company has set up most of its service departments as artificial profit centers. The firm rents a computer for a fixed fee of $15,000 per month, which is charged to the director of the Computer Center, Frank Candor. He in turn charges operating units for use of the computer at $100 per hour. Tom Wright, one of the operating managers, has an acquaintance in a data processing service company that charges only $80 per hour for the same computer that Blue Giant rents.

Managers in Blue Giant are free to buy services inside or outside the firm, so Tom told Frank about the $80 price and indicated that he would use the outside firm if Frank would not reduce his price to $80 per hour.

Required

1. Suppose that Tom's department uses 20 hours of computer time per month and that the Blue Giant machine has idle capacity.
   (a) Is it better for the firm if Frank lowers his price to $80?
   (b) Is it better for Frank to lower his price?
2. Suppose that Tom's department uses 20 hours per month, but that the Blue Giant computer is overloaded and demand exceeds the total time available in a month.
   (a) Is it better for the firm if Frank lowers his price?
   (b) Is it better for Frank if he lowers his price?

10-14 Development of performance report   The Stratton Company is organized by functional areas: sales, production, finance, and administration. The sales department has product managers who are responsible for a particular product and who are evaluated based on the following typical performance report.

Product Zee	Activity Report May 19X4	Manager J. Harrison
Sales (30,000 units)		$300,000
Cost of goods sold		170,000
Gross profit:		130,000
Other expenses:		
Advertising	$32,000	
Travel	17,000	
Depreciation	6,000	
Office expenses	19,000	
Administrative expense	23,000	97,000
Product profit		$ 33,000

The following additional information is available on the procedures for preparing product reports.

(a) Because of problems in the production process, cost of goods sold is $9,000 higher than budgeted.
(b) The product manager spent $18,000 on advertising for the product. The remainder is an allocated share of general advertising costs incurred by the firm.
(c) Depreciation charges consist of the following: 20% on furniture and fixtures in the product manager's office, and 80% for the building in which all the firm's activities take place.
(d) Office expenses include $4,000 allocated from the expenses of the vice president for sales (salaries, data processing, etc.)
(e) Administrative expenses are allocated to each product based on relative sales.

Required
Prepare a revised performance report for product Zee based on the principle of controllability.

Problems

10-15 Evaluation of compensation plans (AICPA adapted)   The Gibson Company pays all its salespeople a 5% commission on gross sales. Although this method has worked well in the past when the firm was primarily concerned with increasing sales and getting its products before the customer, some problems have been developing lately. The following data for two salesmen for last year illustrate the problems.

	Ronald McTavish	James Christy
Gross sales	$230,000	$150,000
Returns and allowances	24,000	6,500
Cost of goods sold—all variable	125,000	68,000
Other costs—all discretionary (travel, entertainment, etc.)	17,000	8,000

Required

1. What are the commissions for each salesman?
2. Does the compensation method encourage them to act in the best interest of the firm? (What other factors should be considered in comparing McTavish and Christy?)
3. What recommendations would you make for changes in the compensation method?

10-16 Cost allocations   The Kaufman Company has three operating departments and several service departments. The costs of service departments are allocated to operating departments on bases determined by the controller.

 The following bases are used:

purchasing department costs—dollar volume of material purchased by the departments
cafeteria costs—number of employees in each department
accounting department costs—total production costs incurred by the departments
building maintenance, security, and other services—square feet of space occupied.

Required

Assuming that the allocations will be made on some bases, criticize the ones used. Do they reflect the extent to which the operating departments influence cost incurrence in the service departments?

10-17 Effects of cost allocations   Performance reports for two months for the supervisor of the assembly department of the Berkey Manufacturing Company are shown below. Maintenance costs are allocated to operating departments by taking the total maintenance costs incurred each month, dividing them by the number of hours worked by maintenance personnel, and multiplying the resulting cost per hour by the number of hours worked in each operating department.

	March			April		
	Budget	*Actual*	*Variance*	*Budget*	*Actual*	*Variance*
Materials used	$1,200	$1,210	$ 10U	$1,500	$1,480	$ 20F
Direct labor	3,400	3,420	20U	4,250	4,220	30F
Maintenance	1,200	900	300F	1,200	1,000	200F
Other overhead	2,000	2,050	50U	2,300	2,350	50U
Totals	$7,800	$7,580	$220F	$9,250	$9,050	$200F

Required

1. How is maintenance expense budgeted? What kinds of occurrences could account for the actual charges, given the allocation method used?
2. How might the performance report be improved?

10-18 Responsibility for rush orders   The Howard Company's sales manager usually requests rush orders from the production department. The production process used by the firm requires a great deal of setup time whenever changes in the production mix are made. The production manager has complained about these rush orders, arguing that production costs are much lower when the process runs smoothly. The sales manager argues that the paramount consideration is to keep the goodwill of the customer and that therefore all sales orders should be made up as quickly as possible.

Required

1. Who is responsible for what under what circumstances?
2. What steps might be taken to effect a satisfactory solution?

10-19 Performance measurement The sales manager of the Warner Company is judged by total sales. Exceeding the sales budget is considered good performance. The sales budget and cost data for 19X3 are shown below.

	Alpha	Beta	Gamma	Total
			Product	
Sales budget	$150,000	$200,000	$450,000 33 1/3	$800,000
Variable costs	75,000 50%	90,000 45%	150,000	315,000
Contribution margin	$ 75,000	$110,000	$300,000	$485,000

Actual sales for the year were as follows:

Alpha	Beta	Gamma	Total
$360,000	$300,000	$180,000	$840,000

Actual prices were equal to budgeted prices, and variable costs were incurred as budgeted (per unit).

Required

1. Did the sales manager perform well? Support your answer with calculations.
2. What suggestions do you have regarding the performance measurement criterion used by the firm?

10-20 Responsibility accounting It is usually not possible to tell whether a cost is the responsibility of a specific manager simply by knowing the object classification of the cost (rent, wages, salaries, shipping, etc.) For each of the following costs, indicate some circumstances under which it would, or would not, be the responsibility of the following: (a) foreman, (b) department manager, and (c) plant manager.

1. Wages of factory workers
2. Rent on equipment
3. Electricity for machinery
4. Cost of materials

10-21 Compensation plan (CMA adapted) The Parsons Company compensates its salespersons with commissions and a year-end bonus. The commission is 20% of a "net profit," which is computed as the normal selling price less manufacturing costs. (Such costs contain some allocated fixed overhead.) The profit is also reduced by any bad debts or sales written by individual salespersons. The granting of credit is the responsibility of the firm's credit department, and credit approval is required before sales are made.

Salespeople can give price reductions which must be approved by the sales vice president. Commissions are not reduced when such price concessions are given.

The year-end bonus is 15% of commissions earned during the year provided that the individual salesperson has achieved the target sales volume. If the target is not reached, there is no bonus. The annual target volume is generally set at 105% of the previous year's sales.

Required

1. Identify which features of the compensation plan would seem to be effective in motivating the salespeople to work in the best interests of the firm. Explain your answers.
2. Identify which features of the plan would seem to be least likely to be effective or may even be counterproductive in motivating salespeople to work in the interests of the firm. Explain your answers.

10-22 Assignment of responsibility The Johns Company is organized by function: sales, production, finance, and administration. The production manager is upset about his latest performance report (see below). He contends that costs of about $8,000 were incurred solely because the sales manager ordered changes in production for rush orders from customers.

Performance Report
Production Department

	Budgeted	Actual	Variance
Controllable costs:			
Materials	$ 80,000	$ 79,000	$(1,000)
Direct labor	160,000	162,000	2,000
Other labor	46,000	53,000	7,000
Idle time*	1,000	4,000	3,000
Other production costs	21,000	20,000	(1,000)
Totals	$308,000	$318,000	$ 10,000

*Wages paid to workers while they are idle, as when machines are being reset because of a change from one product to another.

The report, argues the production manager, shows $3,000 in idle time caused by changing the production process to meet the special orders. In addition, about $5,000 in other labor was for costs incurred to make the necessary changes and the overtime premium paid to workers to get the work finished.

Required

What is wrong and what do you recommend?

10-23 Performance measures Below are six jobs or job titles and the measure by which performance in that job is judged. Comment on each.

Job or Job Title	Performance Measure
(a) Director of the county's medical health program.	The number of patients no longer requiring treatment.
(b) Director of a program to reduce unemployment.	The number of jobs found for persons on the unemployment rolls, as a percentage of the total unemployed persons.
(c) Director of a regional program to rehabilitate substandard housing.	The number of homes now meeting local building codes that had previously been classified substandard.
(d) The operator of a particular machine.	The number of hours the machine is running.
(e) A salesperson.	The dollars of sales orders written divided by the number of customers visited.
(f) A college professor.	The enrollment in the professor's classes.

10-24 Cost allocations and performance measurement   The Edwards Company allocates joint costs to its three products, each of which is the responsibility of a particular manager. The three managers are evaluated based on the pre-tax incomes generated by their respective products. Income statements for a typical month are as follows, in thousands of dollars.

	Product			
	Toasters	Ovens	Dishwashers	Total
Sales	$1,200	$800	$400	$2,400
Variable costs	720	420	150	1,290
Contribution margin	480	380	250	1,110
Joint costs—allocated	450	300	150	900
Income	$ 30	$ 80	$100	$ 210

The manager in charge of toasters believes that if he increases his price from $15 per unit to $20 per unit, sales in units will drop from 80,000 to 40,000. Variable costs per unit would remain the same as they are now. Sales of the other products would not be affected.

Required
1. Determine whether the price increase would benefit the firm, showing calculations.
2. Prepare a new set of income statements based on the manager's estimates. Be sure to reallocate the joint costs based on the new dollar sales figures. Is it in the manager's best interest to raise the price? Comment on the advisability of allocating joint costs the way the firm does it.

10-25 Assignment of responsibility   The controller of the Squiffy Company is authorized to charge the sales departments with any overtime premium paid to production workers when one of the sales managers requests an order that requires overtime. (Overtime premium is the difference between the wage rate paid when workers are on overtime and the regular rate they are paid.) There are four sales managers, each responsible for a different product.

During March, budgeted production is, in total, 10,000 units; capacity production, without overtime, is 12,000 units. An increase in demand for all the company's products is experienced early in the month, and, on March 10, each of the four sales managers requests additional production of 1,000 units. The production manager reports that the extra 1,000 of two products, A and B, were made during regular working hours while the extra production of products C and D was carried out after normal hours when overtime rates were paid. Each unit of any product takes one hour to produce, and overtime premium is $2 per hour.

Required
Which sales manager (s) should be charged with the overtime premium and how much?

10-26 Assigning responsibility and fulfilling company objectives   The Bangor Company has been in operation for 20 years. Growth has been rapid in the past, but is leveling off. The sales manager, who has been with the firm for 17 years, has persuaded the president that the firm should carry large inventories and grant liberal credit terms to increase its sales.

The new controller believes that the large inventories and receivables are too expensive; interest charges are higher than for most comparable firms and debt is higher than most potential lenders find acceptable.

Required

Prepare a brief statement indicating how you would analyze the arguments of the sales manager and of the controller (i.e., what information you would seek). Indicate at least one step you might take to help resolve the argument.

10-27 Performance reporting—alternative organizational structure (CMA adapted) The Cranwell Company sells three products in a foreign market and a domestic market. An income statement for the first month of 19X2 shows the following results.

Sales		$1,300,000
Cost of goods sold		1,010,000
Gross profit		290,000
Selling expenses	$105,000	
Administrative expenses	72,000	177,000
Income		$ 113,000

Data regarding the two markets and three products are given below.

	Products		
	A	B	C
Sales:			
Domestic	$400,000	$300,000	$300,000
Foreign	100,000	100,000	100,000
Total sales	$500,000	$400,000	$400,000
Variable production costs (percentage of sales)	60%	70%	60%
Variable selling costs (percentage of sales)	3%	2%	2%

Product A is made in a single factory that incurs fixed costs (included in cost of goods sold) of $48,000 per month. Products B and C are made in a single factory using the same machinery for both products. The monthly fixed production costs at that factory are $142,000.

Fixed selling expenses are joint to the three products, but $36,000 is separable with respect to the domestic market and $38,000 to the foreign market. All administrative expenses are fixed. About $25,000 is traceable to the foreign market, $35,000 to the domestic market.

Required

1. Assume that the firm has separate managers responsible for each market. Prepare performance reports for the domestic and foreign markets.
2. Assume that the firm has separate managers responsible for each product. Prepare performance reports for the three products.

10-28 Cost allocations, transfer prices, and behavior Several top executives of the Millard Company are discussing problems they perceive in the methods of cost allocation used by the firm. For each of the costs discussed below, indicate what changes would help accomplish the objectives stated by the executives.

(a) Computer cost, which is 95% fixed, is allocated using a transfer price of $100 per hour of use. The executives are concerned that lower-level managers do not make enough use of the computer. The firm is growing rapidly and the executives are worried that other managers will not have the expertise to use the computer when it becomes an essential tool of the manager.

(b) Maintenance costs, which are budgeted at $10 per hour variable and $200,000 per year fixed, are allocated by dividing total incurred cost by total maintenance hours worked and distributing the resulting per-hour cost to operating departments according to the number of hours of maintenance work done in that department. The executives believe that operating managers use maintenance work only when emergencies arise (i.e., when machinery is about to break down). Production has been halted in the past because of repairs on critical machines. The operating managers have been complaining that the per-hour cost is too high.

(c) The firm has a consulting department that provides advice to operating managers on various aspects of production and marketing. The costs of the consulting department are fixed but discretionary, and have been rising in recent years because of heavy demand for the services. The costs are not allocated because it was felt that managers should be encouraged to use the service. One executive commented that the operating managers call the department to find out where to go to lunch.

10-29   Reporting of variances   John Flowers, the assistant controller at the Steiner Company, is impressed with the idea of management by exception. He is looking for ways to use this principle in the operations of the firm. The company uses the following format for reporting budgeted and actual data and variances.

Performance Report
Operations of the Assembly Department
(Clyde Williams, Foreman)

	Budget	Actual	Variance
Material:			
Stock #926-4873	$ 8,000	$ 8,800	$ 800
Stock #926-5436	27,000	31,000	4,000
Direct labor:			
Assemblers	64,000	63,000	(1,000)
Indirect labor:			
Material handling	2,000	2,100	100
Inspection	500	600	100
Maintenance	260	300	40
Setup	90	110	20
Supplies	200	160	(40)
Lubricants	40	30	(10)
Small parts	400	420	20
Totals	$102,490	$106,520	$ 4,030

The budgeted amounts shown in the report are for production achieved. The actual amounts are really actual quantities at budgeted prices because the department managers do not control prices.

John feels that there is too much detail on this report and that the real concern to the manager should be the variance. He proposes to substitute with a report of the following format, showing only the actual results as a percentage of budgeted results.

Performance Report
Operations of the Assembly Department
(Clyde Williams, Foreman)

	Budgeted Results As a Percentage of Actual Results
Material:	
Stock #926-4873	90.9%
Stock #926-5436	87.1
Direct labor:	
Assemblers	101.5
Indirect labor:	
Material handling	95.2
Inspection	83.3
Maintenance	86.6
Setup	81.8
Supplies	125.0
Lubricants	133.3
Small parts	95.2
Total	96.2%

Required

Comment on the reporting method that John is recommending.

10-30 Performance report The controller of the Caldwell Department Store is developing performance analyses for the managers of the store's three major lines—housewares, clothing, and sporting goods. He has prepared the following:

Segmented Income Statement
(In Thousands of Dollars)

	Housewares	Clothing	Sporting Goods	Total
Sales	$900	$1,200	$400	$2,500
Cost of goods sold	500	680	180	1,360
Gross profit	400	520	220	1,140
Other expenses:				
Salaries	60	90	40	190
Advertising	45	60	20	125
Rent	40	40	20	100
Depreciation	20	16	12	48
General and administrative	90	120	40	250
Miscellaneous	60	85	32	177
Total	315	411	164	890
Profit	$ 85	$ 109	$ 56	$ 250

You learn the following about the ways in which the above statements were prepared.

(a) Cost of goods sold is separable.

(b) Salaries expense includes allocated salaries of $75,000 for employees whose work takes them into different departments. The controller believes that relative sales is the best measure of volume to use for allocation.

(c) Advertising is partly allocated. Each department manager is charged at standard market rates for newspaper space, radio time, and television time that he requests. The cost of general advertising ordered by the vice president for sales was $50,000 and was allocated based on sales dollars.

(d) The rent allocation is based on floor space occupied. The three departments occupy 100,000 square feet. The sporting goods department is in the basement, the others on the first floor. Similar property in the city rents for $1.05 per square foot for first floor space, $.80 for basement space. Rent on space occupied by the administrative offices is included in general and administrative expenses.

(e) Depreciation is all for furniture and fixtures within the departments.

(f) General and administrative expenses are allocated based on sales dollars.

(g) Miscellaneous expenses are partly separable, partly allocated. The allocated amounts by department are as follows: housewares, $28,000; clothing, $36,000; and sporting goods, $16,000.

Required

Prepare a new performance report using the principle of controllability. Include a column for unallocated costs, as well as one for each department.

10-31 Transfer prices and behavior All operating departments of the Jacson Company are profit or investment centers, and a number of service departments are artificial profit centers. The maintenance department is an artificial profit center that charges $10 per man-hour for maintenance work that it does for operating departments. The variable cost per man-hour is $4 and fixed costs are $40,000 per month.

The manager of department A, an operating department, has just determined that some changes in the production process can be made. If the changes are made, maintenance requirements will drop from 2,100 man-hours per month to 1,600. However, the variable cost to produce a unit of product will increase from $6 to $7. Department A produces 4,000 units of product per month.

Required

1. Determine the change in monthly profit for department A if the production process is changed.
2. Determine the change in profit of the maintenance department if department A changes its production process.
3. Determine the effect on the firm's monthly profit of the change in department A's production process.

10-32 Responsibility accounting The Svelte Bode Company has produced quality women's swimwear for many years. Two years ago the management decided to undertake a diversification program to reduce the seasonality of the swimwear business. Accordingly, the firm began to produce fur parkas. About five months of the year were given over to producing parkas. Previously the firm had spread swimwear production over the entire year, even though higher carrying costs were incurred and the risks of style obsolescence were greater.

In the last year before parkas were introduced, the firm earned $900,000 on sales of $5,900,000. Fixed costs of production increased $200,000, and general and administrative costs rose $300,000 as a result of introducing parkas. (See income tax statement on page 342.)

The manager of the swimwear segment recently boasted that her profits have increased to more than double previous levels, with profit margins up even more.

Required

Explain, with supporting calculations, how the profits of the swimwear manager increased so substantially. Was the increase due to the manager's skill or to something else?

Income Statement for Svelte Bode Company for 19X7
(In Thousands of Dollars)

	Swimwear	Parkas	Total
Sales	$5,800	$3,000	$8,800
Materials	550	450	1,000
Direct labor	400	150	550
Variable overhead	800	300	1,100
Total variable costs	1,750	900	2,650
Fixed production costs*	700	500	1,200
General and administrative costs (fixed)*	1,400	1,000	2,400
Total costs	3,850	2,400	6,250
Income	$1,950	$ 600	$2,550

*Allocated based on months of production (seven months swimwear, five months parkas).

10-33 Assignment of responsibility   The Peckman Company has one manager in charge of purchasing and another in charge of production. The purchasing manager is responsible for acquiring raw materials at the lowest possible cost consistent with quality standards. The production manager is responsible for meeting production quotas at the least possible cost. The raw materials used by the firm fluctuate in price, and the purchasing manager attempts to take advantage of these fluctuations by buying large quantities when he believes that prices will rise in the near future, and to hold off on purchases when he believes that prices will fall. The production manager has complained that these buying habits adversely affect his performance. He cites the following reasons:

(a) Bottlenecks frequently develop because raw materials are unavailable when the purchasing manager is waiting for better prices.

(b) Efficiency is reduced when large purchases are made: it is difficult to get to needed materials because there is so much stored in a limited space. Workers frequently have to assist the storekeepers to find the required materials.

The production manager suggests that limits be placed on the quantities of materials that can be bought at any one time and that certain minimum levels be set for each type of material so that sufficient quantities will always be available. The purchasing manager feels that these limitations will adversely affect profits because purchases will have to be made at unfavorable times.

Required

1. Discuss the issues involved.
2. How can their responsibilities be separated?
3. What recommendations do you have?

10-34 Cost allocations and performance   Ed Cranston, the new dean of the School of Business at Midstate University, is concerned. It is only early February, and he has just received a statement from the university printing and duplicating service saying that the school has exceeded its budget for duplicating for the academic year. The statement appears as follows.

Printing and Duplicating Department Statement of Budget and Charges
for the School of Business September through January

Annual Budget	Actual Charges	Over (Under)
$4,200	$4,350	$150

An enclosed note states that Ed must either stop using the service or obtain approval of a supplemental budget request from the chief fiscal officer of the university. Ed pulls out his latest statement, from December, and finds that actual charges at that time were $1,830. Since the school was on vacation during a good part of January, he wonders how $2,520 could have been incurred in January.

He finds out that costs for the printing and duplicating department in January were $6,300, of which $700 was for paper, $2,000 for salaries, $2,000 for machine rentals, and $1,600 general overhead (allocated share of all university utilities, depreciation, etc.). A total of 35,000 copies was made in January, a relatively low number because of the vacation period. However, several faculty members in the School of Business had a substantial amount of printing done for scholarly papers that they were circulating to other professors throughout the country. The School of Business was responsible for 14,000 of the 35,000 copies and so was charged $2,520. The charge was computed by dividing total department costs for the month by the number of copies produced ($6,300/35,000) to arrive at a charge to each user of $.18 per copy. Ed also learns that during a typical month about $8,600 in cost is incurred and 150,000 copies are processed. Paper is the only item of variable cost.

Required

Evaluate the transfer pricing system used and recommend changes if you think that any are necessary.

10-35 Allocation of costs—distribution channels The Weisner Company sells its products through wholesalers and retailers. Eric Stern is the manager in charge of wholesale sales and Ralph Pike manages retail sales. Frederick Weisner, the president of the firm, has ordered an analysis of the relative profitability of the two channels of distribution to determine where emphasis should be placed. The following data show last year's operations.

	Wholesalers	Retailers
Sales	$2,000,000	$3,000,000
Cost of sales—all variable	1,600,000	2,000,000
Sales commissions (3% of sales)	60,000	90,000
Managers' salaries	18,000	18,000
Advertising (allocated as a percentage of sales dollars)	12,000	18,000
Selling expenses—salespeople's expenses, delivery, order processing, credit checking (allocated on the basis of number of orders from each group)	80,000	160,000
General expenses (allocated as a percentage of sales dollars)	40,000	60,000
Total expenses	1,810,000	2,346,000
Income	$ 190,000	$ 654,000

The same products are sold to both wholesalers and retailers, but prices to wholesalers are about 20% less than those to retailers.

Required

1. Comment on the reasonableness of the allocation methods used in the analysis.
2. Recast the statement based on the principle of controllability.
3. What further information would help in assigning costs to the responsible managers?

10-36 Allocation of earnings—interaction effects[1] Two students have been hired to grade examination papers in elementary accounting. Jim is a very fast and usually accurate worker who can grade 20

[1]Adapted from Arthur L. Thomas, *Financial Accounting: The Main Ideas*, Belmont, Calif.: Wadsworth Publishing Company, Inc., 1972. Used with permission.

examinations per hour and Jill is always accurate, but somewhat slow. She can grade only 15 papers per hour. Together, by concentrating on the parts that they can each grade best, Jim and Jill are able to grade 50 papers per hour.

The pay for grading is $.20 per paper.

Required:

1. Determine how much Jim and Jill can earn per hour if they grade papers together.
2. If you were Jim, how would you want to divide the pay? Justify your answer.
3. If you were Jill, how would you argue the pay should be shared? Justify your answer.
4. What other possibilities are there for allocating pay?

Cases

10-37 Performance measurement The Tenspeed Company has been in the business of repairing bicycles for many years. Average profits have been $60,000 annually with revenues of $150,000. The firm recently began to sell bicycles and provide free repairs and adjustments for one year after sale. As a result, total profits have increased as shown in the income statement below.

Tenspeed Company Income Statement
for a Typical Year

	Bicycle Sales	Repairs and Adjustments	Total
Revenues	$400,000	$100,000	$500,000
Variable costs	160,000	75,000	235,000
Contribution margin	240,000	25,000	265,000
Separable fixed costs	80,000	15,000	95,000
Income	$160,000	$ 10,000	$170,000

The manager of the repair and adjustment department has complained that his performance looks bad solely because he is charged with the costs of repairing bicycles sold by the firm, while not being credited with any revenue for this work. He contends that he should be credited with revenue of 200% of variable costs of the repair work on sold bicycles, which is consistent with the revenue earned on regular repair and adjustment work.

The bicycle sales manager says that such a markup is too much, but that he is willing to accept a transfer price equal to variable cost of work done on bicycles sold. The mix of work in the repair department is two-thirds regular repairs, one-third repairs on bicycles sold by the firm.

Required

1. Recast the income statement to reflect the repair department manager's position. (Add the revenues credited to the repair department to variable costs of the bicycle sales department.)
2. Recast the income statement to show results if the repair department were credited with revenue equal to the variable cost of repair work done on bicycles sold.
3. What recommendation would you make? Give reasons.

10-38 Performance reports for segments The assistant controller of Octopus Industries, a multinational firm, has been working on the monthly performance report. The report identifies the firm's two products and the two areas in which each is sold—domestic and overseas. He has prepared the following partial report (in thousands of dollars).

| | Domestic | | Overseas | | |
	A	B	A	B	Total
Sales	$100	$150	$80	$70	$400
Variable costs	40	60	32	28	160
Contribution margin	60	90	48	42	240
Separable fixed costs	20	30	14	16	80

At this point the assistant controller is puzzled. There are remaining $120,000 in fixed costs that are not separable both by product and by geographical area. There are $30,000 in fixed costs associated strictly with domestic operations, and $20,000 with foreign operations. But none of these costs can be traced directly to either product A or B. (The firm advertises both products, but the advertisements are only differentiated as being domestic or overseas. There are also administrative expenses that relate to the United States or to overseas, but not to either product specifically.)

In addition, $10,000 of the fixed costs can be related to product A and $15,000 to product B, but not to either foreign or domestic operations. (The firm employs staff personnel who travel extensively in both the United States and overseas, but whose efforts concern only one of the two products.) The remaining $45,000 ($120,000–$30,000–$20,000–$10,000–$15,000) also cannot be broken down and attributed to either product or an individual geographical area.

Required

Prepare two performance reports, one by product, one by geographical area. Separate all costs that you can and determine an incremental profit for each segment. (Each report should include a column for the total activity of the firm.)

10-39 Performance measurement in an automobile dealership   In automobile dealerships the sales managers of new and used cars are commonly evaluated according to the profits on sales of new and used cars, respectively. The new-car sales agreement may include some allowance for a traded-in used car. Assume that the trade-in allowance is based upon what the used-car manager is willing to pay the new-car manager for the car. For example, suppose that the customer wants to buy a new car that has a list price of $5,000, and trade in a used car. If there were no trade-in, perhaps the price of the car would be $4,400. If the used-car manager would give $1,800 for the used car to be traded in, the new-car salesperson would allow up to $2,400 to the customer, because the net price would still be satisfactory. The $2,600 cash paid ($5,000 list price−$2,400 allowed on the old car) is the same as the difference between the $4,400 desired price and the $1,800 that the used-car manager will pay for the car.

Sometimes the used-car manager will offer lower prices than at other times, say if his lot is full and sales are slow. If the used-car manager would pay only $1,500 for the car, the salesperson could give only a $2,100 trade-in allowance to obtain $4,400.

Required

1. Assuming that each manager is evaluated on profits in his respective area, what is the disadvantage to the new-car manager? Is there a disadvantage to the used-car manager?
2. Suppose that the dealership's policy provides that if the new-car manager is unhappy with the price offered by the used-car manager, the former can try to sell the car to another used-car dealer. In the second example, suppose the new-car manager believed that the traded-in automobile could be sold to another used-car dealer for $1,800. The $4,400 deemed acceptable for the new car would be obtained ($2,600 from the customer plus $1,800 from selling the trade-in), so this deal for the new car would be accepted despite the lower bid from the used-car manager. What conflicts could arise under this system? Does the system encourage the managers to act in the best interests of the total firm?

CHAPTER 11

DIVISIONAL PERFORMANCE MEASUREMENT

Chapter 10 sets the general framework for responsibility accounting. Information provided by a responsibility accounting system helps the manager to control operations and provides the basis for higher-level managers to evaluate his performance. This chapter studies these functions in the context of investment centers, which are usually large enough to be divisions[1] of a large firm. Much of what is discussed is also applicable to profit centers, and some to cost centers. This chapter deals with the more autonomous units of a firm—units that may act almost as do independent firms. The investment center concept has been developed largely on the premise that higher-level managers should be evaluated as nearly as possible as if they were chief executive officers of firms. Several criteria can be used to evaluate performance. We shall discuss three of these.

DECENTRALIZATION

It is customary to use the term *decentralized* to refer to firms that make extensive use of investment centers. Individual managers are responsible for and control revenues, expenses, and investment. The horizontal organizational structure that we described in Chapter 10 would be called decentralized, while a vertical organizational structure is usually called centralized. Under any kind of organizational structure, subordinate managers will have responsibilities and exercise control. Thus, in a broad sense, almost any firm could be said to be decentralized. However, the term normally is used only when managers have responsibility for profit and return on investment, rather than for either costs or revenues.

---

[1]The term *division* can refer to any large operating unit of a firm, but in this chapter it refers to an investment center.

In highly decentralized firms, operating units, which are usually called divisions, are almost autonomous; division managers are responsible for both production and marketing, as well as other functions such as personnel and accounting. Normally division managers also prepare capital budgets and submit them to central headquarters for approval. However, division managers usually have no control over long-term financing, which is administered by central headquarters.

Benefits of Decentralization

In a modern business firm of any complexity, it is impossible to operate without delegating some authority to lower-level managers. Given the interdependence of functional areas, conflicts between functional managers are inevitable. Hence it is deemed wise, wherever possible, to make some managers nearly entirely responsible for revenues and costs. Then, when conflicts occur, one of those managers becomes responsible for resolving the problems. When the firm's chief executive is the only manager whose span of responsibility includes both conflicting functions, arbitration and settlement of disputes must necessarily take place at the top. Decentralization allows for conflicts among managers of functional areas to be resolved at relatively low levels within the firm. Top management can also make better evaluations of managerial performance if the interdependencies and conflicts are resolved by having managers fully responsible for the component elements of profit and return on investment.

A benefit that flows from the better ability to evaluate performance and fix responsibility is that top management does not need to be heavily involved in day-to-day decision making. With decentralization, top management can use the principle of management by exception, monitoring the activities of almost autonomous managers.

Decentralization is also advantageous when firms have divisions that operate in different industries. A president or other chief operating officers of a corporation cannot be expected to be knowledgeable about textiles, furniture, appliances, automobile supplies, movies, and sporting goods. Over the past few decades, firms have greatly widened their range of products. Diversification makes it necessary to have divisional managers with broad responsibility. Chief executives can and must manage by exception.

There is evidence to suggest that decentralization is also beneficial from the standpoint of motivation. Experiments in the behavioral sciences suggest that an individual who is involved in the entire production process takes more interest in the work and performs better than one who does the same operation repeatedly. Good performance in a single repetitive task may appear as wasted effort to the worker because the individual cannot control other tasks that affect the quality of the final product. Similarly, a manager who is responsible for virtually all aspects of the operation of a division may feel more in control of his or her performance than if the manager were responsible only for production or sales.

Managing a nearly autonomous division is also good experience in preparing for a chief executive's position with a firm. Such a manager has an appreciation for all aspects of the operations of a firm, instead of only one. The chief executive of Container Corporation of America, in the 1972 annual report, recognizes the advantages of decentralization.

> The corporate organization consists of over 21,000 men and women, working in plants and offices, laboratories, forests and paperboard mills in the U.S. and six other countries. Its 140 plants and mills operate as relatively independent businesses, under a management system that delegates authority and responsibility to local managers. This

decentralized organization, which provides for successful development of local markets, also constitutes an environment which encourages individual self-development. One measure of its success, over the years, is that virtually all of the company's present senior management team is a product of this system.

PERFORMANCE MEASURES

Net Income

The most widely examined (and least understood) result of the accounting process is net income—"the bottom line." To evaluate a division, the income that should be used is the net result of all revenue and expense items controllable by the division manager. This amount may be called **divisional profit**. There are likely to be some costs joint to the divisions, and thus not allocated to individual divisions; therefore the *total profits of all divisions may exceed the total income for the firm*. If a division is a profit center, divisional profit is the most comprehensive measure available for evaluation. If a division is an investment center, divisional profit is not sufficiently comprehensive because it does not indicate the investment required to produce a particular profit. That is, it cannot be concluded that a division earning $1,000,000 is better than one earning $500,000. The problem with the use of divisional profit as a performance measure is that it fails to consider the size of the investment committed to the division. Therefore it is not widely used to measure the performance of investment centers.

Return on Investment

A measure that does take into consideration the relative sizes of divisions is **return on investment (ROI)**. The general form of the computation of ROI is

$$\text{ROI} = \frac{\text{income}}{\text{investment}}$$

ROI can also be used as a criterion for evaluating divisional performance. The income that should be used in divisional performance measurement is *divisional profit*. Similarly, the investment that should be used is investment under the control of the divisional managers. Opinions differ as to the methods to be used in determining the numerator and denominator of the ratio.

ROI is the most frequently used criterion for divisional performance measurement. It has a distinct advantage over divisional profit for this purpose because it is likely that divisions of different sizes will be compared. It allows more equitable comparison of a division returning $100,000 on an investment of $1,000,000 with one earning the same profit on an investment of $5,000,000. ROI makes it possible to compare the efficiency of different-size divisions by relating output (income) to input (investment).

A restatement of the ROI formula helps many managers analyze operating performance and identify actions to improve performance. This variation expands the basic formula income ÷ investment.

$$\text{ROI} = \frac{\text{income}}{\text{sales}} \times \frac{\text{sales}}{\text{investment}}$$

As you can see, the expanded version produces the same final answer because "sales" appears in the numerator of one factor and the denominator of the other and thus cancels out.

The expanded form can help to focus the manager's attention on the two components of ROI. The first, income ÷ sales, is the familiar **return-on-sales** ratio. The second, sales ÷ investment, is called the **investment turnover**. From this expanded version it is clear that an increase in sales, by itself, will not increase ROI because sales cancels out. But a decrease in investment, with other factors remaining the same, will increase ROI (as will an increase in income with other factors held constant). The manager can also determine the effect on ROI of a decision expected to change two factors. Suppose that return on sales is now 15% and investment turnover is 2 times; ROI is now 30% (15% × 2). If the manager is considering changing the product mix to items with lower margins and faster turnover, which would increase turnover to 2½ times, while reducing return on sales to 10%, he or she could see that ROI would fall to 25% (10% × 2½).

The values of the two components of ROI often give clues to the kinds of strategies used by firms or divisions. For example, a single firm might operate both conventional department stores and discount stores. Both kinds of stores may earn the same ROI, but do so using very different strategies.

Assume the following data:

	Conventional Department Store Division	Discount Division
Sales	$2,000,000	$2,400,000
Divisional profit	240,000	192,000
Divisional investment	1,000,000	800,000

The ROI computations are as follows:

$$\text{Conventional store division} \quad \frac{\$240,000}{\$2,000,000} \times \frac{\$2,000,000}{\$1,000,000} = 12\% \times 2 = 24\%$$

$$\text{Discount division} \quad \frac{\$192,000}{\$2,400,000} \times \frac{\$2,400,000}{\$800,000} = 8\% \times 3 = 24\%$$

The discount operations produce a lower return on sales but obtain a higher sales volume for each dollar invested.

While the advantages of ROI in taking into consideration relative sizes and alternative strategies are obvious, absolute size is still of concern to the total firm. Recall from Chapter 8 that the firm was wise if it accepted all proposed investments where expected returns were in excess of cost of capital. It was desirable even when the proposed rate of return was less than that currently being earned. The same general principle prevails in evaluating divisions.

Residual Income

Residual income is a measure of the amount of income that a division produces in excess of the **minimum desired rate of return** for the firm. The minimum desired rate of return is almost invariably established at a management level higher than an individual division. This is because the responsibility for long-term financing rests with the top management of the entire entity and the cost of capital is determined on an entity-wide basis. The minimum desired rate of return should always be equal to or greater than the cost of capital. In general form, residual income (RI) is computed as follows:

$$RI = income - (investment \times desired\ ROI)$$

Application of this third criterion shows that a division with the highest ROI might be less valuable to the firm as a whole than a division with a lower rating using the latter criterion. Suppose that in a given firm Division A produces a $200,000 income on an investment of $1,000,000, an ROI of 20%. Division B of that firm earns a profit of $1,500,000 on an investment of $10,000,000, an ROI of 15%. The desired ROI for the firm is (1) 10%, and then (2) 18%. We could compute the RI for each division in the following manner.

	1 Desired ROI Is 10%		2 Desired ROI Is 18%	
	Division A	Division B	Division A	Division B
Investment	$1,000,000	$10,000,000	$1,000,000	$10,000,000
Net income	$ 200,000	$ 1,500,000	$ 200,000	$ 1,500,000
Desired minimum return (investment × minimum return)	100,000	1,000,000	180,000	1,800,000
Residual income	$ 100,000	$ 500,000	$ 20,000	($ 300,000)

If the minimum desired ROI for the firm is 10%, Division B makes a greater contribution to the firm's profit than does A despite the fact that Division B's ROI is lower than that of A. In this situation we could say that Division B was more valuable to the firm. On the other hand, if the firm has established a minimum ROI of 18% (or, in fact, any rate greater than about 14.5%), Division A contributes more and could be called more valuable.

Generally speaking, using RI as the criterion for evaluating divisional performance, the division rated highest is the one with the greatest positive difference between returns and the minimum desired return. In some ways it is similar to the use of net present values as the criterion for evaluating capital expenditures. Under that criterion, the most desirable (valuable) capital project is the one with the highest net present value after discounting future returns at the cost of capital (or the minimum desired rate of return).

PROBLEMS IN EVALUATION

Whether ROI or RI is used as the evaluation criterion, we still must determine what revenues, costs, and investments are to be included and excluded in the calculations. Essentially, the determination of divisional profit should be made along the lines of responsibility, with controllability as the criterion for inclusion of cost and investment. If a division manager is to be held responsible for earning returns (income) on investment, he or she should have control over both the elements of income and the investment that is required to earn returns.

In computing the income for which the division's manager is responsible, it is necessary to identify variable costs and those fixed costs that we have previously described as separable. Fixed costs that are joint to several divisions should not be used in the computation because the division has no control over them. Opinions differ as to what to include in and how to measure divisional investment. As a start, investment will at least include those assets that are used only by a particular division.

Investment in Assets

Under normal circumstances, most assets can be readily identified with specific divisions. Virtually all plant and equipment, for example, will be under the control of divisions (although it is not uncommon for divisions to share productive assets). Inventory and receivables, which also constitute investment, are most generally under divisional control as long as the divisional manager controls production and credit terms. Cash may or may not be under divisional control. Division managers usually have some cash under their control, but in many cases the central headquarters receives payments directly from customers and pays bills submitted by the divisions.

Some of the firm's assets will inevitably be controlled only at the highest level of management. The central headquarters most probably controls the headquarters building and equipment, most of the firm's investments in the securities of other firms, and such intangible assets as goodwill and organization costs.

Suppose we have analyzed the revenues, costs, and assets of Multiproducts, Inc., and have identified these by divisions as shown in Exhibit 11-1. The firm has three operating divisions, A, B, and C. A central corporate office is also maintained. The board of directors has decided that the minimum desired ROI for the firm is 10%.

Exhibit 11-1
(In Thousands)

| | Divisions | | | | |
	A	B	C	Unassigned	Total
Investment in Assets					
Cash	$ 20	$ 30	$ 60	$ 30	$ 140
Accounts receivable	60	80	90		230
Inventory	100	180	240		520
Prepaid expenses	10	15	20	20	65
Plant and equipment—net of depreciation	200	320	440	60	1,020
Investments	10	—	—	100	110
Total assets	$400	$625	$850	$210	$2,085
Elements of Income					
Sales	$100	$400	$700		$1,200
Variable costs	30	220	400		650
Contribution margin	70	180	300		550
Fixed costs—separable	30	90	140		260
Divisional profit	$ 40	$ 90	$160		290
Fixed costs—joint					80
Income					$ 210

Given the data in Exhibit 11-1, we can compute both ROI and RI for each division and for the firm as a whole. The latter computation should be based on an investment defined as the total assets of the firm. Note that no performance measurement is given for unassigned assets.

| | Divisions | | | Firm as |
	A	B	C	a Whole
Computation of ROI				
Profit of the segment	$ 40,000	$ 90,000	$160,000	$ 210,000
Investment for the segment	400,000	625,000	850,000	2,085,000
ROI (Profit/Investment)	10%	14.4%	18.8%	10.1%
Computation of RI				
Profit of the segment	$ 40,000	$ 90,000	$160,000	$ 210,000
Required return—Investment × minimum return of 10%	40,000	62,500	85,000	208,500
RI (profit − required return)	$ —	$ 27,500	$ 75,000	$ 1,500

Although the firm earns only a bit over 10%, only one division earns so low a rate. *Because of unallocated costs and unassigned assets, it is not only possible but necessary that the divisions earn considerably more than the minimum desired ROI in order for the firm as a whole to do so.* The combined RI of the divisions is consumed by the unallocated costs and unassigned assets, so that although the divisions earn residual income of $102,500 ($0 + $27,500 + $75,000), the firm earns only $1,500 in excess of a 10% return on total assets.

This is why as much cost as possible is often allocated to divisions and virtually all assets are assigned to divisions. Proponents of this approach would say that managers should be made aware that there are substantial costs of running the firm as a whole, which costs each of the divisions must work to offset. These costs are joint to the divisions just as are the unassigned assets. Satisfactory returns must be earned on these joint assets as well as on the separable assets. The effort to make division managers realize that they must consider the performance of the entire firm may be worthwhile, but this particular approach can produce problems. When the costs and assets are joint, any allocation or assignment to divisions will be arbitary and may cause disagreement among the individuals holding divisional responsibility. Thus, the effectiveness of using ROI or RI as a motivational and control technique will be reduced.

Liabilities

As you no doubt learned in financial accounting, from the standpoint of the stockholders, return on equity is generally considered to be more important than return on assets. It is difficult to compute return on equity for the divisions of a single firm. Usually there is no satisfactory way to assign all liabilities to divisions. Some liabilities may be easy to assign; most accounts payable and many accrued expenses would normally present no problems. On the other hand, in a large firm with many divisions the responsibility for deciding on the methods of financing will probably rest with the highest level of management, based on the overall need and problems of the organization. Moreover, it is usually not possible to relate any specific financing alternative taken for a given investment in assets. Nevertheless, we could seek out liabilities that are definitely (not arbitrarily) related to divisions and define divisional investment as controlled assets minus divisional liabilities.

Using any liabilities in the determination of divisional investment will naturally cause the ROI of the divisions to increase. This is true because the denominator in our computation (the investment base) will decline, while the profit (the numerator) would remain the same. If we were to apply this new definition of investment in the example used on page 352, the computations of ROI and RI would be as follows, given the assumptions about identifiable liabilities:

| | | Divisions | | Firm as |
	A	B	C	a Whole
Computation of ROI				
Profit of the segment	$ 40,000	$ 90,000	$160,000	$ 210,000
Total assets	400,000	625,000	850,000	2,085,000
Divisional liabilities (assumed)	60,000	170,000	310,000	540,000
Divisional investment	340,000	455,000	540,000	1,545,000
Unassigned liabilities (assumed)				730,000
Total investment	$340,000	$455,000	$540,000	$ 815,000
ROI	11.8%	19.8%	29.6%	25.8%
Computation of RI				
Profit of the segment	$ 40,000	$ 90,000	$160,000	$ 210,000
Required return—Investment above × minimum return of 10%	34,000	45,500	54,000	81,500
RI	$ 6,000	44,500	$106,000	$ 128,500

Both RI and ROI are higher for all divisions and for the firm as a whole when liabilities are included in the computations.

Fixed Assets

In all computations to this point you have been given the amount of the investment in assets. In Exhibit 11-1, for example, the investments in cash, inventory, and fixed assets were given; there was no mention of how these amounts were reached. There are many views on what constitues an appropriate valuation method to be used in assigning fixed asset investment to divisions. Some of these valuation bases include the following: original cost; original cost less accumulated depreciation; and current replacement cost of fixed assets. The method used to value the assigned assets can have a significant effect on the results obtained by following any of the performance measurement alternatives suggested in this chapter.

Each valuation base has some desirable and some undesirable features. Those who favor the use of original cost recognize that there are several methods for determining the depreciation on fixed assets. (Depreciation can be computed using the straight-line approach or some type of accelerated method, perhaps the sum-of-the-years'-digits). Different depreciation methods produce different depreciation amounts, which lead to different income amounts and also different book values for fixed assets. Thus, it is possible for two divisions in apparently identical circumstances to show quite different ROIs and RIs. Managers advocating the use of original cost for these computations argue that the method of depreciation has nothing to do with the efficiency of operations and hence should not be allowed to affect the performance measure for their divisions. Moreover, often the method of depreciation to be used is not under the control of the division manager.

The use of original cost has a major disadvantage, which is not related to depreciation. Consider that the various performance measure criteria should reflect efficiency in the use of input (investment). Comparisons made on the basis of original costs are flawed because the resulting measures fail to consider differences among divisions related to the ages of assets in use. One could hardly expect a 30-year-old plant to be as efficient as one that is 5 years old. Another drawback to using original cost is that changes in prices may render comparisons invalid. It might cost three times as much to build a given plant now as it cost to build that plant 30 years ago. The division operating with the older plant would most likely show a higher return (if selling prices have appropriately increased to keep up with the times) based on the lower cost than a division that is operating with more expensive but equivalent equipment.

Others advocate the use of current replacement costs for determining asset values in connection with performance measurement. Current replacement cost is the cost of obtaining similar assets in a condition similar to those now in use. The basis for this valuation is that current replacement costs both eliminate the problem of different depreciation methods and allow for changes in prices. Thus, managers are not penalized or rewarded simply because of the depreciation methods used or the respective ages of their divisions. The use of replacement costs assumes, of course, that such information is available. But the normal accounting system does not provide this information, and for many years it was thought that the practical difficulties and associated costs of developing replacement costs were too great to warrant their determination. However, in 1976 the Securities and Exchange Commission began to require that certain organizations under its jurisdiction develop and report selected replacement cost information. As yet, we have seen no reports of this newly available information's being used in divisional performance measurement. If the SEC continues the reporting requirement, however, performance measurements may begin to incorporate this information.

Despite the disadvantages, the most popular approach for determining the value of assets to be assigned to divisions is original cost less accumulated depreciation. This approach seems more reasonable in those situations where the choice of depreciation method is controlled by the central headquarters. The undesirable effects of this valuation method are also less serious where there has been some effort to adopt uniform depreciation methods and uniform useful lives for similar assets throughout the firm.

The Subject of Evaluation–Division or Manager

Suppose the firm has determined what criterion is to be used for evaluation (probably ROI or RI), and what costs and assets are to be included in the computation. With what should the divisional results be compared? How are the comparisons to be interpreted as evidence of performance?

There are several bases on which comparisons can be made; each has its strengths and weaknesses. These bases include comparisons among divisions within the same firm, comparisons with historical results in the same division, and comparisons with industry averages, or with budgets.

Comparisons among divisions within the same firm could provide a ranking of relative profitability and some insight into the relative contributions of divisions. But the ranking should not be used to rank the managers of the respective divisions; different kinds of divisions should be expected to have different ROIs. ROI is generally higher for firms (and divisions) operating in consumer markets than for those selling mostly to other industrial firms. The type of industry dictates, to some extent, the ranking of divisions. Thus, the performance of the division manager may be obscured by intrafirm comparisons. A mediocre manager might be able to earn a respectable ROI in a division operating in a traditionally high-return industry. On the other hand, an excellent manager might be saddled with a division operating in a declining industry (maybe buggy whips), and be doing a great job if he can maintain an ROI of 5%.

Comparisons of current results in one division with historical results in the same division would overcome one difficulty associated with intrafirm comparisons. The differences due to diversities in industries are accounted for to some extent. And, if there is a change in managers, the relative performance of two managers may be compared. On the other hand, historical comparisons suffer from the same objections as do intrafirm comparisons and should be interpreted carefully. That is, there is no way to tell whether historical experience is good or bad. Nevertheless, historical comparisons can indicate relative improvement or decay.

Comparisons of divisional results with industry averages can solve some of the problems associated with other measures of performance. Obviously, differences among divisions due to difference in industry are not allowed to influence the performance measure. A division (and its manager) can be identified as better or worse than firms with which it competes. Such comparisons present their own problems, however, because a division should probably earn a higher ROI than an entire firm operating in the same industry. The division will obtain some benefits from its association with the firm. Even when an entire firm operates in a single industry, a corporate staff will be required and some costs will be incurred that might not be reflected in the operating results for a single division. As the trend to diversification continues, it becomes increasingly difficult to find companies to which the performance of a single division can be compared.

Where budgets are used throughout the organization, a valuable tool exists for assessing the performances of individual division managers. Budgeted data should include an expected ROI or RI by division. Naturally, the usefulness of budgets in performance evaluation depends on the extent to which good budgeting procedures are in effect.

BEHAVIORAL PROBLEMS

ROI

Unlike the approach recommended in Chapter 8, in this chapter we have accepted the use of book values (affected by depreciation) for investment and book income for return in the computation of ROI. Although the use of book value for investment can create problems, it is the measure of investment most commonly used in evaluations of divisional performance. Moreover, over relatively long periods of time, book ROI may well approximate the ROI that would be computed using only cash flows. Recognizing the difficulties of using book ROI, we can still say that the firm should expand if it can earn an ROI in excess of its cost of capital.

The use of ROI as the criterion for divisional performance evaluation can encourage managers to pass up projects that promise returns in excess of cost of capital (or the minimum desired return) if the promised return is lower than the ROI currently being earned by the division. Consider a division manager in a firm that has a 20% minimum desired rate of return. The manager is confronted with an investment opportunity offering a $75,000 incremental profit on a proposed investment of $300,000, for an ROI on the new investment of 25%. (For simplicity, assume that the book rate of return on the proposed investment equals the internal rate of return.) The division is currently producing a profit of $300,000 on an investment of $1,000,000; thus, divisional ROI is currently 30%.

If the performance of the division (and its manager) is to be evaluated on the basis of ROI, the manager would be inclined to reject the new investment opportunity. The manager's decision would be based on the decline in ROI if the investment were made, as can be seen in the following computations:

Investment before new project		$1,000,000
Additional investment for the project		300,000
Total investment		$1,300,000
Divisional profit:		
Current	$300,000	
From new project	75,000	
Total divisional profit		$ 375,000
Divisional ROI after new investment		28.8%

From the point of view of the entire firm, the proposed investment should be undertaken because it promises an ROI in excess of the minimum desired. To encourage the division manager to make the decision that would be advantageous to the firm as well as to the division, the evaluation criterion for the manager's performance must take into account the firm's policy with respect to minimum returns. The residual income approach to evaluation incorporates this important factor.

We shall now apply the RI approach to the situation described. Without the proposed new project, the division would show an RI of $100,000 ($300,000 − 20% of $1,000,000). If the proposed investment were made, RI for the division would increase to $115,000 ($375,000 − 20% of $1,300,000). If the performance of the division manager is being evaluated on the basis of RI, he or she would undertake this project because performance would show improvement. The ROI criterion encourages the maximizing of the ratio of profit to investment. The RI criterion encourages the maximizing of total dollars of profit in excess of the minimum required dollar return.

There is some difficulty with both ROI and RI because the book rate of return does not normally coincide with the internal rate of return. Consider the following example. A project is being considered that requires a $100,000 investment and will provide cash flow before taxes of $40,000 per year for five years. The firm requires a pre-tax return of 25% on investment. The present value of the $40,000 stream of payments discounted at 25% is $107,560 ($40,000 × 2.689). Under the decision rules developed in Chapter 8, the investment is desirable because it promises a return of $107,560 for an investment of $100,000 (a positive net present value of $7,560). Suppose that book values are used in the computation of divisional ROI. The book rates of return for the first two years are as follows if straight-line depreciation is used.

Year	Additional Cash Flow	New Depreciation	Increase in Income	Average Additional Investment*	ROI on Additional Investment
1	$40,000	$20,000	$20,000	$90,000	22.2%
2	40,000	20,000	20,000	70,000	28.6

*Book value at beginning of year plus book value at end of year, divided by two.

The book ROI, on which the manager is likely to be judged, is less than the minimum acceptable return in the first year. This condition may persist for several years, depending on the patterns of cash flows and lives of projects. Possibly the manager will not want to undertake such an investment if his ROI will be penalized for a year or even longer, although his ROI will rise in later years. (As an extreme example, a manager who accepts projects that seriously reduce ROI in the short run may be fired before the anticipated increases in ROI come about. The new manager, with no special effort, will reap the benefits of the former manager's good decision.)

This characteristic of ROI based on book value (rising ROI) is even more pronounced in more realistic situations. It is not entirely realistic to expect an investment to begin producing returns immediately or reach its peak cash flows in the early years. Ordinarily some lead time is required, to build plant, install machinery, test the operation, remove "bugs," and generally get the operation going. If a new product is involved, its sales in the first year or two will probably be substantially lower than those in some later years. It is also not uncommon to incur heavy start-up costs in the opening of a new plant or even the remodeling of an existing one. The returns are likely to increase over the first few years as the plant gains efficiency.

There are two major factors working against the manager who wishes to make substantial investments—lower income in early years, and the natural tendency of ROI to rise as the book value of the investment falls because of accumulated depreciation charges. What can be done to encourage the manager to pursue worthwhile investments?

One way to avoid the first-year drop in ROI and thereby encourage managers to accept desirable investments is to leave the new investment out of the base for calculating ROI until the new project is on stream and running well. A version of this approach is used by Burlington Industries, Inc., which bases ROI calculations on the amount of investment at the end of the previous six months; this eliminates the effects of large amounts of construction in progress.[2] Of course, many major projects will take a relatively long time before they could be said to be "running well."

Another approach is to adopt the policy of amortizing start-up costs over several years instead of reporting them all in the income statement in the first year of an investment's life. A third possibility, seldom observed in practice, is to base depreciation charges on budgeted income to be earned over several years; this would provide lower depreciation in the early years and higher charges in the later years. Although top-level corporate managers may not object to leaving assets out of the base or to amortizing start-up costs, there is not much support for the use of increasing-charge depreciation methods. Perhaps the main rea-

[2]As reported by Donald R. Hughes, then assistant controller of Burlington Industries, Inc., in Thomas J. Burns, ed., *The Behavioral Aspects of Accounting Data for Performance Evaluation* (Columbus, Ohio: College of Administration Science, Ohio State university, 1970), p. 56.

son for lack of interest in such depreciation methods is that they are almost never used in financial accounting, and their use for internal purposes only would require maintaining additional alternative records.

Whatever performance criteria are adopted, it is necessary to apply them in such a way that managers will not be encouraged to take actions that look good in the short run but could possibly cause serious problems in the longer term. A divisional manager probably controls a great deal of discretionary spending for items like job training, management development, and maintenance. By reducing these expenditures, he or she might blow up short-run profits at the expense of the long run.

Transfer Prices

In decentralized firms there may be a great deal of intrafirm buying and selling, which necessitates the setting of transfer prices. Firms in the food industry can have farming operations that supply their own processing plants as well as those of others. A textile mill might sell some of its cloth to divisions within the same firm for further processing and some to outsiders. An automobile manufacturer may establish divisions to produce transmissions or windows, which can be sold to divisions that assemble cars. Transfer prices are also needed if service centers are set up as profit centers.

The determination of transfer prices is of critical importance in division performance evaluation because prices influence both revenues of the selling division and costs of the buying division. A potential source of conflict is created: in their intrafirm transactions, managers would like to buy low and sell high. It is possible that the level of transfer prices could influence managers to take actions that are not in the best interests of the firm.

Transfer pricing policy is of considerable significance in promoting actions consistent with the interests of the total firm.[3] The following examples explore the implications of several pricing policies.

1. *Transfers could be made at full cost plus a markup for the selling division.* This pricing scheme provides no incentive for the selling manager to keep costs down. If a pricing policy were followed that allowed transfer prices at cost plus a given percentage markup, the selling manager would make more profit if he allowed his costs to rise. The manager of the buying division would naturally object that his costs (and hence his apparent performance) could be adversely affected.
2. *Transfers could be made at budgeted costs without any markup.* This pricing policy encourages the selling manager to keep his costs down because he could not pass on unfavorable cost variances and he would not have to reduce his price if favorable cost variances occurred. However, he would be getting no profit, which would not be in keeping with the investment center concept. Of course the manager of the buying division would appreciate this pricing policy.
3. *Transfers could be made at budgeted cost plus a markup.* This method would both encourage the selling manager to keep his costs down and provide him with a profit. Objections to this pricing policy would come from buying divisions and would center on whether the budgeted cost and the markup percentages were too high.

---

[3]It is important to remember, as pointed out in Chapter 10, that changes in transfer prices do not, in themselves, affect the total profits of the firm. It is only if individual managers, acting differently because of a change in transfer prices, make some change in their operations that the total profits of the firm as a whole will be affected.

4. *Transfers could be made at market prices.* This method puts both the buying and selling managers on an independent basis, providing they are free to buy or sell on the outside instead of within the firm. Given this freedom, the managers are in the same position they would be in if they were the chief executives of autonomous firms. This method is generally considered the best. The major difficulty in implementing this policy is that there may not be outside market prices available for the division's products; or the prices that are available may not be representative. For instance, prices available may reflect relatively small transactions, whereas the divisions deal in very large quantities. Under such circumstances, the buying manager might contend that the outside prices are artificially high and that he should pay less than those prices because of the quantities he buys.

5. *Transfers could be made at prices negotiated among the managers.* This method would alleviate the problems that arise with the use of market prices. If there were outside markets, the manager who is dissatisfied with the price being offered could buy or sell in the outside market.

Even when market prices are used, managers must be careful in their analyses. Consider the following budgeted income statement for Division B of a large firm. An outside supplier has just offered the manager of Division A the opportunity to buy, at $9 per unit, a component now supplied by Division B at a price of $11 per unit. The manager of B refuses to meet this price, saying that he will lose money if he sells below cost.

Division B
Budgeted Income Statement

	Sales to Outsiders	Sales to Division A	Total
Sales (10,000 @ $15)	$150,000		
(5,000 @ $11)		$55,000	
Variable costs ($8 per unit)	80,000	40,000	
Contribution margin	70,000	15,000	$85,000
Fixed costs—allocated			
on number of units	22,000	11,000	33,000
Income	$48,000	$ 4,000	$52,000

The manager of Division B has apparently considered his per unit cost to be more than $10. He knows his variable costs are $8. Total production is 15,000 units and fixed costs are $33,000, therefore he has determined a fixed cost per unit of $2.20, yielding a $10.20 average cost. Hence he considers the $9 per unit sales price to be less than his cost. The manager of Division B must determine his best alternative from the choices available—meet the $9 price or lose the business of Division A.

Critical to a correct choice is the nature of the fixed costs. If they are unavoidable, he had best meet the $9 price because it more than covers his variable cost. Abbreviated income statements for Division B under the two alternatives are presented below in support of this decision.

	Do Not Sell to A	Sell to A at $9
Contribution margin:		
Outside sales		
(10,000 units at $7)	$70,000	$70,000
Sales to Division A		
(5,000 units at $1)		5,000
		75,000
Fixed costs	33,000	33,000
Income	$37,000	$42,000

Notice that if the manager of Division B fails to meet the $9 price, he loses *all* of the contribution margin he had been getting from Division A, $15,000. If he lowers the price from $11 to $9, he loses $10,000 in contribution margin ($2 per unit × 5,000 units).

When the division manager decides it is in his best interests to sell to Division A, even at the reduced price, he is also acting in the best interest of the firm as a whole. The variable cost to produce in Division B is $8 per unit; hence the resources of the firm required to obtain the desired component would be $40,000 ($8 × 5,000 units). No funds leave the firm as a result of the $9 transfer price between divisions. If Division A were to purchase the component from an outside supplier, total resources of $45,000 ($9 × 5,000 units) must be relinquished by the firm. Thus, the interdivision transaction requires less of the firm's resources; the best decision of the division manager is also the best decision for the firm. From your study of Chapter 7, you should recognize that the problem being illustrated is really a form of the make-or-buy decision from the point of view of the firm as a whole. The use of transfer prices can obscure the relatively simple analysis required for such decisions, as presented in Chapter 7.

The manager of Division B might believe that the potential outside supplier offering the bargain price to Division A will prove to be unreliable. He may, therefore, turn down the business at this time, believing that the manager of Division A will come back shortly, perhaps even willing to buy at a price higher than he had been paying before.

If some of the fixed costs of Division B are avoidable, the manager of that division can still use the same analytical approach. The incremental income from choosing to sell to Division A (even at the reduced price) is $5,000 ($42,000 − $37,000). If the avoidable fixed costs are greater than $5,000, the manager of Division B would show a larger net income by declining to sell at the reduced price. Suppose that the avoidable fixed costs associated with the sales to Division A were $7,000. Abbreviated income statements under the two choices would show the advantage of rejecting the business from Division A, as follows:

	Do Not Sell to A	Sell to A at $9
Contribution margin, as in prior analysis	$70,000	$75,000
Fixed costs	26,000	33,000
Income	$44,000	$42,000

The manager of Division B has once again made a decision consistent with the best interests of the firm. The firm will avoid costs of $47,000 ($40,000 variable costs for the production of the units to be sold to Division B plus $7,000 fixed costs) while paying the outside supplier only $45,000 (5,000 units at $9).

A slightly different analytical approach is required if the selling division has an alternative outlet for that portion of its production that is currently being sold within the firm. Suppose that all fixed costs of Division B are unavoidable; the original analysis would lead the manager of that division to meet the $9 market price. Assume further that the manager of Division B can sell 5,000 units to a discount store at $10 per unit without affecting sales at regular prices, and that he has capacity for only 15,000 units. Should Division B continue to meet the needs of Division A? In this case, meeting the market price is not advantageous for the manager of Division B or for the firm. The manager of Division B will gain $5,000 from switching his sales to the outside buyer, as follows:

Revenue to be gained from the sale to the discount store (5,000 units × $10)	$50,000
Revenue to be lost from failure to supply the needs of Division A at the market price (5,000 units × $9)	45,000
Net gain to manager of Division B	$ 5,000

For the firm as a whole, the $10,000 contribution margin earned by Division B on the special outside sale [5,000 units × ($10 − $8)] is greater than the $5,000 increase in the firm's variable cost ($8 variable cost of Division B currently being paid versus the $9 price that must be paid to the outside supplier).

Whatever the nature of the proposed intrafirm transaction, a necessary condition to resolution of the problem in the best interest of the firm is that the managers involved in the decision have full information about their costs.

SUMMARY

The evaluation of investment centers, like that of cost centers, requires the determination of what the manager can control. Managers who control both revenues and costs are probably better motivated than those who control only costs. However, the choice of measures of performance may have adverse behavioral consequences. ROI is the most popular measure, but RI is advantageous from a behavioral point of view.

Intrafirm sales and purchases introduce the problem of transfer prices, which is more acute in investment centers than in cost centers. Such prices may encourage managers to take actions not in the best interests of the firm.

KEY TERMS

allocated assets
allocated costs
decentralization
divisional profit
investment center
investment turnover
joint costs

minimum desired rate of return
profit center
residual income (RI)
return on investment (ROI)
return on sales
transfer price

KEY FORMULAS

$$\text{Return on investment (ROI)} = \frac{\text{income}}{\text{investment}}$$

$$\text{Return on investment (ROI)} = \frac{\text{income}}{\text{sales}} \times \frac{\text{sales}}{\text{investment}}$$

$$\text{Return on sales} = \frac{\text{income}}{\text{sales}}$$

$$\text{Investment turnover} = \frac{\text{sales}}{\text{investment}}$$

$$\text{Residual income (RI)} = \text{income} - (\text{investment} \times \text{desired return on investment})$$

REVIEW PROBLEM

The manager of the Bartram Division of United Products Company has given you the following information related to budgeted operations for the coming year, 19X5.

Sales (100,000 units at $5)	$500,000
Variable costs at $2 per unit	200,000
Contribution margin at $3 per unit	300,000
Fixed costs	120,000
Divisional profit	$180,000
Divisional investment	$800,000

The minimum desired ROI is 20%.

Required

Consider each part independently.

1. Determine the division's expected ROI using the formula on the bottom of page 348.
2. Determine the division's expected RI.
3. The manager has the opportunity to sell an additional 10,000 units at $4.50. Variable cost per unit would be the same as budgeted, but fixed costs would increase by $10,000. Additional investment

of $50,000 would also be required. If the manager accepted the special order, by how much and in what direction would his RI change?

4. Of its total budgeted volume of 100,000 units, Bartram expects to sell 20,000 units to the Jeffers Division of United Products. However, the manager of Jeffers Division has received an offer from an outside firm. The outside firm would supply the 20,000 units at $4.20. If Bartram Division does not meet the $4.20 price, Jeffers will buy from the outside firm. Bartram could save $25,000 in fixed costs if it dropped its volume from 100,000 to 80,000 units.

   (a) Determine Bartram's profit assuming that it meets the $4.20 price.
   (b) Determine Bartram's profit if it fails to meet the price and loses the sales.
   (c) Determine the effect on the total profit of the firm if Bartram meets the $4.20 price.
   (d) Determine the effect on the total profit of the firm if Bartram does not meet the price.

Answers to Review Problem

1. 22.5%

$$\frac{income}{sales} \times \frac{sales}{investment} = \frac{\$180,000}{\$500,000} \times \frac{\$500,000}{\$800,000} =$$

$$.36 \times .625 = .225 = 22.5\%$$

2. $20,000

Profit budgeted	$180,000
Minimum required return $800,000 × 20%	160,000
Residual income budgeted	$ 20,000

3. RI would increase by $5,000. This can be determined either by considering the changes in the variables or by preparing new data for total operations. Considering only the changes,

Increase in sales (10,000 × $4.50)	$45,000
Increase in variable costs (10,000 × $2)	20,000
Increase in contribution margin	25,000
Increase in fixed costs	10,000
Increase in profit	15,000
Increase in minimum desired return ($50,000 × 20%)	10,000
Increase in RI	$ 5,000

A new income statement and calculation of new total RI would show the following.

Sales ($500,000 + $45,000)	$545,000
Variable costs (110,000 × $2)	220,000
Contribution margin	325,000
Fixed costs ($120,000 + $10,000)	130,000
Divisional profit	195,000
Minimum desired return ($850,000 × 20%)	170,000
Residual income	$ 25,000

The new $25,000 RI figure is $5,000 more than the original figure based on budgeted operations without the special order.

4. (a) $164,000. If Bartram accepts the lower price, revenue (and hence contribution margin) will be reduced by $.80 per unit for 20,000 units. With no change in fixed costs, the drop in contribution margin, $16,000, means a similar drop in profit. An income statement under the new assumptions would show the following.

Sales [($5 × 80,000) + ($4.20 × 20,000)]	$484,000
Variable costs ($2 × 100,000)	200,000
Contribution margin	284,000
Fixed costs	120,000
Divisional profit	$164,000

(b) $145,000. If Bartram does not accept the lower price, the *full* contribution margin from sales to Jeffers will be lost. The avoidable fixed costs will be saved. The contribution margin lost would be $60,000 (20,000 units at $3) and the fixed costs saved would be $25,000. Hence, divisional profit would drop $35,000 ($60,000 − $25,000) to $145,000 ($180,000 budgeted profit − $35,000).

The answer could also be arrived at by reference to the income statement prepared in part (a). The contribution margin lost would be $44,000 (20,000 × the lower contribution margin of $2.20), with fixed costs savings of $25,000. The net decline in profits would be $19,000 ($44,000 − $25,000), which, when subtracted from the total profit shown in the income statement in part (a), $164,000, equals $145,000.

A third, somewhat longer, approach to the problem would be to prepare an income statement assuming the sales to Jeffers are not made. This approach, too, shows a new divisional profit of $145,000.

Sales $5 × 80,000	$400,000
Variable costs $2 × 80,000	160,000
Contribution margin	240,000
Fixed costs $120,000 − $25,000	95,000
Divisional profit	$145,000

(c) If you concluded that there would be any change in the total profit of the firm as a result of the change in the transfer price, you have forgotten a very important point made in Chapter 10. Changes in transfer prices do not, in themselves, change total profits: only if changes in transfer prices cause managers to change their operations and actions can a change in total profits occur. In this situation, the manager of Bartram Division had planned to sell to Jeffers Division and his income statement was budgeted accordingly. If he accepts the lower price, he will still be selling to Jeffers. Similarly, the manager of Jeffers Division had planned to buy from Bartram Division. He will still buy from Bartram Division, but at a lower price. The only thing that has changed is the transfer price. Hence, the firm's total profit will not change. The reduction in the profit of the Bartram Division (because of the lower contribution margin) will be exactly offset by the increase in the profits of the Jeffers Division (because of that division's lower costs).

(d) The firm would lose $19,000 if Jeffers bought its units from an outside supplier. You should see that from the point of view of the firm as a whole, the decision is basically a make-or-buy decision such as was discussed in Chapter 7. Consider, therefore, the two possible decisions, from the total firm's point of view.

	Decision	
	Buy from Outside Supplier	Make Product Inside (Bartram)
Purchase price (20,000 × $4.20)	$84,000	
Variable cost to product (20,000 × $2)		$40,000
Avoidable fixed costs		25,000
Costs of each decision	$84,000	$65,000

As the above analysis clearly indicates, the decision to produce internally carries a $19,000 advantage.

There is another approach to this problem, taking into consideration the profits of the individual divisions and how those profits would differ from originally budgeted profits if a purchase were made from an outside supplier. Consider that if Jeffers is able to purchase from either Bartram or an outside supplier at a price of $4.20, *its* profits will increase $16,000 (20,000 units × $.80 saved) over what has been budgeted with an original transfer price of $5.00. For this reason, the manager of Jeffers would be eager to obtain the lower price, however this can be accomplished. Consider, now, the position of the manager of the Bartram Division, who has budgeted profits of $180,000. The profit of *his* division will decline $35,000 (budgeted profits of $180,000 − $145,000 profits, computed in part (b), if he does not get the order from Jeffers). For this reason, the manager of Bartram should not want to lose the order from Jeffers. Putting these two changes in divisional profits together, we see that there will be a $19,000 loss (a gain of $16,000 by Jeffers and a loss of $35,000 by Bartram).

The important factor in this second approach is that if each division's manager evaluates his own situation properly, each will make a decision consistent with the good of the firm as a whole. The manager of the Jeffers Division will wisely seek the lower price because it will increase his profits. The manager of the Bartram Division will wisely consider the lower price because failing to do so will decrease his profits.

ASSIGNMENT MATERIAL

Questions for Discussion

11-1 Alternative accounting methods Explain how various cost flow assumptions (last-in-first-out, first-in-first-out, weighted average) could affect the measurement of return on investment for a particular division of a company.

11-2 Variance in performance What implications do you see in the following two contrasting questions?
(a) What is our deviation from plan?
(b) How well are we doing compared with what we could do?

11-3 Replacement costs The Perez Company follows a policy of restating asset values at current replacement cost whenever there is a change in the manager of a division. What advantages are there in such a policy and what problems might its use overcome?

11-4 Performance and decision making Can you see analogies between the recommended accounting in this chapter and that in Chapter 7 on short-term decision making?

11-5 Product-line reporting Financial analysts often express the desire that companies publish annual reports broken down by division or principal lines of activity. They have said they would like to see financial statements broken down by products, or perhaps separated into wholesale and retail business, or maybe separated into government and commercial business. What problems might arise from attempting to fulfill this desire for additional information? What recommendations might you make?

11-6 AMP Incorporated has assets in excess of $200 million and sales of about $300 million. Sales are fairly evenly distributed over six broad markets as follows:

1. Aerospace and military electronics (commercial, military, and private aircraft; military communications; missiles; space vehicles; oceanography; etc.)
2. Commercial and industrial electronics (office equipment, production control systems, medical and educational equipment, security systems, etc.)
3. Computers and data processing (digital and analog computers, printers, time-sharing equipment, etc.)
4. Consumer goods (TV, radio, stereo, organs, washers, dryers, power tools, vending and amusement equipment, etc.)
5. Transportation and electrical equipment (motors and generators, rail and rapid transit equipment, farm equipment, buses, recreational equipment, etc.)
6. Maintenance and repair, utilities, building and construction (airlines, bus lines, mobile homes, electric power companies, etc.)

What problems for divisional performance measurement are created by this variety?

Exercises

11-7 RI, ROI, and volume-cost-profit analysis The following data refer to the DCB division of the Octopus Corporation. DCB sells one product.

Selling price	$ 10
Variable cost	$ 6
Total fixed costs	$100,000
Investment	$400,000

Required

Answer the following questions, considering each independently.

1. If the manager of DCB desires a 20% ROI, how many units must he sell?
2. If 40,000 units are sold, what will ROI be?
3. The minimum desired ROI is 15%. If 45,000 units are sold, what will RI be?
4. The manager desires a 25% ROI and wishes to sell 40,000 units. What price must he charge?
5. The minimum desired ROI is 20% and RI is $30,000. What are sales, in units?

11-8 Comparison of ROI and RI, investment decisions The manager of a large division of a firm has developed the following schedule of investment opportunities. The schedule shows, for each possibility, the amount to be invested and the annual profit to be earned. Currently, investment in the division is $5,000,000 and profits are $1,250,000.

Investment Opportunity	Amount of Investment	Annual Profit
A	$ 500,000	$ 90,000
B	700,000	200,000
C	1,000,000	230,000
D	1,100,000	300,000
E	1,200,000	280,000

Required

1. The division manager wishes to maximize his ROI. (a) Which projects will he select? (b) What ROI will he earn?
2. The manager wishes to maximize RI. Determine which projects he will select and the RI he will earn if the minimum desired ROI is (a) 15%, and (b) 20%.
3. Assuming that the ROI on each project approximates the time-adjusted rate of return discussed in this chapter and in Chapter 8, which policy (maximizing ROI or maximizing RI) is better for the firm? Assume that the minimum desired ROI equals cost of capital.

11-9 Components of ROI   The following data refer to the three divisions of International Enterprises, Inc.

	Huge Division	Giant Division	Colossal Division
Sales	$2,000	$3,000	$5,000
Expenses	1,600	2,700	4,750
Investment	2,500	2,000	1,500

Required

1. Compute ROI for each division, using the ratios of return on sales and investment turnover.
2. Assume that each division could increase its return on sales by one percentage point with the same sales as are currently shown. Recompute ROI for each division and comment on the differences between the results here and those in 1.

11-10 ROI and volume-cost-profit analysis   The following data refer to the operations of the Robust Division of Dynamic Enterprises:

Selling price per unit	$ 20
Variable cost per unit	12
Fixed costs per year	200,000
Investment	500,000

Required

1. Determine the number of units that must be sold to achieve a 20% ROI.
2. The manager has been approached by a firm that wishes to buy 10,000 units per year at a reduced price. Current volume is 40,000 units. If the special order is accepted, fixed costs will increase by $30,000 and investment by $80,000.
   (a) Determine ROI at sales of 40,000 units.
   (b) Determine the lowest price at which the manager can sell the additional 10,000 units without reducing ROI.

11-11 **Performance evaluation criteria**   The Foster Company has four divisions, A, B, C, and D. Operating data for 19X7 are, in thousands, as follows:

	A	B	C	D
Divisional profit	$ 3,000	$ 2,500	$ 6,000	$1,700
Assets employed	$18,000	$14,000	$42,000	$8,000

Required

1. Rank the divisions according to (a) return on investment, (b) residual income if the minimum desired ROI is 10%, and (c) residual income if the minimum desired ROI is 15%.
2. What other information would be helpful in your evaluation of the various divisions?

11-12 **Transfer prices for service work**   The service department of an automobile dealership does two general kinds of work: (1) work on cars brought in by customers; and (2) work on used cars purchased by the dealership for resale. The service manager is often evaluated on the basis of gross profit or some other dollar measure. Because of the evaluation measure, the prices to be charged to the used-car manager for reconditioning and repair work on cars he has bought for resale are particularly important. The used-car manager is also likely to be evaluated by his profits. Thus, he would like the service work done as cheaply as possible. The service manager would naturally like the prices to be the same as those he would charge to an outside customer.

Required

1. What possible transfer prices could be used, and what are their advantages and disadvantages?
2. How might work priorities be incorporated into the pricing policy?
3. What do you recommend?

11-13 **Transfer prices and decisions**   The Grimes Company has two divisions, A and B. A sells its one product to outsiders and to B. B does additional work on the units received from A at additional variable cost of $2 per unit, and sells them to outsiders. Income statements for the coming year are budgeted as follows:

	A	B	Total
Sales:			
To outsiders, 10,000 units	$100,000		$100,000
5,000 units		$75,000	75,000
To B 5,000 units	40,000		40,000
Total sales	140,000	75,000	215,000
Variable costs:			
$6 per unit	90,000		90,000
$8 plus $2 additional cost incurred by B		50,000	50,000
Total variable costs	90,000	50,000	140,000
Contribution margin	50,000	25,000	75,000
Fixed costs	30,000	20,000	50,000
Income	$ 20,000	$ 5,000	$ 25,000

Required

1. Division B can buy the units now supplied by Division A at $7. The manager of Division A refuses to meet the $7 price, and the manager of Division B buys from the outside supplier. If there are no other changes, what will the income for the firm be under the new arrangement?
2. Suppose that if B buys outside, A can sell an additional 3,000 units to outsiders at $10 per unit. Assume Division B must buy all of its requirements from the outside supplier; that is, Division A must lose all of B's business if it sells the additional 3,000 units outside. What should be done?

11-14 Effects of different depreciation methods   The Block Company has four operating divisions; one of these, the Lastec Division, makes plastics. Ralph Remon, the manager of the Lastec Division, is in his first year with the firm and is anxious to make a good showing. He has budgeted capital expenditures of $2,000,000 for the coming year and is trying to decide on a method of depreciation, straight-line or sum-of-the-years'-digits. The assets being purchased have useful lives of four years. Total assets currently employed in the division are $4,000,000, of which $2,000,000 is plant and equipment that is being depreciated at $400,000 per year; the other $2,000,000 consists of current assets.

Ralph expects to show profits, before any depreciation, of $1,600,000 in each of the next four years.

Required

1. Prepare budgeted income statements for the next four years, assuming: (a) the use of straight-line depreciation on the new assets; and (b) the use of sum-of-the-years'-digits depreciation on the new assets.
2. Determine the total assets employed in the division at the ends of each of the next four years under both depreciation methods. Plant and equipment is shown at net book value. Current assets will remain at $2,000,000 over the four years.
3. Compute return on assets for each year.
4. Compute residual income for each year, assuming a 15% minimum desired return.
5. Which depreciation method should Ralph use and why?

11-15 Relationships   For each of the following independent situations, fill in the blanks. In all cases the minimum desired ROI is 20%.

	(a) Income	(b) Investment	(c) ROI	(d) RI
1.	$1,000	$10,000	10%	[1,000]
2.	$2,000	8,000	25%	400
3.	6,000	$20,000	30%	2,000
4.	7,000	$30,000	23.3%	$1,000
5.	$2,000	9,500	23.5%	$300
6.	6,000	20,000	30%	$2,000

Problems

11-16 Performance evaluation criteria   The Hawthorne Company has two divisions, Hi and Lo. The divisional managers are evaluated based on return on investment. Budgeted data for the coming year show as follows:

	Hi	Lo	Total
Sales	$500,000	$ 300,000	$ 800,000
Expenses	300,000	200,000	500,000
Divisional profit	$200,000	$ 100,000	$ 300,000
Investment	$800,000	$1,000,000	$1,800,000

An investment opportunity is available to both divisions. It is expected to return $30,000 annually and requires an investment of $150,000.

Required

1. Given that the divisional managers are evaluated based on ROI, which, if either, of the managers would accept the project? Explain.
2. Assume that the managers are evaluated on residual income. If the minimum desired ROI were 18%, which, if either, of the managers would accept the project? Explain.
3. If the minimum desired ROI were 18%, should the project be accepted from the standpoint of the firm? Explain.

11-17 Components of ROI The managers of two divisions of the Diversified Company were recently discussing their operations. Some of the conversation was as follows: Frank Margin, "I get a good return on sales, about 12%, but my investment is a drag. Turnover last year was only .75 times." Joe Turns, "My problem is margins; turnover is about four times, but return on sales is only 2%."

Required

1. Compute ROI for each division.
2. (a) Assume that Frank Margin's division will maintain the same return on sales. Determine the investment turnover he must achieve to obtain ROI of 18%.
   (b) Assume that Joe Turns' division will maintain its existing investment turnover. Determine the return on sales he must achieve to obtain an ROI of 18%.

11-18 Transfer prices and required profit margins John Roberts, the used-car manager of the Snappy Wheels automobile dealership, is distressed by the firm's transfer pricing policy. Roberts is expected to earn a gross profit of 25% of sales in the used-car operation. He is charged with the trade-in price he sets for a used car plus any reconditioning work that is performed. The charge for reconditioning is based on actual costs by the service department plus a one-third markup over cost (25% on sales). Roberts feels that he is being unduly penalized by the one-third markup. Alan Black, the service manager, is held responsible for earning a 25% gross profit on sales and he argues that it would not be fair to force him to do reconditioning work any cheaper than the work he does on customers' cars.

Roberts has recently been approached by Joe Sharp, the owner of Sharp's Garage, an independent repair shop. Sharp offers to do reconditioning work for Roberts at 20% over cost. The work would be done during Sharp's slack periods and it would generally take about four days longer than work done by the service department, which has no excess capacity.

Required

Should Roberts take his reconditioning business to Sharp?

11-19 Service centers The president of Algon Company has just attended a seminar on the use of profit centers, and he is very enthusiatic about the potential of profit centers for his company. He is especially interested in making some of the service centers within the company into profit centers. It is decided that the maintenance department will be the first to be made into a profit center and it is hoped that the experience gained will be helpful if other service centers are to be converted to profit centers.

A meeting has been called to discuss the setting of prices to be charged by the maintenance department to the units that it serves. The manager of the maintenance department suggests a cost-plus basis for pricing, with labor and materials used plus a 10% markup being charged to the unit asking for maintenance services. He argues that there must be a markup over cost in order to render the department a profit center; otherwise there is no point in changing from the current status—that of a cost center. The managers of operating departments argue that a fee schedule for each kind of maintenance job should be established. They do not like the cost-plus basis, believing that inefficiencies in the maintenance department will be passed along to them.

Required

1. Evaluate each argument.
2. Are there other choices? If so, what?
3. What recommendation can you make?

11-20 Make-or-buy and transfer pricing   Monster Enterprises, Inc. has three divisions, A, B, and C. One of the products of the firm uses components made by A and B, with the final assembly done by C. One unit from A and one from B are required.

Data for the product are as follows:

Selling price (C division)	$60
Variable costs:	
A division	10
B division	14
C division	8
Total variable costs	$32
Volume	10,000 units

Divisions A and B charge Division C $15 and $18, respectively, for each unit. Division C has been approached by an outside supplier who will sell the component now made by Division A at $13 per unit.

Required

1. Prepare partial income statements, down to contribution margin, for A, B, and C based on current operations.
2. Determine whether the offer from the outside supplier should be accepted. If A meets the price offered by the outside supplier, C will continue to buy from A.
3. Suppose that A can sell its entire output of 10,000 units per year at $20 if it performs additional work on the component. The additional work will add $5 to variable cost per unit; fixed costs will be unchanged. Should A meet the outside supplier's price or allow C to buy from the outside supplier? Support with calculations. The capacity of Division A is 10,000 units.

11-21 Goal congruence and motivation   The Rex Company manufactures furniture and related products. The manager of the Redfern Division has been seeking bids on a particular type of chair to be used in a new living room suite she wants to market. No division within the firm can supply the chair because of the unique production process required to make it.

The lowest outside bid is $120 from the Dorfman Chair Company. The Wisner Chair Company has bid $130 and would purchase some of the materials from the Ronson Upholstery Division of Rex Company. The Ronson Division, which has excess capacity, would incur variable costs of $20 for the amount of material needed for one chair and would be paid $38 by the Wisner Company. The manager of the Redfern Division knows that Wisner would buy the materials from Ronson, and that Dorfman would not. Each division manager is evaluated on the basis of return on investment.

Required

1. As manager of the Redfern Division, which bid would you accept, Dorfman's or Wisner's? Explain.
2. As president of the firm, which bid would you like to see accepted? Explain.
3. What recommendation would you make?

11-22 Divisional performance—interactions   The Acme Camera Company has two divisions, film and cameras. The manager of the Film Division, John Kretzmar, has just received a report from his laboratory indicating a breakthrough in a new type of film that produces much clearer pictures. The film can only be used in the X-40, a low-priced camera made by the Camera Division. The film currently sold for the X-40 has a variable cost per roll of $.22 and sells for $.80 per roll. The firm currently sells 2 million rolls per year.

Kretzmar is confident that if he devoted his efforts and facilities to the production and sale of the new film he could sell 2.5 million rolls of the new film at $.70 each. Additionally, he believes, on the basis of several market research studies, that if the Camera Division produced and sold 200,000 more X-40s per year, sales of the new film could reach 4.8 million rolls. The variable cost of the new film is $.10 per roll, additional fixed costs to produce it would be $60,000 per year, and additional investment would be required totaling $300,000.

Sam Brewer, the manager of the Camera Division, is not enthralled with the proposal that he increase production of X-40s. He argues that the camera has a contribution margin of only $4 and that he would have to increase his investment by $3,000,000 and his fixed costs by $300,000 in order to increase production by 200,000 units. He is virtually certain, as is Kretzmar, that the extra units could be sold, but he is well aware also that the firm's minimum desired ROI is 20%.

Required

1. Compute the change in RI for the Camera Division if production and sales of X-40s are increased by 200,000 units to show why Brewer is not anxious to expand his production.
2. If the manager of the Camera Division will not increase production, what is the best action for the Film Division?
3. What is the best action for the firm as a whole?

11-23 RI, ROI, volume-cost-profit analysis, and effects of decisions   The following data refer to the Pratt Division of Standard General National Amalgamated Company. Pratt Division sells only one product.

Selling price	$ 40
Variable costs	$ 24
Total fixed costs	$200,000
Investment	$800,000
Planned sales in 19X9	30,000 units

Required

Answer the following questions, considering each one independently.

1. What is planned ROI for 19X9?
2. The minimum desired ROI is 20% and the division manager wishes to maximize RI. A new customer can be obtained who will buy 10,000 units at $32 each. If the order is accepted, the division will incur additional fixed costs of $40,000 and will have to invest an additional $140,000 in various assets. Should the order be accepted?
3. The minimum desired ROI is 20% and the manager wishes to maximize RI. The division makes components for its product at a variable cost of $4. An outside supplier has offered to supply the 30,000 units needed at a cost of $5 per unit. The units that the supplier would provide are equivalent to the ones now being made and the supplier is reliable. If the component is purchased, fixed costs will decline by $20,000 and assets with book value of $60,000 will be sold at book value. Should the component be bought or made?
4. Again, minimum desired ROI is 20% and the goal is maximization of RI. The manager is considering the introduction of a new product. It will sell for $20, variable costs are $12, fixed costs will increase by $80,000, and sales are expected to be 15,000 units. What is the most additional investment in assets that can be made without reducing RI?
5. Assume the same facts as in 4 above except that investment in the new product is to be $400,000, and that the introduction of the new product will stimulate sales of the existing product. The increase in sales of the existing product is expected to be 2,000 units.
   (a) Should the new product be introduced?
   (b) By how many units must sales of the existing product increase to justify introducing the new product?

11-24 Performance measurement—athletic programs   Haltom University is a medium-sized private university with a religious affiliation. Perhaps prompted by the prospect of declining college enrollment, a number of faculty members at Haltom have become increasingly concerned about the costs of the school's athletic program. The football program has been subjected to particular scrutiny. One professor has assembled the following data and argues, based on these data, that football is clearly a drain on funds needed elsewhere in the university.

19X4 Football Program

Revenue from ticket sales		$300,000
Revenue from concessions		25,000
Total revenue		325,000
Associated costs:		
Tuition for players on scholarship	$120,000	
Room rent in dormitories for players	22,000	
Board and incidentals for players	110,000	
Coaches' salaries	90,000	
Portion of salaries of athletic director, ticket office personnel, attendants, etc.	17,000	
Uniforms, equipment, etc.	10,000	
Total costs		369,000
Net loss on football program		($ 44,000)

Required

1. Comment on each item. Should it be included? If you are uncertain, state the assumptions under which it would be included or excluded.
2. What other information would you want before reaching a decision on the desirability of the football program?

11-25 Transfer prices The following is a budgeted income statement for a division of Weaver, Inc. The division sells to both outsiders and another division within the firm.

Income of Superdivision

	Intercompany Sales to Subdivision	Sales to Outsiders
Sales:		
100,000 units @ $10		$1,000,000
50,000 units @ $ 8	$400,000	
Variable costs ($4 per unit)	200,000	400,000
Contribution margin	200,000	600,000
Fixed costs ($300,000, allocated at $2 per unit)	100,000	200,000
Profit	$100,000	$ 400,000

Required

1. Subdivision has an opportunity to buy all of its requirements from an outside supplier at $7 per unit and will do so unless Superdivision meets the $7 price. The manager of Superdivision knows that if he loses the business of Subdivision, he will not be able to increase his sales to outsiders and his fixed costs will not change. Should Superdivision meet the $7 price from the standpoint of (a) the firm, and (b) Superdivision?
2. Superdivision is offered the opportunity to sell 90,000 units to a chain store at $6.50 each. The price of the 100,000 units now being sold to outsiders would not be affected. However, Superdivision has capacity of 190,000 units and if it could not fill the requirements of Subdivision then

Subdivision would have to buy the units outside at $7. Should Superdivision accept the order, considering (a) the firm, and (b) Superdivision?

3. Suppose now that Subdivision has received the offer from the outside supplier, who will provide as many units as Subdivision wants to buy at $7. Superdivision no longer has the opportunity to sell the 90,000 units to the chain store. The manager of Superdivision believes that if he reduces his prices to outsiders he can increase those sales greatly. His best estimates are that if he reduces the price to $9.20 he can sell 120,000 units, to $8.40, 150,000 units, and to $7.80, 170,000 units. His capacity is 190,000 units. What should be done? How many units should Superdivision sell to outsiders and how many units should it sell to Subdivision at $7?

11-26   ROI, RI, and investment decisions   The manager of the Brandon Division of Greene Industries has been analyzing his investment opportunities. The division currently has profits of $1,250,000 and investment of $5,000,000. The schedule of opportunities is given below.

Investment Opportunity	Annual Profit	Amount of Investment
A	$300,000	$ 900,000
B	300,000	1,600,000
C	240,000	1,200,000
D	280,000	800,000
E	260,000	1,000,000

Required

1. Assume that the manager wishes to earn the highest ROI possible. Determine which projects will be selected and the ROI that will be earned.
2. Assume that the division manager wishes to maximize RI. Determine which projects will be selected and the total RI that will be earned if the minimum desired return is (a) 20%, and (b) 28%.
3. Assuming that the ROI on each project approximates the time-adjusted rate of return discussed in chapter 8, determine which policy is better from the standpoint of the firm: maximizing ROI or maximizing RI. Assume that the minimum desired ROI approximates cost of capital.

11-27   Transfer prices and goal congruence (CMA adapted)   The A. R. Oma Company manufactures a line of men's perfumes and after-shave lotions. The manufacturing process is a series of mixing operations with the adding of aromatic and coloring ingredients. The finished product is bottled and packed in cases of six bottles each.

The bottles are made by one division, which was bought several years ago. The management believed that the appeal of the product was partly due to the attractiveness of the bottles and so has spent a great deal of time and effort developing new types of bottles and new processes for making them.

The bottle division has been selling all of its output to the manufacturing division at market-based transfer prices. The price has been determined by asking other bottle manufacturers for bids on bottles of the appropriate size and in the required quantities. At present, the firm has received the following bids from outsiders, for a year's supply.

Quantity, Cases of 6 Bottles	Price per Case	Total Price
2,000,000	$2.00	$ 4,000,000
4,000,000	1.75	7,000,000
6,000,000	1.6666	10,000,000

The bottle division has fixed costs of $1,200,000 per year and variable costs of $1 per case.

Both divisions are treated as investment centers and their managers receive significant bonuses based on profitability, so the transfer price to be used is of great interest to both of them.

The perfume manufacturing division has variable costs, excluding the cost of bottles, of $8 per case and fixed costs of $4,000,000 annually. The market research group has determined that the following price-volume relationships are likely to prevail during the coming year.

Sales Volume in Cases	Selling Price per Case	Total Revenue
2,000,000	$12.50	$25,000,000
4,000,000	11.40	45,600,000
6,000,000	10.65	63,900,000

The president of the firm believes that the market-based transfer price should be used in pricing transfers. The bottle division has no outside sales potential because the firm does not wish to supply competitors with its own highly appealing bottles.

Required:

1. Of the three levels of volume given, determine the one that will provide the highest profit to the (a) bottle division, (b) perfume division, (c) firm as a whole.
2. Do the results in part 1 contradict your understanding of the effectiveness of market-based transfer prices? Explain why or why not.
3. Make a recommendation to the president of the firm.

11-28 Transfer pricing (CMA adapted)   The manager of the Arjay Division of National Industries, Inc. has been given the opportunity to supply a brake assembly to an aircraft manufacturer. The price that the manufacturer is willing to pay is $50. The manager of Arjay is willing to accept the order if he can break even on it because he has excess capacity and would be able to keep skilled workers busy who would otherwise have to be laid off. Additionally, he believes that there is a good chance of getting more business from the same firm at better prices.

The Bradley Division of National Industries makes a part that would be used in the brake assembly. Bradley is operating at full capacity and producing the part at a variable cost of $4.25. Its selling price is $7.50 to outsiders. None of the division's output is currently being sold internally.

The manager of Arjay decides to offer Bradley a price that would result in breaking even on the order. He determines that the other costs involved in filling the order are as follows, per unit.

Parts purchased outside	$23
Other variable costs	14
Fixed overhead and administration	8
Total, before fitting	$45

He decides to offer the manager of Bradley $5 per fitting, which would bring the total cost per unit to $50, the selling price of the assembly. The firm is decentralized and the managers are evaluated based on ROI.

Required

1. Determine whether the manager of Bradley would be likely to accept the $5 offer from Arjay.
2. Determine whether it would be to the firm's advantage for Bradley to supply the part at $5.
3. As the controller of National Industries, what would you advise be done?

11-29 Developing divisional performances data The Dixon Company has three divisions, X, Y, and Z. The following data regarding operations and selected balance sheet elements have been prepared by the firm's accountant (in thousands):

	X	Y	Z
Sales	$2,000	$3,000	$5,000
Cost of goods sold	1,000	1,400	3,300
Gross profit	1,000	1,600	1,700
Selling and administrative expense	400	900	800
Income	$ 600	$ 700	$ 900
Current assets	$ 400	$ 700	$ 600
Current liabilities	$ 300	$ 200	$ 100
Fixed assets (net)	$2,250	$3,000	$3,750

After determining the costs and assets directly assignable to the divisions, the accountant allocated the remainder in the following way:

(a) Joint cost of goods sold of $1,800 was allocated based on sales dollars.

(b) Joint selling and administrative costs of $1,000 were allocated on the basis of relative sales dollars.

(c) Joint fixed assets of $3,000 were allocated on the basis of relative shares of directly assignable fixed assets of $1,500, $2,000, and $2,500, for X, Y, and Z, respectively.

(d) All current assets except cash (which is held and managed by corporate headquarters) are directly assignable. Cash of $200 is allocated based on sales.

Required

1. Based on the data developed by the firm, rank the divisions based on return on investment in net assets, and residual income. (Assume that the minimum required ROI is 15%.)
2. Recast the statements, computing divisional profit and assets employed without allocations. Rank the divisions on the same bases as in 1 above. Comment on the differences between your rankings.

11-30 Performance evaluation and behavior The manager of the Croydan Division of General Goods, Inc. has been evaluating a proposed investment. His analysis indicates that the project will show an internal rate of return of 23% before taxes, well above the 16% required by the firm. He is, however, concerned with the effect that the investment will have on the book rate of return for his division based on beginning-of-year book value—the basis on which his annual bonus is computed. The following are budgeted for his division for the next three years without considering the effects of the proposed investment (in thousands).

	19X1	19X2	19X3
Sales	$2,600	$2,900	$3,500
Costs	1,600	1,650	2,000
Divisional profit	$1,000	$1,250	$1,500
Invested capital (beginning of year)	$4,000	$4,400	$5,000
ROI	25%	28.4%	30%

Data on the proposed project are as follows:

Cost	$600
Revenues (annually for three years)	500
Costs before depreciation (annually for three years)	200

Straight-line depreciation will be used.

The following analysis is prepared:

	Pro Forma Data		
	19X1	19X2	19X3
Revenues (prior + $500)	$3,100	$3,400	$4,000
Costs (prior + $400)	2,000	2,050	2,400
Divisional profit	$1,100	$1,350	$1,600
Invested capital	$4,600	$4,800	$5,200
ROI	23.9%	28.1%	30.7%

Required

1. Is the investment desirable if the pre-tax rate of return required is 16%?
2. Is it desirable from the standpoint of the manager of the Croydan Division?
3. If your answers to 1 and 2 conflict, can you suggest a reconciliation?

11-31 Transfer pricing The Westfall Division of Bailey Enterprises makes stereophonic speakers and sells them to other firms for use in complete systems. The division has the capacity to make 45,000 speakers per year and cannot increase its production because of shortages of specialized skilled labor. Data for the division's product are as follows.

Selling price		$80
Variable manufacturing costs	$48	
Variable selling costs	8	56
Contribution margin		$24

The division has just lost a customer and volume is projected at 40,000 speakers per year for the next several years. Another division of Bailey, the Leakes Division, is interested in buying speakers from Westfall and combining them into sets to be sold through retail outlets. Leakes currently buys speakers of somewhat higher quality than those made by Westfall at $84 each. The speakers are of better quality than the rest of the components of the set, so the manager of Leakes intends to reduce prices and predicts higher volume if he changes to the lower-quality speakers. Volume of the set in which the speakers would be used is currently 3,500 per year. If the price were reduced from $680 to $600, volume is expected to be 4,500 units per year. Variable costs are currently $460 per set, including the $168 for two speakers now purchased outside. The Leakes Division would buy 9,000 speakers per year from Westfall and the manager has offered a price of $62 per speaker. Westfall would not incur any variable selling expenses on speakers sold to Leakes.

Required

1. Determine whether it would be in the firm's best interests if Westfall sold speakers to Leakes.
2. At the suggested transfer price, would it be in the interests of each of of the managers to have Westfall sell to Leakes?
3. Determine the limits on the transfer price—that is, the highest price that Leakes would be willing to pay and the lowest price that Westfall would accept, assuming that they would not take any action that reduced their division's profits.

Cases

11-32 Divisional performance and accounting methods A divisional manager for McKy Company has been under some criticism for allowing his rate of return to fall in the past two years. He has explained that the division has been making some large investments on which a 30% before-tax rate of return is expected. He complains that the use of straight-line depreciation is hurting his book rate of return, on which his performance is evaluated. Following are comparative income statements and other data for the past three years.

	19X1	*19X2*	*19X3*
Sales	$2,200	$2,900	$3,800
Variable costs	1,200	1,500	1,800
Contribution margin	1,000	1,400	2,000
Discretionary costs	300	500	700
Committed costs (largely depreciation)	300	450	700
Total fixed costs	600	950	1,400
Divisional profit	$ 400	$ 450	$ 600
Invested capital (principally plant and equipment)	$1,000	$1,600	$2,400
ROI	40%	28%	25%
Capital expenditures	$ 200	$ 900	$1,500

Required

1. Explain how the falling ROI (in the years indicated) may not be indicative of poor performance.
2. What possible solutions are there?

11-33 Divisional performance, cost allocations, and dropping a product line Randy Rathman is the manager in charge of two product lines for the Kingston Company. He has just received the following income statement for the three months ended March 31, 19X7. The statement shows Randy's two product lines and the total results for the firm. There are 10 product lines in the firm.

	Product Lines		Total
	A	*B*	*Firm*
Sales	$100,000	$200,000	$2,000,000
Separable expenses:			
Cost of sales	60,000	100,000	1,050,000
Selling and general	29,000	50,000	450,000
Total separable expenses	89,000	150,000	1,500,000
Joint costs (allocated on basis of sales dollars)	15,000	30,000	300,000
Total expenses	104,000	180,000	1,800,000
Income (loss)	($ 4,000)	$ 20,000	$ 200,000

Randy is disturbed by the showing of product line A. He believes that the line is contributing to the joint costs of the firm and should be kept, but is worried about the effect on his performance.

Required

1. Prepare an income statement, assuming that product line A is dropped. Show the effects on both

Randy's and the firm's performance. All separable costs are avoidable. Be sure to reallocate the joint costs to product line B based on its relative percentage of the new sales for the firm. Round to the nearest $500.

2. Comment on the results. Does Randy's performance look better if product line A is dropped? Is it better? Is the decision good for the firm?

11-34 Capital budgeting and performance evaluation Arnold Donald, the manager of the Western Division of Global Enterprises, Inc., is considering an investment opportunity. He can save $10,000 in cash operating costs per year by using a machine that costs $40,000 and has a 10-year life with no salvage value. Arnold calculates the book rate of return in the first year as 15% [($10,000 − $4,000 depreciation)/$40,000]. He therefore decides that the machine is not a wise investment because his curent rate of return is 20% and he is evaluated based on ROI. (His current income is $40,000 and investment is $200,000.)

The seller of the machine offers Arnold the opportunity to lease it at $8,500 per year if Arnold will accept a noncancelable lease for 10 years. Arnold asks your advice and specifically requests that you consider the effect of the lease on book ROI. He wonders whether there will be a significant difference between the ROIs under the lease-purchase alternatives.

Arnold further informs you that the firm's minimum desired ROI before taxes is 12%, which approximates cost of capital.

Required: Advise Arnold regarding his choices. Comment on whether the lease or purchase alternative is better from his standpoint and from the firm's.

11-35 National Automobile Company—A; introduction of a new model The National Auto Company consists of four relatively autonomous divisions. In the past each division has concentrated on a relatively limited range of models designed to appeal to a particular segment of the automobile market. The Kalicak Division has been producing mid-sized cars for many years. They range in price (to dealers) from $4,000 to $5,200.

One day last August, Noel Mack, general manager of the Kalicak Division, was studying some reports prepared by the firm's Market Research Department at central headquarters. Mack had been considering for some time the possibility of bringing out a "stripped-down" version of the division's most popular model, the Panther. He had been hesitant to do so because he feared that sales of the higher-priced Panthers would suffer. The market research reports indicated, however, that lost sales of higher-priced versions would be negligible if a new Panther were introduced and priced to sell to the customer for about $4,100. The lowest price at retail now charged for a Panther is $4,550.

Mack was pleased at the results of the study and instructed his production manager to determine the costs that would be involved in producing 80,000 units of the new model per year—the number of units that the study indicated could be sold. Mack also asked for information about additional investment in equipment, inventories, and receivables that would be necessitated by the higher volume.

A few days later Mack had the additional information. The production manager estimated the cost per unit to be $3,600, composed of the following basic categories.

Variable costs	$3,000
Fixed costs	600
Total	$3,600

The fixed cost per unit included consideration of $10,000,000 in existing fixed costs that would be reallocated to the new model under a complicated formula used by the division's cost accounting department. The additional investment in equipment would be $80,000,000 and in receivables and inventories about $30,000,000.

Mack was reasonably certain that the information he had gathered was as accurate as estimates are likely to be. He consulted with several large dealers and concluded that the model could be priced at $3,800 to dealers. Any higher price would force the dealers to charge more than $4,100, with a consequent decline in volume below the 80,000 per year target.

Like the other divisional managers, Mack is evaluated based on the residual income earned by his division. The minimum desired return is 18%. Income taxes are ignored in determining residual income for the divisions.

Required: Determine whether the new Panther should be brought out.

11-36   National Automobile Company—B; interaction effects of decisions   While mulling over his decision whether to introduce the new Panther model, Noel Mack was eating lunch with Bob Tibbit, general manager of the Hatfield Division, which specializes in compact and subcompact cars. Mack told Tibbit about the study he had ordered and gave a general picture of the results, including the projection of 80,000 units of volume of the new model.

After lunch, Tibbit called Wallace Richards, the chief of market research for the firm and requested more information about the study. Richards said that the study indicated a potential decline in volume of 30,000 units of one of the Hatfield Division's best-selling higher-priced models if Kalicak brought out the new lower-priced model. Tibbit asked why that datum had not been included in the report given to Mack and was told that Mack had only asked for estimates in declines in volume of Kalicak Division cars. Tibbit slammed down the telephone and called his production manager and sales manager. He informed them of the situation and demanded that they quickly collect information.

Several days later, the production manager informed Tibbit that the model in question which sold to retail dealers for $3,400 had unit costs of $2,900 at the division's current volume of 160,000 units per year. There were fixed costs of $500 included in the $2,900 figure. Tibbit asked what savings in fixed costs might be expected if volume were to fall by 30,000 units and was told that the fixed cost per unit would rise to about $560, even though some fixed costs could be eliminated.

Further conversations with other managers revealed that the division's investment could be reduced by about $70,000,000 if the drop in volume were experienced.

Tibbit was visibly distressed by what he had heard. He was concerned with his division's interests, but realized that Mack had the right to operate in accordance with his best interests. He pondered the possibility of going to the firm's executive vice president for advice.

Required:

1. Determine the effects on the Hatfield Division of the introduction of the new Panther.
2. Determine the effects on the firm of the introduction of the new Panther.

11-37   ROI at Burlington Industries, Inc.[4]   Burlington Industries Inc. is a very large and widely diversified manufacturer of textiles and associated products. The organization consists of several largely autonomous divisions, the performances of which are evaluated using, among other measures, ROI and dollar profit. Profit measures are before tax but after a special deduction called the Use of Capital Charge (U. O. C.). The minimum required ROI for a division is the weighted average of the minimum required ROIs for three different types or classes of assets. The three classes are: (1) accounts receivable less accounts payable; (2) inventories; and (3) fixed assets.

The central managers at Burlington believe that the use of different required ROIs recognizes the different risks involved in the different types of asset investment. Fixed assets, which are committed for relatively long periods of time and lack liquidity, should, in their opinion, earn a higher ROI than

---

[4]This problem was adapted from material in a paper presented by Mr. Donald R. Hughes, then assistant controller of Burlington Industries, Inc., at a symposium at Ohio State University. The symposium's papers, and discussions of them, are in Thomas J. Burns, ed., *The Behavioral Aspects of Accounting Data for Performance Evaluation* (Columbus, Ohio: College of Administrative Science, Ohio State University, 1970). We acknowledge gratefully the permission of Professor Burns to adapt the material.

assets committed for a shorter time. Receivables, which are turned into cash in a shorter period of time than inventories, would require a lower ROI. The minimum required ROIs for the three classes are 7% for receivables-less-payables, 14% for inventories, and 22% for fixed assets. These minimums are based on estimates of cost of capital and of relative investment in each class of assets for the firm as a whole.

The following data relate to a hypothetical division of Burlington, stated in thousands of dollars.

Sales	$23,450
Cost of sales	16,418
Selling and administrative expense	1,678
Other expenses, not including U.O.C.C.	1,025
Accounts receivable less accounts payable	2,540
Inventories	3,136
Net fixed assets	3,560

Required

1. Prepare an income statement for the hypothetical division. Use the same basis as is used by Burlington.
2. Compute ROI for the division and the weighted average minimum required ROI.
3. Comment on the method used by Burlington. Does it seem to encourage desirable behavior on the part of managers? Is the use of different minimum ROIs a good idea?

CHAPTER 12

CONTROL AND EVALUATION OF COST CENTERS

Responsibility accounting systems provide the manager with information that helps control operations and evaluate the performance of subordinates. This chapter explains how responsibility accounting is applied to cost centers, how performance standards are set and used, and some problems that arise from their use. The role of standard costs in planning will also be examined, with the major emphasis on development and interpretation of standards for variable costs.

PERFORMANCE CONCEPTS

There are two ways of identifying achievement: as effectiveness or as efficiency. **Effectiveness** relates to whether a particular job was done or an objective achieved. **Efficiency** is a more complex concept of performance because it incorporates the cost required to accomplish the task. If you wish to rid your house of mice, an effective way to do so is to burn it down. This method is quite inefficient because it costs you your house. Setting out traps may keep the mice down to a manageable number; it is not totally effective, but is relatively efficient.

Both total effectiveness and maximum efficiency (least cost) can seldom be obtained. In most situations, trade-offs are required which depend on the relative importance of the two measures. Suppose a firm receives a rush order for its product. To fill the order within the specified time may require the incurrence of more cost than would be normal for the given quantity (overtime premium, disruption of normal production schedule, etc.). The decision to accept or reject the order would depend on the results of an analysis of incremental revenues and costs such as was shown in Chapter 7. If the analysis indicates that the order should be accepted, efficiency would be to some extent forsaken to achieve effectiveness (filling the order).

In this chapter, our concern is primarily with measures of efficiency. We describe techniques for analyzing how well managers have controlled the *acquisition* and *use* of resources in producing a given quantity of output.

STANDARDS AND STANDARD COSTS

A standard is a norm, a criterion by which performance is judged in terms of either effectiveness or efficiency. A standard for effectiveness might be the production of a specified number of units of product. Comparison of the actual production with the standard would indicate whether the manager had been effective. If performance evaluation is to relate to efficiency, the problem is more complex because efficiency is a relationship between input and output. Hence, standards for efficiency must be established for both input and output. The *number* of labor hours expected to be used to produce a unit of product is a standard related to input. Similarly, input standards might be set for the quantities of material required and the variable overhead needed to produce a unit of output.[1] The *prices* to be paid for labor hours, materials, and variable overhead items are also standards related to input. They are standard *prices* or *rates*, while the quantities of inputs required are standard *quantities* (hours, pounds, gallons, etc.).

It is possible to exercise some control and evaluate performance by examining physical measures only. For example, we could compare the number of labor hours used to produce 1,000 units of product with the number expected to be used. And we could compare the pounds of material used with the number of pounds we expected to use. However, it is considered more informative to express expected and actual use in cost terms. How much cost did we incur and does that amount compare favorably or unfavorably with our standards? This approach takes account of the dollar effects of using more or less of an input factor and of paying more or less for the factor than we had planned. While the switch from physical measures to dollars is considered useful, the distinction in the previous paragraph between quantities and prices is still relevant. That is, the dollars of cost (either actual or expected) are influenced by the two separate factors. Hence, in order to express standards in cost terms, we must have both *standard quantities* and *standard prices*.

STANDARD COSTS AND BUDGETS

Before going further it may be helpful to review some of the ideas developed in preceding chapters and see how those ideas apply here.

In Chapter 5 we dealt with the manager's responsibility for planning for profit and for the resources required to achieve the firm's goals. Budgeting can be described as the planning of outputs and inputs. Based on planned outputs (sales and related production), the firm planned its inputs (related cost levels for the various factors involved in achieving

---

[1] Note that a standard for fixed overhead per unit of output is not listed. Since total fixed costs are, by definition, unaffected by changes in volume, the fixed cost per unit will necessarily depend on the number of units produced. Hence, an expected fixed cost per unit can serve as a standard only if the volume of production on which it is based is the volume actually achieved. The discussion of standards by which to evaluate the performance of managers responsible for fixed costs appears later in this chapter.

the planned output levels). Thus, selling costs were planned on the basis of expected sales levels and production costs were planned on the basis of expected production levels. And, because plans do not always coincide with what occurs, we introduced the concept of a **flexible budget allowance**, a budgeted cost allowance that took into consideration some deviation from expectations (e.g., sales or production levels that did not coincide with expectations). The ability to develop flexible budgets derives from the fact that some costs are variable. Thus, if sales levels are not as expected, a flexible budget allowance could be determined for the actual level of sales achieved. If production was not as expected, an appropriate budget allowance could be determined for the achieved level of production. In either case, the budget allowance was adjusted to recognize achieved *output* (sales or production).

The relationship between standard costs and budgets is a very direct and simple one. **Standard costs** are per-unit expressions of flexible budget allowances based on output. If it takes two hours of direct labor to finish one unit of product, and if direct laborers are paid $4 per hour, the standard labor cost of one unit of output is $8. Hence, if 1,000 units are actually produced, the flexible budget allowance is $8,000 (1,000 units × $8 standard labor cost per unit). If the per-unit standard cost of labor is added to the per-unit standards for materials and variable overhead, the total standard variable cost for a unit of product can be found.[2] This standard cost can be used in developing the firm's budget and subsequent flexible budget allowances.

Note, however, that for any of the required input factors (for example, labor), two factors determine its total cost. The first is the quantity of that input used (for example, the number of hours worked by laborers); the second is the cost of a unit of such input (for example, the hourly wage paid to the laborer). Hence, it would be possible to establish a flexible budget allowance that took into consideration inputs rather than outputs. For example, in the situation described above, the flexible budget allowance for total labor cost if 1,000 units of product were produced would be $8,000 (1,000 units × $8 per unit) based on *output*. On the other hand, if a total of 2,100 hours of labor were used during the period, it would be possible to identify a flexible budget allowance based on *input*. This allowance would be $8,400 ($4 per hour × 2,100 hours worked).

In this chapter, we shall use the term *total standard cost* to refer to the flexible budget allowances based on output. As we shall see, however, because the use of separate standards for quantities and prices allows the computation of flexible budget amounts based on inputs, the use of such standards assists in the fixing of responsibility, evaluation of performance, and control of operations.

Illustration of Standard Variable Cost

A manufacturer of wooden packing crates has decided to use standard variable costs to aid in planning and control. After careful study he has determined that if workers are producing at normal efficiency the direct labor time per crate is one-half hour. Also given normal efficiency, 20 feet of lumber should be used per crate. Direct laborers are normally paid $3 per hour and lumber usually costs $.10 per foot. Additionally, variable overhead is expected to be incurred at the rate of $2 per direct labor hour.

---

[2]Again, since fixed costs do not change as production changes, the notion of a standard fixed cost per unit of product is of doubtful value. Other approaches to controlling fixed costs are discussed later in the chapter. More will be said about the treatment of fixed costs in standard cost setting in Chapters 13 and 14.

Using these data the standard variable cost of a crate is computed as follows.

Exhibit 12-1
Standard Variable Costs

Cost Factor	Standard Quantity	× Standard Price	= Standard Cost
Materials	20 feet	$ .10	$2.00
Direct labor	½ hour	$3.00	1.50
Variable overhead	½ hour	$2.00	1.00
Total standard variable cost per crate			$4.50

In practice, there might be several other materials besides lumber; there also might be several kinds of direct labor at different rates. We use a single material and a single type of direct labor so as to focus on the general concepts. The same reason prompts our use of a variable overhead approach that is based on hours of direct labor. Measures of activity other than labor hours could be used for determining the variable overhead rate. The selection of a measure of activity to which to relate overhead requires identification, if possible, of the "casual" factor most associated with overhead incurrence (see Chapter 3, pages 57–60. In a highly automated plant, variable overhead might be related more closely to machine-hours than to labor hours. In complex situations, the rate might be based on several factors and determined by the use of multiple regression analysis, as in Chapter 3. The important thing is to determine some reasonable approach to the identification of an overhead rate which can be translated into a variable overhead per unit of product. We use a single figure for variable overhead for simplicity. There would be a number of costs included in this category, like the variable portions of utilities, supplies, and payroll fringe benefits.

Establishing a standard variable cost per unit gives the manufacturer a tool for both planning and control. The standards, if good, can be used in planning to determine what variable production costs should be for any level of production. When actual production is known, standard cost per unit can be multiplied by the number of units produced to obtain the flexible budget allowance for that level of production. If the standards used are current and reasonable, expected cost can be compared with actual costs to see if performance is favorable. As with previous situations where a comparison is made between budgeted and actual costs, the differences are called **variances**. The next section is devoted to the special problems of computing and interpreting variances when standard costs are used.

VARIANCES

We shall begin the illustration of variance analysis by discussing the possible analysis of direct labor costs. With a single exception, the analysis to be shown here is the same for the other cost factors.

Suppose that in one month 1,000 crates are made. What *should* the direct labor cost be? The total standard direct labor cost, or flexible budget allowance, for 1,000 crates should be $1,500, computed as follows, from data in Exhibit 12-1.

Production	×	standard quantity per unit	=	standard hours allowed	×	standard rate per hour	=	total standard cost
1,000	×	½ hr.	=	500 hrs.	×	$3.00	=	$1,500

The term *standard hours allowed* is used to describe the physical quantity of direct labor that should have been used to produce 1,000 units. We could also have computed the flexible budget allowance for 1,000 crates by simply multiplying the 1,000 crates by the $1.50 standard direct labor cost per crate. The method to be used is largely a matter of convenience.

Suppose now that direct laborers actually worked 480 hours during the month and were paid at a rate of $3.10 per hour. The total actual cost is $1,488, which is 480 hours multiplied by $3.10. We can see that actual costs were $12 less than expected (standard cost of $1,500 from above −$1,488 actual cost), producing a *total variance* of $12. But why? And who is responsible for the difference?

In some types of performance reporting (as in Chapter 10, for example), there is no distinction made between variances in prices paid and in quantities purchased. However, in a large organization there are managers who do not control both prices and quantities. A foreman is not likely to be responsible for wage rates or material prices but only for the quantities of labor and material used.

Because different managers might control different aspects of cost, we want to identify the type of variance involved so that we can identify the manager responsible for the variance. Hence, we want to separate the $12 total variance in the example into two components: (1) the difference due to price; and (2) the difference due to quantity. There are several ways to compute the price and quantity variances and many terms are used to describe such variances. Price variances are sometimes called *rate, budget,* or *spending variances*. Quantity variances are sometimes called *use* or *efficiency variances*. The particular terms that you use are not significant so long as you know which kind of variance is being referred to.

The first computational approach to be illustrated deals with the problem from the point of view of total costs. We will hold one of the variable factors constant (either price or quantity), and see what portion of the total variance is due to the effects of the other factor. Note first that the actual total labor cost can be separated as follows:

Actual input quantity	×	actual rate for input factor	=	actual cost of input factor
480 hrs.	×	$3.10	=	$1,488

To accomplish our objective we need a flexible budget allowance based on our *input* factor, labor. Such a budget allowance is computed below and is $1,440, which is the standard wage rate times the number of hours actually worked.

Actual input quantity	×	standard rate for input factor	=	budget allowance for actual quantity of input factor
480 hrs.	×	$3	=	$1,440

The only difference between these two calculations is related to the rate being used for the input factor.

The difference between the actual cost incurred and this flexible budget allowance is due to the difference between the standard wage rate and the actual wage rate. Both actual cost ($1,488) and the flexible budget allowance ($1,440) are based on 480 hours. Thus, the hours are being held constant. Hence, the $48 difference between the two amounts ($1,488 −$1,440) must be due to the difference in wage rates. The $48 is the rate variance. The variance is said to be *unfavorable,* because the actual cost is greater than the flexible budget allowance for that quantity of input (480 hours).

The variance due to quantity is calculated in much the same way. To accomplish this we calculate the flexible budget allowance based on the actual *output* (1,000 units) as opposed to the actual input (480 hours). Our objective is to determine what the total costs would be, based on output. Such a budget allowance is computed below to be $1,500.

Standard input quantity	×	standard rate for input factor	=	budget allowance for actual quantity of output
1,000 units × ½ hr. per unit = 500 hrs.	×	$3	=	$1,500

Compare this formulation with the one immediately preceding it, where a budget allowance was computed for the actual quantity of the input factor, labor hours. Note that both calculations utilize the standard rate for the input factor: the only difference is related to the quantity of input, labor hours. The $60 difference between the two calculated total costs ($1,500 − $1,440) is due to the difference in the quantity of labor used. This difference is *favorable* because workers worked fewer than the 500 standard hours allowed for 1,000 units of output. The relationships just described are diagrammed in Exhibit 12-2.

Exhibit 12-2
Labor Variances

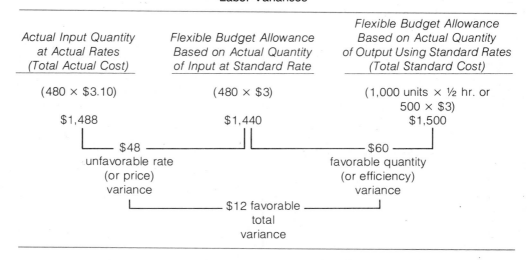

Actual Input Quantity at Actual Rates (Total Actual Cost)	Flexible Budget Allowance Based on Actual Quantity of Input at Standard Rate	Flexible Budget Allowance Based on Actual Quantity of Output Using Standard Rates (Total Standard Cost)
(480 × $3.10)	(480 × $3)	(1,000 units × ½ hr. or 500 × $3)
$1,488	$1,440	$1,500
$48 unfavorable rate (or price) variance		$60 favorable quantity (or efficiency) variance
	$12 favorable total variance	

Our analysis shows that the total variance of $12 can be explained as follows:

Labor rate variance	$48 unfavorable
Labor efficiency variance	60 favorable
Total labor variance	$12 favorable

There is an important point to be observed in Exhibit 12-2. As you move from left to right, the cost figures could be said to become more "standard." The leftmost figure is actual cost, then actual quantity multiplied by the standard rate, and finally, the standard quantity multiplied by the standard rate. Thus, if the number to the left in any pair is larger than the one to right, the variance is unfavorable. If the number to the right is larger than the one to the left, the variance is favorable.

Alternative Computation Methods

We can also accomplish our purpose of isolating variances by dealing with the differences between the standard and actual figures for rate and quantity. For example, the labor rate variance could be computed as follows:

$$\text{Labor rate variance} = \text{actual hours} \times \left(\text{standard rate} - \text{actual rate} \right)$$

$$\$48 = 480 \times (\$3 - \$3.10)$$

Direct laborers were paid $.10 per hour more than standard, and earned this amount over 480 hours.

The same approach could be used to calculate the labor efficiency variance.

$$\text{Labor efficiency variance} = \text{standard rate} \times \left(\text{standard hours} - \text{actual hours} \right)$$

$$\$60 = \$3 \times (500 \text{ hours} - 480 \text{ hours})$$

The firm worked 20 hours fewer than the standard hours required to produce 1,000 units.

When the number inside the parentheses (using these alternative formulations) is negative, as in the rate variance, the variance is unfavorable. When the number inside the parentheses is positive, as in the efficiency variance, the variance is favorable.

You may use either or both methods. The difficulty with this alternative method is that sometimes the actual rate may be a number with several digits after a decimal point. Suppose that workers were paid $1,480 for 480 hours of work. The actual average rate would be $3.083333. . . . You would then have a slight difference between the rate variance computed this way and that computed under the method described earlier. Taking the standard rate multiplied by actual quantity and subtracting this from actual total cost (or vice versa, depending on which is larger) will always yield a precise answer.

In some cases one method might be simpler than the other; fewer computations might be required. If you were told that 6,000 hours were worked by direct laborers at a wage rate $.20 less than the standard rate, you could determine that the labor rate variance was $1,200 favorable ($.20 × 6,000), even though you know neither the total actual cost nor the budgeted amount based on 6,000 hours.

Variable Overhead Variances

We have used labor variances to illustrate the computational procedures. We could as easily have used variable overhead. The computations are the same, extending to the use of direct labor hours if variable overhead is budgeted according to labor hours (as they are in our example).

Assume that variable overhead costs incurred during the month are $980. What are the variable overhead variances? Total standard variable overhead cost for 1,000 units of output is $1,000 ($1 standard cost per crate × 1,000 crates, or 500 direct labor hours at $2 standard rate per hour; refer to Exhibit 12-1). Hence, we know that the total variance is $20 favorable (actual costs of $980 compared with a standard of $1,000).

Exhibit 12-3 shows that actual direct labor hours are used to determine the middle term (the flexible budget based on actual quantity of input), and that standard labor hours are used to determine the right-hand term. (Alternatively, the right-hand term is given by $1 standard variable overhead per unit × 1,000 units.) The rate variance, which is usually called the *spending variance* in overhead analysis, is calculated in the same way as the labor rate variance. The quantity variance is usually called the *efficiency variance* in overhead analysis. It is calculated using the standard variable overhead rate and the actual and standard direct labor hours.

It is possible to compute the spending variance using the alternative calculation method described earlier. However, because we were given only total overhead incurred, we must divide the total cost of $980 by the actual hours of 480 to determine the actual rate

Exhibit 12-3
Variable Overhead Variance

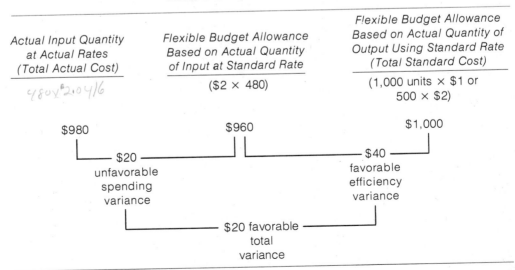

at which the variable overhead was incurred. That rate is about $2.0416 ($980/480). The format of the calculation would be the same as for the computation of the direct labor variance.

$$\frac{\text{Spending}}{\text{variance}} \ = \ 480 \times (\$2.00 - \$2.0416) = \$19.97$$

The variance, $19.97, would be rounded up to $20, the spending variance computed in Exhibit 12-3.

The variable overhead efficiency variance can also be calculated using the standard rate per direct labor hour of $2 and the difference between the actual and standard hours.

$$\frac{\text{Efficiency}}{\text{variance}} \ = \ \$2 \times (500 - 480) = \$40$$

The efficiency variance computed in this manner is the same as that shown in Exhibit 12-3.

The only difference in calculating labor and overhead variances is in the rates; actual and standard direct labor hours are used both for labor and overhead, as long as variable overhead rates are based on direct labor hours. Thus, the variable overhead efficiency variance will always go in the same direction as the labor quantity variance.[3]

This interrelationship is not surprising. Consider some of the costs that might be included in variable overhead. There might be payroll taxes, pensions and other fringe benefits, and many other costs that will be incurred whenever employees work and would vary with the hours worked. The incurrence of these costs is not affected by whether the employees work efficiently or inefficiently. If the employee puts in an hour, the other costs follow. Hence if there are inefficient labor hours (an unfavorable labor efficiency variance), there will be an unfavorable variable overhead variance, and vice versa.

To be complete, the analyses of variable overhead variances would include the computation of variances for each element of cost classified as variable overhead. The analysis would be made the same as the one above. For simplicity, we are grouping all variable overhead into one amount. One reservation on the study of variable overhead and its components—costs such as maintenance, indirect labor, and lubricants—probably have some variable component. A cost cannot be known to be variable, fixed, or mixed by knowing what it is for—its object classification. The cost must be analyzed along the lines shown in Chapters 3 and 5 to determine its behavior.

Materials Variances

Material price variance presents a problem slightly different from its counterparts in labor and variable overhead. Material, unlike labor, may be stored. What is purchased in one

---

[3]In addition, the two variances will bear the same ratio as the ratios of their respective standard rates; if the variable overhead rate is one-half of the direct labor rate, the variable overhead efficiency variance will be one-half of the labor quantity variance.

period is not necessarily used in that period. Consequently, the *material price variance* is calculated based on the quantity of material purchased, not the quantity used. The *material use variance* is calculated the same way as the labor and overhead efficiency variances. Suppose that the firm bought 23,000 feet of lumber and paid $2,390 for it. The average price paid was about $.1039. The standard price per foot of lumber is $.10, as in Exhibit 12-1. Hence, in calculating the material price variance, the flexible budget allowance must be based on what you would expect to pay for the quantity purchased. This would be $2,300 (23,000 feet × $.10 per foot). The material price variance is diagrammed in Exhibit 12-4.

Exhibit 12-4
Material Price Variance

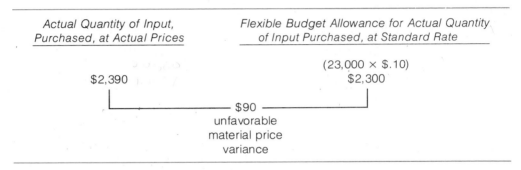

Actual Quantity of Input, Purchased, at Actual Prices	Flexible Budget Allowance for Actual Quantity of Input Purchased, at Standard Rate
$2,390	(23,000 × $.10) $2,300

$90 unfavorable material price variance

Because the purchasing manager's function relates to purchasing, not using materials, the material price variance should be based on the amounts purchased during a period and not the amounts used. If we use the alternative formula, we must remember to use the actual quantity purchased, as follows:

$$
\begin{array}{c}
\text{Material} \\
\text{price} \\
\text{variance}
\end{array}
=
\begin{array}{c}
\text{actual} \\
\text{quantity} \\
\text{purchased}
\end{array}
\times
\left(
\begin{array}{c}
\text{standard} \\
\text{price}
\end{array}
-
\begin{array}{c}
\text{actual} \\
\text{price}
\end{array}
\right)
$$

$$
\$89.70 = 23,000 \times (\$.10 - \$.1039)
$$

The calculated amount, $89.70, is different from the $90 shown in Exhibit 12-4 because of rounding the calculation of the actual price paid per foot.

The material use variance is calculated in the same way as the direct labor and variable overhead efficiency variances. Assume that the firm used 19,500 feet of lumber to make the 1,000 crates. The standard quantity of lumber per crate is 20 feet (Exhibit 12-1), so the total standard quantity for 1,000 crates is 20,000 feet. The standard cost of lumber for 1,000 crates would be $2,000 (which is 20,000 feet at $.10 per foot, or 1,000 crates multiplied by the standard material cost per crate of $2, as shown in Exhibit 12-1). The material use variance is diagrammed in Exhibit 12-5.

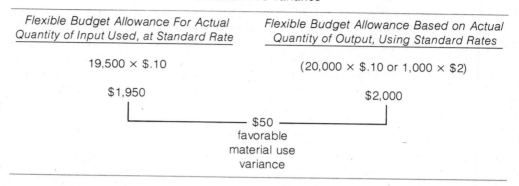

Exhibit 12-5
Material Use Variance

Flexible Budget Allowance For Actual Quantity of Input Used, at Standard Rate	Flexible Budget Allowance Based on Actual Quantity of Output, Using Standard Rates
19,500 × $.10	(20,000 × $.10 or 1,000 × $2)
$1,950	$2,000

$50
favorable
material use
variance

Alternatively, we could calculate the material use variance by using the following formula.

$$\begin{matrix} \text{Material} \\ \text{use} \\ \text{variance} \end{matrix} = \begin{matrix} \text{standard} \\ \text{price} \end{matrix} \times \begin{pmatrix} \text{standard} \\ \text{quantity} \\ \text{for output} \\ \text{achieved} \end{pmatrix} - \begin{matrix} \text{actual} \\ \text{quantity} \end{matrix}$$

$$\$50 \quad = \quad \$.10 \quad \times \quad (20,000 \quad - \quad 19,500)$$

Interaction Effects

Strictly speaking, the methods illustrated do not correctly show the effects on performance due to price differences alone. The price variances are computed using actual quantities. Hence, the managers responsible for the acquisition of resources (materials, labor, overhead) are being assigned responsibility for some of the efficiency or inefficiency of the managers who control the use of resources.

In the example on page 386, standard direct labor hours for 1,000 crates are 500, actual hours 480, and there is a $.10 per hour unfavorable wage rate variance. The rate variance is $48 ($.10 × 480). It can be argued that the manager responsible for wage rates should be charged with a $50 variance ($.10 × 500 standard hours). A person in that position cannot control hours worked and it is unfair to give him credit for the efficient use of workers' time. The manager is responsible for the $.10 per hour excessive cost incurred for labor.

The $2 difference between $48 and $50 is due to interaction of rate and efficiency and is not properly chargeable to either manager. It is a joint variance. The variance due to use of labor is assigned correctly to the manager of resource use; the efficiency variance is calculated based on the standard wage rate. In the earlier computations with this example on page 388, the effects of interaction were assigned to the manager responsible for acquiring labor even though some of the variance was caused by variances from standard hours. In practice, the interaction effect is not likely to be large; it is often ignored and is included in the rate variance.

Interpretation of Variances

We have shown how to isolate the effects of price and quantity differences in variance analysis. We have not identified the *causes* of the variances. It may be obvious that laborers were paid more than or less than the standard rate, but this difference may have occurred for any number of reasons. Isolating a variance is only the first step in analyzing performance. The second step is finding the reason for the variance.

An unfavorable labor rate variance in one department may be due to using higher paid workers from another department. Suppose that to meet a temporary crisis in one department, $4-per-hour workers are shifted to jobs usually done by $3.50-per-hour workers. Workers may have received a raise that had not been taken into consideration in setting the standard. This last variance results from a faulty standard and the standard should be adjusted.

Labor (and therefore overhead) efficiency variances may be caused by any number of factors, some of which may not be controllable by the supervisor in the department where the variance occurs. Suppose that the manager responsible for resource acquisition obtains faulty materials that may necessitate longer production periods, or perhaps bottlenecks in the production process reduce efficiency in departments that deal with the product further along the line. Variances may occur when modifications in the production process cause shorter or longer labor time requirements. The variance in this last situation occurs because standards are not based on the current production process. If the modifications are expected to be permanent, the standard should be adjusted.

Variances are not independent of one another. A favorable material price variance caused by the purchase of an inferior grade of material may be accompanied by unfavorable labor and overhead efficiency variances. An unfavorable material use variance may also result if inferior materials cause more waste than normal.

Isolation of variances is only the first step in cost control. When standards are used and there are variances, managers must decide whether: (1) the amount of the variance is sufficient to warrant investigation; (2) determination of the cause of the variance will lead to corrective action (some variances may not be correctable); and (3) the cost of investigating the cause of the variance and correcting the problem will be less than the cost of a recurrence of the variance.

Investigation of Variances

A variance should be investigated if the inquiry is expected to lead to corrective action that will reduce costs by an amount greater than the cost of the inquiry.

Managers will want to investigate only large variances. Two criteria are generally used to evaluate largeness; absolute size and percentage of standard cost. A variance of $5 is almost certainly not worth investigating, whereas a variance of $100 may or may not be. If the total cost incurred is $500 and standard cost is $400, the $100 variance is 25% of standard. This much of a percentage variance may well be worth investigation, whereas a $100 variance with standard cost of $85,000 may not. Thus, absolute size of a variance is probably less important than its percentage of standard cost.

The cost of investigating variances is difficult to determine. If there are personnel whose job it is to make these investigations, there is not likely to be additional cost because their salaries must be paid in any event. However, with a fixed amount of time to spend on various tasks, it is wise to concentrate on variances that are likely to be correctable and the correction of which may be expected to yield large savings.

Companies sometimes use control charts to decide when a particular variance should be investigated. These charts usually show the cost behavior patterns in the past so that efforts will not be wasted investigating costs that show wide fluctuations. A control chart is shown in Figure 12-1.

FIGURE 12-1   Sample Control Chart

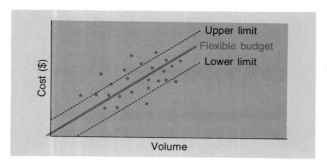

The dots, representing actual costs incurred, are scattered widely. The dotted lines represent the limits within which costs are not investigated. The lines could be set closer to or further away from the flexible budget allowance. The closer the limits, the more variances would be investigated, and vice versa. The wide scattering of costs suggests frequent variances. If the manager believes that the production process is under adequate control and that the variances are unavoidable, wide limits would be set. If the manager thought that the variances were caused by factors that could be corrected, the process would be investigated and perhaps narrow limits would be set. There are many sophisticated ways of developing control charts; you are likely to study some of these in statistics courses.

Management should pay attention to both favorable and unfavorable variances. One might expect that favorable variances could be left alone because as things are going better than expected attention should be focused on unfavorable variances. However, favorable variances in one responsibility area might have unfavorable effects on another segment of the firm. Moreover, favorable variances may be caused by actions that may cause long-run harm to the business. Customers will begin to see reduced quality in the firm's products, and the reputation and subsequent sales of the firm will be hurt. Short-run profits may increase because of lower costs, but long-run profits may suffer.

SETTING OF STANDARDS—A BEHAVIORAL PROBLEM

There are several ways to estimate standards for prices and quantities needed to produce a product. The most common are engineering methods (including time-and-motion studies) and managerial estimates based on experience and knowledge of the production process. These methods apply more to determining quantity standards.

Engineering Methods

Some companies develop standard quantities for materials and labor by carefully examining production methods and determining how much of an input factor is necessary to obtain a finished unit. In time-and-motion studies, which are often used in setting labor quantity standards, an industrial engineer breaks down the movements necessary to perform each task into smaller units. For example, a worker may have to reach into a bin, pick up a part, place it on his bench, drill two holes in specified places, then place the part into another bin. Each individual movement is timed. The total time required to perform the entire task becomes the standard time allowed.

Similarly with material quantities, industrial engineers may study the form and shape of raw materials and the cutting and trimming required. The engineers will then determine how much material will be required per unit, including the material that will be wasted through cutting, trimming, and perhaps spoilage of partly finished units.

Engineering methods may also be applied to some overhead items, such as maintenance. The industrial engineer may be able to identify the necessary components of a desirable maintenance program (much the same as automobile owners do when they set up a schedule for changing oil, tuning the engine, and replacing parts) and estimate the costs of each component. A standard is then established that allows for specified maintenance expense per machine-hour used, with an allowance for other maintenance that occurs because parts break or wear out before they are replaced.

Although some overhead items can be analyzed using engineering methods, it is usually difficult to analyze overhead by starting with a unit of product. Unlike materials and labor, most of overhead is hard to relate directly to single units of product. It is more likely that large amounts of overhead are related to large quantities of product or labor hours. For this reason variable overhead standards are more often developed using methods as illustrated in Chapter 3; high-low, scatter diagram, and regression analysis. Consider the difficulty of trying to determine the cost per labor hour of the wages of materials handlers—men who take partly finished units of product from one work station to another. Only some broad average based on sizeable quantities of production can be used to estimate variable cost of materials handling per direct labor hour.

Managerial Estimates

Some firms cannot use engineering methods. They may then rely on the judgment of managers to determine quantities of input needed to produce a unit of product. This method has several advantages: (1) line managers who are setting the standards are the ones responsible for achieving the standards, and should participate in their setting; (2) line managers may resent staff persons (industrial engineers) intruding into their areas of responsibility; (3) line managers may bring the workers into the process of setting standards, thereby extending participation down to still another level.

What Standard—Ideal, Attainable, or Historical?

What level of performance ought to be considered in developing a standard? Should it be based on what can be done under the best possible conditions? Should it include allowances for waste, fatigue, recurring breakdowns and bottlenecks, that is, currently attainable performance? Should it be based on past performance, an historical measure?

An **ideal standard** is one that could be attained only under perfect conditions. It assumes that laborers continuously work at the peak of their abilities; that materials always arrive at work stations on time; that tools never break; that maintenance on machines never stops production; that no one makes mistakes. In short, an ideal standard is one that is not likely to be achieved under anything like normal working conditions.

Currently attainable performance as a standard is based on expectations about efficiency under normal working conditions. Such a standard makes allowances for unavoidable losses of efficiency due to recurring problems that can never be eliminated. But currently attainable standards are not lax. Performance requirements may be high, but are attainable if everything goes reasonably well.

Historical standards must obviously be based on experience. The use of historical performance as a standard has serious drawbacks. Past inefficiencies will be perpetuated as they become built into the standard. Changes in product design and work methods that drastically affect labor and material requirements may be ignored. Historical achievements have no particular significance and should not be relied upon, *except as they may aid in predicting the future*.

Ideal standards are sometimes argued to be the best choice because they constantly alert managers to deviations from the ideal, and they motivate workers to do the "best possible job." Whether ideal standards really do assist managers in these ways is open to question. A standard that is never attained may cease to have meaning for both manager and worker. The frustrated manager and worker may choose to ignore the standard because they know it is unattainable. Variances using an ideal standard will almost always be unfavorable, therefore the manager has no idea whether his (and the workers') performance is satisfactory based on some reasonable goals.

There is some evidence from the behavioral sciences that motivation is not increased but reduced by the use of ideal standards. Being unattainable goals, ideal standards foster discouragement, lack of commitment to the goal, and distrust of higher levels of management. Research in the behavioral sciences indicates that managers and workers respond well to standards as goals when there has been participation in setting the standards and when the standards are attainable. Such standards may also be used for planning, whereas ideal standards may not. A management that uses ideal standards must still make adjustments in order to plan accurately for expenses, pro forma financial statements, and cash flows.

Additionally, currently attainable standard costs are of more value than ideal standard costs for decision making purposes. Acceptance of special orders, price reductions or increases, promotional campaigns, and other special decisions must be based on *expected* variable costs, not those that could be obtained only under ideal conditions, nor on historical costs that may be outmoded.

Variances and Future Planning: Revision of Standards

When should standards be revised? How often should standards be reviewed? Should variances be incorporated into the planning process or should we continue to assume that standards will be met? Some accountants favor revising standards at frequent intervals because the standards will then more closely reflect currently attainable performance and will therefore also be better for planning. Others advocate less frequent revision because the standards lose their meaning if continually revised; standards will come to represent expected actual results with inefficiencies built in.

The middle group is the most popular. Standards should be revised when the conditions that prevailed when they were set are no longer present. Wage increases, price increases, and changes in work methods would justify changing standards. Several periods of above- or below-standard performance would not justify changing the standards unless some change in conditions would warrant such action. Thus, managers would not have their standard performance levels reduced simply because they could not meet the higher levels.

STANDARD COSTS AND PERFORMANCE REPORTS

Just as with flexible budgets, standard costs serve as bases for performance reporting. A flexible budget prepared on the basis of units produced, rather than hours worked, is the standard cost allowance for performance reporting. The basic concept underlying performance reporting is to report by responsibility. A manager should have the information that is needed to exercise control over operations and should be held responsible only for those costs that he or she can control. However, often the performance of one department will affect that of another. Thus, performance reports usually contain comment sections that provide partial or full explanations of variances; the manager then can concentrate on the variances that need explanation and further improvement.

Exhibit 12-6 on page 398 illustrates a performance report for a cost center. The number of units produced is less than the number budgeted, implying that the manager may have been ineffective because he failed to meet his goal. But failure to meet the production goal may have been caused by a disturbance in a department that has worked previously on the product. In such a case this manager cannot be held responsible for the shortfall in production. If the shortfall is the fault of this manager, shortfalls will appear in other departments that work on the product after this manager's department. The cause of the failure must be determined before the performance of the manager can be evaluated.

This report shows some noncontrollable costs, clearly labeled as such and shown separately. Sample reports in Chapter 10 did not include such costs. We have utilized this format here because noncontrollable costs are usually included in performance reports. The manager is kept aware that such costs exist. This awareness is important in performance reporting for investment centers, as we saw in Chapter 11.

In general, variable costs are controllable whereas many fixed costs are not, at least over short periods of time. Allocated costs are rarely controllable by the department to which they are allocated. Thus, the depreciation on machinery used in the machining department is separable with respect to the department, but not controllable in the short run. The allocated costs are neither controllable nor separable with respect to this department.

CONTROL OF FIXED COSTS

We know from many earlier discussions that total cost per unit of product will change with a change in production because there is a fixed component in the total cost. For product costing purposes, discussed in Chapters 13 and 14, a standard fixed cost per unit is sometimes computed. But for control purposes, the notion of a standard total fixed cost per unit has little meaning. It is the total cost incurred for each element of fixed overhead that is relevant.

Fixed overhead is made up of several components, such as depreciation, property taxes, supervisory and managerial salaries, and the computed fixed component of mixed costs, such as maintenance and power. Each item is budgeted separately for the departments in which they are controllable. The budgeted amount for each element of cost is the standard.

There are, in practice, a number of variances computed for fixed costs, most of which are described in Chapter 13. For the current purpose, the question of cost control, only the budget variance requires comment.

Budget Variances

A **budget variance** is the difference between the fixed cost budgeted and incurred for a particular element of cost for a particular department. Budget variances may occur for many reasons. There may have been changes in the prices for resources (a raise in salaries, an increase in property taxes as a result of a change in rates); some discretionary costs, such

Exhibit 12-6
Departmental Performance Report

Month of May 19X7

Department   Machining   Manager   R. Jones
Date Delivered   6/4   Date Returned   6/6

	Budgeted	Actual	Variance
Production, in units (original budget 11,000 units)		9,000	2,000
Controllable costs, for actual production of 9,000 units:			
Materials, standard of $2	$18,000	$18,800	$800U *
Labor, standard of $3	27,000	28,800	1,800U *
Supplies, standard of $.10	900	880	20F
Repairs	$1,100	$1,200	$100U
Power	900	900	0
Total controllable	$47,900	$50,580	$2,680U
Noncontrollable costs:			
Depreciation Machinery used in department	$1,500	$1,500	0
Heat and light (allocated)	200	220	20U
Other allocated costs	800	860	60U
Total noncontrollable	$2,500	$2,580	$80U

Comments and Explanations * *Faulty materials required more time and created more waste.*

as employee training or travel, might have been increased or decreased by managerial action; and quantities of resources used might have been greater or less than budgeted, as when more or fewer janitors were hired than were budgeted.

Except for the more obvious causes of variances, such as identifiable price changes, the major considerations in analyzing budget variances related to fixed costs are behavioral. A manager who is worried about meeting his budget may have a tendency to postpone incurring discretionary costs (such as employee training). However, where a manager fears that being below budget will lead to a budget cut for the next period, unneccessary costs may be incurred.

A manager can manipulate some discretionary costs to achieve a low total budget variance (total fixed costs incurred less total fixed costs budgeted). If attention is focused only on the totals, critical problems can be obscured. The manager who scrimps on employee training or maintenance is improving short-run performance to the detriment of the long run. This type of undesirable action might escape notice if only the totals were considered.

There are different philosophies about the budgeting of fixed costs. There are advocates of tight budgets, loose budgets, and budgets based on currently attainable performance levels. Our preference is for the use of currently attainable budgets, with the persons whose budgets are being set participating in the determination of what is currently attainable. Likewise, the methods used in setting standard variable costs, historical analysis, engineering methods, and managerial judgment can also be applied to the budgeting of fixed costs.

Fixed Costs on Performance Reports

The performance report shown in Exhibit 12-6 does not distinguish between controllable variable costs and controllable fixed costs. Whereas materials and direct labor can be expected to be variable, the other controllable items could be variable, fixed, or mixed. It is simple to revise such a report to show the fixed and variable components of controllable costs. A revised form of the report appears in Exhibit 12-7.

This report differs from that given in Exhibit 12-6 in only one respect; it shows separately the fixed and variable components of controllable costs. In planning, the manager would want to know whether a variance already experienced is likely to recur. It may be easier to plan for future variances if the fixed and variable controllable costs are separated. If a fixed cost appears to be running $100 per month more or less than budgeted, and this variance is expected to continue, the manager can count on the variance being $100 per month. A direct labor efficiency variance that appears to be 10% of standard cost will be a different dollar amount in each month depending on production. Thus, planning for future operations requires different analyses for the two kinds of costs—fixed and variable.

A PROBLEM AREA: FIXED AND VARIABLE COSTS

In some situations the firm may not be able to isolate the variable overhead variances and the fixed overhead budget variances. This will occur when it is impossible to determine how much of the *actual* overhead costs incurred is fixed and how much is variable. Some overhead costs will be mixed, having both a fixed component and a variable component. For example, a cost like electricity might have both fixed and variable components. For budgeting and planning, the fixed and variable components might be easy to identify by using the

Exhibit 12-7
Departmental Performance Report

Month of May 19X7

Department __Machining__   Manager __R. Jones__
Date Delivered __6/4__   Date Returned __6/6__

	Budgeted	Actual	Variance
Production, in units (original budget 11,000 units)		9,000	2,000
Controllable costs, for actual production of 9,000 units:			
Variable:			
Materials, standard of __$2__	$18,000	$18,800	$800U *
Labor, standard of __$3__	27,000	28,800	1,800U *
Supplies, standard of __$.10__	900	880	20F
Total variable	$45,900	$48,480	$2,580
Fixed:			
Repairs	$1,100	$1,200	$100U
Power	900	900	0
Total fixed	$2,000	$2,100	$100U
Total controllable	$47,900	$50,580	$2,680U
Noncontrollable costs:			
Depreciation __Machinery used in department__	$1,500	$1,500	0
Heat and light (allocated)	200	220	20U
Other allocated costs	800	860	60U
Total noncontrollable	$2,500	$2,580	$80U

Comments and Explanations * _Faulty materials required more time and created more waste._

scatter-diagram or high-low method. And the calculated values might be quite accurate in predicting the total cost that will be incurred at a specified level of activity.

Suppose that electricity is budgeted per month using the following formula: total cost = $2,450 + ($.80 × direct labor hours). The fixed portion is related, perhaps, to lighting and operating machinery that is not turned off when the product is not being produced. The variable portion relates to machinery that is operated only when products are being produced. At the end of a month it would not be possible to tell how much electricity was used for the two major purposes unless the machinery had separate meters. Suppose that production is 4,000 units, and that two standard direct labor hours are required per unit. Total standard hours allowed would be 8,000 (4,000 × 2). The total budgeted cost for electricity would be $8,850, which is $2,450 + ($.80 × 8,000 standard labor hours). If the actual cost were $8,630 or $9,210, it would not be possible to determine the extent to which lighting or machine use was responsible for the total variance.

Consequently, it is often the case that a single variance will be computed for both fixed and variable overhead—a budget variance. This would be done even if it were known that some of the variance was attributable to efficiency or inefficiency. When it is impossible to separate the fixed and variable costs actually incurred, only the one total overhead budget variance may be computed.

Why might a firm not work toward isolating the fixed and variable components of the actual cost? Why, for example, wouldn't the firm in the example above install meters on its machines in order to determine how much electricity related to machines and how much to lighting the factory? The answer is usually that the cost to obtain the additional information would be greater than the benefits to be achieved. True, the firm would have a better idea of why it was experiencing variances. But the cost to install and maintain the meters might be more than the savings that could be achieved through better control. A fundamental principle of managerial accounting is that obtaining additional information is desirable only if the benefits will exceed the costs.

STANDARD COSTS FOR NONMANUFACTURING ACTIVITIES

Standard costs were developed for nonmanufacturing activities long after they were used for manufacturing. Nonmanufacturing activities have certain traits that render the development of standard costs difficult. The measure of output in nonmanufacturing activities is difficult to determine. It is rare that homogeneous physical units flow out of the work done by the product design, legal, accounting, marketing, and general administration departments. There is seldom a definable measure of output because there is no standard product.

Costs associated with administrative and general work also tend to be fixed more than those of manufacturing. Consequently, it might be impossible to develop standard variable costs per unit of output even if the appropriate unit of output could be determined. Therefore, general and administrative activities are usually controlled by budgets, rather than by standard variable costs. Thus the preceding material on control of fixed costs is applicable to nonmanufacturing activities, but, in general, the material on standard variable costs is not.

Despite the difficulties, there have been and will continue to be numerous attempts to develop standards for nonmanufacturing activities. For example, the number of typing strokes per page has been standardized by some organizations as has the number of files processed and the number of books shelved. This is a challenging and important area of managerial accounting.

SUMMARY

The use of standard costs provides a way of controlling and evaluating the activities of cost centers. The manager of a cost center and superiors receive information showing the efficiency of his operation. Comparisons of planned production with actual production indicate whether the manager was effective in performing assigned tasks.

A single manager is not always responsible for both prices and uses of resources, so the separation of total variances into price and use variances assists in assigning responsibility. The same separation is helpful in planning future operations if it can be determined that particular variances are likely to recur.

Standards that are loose may not encourage managers to work efficiently. Standards that are too tight may discourage the manager and he will not accept the standards as legitimate. Participation by managers in the setting of standards can help to overcome some of these problems. It is not usually the case that a manager's performance is strictly a result of his own actions; there are interdependencies among managerial functions. Thus, variances cannot automatically be said to be due to good or bad performance by a single manager, but must be analyzed to determine their causes.

KEY TERMS

currently attainable standards	labor efficiency variance
effectiveness	labor rate variance
efficiency	material price variance
engineered standards	material use variance
flexible budget allowance	overhead efficiency variance
ideal standard	overhead spending variance
	standard costs

KEY FORMULAS

$$\begin{array}{c} \text{Total standard} \\ \text{cost for} \\ \text{input factor} \end{array} = \text{production} \times \begin{array}{c} \text{standard quantity} \\ \text{of input factor} \\ \text{per unit of} \\ \text{production} \end{array} \times \begin{array}{c} \text{standard rate for} \\ \text{input factor per} \\ \text{unit of input} \end{array}$$

$$\begin{array}{c} \text{Total actual cost} \\ \text{for input} \\ \text{factor} \end{array} = \begin{array}{c} \text{actual} \\ \text{input} \\ \text{quantity} \end{array} \times \begin{array}{c} \text{actual price} \\ \text{for input} \\ \text{factor} \end{array}$$

$$\text{Price variance} = \text{actual quantity of input acquired} \times \left(\text{standard price per unit of input} - \text{actual price per unit of input} \right)$$

$$\text{Quantity variance} = \text{standard price per unit of input} \times \left(\text{standard quantity of input required} - \text{actual quantity of input used} \right)$$

REVIEW PROBLEM

The Baldwin Company makes cabinets. One model, the Deluxe, has the following requirements.

Materials (44 feet of wood at $.20 per foot)
Direct labor (4 hours at $7 per hour)
Variable overhead ($5 per direct labor hour)

During June 19X4 the firm made 1,200 Deluxe cabinets. Operating results were:

Material purchases	58,000 feet at $.19	$11,020
Material used	53,200 feet	
Direct labor	4,750 hours at $7.10	$33,725
Variable overhead		$23,900

Required
Compute the standard variable cost per Deluxe cabinet and the variances for June 19X4.

Answers to Review Problem

Standard Variable Cost

Material (44 feet of wood at $.20)	$ 8.80
Direct labor (4 hours at $7 per hour)	28.00
Variable overhead at $5 per direct labor hour	20.00
Total standard variable cost	$56.80

Materials Variances for June 19X4

Actual Cost of Materials Purchased   *Budgeted Cost for 58,000 Feet*

($.19 × 58,000)   ($.20 × 58,000)
$11,020 $11,600

└────────────── $580 ──────────────┘
favorable material
price variance

Alternatively, ($.20 − $.19) × 58,000 = $.01 × 58,000 = $580 favorable.

Budgeted Cost of Materials Used   *Budgeted Cost for 1,200 Units*

($.20 × 53,200)   ($8.80 × 1,200)
$10,640 $10,560

└────────────── $80 ──────────────┘
unfavorable material
use variance

Alternatively, (52,800 − 53,200) × $.20 = 400 × $.20 = $80 unfavorable
╱ standard
quantity
1,200 ×
44 feet

Labor Variances for June 19X4

Direct Labor Cost Incurred   *Budgeted Cost for 4,750 Hours*   *Budgeted Cost for 1,200 Units*

(4,750 × $7.10)   (4,750 × $7)   (1,200 × $28)
$33,725 $33,250 $33,600

└────── $475 ──────┘   └────── $350 ──────┘
unfavorable labor   favorable labor
rate variance   efficiency variance

└────────────── $125 ──────────────┘
unfavorable total
labor variance

Alternatively, the labor rate variance is:

$$4,750 × ($7 − $7.10) = $475 \text{ unfavorable}$$

The labor efficiency variance is:

$$$7 × (4,800 − 4,750) = $350 \text{ favorable}$$
╱ standard
hours
1,200 × 4

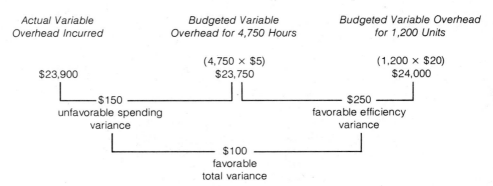

Alternatively, the spending variance could be computed by calculating the actual rate of about $5.032, and subtracting it from the standard rate of $5, then multiplying by 4,750 hours.

$$(\$5 - \$5.032) \times 4,750 = \$152 \text{ unfavorable}$$

The efficiency variance is also given by:

$$\$5 \times (4,800 - 4,750) = \$250 \text{ favorable}$$

Note that because the variable overhead standard is based on direct labor hours, the only difference between the computation of the labor efficiency variance and the variable overhead efficiency variance is the rate used.

ASSIGNMENT MATERIAL

Questions for discussion

12-1 Budgeting and standards · Budgeting aids managers in planning and control. Standard costs are useful for assisting in budgeting and for planning and control in general. What is accomplished by the use of standard costs that is not accomplished by budgeting?

12-2 Interpretation of variances For each of the following situations (a) indicate whether a variance would be expected to occur; (b) state which variance(s) would be affected and in what direction; and (c) state whether an investigation should be undertaken and whether you think corrective action could be taken.

1. Wage rates have risen because a new union contract has been signed.
2. To increase safety, the plant manager has reduced the speeds at which fork-lift trucks carrying materials and semifinished products among work stations can be driven.
3. The firm sells its wasted raw materials, chiefly metals, to a scrap dealer. Lately, revenue from sales of waste has been increasing although production has been steady.
4. Exceptionally heavy rainfall necessitates the drying out of certain materials that are stored outside.
5. The electric utility that supplies the firm with power has been having difficulty with its generators. There are frequent blackouts and brownouts.
6. Many part-time workers must be hired because of a rapid increase in production.
7. The purchasing manager has found a cheaper material that requires more working and creates more waste than did the formerly used material.

12-3 Revising standards Indicate whether each of the events listed below calls for revision in standards and, if so, which standard(s). If possible, indicate the direction of the revision. Assume that currently attainable performance is the basis for all standards.

1. Wage rates have been increased as a result of the signing of a new union contract.
2. Complaints from customers about dullness of a metallic finish on the product have induced the production manager to assign a semiskilled worker to buff the surface.
3. The labor efficiency variance has consistently been unfavorable by anywhere from 2% to 4%.
4. A new material is being used that is more expensive than the old. However, there is less waste and it is easier to handle.
5. The product is a wooden cabinet. Previously, a number of parts of the cabinet had been nailed together. Now those parts are being screwed together.
6. A strike at the plant of a supplier has forced the purchase of some raw materials at higher prices from other sources.
7. Rates for electricity have increased. The plant uses a great deal of electricity for machinery.
8. An overhead crane has been installed to speed the movement of semifinished product from one work station to another.

12-4 The 1973 annual report of Genesco Inc. contains the following paragraphs.

> Genesco's footwear operations consist of divisions which manufacture and wholesale footwear for men, women, and children in a broad range of styles and prices. Also included are the divisions which manufacture leather, soles, heels, adhesives, finishes and other footwear components. During 1973, there were three factors which had a major adverse impact on footwear operations.
>
> **1 The Change in Product Mix.** In fiscal 1972, demand was high for three types of footwear—boots, canvas footwear, and "stitchout/stitchdown" constructions (the casual "jeans shoes"). This consistent demand permitted the plants to operate with high efficiency and low costs. When the product mix shifted in fiscal 1973, the footwear plants made the changeover, but nevertheless experienced start-up costs and temporarily reduced efficiency.
>
> **2 Major Styling and Construction Changes.** In fiscal 1973 the major fashion change was the emphasis on shoe bottoms: high heels, platforms, and clogs. As the footwear plants shifted, this new fashion emphasis necessitated major expansions of shoe bottom preparation departments and the development of new manufacturing techniques. In men's shoes, the advent of high heels introduced a whole new dimension to the men's shoe factories. These styling and construction changes also complicated the manufacturing changeover.
>
> **3 Rising Hide Prices.** Compounding these two factors was a threefold increase in hide prices in a year's time caused by rising world demand. The unstable and unprecedented conditions which prevailed throughout fiscal 1973 affected not only footwear divisions but leather operations as well.
>
> In response to this situation, a significant shift was made to manmade materials. This shift helped hold down costs, although differences between the nature of leather and the synthetic materials created additional manufacturing problems.
>
> Responding to these challenges, footwear manufacturing has been reorganized to reduce the reaction time for future fashion swings. At the same time, the changes and expenses required by these unusual conditions are now largely behind footwear.

What is meant by "efficiency" in the comments on product mix? How would you classify the cost of hides in terms of behavior? What are implications of the "significant shift," as discussed under part 3, for the standard costs used by the company?

12-5 Setting standards The controller of a large manufacturing company said: ''In our company the standard cost is the true cost; actual cost is simply an aberration from true cost.'' Speculate on how the standards might have been set.

12-6 Responsibility for variances (CMA adapted) The Phillips Company used a standard cost system. Variances for each department are calculated and reported to the department manager. The reporting has two major purposes: for use by superiors in evaluating performance, and for use by managers in improving their own operations.

Jake Smith was recently appointed manager of the Assembly Department. He has complained that the system does not work properly and discriminates against his department because of the current practice of calculating a variance for rejected units. The procedures for making this calculation are: (1) all units are inspected at the end of the assembly operation; (2) rejected units are examined to see if the cause of rejection can be assigned to a particular department; (3) units that are rejected but cannot be identified with a particular department are totaled; (4) the unidentifiable rejects are apportioned to each department on the basis of the identifiable rejects. Thus, if a department had 20% of the identified rejects, it would also be charged with 20% of the unidentified rejects. The variance, then, is the sum of the identifiable rejects and the apportioned share of unidentified rejects.

Required
1. Discuss the validity of Smith's claim.
2. Make a recommendation for resolving the problem.

Exercises

12-7 Standard cost computations The Blivet Company makes a single product and has established the standard prices and quantities for a finished unit as follows:

Material	3 lbs. @ $1 per pound
Direct labor	4 hrs. @ $3 per hour
Variable overhead	$4 per direct labor hour (DLH)

The company also has fixed overhead of $100,000 per year.

Required
Fill in the blanks in the following items.
1. The standard cost per unit of finished product is
   (a) _____ for material,
   (b) _____ for direct labor, and
   (c) _____ for variable overhead.
2. At 70,000 hours of direct labor, the total variable overhead cost should be _____.
3. At 80,000 hours of direct labor, production should be _____ units.
4. If 75,000 pounds of material are used, production should be _____ units.
5. At 90,000 hours of direct labor, the total material used should be _____ lbs.
6. If 66,000 pounds of material are used, the total variable overhead cost should be _____, and the total labor cost should be _____.

12-8 Variance computations Below are the standard variable costs for a glotto.

Material	3 lbs. of lotto @ $1 per pound	$ 3.00
Labor	3 hrs. of glueing labor @ $4 per hour	12.00
Variable overhead	$2 per labor hour	6.00
		$21.00

Actual results in March were as follows:

Production	1,000 glottos
Materials purchased and used	3,200 lbs. for $3,520 *1.10 per lb*
Hours of gluing labor worked	3,900 hrs.
Cost of labor	$15,210
Variable overhead incurred	$6,300

Required

Compute all variable cost variances.

12-9 Significance of variances Ann Jackson, the controller for the Stone Company, was recently told by several production managers that ''as long as total costs do not exceed budgeted costs, based on standard prices and quantities, there is no reason to do any investigating or analysis.''

Required

Comment critically on the statement. Cite at least two reasons for not accepting it.

12-10 Variance computations The Trivet Company makes a single product and has developed the following standard cost per unit of finished product:

Material	2 lbs. @ $2	$ 4.00
Direct labor	3 hrs. @ $3	9.00
Variable overhead	$2 per DLH	6.00
Total standard variable cost per unit		$19.00

In 1975, the actual results were as follows:

Direct labor hours worked	75,000
Number of units produced	23,000
Rate paid to direct laborers	$3.10 per hour
Materials purchased	48,000 lbs.
Price paid for materials	$2.05 per pound
Materials used in production	44,000 lbs.
Variable overhead incurred	$146,000

Required

Compute all variable cost variances.

12-11 Revision of standard costs The Clarkson Company manufactures toys. One group of toys consists of small cars, each of which requires the same quantities of materials and direct labor. The cars are packaged and sold in batches of 50. The standard variable cost of a batch is given below.

Materials	$10.00
Direct labor (4 hrs.)	16.00
Variable overhead	12.00
Total standard variable cost	$38.00

The supervisor of the department in which the toys are made is uncertain how to prepare the budget for the coming year. He tells you the following:

(a) Material costs will be higher by an average of 10% because of price increases.
(b) Laborers will get a 5% pay raise at the beginning of the year.
(c) Increased efficiency will result in a 10% reduction in direct labor hours.
(d) The variable overhead rate will increase to $3.20 per direct labor hour.

Required

Prepare revised standard variable costs.

12-12 Relationships Each of the situations given below is independent. The only element of cost being considered is direct labor. Fill in the blanks.

	a	b	c	d	e
Units produced	1,000	8400	4,000	2,000	6000
Actual hours worked	2,800	4,300	7900	6,200	4,000
Standard hours for production achieved	3,000	4200	8,000	6,000	4,200
Standard hours per unit	3	.5	2	3	.7
Standard rate per hour	$2	$10	$4	4	5
Actual labor cost	5712	$41,800	32,200	$24,500	$20,600
Rate variance	$112U	1204F	$600U	$300F	$600U
Efficiency variance	400F	$1,000U	$400F	$800U	1,200U

12-13 Variances Given the following data, compute all variable cost variances.

Standards for a Unit of Product

Material	3 lbs. @ $2 per pound 6
Direct labor	4 hrs. @ $5 per hour 20
Variable overhead	$3 per direct labor hour 12

38

June Activity

Production	2,000 units
Material purchases (all used)	6,500 lbs. for $13,500
Laborers' earnings	7,800 hrs. for $41,000
Variable overhead incurred	$22,500

12-14 Variance analysis The Kuhn Company makes automobile antifreeze. The firm has developed the following formula for budgeting monthly factory overhead costs. Total overhead cost = $122,000 + ($12 × direct labor hours). Other data relating to the cost of a case of the product are given below.

Materials	4 gallons at $.80 per gallon
Direct labor	20 minutes at $6 per hour

During a recent month the firm produced 15,000 cases of product and incurred the following costs.

Materials (purchased and used)	59,500 gallons	$48,200
Direct labor	5,100 hours	$30,600
Overhead		$183,500

Required

Compute the price and quantity variances for materials and direct labor and the total variance for overhead.

12-15 Performance reporting The president of your firm has asked you to investigate some unfavorable variances that arose in one of the departments last month. The following summary of the department's performance report was given to you.

	Budget	Actual	Variance
Production (in units)	2,000	2,500	500F
Costs (based on budgeted production):			
Direct labor	$6,000	$7,000	$1,000U
Supplies	400	650	250U
Repairs	1,000	1,200	200U
Power	800	1,100	300U
Total costs (all variable)	$8,200	$9,950	$1,750U

Required

1. Was performance poor?
2. What suggestions do you have?

12-16 Variances—relationships among accounts Read the following in its entirety and then fill in the blanks.

1. Standard variable costs per unit:
   (a) Materials   3 lbs. @ $ *3.00* $ *19.00*
   (b) Direct labor   *2* hrs. @ $4.00 $ 8.00
   (c) Variable overhead $3 per DLH $ *6.00*
2. Production   8,000 units
3. Material purchases   30,000 lbs. $86,000
4. Material used, at standard prices, 26,000 lbs. *×3* $ *78,000*
5. Direct labor, actual   *14,000* hrs. *56,000÷4* $59,200
6. Material price variance $ 4,000F
7. Material use variance $ *6,000*
8. Direct labor rate variance $ 3,200U
9. Direct labor efficiency variance *14,000× 4=56,000 - 64,000 8000×8* $ *8,000F*
10. Variable overhead spending variance $ 1,200U
11. Variable overhead efficiency variance $ *6,000F*
12. Variable overhead, actual *(14,000×3) 42,000 + 1,200* $ *43,200*

12-17 Standard costs and variances on a machine-hour basis The Wilkens Company is highly automated and uses machine-hours as the basis for setting standard variable costs per unit of product. A unit of product requires two pounds of material costing $3 per pound and 20 minutes of machine time to make. The standard variable overhead rate is $12 per machine-hour. There is no direct labor; all workers are classified as indirect labor and their wages are considered part of variable overhead.

During June, 15,000 units were produced using 4,800 machine-hours. Variable overhead costs incurred were $58,400. Purchases of materials were 34,000 pounds for $105,000 and 31,000 pounds were used.

Required

1. Compute the standard variable cost of a unit of product.
2. Compute the variances for June.

12-18 Investigation of variances   The production manager of the Knowles Company tells you that he exercises management by exception in controlling operations. He examines a performance report and calls for further analysis and investigation if a variance is greater than 10% of total standard cost or more than $1,000. He is not responsible for any rate or price variances, and is therefore concerned only with efficiency variances.

During April, the following occurred:

1. Materials used 4,200 gallons
2. Direct labor hours 6,100
3. Production 1,500 units

The standard cost of a unit of product is as follows:

Materials (3 gals. @ $4)	$12
Direct labor (4 hrs. @ $6)	24
Variable overhead ($8 per DLH)	32
Total standard variable cost	$68

Required

1. Compute the variances for which the production manager is held responsible.
2. Determine which variances should be investigated according to his criteria.

12-19 Determining a base for cost standards   The production manager of the Wingate Company recently performed a study to see how many units of product could be made by a worker who had no interruptions, always had materials available as needed, made no errors, and worked at peak speed for an entire hour. It was found that a worker could make 20 units in an hour under these ideal conditions. In the past, about 15 units per hour was the average. However, some new materials handling equipment had recently been purchased and the manager was confident that an average of 17 units per hour could be achieved by nearly all of the workers.

All workers are paid $5.10 per hour. During the month after the study had been performed, workers were paid $510,000 for 100,000 hours. Production was 1,650,000 units.

Required

1. Compute the standard labor cost per unit to the nearest tenth of a cent based on the following:
   (a) historical performance
   (b) ideal performance
   (c) currently attainable performance
2. Compute the labor efficiency variance under each of the standards in 1 above and comment on the results. Which method of setting the standard would you choose for planning purposes? for control purposes? Explain.

12-20 Investigation of variances   The supervisor of the stamping department is pleased with his performance this past month. His operation showed a favorable material use variance of $1,000. The following data relate to the stamping operation:

Units produced	2,000
Standard costs for materials:	
Libidinum, 3 lbs. @ $3	$ 9
Larezium, 2 lbs. @ $4	8
Total standard material cost	$17

During the month, 5,000 pounds of libidinum and 4,500 pounds of larezium were used.

Required

1. Verify the amount of the material use variance.
2. Did the supervisor do a good job this month? What questions must be answered before coming to a conclusion about the manager's performance?

12-21 Determination of standard costs   The Vernon Company makes its single product, Shine, in the following way.

Materials Dull and Buff are mixed in batches of 500 lbs. Material is used in a ratio of 3 lbs. of Dull for each 2 lbs. of Buff. The mixing is done by two laborers and each batch takes three hours to mix. The resulting mixture is boiled for four hours, which process requires the services of four workers. The mixture that comes out of the boiler yields 4 lbs. of finished product for each 5 lbs. of raw material put in so that the 500 lbs. of material mixed become 400 lbs. of final product. (Evaporation during the boiling process reduces the volume of the output.)

All laborers are paid $4 per hour. Variable overhead is $3 per direct labor hour. Dull costs $1.20 per pound; Buff costs $2 per pound.

Required

Determine the standard variable cost per pound of finished product.

12-22 Cost of investigating variances   The Farnham Company production manager has determined that it costs about $500 (incremental cost) to investigate a variance. About one in four investigations results in corrective action.

Required

Determine what the potential savings should be from the correction of a problem before a variance is investigated.

12-23 Variance analysis   The Cassidy Company manufactures an industrial solvent. The firm budgets its manufacturing costs based on direct labor hours. The production manager is unable to interpret the report that he has just received and asks for your assistance. The report contains the following data.

	Actual Cost at 10,000 Direct Labor Hours	*Budgeted Cost for 10,000 Hours*
Materials used at standard prices	$ 26,000	$ 24,000
Direct labor	67,500	68,000
Indirect labor	27,450	26,500
Other variable overhead	27,400	27,300
Total variable costs	$148,350	$145,800

Production during the period was 48,000 gallons, which would require 9,600 direct labor hours at standard performance.

Required

For each component of cost determine the variance due to efficiency or inefficiency, and that due to spending or price.

12-24 **Bases for standard costs and decisions** The Sewall Company uses very tight standards for determining standard costs for its products. The production manager believes that the use of standards that could be achieved only under ideal conditions helps to motivate foremen and workers by showing them how much improvement is possible and therefore giving them goals to achieve.

The sales manager has criticized the use of such high standards for performance and correspondingly low standard costs because it makes it difficult for him to determine whether business at lower than normal prices should be accepted. In one specific instance, the sales manager was offered the opportunity to sell 4,000 units at $8.50, which is $4 below the normal selling price. The standard variable cost per unit of product is as follows.

Materials (3 lbs. at $.50)	$1.50
Direct labor (½ hr. at $6 per hour)	3.00
Variable overhead ($4 per direct labor hour)	2.00
Total standard variable cost	$6.50

The sales manager was uncertain whether the order should have been accepted because he knew that the standards were never met. It was the extent to which they were not met that bothered him. He asked his assistant to try to determine whether the order would have been profitable. The assistant developed the following information.

Material price and labor rate variances were negligible. However, during a normal month, when 10,000 units were produced, the material use variance, direct labor efficiency variance, and total variable overhead variance were $2,000, $6,000, and $5,200, respectively, all unfavorable.

Required

1. Assuming that the experience of the month presented would have applied when the special order was being made up, should the order have been accepted?
2. Develop new standard variable costs based on currently attainable performance, assuming that the month presented reflected currently attainable performance. Be sure to include both prices and quantities for each input factor.

12-25 **Flexible and static budgets** The Marvel Manufacturing Company is managed by a family; none of its members understand accounting. Ralph Marvel, one of the managers, was elated at the following performance report.

	Budget	Actual	Variance
Production	30,000	26,000	
Direct materials	$ 75,000	$ 72,000	$ 3,000F
Direct labor	45,000	40,000	5,000F
Variable overhead	90,000	86,000	4,000F
Fixed overhead	60,000	60,000	—
Totals	$270,000	$258,000	$12,000F

Ralph showed the report to Susan Roberts, the newly hired assistant controller, saying that one did not need to understand accounting to see that coming in under budget was a good thing.

Required

As Ms. Roberts, what would you say to Mr. Marvel?

12-26   Variance computation and analysis   Your firm makes a product with the following standard costs:

Materials (2 lbs. @ $4)	$ 8
Direct labor (2 hrs. @ $3)	6
Variable overhead ($4 per DLH)	8
Total standard variable cost	$22

The standards have proved to be currently attainable and are generally met within small variances each month. In August the manufacturing vice president brings in a glowing report from the purchasing department. Materials were bought for $3.50 per pound. The new materials were different from the old, but were of equal quality for the finished product. In September the materials bought during August were used with the following results:

Production scheduled	4,000 units
Actual production	3,600 units
Direct labor (8,100 hrs.)	$24,000
Variable overhead	$33,000
Material used	7,920 lbs.

Required

1. Compute all variances that you can.
2. Why may the variances have occurred?
3. Assuming that the experience of September will continue, should the firm continue buying the new material?

12-27   Standard costs, variances, and evaluation (CMA adapted)   The Bergen Company manufactures and sells a single product. The standard variable cost of a unit of product is given below.

Material, 1 lb. plastic @ $2	$ 2.00
Direct labor, 1.6 hrs. @ $4	6.40
Variable overhead	3.00
Total standard variable cost	$11.40

The variable overhead cost is not related to direct labor hours, but rather to units of product because it is felt that production is the causal factor in the incurrence of the variable overhead elements. The elements of variable overhead, based on a yearly volume of 60,000 units of production, are as follows.

Indirect labor, 30,000 hrs. @ $4	$120,000
Supplies, oil, 60,000 gals. @ $.50	30,000
Maintenance costs, variable portion 6,000 hrs. @ $5 per hour	30,000
Total budgeted variable overhead	$180,000

Fixed overhead costs are budgeted as follows, based on 60,000 units of production.

Supervision	$ 27,000
Depreciation	45,000
Other fixed overhead (includes fixed maintenance costs of $12,000)	45,000
Total budgeted fixed overhead	$117,000

During November, 5,000 units were produced and the costs charged were as follows.

Material, 5,300 lbs. used @ $2	$10,600
Direct labor, 8,200 hrs. @ $4.10	33,620
Indirect labor, 2,400 hrs. @ $4.10	9,840
Supplies, 6,000 gals. of oil @ $.55	3,300
Variable maintenance costs, 490 hrs. @ $5.30	2,597
Supervision	2,475
Depreciation	3,750
Other fixed overhead (includes maintenance of $1,100)	3,600
Total	$69,782

Purchases of materials were 5,200 pounds at $2.10 per pound. The firm has divided responsibilities so that the purchasing manager is responsible for price variances for material and oil, and the production manager is responsible for all quantities of materials, labor (direct and indirect), supplies, and maintenance. The personnel manager is responsible for wage rate variances and the manager of the maintenance department is responsible for spending variances.

Required
1. Calculate the following variances:
   (a) material price
   (b) material use
   (c) direct labor rate
   (d) direct labor efficiency
   (e) total variable overhead
   (f) total fixed overhead
2. Prepare a report that details the overhead variances of each element by responsibility. (A convenient method would be to list the managers across the top and under each show the variances for which they should be charged.) You should account for the totals of the variable and fixed overhead variances. That is, the total of your answers to parts (d) and (e) of requirement 1 should be distributed to individual managers.

12-28 Use of unit costs   The foreman of the machining department of the Glenmills Company has just received the following performance report, which was prepared by the new cost accountant.

	Costs per Unit		
	Budget	Actual	Variance
Materials	$ 3.00	$ 2.96	($.04)
Direct labor (1.5 hrs. per unit at standard)	6.00	6.084	.084
Variable overhead:			
Indirect labor	2.40	2.48	.08
Power	.90	.93	.03
Fixed overhead	4.00	4.95*	.95
Totals	$16.30	$17.404	$1.104

*Actual cost incurred divided by actual production in units.

Budgeted production was 12,000 units, actual production was 10,000 units. Budgeted fixed overhead per unit is based on budgeted production. You learn that actual material cost in the report is based on standard prices and that all other actual cost figures are based on actual prices and quantities.

The foreman is not responsible for direct labor rates, which were $3.90 at actual cost. He is also not responsible for variable overhead spending variances, but he is responsible for fixed overhead budget variances.

Required

Prepare a new report including only those items for which the foreman is responsible. You may wish to use a different type of presentation from that shown above.

12-29 Relationships among data   The Dempsey Company uses standard variable costs. Variable overhead rate is based on direct labor hours. The following data are available for operations during April 19X4.

Total production	_____
Actual labor cost	$46,000
Actual materials used	3,200 lbs.
Actual variable overhead	$24,000
Standard labor cost per unit	_____
Standard material cost per unit	$ 4.50
Standard variable overhead cost per unit	_____
Materials purchased	$ 6,800 (4,200 lbs.)
Material price variance	$ 500U
Labor rate variance	$ 4,000U
Variable overhead spending variance	$_____F or U
Material use variance	_____
Labor efficiency variance	$ 2,000U
Variable efficiency variance	$_____F or U
Direct labor hours worked	21,000
Standard labor rate	_____
Standard direct labor hours per unit	20
Variable overhead rate per direct labor hour	$ 1.15

Required

Fill in the blanks. (Hint: You need not do the parts of the problem in the order indicated.)

12-30   Standard costs—alternative raw materials

The Visodane Company manufactures a household cleaner called Kleenall that is sold in 32-ounce (¼ gallon) plastic bottles. The cleaner can be made using either of two basic raw materials—anaxohyde or ferodoxin. Their respective costs are $10 and $8 per pound. Whichever material is used is mixed with water and other chemical agents and is then cooked. The product is then bottled and the bottles are packed into cartons of 20 bottles each.

The basic batch size is made with 1,200 gallons of water, costing $.30 per hundred gallons. The chemical agents other than the raw materials mentioned above cost $120 per batch. If anaxohyde is used, 100 pounds of it are mixed with the water and chemical agents. If ferodoxin is used, 110 pounds are needed. The mixing process takes 3 hours, requiring the services of three laborers.

The mixture is then cooked, for 80 minutes if anaxohyde is used, 90 minutes if ferodoxin is used. One worker is needed for the cooking process. Using either raw material, the output of the cooking process is 1,000 gallons because of evaporation. Bottling and packing requires one laborer working 2 hours.

All laborers are paid $6 per hour. Variable overhead is based on the time required in each process because the high degree of mechanization makes direct labor a poor measure of volume for variable overhead. The overhead per hour for the mixing process is $30, $120 for the cooking process, and $60 for the bottling and packing processes. Bottles cost $.04 each and the cartons cost $.20 each.

Required

1. Compute the standard cost of a carton of 20 bottles of Kleenall, assuming (a) anaxohyde is used; and (b) ferodoxin is used.
2. Suppose that each carton sells for $20 and that cooking time available each month is 1,000 hours. Which material should be used?

12-31   Developing standard costs (CMA adapted)   The controller of the Berman Detergent Company has asked for your help in preparing standard variable costs for the firm's major product, Sudsaway. The firm has never used standard costs and the controller believes that better control would be achieved if a set of standards were to be used. He wants the standards to be based on currently attainable performance.

The following data are available for operations in 19X6.

Materials used 1,350,000 gals. @ $.80 per gallon		$1,080,000
Direct labor 160,000 hrs. @ $5.50 per hour		880,000
Variable overhead:		
Indirect labor	$240,000	
Maintenance and repairs	80,000	
Packaging materials	370,000	
Other variable overhead	480,000	1,170,000
Total variable production costs		$3,130,000

During 19X6, 740,000 cases of Sudsaway were produced. Each case contains 12 bottles of 16 ounces each, a total of 1.5 gallons per case. During 19X6 the firm was using an inferior raw material. During 19X7 the firm expects to pay $.90 per gallon for a better material. Even with the better material, there will still be some shrinkage during production. The controller expects that output of Sudsaway in gallons will be 90% of the raw material put into process.

The firm employed a number of inexperienced workers in 19X6. They worked about 48,000 of the total direct labor hours, which is about 12,000 more than standard hours. During 19X7 the controller expects all workers to be normally productive and to be earning an average wage rate of $5.80.

According to the controller, variable overhead costs were under control during 19X6, given the excessive labor hours worked. Packaging materials were not affected by the excessive labor hours, being related to cases actually produced. Indirect laborers will receive a 10% wage increase early in 19X7.

Required

Prepare standard variable costs, by category of cost, for a case of Sudsaway.

12-32 Standard costs and decisions (AICPA adapted) The Oliver Company produces several kinds of sheet metal products, one of which is an irregularly shaped plate used in making light fixtures. The firm makes two sizes of these plates and sells them to several firms.

The plates are cut from sheets of metal measuring 4 feet long and 12 inches across. Each sheet weighs 2 pounds and costs $1.80. From a single sheet, the firm can cut 25 large plates weighing a total of 1.5 pounds, or 40 small plates weighing a total of 1.4 pounds. The remainder of the metal is sold as scrap for $.60 per pound.

The labor time required to cut plates from a single sheet of metal is 5 minutes for large plates, and 6 minutes for small plates. After the cutting there are several other operations: filing, grinding, and buffing. In one hour, a worker can perform these operations on 200 large plates or 250 small plates. Laborers are paid $6 per hour and variable overhead is $3 per labor hour. In calculating standard cost for materials, the firm deducts the scrap value of metal from the cost of the material.

Required

1. Compute the standard cost of each size plate. Use batches of 1,000 plates to make the calculations.
2. The sales manager of the firm that supplies the metal sheets tells the production manager of Oliver Company that a smaller sheet of metal is available. From the smaller sheet, 20 large plates could be made with only ¼ pound of scrap per sheet. The smaller sheets would cost $1.40 each and the cutting time would be only 3 minutes per sheet. The small plates would still have to be made using the larger metal sheets. The filing, grinding, and buffing operations would not be affected if the smaller metal sheets were used. Determine whether the firm should switch to the smaller sheets of metal to make the large plates.

12-33 Standard costs—joint products The Sigmund Company buys a single raw material and processes it into two intermediate products, guild and stern. Both guild and stern are further processed into final products; neither can be sold at split-off.

The joint process is supervised by one manager, the additional processing of each product is supervised by separate managers. Based on currently attainable performance, it takes six workers three hours to process a one-ton batch of raw material into 800 pounds of guild and 1,000 pounds of stern. The remainder is worthless waste. The raw material costs $360 per ton. All laborers are paid $6 per hour and variable overhead is $4 per direct labor hour.

Still based on currently attainable performance, it takes three workers five hours to complete the processing of an 800-pound batch of guild, and four workers three hours to complete a 1,000-pound batch of stern. When completed, guild sells for $.75 per pound, stern for $.90.

Required

Compute whatever standard costs you think would be helpful to the firm. Explain why you computed the ones you did.

12-34 Incurred costs and performance   The Weldon Oil Company operates a refinery in the northeastern United States. During the winter, about 200 workers are employed as drivers of fuel-oil trucks to deliver oil for heating purposes. Drivers are paid $5 per hour. During the summer there is no need for their services as fuel-oil truck drivers and they are given low-grade jobs in the refinery. Although these low-grade jobs pay only $2 per hour, the drivers are given their usual $5 rate as a matter of company policy.

The manager of the refinery is charged with the $5 wage paid to the drivers while they work in the refinery. The manager of the fuel-oil distribution department bears no charge except when the workers are delivering fuel oil.

The refinery manager does not object to employing the drivers during the summer. Even with this addition to his regular work force he must hire students and other temporary employees in the summer. The manager of the refinery does, however, object to the $5 charge, because he can obtain equally qualified (for those jobs) workers at $2 per hour and he must use the drivers as a matter of firm policy.

Required

Discuss the issues involved and make a recommendation about the charges for the drivers' wages during the summer.

12-35 Standard costs—typing   The Washburn Company employs four typists in its purchasing department. They are paid $140 for a 35-hour week. John Klein, the purchasing manager and the only other employee in the department, has been talking to one of the production supervisors about the use of standard costs.

Mr. Klein believes that standard costs would help him assess the performance of his departmental personnel. Accordingly, he gathers the following data:

(a) Average number of purchase orders typed per week	560
(b) Average lines typed per order	20
(c) Average characters typed per line	20
(d) Average typing strokes per order (20 × 20)	400
(e) Cost of order form	$.20
(f) Salary of purchasing manager—weekly	$350

A standard cost per purchase order was computed, considering typing cost as variable.

Materials	$ .20
Typing labor:	
400 strokes at $0.0025 per stroke	1.00
Total	$1.20

The cost per stroke was computed by determining the total strokes per week (400 per order × 560 orders per week = 224,000) and dividing the total weekly typing cost (4 typists at $140 = $560) by the total strokes.

Mr. Klein knew that the purchase orders varied in the number of strokes required. So to be fair to each typist he decided to evaluate their performance by the number of strokes typed per week. He therefore instructed the typists to keep track of the number of strokes per order and mark the number in the corner of that copy of the order that he kept for his files. He verified the number on about half of the orders the first week of the operation. The following results were obtained during the first week of operations.

Typist	No. of Strokes	No. of Orders	Avg. Strokes per Order
Phyllis Jones	44,850	112	400.4
Barbara Gorman	46,200	115	401.7
Fred Day	45,137	113	399.4
Carol Morris	44,065	110	400.6
	180,252	450	

There were 550 purchase orders turned in during the week for typing.

One of the typists commented to Mr. Klein that it took about 20% of her time to count the number of strokes on the orders. Mr. Klein spent about 7 hours checking the number of strokes on the orders that he reviewed and adding up the total for each typist.

Required

Comment on Mr. Klein's system.

12-36 Determining a standard cost The Renata Tomato Company processes and cans tomato paste. The firm has the capability to can whole tomatoes as well, but has not done so for about a year because of lack of profitability. The production manager and controller were recently discussing the production plan for the next several months. They agreed, on the basis of the information in the schedule below, that the firm should continue to process only tomato paste. The firm has the capacity to process 5,000,000 pounds of tomatoes per month, whether for canning whole or making into paste.

	Whole Tomatoes	Tomato Paste
Selling price per case	$6.00	$5.80
Variable costs:		
Tomatoes*	3.10	2.00
Direct labor	.90	1.00
Variable overhead	1.80	2.00
Packaging	.52	.60
Total variable costs	6.32	5.60
Contribution margin	($ .32)	$ .20

*Whole tomatoes must be grade A tomatoes, which cost 15.5¢ per pound.

Paste is made from grade B tomatoes, which cost $.08 per pound. There are 20 pounds of tomatoes in a case of whole tomatoes, 25 pounds in a case of paste.

A few days after the decision to process only paste had been made, the president of the firm received a call from a large tomato grower. The grower offered to sell Renata as many pounds of tomatoes as it could use for the next six months. The price was to be 9½¢ per pound, and the batches would be mixed A and B grades. The grower would guarantee that at least 40% of the tomatoes would be A grade.

The president told the production manager about the offer. The latter replied that it could cost ½¢ per pound to sort the tomatoes into the two grades, but that there would be no other additional costs if the offer were accepted. The firm's capacity to process 5,000,000 pounds per month would not be affected. The firm can sell all it can produce.

The production and sales managers decided to investigate the probable effects of taking the offer. They agreed that it would be profitable to can whole tomatoes if the price were much less than the current $.155 per pound, but they were uncertain of the effects on the contribution margin of paste. They agreed to ask the controller to prepare a new analysis of relative profitability of the two products.

The controller's analysis showed that paste was now a losing proposition, while whole to-matoes were extremely profitable. The controller's analysis showed the cost of tomatoes for both products at 10¢ per pound, the purchase price and additional sorting cost.

	Whole Tomatoes	Tomato Paste
Price per case	$6.00	$5.80
Variable costs:		
Tomatoes	2.00	2.50
Other variable costs	3.22	3.60
Total variable costs	5.22	6.10
Contribution margin	$ .78	($ .30)

The production manager and sales manager wondered about the wisdom of using the 10¢ per pound cost of tomatoes for both products. "After all," said the sales manager, "aren't we paying more for the A grade tomatoes and less for the B grade? It seems unreasonable to say that they have the same cost." The controller said that other methods were possible, suggesting that the costs could also be assigned based on the ratios of costs of buying the tomatoes already sorted. "If we did it that way," he said, "we would find that if we bought 2,000,000 pounds of grade A tomatoes at 15.5¢ it would cost $310,000. The 3,000,000 grade B tomatoes would cost $240,000 at 8¢. The total cost would be $550,000. The cost of grade B would thus be about 43.6% of the total. So we could assign $218,000 ($500,000 × 43.6%) to the B grade tomatoes in the package deal. That would give a cost per pound of 7.267¢. Doing the same with the A grade produce would give 14.1¢ per pound."

At this point the president entered the room and commented that it seemed to him that the firm was buying $240,000 worth of B grade tomatoes at 8¢ per pound and the rest of the purchase and sorting cost should be assigned to the A grade tomatoes. "That would give $260,000 to the A grade ($500,000 − $240,000), which is 13¢ per pound. Wouldn't that be best?"

Required

1. Determine whether the firm should buy the unsorted tomatoes.
2. Discuss the appropriateness of the methods of determining the standard cost of tomatoes suggested by each of the managers and make a recommendation.

PRODUCT COSTING

Part Five deals with product costing—the determination of unit costs of manufactured products. The study of product costing is important to managers who are not accountants because many reports that managers read incorporate one or another of the methods considered in the following two chapters.

An understanding of cost classification according to behavior and the significance of unit costs is particularly important in interpreting reports of manufacturing firms. Cost allocation is further considered together with its effects—how it can obscure information necessary for planning and decision making. The discussion of product costing methods also takes into consideration the potential behavioral problems associated with such methods. Thus, product costing also has implications for control and performance evaluation.

CHAPTER 13

VARIABLE AND ABSORPTION COSTING, AND STANDARD FIXED COSTS

Throughout this book, we have recommended the contribution margin format of the income statement, where costs are separated by behavior, the contribution margin is highlighted, and fixed costs are then subtracted to obtain the income. We have also consistently noted that the use of a fixed cost per unit, or a total cost per unit, could obscure analysis and possibly lead to poor planning and decision making. Hence, in situations where the costs of units of product were needed, only variable costs per unit were considered.

Accounting information has uses beyond planning and decision making. The accounting system, for example, must serve also for financial reporting and taxation purposes. Income and the costs associated with units of product are of interest for these purposes also. But, as pointed out in Chapter 1, the users of financial accounting reports are different from those of managerial accounting reports. And, because external users are interested in comparisons among firms, financial accounting reports are subject to certain ground rules (generally accepted accounting principles).

For reasons that will not be discussed here, ground rules exist in financial accounting regarding the reporting of income and the costs of units of product. These rules provide that financial accounting reports of income utilize some measure of the *total* per-unit cost of product. (This particular rule also applies to tax accounting.) Under these rules, some type of total cost is associated with each unit of product, whether the unit is sold (cost of goods sold) or still on hand (inventory).

Reports to managers in a nonmanufacturing firm should not be affected by the existence of these special rules. This is true because in such firms the only cost normally associated with a unit of product sold or in inventory is a variable cost, the purchase cost per unit. But application of the rules to a manufacturing firm's accounting would require that both variable and fixed manufacturing costs be associated with a unit of product, whether sold or in inventory. And we know from previous chapters that per-unit total costs can be misleading.

Sometimes, reports to managers of manufacturing firms adhere to the principles explained throughout this book and associate only variable costs with a unit of product. This reporting approach is called **variable costing** or **direct costing**. Often, reports to such managers reflect, instead, adherence to the special rules of financial accounting, and a unit cost is reported, for items sold or still on hand, which includes both fixed and variable manufacturing costs. This reporting approach is called **absorption costing** or **full costing**. Because of the widespread use of absorption costing, it is important that you understand it, how it works, and how to interpret income statements based on it.

This chapter describes and illustrates these two major costing approaches for a manufacturing firm. The initial illustrations point out the critical differences between the two approaches. A refinement of the absorption costing approach, accomplished by the use of a "standard" fixed cost per unit, is also illustrated, and the complications and implications of such a computation are explained.

DESCRIPTION OF METHODS

As stated above, variable and absorption costing are two common approaches used in associating manufacturing costs with units of product. Variable costing assigns only variable manufacturing[1] costs to units of product. Absorption costing assigns both variable and fixed manufacturing costs to units of product. The cost per unit of product is used in two ways: to determine the cost of units on hand (inventory); and to determine the cost of goods sold so as to determine income. Hence, the two costing approaches can be examined for their effects on inventory valuation or their effects on income determination.

We shall illustrate the two approaches by using the data for the Abvar Company for 19X4 and 19X5 as shown in Exhibit 13-1.

Exhibit 13-1

Available Operating Data for Abvar Company
19X4 and 19X5

	19X4	19X5
Sales, 10,000 units at $20 per unit	$200,000	$200,000
Variable manufacturing costs, per unit (includes materials, labor, and variable manufacturing overhead)	$5	$5
Fixed manufacturing costs	$60,000	$60,000
Production, in units	15,000	6,000
Selling and administrative costs:		
Variable, per unit	$1	$1
Fixed	$15,000	$15,000

For simplicity, we have listed only a total for fixed manufacturing costs, or fixed manufacturing overhead, which could include a number of different costs, such as salaries of foremen, depreciation, and the fixed components of mixed costs like maintenance.

[1]The terms *fixed manufacturing cost* and *fixed production cost* are used synonymously in this and the next chapter.

The variable and absorption costing approaches can use either actual costs or, as discussed in Chapter 12, standard costs. When standards are not used, the system is called **actual costing** (variable or absorption). For simplicity we will assume that the costs stated in the exhibit are actual costs. Thus the illustration will show actual variable and actual absorption costing. This approach allows concentration on the critical difference between variable and absorption costing: the treatment of fixed costs.

Inventory Valuation

Under variable costing the inventory at the end of each year will be at $5 per unit, the variable production cost per unit. Under absorption costing, the ending inventory cost per unit will be $5 per unit for variable costs *plus* an amount for fixed cost per unit. The calculations of absorption costing inventory cost per unit are given in Exhibit 13-2.

Exhibit 13-2

Inventory Cost per Unit—Absorption Costing

	19X4	*19X5*
Fixed production costs	$60,000	$60,000
Divided by production in units	15,000	6,000
Equals: fixed cost per unit	$4	$10
Plus: variable cost per unit	$5	$5
Equals: total cost per unit	$9	$15

An alternative method of calculating the inventory cost per unit is to determine total production costs for the year and divide by the number of units produced during the year.

$$
\begin{array}{lll}
\text{Total} & \text{total variable} & \text{total fixed} \\
\text{production} = & \text{manufacturing} + & \text{manufacturing} \\
\text{costs} & \text{costs} & \text{costs}
\end{array}
$$

$$
\begin{array}{ll}
 & (\text{variable cost per} & \text{total fixed} \\
= & \text{unit} \times \text{no. of} + & \text{manufacturing} \\
 & \text{units produced}) & \text{costs}
\end{array}
$$

$$\$135,000 = (\$5 \times 15,000) + \$60,000$$

The total cost per unit is, then, $135,000 divided by the 15,000 units produced, or $9 per unit, as shown in Exhibit 13-2.

We now have a cost to be associated with each unit of product on hand at the end of a period. Exhibit 13-3 shows the calculations of the number of units on hand at the end of each of the years and the total costs to be assigned to those units. We have assumed that there were no units on hand at the beginning of 19X4 and are using the first-in-first-out (FIFO) inventory method.

Exhibit 13-3

Computation of Ending Inventories

	19X4	19X5
Beginning inventory in units	0	5,000
Production in units	15,000	6,000
Units available for sale	15,000	11,000
Sales in units	10,000	10,000
Ending inventory in units	5,000	1,000
Variable costing inventories in dollars ($5 per unit × ending inventory)	$25,000	$ 5,000
Absorption costing inventories in dollars ($9 per unit in 19X4, $15 in 19X5, unit costs from Exhibit 13-2)	$45,000	$15,000

Using the computed amounts for inventories, we can examine the effects of the two costing approaches on income.

Income Determination

In Exhibit 13-4 we show income statements for 19X4 and 19X5 using variable costing. Except for the expanded cost-of-goods-sold section these statements are identical to ones you have been preparing in earlier chapters.

Exhibit 13-4

Income Statements—Variable Costing

	19X4		19X5	
Sales (10,000 × $20)		$200,000		$200,000
Variable cost of goods sold:				
Beginning inventory	$0		$25,000	
Variable production costs:				
15,000 × $5	75,000			
6,000 × $5			30,000	
Cost of goods available for sale	75,000		55,000	
Ending inventories (Exhibit 13-3)	25,000		5,000	
Variable cost of goods sold (10,000 × $5)		50,000		50,000
Gross profit		150,000		150,000
Variable selling and administrative expenses (10,000 × $1)		10,000		10,000
Contribution margin		140,000		140,000
Fixed costs:				
Production	$60,000		$60,000	
Selling and administrative	15,000	75,000	15,000	75,000
Income		$65,000		$65,000

If at some earlier stage in this book, you had been given the same basic information about the sales and costs of Abvar Company for either 19X4 or 19X5, you probably would have prepared statements something like the one below.

Sales (10,000 × $20)		$200,000
Variable costs:		
Production (10,000 × $5)	$50,000	
Selling and administrative (10,000 × $1)	10,000	
Total variable costs		60,000
Contribution margin		140,000
Fixed costs:		
Production	$60,000	
Selling and administrative	15,000	
Total fixed costs		75,000
Income		$ 65,000

Consider this statement carefully. The amounts shown for sales, variable costs, and fixed costs on this income statement are identical with the amounts for those items shown on the income statements in Exhibit 13-4. The only difference is in the detail of cost of goods sold as shown in Exhibit 13-4. More importantly, note that the incomes in both 19X4 and 19X5 are the same. (Thus, the income statement that is shown above could apply to either year.) This equality of income is a critical characteristic of variable costing. *Under variable costing, income does not change if production changes*. Variable cost of goods sold is equal to variable production costs per unit multiplied by the number of units *sold*. Any variable costs incurred to produce units that remain in the ending inventory are shown on the balance sheet as the cost of inventory.

Under absorption costing, reported income *will* be affected by differences in production, even if sales do not change and costs behave according to expectations. Exhibit 13-5 shows income statements using absorption costing.

Exhibit 13-5

Income Statements—Absorption Costing

	19X4		19X5	
Sales (10,000 × $20)		$200,000		$200,000
Cost of goods sold:				
Beginning inventory	0		$ 45,000	
Variable production costs:				
15,000 × $5	$ 75,000			
6,000 × $5			30,000	
Fixed production costs	60,000		60,000	
Cost of goods available for sale	135,000		135,000	
Ending inventories (Exhibit 13-3)	45,000		15,000	
Cost of goods sold		90,000		120,000
Gross profit		110,000		80,000

Selling and administrative expenses:				
Variable (10,000 × $1)	$10,000		$10,000	
Fixed	15,000	25,000	15,000	25,000
Income		$85,000		$55,000

Notice that income was higher in 19X4 than in 19X5. The reason is that production in 19X4 was greater than sales (15,000 units to 10,000 units) while in 19X5 sales were greater than production (10,000 to 6,000). Under absorption costing, income depends not only on sales but also on production. This is true because of the allocation of fixed manufacturing costs to inventory. The amount of fixed cost allocated to inventory depends on the level of production. Under variable costing, the full amount of fixed manufacturing cost is expensed and reduces income in the year the costs are incurred. Under absorption costing, *some* of the year's fixed manufacturing costs are expensed, through cost of goods sold. But, some of those costs are "deferred" as assets on the balance sheet in the sense that those costs are included as part of the cost of the firm's inventory.

Notice also that income under absorption costing was higher than under variable costing in 19X4 ($85,000 compared with $65,000), and that the reverse is true in 19X5 ($55,000 compared with the $65,000 shown in Exhibit 13-4). This is generally true under similar circumstances. *If production is greater than sales, absorption costing produces higher income than variable costing; and if sales are greater than production, variable costing produces higher income.*

The differences between the incomes determined under the two methods relate solely to the fixed costs in the inventories under absorption costing. The *total* fixed manufacturing costs for 19X4 were $60,000 regardless of the method used. Exhibit 13-6 shows how these costs were assigned for 19X4 under the two methods.

Exhibit 13-6

Production Cost Assignments for 19X4

	Variable Costing	Absorption Costing
Total fixed production costs incurred	$60,000	$60,000
Fixed production costs assigned to the ending inventory: 5,000 units at $4 per unit*		20,000
Fixed production costs assigned to expense	$60,000	$40,000

*$9 unit cost – $5 variable cost per unit

The $20,000 difference between the two results above ($60,000 and $40,000) is also the difference between the variable costing and absorption costing incomes for 19X4 ($65,000 and $85,000). Absorption costing income was higher because less fixed cost was assigned to expense. The same $20,000 difference shows up as the difference between the ending inventories under the two methods.

We can do a similar analysis for 19X5, but because of the beginning inventory for 19X5 we need another step. The $20,000 in fixed costs that were assigned, under absorption costing, to inventory cost will become part of the cost of goods sold for 19X5 (Exhibit 13-7).

Exhibit 13-7

Production Cost Assignments, 19X5

	Variable Costing	Absorption Costing
Total fixed production costs incurred	$60,000	$60,000
Fixed production costs assigned to the ending inventory: 1,000 units at $10 per unit*		10,000
19X5 fixed production costs assigned to expense	60,000	50,000
19X4 fixed production costs assigned to expense (included in beginning inventory)		20,000
Total fixed production costs expensed in 19X5	$60,000	$70,000

*$15 unit cost – $5 variable cost per unit

The $10,000 difference between the two results above ($60,000 and $70,000) is also the difference between the variable costing and absorption costing incomes for 19X5 ($65,000 and $55,000).

Summarizing comments. Under both variable and absorption costing, the cost-of-goods-sold section of the income statement will contain variable cost per unit multiplied by the number of units sold. Under absorption costing there will also be fixed costs *included in cost of goods sold,* while under variable costing all fixed costs are deducted as expenses in one place. Under absorption costing, there will be higher inventory cost-per-unit amounts because inventory cost includes some fixed cost as well as the variable cost per unit.

Under both methods, only production costs are included as costs of inventory. Selling and administrative expenses are shown as expenses on the income statement when the costs are incurred.

The two approaches can be said to differ in their definitions of **inventoriable costs** —the costs that are included in inventory. Inventoriable costs are also called **product costs**. Product costs are expensed when the products are sold. The opposite of a product cost would be a **period cost**—a cost that is expensed when incurred.

Interpretation of Results

The interpretation of the results of variable costing based income statements is not new: you have been using such statements all along in this book. If sales increase, income increases by contribution margin per unit multiplied by the number of units of increased sales; if sales decrease, income decreases in like fashion. Under absorption costing that is not true. More-over, the use of percentages is made quite difficult when absorption costing is used in the way we have illustrated it so far. Notice from Exhibit 13-5 that the percentage of gross profit to sales is 55% in 19X4 ($110,000 gross profit divided by $200,000 sales) and only 40% in 19X5 ($80,000 gross profit divided by $200,000 sales). These fluctuating percent-ages make it difficult to determine whether the firm is operating efficiently or not. In the example being used, selling price, variable cost per unit, and total fixed costs have been the same for the two-year period, yet the income results are quite different.

Perhaps the major problem in interpreting income statements prepared using absorp-tion costing is that income changes can be the result of changes in production, in sales, or both.

To illustrate this point let us follow the Abvar Company one more year, into 19X6. In 19X6 the firm incurs costs in the same pattern as before, with variable cost per unit and fixed costs in total being the same as in 19X4 and 19X5. In 19X6 the firm produces 11,000 units and sells 12,000, which gives it a zero inventory at the end of 19X6 (it started 19X6 with 1,000 units). The variable costing income statement would appear as in Exhibit 13-8.

Exhibit 13-8

Income Statement
19X6—Variable Costing

Sales (12,000 × $20)		$240,000
Variable cost of goods sold:		
Beginning inventory (1,000 × $5)	$ 5,000	
Variable production costs (11,000 × $5)	55,000	
Cost of goods available for sale	60,000	
Ending inventory	0	
Variable cost of goods sold		60,000
Gross profit		180,000
Variable selling and administrative expenses (12,000 × $1)		12,000
Contribution margin		168,000
Fixed costs:		
Production	$60,000	
Selling and administrative	15,000	75,000
Income		$ 93,000

The income of $93,000 is $28,000 more than in 19X4 and 19X5, in both of which years income was $65,000 (Exhibit 13-4). The increase is entirely due to selling 2,000 more units with contribution margin of $14 per unit (selling price of $20 − variable production costs of $5 − variable selling and administrative expenses of $1). This result is exactly what you would have calculated at early stages in this book.

Using absorption costing we would obtain the income statement given in Exhibit 13-9 for 19X6.

Exhibit 13-9

Income Statement
19X6—Absorption Costing

Sales (12,000 × $20)		$240,000
Cost of goods sold:		
Beginning inventory (1,000 × $15)	$ 15,000	
Variable production costs (11,000 × $5)	55,000	
Fixed production costs	60,000	
Cost of goods available for sale	130,000	
Ending inventory	0	
Cost of goods sold		130,000
Gross profit		110,000
Selling and administrative expenses:		
Variable (12,000 × $1)	$ 12,000	
Fixed	15,000	27,000
Income		$83,000

The fact that absorption costing income is $10,000 less than variable costing income ($93,000 − $83,000) is due to the $10,000 fixed cost in the beginning inventory and no fixed costs in the ending inventory. Notice especially that the absorption costing income is less than it was in 19X4 even though 2,000 more units were sold in 19X6 than in 19X4. In 19X4 the firm earned $85,000 using absorption costing (Exhibit 13-5). The 19X6 income is higher than the 19X5 income because of a combination of higher sales and higher production.

One more relationship should be mentioned here. The sums of the incomes under variable and absorption costing for the entire three-year period are both $223,000.

	Variable Costing (Exhibits 13-4 and 13-8)	Absorption Costing (Exhibits 13-5 and 13-9)
19X4	$ 65,000	$ 85,000
19X5	65,000	55,000
19X6	93,000	83,000
Total	$223,000	$223,000

The two methods will give equal incomes for any time period when the beginning and ending inventories in dollars are the same for each method—that is, when the beginning and ending inventory under variable costing are the same and when the beginning and ending inventory under absorption costing are the same. In the case of this three-year time period, the beginning inventory for 19X4, the first year, was zero, and so was the inventory at the end of 19X6.

The reason for the equality of incomes when inventories are the same is that cost of goods sold under absorption costing will be equal to production costs incurred, which means fixed costs included in cost of goods sold will be equal to fixed costs incurred. Because fixed costs incurred are all included in expenses for the period using variable costing, when cost of goods sold under absorption costing has fixed costs equal to the incurred amount, the two methods will give the same income. (Beginning inventory is added to production costs to get cost of goods available for sale, and ending inventory is subtracted to get cost of goods sold. Thus, if the beginning and ending inventories are equal, cost of goods sold will equal production costs incurred.)

ABSORPTION COSTING AND STANDARDS

Up to this point we have been dealing with actual cost systems, whether variable or absorption costing was used. As stated earlier, it is possible to use standard costs under either costing approach. You should see that standard costs for variable cost elements (material, labor, and variable overhead) would be the same whether a firm used variable or absorption costing. To avoid the fluctuating unit costs that arise under the absorption costing method, many firms use a **standard fixed cost** per unit, which is based on some level of production longer than a single year. The standard fixed cost per unit is calculated by dividing budgeted fixed production costs by the long-term level of activity, which may be the average expected production over the coming three to five years. This level of activity is usually called **normal activity** or **normal capacity**.

Let us convert our example company, Abvar Company, to standard costing. Since the difference between actual and standard costs as it relates to variable cost elements was fully discussed in Chapter 12, we will concentrate on the fixed cost element only. To avoid interrupting the discussion to deal with variable cost variances, we shall assume that the stated variable costs are also the actual and standard variable costs.

If the Abvar Company expected to produce an average of 12,000 units per year over the next three or four years and budgeted fixed production costs at $60,000 per year, the standard fixed cost per unit based on normal activity would be $5, calculated as follows.

$$\frac{\text{Standard fixed}}{\text{cost per unit}} = \frac{\text{annual budgeted fixed production costs}}{\text{average annual production}}$$

$$= \frac{\$60,000}{12,000} = \$5 \text{ standard fixed cost per unit}$$

Using normal activity for determining the fixed cost per unit is appealing because it incorporates the idea of the long-term total manufacturing cost required to make the product. Advocates of a standard fixed cost based on normal activity point out that the firm may be better able to set prices for its products using some longer-term cost per unit figure than it would using the results of only a single year. Recall that the Abvar Company had a total cost per unit of $9 in 19X4 and $15 in 19X5. Management might have been tempted to raise prices in 19X5, which could have been a poor decision had the price increase resulted in a substantial decline in sales.

Another major advantage of using a standard fixed cost per unit is that although the effects of production on income are not eliminated, they are, as we shall see shortly, at least isolated.

An alternative to normal activity as the basis for calculating a standard fixed cost per unit is **practical capacity**. Practical capacity is the maximum number of units that could be produced by the firm given the usual problems that arise in the production process. Unusual occurrences like strikes or major shortages of materials are not considered in determining practical capacity. Using a term from Chapter 12, where we covered standard variable costs, practical capacity can be defined as the currently attainable production that could be achieved if the firm tried to produce as much as it could.

Advocates of practical capacity as the basis for setting the standard fixed cost per unit argue that the resulting cost per unit eliminates from inventory cost the cost of **idle capacity,** capacity not used in production. To illustrate, suppose that the Abvar Company could produce 20,000 units per year working at full tilt. The standard fixed cost based on practical capacity would be $3 per unit ($60,000 budgeted fixed cost divided by 20,000 units). The $3 standard fixed cost is the *minimum* fixed cost per unit that the firm could incur; at any level of production less than 20,000 units the per-unit fixed cost would be greater than $3. Advocates of the use of practical capacity would say that the $3 minimum possible fixed cost per unit is the appropriate figure for inventory costing (when added to the variable production cost per unit). They would say that if the firm produces fewer than 20,000 units, part of the $60,000 in fixed cost is the cost of having idle production equipment and should not be included in the determination of the inventory cost per unit.

The calculation of a standard fixed cost per unit does not mean that we expect fixed overhead to be *incurred* at the per unit amount we calculated. It merely means that for product costing purposes we shall use the standard fixed cost per unit instead of the actual fixed cost per unit. If the Abvar Company were to use standard fixed cost per unit of $5 based on its normal activity of 12,000 units per year, the cost used to determine inventories would be $10 per unit ($5 fixed and $5 variable).

When standard fixed costs are included in inventory we usually speak of *applying* the fixed production costs to production or of *absorbing* the fixed costs as we produce. We illustrate the working of the method in Exhibit 13-10, which contains the 19X4 and 19X5 income statements for the Abvar Company based on the use of a standard fixed cost per unit of $5. The data are the same as given before, with sales of 10,000 units in both years, production of 15,000 units in 19X4 and 6,000 units in 19X5.

Several important things should be noted as you look at the exhibit. First, consider the manner in which fixed production costs are included. The fixed production costs shown in the cost-of-goods-sold section are $5 per unit multiplied by the number of units produced.[2] The difference between the $60,000 actual fixed production costs incurred and the fixed costs applied in the cost of goods section is shown as an addition to or reduction of income called **overapplied overhead** or **underapplied overhead**. The term *overapplied* is used when the fixed costs applied are greater than the fixed costs incurred, and *underapplied* is

---

[2]In applying fixed production costs in the manner shown we are in effect treating the fixed costs as if they were variable. We are doing this only for product costing purposes, not for planning and control purposes. Thus in any period in which the actual level of production is different from the activity level used to set the standard fixed cost per unit, we will have some difference between the fixed costs *applied* and fixed costs *incurred*.

used when fixed costs applied are less than fixed costs incurred. (The terms *overabsorbed* and *underabsorbed* are also widely used.) Overapplied fixed costs are additions to income and underapplied fixed costs are reductions of income. Thus in 19X4, applied overhead was greater than actual overhead by $15,000 ($75,000 − $60,000); the overapplied overhead must be *added* to arrive at income, because only $60,000 of costs were actually incurred. In 19X5, applied overhead was less than actual overhead by $30,000; the underapplied overhead must be deducted to arrive at income, again because the full $60,000 of costs were actually incurred.

A second important point to notice in Exhibit 13-10 is that the amounts of overapplied or underapplied fixed overhead are exactly equal to the standard fixed cost per unit ($5) multiplied by the difference between actual production and the activity level used to set the standard (12,000 units). This calculation will be used in subsequent sections as a shortcut method.

Exhibit 13-10

Income Statements—Absorption Costing
with $5 Standard Fixed Cost per Unit

	19X4		19X5	
Sales (10,000 × $20)		$200,000		$200,000
Cost of goods sold:				
Beginning inventory	0		$ 50,000	
Variable production costs:				
15,000 × $5	$ 75,000			
6,000 × $5			30,000	
Fixed production costs *applied:*				
15,000 × $5	75,000			
6,000 × $5			30,000	
Cost of goods available for sale	150,000		110,000	
Ending inventory:				
5,000 × $10	50,000			
1,000 × $10			10,000	
Cost of goods sold at standard		100,000		100,000
Standard gross profit		100,000		100,000
Plus: overapplied fixed production costs*		15,000		
Less: underapplied fixed production costs†				30,000
Actual gross profit		115,000		70,000
Selling and administrative expenses				
Variable (10,000 × $1)	$ 10,000		$ 10,000	
Fixed	15,000	25,000	15,000	25,000
Income		$90,000		$45,000

*Total fixed production costs of $60,000 − $75,000 applied
†Total fixed production costs of $60,000 − $15,000 applied

One final important point in Exhibit 13-10 is that the figure called "cost of goods sold at standard" is $10 per unit multiplied by the number of units sold (10,000 units each year). This is one of the advantages of using a standard fixed cost per unit. The firm has, in effect, said that $10 per unit is the production "cost" of a unit *produced and sold*. The cost of goods at standard will always be $10 multiplied by sales in units and it is not necessary to develop an entire cost-of-goods-sold section on the income statement. Cost of goods sold at standard and gross profit at standard can be computed directly by multiplying units sold by the respective figures. The gross profit at standard is $10 (the $20 selling price less the $10 total cost per unit). The income effect of producing a number of units different from the number used to set the standard fixed cost (12,000 per year in this case) is isolated as the overapplied or underapplied fixed production cost. An income statement that takes advantage of this feature of the standard fixed cost is shown below.

		19X4		19X5
Sales (10,000 × $20)		$200,000		$200,000
Cost of goods sold at $10 standard		100,000		100,000
Gross profit at $10 standard		100,000		100,000
Overapplied (underapplied) fixed production costs		15,000		(30,000)
Actual gross profit		115,000		70,000
Selling and administrative expenses:				
Variable (10,000 × $1)	$10,000		$10,000	
Fixed	15,000	25,000	15,000	25,000
Income		$ 90,000		$ 45,000

When a standard fixed cost per unit is used, there is no need to know what the beginning or ending inventories are in order to prepare an income statement. Production must be known so that the amount of overapplied or underapplied overhead can be computed, but it is not necessary that the inventory amounts be known.

Contrast this treatment with Exhibit 13-5 in which the cost-of-goods-sold figure contained both the effects of sales and of production. From the standpoint of a manager who is trying to interpret results, the above treatment seems better than the use of actual absorption costing as illustrated in Exhibit 13-5.

Standard Fixed Costs and Control

The standard fixed cost per unit is not suitable for planning and control purposes. Calculating a standard fixed cost does not mean that fixed costs should be *incurred* at the rate of the standard cost per unit multiplied by the units produced. For control purposes we are interested in the difference between the actual fixed cost incurred and the budgeted fixed costs, that difference being the **budget variance** discussed in Chapter 12.

The total amount of overapplied or underapplied fixed manufacturing overhead is the difference between the actual cost incurred and the cost applied. This total difference contains the budget variance and a difference that is related solely to the fact that actual production may not be the same as the activity level used to set the standard fixed cost. Because the Abvar Company incurred fixed costs equal to budgeted fixed costs, the only cause of overapplied or underapplied overhead was the difference between production and the 12,000 units used to set the standard fixed cost.

Suppose the Abvar Company showed the following results in 19X8 and 19X9. Budgeted fixed costs are again $60,000 for both years.

	19X8	19X9
Units produced	9,000	14,000
Fixed production costs applied at $5	$45,000	$70,000
Fixed production costs incurred	57,000	62,000
Overapplied (underapplied) fixed costs	($12,000)	$ 8,000

The overapplied fixed overhead for 19X9 does not signify good control of fixed costs, nor does the underapplied overhead for 19X8 signify poor control. Control was better in 19X8 than in 19X9 because in 19X8 actual costs were less than budgeted while in 19X9 actual costs were greater than budgeted. To isolate the budget variance from the rest of the overapplied or underapplied cost we use the following format.

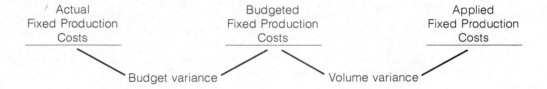

The term **volume variance** is used for the amount of overapplied or underapplied fixed overhead that relates strictly to the difference between units produced and the activity level used to set the standard fixed cost. Filling in the results for 19X8 and 19X9 gives the following:

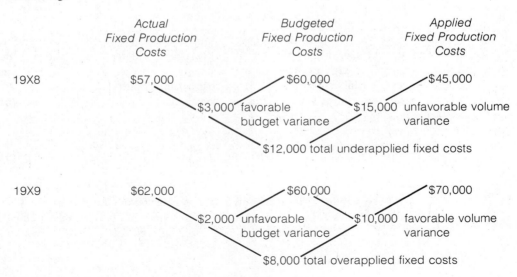

Although the terms "favorable" and "unfavorable" are used to describe the volume variance, we cannot say that a favorable volume variance is a good thing and an unfavorable volume variance a bad thing. The terms are used for convenience in pointing out the direction of the variance; a favorable volume variance is an addition and an unfavorable volume variance is a deduction in computing income. But a volume variance is not a cost when unfavorable nor a negative cost when favorable. It is simply the result of producing more or fewer units than the activity level used to set the standard fixed cost per unit.

We can show this by pointing out that the Abvar Company could use another number of units as its activity level in setting the standard fixed cost per unit. If the firm had used its practical capacity of 20,000 units as the activity level, it would have a standard fixed cost of $3 per unit ($60,000 budgeted fixed costs divided by 20,000 units). Its 19X8 results would then have been:

Fixed costs applied (9,000 units produced × $3)	$27,000
Fixed costs incurred	57,000
Underapplied fixed costs	($30,000)

The budget variance and volume variance would be $3,000 favorable and $33,000 unfavorable, respectively.

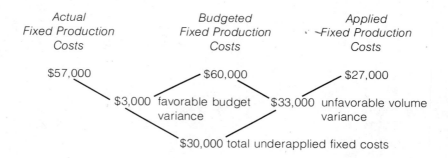

Operations are not affected by the selection of an activity level and the budget variance is the significant figure for control purposes, with budgeted fixed costs being important for planning purposes. The volume variance is simply a result obtained because of the techniques used in setting standard fixed cost per unit figures.

The volume variance can also be calculated directly by using the following formula:

$$\text{Volume variance} = \frac{\text{standard fixed}}{\text{cost per unit}} \times \left(\begin{array}{l} \text{actual} \\ \text{production} \end{array} - \begin{array}{l} \text{level of activity used to set} \\ \text{standard fixed cost per unit} \end{array} \right)$$

The volume variance is favorable if actual production is greater than the level of activity used to set the standard fixed cost per unit, and unfavorable if actual production is less than that used to set the standard. Applying the formula to the results for 19X8 and

19X9 gives the following, which agrees with the calculations made using the format shown above with normal activity as the activity level.

$$19X8 = \$5 \times (9,000 - 12,000) = \$5 \times 3,000 = \$15,000 \text{ unfavorable}$$

$$19X9 = \$5 \times (14,000 - 12,000) = \$5 \times 2,000 = \$10,000 \text{ favorable}$$

Predetermined Overhead Rates

When a firm produces more than one product the standard fixed cost per unit for each product is not usually calculated as we have illustrated. Instead, the calculation is made indirectly, using a **predetermined overhead rate** based on some *input* factor like direct labor hours or machine-hours. Consider a firm that makes two types of tables. Type 101 is a simple table that requires two hours of direct labor time; Type 300 is a more elaborate one that requires six hours of direct labor time. Suppose further that the firm intends to make 25,000 of each type of table on the average over the next four years. Budgeted fixed production costs are $400,000 per year.

One way to determine the standard fixed cost for each type of table would be to use a relative units basis for allocating the fixed production costs. Because an equal number of each is expected to be produced, we could divide the fixed costs evenly between the two tables and calculate a standard fixed cost of $8 for each table.

$$\text{Standard fixed cost for 101} = \frac{\$200,000}{25,000} = \$8$$

$$\text{Standard fixed cost for 300} = \frac{\$200,000}{25,000} = \$8$$

The problem with this kind of allocation is that it does not take into consideration the relative time required to produce each table. A more common approach would be to make the allocations based on the direct labor hours required, as shown in the schedule below.

	Type 101	Type 300
Expected average annual production	25,000	25,000
Multiplied by direct labor hours required	2	6
Equals: total direct labor hours per year	50,000	150,000

The firm expects to work 200,000 direct labor hours per year (50,000 on 101s, 150,000 on 300s). We next divide the budgeted fixed costs by the direct labor hours to get a predetermined overhead rate per direct labor hour.

$$\frac{\$400,000}{200,000} = \$2 \text{ fixed overhead per direct labor hour}$$

The standard fixed costs for each table are calculated by multiplying the *predetermined fixed overhead rate per direct labor hour* by the number of direct labor hours required to make each table.

	Type 101	Type 300
Direct labor hours required per unit	2	6
Predetermined fixed overhead rate per direct labor hour	$2	$ 2
Standard fixed cost per unit	$4	$12

The standard fixed cost of a 300 table is three times that of a 101 table because the 300 requires three times as many direct labor hours. Please notice that all we have done is insert an intermediate step in the calculation of the standard fixed cost per unit. We first developed a predetermined overhead rate by dividing budgeted fixed overhead by normal activity *expressed in direct labor hours* (an input measure) *rather than in units of product* (an output measure). We then used the predetermined overhead rate to determine the standard fixed cost for each model of table.

The firm might even state its *practical capacity in terms of direct labor hours,* rather than in units. In the example being discussed, the firm might have a maximum of 250,000 direct labor hours that can be worked during a year. The practical capacity expressed in direct labor hours would be 250,000 and the predetermined overhead rate using practical capacity would be $1.60 ($400,000/250,000) per direct labor hour. The standard fixed costs for each table would be calculated as follows.

	Type 101	Type 300
Direct labor hours required	2	6
Predetermined overhead rate based on practical capacity	$1.60	$1.60
Standard fixed cost per unit	$3.20	$9.60

For this firm we could not calculate practical capacity in units of product because the number of units would depend on the mix of production. If the firm produced only 101s, it could make 125,000 per year (the 250,000 direct labor hours available divided by the two hours required to make a 101). If only 300s were made, the maximum number would be 41,667 (rounded) which is the 250,000 available direct labor hours divided by the six hours required to make a single unit. The firm can change its production mix, so it is not possible to determine practical capacity in units of product, only in direct labor hours.

When predetermined overhead rates are used there are at least two ways to *apply* overhead. One is to use the actual direct labor hours worked, the other is to use the standard hours worked. We shall illustrate the application and calculation of budget and volume variance using standard direct labor hours.

Let us assume that the table manufacturer has decided to set standard fixed costs based on normal activity of 200,000 direct labor hours. The predetermined fixed overhead rate per direct labor hour is $2, which is $400,000 budgeted fixed costs divided by 200,000 direct labor hours. To make the illustration more complete, we also assume the following results for 19X8. There were no beginning inventories.

	Model 101	Model 300
Standard fixed cost per unit:		
Standard hours required	2	6
Predetermined fixed overhead rate	$2	$2
Standard fixed cost per unit	$4	$12
Standard variable production cost per unit	16	28
Total standard cost	$20	$40
Production in units	22,000	24,000
Sales in units	20,000	18,000
Sales in dollars ($40 per 101, $100 per 300)	$800,000	$1,800,000

Additionally, assume there were no variable cost variances, actual fixed production costs were $385,000, and selling and administrative expenses were $1,100,000. We first calculate the amount of overabsorbed or underabsorbed fixed overhead and break it down into the budget variance and volume variance.

Fixed Overhead Absorbed

	Model 101	Model 300	Total
Units produced	22,000	24,000	
Multiplied by standard fixed cost per unit	$4	$12	
Equals total fixed overhead absorbed	$88,000	$288,000	$376,000

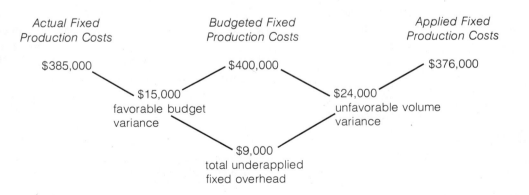

An income statement for 19X8 would appear as follows.

Sales ($800,000 + $1,800,000)		$2,600,000
Cost of goods sold at standard:		
Model 101 [20,000 × $20 ($16 + $4)]	$400,000	
Model 300 [18,000 × $40 ($28 + $12)]	720,000	1,120,000
Standard gross profit		1,480,000
Fixed overhead budget variance	$ 15,000F	
Fixed overhead volume variance	24,000U	
Net fixed overhead underapplied		9,000U
Actual gross profit		1,471,000
Selling and administrative expenses		1,100,000
Income		$ 371,000

SUMMARY OF PROCEDURES

Let us summarize the procedures for preparing income statements based on the three methods that we have examined in this chapter.

Under *variable costing* no special attention is required because variable cost of goods sold is equal to variable production cost per unit multiplied by the number of units sold. Fixed production costs along with any other fixed costs are subtracted from contribution margin.

Under *actual absorption costing* the ending inventory is determined by multiplying the units in inventory by the average per-unit total cost of production for the period. The period's average cost of production (actual total cost per unit) is the sum of all production costs incurred during the period divided by the number of units produced. The fixed cost component of the total unit cost of production is the total fixed cost incurred divided by the number of units produced.

Under *standard absorption costing* the ending inventory is equal to the total standard cost per unit multiplied by the number of units in inventory. The total cost per unit consists of the standard variable cost per unit plus the standard fixed cost, which is the budgeted fixed cost divided by the level of activity selected for use in determining the standard fixed cost per unit. The standard cost of goods sold is the total unit cost (per-unit variable cost + standard fixed cost per unit) multiplied by the number of units sold.

Under standard absorption costing the difference between fixed overhead incurred and fixed overhead applied to production (standard fixed cost × units produced) is deducted or added on the income statement as underapplied or overapplied overhead. This figure is usually shown in two parts: the budget variance and the volume variance.

EVALUATION OF COSTING METHODS

Which costing method provides the best information to managers? Variable costing is not acceptable for *external* financial reporting or for income tax determination. We shall discuss the merits of each method only for internal, managerial purposes.

Advantages of Variable Costing

The basic advantage of variable costing is that it presents information in a form which is most practical for managers—in the form needed for volume-cost-profit analysis.

The separation of fixed and variable costs, and the specific reporting of contribution margin enable the manager to perform volume-cost-profit analysis, which cannot be done by working directly with absorption costing statements. A manager attempting to predict income for a future period would encounter difficulties using an absorption costing income statement for two reasons: (1) he must not only predict sales for that future period, he must also predict production; and (2) he must break down the cost figures into their fixed and variable components (i.e., he must *develop* the information that is *provided* when variable costing is used).

Under variable costing, production has no influence on income. Managers can concentrate on the effects of changes in sales without having to consider the firm's production policy. If sales fall from one period to another, under variable costing income will also fall. If absorption costing is used, it is possible for income to rise in a period of falling sales if production is a good deal higher than sales. Most managers are accustomed to thinking of sales, not production, as the income-generating activity of the firm. Variable costing is therefore more in tune with the basic understanding of income than is absorption costing.

Absorption costing requires making *allocations,* allocations of fixed costs to units of product. We have consistently argued that allocations are unwise for managerial purposes because they obscure volume-cost-profit relationships, can lead to poor decisions, and are not helpful in control and performance evaluation. Absorption costing can therefore be criticized because it does require allocations.

In a multiple-product firm using absorption costing, fixed costs of production will be allocated to the several products, and to the individual units of each product. Many costs that are joint with respect to several products (depreciation on factory building, salary of plant manager, etc.) will be allocated first to products, and then to units of each product. Thus, statements prepared by product or by product line will contain two kinds of allocations, making it extremely difficult to analyze the relative profitability of a product or a product line.

In summary, the information that managers need is provided much more directly by statements prepared under variable costing than under absorption costing. In a firm where absorption costing is used, a manager must often recast the statements he receives in order to perform many of the kinds of analyses needed to carry out his normal functions of planning, decision making, control, and performance evaluation.

Disadvantages of Variable Costing

Advocates of the use of absorption costing argue that variable costing may promote a short-run approach to managerial problems when a long-run approach would be more desirable. Although they would acknowledge the acceptability of variable costing for specific short-run decisions (like the acceptance of special orders), they argue that such analysis in the long run can be harmful. The major objection they have is that if fixed costs are not considered to be costs of product, the firm may tend to set prices too low to cover its fixed costs and earn profits.

If managers become accustomed to using reports prepared using variable costing they could ignore the fixed costs that might be the great bulk of production costs for some firms. Therefore the advocates of absorption costing would argue that it is useful because it makes the manager aware of the need to cover both fixed and variable costs.

There are two counterarguments to the advocates of absorption costing. One is that even absorption costing does not include all costs as product costs. Selling and administrative costs are excluded from inventory under both costing methods. These costs may be extremely significant for many firms. In the same vein, when a standard fixed cost per unit is used, the amount of fixed cost included in product cost (and therefore in inventory) is decided in advance. Some fixed costs will probably be overapplied or underapplied and will not enter into the determination of inventory.

The other counterargument is that it is unnecessary to allocate fixed costs to units in setting prices when the firm faces competition and cannot charge any price it chooses. A firm could analyze the expected volume-price relationships along the lines suggested in Chapter 4 (page 99) and select the best combination of price and expected volume. If a firm does have discretion over prices and can expect to sell about the same volume no matter what price is charged, there would be no harm in using a total cost per unit to set prices. However, firms in these circumstances are much less common than firms that face competition and therefore cannot charge any price they wish.

If absorption costing is to be used it seems better to use a standard fixed cost per unit rather than an actual fixed cost per unit. When a standard fixed cost is used, the income effects of production's being different from sales are isolated in the volume variance. The volume variance tells us what these effects are, but is not helpful for control purposes. The use of standard fixed costs per unit would probably help to alleviate the problem of a manager's changing prices at frequent intervals because total cost per unit is changing as production changes. In Exhibit 13-2 we saw that under actual absorption costing the Abvar Company had total unit cost of $9 and $15 in two periods because of differences in quantities produced. A manager's attempt to raise prices when cost per unit rose might have led to a decline in sales that would have worsened the firm's position.

SUMMARY

Two common approaches are used to prepare income statements for manufacturing firms: variable costing and absorption costing. The difference between them is in what costs are considered to be product costs. Under variable costing only variable production costs are included in inventory; all fixed costs are treated as expenses of the period in which they are incurred. Under absorption costing the cost of a unit of inventory consists of both variable production cost per unit and some amount of fixed cost. Fixed production costs will then be expensed when units are sold (except for underapplied fixed costs that will be expensed in the period incurred). In general, variable costing will produce higher reported incomes than absorption costing when sales are more than production, lower incomes when sales are less than production. When sales are equal to production the two methods will usually produce the same income.

When absorption costing is used it is common practice to employ a standard fixed cost per unit to reduce the effects of different levels of production on the cost-per-unit figure. When a standard fixed cost per unit is used, it is said that fixed manufacturing overhead is being applied to product, which means that fixed production costs are treated like variable costs.

All firms prepare income statements for internal use and must use one of the two basic methods. A manager must understand the implications of both methods in order to be able to interpret the results and see whether the firm is operating according to plan. Budgeted figures should be used for comparison with actual figures to facilitate control over operations.

KEY TERMS

actual absorption costing
idle capacity
inventoriable cost
overapplied (overabsorbed) fixed overhead
period cost
predetermined overhead rate

product cost
standard absorption costing
standard fixed cost per unit
underapplied (underabsorbed)
   fixed overhead
variable costing
volume variance

KEY FORMULAS

Total production costs = total variable manufacturing costs + fixed manufacturing costs

$$\text{Standard fixed cost per unit} = \frac{\text{annual budgeted fixed production costs}}{\text{some measure of capacity}}$$

$$\begin{array}{l}\text{Underapplied (overapplied)} \\ \text{manufacturing overhead}\end{array} = \begin{array}{l}\text{actual fixed} \\ \text{manufacturing cost}\end{array} - \begin{array}{l}\text{applied fixed} \\ \text{manufacturing cost}\end{array}$$

$$\begin{array}{l}\text{Fixed manufacturing} \\ \text{overhead budget variance}\end{array} = \begin{array}{l}\text{actual fixed} \\ \text{manufacturing cost}\end{array} - \begin{array}{l}\text{budgeted fixed} \\ \text{manufacturing costs}\end{array}$$

$$\text{Volume variance} = \begin{array}{l}\text{budgeted fixed} \\ \text{manufacturing costs}\end{array} - \begin{array}{l}\text{applied fixed} \\ \text{manufacturing costs}\end{array}$$

$$\text{Volume variance} = \begin{array}{l}\text{standard fixed} \\ \text{cost per unit}\end{array} \times \left(\begin{array}{l}\text{actual} \\ \text{production}\end{array} - \begin{array}{l}\text{production level used} \\ \text{to set standard fixed} \\ \text{cost per unit}\end{array} \right)$$

REVIEW PROBLEM—INCOME STATEMENT PREPARATION

Try to solve this problem before checking the answers.

Data	Budgeted	Actual
Sales ($10 per unit, 21,000 units)	$210,000	$210,000
Production (in units)	24,000	25,000
Costs:		
Production:		
Fixed	$ 60,000	$ 63,000
Variable (standard is $2 per unit)	$ 48,000	$ 50,000
Selling and administrative:		
Fixed	$ 12,000	$ 12,000
Variable ($1 per unit sold)	$ 21,000	$ 21,000

There were no beginning inventories. Normal activity is 20,000 units; practical capacity is 30,000 units.

Required

Prepare income statements for the period using (1) variable costing; (2) absorption costing using normal activity to determine standard fixed cost per unit; (3) absorption costing using practical capacity to determine standard fixed cost per unit; and (4) actual absorption costing. Show variances separately when appropriate.

Answers to Review Problem

Inventory computations are as follows:

1. Variable costing	$2 per unit	
2. Absorption costing—normal activity		
Variable cost	$2	
Fixed cost	3	($60,000/20,000 units)
Total cost	$5	
3. Absorption costing—practical capacity		
Variable cost	$2	
Fixed cost	$2	($60,000/30,000 units)
Total cost	$4	
4. Actual absorption costing		
Variable cost incurred	$ 50,000	
Fixed cost incurred	63,000	
Total cost incurred	$113,000/25,000 units produced = $4.52	

(1)
Variable Costing

Sales		$210,000
Variable costs:		
Cost of goods sold:		
Beginning inventory	$ 0	
Production costs		
(25,000 @ $2)	50,000	
Cost of goods available for sale	50,000	
Less: Ending inventory		
(4,000 @ $2)	8,000	
Cost of goods sold	42,000	
Selling and administrative expenses		
(21,000 @ $1)	21,000	
Total variable costs		63,000
Contribution margin		147,000
Fixed costs:		
Production costs	63,000	
Selling and administrative expenses	12,000	
Total fixed costs		75,000
Income		$ 72,000

Income Statements—Absorption Costing

	(2) Normal Activity	(3) Practical Capacity	(4) Actual Absorption
Sales	$210,000	$210,000	$210,000
Cost of goods sold:			
Beginning inventory	0	0	0
Production costs:			
Fixed	75,000 (25,000 @ $3)	50,000 (25,000 @ $2)	63,000
Variable	50,000	50,000	50,000
Cost of goods available for sale	125,000	100,000	113,000
Less: ending inventory (4,000 units)	20,000 (@ $5)	16,000 (@ $4)	18,080 (@ $4.52)
Cost of goods sold	105,000	84,000	94,920
Gross profit	105,000	126,000	115,080
Variances:			
Fixed cost budget variance	3,000U	3,000U	
Volume variance	15,000F*	10,000U†	
Total variances	12,000F	13,000U	
Selling and administrative expenses	33,000	33,000	33,000
Total variances and S and A	21,000	46,000	33,000
Income	$ 84,000	$ 80,000	$ 82,080

*(25,000 − 20,000) × $3
†(30,000 − 25,000) × $2

REVIEW PROBLEM—PREDETERMINED OVERHEAD RATE

The King Chair Company produces two types of chairs—the Junior Executive model and the Senior Executive model. Data for 19X4 are given below. There were no beginning inventories.

	Junior Executive		Senior Executive	
Selling price		$100		$250
Variable costs:				
Manufacturing	$30		$80	
Selling	4	34	8	88
Contribution margin		$66		$162
Units produced		8,000		3,000
Units sold		7,600		2,500
Direct labor hours required per unit		2		4

Budgeted fixed production costs are $600,000, selling and administrative expenses $280,000. Actual fixed production costs were $620,000, and fixed selling and administrative expenses were as budgeted. The variable costs for production given above are standard costs. All variable costs were incurred as expected.

The firm uses its normal capacity of 30,000 direct labor hours per year to set standard fixed costs for its products.

Required

1. Determine the predetermined overhead rate for fixed production costs per direct labor hour.
2. Calculate standard fixed costs for each model.
3. Prepare an income statement for 19X4. Show the two fixed cost variances as adjustments to obtain actual gross profit from standard gross profit.

Answers to Review Problem

1. $20 per hour. $600,000 budgeted fixed production costs divided by 30,000 direct labor hours.
2. $40 for the Junior Executive, $80 for the Senior Executive.

	Junior Executive	Senior Executive
Direct labor hours required, per unit multiplied by	2	4
Fixed overhead rate per direct labor hour	$20	$20
equals		
Standard fixed cost per unit	$40	$80

3.

King Chair Company Income Statement for 19X4—Absorption Costing

Sales [(7,600 × $100) + (2,500 × $250)]		$1,385,000
Cost of goods sold:		
Variable production costs [(8,000 × $30) + (3,000 × $80)]		480,000
Fixed production costs*		560,000
Total		1,040,000
Ending inventory [400($30 + $40) + 500($80 + $80)]		108,000
Cost of goods sold (7,600 × $70) + (2,500 × $160)		932,000
Gross profit at standard		453,000
Variances:		
Fixed cost budget variance	$20,000U	
Volume variance†	40,000U	60,000
Actual gross profit		393,000
Selling and administrative expenses:		
Variable [(7,600 × $4) + (2,500 × $8)]	$50,400	
Fixed	280,000	330,400
Income		$ 62,600

*Applied fixed production costs are:

Junior Executive (8,000 × $40)	$320,000
Senior Executive (3,000 × $80)	240,000
Total applied fixed production cost	$560,000

†The volume variance can be calculated in two ways:
(a) It is the difference between budgeted fixed production costs of $600,000 and fixed production costs applied of $560,000. Because application was less than budgeted, the $40,000 difference is unfavorable.
(b) It can be calculated by finding total direct labor hours worked and subtracting that figure from the 30,000 hours used to set the rate of $20 per hour. The difference multiplied by $20 per hour gives the variance.

Model	Units Produced	× Hours per Unit	= Total Hours
Junior Executive	8,000	2	16,000
Senior Executive	3,000	4	12,000
Total hours			28,000
Hours used to set standards			30,000
Variance in hours			2,000
Multiplied by rate per hour			$ 20
Volume variance			$40,000

ASSIGNMENT MATERIAL

Questions for discussion

13-1 Interrelationships with earlier chapters   What similarities and differences do you see between pre-determined overhead rates and flexible expense budgets?

13-2 Overhead application   "Underapplied overhead is a bad sign and overapplied overhead a good sign. This is because the more overhead you apply, the lower your fixed cost per unit." Discuss these statements critically.   *production keeping pace with sale, o.c.*

13-3 Variable and absorption costing   "The trouble with variable costing is that I have to put all of the fixed costs on the income statement right away. But with absorption costing I can put some of them into inventory where they belong and take care of them later when the products are sold." Discuss these statements critically.

13-4 Period costs—product costs   The distinction between product costs and period costs is a major point of contention between the advocates of variable costing and those of absorption costing. Is the distinction important for decision making?

13-5 Variable costing   One argument for variable costing is that fixed manufacturing costs will be incurred regardless of the level of production. Does this argument consider all types of fixed costs?

13-6 Volume variance   Explain the meaning of the volume variance; comment on its significance for planning and control.

Exercises

13-7 Predetermined overhead rates   For each of the following situations, fill in the missing data. The overhead rates are based on budgeted fixed costs and budgeted production for the year.

(a) Fixed Overhead Rate	(b) Budgeted Fixed Overhead	(c) Budgeted Production	(d) Actual Production	(e) Overhead Applied
1. $ 8	$ 80,000	10,000	11,000	$ 88,000 11,000
2. $4	$ 80,000	20,000	22,000	$ 88,000
3. $3	$ 54,000	18,000	15,000	$ 45,000
4. $ 5	$150,000	30,000	28,000	$ 140,000
5. $6	$120,000	20,000	18,000	$108,000

13-8 Absorption costing and variable costing—Five-Year Period Use the following data to prepare income statements on an absorption costing basis and a variable costing basis for the five-year period. There was no inventory at the beginning of year 1.

	1	2	3	4	5
Production	10,000	15,000	10,000	20,000	12,000
Sales	8,000	10,000	13,000	20,000	15,000

Variable cost of production is $5 per unit. Sales price is $10 per unit. Fixed costs are $60,000 (all production costs).

13-9 Determination of standard cost and income The following data pertain to the operations of the Lindsey Company for 19X8.

Normal capacity	200,000 units
Practical capacity	300,000 units
Budgeted production	250,000 units
Actual production	225,000 units
Actual sales ($15 per unit)	200,000 units
Standard variable costs per unit	$5
Fixed costs—budgeted	$1,200,000

During 19X8 there were no variable cost variances; fixed costs incurred were equal to the budgeted amount. There were no beginning inventories and no selling, general, and administrative expenses.

Required

1. Determine the standard total cost per unit assuming that standard fixed cost is based on (a) normal capacity, (b) practical capacity, and (c) budgeted production.
2. Prepare income statements for each of the three bases computed in 1 above.

13-10 Selection of an overhead base The Pruess Company does not now use overhead rates for applying fixed overhead to product. The controller wishes to begin doing so and has developed the following information: budgeted fixed manufacturing overhead for the coming year is $450,000; budgeted production is 100,000 units; budgeted direct labor hours are 60,000; budgeted machine-hours are 75,000.

Required

1. Compute three predetermined rates that could be used by the firm.
2. The results during the year were as follows: fixed manufacturing overhead, $440,000; production 110,000 units; direct labor hours 68,000; machine-hours, 77,000. For each of the rates determined in 1 above, determine (a) the amount of overhead that would be applied to product, and (b) the amount of overapplied or underapplied overhead.

13-11 Standard fixed cost and volume variance The data below refer to the operations of the Hiball Company for 19X8.

Normal capacity	50,000 units
Practical capacity	100,000 units
Budgeted production	60,000 units
Actual production	75,000 units
Fixed costs—budgeted and actual	$300,000

Required

1. Compute the standard fixed cost per unit based on (a) normal capacity, (b) practical capacity, and (c) budgeted production.
2. Compute the volume variances for each of the methods given in 1 above.

13-12 Standard fixed costs and volume variance   For each of the following situations, fill in the missing data. In all cases, the standard fixed cost per unit is based on normal production of 10,000 units.

	(a) Standard Fixed Cost per Unit	(b) Total Budgeted Fixed Costs	(c) Actual Production	(d) Volume Variance (Favorable)
1.	$__	$_____	12,000	($4,000)
2.	$3	$_____	_____	$ 6,000
3.	$__	$40,000	8,000	$_____
4.	$6	$_____	11,000	$_____
5.	$__	$25,000	_____	($7,500)

13-13 Costing methods and product profitability   The Forman Company produces three products in the same plant. Fixed costs are applied to products based on the number of direct labor hours required to make the product. The rate of application is based on budgeted fixed costs of $900,000 and budgeted direct labor hours of 150,000. Per-unit data for the three products are as follows:

	A	B	C
Selling price	$80	$70	$60
Production costs, including applied fixed cost based on predetermined rate	$60	$50	$45
Direct labor hours required for one unit of product	7	6	4

Required

1. Determine variable production costs per unit for each product.
2. Assuming that variable costs of production are the only variable costs, determine which product yields: (a) the highest contribution margin per unit; (b) the highest contribution margin percentage; and (c) the highest contribution margin per direct labor hour.
3. What is the significance of the calculation in 2c?

13-14 Costing methods—effects of changes in production   The following data relate to Elliot Company's one product.

Sales (20,000 units at $10)	$200,000
Production costs:	
Variable ($4 per unit)	
Fixed, budgeted, and actual	$ 60,000

The firm has no beginning inventories and no selling and administrative expenses.

Required

1. Prepare income statements using variable costing assuming that (a) the firm produced 25,000 units, and (b) the firm produced 26,000 units.
2. Prepare income statements using absorption costing. The firm uses a standard fixed cost of $3 per unit based on its normal activity of 20,000 units. Assume production of (a) 25,000 units, and (b) 26,000 units.
3. Prepare income statements using absorption costing and the firm's practical capacity of 30,000 units to set the standard fixed cost of $2 per unit. Assume production of (a) 25,000 units, and (b) 26,000 units.

13-15 Interpretation of results   The president of the Stockley Company has been reviewing the income statements of the two most recent months. She is puzzled because sales rose and profits fell in March, and asks you, the controller, to explain.

	February	March
Sales ($10 per unit)	$100,000	$120,000
Standard cost of sales	60,000	72,000
Standard gross profit	40,000	48,000
Volume variance	4,000	(12,000)
Selling and administrative expenses	(10,000)	(10,000)
Income	$ 34,000	$ 26,000

The standard fixed cost per unit is $4, based on normal capacity of 12,000 units of production per month.

Required

1. Determine production in each month.
2. Explain the results to the president.
3. Prepare income statements based on variable costing.

13-16 Income determination—variable and absorption costing   The following data have been collected for the Ronsen Company, based on activity for the year 19X4.

Sales (110,000 units)	$2,200,000
Production	80,000 units
Variable costs of production	$ 800,000
Fixed production costs	$ 360,000
Beginning inventory	50,000 units
Selling, general, and administrative costs	$ 250,000

Production costs for the prior year were the same as for the current year.

Required

Prepare income statements for the year 19X4 assuming (1) variable costing; (2) absorption costing with 100,000 units being used as the basis to absorb fixed production costs; and (3) absorption costing with 120,000 units being used as the basis to absorb fixed production costs. (Hint: Remember that beginning inventory in dollars will be different for each costing method.)

13-17 Overhead application   The controller of the Williams Company has received the following budgeted amounts for manufacturing overhead costs for 19X7.

	Fixed Amount	Variable Cost per Direct Labor Hour
Indirect labor	$ 55,000	$0.90
Supplies	8,000	.10
Lubricants	12,000	.08
Utilities	32,000	.50
Repairs	18,000	.22
Property taxes	9,000	0
Depreciation	18,000	0
Total	$152,000	$1.80

It is estimated that 80,000 direct labor hours will be worked in 19X7.

Required

1. Compute the predetermined fixed overhead rate per direct labor hour.
2. Assume that 68,000 direct labor hours are worked in 19X7.
   (a) How much fixed overhead will be applied?
   (b) How much variable overhead should be incurred?
   (c) If actual overhead costs are $286,000, how much overapplied or underapplied overhead results from controllable causes (budget variances)?

Problems

13-18 Overhead application and performance evaluation   The Sheffler Company uses predetermined rates for applying fixed production costs to product. Results for several recent months are shown below.

Month	Budgeted Fixed Costs	Units Produced	Incurred Fixed Costs	Applied Fixed Costs
1	$32,000	10,000	$31,000	$30,000
2	26,000	9,000	28,500	27,000
3	31,000	12,000	30,000	36,000
4	27,000	11,000	29,500	33,000

Required

1. Calculate the predetermined rate used to apply fixed costs.
2. Compute the amount of overapplied or underapplied fixed overhead for each month.
3. Comment on the results in 2 above. In which months were the managers exercising good control? poor control? Do the amounts of overapplied or underapplied overhead, by themselves, help in determining whether control was good or poor? What analyses would you suggest?

13-19 The clever president   The Stegman Company has not made a profit for the past few years (see statements below).

	19X3	19X4	19X5
Sales (10,000 units)	$20,000	$20,000	$20,000
Costs (10,000 units)	24,000	24,000	24,000
Net loss	($ 4,000)	($ 4,000)	($ 4,000)

The Board of Directors is looking for a new president to turn the tide. One applicant has offered to take the job for a 50% share of profits, but if losses continue he will personally pay the firm the full amount of the incurred loss.

Variable costs are $1 per unit, fixed costs are $14,000 per year. All costs are for manufacturing. At the end of 19X6, the board anxiously awaited the income statement, which follows:

Stegman Company
Income Statement for 19X6

Sales		$20,000
Costs incurred	$34,000	
Less ending inventory	17,000	17,000
Income		$ 3,000

The president took his $1,500, thanked the board, and left.

Required

What happened? Is the firm now profitable? Would you recommend the president to a failing company?

13-20 Analysis of income statements As the chief financial analyst of Markem Enterprises, Inc., you have been asked by the president to explain the difference between the two income statements prepared for his consideration. One was prepared by the controller, the other by the sales manager. Both used the same data from last year's operations.

	Statement A	*Statement B*
Sales (10,000 units)	$1,000,000	$1,000,000
Cost of goods sold:		
Beginning inventory	0	0
Production costs	600,000	900,000
Ending inventory	(200,000)	(300,000)
Cost of goods sold	400,000	600,000
Gross profit	600,000	400,000
Other costs	500,000	200,000
Income	$ 100,000	$ 200,000

Variable costs of production, the only variable costs, are $40 per unit.

Required

1. Determine which statement was prepared using variable costing, which using absorption costing.
2. Determine (a) fixed production costs; (b) selling and administrative costs; (c) production in units; and (d) cost per unit of inventory for both statements.
3. Which statement do you think was prepared by which manager and why do you think so?

13-21 Allocation and behavior The Brenner Company allocates joint production costs such as depreciation, property taxes, payroll office, and factory accounting on the basis of cost of materials used in each production department. Material costs for the coming year are expected to be $300,000, joint production costs $750,000.

The manager of the fabricating department has developed a new process that requires 10% more materials than the old, but 20% less labor time. Without the new process, she expects to incur materials costs of $60,000 and labor of $50,000 during the coming year.

Required

Would it be desirable to introduce the new process? Consider from the viewpoints of both the firm and the manager of the fabricating department. If your answers conflict, suggest a solution.

13-22 Units costs and performance   The Williams Company produces a single product in three factories around the country. The Westville factory is the newest, having started operations only two years ago. There have been some problems at the Westville factory; start-up costs were higher than expected, and unit costs have remained higher than those of the other two factories.

The sales manager is evaluated based on revenue minus a transfer price of full cost plus a 10% markup from the factory. He is free to order units from any of the three factories. He was recently heard to comment that he would not order anything from the Westville factory except that the others do not have enough capacity to supply his needs. Data from last year's operations are as follows:

	Westville	Eastville	Northville
Capacity in units	200,000	100,000	150,000
Production	80,000	100,000	150,000
Production costs:			
Materials	$160,000	$210,000	$ 320,000
Direct labor	240,000	330,000	475,000
Variable overhead	120,000	160,000	255,000
Fixed overhead	280,000	120,000	225,000
Totals	$800,000	$820,000	$1,275,000
Per unit	$10	$8.20	$8.50

Sales in the latest year were 330,000 units, which equaled production.

Required

1. Determine which factory can make the product for the least cost to the firm.
2. Is the sales manager acting in the best interests of the firm with his policy of purchasing? If not, suggest what changes could be made to bring his actions into line with the firm's interests.

13-23 Overhead application and pricing decisions   The Grendel Company makes high-quality furniture. The firm has just received an offer from a large furniture wholesaler for a single batch of goods. The sale price is $25,000, which is about $10,000 less than would ordinarily be obtained from such a batch. The sales manager is sure that existing sales would be unaffected by the special order and he would like to accept the order if any profit can be made. The production manager provides the following estimates of cost for the order.

Materials	$ 6,000
Direct labor (3,000 hrs.)	9,000
Overhead	15,000
Total	$30,000

The production manager informs you that the overhead cost is based on the firm's overhead application rate of $5 per direct labor hour. The rate includes both fixed and variable overhead and was determined based on 60,000 expected direct labor hours and $300,000 budgeted total overhead costs. The rate last year was $5.50, based on 50,000 direct labor hours and $275,000 total overhead costs. The production manager tells you that the difference in rates is due to the difference in direct labor hours—the cost structure is the same this year as last year.

Required

1. Determine the incremental cost of producing the order. Should the order be accepted?
2. What other factors should be considered in deciding whether to accept this special order?

13-24 Conversion of income statement   The manager of the Morgan Division of Rorshoot Industries has been on the job only a short time, having been hired from another firm. The income statement below, for the third quarter of 19X7, is the first regular report that he has received. He is having some difficulty in understanding it because he is familiar only with variable costing, and he has asked you to convert the statement to a variable costing basis.

Sales		$1,235,000
Cost of sales		710,125
Gross profit		524,875
Operating expenses:		
Selling and administrative	$326,750	
Unabsorbed overhead	66,000	392,750
Income		$ 132,125

From review of internal records you have determined the following additional information.

1. Selling and administrative costs are all fixed.
2. The division sells its one product at $40 per unit.
3. Fixed manufacturing overhead is applied at $4 per unit.
4. There was no fixed overhead budget variance.
5. Production during the quarter was 43,500 units.

Required

Prepare an income statement using variable costing.

13-25 Predetermined overhead rates—multiple products   The controller of the Salmon Company has been working on the development of a new costing system. He believes that the use of standard costs would reduce the cost of recordkeeping and simplify the firm's internal reporting to managers. He has asked your assistance and you have collected the following information relating to the firm's three products.

		Product	
	Model 84	*Model 204*	*Model 340*
Variable production costs	$4	$7	$11
Direct labor hours required	.50	.80	1.50

The firm works 50,000 direct labor hours per year at normal operating level and the controller wishes to use that figure to set the predetermined overhead rate for the budgeted fixed production costs of $300,000.

Operating results for 19X4 are given below. There were no beginning inventories.

	Production in Units	Sales in Units	Sales in Dollars
Model 84	30,000	25,000	$250,000
Model 204	24,000	20,000	$280,000
Model 340	20,000	18,000	$450,000

All production costs were incurred as expected, variable costs per unit and total fixed costs. Selling and administrative expenses were $140,000.

Required

1. Compute standard fixed costs per unit for each model.
2. Compute the ending inventory in dollars for each model.
3. Prepare an income statement for 19X4.

13-26 Effect of costing methods on balance sheet   The McPherson Company has a loan with a large bank. Among the provisions of the loan agreement are (a) the current ratio must be at least 3 to 1, and (b) the ratio of debt to stockholders' equity must be no higher than 75%. The balance sheet at December 31, 19X4 is as follows:

Assets		Equities	
Cash and receivables	$ 460,000	Current liabilities	$ 200,000
Inventory (40,000 units		Long-term bank loan	300,000
at variable cost)	200,000	Stockholders' equity	760,000
Total current assets	$ 660,000		
Fixed assets (net)	600,000		
Total assets	$1,260,000	Total equities	$1,260,000

Current ratio $660,000/$200,000 = 3.3/1
Debt/stockholders' equity $500,000/$760,000 = 65%

The budgeted income statement for 19X5 is as follows:

Sales (100,000 units)		$1,000,000
Variable cost of sales		500,000
Variable manufacturing margin		500,000
Other variable costs (variable with sales)		50,000
Contribution margin		450,000
Fixed costs:		
Manufacturing	$300,000	
Other	50,000	350,000
Income		$ 100,000

Budgeted production is 100,000 units. The president of the firm anticipates substantial expenditures for fixed assets and intends to obtain a new loan to help finance these expenditures. He projects the following pro forma balance sheet for December 31, 19X5.

Assets		Equities	
Cash and receivables	$ 400,000	Current liabilities	$ 240,000
Inventory (40,000 units		Long-term bank loans	460,000
at variable cost)	200,000	Stockholders' equity	860,000
Total current assets	$ 600,000		
Fixed assets (net)	960,000		
Total assets	$1,560,000	Total equities	$1,560,000

He sees that the firm will be in default on both provisions of the loan agreement. (Compute the current ratio and debt/stockholders' equity ratio to verify his finding.) Trying to resolve the problem, he lists the following points:

(a) Plant capacity is 150,000 units.

(b) The firm could perhaps benefit if absorption costing were used.

Required

1. Recast the income statement and balance sheet based on using absorption costing with production of 150,000 units. Assume that all increased production costs are paid in cash.
2. Is the firm safely within the limits of the loan agreement?
3. Is the firm better off using absorption costing?

13-27 Standard costs—multiple products   The Brennan Company makes luggage. For some time, there has been dissatisfaction with the firm's cost information. Unit costs have fluctuated greatly and they have not been useful for planning and control purposes.

Under the present system, unit costs are computed at the end of each month. The costs are determined by allocating all actual production costs for the month to the various models produced, with the allocation based on the relative material costs of the various models.

The controller has decided to develop standard costs for product costing purposes. He has analyzed the material and labor requirements for each model, based on what he believes to be currently attainable performance. The results of his analysis are as follows. (For simplicity, the problem is limited to only three models.)

	Briefcase	Cosmetic Case	Two-Suiter
	#108	#380	#460
Material costs	$12.00	$14.00	$18.00
Labor hours required	.5	.8˙	1.5

Workers are all paid $5 per hour, and the firm usually works about 6,000 labor hours per month. The controller intends to use the 6,000 hours to set his standard fixed cost per unit. His analysis of monthly manufacturing overhead indicates that total overhead behaves according to the formula $48,000 + ($7 × direct labor hours), and he thinks that the $48,000 figure is probably the best for budgeting fixed overhead.

During April the firm had the following results. There were no inventories at April 1.

	#108	#380	#460
Production in units	3,000	2,500	1,200
Sales in units	2,400	1,800	1,000
Sales in dollars	$72,000	$72,000	$70,000

There were no variable cost variances, but fixed production costs were $49,500.

Required

1. Compute the standard cost for each model.
2. Compute the ending inventory of finished goods.
3. Prepare an income statement for April. Selling and administrative expenses were $28,000.

13-28 Interim results, costing methods, and evaluation of performance The Kleffman Company sells a product with a highly seasonal demand. The budgeted income statement for 19X7 is given below.

Budgeted Income Statement for 19X7

Sales (240,000 units)		$2,400,000
Cost of goods sold—at standard:		
Materials	$420,000	
Direct labor	540,000	
Manufacturing overhead	600,000	1,560,000
Gross profit—at standard		840,000
Selling, general, and administrative expenses		420,000
Income before taxes		$ 420,000

Budgeted production is 240,000 units, the number used to set the standard fixed cost per unit. The controller has determined that materials, labor, 40% of manufacturing overhead ($240,000), and $120,000 of the selling, general, and administrative expenses are variable. All fixed costs are incurred evenly throughout the year.

January and February are relatively slow months, each with only about 5% of annual sales. March is the first month of a fairly busy period and production in February is generally high in order to stock up for the anticipated increase in demand. The actual income statements for January and February 19X7 are shown below.

	January	February
Sales (12,000 units)	$120,000	$120,000
Cost of goods sold—at standard	78,000	78,000
Gross profit—at standard	42,000	42,000
Manufacturing variances:		
Variable costs	3,000F	4,000U
Fixed cost—budget	2,000F	3,000U
Fixed cost—volume	9,000U	7,500F
Gross profit—actual	$ 38,000	$ 42,500
Selling, general, and administrative expenses	31,000	31,000
Income	$ 7,000	$ 11,500

Although the president is pleased that performance improved in February, he has asked the controller why there is a difference in profits in the two months, since sales were the same. He also wonders why profits were not about 5% of the amount budgeted for the year, since each month's sales were 5% of the annual budget.

Required

1. Explain to the president why profits in January and February would be expected to be less than 5% of the budgeted annual profit, even though each month's sales were 5% of the budgeted annual amount.
2. Explain to the president why profits differed in the two months. Comment on the president's being pleased that "performance improved in February." Support your answers with calculations.

13-29   Income statements and balance sheets   The Arens Company makes a single product, a microwave oven that sells for $300. The standard variable cost of production is $180 per unit and the only other variable cost is a 10% sales commission. Fixed production costs are $3,600,000 per year, incurred evenly throughout the year. Of that amount, $800,000 is depreciation and the remainder all require cash disbursements. Fixed selling and administrative expenses are $200,000 per month, all requiring cash disbursements.

For inventory costing the firm uses a standard fixed cost of $45 per unit, based on expected production of 80,000 units. However, during 19X6 the firm experienced the following results, by six-month periods.

	January–June	July–December
Sales in units	30,000	40,000
Production in units	32,000	42,000

The firm sells for cash only and pays all of its obligations as they are incurred. Its balance sheet at December 31, 19X5 was as follows.

**Arens Company Balance Sheet as of
December 31, 19X5 (In Thousands of Dollars)**

Assets		Equities	
Cash	$ 400		
Inventory (1,000 units)	225	Common stock	$3,000
Plant and equipment (net)	3,000	Retained earnings	625
Total assets	$3,625	Total equities	$3,625

During 19X6, all costs were incurred as expected, variable costs per unit and fixed costs in total.

Required

1. Prepare income statements for each of the two six-month periods and the year as a whole. (Use thousands of dollars to reduce writing time.)
2. Prepare balance sheets as of June 30 and December 31, 19X6, in thousands of dollars.

13-30   Pricing dispute   The Calligeris Company manufactures brake linings for automobiles. Late in 19X2 the firm received an offer for 10,000 linings from the Phelan Company. Phelan was unwilling to pay the usual price of $5 per lining, but offered to buy the linings at a price that would give Calligeris a $.50 gross profit per lining.

Without consideration of the order, Calligeris expected the following income statement for the year.

Sales (100,000 linings at $5)		$500,000
Cost of goods sold at standard:		
Beginning inventory (20,000 × $4)	$ 80,000	
Variable production costs (100,000 units at $2.50)	250,000	
Fixed production costs at $1.50 per unit	150,000	
Cost of goods available for sale	480,000	
Ending inventory (20,000 × $4)	80,000	
Cost of goods sold at standard		400,000
Standard gross profit		100,000
Volume variance (20,000 × $1.50)	30,000F	
Selling and administrative expenses	50,000	20,000
Income		$ 80,000

The production manager decided that the order could be readily filled from units in the firm's inventory, so no additional production was planned. The firm shipped 10,000 linings to Phelan Company, billing that firm for 10,000 units at $4.50 per lining. No additional costs were incurred in connection with this order.

Required

1. Prepare an income statement for 19X2 assuming that the actual results for the year were as planned except that the additional sale was made to Phelan Company. Do the results show that the firm earned the agreed gross profit?
2. Suppose that you were the controller of Phelan Company. Would you dispute the $4.50 price? If so, why? What price would you propose and why?

13-31 Comprehensive review, budgeting, overhead application The Ruland Company makes and sells a single product. The product sells for $20 and the firm expects sales of 880,000 units in 19X5. The distribution of sales by quarters is expected to be 20%, 25%, 25%, and 30%. The firm expects the following costs in 19X6.

Manufacturing Costs

	Fixed	Variable per Unit
Materials (4 lbs. at $.80)	—	$3.20
Direct labor (.5 hour at $5)	—	2.50
Maintenance	$ 46,000	.20
Indirect labor	422,000	.40
Supplies	316,000	.05
Power	186,000	.10
Depreciation	1,900,000	—
Supervision	310,000	—
Miscellaneous	320,000	.05
Totals	$3,500,000	$6.50

Selling, General, and Administrative Expenses

Salesperson compensation		$2.00
Other salaries and wages	$1,200,000	—
Other expenses, including interest on debt	4,350,000	
Totals	$5,550,000	$2.00

The firm has budgeted production and purchases of raw materials for the four quarters of 19X5 as follows.

Quarter	Production (Units)	Raw Material Purchases (Pounds)
1	210,000	733,000
2	220,000	950,000
3	260,000	904,000
4	210,000	795,000
Totals	900,000	3,382,000

Other information relating to the firm's operations is given below.

1. The firm uses a standard fixed cost of $3.50 per unit for product costing purposes.
2. Sales are collected 60 days after sale.
3. Purchases of raw materials are paid for in the month after purchase.
4. Direct labor costs unpaid at the end of a quarter are about 10% of the cost incurred that quarter. All other manufacturing costs requiring cash disbursements (all but depreciation) are paid as incurred, except for raw material purchases.
5. All selling, general, and administrative expenses require cash disbursements and are paid as incurred except for salesperson's commissions. These are paid in the month after incurrence.
6. The firm has a 40% income tax rate. At the end of any year, the amount of unpaid taxes is about 25% of the total expense for the year.
7. A dividend of $300,000 will be paid to shareholders in 19X5.
8. Purchases of plant assets will total $2,100,000 in 19X5 and will be paid for in cash.
9. You may assume that sales, production, and purchases of raw materials are spread evenly over the months of each quarter (one-third of quarter in each month of the quarter).

The balance sheet at the end of 19X4 appears as follows, in thousands of dollars.

Assets		Equities	
Cash	$ 840	Accounts payable (materials)	$ 240
Accounts receivable	2,800	Accrued commissions	120
Inventory—finished goods		Accrued payroll (direct labor)	64
(146,000 units)	1,460	Income taxes payable	80
Inventory—materials		Long term debt	4,000
(530,000 lbs.)	424	Common stock	7,000
Plant and equipment	16,200	Retained earnings	1,820
Accumulated depreciation	(8,400)		
Total	$13,324	Total	$13,324

Required

1. Prepare a budgeted income statement for 19X5.
2. Prepare a cash budget for 19X5 for the year as a whole only, not by quarter.
3. Prepare a pro forma balance sheet for the end of 19X5.
4. Without preparing new statements, describe the differences there would be in those you have prepared if the firm were using variable costing.

Cases

13-32 Actual costs and pricing policy The sales manager of the Hyland Furniture Company has been complaining to the controller that the firm's pricing policy is doing considerable harm. "I am supposed to charge a price that will provide a 30% markup over cost, but the way our costs behave, I have to readjust the prices all the time. Look at the results from last year [below]. We cannot charge over $100 for one of these chairs that our competitors sell for about $90 to $95. But that is what the president wants me to do in the months when our cost is high. Good grief, we are practically giving them away in the winter when costs are low." The following data refer to a typical chair sold by the firm.

	Chair Model 105	
	October–April	May–September
Production	<u>12,000</u>	<u>4,000</u>
Production costs:		
Materials	$240,000	$ 80,000
Direct labor	180,000	60,000
Variable overhead	120,000	40,000
Fixed overhead ($32,500 per month)	227,500	162,500
Totals	$767,500	$342,500
Per unit (rounded)	$63.96	$85.63
Required selling price @ 130% of cost (even dollars)	$83	$111

Required

Prepare a memorandum to the president, suggesting ways to resolve the problem seen by the sales manager. Provide calculations to support your position.

13-33 What is cost?—consumer action Easy Ed Johnson's Belchfire Auto Agency has been advertising that it will sell cars at $50 over cost and that anyone who can prove that Ed is making more than $50 on a sale will get a $5,000 prize. Phyllis Henley decides to disprove Ed's claim. She obtains the following information from a consumer magazine.

Cost Data from *Consumer Scoop*—Belchfire 8
with Standard Equipment

Invoice cost to dealer	$3,400
Commission to salesman, basic rate per car	100
Variable cost of make-ready services (lubrication, washing, etc.)	40
Total cost to dealer	$3,540

Since Phyllis knows that Ed has been selling this particular model for $3,900, she marches into the showroom and demands a $5,000 prize because she can ''prove'' that Ed is selling this model at $360 over his cost. Ed, with considerable aplomb, summons his accountant, who presents the following information to Phyllis.

Cost Data for the Belchfire 8 with Standard Equipment

Invoice cost to dealer	$3,400
Commission to salesman, basic rate per car	100
Cost of make-ready services	120
General overhead	230
Total cost	$3,850

The accountant points out that Phyllis has failed to consider the ''real'' costs that are incurred in running a large automobile dealership. He states that the make-ready and general overhead costs are based on the total service department cost and total overhead costs divided by the number of cars sold last year (500). General overhead costs are virtually all fixed. Ed pleasantly and politely offers his condolences to Phyllis for having failed to win the $5,000 and invites her back any time she wants to buy a car at $50 over cost.

Phyllis is not at all happy with her reception at Ed's or the data provided by his accountant, and she decides to sue for the $5,000 in the local court.

Required

Assume that Phyllis loses the case at the local level and appeals the decision to a higher court. The trial judge (original decision) has agreed with the explanation of Easy Ed's accountant. Nevertheless, Phyllis argues that Easy Ed is defrauding the populace and owes her $5,000. Her lawyer has asked you to serve as an expert witness. What would your testimony be?

13-34 Costing methods and product profitability   At a recent meeting, several of the managers of the Cornwall Valve Company were discussing the firm's costing and pricing methods. Although there was general agreement that the methods to be used should be helpful to managers in determining which products to emphasize, there was considerably less agreement on which methods would accomplish this.

The sales manager, Ralph Stokes, expressed his preference for product costs based on variable costs only. ''I see no reason to charge a product with fixed costs. Contribution margin is, after all, the critical question in selecting the products to push.''

''I just can't agree with you,'' said Bill Rollo, the production manager. ''If you'd just take a walk through the plant you'd be reminded that men and materials aren't the only things that you need to produce one of our valves. There are tons of machinery that cost money too. Ignoring those costs can only get you into trouble and it sure isn't very realistic anyway. You've *got* to consider the machine time required for each product, and that can only be accomplished by allocating the fixed production costs to products. Machining time is critical, and production costs should be allocated on a machine-hour basis.''

To make his point, Bill put an example on the conference room blackboard. ''Look, let me show you. Let's take just three of our basic products that all require time in the grinding department. That department has a capacity of 1,000 machine-hours a month, and the monthly fixed costs of the department are $10,000.'' Below is the schedule Bill put on the board.

	101–27	101–34	101–56
Selling price	$9.00	$12.50	$17.40
Variable costs	5.00	6.50	8.40
Contribution margin	4.00	6.00	9.00
Fixed costs (see below)	1.00	1.25	2.50
Profit per unit	$3.00	$ 4.75	$ 6.50
Number of valves processed per hour	10	8	4

Bill continued, "Now what I've done is computed a fixed cost per unit by dividing the $10 per-hour fixed cost by the number of valves of each type that we can process in one hour. You can see that what I use the grinding machinery for *does* make a difference. It seems to be that an approach like this is much better for showing what products to emphasize. This shows that the 56 is the best bet and the 27 is the worst."

"But Bill," said Ralph, "we don't disagree. The 56 is a winner because it has the highest contribution margin, and the 27 we wouldn't push because it contributes the least. What are we arguing about?"

Bill was not too happy about having his own example used to counter his argument. He admitted that, in the case he used, the relative rankings of the products were the same as they would be using the contribution margin approach. But he still felt that his method would be more valuable to the sales manager than a simple contribution margin approach, and he looked around the room for support.

"Well, now, it's nice to hear that you two are so interested in the information my staff has to offer," commented Joe Anderson, the controller. "But if you want to be realistic, let's consider something else. We are committed to producing some of each of these valves, though not nearly enough to keep the grinding department operating at capacity. So the big decision isn't really which valve to produce and sell. What we really need to know is which one to produce after we have met the commitments we've made, and the kicker is that we could probably sell all of whatever we produce. The way I see it, we have about 600 hours of grinding time available for discretionary production. So what do we do?"

Bill continued to argue for his approach, and he specifically attacked the question of pricing. "The way we price our products just isn't rational; I know we could do better if we considered the fixed costs the way I said. We should be selling the 27s for $12.50 if we want to make them as profitable as the 56s, and we'd have to jack the price of 34s by $1.75 to equal the profit on the 56s. Okay, okay, I can see you're getting upset about the idea of such increases, Ralph. I know the customers would be unhappy. But if we cater to their needs by producing these models, we ought to get a fair return for doing it."

Required: Determine which valve should be produced once the committed demand is satisfied. Criticize the analyses of the sales manager and the production manager, including their comments about pricing.

13-35 Break-even point—absorption costing   The Tollgate Company expects to produce 190,000 units of product in 19X6. The firm uses a predetermined overhead rate for fixed overhead based on 210,000 units, which is its normal capacity. Over- or underabsorbed overhead is charged to the income statement as a separate item. The firm's selling price is $16 per unit. At the expected level of production the firm expects the following costs.

Variable production costs	$1,330,000
Fixed production costs	630,000
Fixed selling and administrative costs	434,000

In addition, there are variable selling costs of $2 per unit. The firm has no inventory at the end of 19X5.

Required

1. Determine the firm's break-even point assuming that variable costing is used.
2. Determine the number of units that must be sold to break even given that production will be 190,000 units.
3. If your answers to the first two parts are different, explain the difference showing calculations.
4. Would your answer to part 2 be different if the firm had had a beginning inventory of 10,000 units costed at the same per-unit amount that the firm will use in 19X6? Explain why or why not, with calculations.

13-36   Budgeting, cash flow, product costing, motivation   After almost two decades of profitable operations, the Pennywise Company experienced its first loss in 19X6, and all the internal reports during the first eleven months of 19X7 indicated that the company would have a second loss year. At the meeting of the board of directors at the end of December 19X7, the members were given the first draft of the basic operating data for 19X7 which showed a loss. Public announcement of the data would be made shortly after the directors' meeting.

The directors had maintained the dividend record of the company so as not to antagonize the stockholders or give the impression that the recent losses were any more than a temporary setback. Most of the directors had come to realize, by the end of 19X7, that future dividends would be advisable only if the company returned to profitable operations. Consequently, the board members were willing to consider any plans which might help minimize inefficiencies, reduce costs, and build a profitable operation once again.

The chairman of the board (and principal stockholder), Mr. Ira Hayes, had recently attended a conference sponsored by the National Association of Manufacturers on motivating personnel to better performance. Mr. Hayes was not particularly impressed with most of the discussions. He told the personnel manager, Mr. Gray: "Those speakers all seemed to concentrate on qualitative and non-quantifiable issues like working conditions and improving the general atmosphere to promote creativity and individuality. There was the usual lot of noise about implementing methods of 'participatory management,' and the like, and coordinating the efforts of the management team. But really, there wasn't much in the way of concrete suggestions."

Having been closely associated with the company since its founding by Mr. Hayes sixteen years before, Mr. Gray was well acquainted with Mr. Hayes' feelings on the matter of motivation. As Mr. Hayes had said on many occasions, he was convinced that the surest (and easiest) way to really motivate people was to provide monetary incentives of some kind and then let people know exactly what measures would be used to assess their performance. In keeping with this philosophy, Mr. Hayes proposed, at the first board meeting in 19X8, that the company adopt a profit-sharing plan in which all employees could participate. The other members of the board were receptive to the idea and a committee was appointed to draw up a plan.

According to the plan devised by the committee, the company would set aside cash equal to a certain percentage of before-tax profits. The cash would be distributed to all employees on the basis of a pre-established formula. Or, more correctly, a set of such formulas was needed because the performances of employees in different areas of the company had to be measured in different ways. Mr. Ira Hayes Jr., the president, wanted to provide his own incentives to encourage better performance by sales and production personnel. He gave the sales and production manager, individually, several long and enthusiastic pep-talks on expanding their respective areas to higher levels. He further authorized an expenditure for $450,000 on a nationwide advertising program.

Production in the plant reached the normal capacity of 1,875,000 units for the year 19X8. At the board meeting in early 19X9, the president remarked: "Back in the black again. The field people did a great job pushing sales up by almost 17%." (Exhibit 2 shows the data presented to the board at that meeting; Exhibit 1 shows the basic data available to the directors at the meeting discussed in the first paragraph of the case.)

The board was pleased with the results of their new plan and with its apparent immediate effectiveness. There was, in fact, much optimistic talk at the meeting about the effect that the new plan would have on 19X9 operations, especially because the special sales campaign would probably not be repeated regularly. The board voted to continue the plan for at least one more year. After the vote, Mr. Hayes Jr. suggested that it would probably be good for employee relations if the board would announce soon when the pool for profit sharing would be distributed in cash to the employees because the dividend announcement had already been widely publicized. In an outer room, the sales manager, the production manager, and the controller were discussing the advantages and disadvantages of nepotism and of nonoperating management on the board of directors.

The questions provided below are not designed to limit your discussion or specifically direct your analysis. Nor is there any particular significance to the order in which they are listed; you will find it worthwhile to answer the first one first because it may provide some clue as to how you might proceed. It would probably be inefficient to answer each of the questions directly and in order because some are interrelated, but you may want to incorporate some comments about each of them in your answer.

1. What is the company's break-even point?
2. What is the company's system for implementing the management functions of planning and control?
3. Are profits likely to continue?
4. Has the profit-sharing plan contributed to efficiency? to cost reduction? to a return to profitable operations?
5. Should the board announce a cash distribution to employees relatively soon?

Exhibit 1
Pennywise Company
Operating Data for 19X7

Part A: Condensed Statement of Income

Sales (1,200,000 units at $12 per unit)	$14,400,000
Cost of goods sold	11,760,000
Gross margin on sales	2,640,000
Selling and administrative expenses	3,630,000
Net operating loss for the year 19X7	($ 990,000)

Part B: Miscellaneous Operating Data

Normal operating capacity, in units		1,875,000
Fixed costs:		
Manufacturing		$ 6,000,000
Selling and administrative		750,000
Variable costs, per unit:		
Manufacturing	$4.80	
Selling and administrative	$2.40	

Exhibit 2
Pennywise Company
Operating Data for 19X8

Sales (1,406,250 units at $12)		$16,875,000
Cost of goods sold:		
Fixed costs	$ 6,000,000	
Variable costs (1,875,000 @ $4.80)	9,000,000	
	15,000,000	
Less: ending inventory (468,750 units @ $8.00)	3,750,000	
		11,250,000
Gross margin on sales		5,625,000
Selling and administrative expenses:		
Fixed costs	1,200,000	
Variable costs (1,406,250 @ $2.40)	3,375,000	
		4,575,000
Operating profit before taxes and allowance for profit-sharing pool		1,050,000
Provision for profit-sharing pool		210,000
Operating profit before taxes		840,000
Provision for federal income taxes		420,000
Net income for the year 19X8		$ 420,000
Dividends to common stockholders (@ $.20)		$ 200,000

CHAPTER 14

PRODUCT COSTING: PROCESS, JOB ORDER, STANDARD

In this chapter we consider the development of methods of recording and accounting for costs in order to (1) provide unit costs for inventory determination and financial reporting, and (2) enable managers to identify deviations from budgeted results at an early point in time so that investigation and corrective action can be immediately initiated. We shall describe and illustrate the general pattern of accounting for costs and then proceed to refinements of the basic pattern that assist in control.

COST FLOWS IN A MANUFACTURING FIRM

Manufacturing processes take time. At any particular time there are likely to be some finished units on hand, and other units of product in various stages of completion. Thus, manufacturing firms will normally have three kinds of inventory: finished goods, semifinished goods (called Work in Process Inventory), and some materials that have not yet been put into the manufacturing process (called Raw Materials Inventory).

Costs incurred are first recorded in descriptive accounts such as Direct Labor, Supplies, and so on. The account, Work in Process Inventory, is used to collect and accumulate all costs considered to be product costs. Under absorption costing, materials, direct labor, and overhead (either actual or applied) will be put into Work in Process. Under variable costing only the variable costs of manufacturing will be put into that account.

As units are completed, their costs are taken out of Work in Process Inventory and put into Finished Goods Inventory. As goods are sold, the costs are taken out of Finished Goods Inventory. As goods are sold, the costs are taken out of Finished Goods Inventory and put into the Cost of Goods Sold account. These flows are diagrammed in Figure 14-1.

TYPES OF COST SYSTEMS

Within the general framework shown in Figure 14-1, there are several methods or systems that are in general use. We shall describe three of these methods, then illustrate each of them.

FIGURE 14-1   Flow of Costs in a Manufacturing Firm

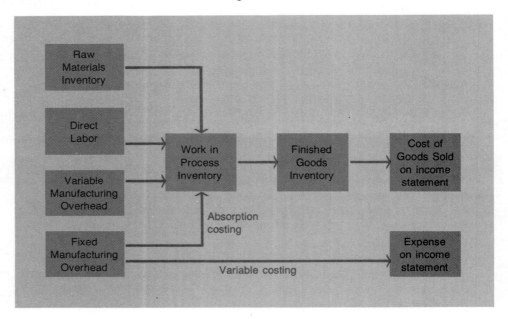

Process Costing

There is a great deal of variety in manufacturing operations. At one end of a spectrum are firms whose factories mass produce a single, homogeneous product in more or less continuous processes. Producers of sugar, bricks, cement, and some chemicals make the same product over and over. A maker of instant coffee puts raw coffee beans through roasting, mixing, grinding, and freezing processes. Firms that make their products this way can use **process costing**. In general, under process costing the firm accumulates costs by process and obtains per-unit costs by dividing the cost of the process by the number of units produced. The result is an average cost per unit.

Let us give a very brief, simplified example. A firm puts 100,000 units of product through two processes during a month and incurs total costs for the processes as follows: process I, $380,000; process II, $860,000. The cost per unit for finished goods would be calculated as shown below.

$$\text{Unit cost for process} \quad = \quad \frac{\text{total costs charged to process}}{\text{units processed}}$$

For our example,

$$\text{Process I} \quad = \quad \frac{\$380,000}{100,000} \quad = \quad \$\ 3.80$$

$$\text{Process II} \quad = \quad \frac{\$860,000}{100,000} \quad = \quad \underline{\quad 8.60\quad}$$

Total per-unit cost $\qquad\qquad\qquad\qquad\qquad\qquad \underline{\underline{\$12.40}}$

The cost-per-unit figures will contain fixed costs if the firm is using absorption costing. Thus, there is an allocation of fixed costs to units. Additionally, fixed overhead included in the total costs, above, could be either actual or applied, depending on whether the firm uses predetermined overhead rates as discussed in Chapter 13. (Please remember that we are describing systems for *product costing*, not for control and planning. Both financial and tax accounting require the absorption approach to product costing.)

Process costing is used, then, by firms that make virtually the same kind of unit of product all of the time. Use of the averaging method of determining unit costs is appropriate in those circumstances.

Job Order Costing

At the other end of the spectrum of manufacturing operations are firms that make products one at a time or in batches. These products are usually somewhat different; sometimes they are made to customer order and the firm might never make the same kind of unit twice. Buildings, bridges, airplanes, books, and large pieces of machinery like cranes and derricks are made one at a time or in identifiable batches.

Such firms cannot determine unit costs by dividing the costs of a production process by units produced. Consider a printer who produces 200,000 books during a particular month. Some of the books might have 800 pages, some 200. The 800-page books require more paper, more ink, and more press time than the 200-page books. An average cost per book (total costs divided by the number of books produced) would be meaningless.

Job order costing is used by firms that do not make homogeneous products. Under job order costing the firm accumulates costs for each unit or batch of units that it produces. The printer will keep track of the paper, labor time, and press time of each batch of books. A builder will keep track of materials and labor time used on each building being worked on during a period. Overhead will be applied using labor hours or some other causal factor.

Job order firms require information about *this* unit or *that* batch of units. Process cost firms do not: it would be impossible to determine the cost of a *particular* pound of sugar or gallon of orange juice. So long as the units are the same, no harm comes from calculating an average cost per unit.

There are many borderline cases—firms that could use either method. A furniture manufacturer might produce the same kinds of units, like chairs of a particular model, over and over again. If the chairs are made in batches as orders are received, the firm could employ job order costing. But if the firm generally makes a single model for a month or so, a form of process costing could be used. Costs could be accumulated by process (cutting, assembling, upholstering) for the period during which only one type of chair is being made. An average cost per unit could then be computed because the units made during the period are all the same.

Standard Costing

We have already discussed the use of standard costs for control purposes. Standard costs are also widely used for product costing. Under standard costing the firm does not calculate an actual cost per unit. Instead, the standard cost of a unit is used for determining inventory and cost of goods sold. Actual costs are accumulated and used for computing variances, but do not enter into the determination of per-unit costs.

Standard costing offers some distinct advantages over actual costing. We can illustrate one major advantage by considering a firm that makes bolts. The firm might make 200 different types and sizes of bolts. Bolts would vary in length, thickness, shape of head, and number of threads. The material requirements would vary from bolt to bolt, as would the machine time required for cutting, putting on the threads, and putting on the head.

The firm could not use process costing because of the wide variety of units. Job order costing would be impractical and costly. The time spent keeping track of machine time needed to put heads on a particular batch of bolts would be better spent in making more bolts.

The use of standard costs would be extremely efficient, much less costly, and would provide better information for managerial purposes. The firm would determine the number of bolts of each type and size produced and sold. Cost of goods sold would be the grand total of the standard costs for each type of bolt multiplied by the number of bolts sold. Inventory would be the grand total of the standard cost for each type of bolt multiplied by the number of that type still on hand. Thus, if the firm had only two types of bolt on hand at the end of a period, the calculation of inventory would be as follows, using the assumed data.

Type of Bolt	Standard Cost per Bolt	×	Quantity on Hand	=	Inventory Amount for Type of Bolt
L-50	$.05		20,000		$1,000
M-80	.15		30,000		4,500
Total inventory					$5,500

Standard costing is also useful for single-product firms, including ones that could use process costing. Job order firms could also use standard costs, provided they make standard products whose materials and labor requirements do not change frequently. A significant advantage of standard costing is that it integrates the product costing and control aspects of an accounting system. Developing information is costly and it usually pays to use the same information for several purposes, provided that it is relevant for those purposes. We shall see this point illustrated shortly in our example of standard process costing.

COSTING METHODS ILLUSTRATED

From the description of the various costing methods we can see that there are two basic possibilities for process costing: actual process costing and standard process costing. When the products of a job order firm differ significantly from batch to batch, the establishment of meaningful standards is not possible. And, because it is very difficult to determine the actual overhead for any single job, actual job order costing is seldom practicable for all three cost elements (material, labor, and overhead). A common costing approach for job order firms is to use actual costing, but with a predetermined overhead rate such as was discussed in Chapter 13.

The procedures followed and journal entries made to effect the flow of costs are not significantly different for the various costing methods. The entries formalize the cost flows portrayed in Figure 14-1. Materials, labor services, and overhead items are purchased from outside the firm; transfer of these factors to production is reflected through a Work in Process account; and completed work is transferred to Finished Goods until a sale is made. The flows and the *general* form of the journal entries are the same for each of the costing methods, though each method has one or more special procedures required to accomplish its objective. We shall illustrate the three most common methods: actual and standard process costing, and actual job order costing with a predetermined overhead rate.

Illustration of Actual Process Costing

We begin with a simplified example of cost flows in a firm that operates a single process, then proceed to show some refinements in the basic pattern. The Mason Company produces wooden cabinets on an assembly line. Only one type of cabinet is made. Workers at various stations along the line put the frame together, add doors, and sand the surfaces. During 19X5 the firm had the experience described below. We omit explanations of journal entries because the transactions describe the entries. There were no beginning inventories.

Purchase of materials: The firm bought 1,400,000 feet of wood at $.095 per foot.

1.	Materials Inventory (1,400,000 × $0.95)	$133,000	
	Cash or Accounts Payable		$133,000

Materials put into process: The firm used 1,300,000 feet of wood in making cabinets.

2.	Work in Process Inventory (1,300,000 × $.095)	$123,500	
	Materials Inventory		$123,500

Direct labor incurred: The firm paid direct laborers $344,400 for 82,000 hours of work at $4.20 per hour. The cost was charged to work in process.

3(a).	Direct Labor	$344,400	
	Cash		$344,400
3(b).	Work in Process Inventory	$344,400	
	Direct Labor		$344,400

Overhead costs incurred: The firm incurred the following overhead costs. For brevity we list only a few individual items, lumping the bulk of overhead costs into the "Other" category.

Variable overhead:		
	Indirect labor	$ 84,000
	Supplies	12,000
	Other	155,300
Total variable overhead		$251,300
Fixed overhead:		
	Supervision	$ 74,000
	Depreciation	96,000
	Other	291,000
Total fixed overhead		$461,000

Overhead costs are first recorded by type of cost.

4.	Indirect Labor	$ 84,000	
	Supplies	12,000	
	Other Variable Overhead	155,300	
	Supervision	74,000	
	Depreciation	96,000	
	Other Fixed Overhead	291,000	
	Accumulated Depreciation		$ 96,000
	Cash, Accrued Payables		616,300

Overhead costs are not usually put directly into Work in Process Inventory. Instead, they are gathered together into an account called Manufacturing Overhead, or into two such accounts: one for variable overhead and one for fixed overhead.

5(a).	Variable Manufacturing Overhead	$251,300	
	Indirect Labor		$ 84,000
	Supplies		12,000
	Other Variable Overhead		155,300

5(b).	Fixed Manufacturing Overhead	$461,000	
	Supervision		$ 74,000
	Depreciation		96,000
	Other Fixed Overhead		291,000

The manufacturing overhead accounts are for convenience and are especially helpful when standard costing is used, as we shall show shortly. The amounts put into the manufacturing overhead accounts are now transferred to Work in Process Inventory.

6.	Work in Process Inventory	$712,300	
	Variable Manufacturing Overhead		$251,300
	Fixed Manufacturing Overhead		461,000

Production: During the year the firm finished 40,000 cabinets and transferred them to the storage area for finished goods. Another 3,000 units were still in process at the end of 19X5. These 3,000 units were two-thirds finished. That is, on the average, the units remaining in process had two-thirds of the materials and two-thirds of the labor required to make a finished cabinet.

To transfer the cost of finished units to Finished Goods it is necessary to know the per-unit cost of a cabinet. But we cannot compute the unit cost by dividing the total costs by 40,000 cabinets (the number finished) because another 3,000 units had some work done on them. Nor can we use 43,000 cabinets (the number worked on) because 3,000 of them are not finished. To calculate the per-unit cost of a cabinet we must calculate what is called **equivalent production.** The equivalent production is the 40,000 units completed plus the *equivalent* of the 3,000 units that are only two-thirds complete. Thus,

$$\begin{array}{l} \text{Equivalent} \\ \text{production} \end{array} = \begin{array}{l} \text{units} \\ \text{completed} \end{array} + \left(\begin{array}{l} \text{units in} \\ \text{ending inventory} \end{array} \times \begin{array}{l} \text{percentage} \\ \text{complete} \end{array} \right)$$

In this case,

$$\text{Equivalent production} = 40,000 + (3,000 \times \tfrac{2}{3}) = 42,000 \text{ units}$$

The 42,000 equivalent production figure is used to determine the cost per unit. At this point we have $1,180,200 in the Work in Process Inventory account, composed of the following costs. The numbers in parentheses refer to journal entries.

Materials (2)	$ 123,500
Direct labor (3b)	344,400
Variable overhead (6)	251,300
Fixed overhead (6)	461,000
Total	$1,180,200
Divided by equivalent production	42,000
Equals cost per unit	$28.10

The $28.10 cost per unit is used for the transfer to Finished Goods Inventory.

7.	Finished Goods Inventory (40,000 × $28.10)	$1,124,000	
	Work in Process Inventory		$1,124,000

Sales: The firm sold 35,000 cabinets at $40 each.

8(a).	Cash or Accounts Receivable (35,000 × $40)	$1,400,000	
	Sales		$1,400,000
8(b).	Cost of Goods Sold (35,000 × $28.10)	$ 983,500	
	Finished Goods Inventory		$ 983,500

Selling and Administrative Expenses: The firm incurred $340,000 in selling and administrative expenses.

9.	Selling and Administrative Expenses	$340,000	
	Cash, Accrued Payables		$340,000

At this point the accounts for direct labor, variable overhead, and fixed overhead would all have zero balances. The other key accounts would show the following.

Work in Process Inventory

(2)	$ 123,500		
(3b)	344,400		
(6)	712,300	1,124,000	(7)
	1,180,200	1,124,000	
Bal.	$ 56,200		

Finished Goods Inventory

(7)	$1,124,000	$983,500	(8b)
Bal.	$ 140,500		

Cost of Goods Sold

(8b)	$ 983,500		

Materials Inventory

(1)	$133,000	$123,500	(2)
Bal.	$ 9,500		

An income statement for the Mason Company is shown in Exhibit 14-1, which appears on page 479 along with a standard costing income statement that we shall develop in the next section.

Illustration of Standard Process Costing

To highlight the differences between actual and standard process costing we shall use the same transactions for the Mason Company, but assume that the firm uses standard costing. The standard cost for a cabinet is given below.

Materials (30 feet of wood at $.10 per foot)	$ 3
Direct labor (2 hours at $4 per hour)	8
Variable overhead ($3 per direct labor hour)	6
Fixed overhead*	9
Total standard cost	$26

*Based on *budgeted* fixed overhead of $450,000 and normal capacity of 50,000 cabinets ($450,000/50,000 = $9).

One major objective of using a standard costing system is the isolation of variances at the earliest possible time. Timely determination of variances helps in control because the sooner it is known that a variance has occurred, the sooner investigation and corrective action can be taken.

For ease in reference, we calculate all variances below. The variances will later be recorded in journal entries. Notice that equivalent production of 42,000 units is used to determine total standard costs.

Materials Variances

Price variance [1,400,000 feet at $.005 ($.10 − $.095)]	$	7,000 favorable
Use variance [1,300,000 − (42,000 × 30 feet)] × $.10		4,000 unfavorable

Direct Labor Variances

Rate variance [82,000 hours × ($4.20 − $4)]	$16,400 unfavorable
Efficiency variance [82,000 hours − (42,000 × 2)] × $4	8,000 favorable

Variable Overhead Variances

Spending variance [$251,300 − (82,000 × $3)]	$ 5,300 unfavorable
Efficiency variance [82,000 hours − (42,000 × 2)] × $3	6,000 favorable

Fixed Overhead Variances

Budget variance ($461,000 − $450,000)	$11,000 unfavorable
Volume variance [(50,000 − 42,000) × $9]	72,000 unfavorable

Purchase of materials: The 1,400,000 feet of wood were bought at $7,000 under the standard price. We isolate the material price variance at the time of purchase as follows.

1.	Materials Inventory (1,400,000 × $.10)	$140,000	
	Material Price Variance		$7,000
	Cash or Accounts Payable		133,000

Materials put into process: The 1,300,000 feet of wood put into process were 40,000 feet above the standard. The material use variance is isolated as soon as possible as shown below.

2.	Work in Process (1,260,000 × $.10)	$126,000	
	Material Use Variance	4,000	
	Materials Inventory		$130,000

Notice that materials are carried in Materials Inventory at standard cost and are taken out at standard cost, which simplifies recordkeeping, especially if materials are purchased at different prices.

Direct labor incurred: The direct labor rate variance can be isolated at the time direct laborers are paid and the efficiency variance is isolated when direct labor costs are transferred to work in process.

3(a).	Direct Labor (82,000 × $4)	$328,000	
	Direct Labor Rate Variance	16,400	
	Cash		$344,400
3(b).	Work in Process Inventory (42,000 × 2 × $4)	$336,000	
	Direct Labor Efficiency Variance		$8,000
	Direct Labor		328,000

Overhead costs incurred: The initial recording of overhead costs and their transfer to Manufacturing Overhead accounts is the same as in the actual process costing example, except that spending or budget variances are isolated. The variable overhead efficiency variance and volume variance are isolated when overhead is transferred to work in process.

4.   Same as on page 474.

5(a).	Variable Manufacturing Overhead		
	(82,000 hours × $3)	$246,000	
	Variable Overhead Spending Variance	5,300	
	Indirect Labor		$84,000
	Supplies		12,000
	Other Variable Overhead		155,300
5(b).	Fixed Manufacturing Overhead		
	(budget of $450,000)	$450,000	
	Fixed Overhead Budget Variance	11,000	
	Supervision		$74,000
	Depreciation		96,000
	Other Fixed Overhead		291,000
6(a).	Work in Process Inventory (42,000 × $6)	$252,000	
	Variable Overhead Efficiency Variance		$6,000
	Variable Manufacturing Overhead		246,000

6(b). Work in Process (42,000 × $9)	$378,000	
Fixed Overhead Volume Variance		
(8,000 × $9)	72,000	
Fixed Manufacturing Overhead		$450,000

Production: the 40,000 units *completed* are transferred to finished goods at the standard cost of $26 per unit, leaving Work in Process Inventory with the standard cost of the uncompleted units.

7. Finished Goods Inventory (40,000 × $26)	$1,040,000	
Work in Process		$1,040,000

Sales: Cost of goods sold is recorded using the standard cost of the 35,000 units sold.

8(a). Cash or Accounts Receivable		
(35,000 × $40 selling price)	$1,400,000	
Sales		$1,400,000
8(b). Cost of Goods Sold (35,000 × $26)	$910,000	
Finished Goods Inventory		$ 910,000

Selling and administrative expenses: The $340,000 in selling and administrative expenses would be recorded the same as in entry 9 on page 475.

At this point the accounts for direct labor, variable overhead, and fixed overhead would all have zero balances. The other key accounts would appear as follows.

Work in Process Inventory

(2)	$ 126,000		
(3b)	336,000		
(6a)	252,000		
(6b)	378,000	$1,040,000	(7)
	1,092,000	1,040,000	
Bal.	$ 52,000		

Finished Goods Inventory

(7)	$1,040,000	$910,000	(8b)
Bal.	$ 130,000		

Cost of Goods Sold

(8b)	$910,000	

Materials Inventory

(1)	$140,000	$130,000	(2)
Bal.	$ 10,000		

What are the differences between the results under actual process costing and those under standard process costing? One major difference is that inventories are shown at standard costs. Materials Inventory contains $10,000, which is the standard price of $.10 per foot multiplied by the 100,000 feet on hand (1,400,000 purchased − 1,300,000 used in production). Work in Process Inventory is $52,000 which is the standard cost of the 2,000 *equivalent units* on hand (3,000 units two-thirds finished) at $26 per unit (2,000 × $26). Finished Goods Inventory shows 5,000 units (40,000 finished − 35,000 sold) at the standard cost of $26 per unit (5,000 × $26 = $130,000). Cost of Goods Sold is also at standard cost. The $910,000 is 35,000 units at $26 per unit.

The variances have all been isolated in individual accounts. The material price and labor rate variances were isolated as soon as they were known, which was when the materials were purchased and direct labor was paid for. As production proceeded throughout the year, Work in Process Inventory was charged with the standard cost of inputs put into process so that it always contained the standard cost of the units in process.

In a more realistic situation, where a number of supervisors and managers were responsible for controlling costs, the variance accounts would have subsidiary accounts or other records pertaining to each responsible manager. Thus, the labor efficiency variance might have a number of components related to the use of direct labor by a number of managers in charge of groups of laborers.

The income statement for Mason Company if it uses standard process costing is shown in Exhibit 14-1 alongside the statement for actual process costing. Since fixed manufacturing costs were applied to production in both cases, the statements reflect absorption costing.

Exhibit 14-1
Income Statements for Mason Company—Absorption Costing

	Actual Process Costing		Standard Process Costing
Sales (8)*	$1,400,000		$1,400,000
Cost of goods sold (8)	983,500		910,000
Gross profit	416,500		490,000
Manufacturing variances:			
Material price (1)		$ 7,000F	
Material use (2)		4,000U	
Direct labor rate (3)		16,400U	
Direct labor efficiency (3)		8,000F	
Variable overhead spending (5)		5,300U	
Variable overhead efficiency (6)		6,000F	
Fixed overhead budget (5)		11,000U	
Fixed overhead volume (6)		72,000U	87,700U
Actual gross profit			402,300
Less: selling and administrative expenses (9)	340,000		340,000
Income	$ 76,500		$ 62,300

*Figures in parentheses indicate journal entry numbers from the earlier illustrations.

The illustrations of actual and standard process costing incorporated two assumptions that served to simplify the exposition. First, it was assumed that there was no beginning inventory of units in process in order to simplify the computation of equivalent production. Second, the firm was said to operate only one process, which served to avoid the problem of transferring costs and units from one operating department to another within the firm. In a realistic situation, neither of these complications can usually be avoided, and we shall briefly discuss in the next two sections how to deal with these practical complications.

Equivalent Production—Beginning and Ending Inventories

We have illustrated the concept of equivalent production when there are ending inventories of work in process. When there are also beginning inventories of semifinished units an additional step is needed to determine equivalent production.

Assume that a firm starts a month with 4,000 units that are 40% complete and has total costs of $21,000 in the Work in Process account. During the month the firm completes 10,000 units, including those in the beginning inventory, and has another 3,000 units on hand at the end of the month. These units are 60% complete. Production costs incurred during the month are $114,770. There are two ways that equivalent production can be calculated: one is the weighted average method, which is most frequently used for product costing purposes; the other is a first-in-first-out method which is more suitable for control purposes. Using the weighted average method

$$\begin{array}{c}\text{Equivalent}\\\text{production—}\\\text{weighted}\\\text{average}\end{array} = \begin{array}{c}\text{units}\\\text{completed}\end{array} + \left(\begin{array}{c}\text{units in}\\\text{ending}\\\text{inventory}\end{array} \times \begin{array}{c}\text{percentage}\\\text{complete}\end{array}\right)$$

and the per-unit cost can be computed as

$$\begin{array}{c}\text{Cost per}\\\text{unit—}\\\text{weighted}\\\text{average}\end{array} = \frac{\begin{array}{c}\text{cost of beginning}\\\text{inventory}\end{array} + \begin{array}{c}\text{costs incurred}\\\text{during the period}\end{array}}{\text{equivalent production—weighted average}}$$

For our example,

$$\begin{array}{c}\text{Equivalent}\\\text{production}\end{array} = 10,000 + (3,000 \times 60\%) = 11,800$$

and

$$\begin{array}{c}\text{Cost per}\\\text{unit}\end{array} = \frac{\$21,000 + \$114,700}{11,800} = \frac{\$135,700}{11,800} = \$11.50$$

We do not have to consider the *units* in the beginning inventory in making the calculation because they are already included in the 10,000 units completed during the period. We do have to consider the *cost* of the beginning inventory.

Essentially, then, the only difference in calculating cost per unit that arises when there are beginning inventories, as opposed to only ending inventories, is that the cost of the beginning inventory is added to the cost incurred during the period. But under the weighted average method the calculation of equivalent production is exactly the same whether or not there are beginning inventories.

The cost-per-unit figure given by the weighted average method is not suitable for control purposes. Even if the firm uses variable costing and therefore includes only variable costs in the calculation of cost per unit the method mixes performance in the current period with performance in prior periods.

Some firms may use actual process costing for product costing purposes, but may also compute variances from standard performance for control purposes. To do so the firm can use a first-in-first-out (FIFO) method of determining equivalent production and unit costs. The calculation requires that we consider only the costs incurred during the period and that we remove the equivalent units from the beginning inventory to determine FIFO equivalent production for the period.

In general terms,

$$\begin{array}{l}\text{Equivalent} \\ \text{production—} \\ \text{first-in-} \\ \text{first-out}\end{array} = \begin{array}{l}\text{units} \\ \text{completed}\end{array} + \left(\begin{array}{l}\text{units in} \\ \text{ending} \\ \text{inventory}\end{array} \times \begin{array}{l}\text{percentage} \\ \text{complete}\end{array}\right) - \left(\begin{array}{l}\text{units in} \\ \text{beginning} \\ \text{inventory}\end{array} \times \begin{array}{l}\text{percentage} \\ \text{complete}\end{array}\right)$$

Using the data from the previous example, we would calculate equivalent production as follows. Recall that the beginning inventory was 4,000 units 40% complete.

$$\begin{array}{l}\text{Equivalent} \\ \text{production—} \\ \text{FIFO}\end{array} = 10,000 + (3,000 \times 60\%) - (4,000 \times 40\%) = 10,200 \text{ units}$$

The FIFO per-unit cost would be computed by dividing the current production costs by the FIFO equivalent production. In general terms,

$$\begin{array}{l}\text{Current cost} \\ \text{per unit—} \\ \text{FIFO}\end{array} = \frac{\text{costs incurred during the period}}{\text{equivalent production—FIFO}}$$

In this case,

$$\text{Cost per unit—FIFO} = \frac{\$114,700}{10,200} = \$11.25 \text{ (rounded)}$$

Suppose further that the firm has established a standard variable cost of $6 per unit and that the costs incurred during the period can be analyzed as follows.

Fixed production costs	$ 55,000
Variable production costs	59,700
Total	$114,700

Based on 10,200 units of work done during the current period we would have total standard variable costs of $61,200 ($6 × 10,200). Because actual variable costs were $59,700, there were total favorable cost variances of $1,500 ($61,200 − $59,700). These variances could be analyzed along the lines shown in Chapter 12 if we had more information about the makeup of the standard cost and actual costs.

Multiple Processes

If the firm operates more than one process the basic pattern of cost transfers requires that costs be moved from one Work in Process account to another as goods are moved from one process to another. (Eventually the goods will be transferred to finished goods.) The basic entries remain the same, but with more work in process accounts.

The one complication that is created by multiple processes is that a unit cost must be computed separately for each process. Because of the possibility of different amounts of equivalent production in each process, it is inappropriate to determine unit costs by dividing total production costs by equivalent production for one process. This will become clear as we develop an example.

The Fisher Company manufactures a product that requires two processes. Data for July are given below. There were no beginning inventories in either process.

	Process I	Process II
Units completed and sent to process II	16,000	
Units completed and sent to finished goods		16,000
Ending inventory	2,000	0
Percentage complete	60%	
Equivalent production [16,000 + (2,000 × 60%)]	17,200	16,000
Total costs of process	$247,680	$201,600
Unit cost of process:		
$247,680/17,200	$14.40	
$201,600/16,000		$12.60

When the units produced by process I are transferred to process II, the following journal entry would be made.

Work in Process—II (16,000 × $14.40)	$230,400	
Work in Process—I		$230,400

And the transfer to finished goods would be made up of the $230,400 cost transferred from process I to process II plus the $201,600 incurred in process II.

Finished Goods Inventory (16,000 × $27)	$432,000	
Work in Process—II		$432,000

The $27 unit cost shown in the journal entry above is the sum of the unit costs of the two processes, $14.40 in process I and $12.60 in process II. Notice that we have two different equivalent production amounts for the two processes and therefore cannot make a single computation of per-unit costs.

Illustration of Job Order Costing

Job order firms can use standard costing if they produce the same products over and over as a manufacturer of standard lines of furniture might do. However, if the products differ from batch to batch, it may not be possible to use standard costs. It would still be possible, and desirable, to apply overhead based on predetermined rates, because trying to determine the actual overhead on a particular batch is virtually impossible.

One unfortunate characteristic of job order costing is that it requires a great deal more recordkeeping than do other methods. Job order firms will have to keep track of materials used for *each* order, or batch, of goods. The laborers who work on the different batches will turn in time tickets indicating how much time they spent on each order, and overhead will have to be applied to each order.

We shall illustrate job order costing using the Ehrens Company, a manufacturer of heavy equipment used in mining. The machines are made to customer specifications. The firm uses actual costing for material and labor and a predetermined rate for manufacturing overhead. The accountant for Ehrens Company has analyzed the behavior of overhead costs using regression analysis and has come up with the following formula: total overhead = $300,000 + ($3 × direct labor hours). These amounts have been used for budgeting purposes. Because the firm expects to work 60,000 direct labor hours at normal capacity, the predetermined overhead rate is $8, calculated as follows.

Variable overhead rate per direct labor hour		$3
Fixed overhead budgeted	$300,000	
Direct labor hours at normal capacity	60,000	
Fixed overhead rate ($300,000/60,000)		5
Total overhead rate		$8

During 19X6 the firm worked on only three jobs: L-101; L-102; and L-103. The first two were completed and sold and L-103 was still unfinished at the end of the year. Data on the three jobs are given below.

	L-101	L-102	L-103	Totals
Direct labor at $6 per hour	$ 84,000	$168,000	$ 96,000	$ 348,000
Material used	110,000	120,000	98,000	328,000
Overhead at $8 per direct labor hour*	112,000	224,000	128,000	464,000
Total costs charged to jobs	$306,000	$512,000	$322,000	$1,140,000

*Direct labor hours are: L-101, 14,000 ($84,000/$6); L-102, 28,000 ($168,000/$6); and L-103, 16,000 ($96,000/$6). These amounts multiplied by the $8 overhead application rate give the overhead figures shown.

Assume further that actual overhead was $470,000, which gives a total of $6,000 in underapplied overhead ($470,000 − $464,000 applied) and that sales were $1,150,000, and selling and administrative expenses $195,000.

In the journal entries below we show only those entries involving Work in Process and Finished Goods Inventory. The entries to record the incurrence of costs and to record sales are already familiar. Ehrens Company uses a single account for manufacturing overhead. The firm cannot distinguish incurred variable overhead from incurred fixed overhead.

1.	Work in Process Inventory	$1,140,000	
	Materials Inventory		$328,000
	Direct Labor		348,000
	Manufacturing Overhead		464,000

To record costs put into work in process.

2.	Finished Goods Inventory ($306,000 + $512,000)	$818,000	
	Work in Process Inventory		$818,000

To record completion of jobs L-101 and L-102 and their transfers to finished goods.

3.	Cost of Goods Sold	$818,000	
	Finished Goods Inventory		$818,000

To record cost of sales of L-101 and L-102.

At this point the Work in Process Inventory account would show $322,000, the accumulated costs of job L-103, which is not yet complete ($1,140,000 − $818,000). The Manufacturing Overhead account would show $6,000 as follows:

Manufacturing Overhead

Incurred	$470,000	$464,000	Applied
Balance (underapplied)	$ 6,000		

Following the analytical approach developed in Chapter 13, the $6,000 balance can be analyzed into spending (budget) and volume variance components as follows:

Total budget variance, fixed and variable overhead:	
Actual overhead incurred	$470,000
Budgeted overhead for actual volume, using the company's cost formula	
$300,000 + ($3 × 58,000 hrs.)	474,000
Total budget variance, favorable	$ 4,000
Volume variance:	
Fixed overhead budgeted	$300,000
Fixed overhead applied $5 × 58,000 hrs.	290,000
Volume variance, unfavorable	$ 10,000

Cost control seems to have been good because the budgeted overhead amount was more than actual overhead incurred. Because we do not have information about standard hours, we cannot determine whether labor was used efficiently or not. But since the firm does not make a standard product, the notion of a standard number of hours per machine is at best an approximation based on the estimates of required time when the orders were accepted.

An income statement for the Ehrens Company would appear as follows.

Sales		$1,150,000
Cost of goods sold		818,000
Gross profit		332,000
Less:		
Underapplied overhead	$ 6,000	
Selling and administrative expenses	195,000	201,000
Income		$ 131,000

SUMMARY

The flow of costs through manufacturing firms can be accounted for using several methods or systems, the most common being process costing and job order costing. Firms using either of these methods also use either actual or standard costs, with the nature of the manufacturing operation determining the extent to which standards can be meaningfully employed.

The calculation of unit costs under process costing is complicated somewhat by the existence of incomplete units in the inventories at the beginning and/or end of the period. The concept of equivalent production was developed to overcome this problem. Two calculations of equivalent production are possible, depending upon whether the unit cost to be computed is based on a weighted average or is to reflect a first-in-first-out cost flow. The latter is usually more suitable for cost control purposes.

The journal entries to reflect cost flows are more complex when standard costs are used, because the entries provide for the isolation of variances into separate accounts. But the basic accounting for the flows of costs does not differ significantly whether the firm uses process or job order costing and actual or standard costs.

KEY TERMS

equivalent production
finished goods inventory
job order costing (actual or standard)

process costing (actual or standard)
raw materials inventory
work in process inventory

KEY FORMULAS

$$\text{Unit cost for process} = \frac{\text{total costs charged to process}}{\text{units processed}}$$

$$\text{Equivalent production—} \atop \text{weighted average} = \text{units} \atop \text{completed} + \left(\text{units in} \atop \text{ending inventory} \times \text{percentage} \atop \text{complete} \right)$$

$$\text{Equivalent} \atop \text{production—} \atop \text{first-in-first-} \atop \text{out} = \text{units} \atop \text{completed} + \left(\text{units} \atop \text{in} \atop \text{ending} \atop \text{inventory} \times \text{percentage} \atop \text{complete} \right) - \left(\text{units} \atop \text{in} \atop \text{beginning} \atop \text{inventory} \times \text{percentage} \atop \text{complete} \right)$$

$$\text{Cost per} \atop \text{unit—} \atop \text{weighted} \atop \text{average} = \frac{\text{cost of} \atop \text{beginning inventory} + \text{costs incurred} \atop \text{during the period}}{\text{equivalent production—weighted average}}$$

$$\text{Cost per} \atop \text{unit—} \atop \text{first-in-first-} \atop \text{out} = \frac{\text{costs incurred during the period}}{\text{equivalent production—first-in-first-out}}$$

REVIEW PROBLEM—PROCESS COSTING

The Stambol Manufacturing Company makes a single type of chemical solvent. Data for April 19X8 are given below. The solvent is mixed first, then distilled.

	Mixing Department	Distilling Department
Beginning inventory of work in process	$ 6,000	0
Materials used	$485,000	0
Direct labor incurred	$648,000	$355,000
Overhead incurred	$604,000	$245,000
Gallons completed and sent to distilling	800,000	
Gallons completed and sent to finished goods		800,000
Gallons in ending inventory (75% complete)	40,000	0

Required

1. Determine equivalent production and cost per unit for each department. Use the weighted average method.
2. Determine the cost of the ending inventory of work in process in the mixing department.
3. Prepare T-accounts for Work in Process Inventory for each department. Check the ending balance for the mixing department with your answer to part 2.
4. Assume that there was no inventory of finished product at the beginning of April. During April, 730,000 gallons were sold, 70,000 remained in ending finished goods inventory. Determine cost of goods sold and the cost of the ending inventory of finished product.

Answers to review problem

1. Equivalent production and cost per unit

Equivalent Production

	Mixing Department	Distilling Department
Gallons completed	800,000	800,000
Equivalent production in ending inventory (40,000 × 75%)	30,000	0
Equivalent production for April	830,000	800,000

Cost per unit—weighted average

	Mixing Department	Distilling Department
Beginning inventory of work in progress	$6,000	$0
Costs incurred:		
Materials	485,000	0
Direct labor	648,000	355,000
Overhead	604,000	245,000
Totals	$1,743,000	$600,000
Divided by equivalent production	830,000	800,000
Equals cost per unit	$2.10	$.75

Total unit cost equals $2.85 ($2.10 + $.75)

2. Ending inventory in mixing department, $63,000 (30,000 × $2.10)

3.
Work in Process Inventory— Mixing Department

Beginning balance	$6,000		
Materials	485,000		
Direct labor	648,000		
Overhead	604,000	$1,680,000	transferred out (800,000 × $2.10)
	1,743,000	1,680,000	
Ending balance	$ 63,000		

The $63,000 equals the answer to part 2.

Work in Process Inventory— Distilling Department

Transferred from mixing department	$1,680,000		
Direct labor	355,000		
Overhead	245,000	$2,280,000	transferred to finished goods (800,000 × $2.85)
	2,280,000	2,280,000	

The ending balance is zero. There is no physical inventory and therefore no dollar cost.

4. Cost of goods sold is $2,080,500, which is 730,000 gallons multiplied by $2.85. Ending inventory of finished goods is $199,500, which is 70,000 gallons (800,000 − 730,000) multiplied by $2.85.

REVIEW PROBLEM—STANDARD PROCESS COSTING

The Sterling Company uses a standard cost system. The standard cost of one of its products is given below. To reduce computations we have assumed that there is no variable overhead.

Materials (2 gallons at $2)	$4
Direct labor (½ hour at $6)	3
Fixed overhead	3
Total standard cost	$10

The standard fixed overhead per unit was determined on the basis of the firm's normal activity of 30,000 units per year and budgeted fixed overhead of $90,000. There were no beginning inventories. During 19X6 the following events occurred.

1. The firm started and completed 28,000 units. There was no ending inventory of work in progress.
2. Material purchases were 70,000 gallons at $2.02, a total of $141,400.
3. Material use was 58,500 gallons.
4. Direct laborers worked 13,800 hours and were paid $83,490, for an average hourly rate of $6.05.
5. Fixed overhead incurred was $91,600, consisting of $15,000 in depreciation expense and $76,100 in other fixed overhead paid in cash.

Required

Prepare journal entries to record the above events. Isolate variances at the earliest possible time. You will find it helpful to calculate variances first.

Answer to review problem

Calculations of Variances

Materials variances:
Price variance [70,000 gals. × ($2.02 − $2)] $1,400U
Use variance [$2 × (58,500 − 56,000*)]   5,000U

Direct labor variances:
Rate variance [13,800 hrs. × ($6.05 − $6)] $ 690U
Efficiency variance [$6 × (14,000† − 13,800)]   1,200F

Fixed overhead variances:
Budget variance ($91,600 − $90,000) $1,600U
Volume variance [$3 × (30,000 − 28,000)]   6,000U

*56,000 standard gallons is 28,000 units × 2 gallons per unit
†14,000 standard hours is 28,000 units × ½ hour per unit

1. Finished Goods Inventory (28,000 × $10) $280,000
        Work in Process Inventory $280,000

    To transfer standard cost of 28,000 units. (Notice that we don't need to know actual costs because transfers are always at standard.)

2. Materials Inventory (70,000 gals. × $2) $140,000
    Material Price Variance (70,000 × $.02)   1,400
        Cash, Accounts Payable $141,400

    To record purchases of materials and isolate material price variance.

3. Work in Process Inventory (56,000 gals. × $2) $112,000
    Material Use Variance (2,500 gals. × $2)   5,000
        Materials Inventory (58,500 gals. × $2) $117,000

    To record standard cost of materials used for 28,000 gallons of product, isolate material use variance, and record cost of materials used at standard price.

4. Direct Labor (13,800 hrs. × $6) $82,800
    Direct Labor Rate Variance (13,800 hrs. × $.05)   690
        Cash $83,490

    To record direct labor at standard rate of $6 per hour, isolate direct labor rate variance, and record actual cost of direct labor.

    Work in Process Inventory (14,000 × $6) $84,000
        Direct Labor Efficiency Variance (200 hrs. × $6) $1,200
        Direct Labor (13,800 hrs. × $6)   82,800

    To record standard cost of direct labor for 28,000 units of product and isolate direct labor efficiency variance.

5. Depreciation Expense $15,000
    Other Fixed Overhead   76,600
        Accumulated Depreciation $15,000
        Cash   76,600

    To record incurred fixed overhead costs.

    Fixed Manufacturing Overhead, at budgeted amount $90,000
    Fixed Overhead Budget Variance   1,600
        Depreciation Expense $15,000
        Other Fixed Overhead   76,100

    To close expense accounts to fixed overhead and isolate budget variance.

    Work in Process Inventory (28,000 units × $3) $84,000
    Volume Variance (2,000 units × $3)   6,000
        Fixed Manufacturing Overhead $90,000

    To record standard cost of units completed and isolate volume variance.

APPENDIX: EQUIVALENT PRODUCTION— ADDITIONAL REFINEMENTS

Throughout Chapter 14 we assumed that a single figure for percentage of completion of units applied to all cost factors. Thus, if we said that units on hand were 60% complete, we were saying that 60% of the total required materials were in process and that 60% of total required labor and overhead had been performed. This assumption does not usually hold in real situations.

In some processes, materials are put into process at the beginning and labor is performed later. Therefore, at any point in the process prior to final completion, the units will be 100% complete with respect to materials and partially complete with respect to labor and overhead. The same situation holds with a product that goes through more than one process. Any units on hand are complete with respect to the costs incurred in prior departments, and partially complete with respect to the work of the current department.

The fact that units can be at different stages of completion with respect to different cost factors does not create serious accounting problems. It only requires that we compute unit costs for each type of cost factor, rather than for all costs as a whole. We shall illustrate the accounting with the following example. A firm makes a single type of chair. The parts of the chair are assembled in one department, then transferred to the sanding department. After sanding, the chairs are transferred to finished goods. At the beginning of March the firm had no inventories. During March the following events occurred.

Unit Data

	Assembly	Sanding
Units completed	2,400	1,800
Units on hand at March 31	500	600
Percentage of completion:		
Materials	100%	
Prior department costs	—	100%
Labor and overhead	40%	60%

Using these data we can calculate equivalent production for the different cost factors as follows.

Assembly

	Materials	Labor and Overhead
Units finished	2,400	2,400
Ending inventory: 500 × 100%	500	
500 × 40%		200
Totals	2,900	2,600

Sanding

	Prior Department Costs	Labor and Overhead
Units finished	1,800	1,800
Ending inventory: 600 × 100%	600	
600 × 60%		360
Totals	2,400	2,160

Notice that we have four different figures for equivalent production, two cost factors in each of the two departments. These figures will be used in determining the unit costs.

Cost Data

	Assembly	Sanding
Materials	$34,800	—
Labor and overhead	10,920	$17,280
Prior department costs		?

Our next step is to determine the cost per unit for each factor in the assembly department. The total cost per unit in that department will be used to make the journal entry transferring the cost of the 2,400 units sent to the sanding department. The total transferred to sanding will be treated as raw materials by the sanding department. The unit cost calculations are given below.

Cost per Unit—Assembly

	Materials	Labor and Overhead
Cost incurred	$34,800	$10,920
divided by		
Equivalent production	2,900	2,600
equals		
Cost per unit	$12.00	$4.20

Total unit cost = $16.20 ($12.00 + $4.20)

The $16.20 cost per unit would be used to make the entry transferring the cost of the 2,400 completed units to the sanding department.

Work in Process—Sanding (2,400 × $16.20)	$38,880	
Work in Process—Assembly		$38,880

The $16.20 will be used in determining the unit cost for transferring finished units from the sanding department to finished goods inventory, along with the cost per unit incurred in the sanding department. The calculations are given below.

Cost per Unit—Sanding

		Prior Department Costs	Labor and Overhead
Cost		$38,880	$17,280
	divided by		
Equivalent production		2,400	2,160
	equals		
Cost per unit		$16.20	$8.00

Total unit cost = $24.20 ($16.20 + $8.00)

The transfer to finished goods inventory of the 1,800 units completed would be recorded in the following journal entry.

Finished Goods Inventory (1,800 × $24.20)	$43,560	
Work in Process—Sanding		$43,560

The inventories of work in process for the two departments reflect the differing quantities of cost factors. The 500 units in the assembly department's ending inventory would have a cost of $6,840, calculated as follows.

	Materials	Labor and Overhead
Equivalent units in ending inventory:		
500 × 100%	500	
500 × 40%		200
Costs per unit	$12.00	$4.20
Inventory	$6,000	$840

Total inventory = $6,840 ($6,000 + $840)

Similarly, the inventory in process in the sanding department has two different unit costs, one for costs of the sanding department, one for costs of the assembly department transferred.

	Prior Department Costs	Labor and Overhead
Equivalent units in ending inventory:		
600 × 100%	600	
600 × 60%		360
Costs per unit	$16.20	$8.00
Inventory	$9,720	$2,880

Total inventory = $12,600 ($9,720 + $2,880)

We can verify these figures by looking at the work in process accounts for the two departments.

Assembly Department—Work in Process Inventory

Materials used	$34,800		
Labor and overhead	10,920	$38,880	transferred to sanding department
	45,720	38,880	
Ending inventory	$ 6,840		

Sanding Department—Work in Process Inventory

Transferred from assembly department	$38,880		
Labor and overhead	17,280	$43,560	transferred to finished goods
	56,160	43,560	
Ending inventory	$12,600		

Let us now take the firm one month further to show the effects of beginning inventories. Beginning inventories are treated the same as they were in the chapter: the cost is added to costs incurred during the period to determine cost per unit. The only difference is one that you might expect: the cost factors must be separated into their individual components because of the different percentages of completion. The following data are for April.

	Assembly	Sanding
Materials	$20,400	
Labor and overhead	$ 8,400	$16,809
Units finished	2,100	2,200
Ending inventory	300	500
Percentage complete:		
Materials	100%	—
Prior department costs	—	100%
Labor and overhead	70%	40%

As in the chapter, using the weighted average method we do not need to consider the units in the beginning inventories, only the costs. The cost-per-unit calculations are given below, beginning with equivalent production.

Assembly

	Materials	Labor and Overhead
Units finished	2,100	2,100
Ending inventory: 300 × 100%	300	
300 × 70%		210
Totals	2,400	2,310

Sanding

	Prior Department Costs	Labor and Overhead
Units finished	2,200	2,200
Ending inventory: 500 × 100%	500	
500 × 40%		200
Totals	2,700	2,400

We can now calculate the unit costs by using the beginning inventories for each cost factor plus the costs incurred during the period. We begin with the assembly department in order to determine the amount to be transferred to the sanding department.

Cost per Unit—Assembly

	Materials	Labor and Overhead
Beginning inventory	$ 6,000	$ 840
Incurred during April	20,400	8,400
Totals	26,400	9,240
divided by		
Equivalent production	2,400	2,310
equals		
Cost per unit	$11.00	$4.00
Total unit cost = $15.00 ($11.00 + $4.00)		

The $15 unit cost is used to transfer the 2,100 completed units to the sanding department in the following journal entry.

Work in Process Inventory—Sanding ($15 × 2,100)	$31,500	
Work in Process—Assembly		$31,500

We can now determine the unit cost added in the sanding department.

Cost per Unit—Sanding

	Prior Department Costs	Labor and Overhead
Beginning inventory	$ 9,720	$ 2,880
Incurred during April	31,500	16,809
Totals	$41,220	$19,689
divided by		
Equivalent production	2,700	2,400
equals		
Cost per unit	$15.27 (rounded)	$8.20 (rounded)
Total unit cost = $23.47 ($15.27 + $8.20)		

The $23.47 is used to transfer the cost of the 2,200 units completed and sent to finished goods.

Finished Goods Inventory ($23.47 × 2,200)	$51,634	
Work in Process Inventory—Sanding		$51,634

We can now calculate the ending inventories and show the work in process accounts for the two departments. In the assembly department the 300 units on hand at the end of April would have a total cost of $4,140, calculated as follows.

	Materials	Labor and Overhead
Equivalent units in ending inventory:		
300 × 100%	300	
300 × 70%		210
Costs per unit	$11	$4
Inventory	$3,300	$840
Total inventory = $4,140 ($3,300 + $840)		

And for the sanding department we have:

	Prior Department Costs	Labor and Overhead
Equivalent units in ending inventory:		
500 × 100%	500	
500 × 40%		200
Costs per unit	$15.27	$8.20
Inventory	$7,635	$1,640
Total inventory = $9,275 ($7,635 + $1,640)		

The work in process accounts for the two departments would appear as shown below.

Work in Process Inventory—Assembly

Beginning inventory	$ 6,840		
Incurred in April:			
Materials	20,400		
Labor and overhead	8,400	$31,500	transferred to sending
	35,640	31,500	department
Ending inventory	$ 4,140		

Work in Process Inventory—Sanding

Beginning inventory	$12,600		
Transferred from			
assembly department	31,500		
Labor and overhead	16,809	$51,634	transferred to finished goods
	60,909	51,634	
Ending inventory	$ 9,275		

ASSIGNMENT MATERIAL

Questions for discussion

14-1 **"True" fixed cost**   Is there any meaning to the statement that there is a "true" fixed cost per unit of product? Discuss.

14-2 **Kinds of standards**   If you were the president of a manufacturing firm, which of the following kinds of income statement would you prefer to receive and why?
(a) One showing actual costs only.
(b) One showing standard costs and variances, with standard costs based on ideal standards.
(c) One showing standard costs and variances with standard costs based on currently attainable standards.

Exercises

14-3 **Overhead rates, standard cost income statement.**   The following data pertain to the operations of the Dickson Company for 19X5.

Budgeted production	100,000 units
Actual production	90,000 units
Budgeted costs—manufacturing:	
Materials	$ 400,000
Direct labor	300,000
Variable overhead	300,000
Fixed overhead	200,000
Actual costs:	
Materials	$ 350,000
Direct labor	280,000
Variable overhead	290,000
Fixed overhead	220,000
Administrative	300,000
Actual sales (60,000 units)	$1,200,000

There were no beginning inventories. The firm uses standard costs based on budgeted production.

Required
Prepare a standard cost income statement. Show variances separately for each category of manufacturing cost.

14-4 **Standard cost system—journal entries**   The Watson Company makes a single product. Its standard cost is given below.

Materials (2 lbs. @ $4)	$ 8
Direct labor (3 hrs. @ $5)	15
Variable overhead ($6 per direct labor hour)	18
Fixed overhead (based on normal capacity of 50,000 units)	10
Total standard cost	$51

At the beginning of 19X9 there were no inventories. During 19X9 the following events occurred:

(a) Material purchases were 120,000 lbs. for $455,000.
(b) Direct laborers were paid $790,000 for 151,000 hours of work.
(c) Variable overhead of $895,000 was incurred.
(d) Fixed overhead incurred was $490,000.
(e) Materials used were 95,000 lbs.
(f) Production was 48,000 units. All units started were finished.
(g) Sales were 45,000 units at $100 each.

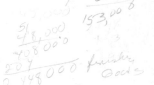

Required

1. Prepare journal entries to record the above events. Isolate variances as early as possible. Assume that the department managers are responsible for all variances except material price and direct labor rate.
2. Calculate ending inventory and cost of goods sold assuming (a) standard process costing, and (b) actual process costing.

14-5 Relationships Answer the questions for each of the following independent situations.

1. The standard fixed cost per unit is $4 based on budgeted fixed overhead of $300,000. The beginning inventory was 20,000 units, sales were 90,000 units and the ending inventory was 15,000 units.
   (a) What was the volume variance?
   (b) What would have happened to income if 1,000 more units had been produced, but not sold?
2. A firm sells its one product for $10. All of its costs are fixed manufacturing costs, which are budgeted at $300,000. Last year the firm showed a standard gross profit of $160,000, selling 40,000 units, and an income of $58,000. Fixed costs were incurred as budgeted.
   (a) What is the standard fixed cost per unit?
   (b) What was the volume variance?
   (c) What was production in units?
   (d) What would income have been under variable costing?
3. A firm uses a standard fixed cost per unit of $8 and has variable costs of $12 per unit. All costs are for manufacturing. Last year the firm earned $332,000 and had an unfavorable volume variance of $72,000. Sales were 101,000 units. There was no change in inventories over the year and all costs were incurred as budgeted.
   (a) What is the selling price of the product?
   (b) What volume was used to set the standard fixed cost per unit?
   (c) What were budgeted fixed costs?

14-6 Analysis of income statements The controller of the Anderson Company has prepared income statements on three different bases: (1) variable costing; (2) absorption costing with normal capacity of 40,000 units used to set the standard fixed cost per unit; and (3) absorption costing with practical capacity of 60,000 units used to set the standard fixed cost per unit. The same operating data were used in all three statements. There were no beginning inventories.

	A	B	C
Sales (45,000 units)	$900,000	$900,000	$900,000
Cost of sales, at standard	810,000	720,000	540,000
Standard gross profit	90,000	180,000	360,000
Volume variance	60,000	(40,000)	—
Actual gross profit	150,000	140,000	360,000
Other expenses	80,000	80,000	320,000
Income	$ 70,000	$ 60,000	$ 40,000

Required

1. Determine which statements were prepared using which method.
2. Determine the variable production costs per unit, total fixed production costs, and the standard fixed cost per unit under the two absorption costing methods.
3. Determine the number of units produced.
4. Determine the change, if any, in income that would occur under each costing method if (consider each independently):
   (a) production was increased by one unit, but sales remained the same.
   (b) sales increased by one unit, but production remained the same.
   (c) sales and production were both increased by one unit.

14-7 Predetermined overhead rates—job order costing   The Walton Company uses predetermined rates for fixed overhead, based on machine-hours. The following data are available relating to 19X5:

Budgeted fixed factory overhead cost	$80,000
Budgeted machine-hours	50,000
Actual fixed factory overhead cost incurred	$85,000
Actual machine-hours used	55,000

Jobs worked on:

Job No	Machine-hours used on job:
12	12,000
13	18,000
14	15,000
15	10,000

Required

1. Compute the predetermined overhead rate to be used for the year.
2. Determine the overhead to be applied to each of the jobs worked on during the year.
3. Determine the budget variance.
4. Determine total over- or underapplied overhead at the end of the year.

14-8 Process costing—unit costs   The Valley Manufacturing Company uses a process costing system. The following data apply to July 19X9.

		Units
Beginning inventory, 30% complete		2,000
Finished during July		84,000
Ending inventory, 60% complete		6,000
Production costs:		
Cost in beginning inventory	$2,700	
Incurred during July	$369,600	

Required

1. Compute the cost per unit of the units finished during the period, using the weighted average costing method.
2. Compute the amount of ending work in process inventory in dollars.
3. Prepare a T-account for Work in Process Inventory.

14-9 Process costing   The Berke Manufacturing Company makes a single product, a chemical called Argot. The product is made in two processes, mixing and boiling. The following data apply to May 19X7. There were no beginning inventories.

	Mixing	Boiling
Barrels completed during May	42,000	42,000
Barrels on hand at May 31	4,000	—
Percentage complete	60%	
Production costs incurred	$37,740	$15,120

Required

1. Compute the cost per barrel for each process.
2. Compute the amount of ending work in process inventory in the mixing department.
3. The firm had no finished product on hand at the beginning of May. Of the 42,000 gallons finished during May, 34,000 were sold. Compute cost of goods sold and ending inventory of finished goods.

14-10 Job order costing   The Wisconsin Machinery Company makes large industrial machines. The firm uses a job order cost system with overhead applied to jobs at $15 per direct labor hour. Direct laborers are paid $8 per hour. The following data apply to jobs worked on in March 19X4.

	4-22	4-23	4-24	4-25
Costs in beginning inventory:				
Materials	$ 34,000	0	0	0
Direct labor	48,000	0	0	0
Overhead	90,000	0	0	0
Total	$172,000	0	0	0
Costs incurred in March:				
Materials	$11,000	$46,000	$60,000	$ 9,000
Direct labor	24,000	32,000	44,000	12,000

Job 4-22 was completed and sold in March. Jobs 4-23 and 4-24 were also completed and sold. Job 4-25 was not finished at the end of March. Total overhead incurred during March was $225,500.

Required

1. Compute the amounts of overhead to be applied to each job.
2. Compute the amount of over- or underapplied overhead for March.
3. Compute cost of goods sold for March and the inventory at March 31.
4. Sales revenue from the three jobs sold was $840,000 and selling and administrative expenses for March were $130,000. Prepare an income statement for March.

14-11 Analysis of income statement—standard costs   The following income statement and other data are for the Bourque Manufacturing Company for 19X6.

Bourque Manufacturing Company
Income Statement for 19X6

Sales (20,000 units @ $40)		$800,000
Cost of goods sold—at standard		440,000
Standard gross profit		360,000
Variances:		
Materials	$ 3,000U	
Labor	3,000U	
Variable overhead	3,000U	
Fixed overhead:		
Spending variance	5,000F	
Volume variance	10,000F	
		6,000F
Gross profit		366,000
Selling, general, and administrative expenses		220,000
Income		$146,000

The company uses standard costs and has established the following standards for a unit of finished product:

Materials (10 lbs.@ $1)	$10
Direct labor (2 hrs. @ $4)	8
Variable overhead ($1 per direct labor hour)	2
Fixed overhead	2
Total	$22

The standard for fixed overhead is based on a normal capacity of 20,000 units. During the year 19X6, 51,000 direct labor hours were worked and 248,000 lbs. of material were used.

Required

1. Based on the information provided, determine the following:
   (a) Number of units produced
   (b) Material use variance
   (c) Material price variance
   (d) Direct labor efficiency variance
   (e) Direct labor rate variance
   (f) Variable overhead efficiency variance
   (g) Variable overhead spending variance
   (h) Fixed overhead incurred
2. Prepare an income statement based on variable costing.
3. Prepare an income statement based on absorption costing, using practical capacity of 40,000 units for fixed overhead application.

14-12   Process Costing (Related to Appendix)   The Hittite Company makes a water-soluble paint. All materials are put into process and are then mixed for several hours. Data for July are given below.

Unit Data

Gallons completed in July	130,000
Gallons in ending inventory	24,000
Percentages completed:	
Materials	100%
Labor and overhead	75%

Cost Data

	Materials	Labor and Overhead
Beginning inventory	$3,200	$9,600
Incurred during July	$29,140	$82,160

Required

1. Using the weighted average method, compute equivalent production for (a) materials, and (b) labor and overhead for the month of July.
2. Compute unit costs for each cost factor using the weighted average method.
3. Prepare the journal entry to transfer the cost of finished gallons to finished goods inventory.
4. Prepare a T-account for Work in Process Inventory.
5. Prove that your ending balance in Work in Process, from part 4, is correct.

Problems

14-13 Costing methods and pricing The sales manager and the controller of the Emerson Company were discussing the price to be set for a new product being brought out by the firm. They had accumulated the following data.

Variable costs	$8 per unit
Fixed costs	$80,000 per year

The sales manager had set a target volume of 10,000 units per year. She determined that average fixed cost would be $8 per unit, bringing average total cost per unit to $16. The firm follows a policy of setting prices at 200% of cost, so the sales manager stated that the price would be $32 per unit.

The controller said that $32 seemed high, especially as competitors were charging only $30 for essentially the same product. The sales manager agreed, stating perhaps only 8,000 units per year could be sold at $32. However, she was convinced that the price should be set at 200% of cost. She added that it was unfortunate that fixed costs were so high, because she felt that 10,000 units could definitely be sold if the price were $30, and probably 12,000 at $28. However, it would not be possible to achieve the desired markup at those prices.

Required

1. Point out the fallacies in the reasoning of the sales manager. (You might wish to show what would happen at the $32 price. Would the firm achieve the desired markup?)
2. Determine which of the three prices ($32, $30, $28) will give the highest annual profit.

14-14 Equivalent units and standard costs The production manager of the Kneehi Company has just received his performance report for June 19X9. Among the data included are the following:

		Costs	
	Budgeted	Actual	Variance
Material	$10,000	$11,500	$1,500U
Direct labor	20,000	21,300	1,300U
Variable overhead	15,000	15,400	400U
Fixed overhead	18,000	18,800	800U
Totals	$63,000	$67,000	$4,000U

The budgeted amounts are based on 2,000 units, the number actually completed during June. The production manager is upset because 800 half-finished units are still in process at the end of June and are not counted as part of production for the month. However, at the beginning of June, there were 300 units one-third completed.

Required

1. Compute production in equivalent units on a first-in-first-out basis.
2. Prepare a new performance report.

14-15 Process costing—journal entries The Swanson Company makes a single type of pump on an assembly line. The firm uses process costing and applies manufacturing overhead at the rate of $12 per direct labor hour. Inventories at the beginning of 19X6 were as follows.

Raw material	$ 34,000
Work in process	67,000
Finished goods	125,000

During 19X6 the following transactions took place.

1. Material purchases were $286,000.
2. Wages earned by direct laborers for 35,000 hours were $289,000.
3. Raw materials costing $271,000 were put into process.
4. Other manufacturing costs incurred were:

(a) Indirect labor	$ 46,000
(b) Supervision and other salaries	182,000
(c) Utilities and insurance	23,500
(d) Depreciation	72,000
(e) Other miscellaneous costs	112,000

5. Transfers from work in process to finished goods were $863,000.
6. Sales were $1,314,000.
7. Cost of goods sold was $818,000.
8. Selling and administrative expenses were $387,000.

Required

1. Prepare journal entries to record the above events.
2. Determine the ending balances in each inventory account.
3. Prepare an income statement for 19X6.

14-16   Product costing and volume-cost-profit analysis   The president of the Landry Company asked you for assistance in analyzing the firm's revenue and cost behavior. You gathered the following data relating to the firm's only product.

Selling price		$10
Variable costs:		
Production	$4	
Selling	2	6
Contribution margin		$ 4
Fixed production costs	$120,000 per month	
Fixed selling and administrative expenses	$ 30,000 per month	

You calculated the firm's break-even point as 37,500 units per month and the volume required to earn the president's target profit of $8,000 per month as 39,500 units.

Three months after you provided the analysis, the president called you. On arriving at his office he gave you the following income statements.

	April	May	June
Sales	$380,000	$395,000	$420,000
Cost of goods sold	243,200	269,300	316,125
Gross profit	136,800	125,700	103,875
Selling and administrative costs	106,000	109,000	114,000
Profit (loss) before taxes	$ 30,800	$ 16,700	($ 10,125)

The president is extremely upset at the results. He asks why your analysis does not hold, particularly because he has been assured by the production manager that variable costs per unit and fixed costs in total were incurred as expected during the three months. The sales manager has also assured the president that selling prices and variable costs per unit, as well as fixed costs in total, were as expected.

After a few minutes you talk to the controller, who tells you the firm uses actual absorption costing and produced the following quantities of product during the three months: April, 50,000 units; May, 40,000 units; June, 32,000 units. There were no inventories on hand at the beginning of April.

Required

Explain the results to the president. Show calculations of the determination of cost of goods sold for each month.

14-17   Standard costs—performance evaluation   The Topham Company is opening a new division to make and sell a single product, the Wally. The product is to be made in a factory that has a practical capacity of 150,000 units per year, but production is expected to average 120,000 units after the first two years of operation. During the first two years, sales are expected to be 80,000 and 100,000 respectively, with production being 100,000 and 110,000 in those years.

The product is to sell for $20, with variable manufacturing costs of $8. Fixed production costs are expected to be $360,000 annually for the first several years. Selling and administrative costs, all fixed, are budgeted at $300,000 annually.

Ronald Yost, the controller of the firm, has suggested that the normal capacity of 120,000 units be used to set the standard fixed cost per unit. The other managers agree that Ron's idea is sound and Bill Roberts, the controller of the new division, is given the task of developing budgeted income statements based on the data given.

The operations of the first year are summarized below.

Sales (78,000 units)	$1,560,000
Production	115,000 units
Costs incurred:	
Variable production costs	$ 930,000
Fixed production costs	370,000
Selling and administrative costs	300,000

Required

1. Prepare a budgeted income statement based on the expected results in the first year of operations.
2. Prepare an income statement based on actual results.
3. Comment on the results. Was performance better than expected or worse? Explain.

14-18   Process costing (Related to Appendix)   The Stockton Company makes a chemical spray that goes through two processes. Data for February are given below.

	Mixing Department	Boiling Department
Gallons transferred to Boiling Department	75,000	
Gallons transferred to finished goods		68,000
Gallons on hand at end of month	9,000	15,000
Percent complete:		
Prior department costs	—	100%
Materials	100%	—*
Labor and overhead	60%	40%
Costs incurred during February		
Materials	$18,480	—
Labor and overhead	$32,160	$25,900
Beginning inventories		
Gallons	8,000	8,000
Costs:		
Materials	$ 1,680	$ 6,350
Prior department costs	—	$ 6,350
Labor and overhead	$ 4,020	$ 2,220

*No material is added in this department.

Required

1. Determine the weighted average equivalent production by cost category (materials, prior department costs, labor and overhead) for each department.
2. Determine the per-unit cost by category for the Mixing Department.
3. Prepare the journal entry to record the transfer from the Mixing Department to the Boiling Department.
4. Determine the cost per unit by cost category for the Boiling Department.

5. Prepare the journal entry to record the transfer of product from the Boiling Department to finished goods.
6. Prepare the T-accounts for work in process inventories for each department. Verify the ending inventory balances.

14-19 **Standard cost income statement—relationships and variances**   The following income statement is for the Rider Company for 19X6.

Sales (200,000 units)		$2,000,000
Cost of sales:		
Materials	$300,000	
Direct labor	400,000	
Overhead	600,000	1,300,000
Standard gross profit		700,000
Less: Manufacturing variances		
Materials	$ 12,000U	
Direct labor	18,000F	
Variable overhead budget	4,000U	
Variable overhead efficiency	8,000F	
Fixed overhead budget	7,000F	
Other underabsorbed overhead	20,000U	3,000U
Actual gross profit		697,000
Selling and administrative expenses		600,000
Income		$ 97,000

Other data are as follows:

(a) There were no beginning inventories.
(b) Fixed overhead absorbed per unit is $2, based on budgeted production of 250,000 units, and budgeted fixed costs of $500,000.
(c) The standard direct labor rate is $4 per hour.
(d) Variable overhead standard cost is based on a rate of $2 per direct labor hour.
(e) Direct laborers worked 116,000 hours.
(f) The standard price for materials is $.50 per pound.
(g) Material purchases were 800,000 lbs. at $3,000 over standard price.

Required

Determine the following:

1. Standard cost per unit, including standard prices and quantities for each element of cost.
2. Standard variable cost per unit.
3. Production for the year.
4. Ending inventory at standard cost.
5. Fixed overhead costs incurred.
6. Cost of materials purchased.
7. Material use variance.
8. Pounds of material used in production.
9. Direct labor efficiency variance.
10. Direct labor rate variance.
11. Direct labor costs incurred.
12. Variable overhead costs incurred.
13. Amount by which income would have increased if one more unit had been sold, no more produced.
14. Amount by which income would have increased had one more unit been produced at standard cost and sold.

14-20 Interpretation of standard cost statement The following income statement represents the operations of the Thomas Company for June.

Sales (20,000 units)		$200,000
Standard cost of sales		120,000
Standard gross profit		80,000
Manufacturing variances:		
Materials	$2,000U	
Direct labor	1,000F	
Overhead budget	1,000U	2,000U
		78,000
Volume variance		24,000U
Gross profit—actual		54,000
Selling, general, and administrative costs		48,000
Income		$ 6,000

Variable manufacturing costs at standard are 50% of total standard manufacturing cost. Standard fixed costs per unit are based on normal activity of 30,000 units per month.

Required

1. What are fixed and variable standard costs per unit?
2. What are monthly fixed manufacturing costs?
3. How many units were produced in June?
4. If beginning inventory of finished goods was $60,000 at standard cost, how much is ending inventory at standard cost? (Hint: Prepare an expanded cost-of-goods-sold section.)
5. Assume that fixed costs remain the same in total as computed in 2 above. There were no beginning inventories and standard fixed cost per unit is now based on practical capacity of 40,000 units per month. Prepare a new income statement based on the production of the number of units computed in 3 above.

14-21 Standard costs, budgets, variances, journal entries The following data relate to the operations of the Warner Company for 19X2.

Budgeted sales (100,000 units)	$1,000,000	
Budgeted production	140,000	units
Budgeted costs:		
Materials (2 lbs. per unit)	$ 210,000	
Direct labor (1 hour per unit)	420,000	
Variable overhead ($1 per direct labor hour)	140,000	
Fixed overhead—manufacturing	300,000	
Selling and administrative (all fixed)	180,000	

The firm uses a standard cost system; the production costs above are based on standard cost per unit. Standard fixed cost per unit is based on 150,000 units of production at practical capacity. The inventory of finished goods at December 31, 19X1 is 13,000 units at standard cost. There were no inventories of work in process or materials at December 31, 19X1.

Actual results for 19X2 are as follows:

Sales (95,000 units)	$950,000
Production	130,000 units
Materials purchased (250,000 lbs.)	$192,500
Materials used	236,000 lbs.
Direct labor (133,000 hours)	$402,000
Variable overhead	128,000
Fixed overhead	285,000
Selling and administrative expenses	175,000

Required

1. Prepare a budgeted income statement for 19X2.
2. Prepare all necessary journal entries to record events in 19X2. The production manager is responsible for all variances except material price and labor rate.
3. Prepare an income statement for 19X2.

14-22 Process cost—comparison of actual and standard costing The president of the Wilberforce Company has asked for your assistance. The firm now uses a process costing system. He would like to know whether standard costing could be used by his firm and how it would work. He provided the following data related to operations in July 19X7. There were no beginning inventories.

1. Material purchases were $39,600 for 12,000 pounds ($3.30 per pound).
2. Payments to direct laborers were $28,850 for 7,300 hours of work.
3. Variable overhead costs incurred were $58,510.
4. Fixed overhead costs incurred were $86,500.
5. Material use was 11,000 pounds.
6. Units completed totaled 7,200. Units in process at the end of July 19X7 were 500, 40% complete.
7. Sales were 6,500 units at $50 per unit.
8. Selling and administrative expenses were $106,000.

If the firm were to use standard costing, the following data were considered appropriate.

Materials (1.5 lbs. at $ 3.20)	$ 4.80
Direct labor (1 hr. at $4)	4.00
Variable overhead at $8 per direct labor hour	8.00
Fixed overhead at $12 per direct labor hour	12.00
Total standard cost	$28.80

The fixed overhead per unit figure is based on normal capacity of 7,000 direct labor hours per month.

Required

1. Prepare journal entries using process costing.
2. Prepare an income statement for July using process costing.
3. Prepare journal entries using standard costing.
4. Prepare an income statement using standard costing.

14-23 Special order The Western Corn Oil Company has found that its sales forecast for 19X6 was too high by about 40,000 cases of oil. Because the production budget was not revised, inventory is expected to be about 40,000 cases above normal at year end. In early December the sales manager was offered the opportunity to sell 25,000 cases at $4.80, well below the normal price of $8. Regular sales would not be affected if the order were accepted. He asked the controller for an analysis indicating whether the order should be accepted and was given the partial income statements shown below. The controller said that because there would be no effect on general and administrative expenses, it was only necessary to determine the unfavorable effect on gross profit.

Expected Income Statements

	Without Order	With Order
Sales	$2,400,000	$2,520,000
Standard cost of sales, $6 per case	1,800,000	1,950,000
Standard gross profit	$ 600,000	$ 570,000
Volume variance	(120,000)	(120,000)
Actual gross profit	$ 480,000	$ 450,000

The sales manager was puzzled and asked the controller about the volume variance. The controller replied that the volume variance related to production, not sales, and that production would not be increased because inventory was already too high. He said that the volume variance resulted because the firm used 400,000 cases on which to base the standard fixed cost and actual production was expected to be only 340,000 cases.

Required

1. Determine whether the order should be accepted.
2. Prepare new income statements, down to actual gross profit, using variable costing.
3. Prepare a new partial income statement assuming that production would be increased by 25,000 cases if the order were accepted.

14-24 Job order costing—standards and variances The Carlson Company makes a variety of types of furniture. The firm has established standard variable costs for some of its high-volume models like the ones described below.

	Chair Model 803	Sofa Model 407
Materials:		
Wood	$ 24	$ 58
Fabric	46	92
Other	13	21
Total materials	83	171
Direct labor at $5 standard rate per hour	65	90
Variable overhead at $8 per direct labor hour	104	144
Total standard variable cost	$252	$405

During June the firm worked on two job orders. Order 82 was for 80 units of model 803, order 83 was for 50 units of model 407. Both jobs were finished and sold for $97,000.

Cost data are as follows:

Materials used, at standard prices:

Wood	$ 4,855
Fabric	8,360
Other	2,090
Direct labor, 2,050 hours at $5 per hour	10,250
Variable overhead incurred	16,850

Fixed production costs were incurred as budgeted, $24,600. Selling and administrative expenses were $18,700. There were no material price variances.

Required

1. Determine the standard cost of each job order, by individual cost category.
2. Determine the following variances: material use, by type of material; direct labor efficiency; variable overhead budget; variable overhead efficiency.
3. Prepare an income statement for June using standard variable costing. Show the variances calculated in part 2 as a single lump sum.

14-25 Job order costing and decisions   Last month the Marchmont Furniture Company began work on a large number of custom-made chairs ordered by a retail store in New Jersey. When the work was nearly complete the retailer went bankrupt and would not be able to pay for the chairs. The sales manager of Marchmont immediately began to call other stores in an effort to sell the chairs. The price orginally agreed on was $210,000, but the best price that the sales manager could get if the chairs were finished according to the original specifications is $140,000. This offer was obtained from the Z-Store chain. The Randle Company, which also operates a chain of stores, offered $158,000 for the chairs provided that some different upholstery and trim were used. The sales manager talked to the production manager about the order and got the following information.

	Costs Accumulated to Date
Materials	$ 31,500
Direct labor (7,000 hours at $5)	35,000
Factory overhead at $10 per hour	70,000
Total accumulated costs	$136,500

The factory overhead rate includes $4 variable overhead and $6 fixed overhead. The additional work required to complete the chairs was estimated as follows by the production manager.

	Original Specifications	Randle's Specifications
Materials	$4,100	$9,000
Direct labor hours	800 hours	1,800 hours

Required

1. Using the firm's costing method, determine the total costs that would be charged to the job assuming (a) the work is completed based on the original specifications, and (b) the chairs are modified as required by Randle Company.
2. Determine which offer the firm should accept.

14-26 Incorporating variances into budgets   The Viner Company is developing its budgets for the coming year. The firm uses the standard costs shown below for its final product.

Materials	3 gals. @ $3	$ 9
Labor	4 hrs. @ $5	20
Variable overhead	$6 per DLH	24
Total standard variable cost		$53

Budgeted fixed manufacturing costs are $300,000. Selling, general, and administrative expenses, all fixed, are budgeted at $400,000. Generally, there is about a 10% variance over standard quantity for materials, which usually cost 5% less than the standard price. Direct laborers will receive a 6% wage increase at the beginning of the year, and labor efficiency is expected to be 4% better than standard. An unfavorable variable overhead spending variance of 5% is expected. Sales for the year are budgeted at 20,000 units at $100; production schedules indicate planned production of 24,000 units. There are no beginning inventories. The purchases of raw material are budgeted to be equal to expected material use.

Required

1. Determine the expected variable cost variances for the year.
2. Prepare an income statement for the coming year based on the information given.

14-27 Costs and decisions   "You're fired!!" was the way your boss, the controller of the Saran Bathing Suit Company, greeted you this morning. His ire was based on the two income statements shown below. A few months ago you recommended accepting an offer from a national chain for 10,000 suits at $12 each. At that time, inventories were getting too high because of slow sales. Things have not improved noticeably since then. Your recommendation was based on the variable production costs of $10 per unit, which are the only variable costs. The total standard cost of $16 per suit includes $6 in fixed costs, based on normal production of 130,000 units.

Income Statements for 19X4

	If Special Order Had Not Been Accepted	Actual, with Special Order
Sales: 100,000 × $25	$2,500,000	$2,500,000
10,000 × $12		120,000
Total sales	2,500,000	2,620,000
Cost of sales at standard cost of $16	1,600,000	1,760,000
Standard gross profit	900,000	860,000
Volume variance (20,000 @ $6)	120,000U	120,000U
Actual gross profit	780,000	740,000
Selling and administrative expenses	710,000	710,000
Income	$ 70,000	$ 30,000

"Your stupidity cost us $40,000, you jerk!! Now clean out your desk and scram."

Required

Prepare an argument that will get your job back.

14-28 Departmental overhead rates   The Jurgenson Company makes a number of different types of electric motors. The motors go through three departments, fabrication, machining, and assembly. The firm has been using a predetermined rate for variable overhead, but the results have not been satisfactory. The firm prices its motors at 250% of variable cost and has been finding that some models sell poorly, some well.

The variable overhead rate was calculated in the following way. The chief cost accountant determined the amounts of total variable overhead and direct labor hours in the three departments and based the rate on the weighted average. The schedule below shows the derivation of the rate, based on an average month's operations.

Department	Direct Labor Hours Worked	Total Variable Overhead
Fabrication	6,000	$ 48,000
Machining	10,000	60,000
Assembly	14,000	42,000
Totals	30,000	$150,000

Weighted average variable overhead rate = $5 per direct labor hour ($150,000/30,000).

The following schedule shows the determination of prices for two models, the 136 and the 260, for lots of 100 motors.

	Model 136	Model 260
Materials	$ 350	$410
Direct labor ($4 per hour)	320	260
Variable overhead ($5 per hour)	400	325
Total variable cost	$1,070	$995
Multiplied by 2.5 (250%) equals price per 100	$2,675	$2,487.50

The direct labor requirements in hours for each model, by department, are given below.

	Model 136	Model 260
Fabrication	40	5
Machining	25	10
Assembly	15	50
Total direct labor hours	80	65

The chief cost accountant realizes that the variable rates per direct labor hour are different among the departments. But he believes that it is simpler to use the weighted average rate. He also believes that it would make little difference to use individual departmental rates.

Required

1. Compute the variable costs of each model using variable overhead rates based on the individual departmental rates.
2. Compute the selling prices that the firm would charge if it used the data given in part 1.
3. Do you think that the firm is wise to use the weighted average variable overhead? Why or why not?

14-29 Product costing, variances, Part A   The Sluggem Company makes baseball bats that sell for $25 per dozen. The standard variable production costs per dozen are as follows:

Materials (40 ft. of wood at $.15 per foot)	$ 6
Direct labor (⅓ hr. at $6 per hour)	2
Variable overhead ($9 per direct labor hour)	3
Total standard variable cost per dozen	$11

Budgeted fixed production costs are $800,000 per year. During 19X6 the firm had the following operating results.

Sales (130,000 dozen)	$3,250,000
Production	140,000 dozen bats
Production costs:	
Material purchased (6,000,000 ft.)	$930,000
Material used (5,800,000 ft.)	
Direct labor (48,000 hrs.)	$276,000
Variable overhead	$440,000
Fixed production costs	$780,000
Selling and administrative expenses, all fixed	$840,000

There were no beginning inventories. The president of the firm would like to have two income statements: (1) a statement based on standard variable costing with all variances shown as expenses of the period; (2) a statement based on standard absorption costing, with normal activity of 160,000 dozen bats used to set the standard fixed cost. In both statements, all identifiable variances are to be shown separately (price and quantity variances for variable production costs, budget and volume variances, for fixed production costs, where applicable).

Required: Prepare the statements requested by the president.

Part B   During 19X7 the firm produced 150,000 dozen bats and sold 140,000 dozen at $25 per dozen. The same standards and budgets were in effect in 19X7 as had been in 19X6. Actual costs incurred were as follows.

Material purchased (6,200,000 ft.)	$920,000
Material used (5,950,000 ft.)	
Direct labor (49,500 hrs.)	$295,000
Variable overhead	$450,000
Fixed production costs	$810,000
Selling and administrative expenses, all fixed	$870,000

Required: Prepare income statements using the same bases as those in Part A.

14-30 **Comprehensive problem in costing methods, Part A**   The following data relate to the Gagner Company operations for 19X5.

	Budgeted	Actual
Production (units)	200,000	180,000
Sales (units)	190,000	160,000
Direct materials	$400,000	$375,000
Direct labor	$600,000	$580,000
Variable overhead	$400,000	$395,000
Fixed overhead	$200,000	$208,000
Selling, general, and administrative expenses	$700,000	$700,000

There were no beginning inventories; sales prices averaged $15 per unit; practical capacity is 250,000 units.

Required

1. Prepare income statements based on the following costing methods:
   (a) actual absorption costing
   (b) standard absorption costing—fixed overhead based on budgeted production (show the total variance for each element of cost)
   (c) standard absorption costing using practical capacity as the fixed overhead allocation base
   (d) standard variable costing
   (e) actual variable costing
2. Compare and contrast the results obtained in 1 above.

Part B   The following data relate to 19X6:

	Budgeted	Actual
Production (units)	150,000	190,000
Sales (units)	140,000	200,000
Direct materials	$300,000	$400,000
Direct labor	$450,000	$590,000
Variable overhead	$300,000	$410,000
Fixed overhead	$200,000	$215,000
Selling, general, and administrative expenses	$700,000	$720,000

Selling prices again averaged $15 per unit.

Required

1. Prepare income statements for 19X6, using each of the methods used in Part A.
2. Describe and explain the major differences between the results of 19X5 and of 19X6 under each method.

14-31 **Standard costs and product profitability**   The Tucumcary Office Products Company makes three sizes of file folders. The firm has practical capacity of 50,000 machine-hours per year and uses that figure to set standard fixed costs for each size of folder. At the beginning of 19X6 the controller had prepared the following data regarding the three sizes of folders (all data per carton of 50 folders).

	Two-inch	Three-inch	Four-inch
Selling price	$17.00	$24.00	$31.00
Standard variable costs	8.00	11.00	16.00
Standard fixed costs	4.80	6.40	9.80
Total standard costs	12.80	17.40	25.60
Standard gross profit	$ 4.20	$ 6.60	$ 5.40
Expected sales in cartons	44,000	25,000	30,000
Machine-hours required per carton	.3	.4	.6

The sales manager has informed the controller that he has been approached by a large office supplies chain. The chain wants to buy 24,000 cartons of a six-inch folder and is willing to pay $40 per carton. The sales manager had discussed the offer with the production manager who stated that the folders could be made using the existing equipment. Variable costs per carton would be $19 and .8 machine-hours would be required per carton.

Because the chain would take not fewer than 24,000 cartons, the sales manager was fairly sure that the firm would not have the capacity to fill the special order and still manufacture its other products in the volumes required by the expected sales. He therefore asked the controller to develop data on the proposed order and to decide which of the existing products should be partially curtailed. The controller then prepared the following analysis, which is incomplete because he was called away before finishing it. The sales manager was not sure how to proceed from this point and asked you to help him make the decision.

	Six-inch Folder
Selling price	$40.00
Standard variable cost	19.00
Standard fixed cost	12.80
Total standard cost	$31.80
Standard gross profit	$ 8.20

The controller has also prepared the following analysis of budgeted profit for the year.

	Two-inch	Three-inch	Four-inch	Total
Standard gross profit per carton	$ 4.20	$ 6.60	$ 5.40	
Expected volume	44,000	25,000	30,000	
Total expected gross profit—standard	$184,800	$165,000	$162,000	$511,800
Expected volume variance				140,800
Expected actual gross profit				371,000
Budgeted selling and administrative expenses, all fixed				327,000
Budgeted profit before taxes				$ 44,000

The firm generally manufactures about as many cartons of each size of folder as it sells. Because it rarely experiences differences between standard and actual machine-hours for given levels of production, it computes its volume variance based on the difference between 50,000 hours and actual hours worked.

Required

Prepare an analysis for the sales manager showing him whether the special order should be accepted and for which products, if any, production and sales should be reduced.

14-32   Review problem   Sally Ann Frocks is a manufacturer of dresses. Its relevant range is 1,500 to 5,000 dresses per month. For the month of May 19X5, it has prepared the following forecast.

Sales (2,500 dresses @ $30 each)
Variable manufacturing costs per dress:
   Materials (3 yds. @ $2 per yard)
   Direct labor (2 hrs. @ $.50 per hour)
   Variable overhead ($1 per direct labor hour)
Fixed manufacturing overhead ($3,000)
Variable selling costs (commissions at 10% of sales)
Fixed selling and administrative costs ($6,000)

Inventories:
   May 1, 19X5   none
   May 31, 19X5   materials 500 yards, finished dresses 500

Normal capacity is 3,000 dresses per month, which is the basis for overhead application.

Required

Answer the following questions.

1. What is practical capacity?
2. What is budgeted production for May?
3. How many yards of materials should be purchased during May?
4. How many hours does it take to produce a dress?
5. What are total variable manufacturing costs per dress?
6. What are total manufacturing costs per dress?
7. What is contribution margin per dress?
8. What is the cost per dress of the ending inventory if variable costing is used?
9. What is the cost per dress of the ending inventory if absorption costing is used without a predetermined fixed overhead rate?
10. What is the cost to produce one additional dress?
11. What is the cost to produce and sell an additional dress?
12. What is the predetermined fixed overhead rate per direct labor hour?
13. What are total budgeted manufacturing costs for May?
14. Give a formula for total manufacturing costs in the range of 1,500 to 5,000 dresses per month.
15. What would the predetermined fixed overhead rate be per direct labor hour if practical capacity were used as the base?
16. What is budgeted net income for May?
17. What is the break-even point, in dresses?
18. By how much could budgeted sales fall before a loss was incurred?
19. By how much would income increase for each unit sold above budgeted volume?

14-33 Comprehensive review The McLeod Company produces and sells a single product, the Winser. Standard manufacturing costs for a unit of Winser, which sells for $20, are as follows:

Materials:	
Wyn (2 lbs. @ $1 per pound)	$2.00
Luz (1 yd. @ $.50 per yard)	$0.50
Forming labor (½ hr. @ $6 per hour)	3.00
Variable overhead ($4 per hour of forming labor)	2.00
Fixed overhead ($7 per hour of forming labor)	3.50

The standard for fixed overhead is based on normal productive capacity of 10,000 units. The company has also established standards for marketing and administrative costs as follows, based on a normal sales volume of 10,000 units:

Marketing costs:	
Variable	$2.50 per unit sold
Fixed	$2.50 per unit sold
Administrative costs:	
Fixed	$1.50 per unit sold

The balance sheet of the McLeod Company at December 31, 19X0 is shown below. The last column in the balance sheet indicates the budgeted change in each balance sheet item for 19X1. A budgeted statement of cash flows for 19X1 is also provided.

McLeod Company Balance Sheet

Assets

		December 31, 19X0	19X1 Budgeted Change
Current assets:			
Cash		$ 31,000	$ − 7,000
Marketable securities		—	+ 8,000
Accounts receivable, net of allowance			
for doubtful accounts		40,000	+ 15,000
Inventories			
Finished product	$ 55,000		0
Raw materials	20,000		+ 5,000
		75,000	
Prepaid expenses		4,000	− 1,000
Total current assets		150,000	
Property, plant, and equipment:			
Land	50,000		0
Building, net of accumulated depreciation	100,000		− 8,000
Equipment, net of accumulated depreciation	100,000		− 18,000
		250,000	
Total assets		$400,000	

Equities

Current liabilities:			
Accounts payable		$ 45,000	+ 5,000
Notes payable		30,000	0
Total current liabilities		75,000	
Long-term liabilities:			
Bonds payable		150,000	− 10,000
Total liabilities		225,000	
Stockholders' equity:			
Common stock	100,000		0
Retained earnings	75,000		− 1,000
Total stockholders' equity		175,000	
Total equities		$400,000	

McLeod Company Budgeted Cash Flows for 19X1

Sources of cash:		
Operations		$ 25,000
Uses of cash:		
Dividends	$ 10,000	
Purchases of equipment	4,000	
Retirement of bonds	10,000	
Purchase of marketable securities	8,000	
		32,000
Decrease in cash balance		$ 7,000

For the year 19X1, the company planned to produce and sell 8,400 units of Winser, and succeeded in achieving the production and sales goals. A total of 17,000 lbs. of Wyn and 8,000 yds. of Luz were used and 4,400 hours were worked by forming laborers. At the end of 19X1, the following income statement was prepared:

McLeod Company Income Statement for 19X1

	Budget	*Actual*	*Difference*
Sales	$168,000	$172,200	$4,200F
Variable costs:			
Wyn	16,800	18,500	1,700U
Luz	4,200	4,000	200F
Forming labor	25,200	24,500	700F
Manufacturing overhead	16,800	18,000	1,200U
Marketing overhead	21,000	21,000	—
Fixed costs:			
Manufacturing	35,000	34,000	1,000F
Marketing	25,000	23,000	2,000F
Administrative	15,000	15,000	0
Total costs	159,000	158,000	1,000F
Income	$ 9,000	$ 14,200	$5,200F

Required

On the basis of the information provided, complete the following sentences.

1. The budgeted return on average owners' equity is $_____ divided by $_____.
2. The budgeted cash to be received from customers (ignoring bad debts) is $_____.
3. The budgeted raw material purchases are $_____.
4. Budgeted expiration of prepaid expenses exceeds new prepayments by $_____.
5. The budgeted change in equipment can be explained by a purchase of equipment of (a) $_____and depreciation charges of (b) $_____.
6. The budgeted increase in working capital is $_____.
7. The budgeted working capital from operations is $_____.
8. The budgeted pounds of Wyn used for production are _____.
9. The total budgeted standard costs of Wyn are $_____.
10. The material use variance for Wyn for 19X1 is $_____.
11. The material price variance for Wyn for 19X1 is $_____.
12. The budgeted yards of Luz to be used for production are _____.
13. The total budgeted standard cost of Luz is $_____.
14. The material use variance for Luz is $_____.
15. The material price variance for Luz is $_____.
16. The total budgeted standard cost of forming labor is $_____.
17. The labor rate variance is $_____.
18. The labor efficiency variance is $_____.
19. The number of labor hours reported as inefficient is _____
20. The total budgeted manufacturing cost for 19X1 is $_____.
21. The efficiency variance for variable manufacturing overhead is $_____.
22. The spending variance for variable manufacturing overhead is $_____.
23. The budget variance for fixed manufacturing overhead is $_____.
24. The predetermined fixed overhead absorption rate for fixed manufacturing overhead was calculated by dividing $_____ by _____ units.
25. The volume variance for fixed manufacturing overhead is $_____.
26. If the predetermined overhead rate for fixed manufacturing overhead had been set at 8,800 units rather than at the normal capacity of 10,000, the volume variance would have been $_____.
27. If the predetermined overhead rate for fixed manufacturing overhead had been calculated by using 7,000 units of Winser, the rate would have been $_____ per hour of labor.
28. The amount of total manufacturing overhead in the 8,400 units of product transferred to finished goods is $_____.
29. The reported variance most likely attributable to the purchasing department is _____ variance.
30. From the budgeted cash flows, it _____(is, is not) possible to determine that for any time period during the year, cash inflows from normal operations are greater than cash outflows from such normal operations.
31. An unfavorable labor efficiency variance _____.
    (a) is always attributable to poor supervision or inept laborers.
    (b) could result from excess time spent in processing substandard materials.
    (c) must be investigated, regardless of the cost of the investigation.
    (d) could not be self-correcting.
    (e) could not be attributable to action by the purchasing department.
32. The predetermined total manufacturing overhead absorption rate is $_____ per hour of forming labor.
33. Of the sales, cash, direct labor, direct materials, and manufacturing overhead budgets, the one most likely to be prepared first would be the _____ budget.
34. The total cost of producing one more unit of Winser than budgeted would be _____.
35. The cost of producing and selling one more unit of Winser than budgeted would be _____

Cases

14-34 **Cost justification** The following material is taken from a column by Rowland Evans and Robert Novak that appeared in the July 8, 1976 *Knickerbocker News* (Albany, New York). At that time, the federal election laws required that candidates for the presidency limit spending before their parties' conventions to $13 million.

> When Treasury Secretary William Simon traveled to Raleigh, N.C., last Jan. 20 to address the state Chamber of Commerce and then a President Ford Committee (PFC) reception, the taxpayers' bill was $2,310. The reimbursement to Uncle Sam from the PFC for political expenses: $17.44. . . .
>
> The method used for Simon's Jan. 20 journey to North Carolina, an important primary state, is the model. The Air Force charged $2,310 for a Jetstar carrying Simon and seven others (including aides and Secret Service agents) to North Carolina. Since Simon occupied only one of eight seats, his share of the cost is $288.75. The 30 minutes spent at the PFC reception amounted to only 5 per cent of the portal-to-portal time from Washington. So, 5 per cent of $288.75 is $14.44. Add $3 for the share of meals, and the cost to the PFC is $17.44.

Required

1. Suppose that you had been engaged as a consultant to Mr. Ronald Reagan, who was President Ford's opponent in that campaign for the Republican nomination. What would you say about the method used to determine the cost billed to the PFC? What other information would you seek?
2. Suppose that you were engaged as a consultant to the PFC. How would you defend the $17.44 charge?

14-35 **Cost justification** Many states operate Medicaid and other programs designed to provide health services for their citizens. Sometimes these services are reimbursed by the state on a cost-plus basis. The following testimony took place at a hearing of the State Senate committee on nursing home costs. Nursing home care is one of the many types of health services covered by Medicaid programs. In most cases, the nursing homes are privately owned and operated.

> *Senator:* Now, as I understand it, the state pays you for the costs to run the home plus 10% of cost, but you are allowed a maximum profit of 15% return on investment. Is that correct?
>
> *Nursing Home Manager:* That's right. And we have a very big investment in the home. About $70,000 per bed in building and equipment alone, which does not count our major asset, those dedicated employees. Now, a lot of hospitals and nursing homes try to get away with less, but we want our guests to have the finest possible accommodations.
>
> *Senator:* I see by the drawings of the building that about 60% of the space is devoted to offices. Your own office is 40 by 35 feet and has a fireplace, two couches, 12 chairs, and a Louis XIV desk. Is that, too, correct?
>
> *Nursing Home Manager:* Well, Senator, I do need a lot of space for conferences and other activities. For example, I often hold small social functions in my office for staff personnel. It helps to keep up morale, which is very important.
>
> *Senator:* Commendable. Now about these charges for laundry.
>
> *Nursing Home Manager:* We are very proud of our cost-cutting efforts there, Senator. We used to do the laundry ourselves, but it was costing too much. My brother-in-law's firm does it for only $.60 per pound. Why, in 19X7 it cost us $117,000 to process 100,000 pounds of laundry. Soap and detergents were $12,000, power and water amounted to $8,000, salaries were $35,000, depreciation on our equipment was

$7,000, and depreciation on the building was $55,000. Of course, the building depreciation is only for the basement, where the laundry was located. We don't use that space now that we have the laundry done outside. Now in 19X8 it cost us $121,000 to process 120,000 pounds of laundry, which is $.91 per pound. We could have processed about 340,000 pounds with the equipment and personnel we had, but we knew we would never get that high, so we sold the equipment to the laundry service that we use now. We took a pretty big loss on that sale, as a matter of fact. Now we are sending out about 200,000 pounds of laundry per year.

Senator: I see. I wonder if you could explain to us the $350,000 management fee that was charged to the home for 19X8.

Nursing Home Manager: I'm glad you asked about that, Senator. Did you notice that it has gone down since the prior year? You see, our home is owned by a large corporation and it has opened several new homes, so naturally that cuts down on our share of the fee. The fee is based on the number of guests served.

The home office of the corporation incurs a lot of costs on behalf of all of the homes. You remember, for example, Senator, the large press party given to announce the opening of several new homes and the overall plans for growth and improved services to guests. I believe you were quite impressed at the time with the corporation's plans.

Senator: Well, yes, that's true. I do think it is wise to get to know more about the people you deal with; it gives you an idea of what type of people they are. But I have one last thing I'd like to cover here, the fees for laboratory tests. They seem to be awfully high for an operation the size of yours.

Nursing Home Manager: I suppose they could appear so. But we are concerned about the health of our guests and so we test their blood every day. You can't be too careful, you know. I know that a lot of the homes wouldn't do that $5 test for bubonic plague, but you never can tell when an outbreak might occur.

Senator: Frightful thing, the plague. Well, I think that about covers everything I wanted to get to. And I must say that you were very well prepared for your testimony here.

Nursing Home Manager: Thank you, Senator. It has been a pleasure to clear up these little points for your committee.

Required: Comment on the practices described.

14-36 Costing methods and evaluation of results   Warren Progman, the new manager of the Oliver Division of General Products Company, was greatly displeased at the income statements that his controller, Hal Gannon, had been giving him. Progman had recently been placed in charge of the division because it had not been showing satisfactory results. Progman was upset because although sales had risen in each of the last two months, profits had not kept pace. The income statements for the last three months are given below.

	March	April	May
Sales	$360,000	$440,000	$560,000
Cost of sales	198,000	264,000	381,000
Gross profit	162,000	176,000	179,000
Other expenses	142,000	150,000	162,000
Profit before taxes	$ 20,000	$ 26,000	$ 17,000

Progman asked Gannon why profits had actually declined when sales had, in fact, increased, and why a substantial increase in sales from March to April had produced only a small increase in profits. Gannon's reply was simply that operations had gone according to plans that Progman had set, and that the problems that Progman wanted to know about were due to the method of accounting for product costs and the relationships of sales to production.

Progman was unimpressed with this explanation and rather testily pointed out that he had been put in charge of the division to "turn it around," and he was not about to let accounting conventions give the corporate management second thoughts about placing him in charge. Gannon, who was fully aware of the claims Progman had made when being considered for the manager's job, had not liked Progman from the start. To the suggestion that accounting conventions were standing in the way of Progman's performance, Gannon replied only that the reports for all divisions were prepared from the same uniform accounting system and in the form required for corporate reporting. He told Progman that the reports were prepared using generally accepted accounting principles, which was necessary because the corporation was publicly held and had to issue reports to shareholders. He did not tell Progman that he believed the methods used by the firm for external reporting were inappropriate for internal purposes.

Later, at lunch with Frank Holloway, the division's sales manager, Gannon related the conversation that he had had with Progman. Holloway, who had also wondered about the firm's accounting methods, asked Gannon why he didn't just explain the statements to Progman. "Not on your life," said Gannon. "I see no reason to help that braggart. Let *him* explain to the top brass why things aren't going the way he said they would if he were put in charge instead of me."

"Actually," Gannon continued, "what he's worried about just isn't a difficult problem. Cost of sales included both standard cost and the adjustment needed when production for the month did not equal the 25,000-unit volume that was used to set the standard fixed cost of $9 per unit. In fact, things have gone very well. We have had no variances at all except for volume. Selling prices have held very well at $20 per unit, and the division is doing much better now. But would I like to be there when the brass asks Progman why things are not going so well! Why, even production in April was right on target at 25,000 units budgeted."

Required

1. Explain the results in the three-month period. You may wish to compute standard fixed costs per unit and production in each month.
2. Prepare income statements for the three months using variable costing.

14-37   Costing methods and evaluation of performance   Ralph Sampson is the manager of the Wallace Division of Fizer Industries, Inc. He is one of several managers being considered for the presidency of the firm, as the current president is retiring in a year.

All divisions use standard absorption costing for inventories; normal capacity is the basis for application of fixed overhead. Normal capacity in the Wallace Division is 40,000 units per quarter, and quarterly fixed overhead is $500,000. Variable production cost is $50 per unit. Ralph has been looking at the report for the first three months of the year and is not happy with the results.

Wallace Division Income Statement for First Quarter

Sales (25,000 units)		$2,500,000
Cost of goods sold:		
Beginning inventory (10,000 units)	$ 625,000	
Production costs applied	1,562,500	
Total	$2,187,500	
Less: ending inventory	625,000	1,562,500
Gross profit		937,500
Volume variance		187,500U*
Selling and general expenses		500,000*
Income		$ 250,000

*deductions

The sales forecast for the second quarter is 25,000 units. Ralph had budgeted second-quarter production at 25,000 units, but changes it to 50,000 units which is practical capacity for a quarter. The sales forecasts for each of the last two quarters of the year are also 25,000 units. Costs incurred in the second quarter are the same as budgeted, based on 50,000 units of production.

Required

1. Prepare an income statement for the second quarter.
2. Does the statement for the second quarter reflect Ralph's performance better than that for the first quarter? Can you make any suggestions for reporting in the future? Do you think Ralph should be seriously considered for the presidency of the firm? Why or why not?

PART SIX

SPECIAL TOPICS

The last part of this book is devoted to three special topics that are often treated in managerial accounting courses but which are also frequently covered as parts of other courses.

Chapter 15 introduces the use of quantitative decision-making techniques that are increasingly being employed in approaching real-world problems. Chapter 16 covers the statement of changes in financial position, including both cash flow and working capital flow. Chapter 17 is an introduction to financial statement analysis. The chapter is geared primarily to the uses of financial statements by creditors and stockholders.

CHAPTER 15

QUANTITATIVE METHODS AND MANAGERIAL ACCOUNTING

Throughout this book we have discussed the use of quantifiable data and the need to consider nonquantifiable consequences of decisions. In recent years much attention has been given to refining the uses of quantifiable data in the decision-making process. For the most part, these refinements are aimed at determining the best course of action in complex situations. When the proposed solution to a problem results in the maximum profit, it is called an optimal solution; a technique used to find the optimal solution is called an optimizing technique.

We believe that any manager, especially a managerial accountant, should be aware of the kinds of techniques that are now coming into widespread use, even if he or she does not understand the mathematics that underlie them.

The manager will have to describe the problem to a specialist and assist in getting "bugs" out of the solution, and it is the manager who should be able to suggest possible changes if the solution does not seem to be working out. To work effectively with the specialist, the manager must understand how to talk to the specialist; he or she must comprehend what the specialist is saying and grasp the basics of the solution being offered.

All of the techniques discussed here have limitations. It is essential that the manager know and understand those limitations in order that he has some place to start looking if things begin to go wrong.

QUANTITATIVE METHODS—AN OVERVIEW

The term *quantitative methods* describes sophisticated mathematical techniques in the solution of managerial problems. Other terms are operations research, model building, and quantitative analysis. You have been using quantitative methods throughout this book. Volume-cost-profit analysis uses simple algebra; budgeting uses mathematically stated relationships among variables (collections on receivables are 40% of the current month's sales, 60% of the preceding month's sales); and capital budgeting utilizes present values.

Almost all the analytical techniques in this book rely on assumptions. We assumed conditions as to price, costs, demand, and so on. Often, quantifiable factors were stated as equations [net income = (sales price × units sold) − (variable costs × units sold) − fixed cost].

Operations research techniques or models are used in the same way. Quantifiable factors related to a decision are determined, relationships among the factors are expressed in equations, and the equations are solved to obtain the answer. The major difference between operations research models and the techniques you have been using is the level of complexity.

In one respect all the quantitative methods are the same; a solution will be only as good as the assumptions made about future conditions. If these conditions do not turn out to be true, the optimal solution will not be realized. Hence, when assumptions about future conditions are being set, there must be close cooperation and communication between manager and specialist.

STATISTICAL DECISION THEORY

We introduced the concept of **expected value** in Chapter 5. We applied the concept to sales forecasting under conditions in which managers believed that several possible outcomes were possible and were able to assign probabilities to each of these outcomes. The concept is applicable to many other situations, which we illustrate here. Following these illustrations we discuss some questions involving the ways probabilities are developed.

Suppose your firm is considering alternative methods of acquiring computer time. You have identified three feasible choices:

(a) You can rent one make of computer for a flat rate of $6,000 per month, using as much computer time as you need.

(b) You can rent another make of computer for $2,000 per month plus $40 per hour of use.

(c) You can use the computer at a service bureau (a firm that rents computer time to others) for $80 per hour.

Study of the three computers indicates that all will meet your computing needs, and you have assessed the likelihood of your needs as follows:

(1) Event (Estimated Hours of Computer Time Needed per Month)	(2) Estimated Probability of Occurrence	(1) × (2) Expected Value
30	.10	3
60	.15	9
100	.25	25
150	.30	45
200	.20	40
	1.00	122

The expected value required is 122 hours. You can now compare the costs related to the three choices at 122 hours as follows:

Alternative	Cost
(a) Rent for $6,000 per month	$6,000
(b) Rent for $2,000 plus $40 per hour	
122 hours at $40 per hour = $4,880 + $2,000	$6,880
(c) Buy time from the service bureau at $80 per hour	
122 hours × $80 per hour	$9,760

Renting the computer for $6,000 per month is the least-cost choice.

    Sometimes the costs of choices can be directly associated with the probabilities of occurrence. You could have computed the expected values of the costs of each outcome in the problem above. The situation for choice (b) could have been analyzed as follows:

(1) Hours Required	(2) Probability	(3) Conditional Value*	(2) × (3) Expected Value
30	.10	$ 3,200	$ 320
60	.15	4,400	660
100	.25	6,000	1,500
150	.30	8,000	2,400
200	.20	10,000	2,000
	1.00		$6,880

*Cost incurred if the event in column 1 occurs.

The cost for choice (c) would have been computed as follows:

Hours Required	Probability	Conditional Value	Expected Value
30	.10	$ 2,400	$ 240
60	.15	4,800	720
100	.25	8,000	2,000
150	.30	12,000	3,600
200	.20	16,000	3,200
	1.00		$9,760

Choice (a) has the same cost no matter what the hourly rate. Therefore, the expected value is 100% certain to be $6,000.

Variance Investigation

As illustrated in Chapter 12, a variance should be investigated when the expected savings from investigation are more than the cost of the investigation. The expected value framework is helpful in deciding whether or not to investigate.

Assume that a $300 variance has occurred that is expected to continue for six months if not corrected. An investigation to identify the exact cause of the variance will cost nothing. The chances are about 80% that even after identifying the cause, the variance cannot be corrected. The expected values of the costs of investigating and not investigating are summarized below.

Choice 1—Do Not Investigate

A certain cost of $300 for six months $1,800

Choice 2—Conduct an Investigation

Possible Outcome	Probability of Outcome	Cost Associated with Outcome	Expected Value	
Cause is correctable	.20	0	0	
Cause is not correctable	.80	$1,800	$1,440	
Total	1.00			$1,440

It is worthwhile to investigate the variance; it costs nothing to investigate and there are potential savings of $360 ($1,800 − $1,440). In this instance, the expected values are really expected costs. The decision to investigate is the least-cost one.

The $360 difference ($1,800 − $1,440) has special significance; it is the maximum amount you would be willing to spend to investigate if the variance could be corrected. The amount is called the **value of perfect information,** which is generally defined as the difference between: (1) the expected values of alternatives, given the existing information; and (2) the expected values of alternatives when you know in advance what event will occur.

To confirm that the computed difference is the maximum you would pay to investigate the variance, suppose that it will cost $360 to investigate. What would be the expected values (costs) of the two choices?

Choice 1—Do Not Investigate

A certain cost of $300 for six months $1,800

Choice 2—Conduct an Investigation

Possible Outcome	Probability of Outcome	Cost Associated with Outcome	Expected Value	
Cause is correctable	.20	$ 360*	$ 72	
Cause is not correctable	.80	2,160†	1,728	
Total	1.00			$1,800

*The cost to investigate will be incurred.
†The cost to investigate plus the cost of the continued variance will be incurred.

Thus, the expected cost of both choices is the same.

Let us introduce two modifications of the variance investigation circumstances: (1) the cost to investigate the variance is $200; and (2) the variance has a 30% probability of not continuing. (This second condition could exist if the disturbance is caused by a random factor in the production process so that no corrective action is necessary.) Two methods of solving this problem are the usual expected value table and the *decision tree*. The latter is a commonly used device that offers a graphical representation of the problem.

Choice 1—Do Not Investigate

Possible Outcome	Probability of Outcome	Cost Associated with Outcome	Expected Value	
Variance is random, will stop without action	.30	0	$ 0	
Variance will continue	.70	$1,800	1,260	
Total	1.00			$1,260

Choice 2—Conduct an Investigation

Possible Outcome	Probability of Outcome	Cost Associated with Outcome	Expected Value	
Variance is random, will stop without action	.30	$ 200	$ 60	
A problem exists that can be corrected	.14*	200	28	
A problem exists that cannot be corrected	.56†	2,000	1,120	
Total	1.00			$1,208

*The 20% chance of being able to take corrective action now applies to only 70% of the cases. The probability thus becomes 70% × 20%, or 14%. (Remember the total probabilities must be 1.0.)
†Same reasoning as in above note except that the probability of there being an uncorrectable problem is 70% × 80%, or 56%.

Under these new conditions, the investigation should be undertaken because the expected value (expected cost) of investigating is smaller than that of not investigating.

The decision tree shown in Figure 15-1 works in essentially the same way as the tabular format, but has the advantage of allowing a step-by-step determination of probabilities when there are several possible events within other events (the 80% − 20% probabilities within the 70% probability).

Using either format, the expected cost of investigating is less than the expected cost of not investigating. The difference between the expected costs of the two choices is smaller now than it was before ($52 as opposed to $360). This makes sense because now there is a 30% chance that you do not have to do anything and the variance will stop anyway. This condition should make the investigation less attractive, as does the fact that it now costs you something to investigate.

FIGURE 15-1

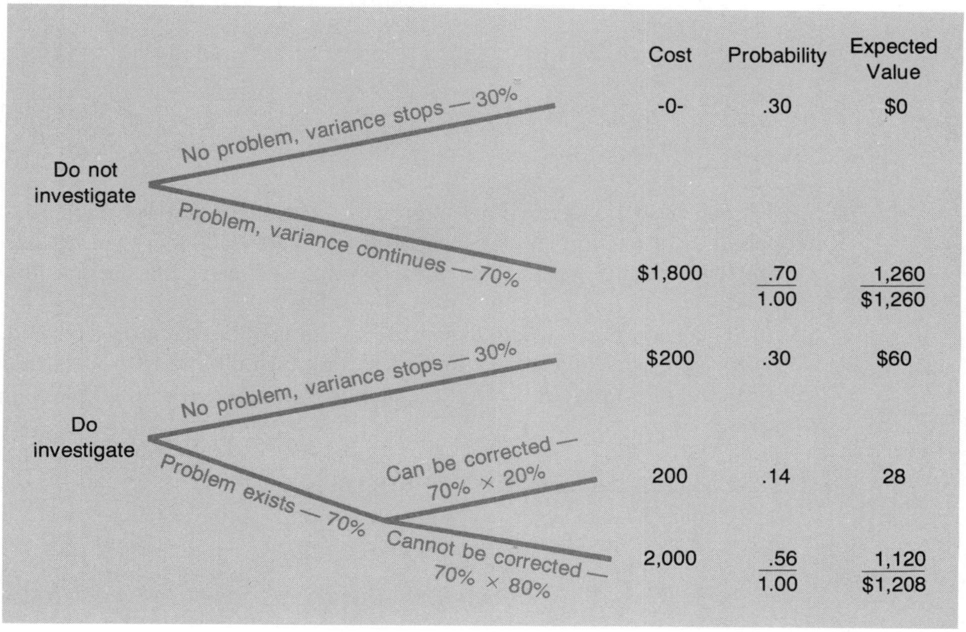

	Cost	Probability	Expected Value
Do not investigate — No problem, variance stops — 30%	-0-	.30	$0
Problem, variance continues — 70%	$1,800	.70 / 1.00	1,260 / $1,260
Do investigate — No problem, variance stops — 30%	$200	.30	$60
Problem exists — 70% — Can be corrected — 70% × 20%	200	.14	28
Cannot be corrected — 70% × 80%	2,000	.56 / 1.00	1,120 / $1,208

Capital Budgeting Application

Firms are frequently confronted with investment opportunities that promise either high rewards (high net present values) or large losses (high negative net present values). Such opportunities are called risky because they involve potential loss, but they can also be rewarding. (Chapter 3 discusses cost structure and risk; the substitution of fixed costs for variable costs could be either beneficial or disastrous, depending on the future levels of sales.) Consider a manufacturer of toys who is trying to decide whether to market a new toy. The manufacturer believes that the toy has a chance to be a big seller, but could also not strike public fancy.

Assume the following possibilities for net cash flows after taxes in the two circumstances described: the toy sells well; the toy is a flop. The required investment is $20,000.

Annual Net Cash Flows after Taxes

	Sells Well	Flops
Years 1–5	$15,000	$1,000

What should the manufacturer do? A common approach is to find the expected value of the future cash flows based on the probabilities of their occurrences. The expected value is the sum of the individual flows under the possibilities stated, multiplied by the probability of occurrence. Assume that the marketing group believes there is a 60% chance of the toy's being a big seller and a 40% chance of its being a flop.

	Cash Flow ×	Probability of Occurrence =	Expected Value
Sells Well	$15,000	.60	$9,000
Flops	1,000	.40	400
Totals		1.00	$9,400

The cash flows are now expressed as an expected value of $9,400 based on the probabilities of occurrence of each situation. The $9,400 can then be discounted at cost of capital to determine whether the present value is greater than or less than the investment required.

There are times when it may be unwise to rely solely on expected values. Suppose you were given the following choices: (1) take $10,000 now; or (2) flip a coin, heads you get $40,000, tails you lose $20,000. Compute the expected values (assuming an honest coin, of course).

Choice 1—A certain gain of $10,000.
Choice 2—An expected value of $10,000, as indicated below.

Event	Probability	Conditional Value	Expected Value
Heads	.5	$40,000	$20,000
Tails	.5	−20,000	−10,000
	1.00		$10,000

At first glance, the two choices are equally valuable, since both provide an expected value of $10,000. But as with most decisions, nonquantifiable factors would influence your decision. In this case, unless you have a great deal of money, you would probably not select choice 2. The difficulty with relying solely on the expected value may be described, though in an oversimplified fashion, like this: the expected value concept is based on probabilities, and probability theory is based on mathematical laws that assume large numbers of situations. If you had 100 or 1,000 chances to play the coin flip game just described, it would not matter much whether you took the $10,000 or tossed the coin. You could expect to win about 50 times, lose about 50 times. But with only one try, you are staking a great deal on only one coin toss.

Operations researchers have tried to incorporate such considerations into the simple expected value model by attaching "utilities" to the various outcomes. Utility represents the degree of "better-offness" or "worse-offness" associated with the events. Using utilities, operations researchers have tried to recognize that generally it detracts more from your well-offness to lose $20,000 than is added by winning $40,000 when you could simply take $10,000 and quit. But assigning values to the utilities remains a matter of judgment, and assigned values may differ markedly depending on who is doing the choosing.

The use of statistical probabilities can provide more rational evaluations of the consequences of decisions than guesswork. Provided that the limitations of the analysis are accepted, more effective decisions can be made.

The expected value concept is often applied in situations in which the firm has several available strategies with probabilities attached to the outcomes of each. A typical application would be a firm's decision on how many units of a product should be bought or made when there are given probabilities for sales and the unsold units are discarded or sold at substantial losses.

For example, suppose that a florist must decide how many units of a particular corsage should be bought for the coming week. All of the units must be bought in advance and no additional purchases are possible. Unsold corsages will have to be discarded. The florist has estimated the demand for the corsage as follows. We shall assume no other outcomes are possible.

Demand in Units	Probability of Demand
4,000	20%
8,000	50%
12,000	30%

The variable cost per corsage is $6 and the selling price is $10. Please notice the difference between this situation and the one described on page 529. Here, the firm must produce a specific number of corsages, and so if the demand does not at least equal the number produced, the firm has a loss of $6 per unit in discarding the corsages. The approach to this kind of problem is to prepare a **payoff table** which shows the outcomes of each possible strategy. We assume that the florist will buy either 4,000, 8,000, or 12,000 units. The conditional payoffs of each of those strategies is computed in Exhibit 15-1.

Exhibit 15-1
Payoffs of Various Strategies—Conditional Values

Action: Purchases of

Event: Demand	4,000	8,000	12,000
4,000	$16,000	($ 8,000)	($32,000)
8,000	16,000	32,000	8,000
12,000	16,000	32,000	48,000

The values are computed as follows. Each individual entry is the contribution margin that would be gained, or lost, given the combination of sales and purchases. Thus, if the firm bought 4,000 units, it would sell 4,000 units no matter what the demand because it could not buy any more even if it learned that 8,000 or 12,000 units would be demanded by buyers. Hence, if purchases are 4,000 units, the firm will earn a $16,000 contribution margin by selling 4,000 units ($4 per unit × 4,000 units) and will lose nothing by having to discard units made but not sold.

If the firm buys 8,000 units and can only sell 4,000, it will incur costs of $48,000 (8,000 × $6) and earn revenues of only $40,000 (4,000 × $10), thus losing $8,000. Or, put another way, the firm would earn $16,000 contribution margin on the 4,000 units sold, but would sustain losses of $6 per unit for the 4,000 units not sold and discarded. If the firm did sell 8,000 units, it would earn revenues of $80,000, have costs of $48,000, and show a contribution margin of $32,000 ($4 × 8,000). The same contribution margin would be earned if the firm could have sold 12,000 units, but only sold 8,000 because only 8,000 were purchased.

The next step is to compute the expected value of each possible outcome, using the probabilities of demand. The strategy with the highest expected value should be picked.

Exhibit 15-2
Expected Values of Strategies

| | | Action: Purchases of | | | | | |
| | | 4,000 | | 8,000 | | 12,000 | |
Demand	Probability	CV*	EV†	CV*	EV†	CV*	EV†
4,000	20%	$16,000	$ 3,200	($ 8,000)	($ 1,600)	($32,000)	($ 6,400)
8,000	50%	16,000	8,000	32,000	16,000	8,000	4,000
12,000	30%	16,000	4,800	32,000	9,600	48,000	14,400
Expected values			$16,000		$24,000		$12,000

*Conditional values from Exhibit 15-1.
†Conditional value multiplied by probability.

The best strategy to follow, using the expected value criterion, would be to buy 8,000 units. The safest strategy would be to buy 4,000 units, in which case the firm would be assured of a $16,000 contribution margin provided that sales could not go below 4,000 units. Notice that the expected value of the strategy of producing 4,000 units is equal to the conditional value of each outcome: demands of 4,000, 8,000, and 12,000. This should not be surprising because the firm will sell 4,000 units if it buys only that many. The problem with that strategy is that the firm loses contribution if it could have sold more than 4,000 units.

The outcomes of the strategy of buying 12,000 are much more dispersed than the others, which is also to be expected. The more you buy *and* sell, the higher the contribution margin; but the more you buy and *don't* sell, the greater the loss for having to dispose of unsold units.

This type of analysis is usually applied to situations in which the firm is continually making decisions about production or purchasing. Examples would be firms that sell perishable goods. A vendor of fresh fruits and vegetables must buy them in advance and cannot keep unsold quantities in stock.

The value of perfect information can also be computed from payoff tables. It is, in this application, the difference between the amount of contribution margin that would be earned if the firm knew how many units would be demanded and therefore purchased exactly that many, and the expected value of the strategy it would follow using only probabilities.

If the firm knew in advance how many corsages would be demanded, it would buy exactly that many and would have the following expected value of contribution margin, selling 4,000 units in 20% of the weeks, 8,000 units in 50% of the weeks, and 12,000 units in 30% of the weeks.

Sales	Contribution Margin, Conditional Value (Exhibit 15-1)	Probability	Expected Value
4,000	$16,000	20%	$ 3,200
8,000	32,000	50%	16,000
12,000	48,000	30%	14,400
Expected value			$33,600

Notice that the expected values correspond to those in Exhibit 15-2 for the entries in the same row and same column. That is, the entry in the row for 4,000 here is $3,200 as in the 4,000 row and column in Exhibit 15-2. In the 8,000 row, 8,000 column is $16,000; and in the 12,000 row 12,000 column is $14,400. The same is true of the conditional values.

In this case, then, the value of perfect information is $9,600 ($33,600 − $24,000). We can make this clear by showing the expected sales for a 10-week period, following the strategy of buying 8,000 units each week and following the optimal strategy when we know in advance what the week's demand will be.

During the 10-week period we would expect to sell 4,000 corsages twice (20% × 10 weeks); 8,000 corsages five times; and 12,000 corsages three times. If we follow the strategy of buying 8,000 each week we would have losses of $8,000 twice and gains of $32,000 eight times. (When we sell only 4,000 corsages we lose $8,000, and when we sell 8,000 we gain $32,000, from Exhibit 15-1.) Our total contribution margin for the 10-week period would then be $240,000, which is ($32,000 × 8) − ($8,000 × 2). If we followed the optimal strategy, we would buy and sell 4,000 corsages twice, buy and sell 8,000 corsages five times, and buy and sell 12,000 corsages three times. The contribution margin for the period would be as follows.

Sales	Number of Weeks	× Contribution Margin per Week	= Total
4,000	2	$ 16,000	$ 32,000
8,000	5	32,000	160,000
12,000	3	48,000	144,000
Total			$336,000

The difference between the expected contribution margin with perfect information ($336,000) and using the optimal strategy without having perfect information ($240,000) is $96,000, which is 10 times (for 10 weeks) the value of $9,600 that we calculated before.

In the real world it is difficult to obtain perfect information, but the concept is still valuable. Some additional information can almost always be obtained at a price—test-marketing of new products is an example of an effort to obtain more information. The question is whether the information gained would result in a change in your strategy, whether your decisions would be better if you did obtain the information, and whether the cost is less than the added benefits.

Developing Probabilities

The probabilities to be used in computing expected values can be intuitive and judgmental, or can be developed by using more objective, sophisticated statistical techniques.

At one extreme, probabilities might be "best estimates" of experienced managers. There might be some historical basis for the estimates, as when managers have developed rules of thumb through past experience and believe that the current situation is similar to previous situations. For example, if a machine is not operating at peak efficiency the manager might believe that the probability is about 60% that an internal part is wearing out, 40% that some random factor is at work that will not continue. Tearing down the machine to examine and perhaps replace the part could be very costly both in labor and in lost production while the machine is idle. The manager might decide to wait for another week or so to get a better idea.

At times the manager may have fairly objective probabilities based on the presence or absence of external factors. A good example is provided by a firm whose business depends greatly on the weather. A firm that sells hot dogs and soft drinks at baseball parks might be able to develop probabilities of sales based on weather reports. The hotter the day is expected to be, the more soft drinks the firm can expect to sell. Of course, the validity of the manager's estimates depends on the validity of the weather forecasts relied on.

Finally, firms will often try to narrow down the range of estimates by getting additional information and using statistical techniques to evaluate the information. One common example is in the area of market research. A firm might be considering the introduction of a new product that would require a nation-wide advertising and promotional campaign. Because such campaigns can be very costly, the firm might test-market the product using a regional promotional campaign. The area or areas selected should be fairly representative of the entire country for the results to be useful. After the small-scale campaigns are underway the managers can analyze the information and gain a better perspective on probable nation-wide sales. You may study some of these techniques in later courses in marketing and statistics.

INVENTORY CONTROL MODELS

Inventory is one of the most important assets of the firm. It usually makes up a large proportion of the current assets, and its level will have a significant effect on the rate of return earned by the firm.

The ideal situation would be to immediately sell the merchandise that had just arrived. In a manufacturing firm, the ideal would be to sell all output as soon as it was finished. In these ideal cases, the investment in inventory awaiting sale is minimized—at zero.

However this is rarely possible because of the leads and lags between purchases or production and sales; most firms must stock inventory well in advance of its being sold. In most retail businesses, there must be a supply sufficient to attract customers. Yet, if too large an inventory is carried, excessive carrying costs will be incurred. There are costs related to carrying inventory in a manufacturing firm also, but, in addition, failure to have sufficient inventory can result in production delays, idle workers, and dissatisfied customers. Thus, there has been considerable research in the area of inventory control.

The Problem

Inventory has three basic kinds of costs associated with it: the costs of ordering; the costs of having inventory on hand; and the costs of not having enough inventory on hand. Examples of specific costs in each of these categories are given in Exhibit 15-3.

We are seeking an inventory level that will minimize total costs. A major difficulty is that the three types of costs are not independent. The more you order at one time, the lower the ordering costs. But the more you order, the higher is your average inventory, thus increasing the carrying costs. On the other hand, the higher your average inventory, the less likely you are to lose profits on sales (incur opportunity costs).

Exhibit 15-3

Costs of Ordering

1. Processing of the order
2. Forms used
3. Time spent (opportunity cost)
4. Order follow-up time

Costs of Carrying Inventory

1. Space used
2. Wages of personnel in storage section
3. Personal property taxes
4. Fire and theft insurance
5. Clerical costs
6. Risks of obsolescence and deterioration
7. Cost of capital on investment (recall Chapter 8)
8. Handling

Costs of Not Having Enough Inventory

1. Lost contribution margin from sales
   (a) Particular sales are lost because a customer could not get what he wanted.
   (b) Later sales may be lost because the dissatisfied customer does not return and other customers may not come because of word-of-mouth notification that your selection is inadequate.
2. Quantity purchase discounts lost if your policy does not permit large purchases.
3. Bottlenecks in production because of the lack of one material.

In any particular situation, one or more of the costs listed in Exhibit 15-3 may not be relevant to the solution of the cost minimization problem. For example, there is no storage cost if the firm has large amounts of space with no alternative uses. The costs to be considered are only those that will change with the level of inventory held. If insurance premiums are based on the quantity of goods carried, they are relevant. If the premium is a flat amount no matter how much inventory is carried (unlikely, but possible), it is irrelevant. Only variable or incremental costs are relevant in determining the desired level of inventory.

Serious difficulties are encountered in dealing with the items shown as costs of carrying too little inventory (usually called stockout costs). These costs are opportunity costs and are not normally shown in accounting records. For this reason they may be inadvertently ignored, or their significance may be downplayed. Such costs are as real as those that are recorded and can, in a given situation, be far greater than recorded costs. When goods have relatively high contribution margins, the cost of stockouts could well exceed by several times the total costs associated with carrying inventory sufficient to ensure against stockouts.

We shall deal with the problem of minimizing costs in two stages: (1) the manager must determine when to order, that is, how low inventory can get before a new supply is ordered; and (2) the manager must determine how much inventory to order at a time (how often to order). Ordering only as much as you need and at exactly the right time will minimize costs.

When to Order–The Reorder Point

How low should we allow inventory to get before ordering more? The answer to this question is called the **reorder point**. It can be expressed either in units or dollars. In determining the reorder point, we are trying to minimize the total costs of being out of stock when the item is needed for production or sale, and the cost of carrying the inventory.

Determination of the reorder point is based on two things: the amount of inventory that can be expected to be used or sold between the times of placing the order and receiving the new stock; and **safety stock**. Safety stock is the quantity of inventory that serves as a cushion in case the order comes in late or use is greater than normal from the time the order is placed to the time it is received.

The period of time between placing an order and its receipt is called **lead time**. The lead time in days multiplied by the expected daily use of inventory is one component of the reorder point; the other is the safety stock. Suppose it takes 10 days to receive an order, daily use of the part is 20 units, and no safety stock is provided. The reorder point is 200 units (20 units × 10 days). If your predictions are accurate, you will not run out of inventory. As you use the last unit, the new units will have just come in. If the manager believes that a safety stock of 100 units is desirable, the reorder point will be set at 300 units (200 + 100). Then, if the order is late in arriving, or there is an unexpected need for more than 20 units on one or more days, there will be enough stock to last until the order is received. The behavior of inventory for this situation is depicted in Figure 15-2. It is assumed in that graph that 800 units are ordered at a time.

In some cases, expected daily use will be computed by reference to annual use and the number of working days during a year. Suppose that the records reveal the annual use to be $60,000 (at cost), that there are 200 working days in the year, that lead time is 15 working days, and a safety stock of $5,000 is desired. The reorder point in dollars would be $9,500, computed in the following manner.

FIGURE 15-2   Behavior of Inventory Level

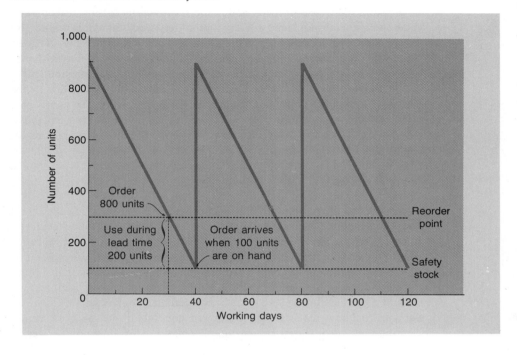

Inventory reorder point = safety stock + (daily use × lead time)

Average daily use can be estimated at $300 ($60,000/200 days). With a lead time of 15 days, the reorder point before considering safety stock is $4,500 ($300 × 15 days). Adding the safety stock of $5,000 yields the $9,500 reorder point.

Determination of Safety Stock

One of the most critical aspects of inventory management is deciding on the safety-stock level. The costs of not having enough inventory are most closely related to the amount of safety stock carried.

Safety stock is required because two factors are uncertain: lead time and use during the lead time. If both factors were known, there would be no reason to carry safety stock. Suppose that normal lead time is determined to be 10 days but can be as long as 15 days. Suppose that average daily use is $300 but can be as high as $420. Based only on the averages, the reorder point before consideration of safety stock is $3,000 (10 days × $300). But using the extreme possibilities for lead time and daily use, the computed reorder point is $6,300 ($15 days × $420). If we reorder when inventory is $6,300, we are certain to never run out. But the cost of carrying so much inventory might be prohibitive. Moreover, while we might expect to occasionally experience 15-day lead time or daily use of $420, it is unlikely that both would be encountered at the same time. Hence, a compromise is in order. We would select a reorder point between $3,000 (no safety stock) and $6,300 ($3,300 safety stock). To arrive at the compromise, we might investigate how often lead time exceeds 10 days and daily use exceeds $300, and the importance of the item in the production or sales picture. We would tend to carry more safety stock for a high-selling, high-contribution-margin item, than for an item with the opposite characteristics. We would generally set a higher safety stock for a part that is used in the production of several of the firm's major products than might be set for a part used in only one, not particularly popular product.

In practice, detailed analyses might be made for only a few items of especial importance. Low-cost, nonessential items might be given reorder points based solely on the intuition of an experienced manager. It can be very expensive to make extended studies of the flows of inventory items. Extensive analysis should not be undertaken unless the potential benefits exceed the investigative costs.

How Much to Order—The Economic Order Quantity

The answer to the question "how much to order at a time?" is called the **economic order quantity** (EOQ). (The question is often stated in terms of how often an order should be placed.) Our examples use firms that do not manufacture the item but order it from a supplier. The analysis would, however, be the same if the item were produced internally.

In determining how much to order at a time, we are trying to minimize the sum of the costs of ordering and the costs of carrying inventory. Suppose that a firm uses 12,000 units of a product during a year. ("Uses" can mean either sells or uses in some other way. Supplies and raw materials are used, but not "sold" in the usual sense.) The firm has identified incremental costs of carrying inventory at $.60 per unit per year. The incremental cost of placing an order has been determined to be $250 (including incremental clerical costs, forms, data processing, delivery, etc.).[1] If use is even throughout the year, we can prepare a schedule showing how ordering costs and carrying costs would behave as the number of orders changes. The assumption that use is even throughout the year is critical to the EOQ model. If use varies from month to month or week to week, the model will not give the correct solution.

The cost of carrying inventory is based on the average number of units held in addition to safety stock. The cost of carrying safety stock should be excluded because it is the same under all alternative ordering schemes. Since we have relatively even use throughout the year, the average inventory will be one-half of the order size, as can be seen by considering the possible inventory levels. The highest level occurs when an order has just been received; inventory equals safety stock plus the order size. The lowest point occurs just prior to the receipt of the order, when inventory equals safety stock.

Carrying costs are treated as variable with the level of inventory, so the incremental carrying costs are the cost per unit per year multiplied by the average number of units in inventory above the safety-stock level. The costs for our example are shown in Exhibit 15–4. The EOQ is 3,000 units ordered four times a year. When solving for EOQ in this way, you know you have reached the answer when the total cost begins to rise after having fallen. Figure 15-3 shows the behavior of each element of cost and total cost as the number of orders increases. The total cost does not change very much over a fairly wide range. In the example, the costs of ordering three, four, and five times per year are fairly close together. This phenomenon occurs because one component of cost is rising while the other is falling.

---

[1]If we were dealing with a manufactured item, the costs to be considered would be those of setting up to make a batch of the product (for example, changing dies, and idle time during the changeover).

Exhibit 15-4
Determination of EOQ

(a) Number of Orders per Year	(b) Number of Units Ordered 12,000/(a)	(c) Average Inventory (b)/2	(d) Annual Ordering Costs $250 × (a)	(e) Annual Carrying Costs 60¢ × (c)	(f) Total Annual Costs (d) + (e)
1	12,000	6,000	$ 250	$3,600	$3,850
2	6,000	3,000	500	1,800	2,300
3	4,000	2,000	750	1,200	1,950
4	3,000	1,500	1,000	900	1,900
5	2,400	1,200	1,250	720	1,970

We can also approach the problem by examining the costs based on the number of units ordered at a time. We know from Exhibit 15-4 the costs of ordering 12,000, 6,000, 4,000, 3,000, and 2,400 units at a time. We add 3,500 units and 2,800 units and determine the results, which are shown in Exhibit 15-5 (page 540). The number of orders per year is not even for either alternative; this means that you might order three times in one year, four times the next year. The ordering cost computed based on fractional orders is an average annual ordering cost, not the cost to order in any one particular year. Neither of the order sizes in Exhibit 15-5 produces a more economical result than the one produced with an order size of 3,000 units as shown in Exhibit 15-4.[2]

FIGURE 15-3 Behavior of Inventory Costs

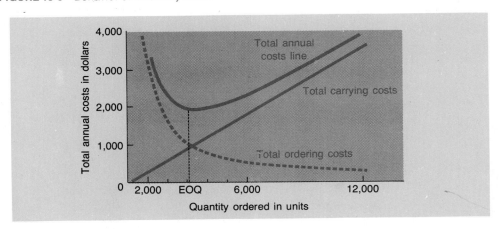

[2]The lowest possible cost that we could incur is $1,898.60. The exact EOQ is given by the formula, $EOQ = \sqrt{2CD/k_u}$, where C is the incremental order cost, D is the number of units used in a year, and k_u is the annual carrying cost per unit. Applied in the example, $EOQ = \sqrt{2 \times \$250 \times 12,000/\$.60} = 3,162$ units (rounded), or 3.8 orders per year (12,000/3,162). The costs would be as follows: order costs $950 (3.8 × $250); carrying costs $948.60 ($.60 × 1,581). The difference in cost between the exact EOQ and the cost based on ordering 3,000 units at a time is only $1.40 per year.

Exhibit 15-5
Annual Costs of Ordering and Carrying
for Order Sizes of 3,500 and 2,800 Units

(a)	(b)	(c)	(d)	(e)	(f)
			Average		*Average*
	Number of		*Annual*	*Annual*	*Annual*
Number of	*Orders*	*Average*	*Ordering*	*Carrying*	*Total*
Units	*per Year*	*Inventory*	*Costs*	*Costs*	*Costs*
Ordered	*12,000/(a)*	*(a)/2*	*$250 × (b)*	*$.60 × (c)*	*(d) + (e)*
3,500	3.43	1,750	$ 857.50	$1,050	$1,907.50
2,800	4.29	1,400	1,072.50	840	1,912.50

Another technique that determines EOQ uses dollars of inventory rather than units, and carrying costs as a percentage of dollar costs instead of per unit. The method is no different from the one illustrated above: it applies in situations in which it may not be feasible to compute in units. A manager in a hardware store may not wish to keep track of individual items such as screws and nails of various sizes; instead he may wish to order a batch of various sizes when the dollar amount of inventory reaches a reorder point. While it would be possible to keep track of every single kind of item in a hardware store, it would cost more to keep such records than the benefits that could be gained.

We shall continue to use the same example; however, we will now express the annual use of the item in dollars. Assume that each unit costs $4; then the annual use is $48,000 (12,000 × $4). The carrying costs are now 15% of cost ($.60/$4). In Exhibit 15-6 only dollar amounts are used. The costs are exactly the same as those computed in Exhibit 15-4.

Exhibit 15-6
Determination of EOQ
(In Dollars)

(a)	(b)	(c)	(d)	(e)	(f)
	Dollar Amount		*Annual*	*Annual*	*Annual*
Number of	*Ordered*	*Average*	*Ordering*	*Carrying*	*Total*
Orders	*at Cost*	*Inventory*	*Costs*	*Costs*	*Costs*
per Year	*$48,000/(a)*	*(b)/2*	*$250 × (a)*	*15% × (c)*	*(d) + (e)*
1	$48,000	$24,000	$ 250	$3,600	$3,850
2	24,000	12,000	500	1,800	2,300
3	16,000	8,000	750	1,200	1,950
4	12,000	6,000	1,000	900	1,900
5	9,600	4,800	1,250	720	1,970

If use is given in dollars and carrying costs as a percentage of dollar costs, the formula described on page 539 cannot be used. The formula can be used to find the exact EOQ when data are given in units.

LINEAR PROGRAMMING

In Chapter 7 we noted that profits are maximized when the firm produces the combination of products that maximizes the contribution margin per unit of the fixed resource. In the example given, page 217, only one resource was fixed, machine-hours available. In real situations it is likely that several resources will be fixed and that there will be many products from among which to choose. There is also often a constraint on the production of alternative products because it is unlikely that very large quantities of any single product can be sold at the same prices as smaller quantities.

In situations in which several constraints are present and several products can be produced, **linear programming** can be used to determine the combination of products that will maximize profits. Linear programming can also be used to find the combination of input factors that minimizes the cost of performing a certain activity. A cattle feeder can determine the least-cost method of mixing various feeds to provide a specific level of nourishment for his cattle. Or, a firm with several factories and warehouses can determine the least-cost method of getting the required quantities of product to the warehouses from the factories.

The mathematics involved in linear programming is complex and will not be dealt with in this book. You should be able to recognize the kinds of problems that can be solved with linear programming, understand the formulation of the problem, and see what is being done when the problem is solved.

Essentially, linear programming is the solving of a system of simultaneous linear equations that includes an **objective function** specifying what is to be maximized (usually contribution margin) or minimized (usually cost). The rest of the equations state the **constraints.**

A firm produces two products, X and Y. Both products require time in two production departments, the assembly department and the finishing department. Data on the two products are given below.

	X	Y
Hours required in assembly department	2	4
Hours required in finishing department	3	2
Total hours required	5	6
Variable cost per hour, both departments, labor and overhead	$ 5	$ 5
Total variable labor and overhead	$25	$ 30
Materials	15	30
Total variable cost	$40	$ 60
Selling price	$65	$100
Contribution margin	$25	$ 40

The firm has available, per week, 100 hours in the assembly department, 90 hours in the finishing department. Using these data we can formulate the linear program in the following steps:

Step 1. Formulate the objective function, which in this case is to maximize total contribution margin per week.
Maximize: contribution margin = $25X + $40Y, where X and Y stand for the numbers of units of each product that will be produced.

Step 2. Formulate the constraints as inequalities:

$2X + 4Y \leqslant 100$

$3X + 2Y \leqslant 90$

The symbol $\leqslant$ is read *is equal to or less than*. Each inequality describes the constraint on available time in a department. The first one states that the number of units of X multiplied by 2, plus the number of units of Y multiplied by 4, cannot exceed 100, which is the available capacity of the assembly department. The second inequality states that the number of units of X multiplied by 3, plus the number of units of Y multiplied by 2 cannot exceed 90, the number of hours available in the finishing department. We shall return to these in a moment. First, there are two other constraints that might not seem obvious at first glance, but are required. They are "non-negativity" constraints.

$X \geqslant 0$

$Y \geqslant 0$

The symbol $\geqslant$ is read *is equal to or greater than*. The reason for these constraints is that if they were not introduced, it would be possible to "unproduce" a product.

At this point we can show the entire set of equations and inequalities that would be used if we were going to solve the problem using mathematical techniques.

Maximize: contribution margin = $\$25X + \$40Y$
Subject to the constraints:

$$
\begin{aligned}
2X + 4Y &\leqslant 100 \\
3X + 2Y &\leqslant 90 \\
X \quad\;\; &\geqslant 0 \\
Y &\geqslant 0
\end{aligned}
$$

Step 3. Draw the lines representing constraints on a graph. The constraints on the capacities of the two departments are shown in Figure 15-4. The nonnegativity constraints are implicit because we show only the upper right-hand side of the graph, where production of both products is zero or positive.

Drawing the lines representing the capacity constraints can be done intuitively. For example, the assembly constraint is $2X + 4Y \leqslant 100$. Thus if only product X is made, maximum production is 50 units, which is 100/2. If only Y is made, maximum production is 25 units, which is 100/4. Hence, the points on the axes are determined and the line is drawn to connect them. Each point on the line represents a possible combination of production.

For example, assembling 30 units of X would require 60 hours of assembly time. There would be 40 hours left $(100 - 60)$ to assemble units of Y. In that time, 10 units of Y could be assembled. Notice on the graph that the point $30X$, $10Y$ is not inside the shaded area, the area of feasible, possible solutions. Though the firm can assemble that combination of units, it cannot finish that combination because the point $30X$, $10Y$ lies above the line

FIGURE 15-4   Linear Programming: Graphic Solution of Constraints on Capacity

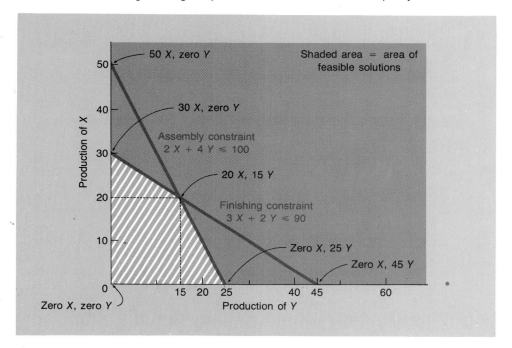

representing the finishing department constraint. All points within the area of feasible solutions are achievable combinations of production, all points outside the area are unachievable.

Step 4. Determine the contribution margin at all of the corners in the area of feasible solutions. In linear programming an optimal solution always occurs at a corner, an intersection of two lines. The axes are considered to be lines.[3]

Corner		Production		Contribution Margin		Total Contribution
X	Y	X	Y	X	Y	Margin
0	0	0	0	0	0	0
30	0	30	0	$750	0	$750
20	15	20	15	$500	$600	$1,100
0	25	0	25	0	$1,000	$1,000

The corner 20X, 15Y produces the best solution.

In certain cases it is possible to solve for the intersections of constraints using simultaneous equations.[4] This enables you to find the intersection of two constraints without having to draw an accurate graph. Using the illustration in the text, we turn the inequalities into equations.

---

[3]There may be other solutions that also yield the best possible result, but none yields a better result than is achieved at an intersection.

[4]The most widely used technique for solving large linear programming problems is called the *simplex method*. It requires finding solutions to a set of simultaneous equations until the optimal solution is found.

(1) $2X + 4Y = 100$
(2) $3X + 2Y = 90$

Multiplying equation (2) by 2 and subtracting equation (1) we obtain:

$4X = 80$
$X = 20$

Substituting 20 for X in equation (1) gives:

$40 + 4Y = 100$
$4Y = 60$
$Y = 15$

This approach is helpful in some cases, but the introduction of additional constraints warrants the use of the more complex approach.

Many other types of constraints are possible. Figure 15-5 shows the graph when the sales of product X are assumed to be limited to 16 units per week because of market conditions. The formerly optimal solution of $20X$, $15Y$ is no longer feasible. Two new corners have been created, $16X$, zero Y; and $16X$, $17Y$. Clearly, $16X$ and zero Y is less desirable than $16X$ and $17Y$. The question is now whether $16X$, $17Y$ is better than zero X, $25Y$, which was the second best solution in the original problem.

FIGURE 15-5 Linear Programming: Graphic Solution of Constraints on Capacity and on Sales of X

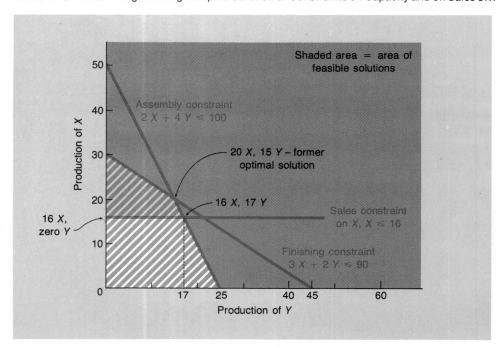

At $16X$, $17Y$, total contribution margin per week is $1,080, ($25 $\times$ 16) + ($40 $\times$ 17). This is better than the $1,000 that would be earned producing only 25 units of Y.

The constraint of the finishing department is no longer critical. It now lies completely outside the area of feasible solutions and therefore does not get full utilization. The finishing department will have 8 hours of unused capacity because 16 units of X and 17 of Y can be finished in 82 hours.

$$
\begin{array}{rl}
3X + 2Y \leq & 90 \\
3 \times 16 = & 48 \\
2 \times 17 = & \underline{34} \\
\text{Total} & 82
\end{array}
$$

Management would consider reducing the available capacity of the finishing department if it expected the constraint on sales of X to continue and if there would be savings in cost accompanying a reduction in capacity. Linear programming does not consider fixed costs, but in a situation like the one described, the firm should consider the possibility of reducing capacity.

Sensitivity Analysis

Sensitivity analysis, the testing of a solution to see whether it would change if one or more of the variables were to change, is an important part of decision making. Let us consider the original problem we discussed, in which there was no constraint on the sales of product X. The manager of the firm might expect the price of product X to fall, which would lower its contribution margin. Total contribution margin would also fall so long as the firm stayed with its original plan to produce 20 units of X and 15 of Y. At some point the drop in contribution margin would make it more profitable for the firm to produce 25 units of Y, none of X, than to continue with the original plan.

The manager is interested in knowing how far the contribution margin of product X would have to fall before he should stop producing product X. He can make that determination in the following way. If he produces 25 units of Y, none of X, the firm will earn $1,000 contribution margin per week. Therefore, when the total contribution margin from producing 20 units of X and 15 of Y drops to $1,000 he would be indifferent between the two mixes.[5] Total contribution margin at the optimal solution is now $1,000, which is $100 more than that earned if 25 units of Y are produced. Therefore, if the contribution margin from X drops by more than $100, when 20 units of X are made, it would pay the firm to stop producing X. Because 20 units are being produced, a drop of more than $5 per unit ($100/20) would make it more profitable to produce only 25 units of Y. A $5 drop would put contribution margin for a unit of X at $20.

We can also solve this problem using the following equation, where ? equals the contribution margin of X, per unit, that would make the firm indifferent between producing $20X$, $15Y$ and zero X, $25Y$.

$$
\$40 \times 25 = (\$40 \times 15) + (? \times 20)
$$

---

[5] In fact, any combination of production along the line representing assembly capacity, from $20X$, $15Y$ down to zero X, $25Y$ would give the same total contribution margin per week.

This equation says simply that when contribution margin per week from producing 25 units of Y, none of X, equals that earned from producing 15 units of Y, 20 of X, the manager is indifferent. Solving for ?,

$$
\begin{aligned}
\$1,000 &= \$600 \quad + \quad (? \times 20) \\
\$400 &= ? \times 20 \\
? &= \$20
\end{aligned}
$$

Consequently, if the contribution margin per unit of product X went below \$20, the firm would stop producing X, devoting its facilities instead to making Y.

Similarly, a rise in the price and contribution margin per unit of Y would tend to make the firm more likely to stop producing X and produce more of Y. The equation below states that when the contribution margin of 25 units of Y equals that of 15 units of Y plus 20 units of X, the firm would earn the same with either production mix. ? represents contribution margin per unit of Y.

$$
\begin{aligned}
? \times 25 &= (? \times 15) \quad + \quad (\$25 \times 20) \\
? \times 25 &= (? \times 15) \quad + \quad \$500 \\
? \times 10 &= \$500 \\
? &= \$50
\end{aligned}
$$

If contribution margin of product Y goes above \$50 per unit, the firm will earn more total contribution margin producing 25Y, zero X, than 15Y, 20X.

Shadow Prices

A manager who has solved a linear programming problem might wish to know whether it would be beneficial to add capacity in a particular department. He would be interested in the value to the firm of adding, say, an hour per week of assembly time. The value of adding an additional hour of capacity is the additional contribution margin that could be earned. This amount is called the shadow price of the resource.[6]

A **shadow price** is an opportunity cost: the cost of not having an additional unit of capacity. It can also be interpreted as the value of the last hour, the amount of contribution margin that would be lost if the firm had one hour fewer than it actually does have.

We shall calculate the shadow price of the assembly constraint using our original illustration in which there was no constraint on the sales of product X. To make it easier to show graphically, we shall add 8 hours of capacity to the assembly department, rather than 1 hour. Figure 15-6 shows the new assembly constraint. It also shows the former optimal solution, where the assembly constraint and finishing constraint lines intersected when capacity in the assembly department was 100 hours per week. Notice that the new corner, 18X, 18Y shows the firm making fewer units of X than before, but more units of Y. Because the contribution margin of Y is higher than that of X the firm would be willing to give up 2 units of X $(20 - 18)$ to add 3 units of Y $(18 - 15)$.

[6]Stated generally, a shadow price is the value of being able to relax any constraint by one unit. A unit could be an hour, or it could be a unit of product. For example, in the illustration in which sales of X were limited to 16 units per week, a shadow price could be computed for that constraint. It would be the difference between contribution margin at 16X, 17Y and at the optimal solution if 17 units of X could be sold.

FIGURE 15-6   Linear Programming: Graphic Solution of Increased Assembly Capacity

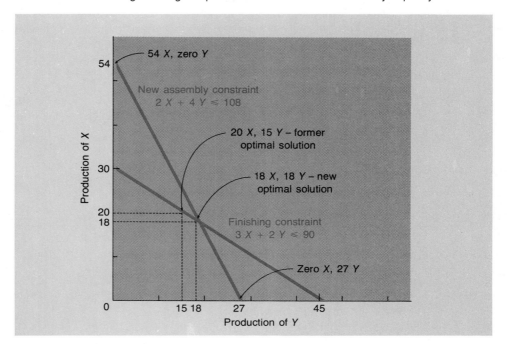

Checking the new corners for the optimal solution, we have:

Corner		Production		Contribution Margin		Total Contribution
X	Y	X	Y	X	Y	Margin
18	18	18	18	$450	$ 720	$1,170
0	27	0	27	0	$1,080	1,080

The new optimal solution of 18X, 18Y has total contribution margin of $1,170 per week. That is $70 higher than the $1,100 earned under the optimal solution of 20X, 15Y when the assembly department had 100 available hours. Therefore the firm would be willing to pay up to $70 per week to get an additional 8 hours of assembly capacity.

The shadow price is $8.75, which is $70/8 hours. If we had used 101 hours, we would have had contribution margin of $1,108.75. We would also have had a noninteger solution, with fractional units of both products being made. In linear programming, capacity is fixed for the planning period (a week, day, month, or year). In the long run the firm can add to capacity or reduce it. Shadow prices give an idea of the value of adding capacity and are important information for long-run planning.

SUMMARY

The use of statistical decision theory allows the manager to incorporate the effects of uncertainty regarding future results into his or her analysis. Inventory control models provide more rational ways of evaluating inventory policy than do guesses and intuitive methods. Linear programming is a useful tool when the manager must decide how best to use existing resources.

Much of the information needed for using these techniques is supplied by the managerial accountant. Therefore, he or she must be aware of the objectives and information requirements of such techniques. The managerial accountant will sometimes have to assist in formulating the problem and must therefore be aware of the capabilities and limitations of the techniques available.

KEY TERMS

decision tree	reorder point
economic order quantity	safety stock
expected value	shadow prices
lead time	value of perfect information
linear programming	

KEY FORMULAS

Economic order quantity $= \sqrt{\dfrac{2(\text{incremental order cost})(\text{no. of units used in a year})}{\text{annual carrying cost per unit}}}$

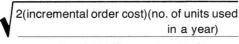

Inventory reorder point = safety stock + (daily use × lead time)

REVIEW PROBLEM—EXPECTED VALUES

In March the Grauger Company experienced an unfavorable cost variance of $2,000. Based on his experience and judgment, the production manager believes that there is a 40% probability of the variance being due to random causes and therefore not continuing. There is a 60% probability that there is some difficulty in the production process and that the variance will continue at $2,000 per month for the next two months. Investigating the variance would cost $800. If the variance is investigated, and something is wrong with the process, there is a 70% probability that corrective action could be taken, a 30% probability that nothing can be done.

Required: Determine the expected costs of investigating and of not investigating the variance.

Answers to review problem

1. Expected Cost of Investigating

Event	Cost	Probability	Expected Value
Variance is random and will not continue	$ 800	.40	$ 320
Variance is caused by problem in process that can be corrected	$ 800	.42*	336
Variance is caused by problem that cannot be corrected	$4800	.18†	864
Expected cost of Investigating		1.00	$1,520

*60% × 70%
†60% × 30%

2. Expected Cost of Not Investigating

Variance is random	0	.40	0
Variance is caused by problem in process and will continue	$4000	.60	$2,400
Expected cost of not investigating		1.00	$2,400

The variance should be investigated because the expected cost to investigate is less than that of not investigating.

REVIEW PROBLEM—INVENTORY CONTROL

The following data apply to one of the products of the Tebbetts Company.

Annual use	12,000 units
Annual carrying cost	$.80 per unit
Order cost	$300 per order
Safety stock	500 units

There are 200 working days per year and the lead time is 12 days.

Required

1. Determine the reorder point.
2. Determine the total annual cost of ordering (a) twice a year, (b) three times a year, (c) four times a year, and (d) five times a year.

Answers to review problem

Safety stock	500	
Use during lead time	720	12 × (12000/200)
	1,220	

	(a)	(b)	(c)	(d)
1. Orders per year	2	3	4	5
2. Order cost at $300 each	$ 600	$ 900	$1,200	$1,500
3. Quantity ordered 12,000/orders per year	6,000	4,000	3,000	2,400
4. Average inventory quantity ordered/2	3,000	2,000	1,500	1,200
5. Carrying cost average inventory × $.80	$2,400	$1,600	$1,200	$ 960
6. Total cost order cost and carrying cost	$3,000	$2,500	$2,400	$2,460

The lowest cost is achieved by ordering 3,000 units four times per year. In fact, in this case the exact EOQ is 3,000 units. We can tell this because the carrying costs and order costs are exactly the same, $1,200. The lowest total cost is achieved when carrying costs and order costs are the same. We can verify this by using the EOQ formula from page 539.

$$\text{EOQ} = \sqrt{\frac{2 \times \$300 \times 12000}{\$.80}} = \sqrt{\frac{\$7,200,000}{\$.80}} = \sqrt{9,000,000} = 3,000$$

ASSIGNMENT MATERIAL

Questions for discussion

15-1 Optimum order size—changing conditions Explain the effect that each of the following would tend to have on the optimum order size for product X at Company A.

(a) Leading banks in the country have announced a reduction in the prime interest rate.
(b) The selling price of product X declines with no change in its purchase cost.
(c) The company is located in a high-crime, inner-city area.
(d) The city in which Company A is located increases the personal property tax rate.
(e) There is a substantial increase in the demand for product X.
(f) The company decides to change from the straight-line method of depreciating its warehouse to the sum-of-the-years'-digits method.

15-2 Inventory costs In the 1972 annual report of Pitney Bowes, the following appeared under the heading of Operational Improvements.

> The control of inventories of products and parts, and their attendant costs, was improved during the year, in part as the result of improved forecasting of market needs and the institution in the United States of a more efficient distribution system. Under this system, a new facility constructed in Newtown, Connecticut, serves as a national distribution center for business equipment products, parts, and supplies. Shipments are made from this center to five regional distribution centers strategically located across the country.

Required: The centralized distribution center must have increased some costs and decreased some others. Which costs probably increased and which decreased?

15-3 Reorder point   Indicate how each of the following factors, considered independently, would influence your establishing the reorder point for inventory (relatively high, relatively low, or no effect). Explain.

1. Your firm has very low fixed costs, very high variable costs (about 85% of sales).
2. Your product is stored in specially designed and built freezers that cost a great deal of money.
3. Your product is ice cream, sold from a store located in a large shopping center.
4. Your suppliers have seen falling profits because of intensive competition.
5. Your major supplier is having difficulties because two factions of its stockholders have been fighting for control.

Exercises

15-4 Inventory control   The Ridley Company uses $60,000 (at cost) of a particular raw material during the year. The material is used evenly throughout the year. Order costs are $400 per order, and carrying costs for inventory are 18% of carrying value. The firm carries a safety stock of $3,000 (at cost), has a lead time of 10 days, and works 300 days per year.

Required

1. Determine the reorder point.
2. Prepare a table to determine the economic order quantity.

15-5 Variance investigation   The Cole Company's controller has determined that it costs $300 to investigate a variance and that in one out of four cases investigated corrective action is possible. A variance of $1,000 unfavorable has been experienced. The production process will be changed after next month, so any savings would be only for one month if corrective action can be taken. Should the variance be investigated?

15-6 Inventory control   Using the following data, determine the economic order quantity and the reorder point for part A.

Cost per unit	$10
Use per year	10,000 units
Carrying costs	15% of cost
Order costs	$300 per order
Lead time	10 days
Safety stock	300 units
Working days in a year	200

Round your computations to even units and dollars.

15-7 New products—expected values and risk   The sales manager of the Happy Toy Company is considering two new toys. One is a doll, the other a game. She has, on the basis of market research and experience, formulated the following tables of cash flows and probabilities.

	Doll		Game	
Event	Cash Flow	Probability	Cash Flow	Probability
Big success	$20,000	.2	$38,000	.3
Fair success	14,000	.6	19,000	.4
Flop	8,000	.2	(10,000)	.3

Required

1. Determine the expected values of cash flows associated with each new toy.
2. Which one would you select, and why?

15-8 Linear programming—formulation of problem   The Garson Company makes three products, A, B, and C. Their respective contribution margins are $60, $70, and $80. Each product goes through three processes: cutting, shaping, and painting. The numbers of hours required by each process for each product are shown below.

Hours Required in Each Process

Product	Cutting	Shaping	Painting
A	2	3	5
B	1	5	3
C	5	2	3
	400	300	300

The following numbers of hours are available per month in each process: cutting, 400; shaping, 300; and painting, 300.

Required

Formulate the objective function and constraints to determine the optimal production policy.

15-9 Cost structure and probabilities   The production manager of the Omega Company is considering modifying one of his machines. The modification will add $10,000 per month to the cost of running the machine, but will reduce variable operating costs by $.20 per unit produced. The modification itself costs nothing and the machine can be returned to its regular operating method at any time.

The product produced on the machine has an uncertain demand; the best estimates available are as follows:

Monthly Demand	Probability
25,000	.25
40,000	.30
60,000	.35
70,000	.10

Required

1. Determine the number of units that must be produced to justify the modification.
2. Determine the expected value of making the modification. Should it be made?

15-10 Payoff table   The Campus Program Company sells programs for football games. The owner of the firm believes that the following data reflect the pattern of sales.

Quantity Sold (Cases)	Probability
100	20%
150	50%
200	30%

The owner is uncertain of the number of cases of programs to order. He must order one of the quantities given above. A case of programs sells for $200 and the purchase price is $100. Unsold programs are thrown away.

Required

Construct a payoff table to determine the number of cases of programs the firm should order.

Problems

15-11   Expected values—a law firm   The firm of Ambu, Lance, and Chaser has been approached by Hirt, a victim of a whiplash injury suffered in an automobile accident. He wants the firm to represent him in a court suit, with the firm's fee being one-third of the total judgment given by the court.

An analyst in the firm states that 1,500 hours would be needed to prepare and try the case, with the opportunity cost being $40 per hour. Based on experience with similar cases, he believes that the following judgments and associated probabilities are reasonable estimates on which to decide whether to accept the case.

Judgment for Hirt	Probability of Judgment
0	20%
$180,000	30%
$300,000	25%
$420,000	25%

Required: Determine whether the firm should accept the case.

15-12   Inventory control   Blitzen Industries makes products in individual production runs, because all its products must go through one particular machine. Each time a new production run is set up, the firm incurs incremental costs of $800.

The cost to carry a unit of product A is $2 per year, including taxes, insurance, spoilage, and the required return on investment. Sales of product A are 12,000 units per year.

Required

1. Determine the number of times that A should be made in a year.
2. The firm carries a safety stock of 300 units of A, the working year is 200 days, and production of a batch requires eight days. At what inventory level will a production run be made?

15-13   Variance investigation   The Edwards Company has just experienced a $2,000 unfavorable variance. The production supervisor believes that there is a 30% chance that the variance was a one-time thing and will not continue. He believes that if an investigation is made, the chance of correcting the variance is 40% and of not correcting it is 60%. It costs $600 to investigate a variance. The most that will be lost if the variance continues is $2,800.

Required

Compute the expected costs of investigating and not investigating the variance. Determine whether an investigation should be made.

15-14   Linear programming   The Fast Class Company makes two products, the Fast and the Class. Fasts sell for $12 and have variable costs of $5. Classes sell for $14 and have variable costs of $6. Both products are put through two processes—cutting and forming. Each unit of Fast requires two hours of cutting and four hours of forming. Each unit of Class requires three hours of cutting and two of forming. The firm has available 300 hours of cutting time and 240 hours of forming time per month.

Required

1. Determine the number of Fasts and Classes that should be produced each month.
2. Determine the total contribution margin that will be earned per month.

15-15 Product selection with probabilities   The Henson Electronics Company is trying to decide which of three products to introduce for the coming season. It is felt that only one should be brought out because the firm is relatively small and needs to concentrate its promotional effort. Information about the products being considered is given below.

	Radio	Toaster	Coffee Maker
Selling price	$12.00	$20.00	$27.00
Variable cost	3.00	4.00	12.00
Contribution margin	$ 9.00	$16.00	$15.00
Sales forecasts in units, with probabilities in	25,000 (20%)	12,000 (10%)	18,000 (30%)
parentheses	40,000 (40%)	19,000 (25%)	22,000 (35%)
	50,000 (30%)	28,000 (50%)	29,000 (35%)
	70,000 (10%)	38,000 (15%)	

Required

1. Compute the expected values of contribution margins for the three products.
2. Which product would you select and why?

15-16 Inventory control—effects of errors in policy   The purchasing manager of the Kensington Company buys one of its principal products in batches of 2,500, based on his personal judgment. Data for the product are:

Order cost	$800
Carrying cost, annual per unit	$2
Annual demand	20,000

Required

1. Determine the EOQ using the formula on page 539.
2. Determine the cost to the firm of not following the optimal purchasing policy. That is, determine the difference between total costs under the existing policy and under the optimal policy.
3. Determine how high the carrying costs would have to go to make the EOQ 2,500 units.
4. Determine how low order costs would have to go to support an EOQ of 2,500 units, assuming that the carrying costs are $2.

15-17 Inventory control—determination of incremental costs   The Rankin Company currently has no stated inventory policy; the sales manager and controller have asked you to assist in preparing a policy. Two of the factors to be determined are the cost of carrying inventory and the cost of ordering. The following information pertains to the firm's only product.

Cost per unit	$80
Sales per year	15,000 units
Required return on investment	13%
Insurance	$500 per year plus $1 per unit of average inventory
Taxes	$2 per unit of average inventory
Spoilage	2% of average inventory will become unsalable due to spoilage
Storage	The firm leases a warehouse that holds 20,000 units. Rent is $1,000 per year
Costs of purchasing department:	
Salaries	$12,000 per year fixed, plus $40 per order
Forms, postage	$10 per order

In addition, each time an order is received, the firm hires men from a local employment service to unload the order. On any size order, three men are hired at $30 each per day.

Required

Determine the economic order quantity using the formula on page 539. Be sure to determine which costs shown above are relevant to the analysis, which are not.

15-18 Special order decision—probabilities The sales manager of the Schieren Company has been approached by a chain store that would like to buy 10,000 units of the firm's product. The sales manager believes that the order should be accepted because the price offered is $6 and variable costs of production are $5.

In a conversation with the production manager, the following information was developed by the sales manager. (1) Sufficient capacity exists to meet the special order. (2) Prices for materials and wage rates are expected to increase by the time the order would be manufactured, but the amounts of the increases are not certain. The best estimates of the probabilities are as follows:

New Variable Cost	Probability
$5.20	.30
5.70	.40
6.60	.30

Required

1. Determine whether the special order should be accepted based on the data given.
2. What other factors might be taken into consideration in reaching a decision?

15-19 Standard costs with fluctuations The Corman Company produces its major product under uncertain conditions. Due to differences in the quality of raw materials received from suppliers, it may take anywhere from 8 pounds to 10 pounds of material to make a unit of product. The production manager believes that it is foolish to try to set standard costs for materials under present circumstances of the firm. As the controller, you are reluctant to forego completely the opportunity to collect information that could aid in the control process; you decide to make further investigation.

You find that the production manager is essentially correct about the fluctuations in the amount of raw material required. However, the quantity of materials required is 8 pounds about 20% of the time, 9 pounds about 70% of the time, and 10 pounds only 10% of the time.

Required

1. Can standard costs for materials be developed that will aid in both control and planning?
2. What would you suggest as a standard quantity for materials?

15-20   Cost of investigating a variance   The Chapman Company production manager has been trying to decide whether a particular variable overhead variance should be investigated. The variance was $300 unfavorable this past month, and it is expected that the variance will continue at the rate of $300 for five more months if nothing is done. The estimated cost to investigate the variance is $600 and the chances are four out of five that nothing can be done to correct the variance even if its cause could be isolated. If the variance is investigated and found to be correctable, the total savings, not considering the cost of the investigation, will be $1,500 (the total cost of the variance over the next five months).

Required: Determine whether the variance should be investigated.

15-21   Expected values and utilities   The sales manager of the Winston Toy Company has been studying a report prepared by an outside consultant. The consultant had been asked to study the advisability of the firm's bringing out a new doll that would be quite different from anything else on the market. The report indicated that there was considerable variation in expectations of sales of the new doll. The consultant concluded that there was about a 60% chance of selling 50,000 dolls and a 40% chance of selling only 10,000 dolls.

The doll would be priced at $12, with variable costs of $8. Incremental fixed costs, primarily for advertising, would be $120,000.

The sales manager decided, on the basis of the expected value of profit, that the doll should be introduced, but the president of the firm was leery. The president said there was a good chance the doll would lose money and the firm had had too many duds in recent years. After some discussion, the president decided that losing a dollar was twice as bad as earning a dollar was good. He instructed the sales manager to prepare a new analysis incorporating his utility, although he did not call it that.

Required

1. Prepare a schedule showing the expected value of profit without consideration of the president's views.
2. Prepare a new schedule in which the president's views are incorporated. Determine whether the doll should be brought out.

15-22   Variance investigation   The Richter Company has experienced an unfavorable variance of $2,000 in May. The production manager has found from past data that 30% of the time a variance of this size is experienced there is nothing wrong with the process and the variance stops. When there is a problem with the process, 60% of the time the variance continues for two additional months, at $2,000 per month and 40% of the time it continues for three additional months, also at $2,000 per month.

Investigating the variance would cost $800. If there is a problem with the production process, it can be corrected 40% of the time. The other 60% of the time nothing can be done. The 40% and 60% probabilities apply both to variances that would continue for two additional months and to those that would continue for three additional months. Once the investigation has been carried out, if it has been determined that the cause of the variance can be corrected, correcting it costs an additional $600.

Required

1. Determine the expected cost of not investigating the variance.
2. Determine the expected cost of investigating the variance.

15-23   Capital budgeting probabilities   The following estimates and probabilities have been prepared by the production manager of the Hector Company. They relate to a proposed $60,000 investment in a machine that will reduce the cost of materials being processed by the firm. The cost of capital is 16%. Ignore taxes.

Annual Cash Savings		Useful Life	
Event	Probability	Event	Probability
$20,000	.30	9 years	.40
14,000	.30	8 years	.40
12,000	.40	6 years	.20

Required

1. Compute the expected values of annual cash savings and useful life. Determine whether the machine should be purchased.
2. The production manager wishes to see whether the machine would be a good investment if each of his most pessimistic estimates, but not both at the same time, came true. Determine whether the investment would be desirable if (a) the useful life is the expected value computed in 1 above, and annual cash flows are only $12,000; (b) the annual cash flows are equal to the expected value computed in 1, and the useful life is only six years.

15-24   Expected values   The managers of the Hawkins Company are trying to decide how to operate in the coming year. The firm rents a machine that performs essential operations on the product; the rental period is one year. The product sells for $10 per unit and has variable costs of $1.

There are three machines available; operating and other data are summarized below.

Machine	Productive Capacity	Annual Rental
Standard	11,000 units	$50,000
DeLuxe	12,000	54,000
Super	13,000	55,500

The sales forecast for the coming year has been based on the 10,000 units sold the prior year; it is expected that demand for the product will increase, but the size of the increase is uncertain. The best estimates are as follows:

Sales in Units	Probability
11,000	.30
12,000	.50
13,000	.20

Required: Determine the best course of action for the firm to take and defend your answer.

15-25   Inventory control—quantity discounts   Alexander Company buys one of its principal products from the Zephyr Company in batches of 2,000. The product costs Alexander $10 and annual demand is 20,000 units. Annual carrying costs are $1.60 per unit, which includes a required rate of return of 10% (all other carrying costs are related to units, not cost), and incremental ordering costs are $160 per order. The current batch size is the EOQ for this product.

Zephyr sells this product only to Alexander and has to set up a production run every time an order is received. There are no carrying costs because Zephyr maintains no inventory, and set-up costs are $1,000 per production run. The production manager of Zephyr asked the sales manager whether it might not be a good idea to offer Alexander a price reduction if Alexander would agree to buy half as often, and double the usual quantity each time.

After some discussion, it was agreed that Alexander would be offered a $.20 price reduction for buying in batches of 4,000 units or more.

Required

1. Compute the annual gain or loss to both Alexander and Zephyr if the price reduction is granted.
2. Suppose that Zephyr offers to supply all 20,000 units at a single time. Determine the lowest price per unit that Zephyr could charge and not reduce its income below the level it would earn supplying the product in batches of 4,000.
3. Determine whether Alexander should buy all of its annual requirements at once, at the price you computed in part 2. (Assume that Alexander would still get the $.20 reduction if it decided to buy 4,000 units at a time.)

15-26 Inventory policy—opportunity cost of lost sales   The Frankel Company carries several products, one of which is the Mytie, which has very heavy carrying costs due to perishability. The Mytie has a contribution margin of $12 per unit, with carrying costs of $4 per unit per year. Sales of Myties are unusual. Only one customer buys them. He comes in every working day and requests either 30, 40, or 50 units. If the firm cannot fill his entire order, the customer goes to a competitor across the street. While the sales manager cannot predict how many units will be ordered on a given day, she does know that the order is for 30 units 20% of the time, 40 units 60% of the time, and 50 units 20% of the time. The lead time for ordering Myties for the Frankel Company is one day. The working year is 200 days.

Required

1. Compute the expected value of one day's sales of Myties.
2. Using the expected value of potential sales, compute the reorder point, assuming that no safety stock is kept.
3. Myties are ordered 20 times a year. How many times will the firm be unable to sell as many Myties as it could because not enough are in stock? What is the lost contribution margin per year due to lost sales?
4. The firm is studying the possibility of carrying a safety stock.
   (a) How much safety stock would have to be carried to eliminate the opportunity cost of lost sales?
   (b) How much would it cost the firm to carry this amount of safety stock?
   (c) Would it be worthwhile to carry that much safety stock?

15-27 Payoff table   *The Evening News* is a large metropolitan newspaper. The paper is sold through dealers who are charged $.20 per copy that they sell. Unsold copies are returned to *The News* and full credit is given. The unsold copies are sold as waste paper for $.02 each.

The News is currently printed in daily batches of 500,000. Management is considering a change in this policy and has asked for your help. A recent study showed the following results.

Papers Returned	Percentage of Time
100,000	20%
50,000	20%
-0-	60%

The study also indicated that when 500,000 copies were all sold, there were often more papers demanded. The demand could not be met because of the limit of 500,000 copies available. The best estimates are that 25% of the time 500,000 copies are demanded, 25% of the time 550,000 are demanded, and 10% of the time 600,000 papers could be sold if they were available.

The variable cost of producing a paper is $.10.

Required

1. Determine the best strategy for *The Evening News*.
2. Determine the value of perfect information.

15-28 Linear programming, graphical solution   The Salinas Furniture Company makes two types of sofas, traditional and modern. Because of their different types of construction they require different amounts of machine time and skilled labor time. The firm has available, per week, 1,000 hours of skilled labor and 1,200 hours of machine time. The variable costs associated with skilled labor, including both wages and variable overhead, are $7 per hour; for machine time, the variable costs are $6 per hour. The firm can sell all of the modern sofas it can make, but only 200 traditional sofas per week.
Additional data on the two sofas are as follows.

	Traditional	Modern
Selling price	$240	$180
Material costs (the only other variable cost)	$ 80	$ 60
Labor hours required, per unit	4	2
Machine-hours required, per unit	3	4

Figure 1 plots the above constraints.

FIGURE 1

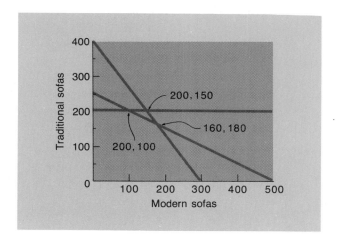

Required

1. Determine the number of each sofa that should be produced each week.
2. Assuming that the price of modern sofas remains constant, at what price for traditional sofas would the firm increase its production of traditional sofas and reduce that of modern sofas?

15-29 Expected values—capital budgeting   The Fleming Company is planning to build a factory to manufacture a new product. The product and the factory are expected to have useful lives of 10 years. No salvage value is expected for any of the components of the factory. The firm's marketing research staff has studied the potential demand for the product and has provided the following information.

	Expected Annual Demand	Probability of Demand
	200,000 units	60%
	250,000 units	40%

The firm can build a factory with capacity of either 200,000 or 250,000 units. Data on the two possible factories are given below.

Capacity	Total Cost, All Depreciable Assets	Annual Fixed Costs Requiring Cash
200,000	$1,500,000	$300,000
250,000	1,800,000	380,000

The product will sell for $5 and have variable costs of $1. The tax rate is 40% and cost of capital is 16%. Straight line depreciation would be used for tax purposes.

Management has decided to base its decision on net present value. The factory that shows the greater favorable difference between the present value of the expected value of future cash flows and the investment required will be built.

Required

Prepare analyses of the expected values of future cash flows under the two investment possibilities. Determine which factory should be built.

CHAPTER 16

STATEMENT OF CHANGES IN FINANCIAL POSITION

We have seen throughout this book that the accounting information system must serve the needs of both financial and managerial accounting. In many cases, information prepared for distribution outside the firm is used, in the same or somewhat different form, by the firm's managers, who may, for example, utilize the data from income statements and balance sheets for such purposes as performance measurement and budgeting.

A third formal statement commonly used in financial accounting is the statement of changes in financial position.[1] This statement is closely related to the cash budget, which is used for managerial accounting purposes (see Chapter 6). This chapter discusses the use and development of the statement of changes in financial position in its two most common forms.

THE INTEREST IN RESOURCE FLOWS

Creditors, investors, and others interested in a particular firm are aware, as are the firm's managers, that the profitability of current operations is but one of the factors important to the survival and growth of the firm. Also of importance are the current flows of financial resources to the firm and the uses to which those resources are put. The firm's managers develop a cash budget to anticipate potential deficiencies of resources for carrying out the firm's plans. Sometimes deficiencies are resolved by obtaining additional resources; sometimes planned activities are curtailed. In either case, the firm's operations involve a balancing of resources available and resources needed. How the managers accomplish this balancing is of interest to both creditors and investors.

The flows of resources into the firm provide the means for repaying debts, bringing out new products, replacing worn-out equipment, etc. These inflows constitute the firm's **financing activities.** The use of available resources, called the **investing activities** of the firm, affects its future. As we saw in Chapters 8 and 9, the firm's decision to invest in new or replacement equipment affects the future profitability of the firm. Timely repayments of debt help to preserve credit standing and access to additional resources. Hence the creditor

---

[1]Since the publication of *Accounting Principles Board Opinion No. 19* (New York: American Institute of Certified Public Accountants, 1971), the statement of changes in financial position has been a required part of any set of financial statements purporting to show financial position and results of operations.

and investor's interest in the firm's resource flows: Where did the firm obtain the resources to support its current outlays for long-term investments? Is the firm making significant investments for the future?

The current year's income statement can show the *current* effects of past financing and investing activities. It can show the current revenues and expenses from past investment, the current interest on all borrowing, and the current return to stockholders. The current year-end balance sheet shows the cumulative financing and investing activities of the firm —assets the firm still has, the total remaining unpaid on borrowings, the accumulated stockholders' investment. A statement of changes in financial position is needed because neither of the other statements provides enough data on the firm's current investing and financing activities, which clearly affect the future of the firm. Though such a statement is, like the other formal statements, after-the-fact or historical in nature, it provides the external observer with further information with which to assess the decisions and performance of the firm's managers and to gain some insight into the firm's prospects.

Cash Flows and the Formal Resource Statement

The formal statement of resource flows (the statement of changes in financial position) may differ from the actual cash flows that would be shown as part of a typical cash budget (Chapter 6) in three ways: in format or classification scheme, in the definition used for *resources*, and in the types of transactions reported.

To meet the information needs of creditors and investors, the formal statement of resource flows is designed to show its relationship to the formal income statement. Hence, net income, an amount not specifically identified in the typical cash budget (showing either budgeted or actual flows), is shown as a separate item on the formal resource statement. Since, as you know, net income is not the same as cash, the separate reporting of this item necessitates several explanatory steps to show the actual cash flow from the firm's operating activities of the period.

The second way in which a formal statement of resource flows may differ from a typical cash budget involves a difference in the concept of *resources*. Although cash is an extremely important asset and the firm cannot get along without it, both managers and external persons recognize that cash flows alone do not necessarily reflect the firm's investing and financing activities. For example, a financial manager would be concerned that temporarily available cash in excess of immediate needs be invested for short periods in highly liquid, income-producing securities such as government bonds. He would view the firm's immediately usable "resources" as cash and these securities. A formal statement of resource flows sometimes reflects this point of view.

An even broader concept of resources is commonly found in formal statements of resource flows. Under this concept, resources are defined as **working capital** (current assets − current liabilities). Reported resource inflows (or outflows) are those transactions or events that give rise to increases (decreases) in working capital rather than cash or the combination of cash and short-term investments. There are at least two reasons to extend the concept of resources beyond cash or near-cash items.

First, because cash is of critical importance, it is not only wise to know something about what is happening to cash, but also to know about the prospects for cash flows over the near future. For the most part, current assets and liabilities are known items that will be turned into cash or require the use of cash within a year. Managers, accountants, and external users of financial statements believe that looking at flows of working capital, which encompasses cash-to-be-received and cash-to-be-paid, affords a broader view of the firm's liquidity than an examination of cash alone.

A second reason for the use of the working capital concept in a statement of resource flows is that such statements are usually prepared for relatively longer time periods than are the detailed cash budgets used by the firm's managers. Such statements most often report flows for a year, or perhaps a quarter, as opposed to the monthly, weekly, or even daily reports needed by managers to plan and control day-to-day operations. With longer periods of time, the importance of the timing of the actual flows of cash declines relative to the total flows of cash. Remember, for example, that in some of the cash budgets studied in Chapter 6, the total inflows for a six-month or one-year period were adequate to cover any short-term borrowing necessitated by temporary imbalances between inflows and outflows for shorter periods. Relatively short-term timing differences between making a sale and collecting cash, or purchasing inventory and paying cash, can be removed from the resource-flow picture over a longer period by using the working capital concept. Working capital includes normal short-term receivables and payables, and inventory. It is not unusual for a firm to apply the working capital concept in an internal resource flow statement prepared as part of the budgeting process. But these statements do not replace the firm's detailed cash budgets and usually cover a longer period of time.

Thus, a statement of resource flows can be based on flows of cash, cash and short-term investments, working capital, or even some other concept of resources. Regardless of the concept used, items included in the definition of resources are often referred to as *funds*. (For some years the statement now called the statement of changes in financial position was called the *funds flow statement* or simply the funds statement.) You will still see the term *funds* used in many published financial statements and we use it interchangeably with *resources*.

The final way in which a formal statement of resource flows may differ from a firm's cash-based resource statement involves the reporting of transactions and events that, no matter what the concept of resources used, do not technically change resources. For example, suppose that a firm issued a ten-year note payable in a transaction to acquire machinery. Since no cash was involved, a report of the firm's cash flows would not include this transaction. And, since neither the machinery nor the ten-year note payable would affect working capital, a report of the firm's resource flows using the working capital concept would also omit this transaction. Yet the acquisition of machinery is obviously an investment by the firm; and the issuance of the note is a financing activity of the firm. So that *all* important investing and financing activities of the firm will be reported, a formal statement of resource flows will include information about significant transactions that did not technically affect resources as defined for that statement.

Categories of Resource Flows

Because the statement of changes in financial position is a formal financial statement, distributed and used outside the firm, the format and content of the statement are governed by generally accepted accounting principles, the ground rules of financial accounting.

Regardless of the concept of resources used, there are very few firm rules to be applied in the presentation of a formal statement of changes in financial position. The first such rule involves the basic format of the statement and is quite simple. The statement should have two basic parts: *resource inflows*, often called *funds provided*, and *resource outflows*, often called *funds used* or *funds applied*. The second rule requires the reporting of a single net flow relating to the firm's basic operating activities. This single flow is identified as *funds or resources provided by operations*, if resources were increased as a result of such activities, or as *funds used for operations*, if resources were decreased as a result of such activities. The third rule is that the statement must show those financing and investing activities that did not affect resources under whatever definition is being used. Such activities are primarily the acquisition of assets through the issuance of long-term debt or stock and the liquidation of long-term debt through the issuance of stock.

Although there is no absolute requirement to do so, it is perhaps universal practice, as explained in the preceding section, to clearly and specifically report the firm's net income in connection with its funds flow from operations. Because net income is not likely to represent the operating resource flows of the firm under any of the common definitions of resources, the formal statement invariably includes a section that explains the difference between net income and resources provided by operations.

A skeleton outline of a formal statement of changes in financial position is presented in Exhibit 16-1. Since a firm's normal operations are expected, under normal circumstances, to produce a net inflow of resources rather than a net outflow, the outline shows that funds were provided by operations (that is, that resources were increased).

The section of the statement entitled "Adjustments for items that affected net income but did not affect resources in the same way" contains the explanation of the difference between net income and the resources flowing from operations. The content of this section will depend, to some extent, on the concept of resources used to develop the statement. The

Exhibit 16-1
Example Company
Statement of Changes in Financial Position
for the Year 19X7

Resources provided by:

Operations:

    Net income   quto. Dml

    Adjustments for items that affected net income but did not affect resources in the same way:

        _aeyo aoiou dxpo quto au   ıoiou dxp

        ıoiou dxpo guto auoi bxg   ıxop qutc   ɔmbent d

    Funds provided by operations   _aeyo aoi

Other sources:

        ıxop quto auoi. Dtnsti px   aeyo aoi

        quto. Cmbent dtnsti pxrn: _aeyo aoi   ıoiou dxp

Total resources provided during the year   ıxop qutc

Resources used for:

        ɔmbent dtnsti pxrnxo. D: quto. Dml

        ɔmbent dtnsti. Aoiou dxp   ɔmbent d

Total resources used during the year   quto. Cmt

Net increase in resources   ɔmbent d

Other financing and investing activities:

        _aeyo aoiou dxpo quto av   ıoiou dxp

        ıoiou dxpo quto auoi bxy   ıxop qutc

concept of resources also determines, to a degree, what items will be shown as resources provided by other sources, as resources used, and as other financing and investing activities. But in most cases, it makes little difference in these sections whether the cash or the working capital concept of resources is used.

With this basic outline in mind, we shall show the development of a formal statement of changes in financial position using the cash concept and the working capital concept of resources. The same basic data will be used in both cases.

Data for Illustration

We shall illustrate the preparation of a formal statement of changes in financial position with the USL Corporation, a retailing firm. Because the statement describes changes in the balance-sheet items during the period and relates directly to the income statement for the period, we have provided these financial statements for the company in Exhibits 16-2 and 16-3. Let

Exhibit 16-2
USL Corporation
Balance Sheets as of December 31

	19X5	19X4	Increase (Decrease)
Current assets:			
Cash	$ 239,500	$ 360,000	($120,500)
Accounts receivable	280,000	150,000	130,000
Inventory	190,000	100,000	90,000
Total current assets	709,500	610,000	
Noncurrent assets:			
Plant and equipment, at cost	890,000	600,000	290,000
Less: accumulated depreciation	115,000	60,000	55,000
Total noncurrent assets	775,000	540,000	
Total assets	$1,484,500	$1,150,000	
Current liabilities:			
Accounts payable	$ 85,000	$ 55,000	30,000
Accrued expenses	50,000	5,000	45,000
Total current liabilities	135,000	60,000	
Bonds payable, due 19X9	100,000	100,000	—
Total liabilities	235,000	160,000	
Owners' equity:			
Common stock	860,000	800,000	60,000
Retained earnings	389,500	190,000	199,500
Total owners' equity	1,249,500	990,000	
Total equities	$1,484,500	$1,150,000	

Exhibit 16-3
USL Corporation
Combined Statement of Income and Retained
Earnings for the Year 19X5

Sales		$1,000,000
Cost of goods sold:		
Beginning inventory	$100,000	
Purchases	540,000	
Cost of goods available for sale	640,000	
Less: ending inventory	190,000	
Cost of goods sold		450,000
Gross profit		550,000
Operating expenses:		
Depreciation	56,000	
Other operating expenses	264,500	
Total operating expenses		320,500
Net income		229,500
Retained earnings at the beginning of the year		190,000
		419,500
Dividends declared and paid during the year		30,000
Retained earnings at the end of the year		$389,500

Exhibit 16-4
USL Corporation
Final Cash Budget for 19X5

	Quarter				Total for the Year
	One	Two	Three	Four	
Beginning balance					$ 360,000
Receipts:					
From sales to customers	rnxo	ɔ. Px	ɔi bx	‹o bɔ	870,000
Sale of equipment	‹o bɔ	rnxc	ɔ. Px	xpo	9,000
Issue of new stock	‹po	‹o bɔ	rnxc	o qu	60,000
Total receipts	o qu	po q	o bɔ	oi bx	939,000
Total available	ɔi bx	ɔuoi	po q	o. Pɔ	1,299,000
Disbursements:					
For purchase of merchandise	rnxc	ɔi bx	ɔuoi	po ɔ	510,000
For operating expenses	‹o bɔ	ɔ. Pɔ	ɔi bx	ɔ qu	219,500
For new equipment	po c	rnxo	ɔ. Pɔ	ɔi bx	300,000
Dividends	ɔuoi	‹o bɔ	‹nxo	ɔ. Px	30,000
Total disbursements	ɔi bx	‹po	o bɔ	rnxc	1,059,500
Balance at end of period	o. Pɔ	o qu	rnxo	o bɔ	$ 239,500

us also assume that the company's actual detailed cash flows corresponded to its budgeted flows as they appear in Exhibit 16-4. The cash flows in individual quarters within the year are omitted from the exhibit because we are interested in the resource flows for the entire year.

RESOURCES AS CASH

From the comparative balance sheets we can see that USL's cash decreased by $120,500 during the year. Our objective is to develop a formal statement identifying the basic sources of cash inflows and the basic purposes of cash outflows that produced this decrease.

By referring to the company's final cash budget (Exhibit 16-4) we could readily determine the various major components for the formal statement. The net cash flow from operations would be $140,500, determined as follows:

Operating Cash Flows for 19X5

Inflows—receipts from customers		$870,000
Outflows:		
Purchases of merchandise	$510,000	
Payments for operating expenses	219,500	
		729,500
Net cash inflow from operations		$140,500

The remaining cash inflows (from the sale of equipment and the issuance of stock) would be "other" (nonoperating) sources of cash. The other cash outflows (for dividends and purchases of equipment) would be resource uses (nonoperating). But a formal statement of changes in financial position normally shows not only the identification of the major components but also a direct link with the income statement. That is, the net flow from operations is reported with specific reference to net income, and the statement shows how the net flow from operations is derived from the amount reported as net income. This derivation is sometimes called a reconciliation of net income and cash flow from operations and provides the content of the section of the formal statement entitled "adjustments."

Reconciliation of Net Income and Cash from Operations

It is not a difficult task to derive the net operating cash flow from the net income if you keep in mind the makeup of the income statement and the basic facts underlying a cash budget. Why are the revenues on the income statement not the same as the cash collections from customers as shown on the cash budget? Why are the cost of goods sold and operating expenses not the same as the cash disbursed for purchases and expenses as shown on the cash budget?

The difference between sales and cash receipts has two causes. (1) Early in the year, cash was received from customers for sales made in the prior year. These amounts constituted the beginning balance in accounts receivable. (2) Late in the year, sales were made but the cash was not collected in the same year. Amounts still due from these sales constitute the accounts receivable at the end of the year. Thus, net income reflects sales made this year regardless of the period in which cash was collected, and cash receipts reflect cash collected this year for sales regardless of the period in which the sales were made. Hence, to move from the amount of net income to the cash flow, we must (1) add the cash receipts on accounts receivable at the beginning of the year, and (2) subtract the accounts receivable at the end of the year. In the case of USL Corporation, we would add $150,000 and subtract $280,000, or we can simply subtract the increase of $130,000. This will be the first "adjustment" on the formal statement. (You may want to look briefly now at the formal statement shown in Exhibit 16-5.)

Let us consider next the difference between cost of goods sold ($450,000) and the amount of cash disbursed for merchandise ($510,000). Two major factors are responsible for this difference.

First, the beginning and ending inventory affect cost of goods sold for the year regardless of the period in which payment for that merchandise occurred. In USL's case, the beginning inventory increased cost of goods sold by $100,000, and the ending inventory decreased cost of goods sold by $190,000. Cost of goods sold was lower and hence net income was higher by $90,000 ($190,000 − $100,000) because of consideration of inventory items with no regard whatever for the timing of cash payments for those items. Thus, net income reflects the effects of inventories, and cash payments for merchandise reflect payments regardless of whether the items are on hand. Hence, to remove from the amount of net income the effect of inventories which have no direct relationship with cash flows, we must add the beginning inventory, and subtract the ending inventory. Or, we can simply subtract the $90,000 increase in inventory. This is the second adjustment in the formal statement.

The second reason for the difference between the cost of goods sold and the actual cash outflows for merchandise is the fact that cost of goods sold shows the purchases made this year regardless of when the purchased merchandise was paid for. From our knowledge of cash budgets we know two things. (1) In the early part of the year, cash was paid for purchases made in the prior year. The amounts of these payments can be found by referring to the beginning balance in accounts payable. (2) Late in the year, purchases were made but the cash was not disbursed. Amounts still unpaid for these purchases constitute the ending balance in accounts payable. Thus cost of goods sold is higher than cash payments, and net income is lower than cash inflows from operations because of the timing difference in the payment of purchases. To move from the amount of net income to the cash operating flow for the year we must (1) subtract the cash payments on accounts payable at the beginning of the year, and (2) add the amount not yet paid (the ending accounts payable). In the case of USL, we would subtract $55,000 and add $85,000, or we can simply add the $30,000 increase in accounts payable. This will be the third adjustment.

Let us now consider the difference between operating expenses and cash disbursements for such expenses. One reason for the difference is well known to you. Operating expenses on the income statement include depreciation, which does not appear in the cash budget because it does not involve a cash disbursement. Depreciation expense reduced net income without having any effect on cash flows this period. Hence, to remove from net income the effect of depreciation expense we must add the amount of depreciation (in USL's case, $56,000). This is the fourth adjustment.

There is a second reason for the difference between the operating expenses and cash disbursements for such expenses. Again, as we saw from preparing cash budgets: (1) in the early part of the year cash will be paid to liquidate liabilities for expenses of the prior year (called accrued expenses); and (2) in the later part expenses will be incurred for which cash will not be disbursed until the next year. Thus, net income for the current period has been reduced by this year's expenses regardless of the year in which the expenses were paid for, while disbursements of the year include only current payments for expense items regardless of the year in which the expense was incurred. Hence, to move from the amount of net income to the net cash flow, we must (1) subtract the cash payments for expenses accrued at the beginning of the year, and (2) add the expenses accrued at the end of the year. In the case of USL, we would subtract $5,000 and add $50,000, or we could simply add $45,000. This final adjustment explains the difference between net income and the cash flow from operations; the reconciliation is now complete and the remainder of the statement can be prepared.

The Formal Statement

The formal statement of changes in financial position, using the cash concept of resources, is shown in Exhibit 16-5. Because such statements can apply different definitions of resources, the title of the statement specifically refers to the resource definition used.

Exhibit 16-5
USL Corporation
Statement of Changes in Financial Position—Cash Basis
for the Year 19X5

Resources provided by:		
Operations:		
Net income		$229,500
Adjustments for items that affected net income but did not affect resources in the same way:		
Increase in accounts receivable	($130,000)	
Increase in inventory	(90,000)	
Increase in accounts payable	30,000	
Depreciation for the year	56,000	
Increase in accrued expenses	45,000	
Total adjustments		(89,000)
Funds provided by operations		140,500
Other sources:		
Issuance of common stock	60,000	
Sale of plant and equipment	9,000	
Funds provided by other sources		69,000
Total resources provided during the year		209,500
Resources used for:		
Purchase of plant and equipment	300,000	
Dividends	30,000	
Total resources used during the year		330,000
Net decrease in cash resources		$120,500

The five adjustments appearing in the reconciliation of net income and funds provided by operations are listed in the order in which they are discussed in the preceding section. It is almost universal practice, however, for the depreciation adjustment to be shown first.

Reviewing all of the adjustments, you can see that four of them are quite different from the fifth. The depreciation adjustment is required because depreciation expense, as shown on the income statement, has no relation at all to the operating inflows or outflows of funds for the period; it does not even appear in the cash budget. The other four adjustments (for the changes in accounts receivable and payable, inventory, and accrued expenses) all directly relate to specific operating flows that do appear in the cash budget for the period. The adjustments are needed because of relatively short-term timing differences between cash flows and appearance on the income statement. Once you understand the reasoning for the treatment of these changes in the reconciliation you may find the following general rules helpful. If the change is a decrease in a current asset item or an increase in a current liability item, the change is added to net income in the reconciliation. If the change is an increase in a current asset item or a decrease in a current liability item, the change is subtracted from net income in the reconciliation.

Note that the net change in cash as shown on the formal statement (a decrease of $120,500) agrees with the decrease in cash as shown in the comparative balance sheets (Exhibit 16-2). The two statements are thus linked together, with the statement of changes in financial position describing the cash inflows and outflows that contributed to the decline in the resource, cash, shown on the balance sheet. The name, "changes in financial position," is derived from this link with the balance sheet, which is called, on occasion, a statement of financial position.

Note also that the amount shown as cash provided by operations ($140,500) is exactly the same as we computed on page 567 by reference to the firm's actual cash flows. Obviously, the method used on page 567 is less laborious than the reconciliation approach discussed in detail in the preceding section and shown in Exhibit 16-5. Nevertheless, it is almost universal practice to present such a reconciliation. The statement can then be directly linked to the balance sheet (through the cash balance) and to the income statement (through the reference to net income).

Working Without the Cash Budget

Because of the availability of the information on the year's actual cash flows for USL Corporation, it was relatively easy to identify the cash flows related to operations and determine the existence of other cash flows (sales and purchases of equipment, etc.). Note, however, that we could actually have *computed* the cash flow from operations by simply following the procedures used in the reconciliation. That is, we did not need the actual cash flow information. When actual flow information is not available, it is usually still possible to determine the other (nonoperating) flows by studying the other financial statements.

Look again at the comparative balance sheets in Exhibit 16-2. Almost every item on the balance sheet showed a change between the two years. We know that the changes in accounts payable, accounts receivable, inventory, accrued expenses, and part of the change in accumulated depreciation relate to operations. What brought about the other changes? They must be related to other financing and investing activities of the firm. By applying a little common sense, we can reach tentative conclusions about the nature of those other activities, and then, with a few inquiries, we can complete the formal statement.

Below is a summary of the changes in balance-sheet items other than those related to normal operations.

Item	Change Increase (Decrease)
Retained earnings	$199,500
Common stock	60,000
Accumulated depreciation	55,000
Plant and equipment	290,000

The combined statement of income and retained earnings (Exhibit 16-3) tells us that the change in retained earnings is due to the net income and the payment of dividends. So we know that there was a nonoperating outflow of cash for dividends. The increase in common stock must have been brought about by the issuance of additional stock; whether or not the stock was issued for cash can be determined by inquiry. If for cash, we can include the issuance among the nonoperating sources of cash in our formal statement. If the stock was issued in return for plant and equipment, we have a financing and investing activity that did not affect cash and should be reported separately in the final section of the formal statement.

The increase in accumulated depreciation requires a little more analysis. From the income statement we know that the depreciation for the year was $56,000, which *should* have increased accumulated depreciation by the same amount. Since the increase is only $55,000, something must have happened during the year to decrease accumulated depreciation by $1,000. From your knowledge of financial accounting you know that accumulated depreciation decreases when a depreciable asset is sold.[2] You could conclude, then, that some asset was sold and could then inquire further as to its cost and selling price. Let us assume we learn that some equipment that had cost $10,000 and had accumulated depreciation of $1,000 was sold for $9,000. The $9,000 would be reported as cash provided by other sources.

Plant and equipment was decreased by $10,000 when equipment was sold, as we determined above. Yet over the year plant and equipment increased by $290,000; therefore, there must have been a total addition to plant and equipment of $300,000. Here again, inquiry would determine whether or not the acquisition involved only cash. If only cash was involved (as in USL's case), this outflow would show as a use of resources. If the acquisition involved both cash and, say, common stock issued during the year, the formal statement would show both.

It is possible, as we have shown, to develop the information for a statement of changes in financial position by analyzing the other formal financial statements and asking a few questions. For the managers of the firm with access to information about actual cash flows, the task is relatively easy. Without access to information about actual flows, the task is still not impossible. And for anyone—manager, investor, or creditor—presented with a complete formal statement of changes in financial position, the main task is to understand

---

[2]The cost of the asset is removed from the asset account, and the accumulated depreciation on that asset is removed from the Accumulated Depreciation account.

its contents and implications. Before discussing the information presented in the statement we will develop another statement based on the working capital concept of resources.

RESOURCES AS WORKING CAPITAL

A statement of changes in financial position based on the working capital concept of resources must meet the same four general requirements as the statement based on the cash concept. The statement must show (1) both inflows and outflows of resources, (2) the resources provided by operations, (3) the firm's net income and its relationship with (reconciliation to) resources provided by operations, and (4) other financing and investing activities that did not involve resources as defined.

The objective of a statement using the working capital concept is to describe the inflows and outflows of resources now described as working capital. Because cash is a part of working capital, changes in cash may change working capital. But many changes in cash do not affect working capital at all. For example, collections of accounts receivable or payments of accounts payable do not affect the amount of the firm's working capital. Purchases of inventory on account do not affect total working capital, nor do payments of accrued expenses.

You should recognize that these examples were among several factors involved in the reconciliation of reported net income and the cash flows from operations. When the concept of resources is broadened from cash to working capital, the statement of changes in financial position is less complex, primarily because the reconciliation of net income and resources provided by operations is less complex.

Reconciliation of Net Income and Working Capital from Operations

Most of the factors that create differences between the components of net income and the increases and decreases in cash do not create differences between those components and the increases and decreases in working capital.

As an example, consider the difference between reported revenues and cash receipts from customers. The difference is totally related to the accounts receivable at the beginning and the end of the year. In our reconciliation of net income and cash from operations we had to add the collections of prior years' accounts receivable because these collections increased cash this year without increasing this year's income. But both cash and accounts receivable are current assets and hence components of working capital. The collection of cash on old accounts receivable does not increase working capital this year. Cash goes up and accounts receivable go down; there is no increase (inflow) of working capital. Similarly, in our reconciliation of net income and cash from operations we had to subtract the amounts relating to sales for which no cash was collected this year; we did this because net income had been increased by such sales while cash had not. But the sale of merchandise on account this year increases both net income *and* working capital this year: sales (and net income) go up, and working capital, in the form of accounts receivable, goes up.

Look again at the reconciliation of net income and cash flow from operations (Exhibit 16-5). Almost all of the adjustments involve items that are not cash but part of working capital. In a statement of resource flows based on the working capital concept, these adjustments are not necessary because the components of net income reflect increases or decreases consistent with the increases or decreases in working capital.

Let us illustrate by analyzing one more of the adjustments, that for the change in accrued expenses. We had to subtract from net income the accrued expenses at the beginning of the year because cash was used to pay for them even though they were not included in this year's expenses. But this payment for last year's expenses reduced neither income nor working capital. (The payment reduced current liabilities and current assets by the same amount.) Hence, in reconciling net income and working capital from operations, the cash payment of the previous year's accrued expenses is irrelevant and no adjustment is required. Neither is there a need to adjust for the accrued expenses at the end of the year. Net income was reduced because of the recognition of these expenses, and working capital was also reduced because a current liability was increased.

Analysis would also show that any of the adjustments related to components of working capital are not needed to reconcile net income and working capital from operations. Are there *any* differences between net income and working capital provided by operations? Without looking at the adjustments you should be able to develop a *general* answer to the question. The only differences between net income and working capital provided by operations must result from items that affected net income but did not have a similar effect on working capital.

Very few items meet this description. The most obvious is depreciation expense, which reduces net income but does not involve any components of working capital. For USL Corporation, the only difference between net income and working capital from operations is depreciation expense. In other cases, expenses similar to depreciation (depletion of natural resources, amortization of intangible assets such as franchises or patents) would fit the description and thus qualify as adjustments.[3]

The Formal Statement

With respect to nonoperating flows of resources, all other items appearing in the statement of changes in financial position under the cash concept would also appear in the statement based on the working capital concept. In each item, cash and working capital were both affected by the same amount. A formal statement using the working capital concept appears in Exhibit 16-6.

The statement shows that working capital increased during the year by $24,500. Is this correct? To prove this we can refer to the comparative balance sheets and compute the change in working capital during the year. A schedule computing the change is shown in Exhibit 16-7. The schedule shows that working capital did indeed increase by $24,500, from $550,000 at December 31, 19X4, to $574,500 at December 31, 19X5.[4] Thus, this formal statement, like the one prepared using the cash concept of resources, is directly linked to the balance sheet (through the working capital change) and to the income statement (through the reference to net income).

We noted earlier that an individual trying to develop the cash basis statement of changes in financial position may not have immediate access to the details of actual cash flows for the period but could still, with careful analysis and some inquiries, accomplish

---

[3]Those familiar with the accounting for bonds payable and income taxes should recognize that bond discount or premium amortization and deferred taxes would also qualify as adjustments.

[4]In published financial statements, which are governed by *Accounting Principles Board Opinion No. 19,* a schedule of working capital such as that shown in Exhibit 16-7 is required to be presented when the working capital concept of resources is used in the preparation of the statement of changes in financial position.

Exhibit 16-6
USL Corporation
Statement of Changes in Financial Position—Working Capital Basis
for the Year 19X5

Resources provided by:		
Operations:		
Net income		$229,500
Adjustment for items that affected net income but did not affect resources in the same way:		
Depreciation for the year		56,000
Funds provided by operations		285,500
Other sources:		
Issuance of common stock	$ 60,000	
Sale of plant and equipment	9,000	
Funds provided by other sources		69,000
Total resources provided during the year		354,500
Resources used for:		
Purchase of plant and equipment	300,000	
Dividends	30,000	
Total resources used during the year		330,000
Net increase in working capital resources		$ 24,500

Exhibit 16-7
USL Corporation
Schedule of Working Capital
at December 31

	19X5	19X4	Increase (Decrease) in Working Capital
Current assets:			
Cash	$239,500	$360,000	($120,500)
Accounts receivable	280,000	150,000	130,000
Inventory	190,000	100,000	90,000
Total current assets	709,500	610,000	
Current liabilities:			
Accounts payable	85,000	55,000	(30,000)
Accrued expenses	50,000	5,000	(45,000)
Total current liabilities	135,000	60,000	
Working capital	$574,500	$550,000	$ 24,500

the task. The same applies to a formal statement using the working capital concept of resources. The comparative balance sheets would be studied to identify changes that have occurred, and the statement of income would be reviewed for clues to the reasons for the changes. With the answers to a few careful questions (such as those raised in the analysis of the cash basis statement), a statement not significantly different from that in Exhibit 16-6 could be developed.

OPERATING FLOWS—A SPECIAL PROBLEM

In illustrating the development of a statement of changes in financial position under either concept of resources, very common transactions were used. For example, depreciation was the only item shown as affecting income and not affecting one of the current asset or liability accounts. Stock was issued for cash and equipment was acquired for cash. The sale of plant and equipment was assumed to be at book value, so no gain or loss appeared in the income statement.

Of the transactions used, the one least likely to occur in a more realistic situation is the sale of a plant asset at its book value. If the asset has been held for some time, it is highly unlikely that its current market value is equal to its original cost, or, in the case of a depreciable asset, to its undepreciated cost. Depreciation is, as you know from financial accounting, a process of cost allocation and not a valuation process.

When a noncurrent asset is sold at any price other than its book value, the gain or loss on the sale will appear in the income statement. The cash or working capital flow associated with the sale will be equal to its selling price, while net income will be affected by only the gain or loss on the sale. Such a transaction produces an inflow of resources but the inflow is not related to operations; the gain or loss produces a change in net income, but not because of operations. In a reconciliation of net income with resources provided by operations, the effect of the gain or loss must be removed from net income. Whatever resources are provided by the sale will be shown under "other sources of funds."

For example, suppose a particular long-term investment that had cost $30,000 was sold during the year for $45,000 in cash. The resources (cash or working capital) provided by this sale were $45,000 and this amount should be reported as an other (nonoperating) source of funds. But the $15,000 gain on the sale must be included in the net income for the year. Hence, net income has been increased by $15,000 as a result of a nonoperating inflow of resources of $45,000. In the statement of changes in financial position for this firm, the $15,000 gain would be *subtracted* from net income as one of the adjustments to arrive at funds from operations, and the total selling price, $45,000, would appear as a nonoperating source of funds.

If the sale of a noncurrent asset results in a loss rather than a gain, the same line of reasoning would lead to an adjustment of net income that *added* the loss. For example, suppose that the long-term investment described above as costing $30,000 was sold for $20,000 during the year. Net income will have been lower because of the $10,000 loss sustained on the sale. Yet there would have been no outflow of resources at all; rather, the sale would have produced a $20,000 inflow of resources. In the firm's statement of changes in financial position, the $10,000 loss would be added to net income as one of the adjustments to arrive at funds from operations in order to remove the effect of this nonoperating transaction. The $20,000 inflow of resources as a result of the sale would be shown among the nonoperating sources of funds.

Exhibit 16-8 contains a statement of changes in financial position for a company that sustained both a loss and a gain as a result of sales of noncurrent assets. Note that this statement is not significantly different from previous examples except that provision has been made for the additional adjustments to net income.

Exhibit 16-8
Lenseth Company
Statement of Changes in Financial Position—Working Capital Basis
for the Year 19X7

Resources provided by:		
Operations:		
Net income		$203,000
Adjustments for items that affected net income but did not affect resources in the same way:		
Depreciation for the year	$25,000	
Loss on sale of equipment	12,000	
Gain on sale of investment in stock of Girard Company	(15,000)	
Total adjustments		22,000
Funds provided by operations		225,000
Other sources:		
Sale of equipment	13,000	
Sale of investment in the stock of Girard Company	45,000	
Funds provided by other sources		58,000
Total resources provided during the year		283,000
Resources used for:		
Dividends	143,000	
Purchases of new equipment	110,000	
Total resources used during the year		253,000
Net increase in working capital resources		$ 30,000
Other financing and investing activities:		
Issuance of long-term notes for new equipment		$180,000

CONCLUDING COMMENTS

The headings and descriptions used in the various parts of a statement of changes in financial position may vary from company to company. A company may use the words *cash, working capital, resources,* or *funds* where we have used other terms. The heading "Adjustments for items that affected net income but did not affect resources in the same way" is actually a relatively uncommon description for the items used to reconcile net income and resources provided by operations. A more common heading would be "Adjustments for items that did not affect working capital." If the only adjustment were for depreciation or similar items, a heading more descriptive of the adjustments is used, such as "Adjustments for noncash expenses."

The title used for the adjustments section should be descriptive of the purpose of the adjustments. A common misconception has arisen over the years that depreciation is a source of funds. This misconception is understandable when we consider that depreciation is added to net income to arrive at funds provided by operations. The misunderstanding has not been reduced by carelessly prepared funds statements that provide no heading at all for the adjustments but simply list the individual adjustments, starting with depreciation, after the net income. As you know, depreciation is neither a use nor a source of funds. It requires no current outlay of cash or working capital; an outflow of funds occurred at the time the depreciating asset was acquired. It brings in neither cash nor working capital; funds are provided by revenues.

There is, as a matter of fact, one sense in which it could be said that depreciation *influences* current funds flows. Because depreciation is deductible for tax purposes, a firm's income tax payment (which is an operating use of funds) is lower than it would have been had there been no depreciation to deduct. Hence the net funds from operations are larger than would be the case had there been no depreciation. But if the firm had no revenues and still had depreciation, there would be no funds from operations. Thus, depreciation can help the firm *retain* funds, but only when there is some source producing an inflow of funds to be retained.

Because the statement of changes in financial position is required for companies that distribute their financial statements publicly, it will normally be prepared by the firm's accountants (as are the balance sheet and income statement). The actual development of the statement can involve many complex problems that are considered in other, more advanced accounting courses. Nevertheless, the nonaccountant, inside or outside the firm, must have a basic understanding of the development of the statement and of the alternative concepts of resources on which the statement is based.

SUMMARY

Information on flows of working capital or cash is important to readers of financial statements. The statement of changes in financial position provides information on the sources and uses of the firm's financial resources. This information can be used to determine how the firm was financed, whether from internal generation of resources, from long-term creditors, from stockholders, or from combinations of all of these sources. The information in the statement also enables the reader to determine how the firm used its financial resources, whether it bought plant assets, retired long-term debt, paid dividends to its stockholders.

Either one of two approaches to preparing the statement are commonly used, a working capital basis or a cash basis. The reader can convert a statement from one basis to the other by using data from comparative balance sheets.

KEY TERMS

current asset	investing activities
current liability	operating activities
financing activities	statement of changes in financial position
funds provided by operations	working capital

KEY FORMULA

Working capital $= $ current assets $-$ current liabilities

Comparative balance sheets and a combined statement of income and retained earnings for the Harold Company are given below.

The following additional information is also available to you.
1. Common stock was issued for $200 cash this year.
2. Investments costing $40 were sold at a gain of $30.
3. Equipment costing $30 and with accumulated depreciation of $20 was sold for $10.

Required

1. Determine the cash provided by operations.
2. Prepare a statement of changes in financial position using the cash concept of resources.
3. Determine the change in working capital for the year 19X7.
4. Determine the amount of working capital provided by operations for the year 19X7.
5. Without preparing a formal statement, reconcile the change in working capital as computed in part 3, with the working capital provided by operations, as computed in part 4.

Harold Company
Balance Sheets at December 31

	19X7	19X6	Change Increase (Decrease)
Current assets:			
Cash	$ 205	$ 190	$15
Accounts receivable	420	430	(10)
Inventory	350	310	40
Total current assets	975	930	
Investments	120	160	(40)
Plant and equipment	2,500	2,250	250
Accumulated depreciation	(800)	(720)	80
Total assets	$2,795	$2,620	
Current liabilities:			
Accounts payable	$ 210	$ 220	(10)
Accrued expenses	65	70	(5)
Total current liabilities	275	290	
Long-term debt	100	250	(150)
Total liabilities	375	540	
Owners' equity:			
Common stock, no par value	1,800	1,600	200
Retained earnings	620	480	140
Total owners' equity	2,420	2,080	
Total equities	$2,795	$2,620	

Harold Company
Combined Statement of Income and Retained Earnings*
for the Year 19X7

Sales		$1,950
Cost of goods sold:		
Beginning inventory	$ 310	
Purchases	890	
Cost of goods available for sale	1,200	
Less: ending inventory	350	
Cost of goods sold		850
Gross profit on sales		1,100
Operating expenses:		
Depreciation	100	
Other operating expenses	300	
Total operating expenses		400
Operating income		700
Other income—gain on sale of investments		30
Net income		730
Retained earnings at December 31, 19X6		480
		1,210
Dividends declared and paid		590
Retained earnings at December 31, 19X7		$ 620

*In a practical situation, income taxes would probably be shown as a separate
expense at the bottom of the income statement (just before net income).

Answers to Review Problem

1. Because we do not have access to information about the firm's actual cash flows for the year, we must compute the cash flow from operations by making the adjustments to net income.

    Review of the company's income statement reveals the need for three adjustments: (a) depreciation, a noncash expense, has reduced income; (b) the sale of a long-term investment, a *nonoperating* transaction, has increased income to the extent of the gain on the sale; and (c) the change in inventory, which is not directly related to cash flows, has increased net income. The change in inventory (an increase) produced an increase in net income because the ending inventory, which reduced cost of goods sold and hence increased income, was greater than the beginning inventory, which increased cost of goods sold and hence decreased income.

    We can then turn to the comparative balance sheets for any other facts that might cause the reported components of net income (revenues, cost of goods sold, and operating expenses) to be different from the actual cash flows relating to operations. Review of the comparative balance sheets reveals the need for three additional adjustments: (d) the change in accounts receivable means there is a difference between the cash inflows from operations and the reported revenues; (e) the change in accounts payable means there is a difference between cash outflows for operations and the reported cost of goods sold because there is a difference between cash outflows for purchases and the reported purchases; and (f) the change in accrued expenses means that there is a difference between the operating cash outflows for expenses and the reported operating expenses.

    Changes in the other balance-sheet items, though they may have affected cash, would not have given rise to operating cash flows. If such changes affected net income, their effect should be eliminated from net income as we compute the cash flow from operating activities. Let us look at the other balance-sheet changes.

A change in investments would be a nonoperating change, a sale or purchase. A cash flow from such a change would not result from operations. We have already recognized that net income must be adjusted to remove the effect of the sale of investments on net income (adjustment (b) above). A change in plant and equipment too would be a nonoperating change, a sale or purchase. The income statement shows no evidence that either type of nonoperating change affected net income. The only operations-related effect of a change in accumulated depreciation is the depreciation for the year, which has no effect on cash flow from operations. We have already identified an adjustment (a) to remove the effect of the depreciation expense from the net income.

The changes in long-term debt and common stock, whatever their causes, would give rise to nonoperating flows. Again, there is no evidence (such as a gain from retirement of debt) in the income statement that such nonoperating changes affected net income. The change in retained earnings is explained by net income, which we have already considered, and the payment of dividends, which is a nonoperating flow that did not affect net income.

Thus, we can compute the cash provided by operations by starting with net income and making the six adjustments (a) through (f).

	Net income		$730
	Adjustments for items that affected net income but did not affect cash the same way:		
(a)	Depreciation for the year	$100	
(b)	Gain on sale of long-term investment	(30)	
(c)	Increase in inventory	(40)	
(d)	Decrease in accounts receivable	10	
(e)	Decrease in accounts payable	(10)	
(f)	Decrease in accrued expenses	(5)	
	Net adjustment		25
	Cash provided by operations		$755

2. In part 1, the information needed for one section of the formal statement, cash provided by operations, was developed. Our objective now is to find any other inflows or outflows of cash (nonoperating flows). For this information we refer again to the balance-sheet changes that did not affect the cash flow from operations. The changes, already discussed briefly, are summarized below.

Item	Change Increase (Decrease)
Investments	($40)
Plant and equipment	250
Accumulated depreciation	80
Long-term debt	(150)
Common stock	200
Retained earnings	140

Let us examine each of these changes carefully.

The decrease in investments was the result of a sale which produced a gain of $30. Since the investments that were sold cost $40 (the amount of the decrease), the proceeds from the sale must have been $70. Hence we have a nonoperating cash inflow of $70 to be reported on the statement.

The normal reason for an increase in plant and equipment would be a purchase of new equipment. Remember, however, that each change shown in the comparative balance sheets is a *net* change which could be the result of more than one transaction. We already know that during the year the company sold equipment that originally cost $30. This transaction would have *reduced* plant and equipment by $30. Thus, the purchases of new plant and equipment must have been enough to offset this decrease and produce a net increase in plant and equipment of $250, or $280 ($250 + $30). We have, then, two transactions: sale of equipment and purchase of equipment, both of which involve nonoperating cash flows. The old equipment was sold for $10, which amount should be reported as a nonoperating cash inflow. The new equipment must have cost $280, reported as a nonoperating use of cash.

Depreciation, as we know, neither produces nor uses cash. Hence, the change in accumulated depreciation is not a cash inflow or outflow. We can explain the change from what we already know about the firm's activities for the year. Accumulated depreciation increased by $100 because of the current year's depreciation expense as shown on the income statement. Accumulated depreciation decreased by $20 because an asset on which depreciation of $20 had accumulated was sold. The net change is an increase of $80 (an increase of $100 offset by a decrease of $20). We already identified, in our analysis of plant and equipment, that a nonoperating cash inflow of $10 should be reported in connection with the sale of equipment.

The normal reason for a decline in long-term debt is that some of the debt was repaid. Such a repayment would be a nonoperating outflow or use of cash. Since we have no evidence to indicate some other reason for the decrease, we shall report the decline as a nonoperating use of cash in the amount of $150.

Common stock increased by $200 during the year; the normal explanation for such an increase is that additional shares of stock were issued. This conclusion is confirmed by the information obtained at the beginning of the problem, and we can include among the nonoperating sources of cash the issuance of additional stock for $200.

The lower portion of the combined statement of income and retained earnings reports that the net change in retained earnings resulted from an increase because of net income and a decrease because of dividends. The net income is an operating source of cash and we have already dealt with cash from operations. The payment of dividends should be reported on our statement as a $590 nonoperating use of cash.

Having analyzed and explained all the changes in balance sheet accounts during the year, we can incorporate our conclusions into a formal statement of changes in financial position, as shown below.

Harold Company
Statement of Changes in Financial Position—Cash Basis
for the Year 19X7

Resources provided by:		
Operations:		
Net income		$730
Adjustments that affected net income but did not affect cash the same way:		
Depreciation for the year	$100	
Gain on sale of long-term investment	(30)	
Increase in inventory	(40)	
Decrease in accounts receivable	10	
Decrease in accounts payable	(10)	
Decrease in accrued expenses	(5)	
Net adjustment		25
Cash provided by operations		755

Other sources:			
Sale of investments		70	
Sale of equipment		10	
Issuance of common stock		200	
Total cash from other sources			280
Total cash provided during the year			1,035
Resources used for:			
Acquisition of plant and equipment		280	
Retirement of long-term debt		150	
Dividends on common stock		590	
Total cash used during the year			1,020
Net increase in cash			$ 15

3. Although this requirement could be completed on a less formal basis, below is a schedule of working capital such as might appear as part of a statement of changes in financial position prepared on a working capital basis. The amounts are taken directly from the comparative balance sheets.

Harold Company Schedule of Working Capital
at December 31

	19X7	19X6	Change in Working Capital Increase (Decrease)
Current assets:			
Cash	$205	$190	$15
Accounts receivable	420	430	(10)
Inventory	350	310	40
Total current assets	975	930	45
Current liabilities:			
Accounts payable	210	220	10
Accrued expenses	65	70	5
Total current liabilities	275	290	15
Working capital	$700	$640	$60

4. From part 1 we already know those items that caused a difference between net income and cash from operations. Cash is one component of working capital. If any of the items already identified is also a part of working capital, the difference between net income and working capital from operations would disappear. Reviewing the list of adjustments in the cash basis statement of changes in financial position, we see that the last four relate to changes in other working capital accounts. Hence, the only adjustments still needed are the first two, and we can compute working capital from operations as follows:

Net income		$730
Adjustments for items that affected net income but did not affect working capital in the same way:		
Depreciation for the year	$100	
Gain on sale of investments	(30)	
Net adjustment		70
Working capital provided by operations		$800

5. The total change in working capital was an increase of $60. Although the working capital provided by operations was $800, there were other sources of working capital during the year, and the company used working capital for various reasons. We can refer to the cash basis statement of changes in financial position which was prepared earlier. Those nonoperating transactions which provided or used cash resources during the year also provided or used working capital resources during the year. (This might not always be the case, but it is true for the Harold Company this year.) Without preparing a formal statement of changes in financial position based on the working capital concept, we can reconcile the $800 and the $60 as follows:

Funds provided by operations		$ 800
Funds provided by other sources:		
Sale of investments	$ 70	
Sale of equipment	10	
Issuance of common stock	200	280
		1,080
Funds used for:		
Dividends	590	
Debt retirement	150	
Acquisition of plant assets	280	1,020
Increase in working capital		$ 60

APPENDIX: A WORKSHEET APPROACH TO PREPARING STATEMENTS OF CHANGES IN FINANCIAL POSITION

The commonsense approach to preparing the statement of changes in financial position used in the chapter can be supplemented with a more systematic approach, the use of a worksheet. The worksheet does not replace a basic knowledge of accounting; rather it organizes the elements of the statement and serves as a means to account for all its necessary components.

The worksheet technique is especially helpful when the problem is complex and data are missing. You know from the chapter and the review problem that you sometimes have to make judgments about the most probable cause of a change in a noncurrent account like accumulated depreciation, bonds payable, or common stock. The use of a worksheet enables you to determine more systematically whether you have considered all of the transactions that affect the statement.

The rationale of the worksheet is straightforward. It is used to *reconstruct* the transactions that affected working capital or cash during the year and to identify the effects of those transactions as sources and uses of funds. We shall use the data from the review problem on pages 578–579 to illustrate the preparation of a worksheet for a working capital basis statement of changes in financial position.

PREPARING THE WORKSHEET

The worksheet is prepared in two basic steps. First, the beginning and ending balances of all noncurrent accounts and of a single summary account for working capital for Harold Company are entered as shown in the partially completed worksheet in Exhibit 16-9. The lower part of the worksheet will then serve as the basis for preparing the formal statement after the transactions for the year have been entered in the two middle columns.

Exhibit 16-9
Harold Company Worksheet for Statement of Changes in
Financial Position for Year Ended December 31, 19X7

	Beginning Balance		Analyses of Transactions		Ending Balance	
	Dr.	Cr.	Dr.	Cr.	Dr.	Cr.
Noncurrent accounts:						
Investments	160				120	
Plant and equipment	2,250				2,500	
Accumulated depreciation		720				800
Long-term debt		250				100
Common stock		1,600				1,800
Retained earnings		480				620
Subtotal	2,410	3,050			2,620	3,320
Various working capital acccounts						
(net debit balance)	640				700	
Working capital provided by operations:						
Net income						
Adjustments:						
Depreciation						
Other sources of working capital:						
Uses of working capital:						
Totals	3,050	3,050			3,320	3,320

Please notice a couple of points about the worksheet. First, it is set up in debit-credit form. The total debits are equal to the total credits at both the beginning and end of the year, reflecting a basic accounting formula. Second, working capital is shown as a single figure; the individual current assets and current liabilities are not shown. The reason for using this summary account is that we do not care about *particular* current assets and current liabilities, only about the net amount of working capital. The single summary amount can be derived in the manner shown in part 3 of the review problem (page 582).

Notice also that we have filled in part of the bottom of the worksheet. We would not normally know exactly what items the statement will contain, but we can be fairly sure that there will be an operations section which includes net income and depreciation. We can also be reasonably confident that there will be some other sources and uses. As we reconstruct the year's transaction we shall fill in appropriate titles for the individual sources and uses.

The second step in preparing the worksheet is to reconstruct the transactions that affected working capital over the year. This is done by working with the information available and making the most plausible assumptions about items for which information is not available. The reconstruction is done in journal entry form.

As we make the journal entries we shall be accounting for the changes in noncurrent accounts and in working capital at the same time. Again, because we are not concerned with particular current asset and current liability accounts we shall use the account title Various Working Capital Accounts to designate sources and uses of working capital that will appear on the formal statement.

Reconstruction of Transactions

We shall begin the reconstruction of transactions by considering retained earnings. We know that net income for the year was $730 and that dividends were $590. Net income, of course, is not a single transaction, but rather the net effect of a great many transactions affecting a number of working capital and noncurrent accounts. In journal entry form we show the effect of net income on working capital.

| 1. | Various Working Capital Accounts | $730 | |
| | Retained Earnings | | $730 |

To record net income as a source of working capital.

Dividends are recorded in the following entry.

| 2. | Retained Earnings | $590 | |
| | Various Working Capital Accounts | | $590 |

To record dividends as a use of working capital.

Common stock: We know that the Harold Company issued $200 of common stock for cash. However, even if we did not know that, we would still assume that the $200 increase in the Common Stock account was the result of an issuance. Again, because we are concerned with working capital, the fact that cash was received for the stock is not important. The entry below recognizes the issuance.

| 3. | Various Working Capital Accounts | $200 | |
| | Common Stock | | $200 |

To record issuance of common stock as a source of working cpaital.

Long-term debt: The balance sheets of Harold Company and the partially filled-in worksheet tell us that long-term debt decreased by $150. The most likely explanation is that there was a retirement of long-term debt. The entry below gives effect to that transaction.

| 4. | Long-Term Debt | $150 | |
| | Various Working Capital Accounts | | $150 |

To record retirement of long-term debt as a use of working capital.

Accumulated depreciation and plant and equipment: These two accounts have to be considered together because the sale of equipment affected both of them. The sale of equipment with a cost of $30 and accumulated depreciation of $20 for its book value of $10 is recorded in entry 5.

5. Various Working Capital Accounts $10
    Accumulated Depreciation   20
        Plant and Equipment $30

    To record sale of plant assets as a source of working capital.

We must also give effect to depreciation expense, which did not use working capital, but was included in the determination of net income.

6. Adjustments $100
        Accumulated Depreciation $100

    To record depreciation as an adjustment that did not affect working capital the same way it affected net income.

These two entries fully account for the change in accumulated depreciation, but not for the change in plant and equipment. Plant and equipment began with a balance of $2,250 and increased to $2,500, a change of $250. The $30 credit made in entry 5 tells us that the firm must have added $280 in plant assets. This inference is recorded in entry 7.

7. Plant and Equipment $280
        Various Working Capital Accounts $280

    To record purchases of plant assets as a use of working capital.

Investments: The only noncurrent account left is investments, which decreased by $40, from $160 to $120, as the result of a sale of investments. The sale brought a price of $70, giving a $30 gain. We know that the formal statement must show the $70 price as an "other source," not as an operating source. We also know that the gain was included in the determination of net income and must therefore be subtracted in the adjustments section. In journal entry form we can take care of this transaction by showing a debit to working capital of $70 for the selling price and a credit to income adjustments of $30 for the gain. The credit will then become a deduction in the operations section of the formal statement.

8. Various Working Capital Accounts $70
        Investments $40
        Adjustments   30

    To record a $70 source of working capital from the sale of investments and a $30 adjustment in working capital provided by operations from the gain on the sale.

At this point all of the accounts are fully reconciled. The completed worksheet appears in Exhibit 16-10. The lower part of the worksheet provides all of the information needed to prepare a formal statement. The debit entries are either sources of working capital or adjustments in the operations section, the credit entries are either uses of working capital or adjustments in the operations section.

Exhibit 16-10

Harold Company Worksheet for Statement of Changes in
Financial Position for the Year Ended December 31, 19X7

	Beginning Balance		Analyses of Transactions		Ending Balance	
	Dr.	Cr.	Dr.	Cr.	Dr.	Cr.
Noncurrent accounts:						
Investments	160			40 (8)	120	
Plant and equipment	2,250		280 (7)	30 (5)	2,500	
Accumulated depreciation		720	20 (5)	100 (6)		800
Long-term debt		250	150 (4)			100
Common stock		1,600		200 (3)		1,800
Retained earnings		480	590 (2)	730 (1)		620
Subtotal	2,410	3,050			2,620	3,320
Various working capital accounts						
(net debit balance)	640				700	
Working capital provided by operations:						
Net income			730 (1)			
Adjustments:						
Depreciation			100 (6)			
Gain on sale of investments				30 (8)		
Other sources of working capital:						
Issuance of common stock			200 (3)			
Sale of investments			70 (8)			
Sale of equipment			10 (5)			
Uses of working capital:						
Dividends				590 (2)		
Retirement of debt				150 (4)		
Purchases of plant assets				280 (7)		
Totals	3,050	3,050	2,140	2,140	3,320	3,320

16-1 Depreciation and working capital It is often said that working capital, or cash, generated by operations consists of net income and depreciation. Explain why this statement is or is not true.

16-2 Net income and cash flow The Bryant Machine Shop was started by Walter Bryant five years ago. The firm has been fairly profitable and Mr. Bryant has been withdrawing cash in an amount equal to net income for each year. He has taken out an amount equal to nearly half of his original investment of $80,000, which was used mainly to purchase machinery. Mr. Bryant's customers pay cash on completion of work. He keeps very little inventory and pays his bills promptly. He is puzzled because the cash balance continues to increase despite his withdrawals. Can you offer any explanation for the increase in cash?

16-3 Net income and working capital Suppose that a large retail chain and a railroad earned the same net income. Which firm would you expect to show the higher working capital provided by operations? Explain your answer.

16-4 Explanation of cash-based statement You have provided the president of the Ralston Company a full set of financial statements, including a statement of changes in financial position on a cash basis. He understands everything except some of the adjustments in the operations section of the statement of changes in financial position. He has three specific questions.

1. "Why do you subtract the increase in accounts receivable? We don't pay out cash for our accounts receivable, we collect it."
2. "And the inventory, which you show as an addition because our inventory decreased during the year. We sure didn't get any cash because our inventory decreased. In fact, the decrease means that we have less to sell next year and will have to spend more cash to replenish our supply. So why add it back to net income?"
3. "Our accrued expenses increased and you showed this as a source of cash? Look, we had especially heavy payroll costs at the end of the year and we paid them the third day of the new year. So it seems to me that we had to use more cash because of the increase, not less."

Required
Explain each of the items to the president.

Exercises

16-5 Relationships Answer the questions for each of the following independent situations.

1. At year end the ABC Company had current assets of $80,000, which were $12,000 higher than at the beginning of the year. Working capital at year end was $36,000, which was $4,000 lower than at the beginning of the year.
   (a) What were current liabilities at the end of the year?
   (b) What were current liabilities at the beginning of the year?
2. Noncurrent assets of the NMO Company increased by $120,000 and noncurrent equities (equities other than current liabilities) declined by $30,000 over the past year. What was the change in working capital over the year?
3. Working capital of the XYZ Company increased by $50,000 over the past year. Current assets other than cash increased by $35,000 and current liabilities decreased by $7,000 over the year. What was the change in cash over the year?
4. Working capital provided by operations was $90,000. Current assets other than cash increased by $12,000 and current liabilities increased by $18,000 over the year. What was cash provided by operations?
5. Working capital provided by operations was $60,000 and depreciation expense was $32,000. What was net income?

16-6 Working capital—operations The Drew Company had net income of $400,000 in 19X6. The following were included in the determination of net income.

1. Depreciation expense of $65,000.
2. Amortization of intangible assets of $12,000.
3. Loss on sale of plant assets of $4,000.
4. On one sale for $24,000, the customer gave Drew Company a five-year note bearing 9% interest.

Required
Compute the amount of working capital provided by operations.

16-7 **Cash from operations**   The Drew Company (exercise 16-6) experienced the following changes in its current accounts during 19X6.

Accounts receivable	+$18,000
Inventory	−$13,000
Accounts payable	−$17,000
Accrued expenses	+$11,000

All other data are given in the previous exercise.

Required

Determine cash provided by operations.

16-8 **Converting cash flow to income**   The following data were prepared by the controller of the Boyd Company. They relate to 19X7.

Cash collections from customers		$810,000
Payments to suppliers of merchandise	$470,000	
Wage and salary payments	160,000	
Other payments of operating expenses	90,000	720,000
Cash provided by operations		$ 90,000

Other data taken from the firm's records show the following.

1. Accounts receivable increased by $15,000.
2. Accounts payable decreased by $8,000.
3. Inventory remained constant.
4. Accrued wages and salaries increased by $3,000.
5. Depreciation expense was $35,000.

Required

Determine net income for 19X7.

16-9 **Reconciliation of net income and cash from operations**   Select from the list below those items that would be relevant to a reconciliation of net income and cash from operations, and prepare such a reconciliation.

Gain on sale of long-term investment	$133,500
Increase in accounts receivable	14,300
Increase in land	48,000
Increase in accrued expenses payable	6,800
Decrease in inventory	21,700
Decrease in accounts payable	12,000
Decrease in prepaid insurance	1,500
Increase in common stock	85,000
Net income	124,800
Depreciation of buildings for year	48,000
Decrease in cash	14,000
Cash received from sale of long-term investment	228,800
Cash provided by operations	43,000

16-10 Reconciliation of net income and working capital from operations   Using the relevant information from 16-9, prepare a reconciliation of net income and working capital from operations.

16-11 Analysis of noncurrent accounts   The following data were taken from the records of the Miller Mining Company.

	End of Year	
	19X6	19X5
Plant and equipment	$2,240,000	$1,980,000
Accumulated depreciation	(980,000)	(740,000)
Mineral properties, net of depletion	3,750,000	2,950,000

Additional information you have gathered is that plant and equipment costing $240,000 and with accumulated depreciation of $90,000 was sold for $80,000 and that depletion expense related to mineral properties was $440,000. The only other transactions affecting the accounts shown were depreciation expense, purchases of plant and equipment, and purchases of mineral properties.

Required

1. Determine the amount of working capital provided by sales of plant and equipment.
2. Determine the gain or loss to be added back or subtracted in the operations section of the statement of changes in financial position.
3. Determine the amount of depreciation expense to be added back to net income in the operations section of the statement.
4. Determine the amount of working capital used to buy plant and equipment.
5. Determine the amount of working capital used to buy mineral properties.

16-12 Working capital—transactions   The Fisher Company began 19X4 with $80,000 in working capital. During 19X4 the following occurred.

1. Net income was $60,000.
2. Depreciation expense was $15,000.
3. The firm retired bonds that were due in 19X9. The amount of cash spent to retire them was equal to their book value of $30,000.
4. The firm paid $90,000 for plant and equipment.
5. The firm declared dividends of $8,000, to be paid in January 19X5.
6. The firm wrote off as expense the book value of some long-term investments in stock of companies that went bankrupt in 19X4. The expense was $34,000.

Required

Prepare a statement of changes in financial position on a working capital basis.

16-13 Effects of transactions   Determine the effect of each transaction listed below on (a) working capital and (b) cash. Show the amount of the change and its direction (+ or −). Some transactions might have no effect on one or both.

1. Common stock was issued in exchange for equipment. The agreed price was $300,000.
2. A dividend payable in cash of $120,000 was declared, but not paid.
3. The dividend in 2 was paid.
4. An account receivable of $10,000 was written off against the allowance for doubtful accounts.

5. Marketable securities classified as a current asset were sold for $30,000 cash. They had been shown at their cost of $27,000.
6. A customer who owed the firm $12,000 on account receivable gave the firm equipment with a fair market value of $12,000 in settlement of the receivable.
7. Interest payable was accrued in the amount of $14,000.
8. The interest payable in 7 was paid.
9. The firm bought 100 shares of its own stock for the treasury. The cost was $4,600, paid in cash.
10. Inventory with a cost of $18,000 was written off as obsolete.
11. Plant assets that had cost $45,000 and were one-third depreciated were sold for $12,000 cash.

16-14 Working capital flow (Related to Appendix)   The most recent income statement and condensed comparative balance sheets for the Stout Company are given below.

Stout Company Balance Sheets as of June 30

Assets	19X6	19X5
Current assets	$ 325	$ 350
Plant and equipment	1,290	1,110
Accumulated depreciation	(640)	(590)
Totals	$ 975	$ 870

Equities		
Current liabilities	$ 210	$ 195
Long-term debt	200	150
Common stock	300	300
Retained earnings	265	225
Totals	$ 975	$ 870

Stout Company Income Statement
Year Ended June 30, 19X6

Sales		$1,240
Cost of sales		710
Gross profit		530
Operating expenses:		
Depreciation	$ 50	
Other operating expenses	240	290
Net income		$ 240

The firm declared and paid dividends of $200. There were no sales or retirements of plant assets. Plant assets were bought for $180 cash and $50 in long-term debt was issued to ease a cash shortage.

Required

1. Determine the change in working capital over the year 19X6.
2. Prepare a worksheet for a statement of changes in financial position.

16-15 Statement preparation—cash basis Below is a list of items that would appear in the statement of changes in financial position for Brillan Company for the year 19X8.

Net income for the year	$346,000
Dividends paid during the year	125,000
Proceeds from sale of a ten-year bond issue	300,000
Amortization of the company's patents	7,000
Depreciation expense	156,000
Cash received on sale of land	80,000
Decrease in inventory	6,000
Increase in accounts receivable	81,000
Loss on the sale of land	20,000
Increase in accrued expenses	11,000
Cash purchase of new equipment	500,000
Cash purchase of a long-term investment	158,000
Decrease in income taxes payable	24,000
Increase in accounts payable	54,000
Purchase of land and buildings by giving a twenty-year note	200,000

Required: Prepare a cash basis statement of changes in financial position using all the items given. (Hint: the change in cash was an increase of $92,000.)

16-16 Statement preparation—working capital basis Using the information given in 16-15, (1) prepare a statement of changes in financial position using the working capital concept, and (2) verify the change in working capital, which was an increase of $126,000.

Problems

16-17 Working capital flows—balance sheets Condensed comparative balance sheets and other data pertaining to the LMN Company are given below.

LMN Company
Balance Sheets as of December 31

	19X5	19X4
Current assets	$ 78,000	$ 84,000
Investments	60,000	110,000
Plant and equipment	450,000	400,000
Accumulated depreciation	(250,000)	(220,000)
Total assets	$338,000	$374,000
Current liabilities	$ 32,000	$ 36,000
Long-term debt	30,000	100,000
Common stock, no par value	210,000	180,000
Retained earnings	66,000	58,000
Total equities	$338,000	$374,000

Other Data

1. Net income was $21,000 in 19X5. Dividends were $13,000.
2. No plant assets were sold or retired in 19X5.
3. Investments costing $50,000 were sold for $55,000.
4. Depreciation included in expenses for the year was $30,000.

Required

1. Determine the change in working capital for the year 19X5.
2. Prepare a statement of changes in financial position on a working capital basis. When information is unavailable, make the most likely assumption about a change in a noncurrent account.

16-18 Working capital and cash—transactions   The transactions of the Martin Company for 19X6 and other selected data are given below.

1. Sales, all on account, were $600,000.
2. Cost of goods sold was $280,000.
3. Depreciation expense was $40,000.
4. Other operating expenses, all paid in cash, were $210,000.
5. Equipment was purchased for $120,000 cash.
6. Long-term investments were sold at an $8,000 gain. They had cost $57,000.
7. Common stock was issued for cash of $200,000.
8. A building that had cost $80,000 and had accumulated depreciation of $72,000 was destroyed by fire. There was no insurance coverage.
9. Over the year, the following changes occurred in the current accounts of the firm.

Cash	+$210,000
Accounts receivable	+ 15,000
Inventory	+ 20,000
Accounts payable	− 10,000

Required

1. Determine net income for the year.
2. Prepare a statement of changes in financial position on a working capital basis. The change in working capital can be determined from the information in item 9.
3. Prepare a statement of changes in financial position on a cash basis.

16-19 Balance sheet   The following condensed balance sheet and statement of changes in financial position for the Quatro Company are available. Notice that working capital is shown as a single figure.

Quatro Company Balance Sheet
as of June 30, 19X7

Working capital	$50,000		
Investments	80,000	Long-term debt	$90,000
Plant and equipment	280,000	Common stock, no par	100,000
Accumulated depreciation	(160,000)	Retained earnings	60,000
Totals	$250,000		$250,000

Quatro Company Statement of Changes
in Financial Position Year Ended June 30, 19X8

Resources provided by:		
Operations:		
Net income		$ 34,000
Adjustments:		
Depreciation		18,000
Working capital provided by operations		52,000
Other sources:		
Sales of investments		30,000
Sale of common stock		40,000
Total resources provided		$122,000
Resources used for:		
Dividends	$14,000	
Purchases of plant assets	80,000	
Retirement of long-term debt	20,000	114,000
Increase in working capital		$ 8,000

Investments were sold at book value. No plant assets were sold or retired.

Required

Prepare a balance sheet for Quatro Company as of June 30, 19X8. Show working capital as a single figure.

16-20 Balance sheet   Refer to the data in problem 16-19. Assume that the balance sheet given is for June 30, 19X8, instead of June 30, 19X7. The statement of changes in financial position is still for the year ended June 30, 19X8. Prepare the balance sheet for June 30, 19X7. That is, instead of preparing the ending balance sheet, you are to prepare the beginning balance sheet.

16-21 Cash flow   As you were walking down the hall to your office at the Complan Company, you met the president of the firm. He was disturbed at the latest financial statements and wanted your help. He explained that the firm was faced with a serious shortage of cash even though profits were high and working capital increased. He showed you the following condensed financial statements. All data are in thousands of dollars.

Complan Company Balance Sheets as of December 31

Assets	19X7	19X6	Change
Cash	$25	$380	($355)
Accounts receivable	990	860	130
Inventory	1,445	1,200	245
Plant and equipment (net)	3,850	3,370	480
Totals	$6,310	$5,810	
Equities			
Accounts payable	$190	$280	($90)
Accrued expenses	110	200	(90)
Long-term debt	2,250	2,200	50
Common stock	2,080	2,080	0
Retained earnings	1,680	1,050	630
Totals	$6,310	$5,810	

Complan Company Income Statement for 19X7

Sales	$6,720
Cost of sales	3,850
Gross profit	2,870
Operating expenses	2,140
Net income	$730

The president told you that it had been touch-and-go whether the firm would have enough cash to pay a $100,000 dividend that had been declared when the directors realized that the firm was having an excellent year. In order to pay the dividend, the firm had to increase its long-term borrowings by $50,000. "We made $730,000," he went on, "and had depreciation expense of $150,000. We did buy $630,000 worth of plant assets, but I figured that our cash would stay about the same as it was last year. Look at this stuff and tell me what happened."

Required

Answer the president by preparing a statement of changes in financial position on a cash basis.

16-22 Working capital—comprehensive problem (Related to Appendix) . Condensed comparative balance sheets and other data for the Rhonda Company are given below.

Rhonda Company Balance Sheets

	End of Year	Beginning of Year
Current assets	$130,000	$100,000
Investments, long-term	100,000	140,000
Plant and equipment	450,000	400,000
Accumulated depreciation	(110,000)	(80,000)
Intangible assets	54,000	60,000
Total assets	$624,000	$620,000
Current liabilities	$ 45,000	$ 90,000
Long-term debt	140,000	200,000
Common stock, $10 par value	80,000	50,000
Paid in capital	270,000	220,000
Retained earnings	89,000	60,000
Total equities	$624,000	$620,000

Other Data

1. The change in working capital was an increase of $75,000.
2. Net income was $41,000, dividends were $12,000.
3. Sales of plant assets for $12,000 resulted in a loss of $10,000. The assets had cost $40,000 and had accumulated depreciation of $18,000. Purchases of plant were $90,000. Depreciation expense for the year was $48,000.
4. Amortization of intangible assets was $6,000.
5. Investments costing $40,000 were sold for $51,000.
6. Long-term debt in the amount of $60,000 was retired.
7. Common stock was sold for a total price of $80,000 cash.

Required

1. Prepare a worksheet to reconstruct the events of the year and make the necessary entries.
2. Prepare a formal statement of changes in financial position on a working capital basis.

16-23 **Treatment of transactions** For each of the following transactions, explain how it would be reflected on a statement of changes in financial position prepared on (a) the working capital basis, and (b) the cash basis. Be specific.

1. Depreciation expense was $340,000.
2. A $110,000 dividend, payable in cash, was declared late in the year and will be paid early next year.
3. Fixed assets costing $380,000 with accumulated depreciation of $170,000 were sold for $80,000 cash.
4. Long-term investments were written off because the firms issuing the securities went bankrupt. The write-off was $220,000.
5. The firm issued long-term debt in exchange for land. The value of the land was $640,000, which equaled the value of the debt.
6. Near the end of the year the firm sold a parcel of land for $300,000, which was $60,000 more than its cost. The buyer gave the firm a five-year, 8% note for $300,000.
7. The firm was required to pay $50,000 in settlement of a dispute relating to its income tax return of three years ago. The firm debited retained earnings for $50,000.

16-24 **Statements from limited data** The following *changes* in the balance sheet accounts of the Rohmer Company occurred during 19X8.

		Change	
Account	Debit	Credit
Cash	$120	
Accounts receivable		$180
Inventory	120	
Plant and equipment	350	
Accumulated depreciation		90
Accounts payable	80	
Accrued expenses		30
Long-term debt	15	
Common stock		200
Retained earnings		185
Totals	$685	$685

The firm had net income of $225 and paid dividends of $40. No plant assets were sold or retired.

Required

1. Prepare a statement of changes in financial position on a working capital basis. In the absence of available information, make the most reasonable assumption about the cause of a change. Be sure to find the change in working capital first.
2. Prepare a statement of changes in financial position on a cash basis.

16-25 **Working capital and net income** Walter Rimstone, the president of Piedmont Enterprises, was recently talking to his banker. The banker had just received Piedmont's most recent financial statements and was disturbed by the decline in working capital, which he called "deterioration of the current position." Mr. Rimstone said that he was surprised because the year had been the best in the firm's history. Condensed financial statements are given below.

Piedmont Enterprises Balance Sheets
as of June 30 (In Thousands)

	19X5	19X4
Current assets	$120	$160
Plant and equipment	740	560
Accumulated depreciation	(140)	(110)
Total assets	$720	$610
Current liabilities	$ 55	$ 48
Long-term bank loan	110	125
Common stock	200	200
Retained earnings	355	237
Total equities	$720	$610

Piedmont Enterprises Income Statement for 19X5

Sales	$840
Total expenses, including $30 depreciation	590
Net income	$250

Mr. Rimstone asks you to figure out why working capital declined in the face of record income.

Required

Prepare a statement of changes in financial position on a working capital basis. Make whatever reasonable assumptions you think are appropriate when information is lacking.

16-26 **Cash flow and income** The Hamer Company is currently negotiating a bank loan with the Eighteenth National Bank of Mardel. The bank officers would like a statement showing the estimated cash flow that the Hamer Company expects in the coming year. They need this information to be able to decide on the likelihood that Hamer Company will be able to repay the loan of $100,000 at the end of the year. Hamer Company's current balance sheet is given below, along with other data.

Hamer Company Balance Sheet
as of December 31, 19X6

Cash	$ 15,000	Accounts payable	$ 48,000
Accounts receivable	110,000	Wages and salaries payable	12,000
Inventory	130,000	Common stock	300,000
Plant and equipment	750,000	Paid in capital	250,000
Accumulated depreciation	(300,000)	Retained earnings	95,000
Totals	$705,000		$705,000

Other Data

1. Sales for 19X7 are expected to be $1,030,000. Accounts receivable are expected to be $140,000 at the end of 19X7.
2. Cost of goods sold is expected to be $480,000 and year-end inventory is expected to be $150,000.

3. Accounts payable are expected to be $15,000 higher at the end of 19X7.
4. Wages and salaries payable are expected to be $22,000 at the end of 19X7, with wages and salary expense expected to be $215,000 for 19X7.
5. Depreciation expense for 19X7 is expected to be $60,000.
6. Other expenses, all to be paid in cash, are expected to be $95,000, including the interest on the loan being negotiated.
7. Cash expenditures for plant and equipment are expected to be $140,000 in 19X7.
8. The firm expects to pay a dividend of $30,000 in 19X7.

Required

1. Determine the expected net income for 19X7, including as an expense the interest on the loan.
2. Prepare a statement of changes in financial position on a cash basis for the expected transactions of 19X7. Include the bank loan as a source of cash, but not as a use. Determine whether the firm will be able to repay the loan on January 1, 19X8.

16-27 Working capital and cash requirements   The Pittston Valve Company is expanding its plant to meet increased demand for its products. The expansion will enable the firm to increase its annual sales by $2,000,000. Additional expenses will be $1,700,000, including $140,000 in depreciation. During the first year of operation of the expanded plant, accounts receivable are expected to rise by $600,000 and inventory by $450,000 to support the higher sales levels. Accounts payable will increase by about half of the increase in inventory. In later years these accounts will remain at their higher levels, but will not increase any further.

Required

1. Determine the amount of working capital that is expected to be provided by operations related to the expansion for the first year and the second year.
2. Determine the amount of cash expected to be provided by operations related to the expansion for the first year and the second year.

16-28 Comprehensive problem (Related to Appendix)   Comparative balance sheets and an income statement for the RJM Company are given below. All data are in millions of dollars.

RJM Company Balance Sheets June 30

	19X7	19X6
Cash	$ 9.5	$ 28.7
Accounts receivable	125.8	88.6
Inventories	311.4	307.0
Prepayments	12.6	11.4
Total current assets	459.3	435.7
Investments	68.3	71.8
Plant and equipment	1,313.9	1,240.6
Accumulated depreciation	(753.1)	(687.4)
Intangible assets	42.5	46.2
Total assets	$1,130.9	$1,106.9
Accounts payable	$62.6	$59.8
Taxes payable	32.4	29.6
Accrued expenses	38.9	52.6
Total current liabilities	133.9	142.0
Long-term debt	505.3	496.2
Common stock, no par value	384.2	377.4
Retained earnings	107.5	91.3
Total equities	$1,130.9	$1,106.9

RJM Company Income Statement for 19X7

Sales and other revenue		$896.3
Expenses:		
Cost of goods sold	$493.2	
Depreciation	69.3	
Amortization	3.7	
Other expenses	288.5	854.7
Net income		$ 41.6

Sales and other revenue includes a gain of $.8 million on sale of investments. Amortization expense is related to intangible assets. Other expenses include losses of $1.3 million on sales and other disposals of equipment. These assets had cost $9.6 million and had accumulated depreciation of $3.6 million. Long-term debt and common stock were issued for cash.

Required

1. Prepare a worksheet for a statement of changes in financial position on a working capital basis.
2. Prepare the section on operations only for a cash flow basis statement of changes in financial position.

CHAPTER 17

ANALYZING FINANCIAL STATEMENTS

Relationships among selected items in the firm's financial statements are often of interest to the firm's managers. We saw in Part One of this book that managers may plan for profits with some target return on sales in mind. Some managers utilize selected ratios or relationships within financial statements to assist them in long-term financial budgeting, as we saw in Chapter 6. Among the criteria for evaluating divisional performance is return on investment, a basic relationship between two financial statement items. This chapter explores more fully, and from a different point of view, some of the most commonly considered relationships among items in financial statements.

The topic is approached from the point of view of the financial analyst, an individual outside the firm but interested, for various reasons, in the firm's activities. The financial analyst's conclusions, opinions, and recommendations can affect the firm's ability to obtain credit, sell stock, and secure new contracts. Therefore, the manager must be aware of the financial analyst's viewpoint.

THE PURPOSE AND APPROACH OF THE ANALYST

Financial analysts use financial statements in decision making. Banks that provide short-term loans, insurance companies that buy long-term bonds, brokerage firms that make recommendations to their customers, mutual funds that buy common stock—all of these and many other institutions will employ financial analysts who provide information that will help in making decisions about individual firms. Individual investors also perform financial analyses in making their investment decisions.

The thrust of financial analysis is to the future. Analysts want to know what to expect from a firm—whether it is likely to be able to pay its bills, repay loans with interest, pay dividends on stock, or expand into new areas. What has happened in the past is of concern only insofar as it can be considered a reliable guide to the future. For example, a firm might have an extremely impressive history with regular growth in net income and sales, financial stability and capable management. But if its major product becomes illegal (e.g., the insecticide DDT), or obsolete (e.g., early types of computers), the firm's prospects would be severely impaired. Nevertheless, the analyst approaches his task with the assumption that what has held true in the past is likely to continue unless his information indicates otherwise. He will continually be on the lookout for any signs of changes in the future.

The viewpoint of the financial analyst is also used by managers within the firm. The vice president of finance might be considering the issuance of a considerable amount of long-term debt to finance plant expansion. On the basis of analyses described later in this chapter, she might conclude that the firm would be better off if common stock were issued instead of debt. This conclusion could be based on her assessment of the probable response of investors who might feel that the firm cannot afford to take on additional debt. The determination of an appropriate balance between debt and equity financing is critically important to the firm and a matter of continual concern to internal financial managers.

GENERAL METHODS OF ANALYSIS

Financial analysis consists of a number of interrelated activities. Among the most important are considerations of ratios and trends and the comparison of ratios and trends against some norms. (A norm is a standard for comparison, which could be an average value for a particular industry or an average value for all firms in the economy.) Trends are of interest, of course, as clues to what the future holds.

Areas of Analysis

Different types of investors are interested in different aspects of a firm. Short-term creditors such as suppliers and banks considering loans of relatively short duration (ninety days or six months) are concerned primarily with the firm's short-term prospects. They want to know whether there is a significant danger that the firm will not be able to pay its obligations in the near future. Banks, insurance companies, pension funds, and other investors considering relatively long-term commitments (ten-year loans) are also concerned with the firm's short-term prospects, but are more concerned with its long-term outlook. If such investors are satisfied that there are no short-term problems with a firm, they still might not make a loan unless they were reasonably sure that the firm had good prospects for long-term financial stability and could be expected to repay the loan and interest on it.

The current stockholders of a firm, and potential individual or institutional stockholders, are also interested in both the short-term and long-term prospects of the firm. But they are concerned with more than the firm's ability to repay loans and make interest payments. They are interested in its potential profitability, its ability to earn satisfactory profits and pay dividends. Along with profitability comes the likelihood that the market price of the stock will increase and provide its owners with capital gains.

We have divided the discussion of these aspects of the prospects of a firm into three major areas: liquidity; solvency; and profitability. For the most part we shall be working with ratios, the results of dividing numbers by other numbers. Financial analysts use ratios primarily because they can be used to compare firms of different sizes and can serve as benchmarks or norms against which the firm can be evaluated.

Sample Financial Statements

In our discussion we shall use the financial statements and some additional financial information about the Graham Company (Exhibit 17-1). The analysis has actually begun in the exhibit because it shows the percentages of sales for each item on the income statement and

Exhibit 17-1
Graham Company Balance Sheets as of December 31

	19X6		19X5	
	Dollars	*Percent*	*Dollars*	*Percent*
Current assets:				
Cash	$ 80,000	5.2%	$ 50,000	3.6%
Accounts receivable	180,000	11.6	120,000	8.7
Inventory	190,000	12.2	230,000	16.7
Total current assets	450,000	29.0	400,000	29.0
Plant and equipment—cost	1,350,000	87.1	1,150,000	83.3
Accumulated depreciation	(340,000)	(21.9)	(250,000)	(18.1)
Net plant and equipment	1,010,000	65.2	900,000	65.2
Other assets	90,000	5.8	80,000	5.8
Total assets	$1,550,000	100.0	$1,380,000	100.0
Current liabilities:				
Accounts payable	$ 110,000	7.1%	$ 105,000	7.6%
Accrued expenses	40,000	2.6	15,000	1.1
Total current liabilities	150,000	9.7	120,000	8.7
Long-term debt	600,000	38.7	490,000	35.5
Total liabilities	750,000	48.4	610,000	44.2
Common stock, 22,000 shares	220,000	14.2	220,000	15.9
Paid in capital	350,000	22.6	350,000	25.4
Retained earnings	230,000	14.8	200,000	14.5
Total stockholder equity	800,000	51.6	770,000	55.8
Total equities	$1,550,000	100.0	$1,380,000	100.0

Graham Company Income Statements

	19X6		19X5	
	Dollars	*Percent*	*Dollars*	*Percent*
Sales	$1,300,000	100.0%	$1,080,000	100.0%
Cost of goods sold	800,000	61.5	670,000	62.0
Gross profit	500,000	38.5	410,000	38.0
Operating expenses	280,000	21.6	210,000	19.4
Income before interest and taxes	220,000	16.9	200,000	18.6
Interest expense	48,000	3.7	42,000	3.9
Income before taxes	172,000	13.2	158,000	14.7
Income taxes at 40% rate	68,800	5.3	63,200	5.9
Net income	$ 103,200	7.9%	$ 94,800	8.8%

Other information:

> Dividends declared and paid were $73,200 in 19X6, $63,000 in 19X5.
> Operating expenses include depreciation of $90,000 in 19X6, $75,000 in 19X5.

---

the percentage of total assets or total equities for each balance sheet item. These percentage statements, or *common size statements*, are used to spot trends. They can sometimes help an analyst to see signs of either trouble or improvement.

Some of the more important percentages on the income statement are the *gross profit ratio*, which is gross profit divided by sales, and the ratio, *return on sales*, which is net income divided by sales. These ratios for Graham Company in 19X6 are 38.5% and 7.9% respectively. The gross profit ratio improved in 19X6 over 19X5, but return on sales declined.

The balance-sheet ratios are used to see whether the proportions of particular assets or liabilities are increasing or decreasing, and whether they are within reasonable bounds. We shall explore balance-sheet ratios in more detail later in the chapter.

LIQUIDITY

Liquidity can be defined as the ability of a firm to meet its short-term liabilities. The more liquid a firm, the more likely it is to be able to pay its employees, suppliers, and holders of its short-term notes payable. Analysis of liquidity is most important to short-term creditors, but is also of concern to long-term creditors and stockholders. Even if a firm has excellent long-term prospects, it could fail to realize them because it was forced into bankruptcy when it could not pay its short-term liabilities. In order to get to the long term, a firm has to get through the short term.

Working Capital and the Current Ratio

Working capital is, as we know from earlier chapters, the difference between current assets and current liabilities. It is a very crude measure of liquidity. The Graham Company had the following amounts of working capital at the ends of 19X5 and 19X6.

	19X6	*19X5*
Current assets	$450,000	$400,000
Current liabilities	150,000	120,000
Working capital	$300,000	$280,000

We see that working capital increased, but this does not necessarily mean that the firm became more liquid. For one thing, working capital is a measure of absolute size and both major components of working capital were higher at the end of 19X6 than at the end of 19X5. Most analysts will look at changes in working capital only as a rough indication of changes in liquidity and will supplement their analysis with several other calculations.

The **current ratio** is a measure of relative liquidity, which takes into account different absolute sizes. It can be used to compare firms that have different total current assets and liabilities.

$$\text{Current ratio} = \frac{\text{current assets}}{\text{current liabilities}}$$

The Graham Company has current ratios of 3.33 to 1 in 19X5 ($400,000/$120,000) and 3 to 1 in 19X6 ($450,000/$150,000). We would therefore say that, on the basis of the current ratio, the firm seemed to become less liquid at the end of 19X6. There is a very good reason for saying "seems to be less liquid." One major problem that arises with the use of any ratio, but especially the current ratio, is that of *composition*. The composition problem is the makeup of current assets and current liabilities. How close are the current assets to being converted into cash and how soon must the current liabilities be paid? You know already that current assets are listed in the order of their liquidity, from cash, the most liquid, to prepaid expenses. (In fact, prepaid expenses will not be converted into cash, so technically they are not liquid at all.)

Quick Ratio (Acid-Test Ratio)

The **quick ratio**, or **acid-test ratio**, is computed by dividing cash plus accounts receivable plus marketable securities by current liabilities. Thus it is similar to the current ratio but with inventories and prepayments eliminated from the numerator. Only those assets (called *quick assets*) that are cash or "near cash" are included, so that the ratio gives an indication of debt paying ability in the very, very near term.

$$\text{Quick ratio} = \frac{\text{cash} + \text{marketable securities} + \text{receivables}}{\text{current liabilities}}$$

The Graham Company had no marketable securities at the end of either year, hence its quick ratios are as follows:

19X5 $\dfrac{\$50,000 + \$120,000}{\$120,000} = 1.42$

19X6 $\dfrac{\$80,000 + \$180,000}{\$150,000} = 1.73$

Here we see that Graham Company seems to have increased its liquidity because its quick ratio increased. We could say that the firm was better able to meet current liabilities at the end of 19X6 because the ratio of its most liquid assets to its current liabilities has increased. We would still like to know more. For example, we would want to know how soon its current liabilities have to be paid, and how rapidly the firm can expect to turn its receivables and inventory into cash. The payment schedules for current liabilities cannot be determined simply by examination of financial statements, but we can gain some insight into the liquidity of receivables and inventory.

Current Asset Activity Ratios

Neither the acid-test ratio nor the current ratio indicates the time within which the firm expects to realize cash from its receivables and inventories. Nor does either tell us the time within which the firm must pay its various current liabilities. Two ratios are commonly used to determine how quickly the firm's receivables and inventories are likely to be turned into cash.

Accounts Receivable Turnover. This ratio is calculated by dividing credit sales for the year by average accounts receivable.

$$\text{Accounts receivable turnover} = \frac{\text{credit sales}}{\text{average receivables}}$$

In general, average receivables are defined as the beginning balance plus the ending balance, divided by two. This simple averaging procedure is satisfactory so long as there are no extremely high or low points during the year (including the end of the year). If a firm has widely fluctuating receivable balances, it would be better to take a monthly average instead of using only the beginning and ending balances for the year. For illustrative purposes we assume that all of Graham Company's sales are on credit. Because we do not have the beginning balance for 19X5, we can only calculate the turnover for 19X6 for the Graham Company.

$$\frac{\$1,300,000}{(\$120,000 + \$180,000)/2} = \frac{\$1,300,000}{\$150,000} = 8.67 \text{ times}$$

Receivable turnover is a measure of how rapidly the firm collects its receivables. In general, the higher the turnover the better. Analysts will sometimes make a different but related calculation called number of **days' sales in accounts receivable.** This figure indicates the average collection period for accounts receivable and is calculated as follows:

$$\text{Days' sales in accounts receivable} = \frac{\text{ending balance of accounts receivable}}{\text{average daily credit sales}}$$

Average daily sales is simply credit sales for the year divided by 365. For the Graham Company, assuming that all sales are on credit, we have average daily credit sales of about \$3,562 (\$1,300,000/365).

$$\text{Days' sales in receivables} = \frac{\$180,000}{\$3,562} = 51 \text{ days}$$

The Graham Company's accounts receivable are, on the average, 51 days old. The firm therefore will probably collect all of its outstanding receivables by about 51 days after the balance-sheet date.

These two ratios are interrelated. If receivables at the beginning and end of the year were the same, we could calculate days' sales in receivables by dividing the number of turnovers into 365 days. In this case we would get about 42 days (365/8.67 turnovers), which is somewhat less than the 51 days we calculated before. The difference arises because the beginning balance in receivables was a good deal lower than the ending balance. Similarly we could divide the number of days' sales in receivables into 365 days to get the turnover. Again, the result would be different from our previous calculation of 8.67 because of the lower beginning balance.

The faster customers pay, the better. An increase in turnover (or decrease in days' sales in receivables) indicates that the firm is becoming more efficient in collecting its accounts. Of course, if the firm loses sales because of too tight credit policies, its turnover might be high, but it could be losing profits because of lower sales.

Inventory Turnover. We can make about the same type of analysis of the firm's inventory. Inventory turnover is calculated as follows:

$$\text{Inventory turnover} = \frac{\text{cost of goods sold}}{\text{average inventory}}$$

Again, average inventory is usually considered to be the sum of the beginning and ending balances divided by two. If the firm has higher inventories and lower inventories for significant portions of the year because of seasonal business, it would be better to use monthly figures to determine the average.

Graham Company's inventory turnover for 19X6 is about 3.8 times, calculated as follows:

$$\frac{\$800,000}{(\$230,000 + \$190,000)/2} = \frac{\$800,000}{\$210,000} = 3.8$$

This measure indicates the efficiency with which the firm uses its inventory. Turnover of inventory is critical for many businesses, especially those that sell at relatively low markups over cost and depend on high volumes of sales to earn satisfactory profits. Discount stores and food stores rely heavily on rapid turnover of inventory to keep up their profitability. Other firms, like jewelry stores, with very high markups over cost do not need such rapid turnovers to be profitable.

Investment in inventory can be very expensive. Some costs—insurance, personal property taxes, interest on the funds tied up in inventory, and obsolescence—can be very high. Therefore, a firm would prefer to keep its inventory as low as possible. The problem is that if inventory is too low, particularly in firms like retail clothing stores, sales might be lost because customers cannot find what they want. Such firms must balance the need to maintain fairly high inventories to keep sales up with the additional costs of having high inventories.

Analysts will also sometimes calculate the number of **days' sales in inventory,** which is a measure of the supply that the firm maintains. This ratio is calculated as follows:

$$\text{Days' sales in inventory} = \frac{\text{ending inventory}}{\text{average daily cost of goods sold}}$$

Average daily cost of goods sold is simply cost of goods sold for the year divided by 365. For the Graham Company this figure is $2,192 ($800,000/365) and the number of days' sales in inventory is about 87 ($190,000/$2,192).

Ratios and Evaluations

The calculating of ratios is a starting point, no more. A number of factors besides the magnitudes of ratios must be considered in an evaluation of a company.

Comparisons are critical to evaluation. The ratios for a firm must be compared with ratios calculated for that firm in prior years, and trends must be evaluated. Is the firm becoming more or less liquid? Have its credit policies been loosened up, thus producing a lower turnover of receivables?

The ratios for a firm must also be compared, if possible, with similar firms, or with the industry as a whole. Are the firm's ratios moving in the same direction as those in industry? Are they generally consistent with those for the industry? An electric or gas utility, which carries little or no inventory and has fairly stable cash receipts from its sales, could afford to have a much lower current ratio than a manufacturing company. Grocery stores would be expected to have a higher inventory turnover than manufacturers of heavy equipment. Though occasionally you may hear someone say that a particular ratio, such as a 2 to 1 current ratio, is normal, such a ratio is normal only for some firms in some industries.

Industry comparisons become more difficult as a firm diversifies its operations, a major trend over the last few decades. Some extremely diversified firms may operate in 15 or more different industries. A more recent trend, one welcomed by financial analysts, is increased public disclosure of detailed information about the various segments that make up diversified companies. Such additional disclosure has helped analysts to make comparisons that were not possible when only overall results were available.

Even comparisons with very similar companies can be misleading. The fact that one firm shows up better than another in virtually all measures of liquidity does not necessarily mean that it is better than the other. A company may have, for example, a degree of liquidity unjustified in its circumstances. Too much cash is not as bad as too little cash, but having excessive cash may also be unwise. Cash does not earn profits unless it is used for something. Nevertheless, it is difficult to judge whether, in any but the most extreme cases, a firm has an excessive investment in cash, receivables, or inventory.

One of the most important factors to consider in making comparisons of ratios among companies is the possibility that differing methods of accounting are creating (or masking) differences. For example, the accounting method used for inventory determination has a significant influence on both the current ratio and inventory turnover. Two firms identical in all respects except that one uses LIFO and one uses FIFO can show quite different ratios. If prices have generally been rising, the LIFO firm will show a lower inventory amount, a lower current ratio, and a higher inventory turnover. The longer the price trend has continued and the longer the firm has been using LIFO, the more marked the effect of the difference in inventory methods. Accounting methods may also have significant impacts on profitability ratios, which will be discussed in the next section.

Though the components of a ratio may be the accumulated results of many transactions, the analyst must remember that a single transaction can change a ratio. The effect of a single transaction such as the payment of cash for current liabilities is of particular relevance in reviewing liquidity. Such a transaction reduces both cash and current liabilities and has no effect on the total working capital, but can improve the current ratio. We can illustrate this by looking at the ratios for Graham Company at the end of 19X6 and assuming that it paid current liabilities of $30,000 just before the end of the year. Its current assets before the payment would have been $480,000 ($450,000 + $30,000), and its current liabilities $180,000 ($150,000 + $30,000), giving a current ratio of 2.67 to 1, which is lower than the 3 to 1 we calculated earlier. Before the payment the acid-test ratio would have been 1.6 to 1 [($80,000 + $180,000 + $30,000)/($150,000 + $30,000)], which is also lower than the ratio calculated earlier (1.73 to 1). Actions taken to improve ratios in this manner are sometimes called "window dressing." This particular type of window dressing is possible only if the current ratio and acid-test ratio are greater than 1 to 1. If they are less than 1 to 1, paying a current liability will reduce them.

PROFITABILITY

Profitability can be measured in absolute dollar terms, like net income, or it can be measured using ratios. Profitability measures that use ratios are usually expressed as returns on investment. The two most common ratios of return on investment are return on assets and return on common stockholders' equity.

Return on Assets (ROA)

Return on assets can be calculated in several ways. We shall use the following:

$$\text{ROA} = \frac{\text{net income} + \text{interest expense}}{\text{average total assets}}$$

Average total assets is generally the sum of the beginning and ending balance-sheet totals divided by two. We add back interest expense because we are trying to determine how profitably the firm uses its assets, regardless of how it financed those assets. We are interested here in the operating efficiency of the firm. Net income will be higher if the firm has no long-term debt and therefore no interest expense, but the interest expense (or lack of it) does not change the firm's operating efficiency. To measure operating efficiency we want to eliminate the expense that relates only to the way in which the firm is financed.

Income taxes could also be added back to net income because they depend on factors other than operating efficiency; interest expense is tax deductible and therefore income taxes will be affected by the amount of debt in the firm's capital structure. Some analysts prefer to leave income taxes in, adding back only interest expense; some prefer to add back only the after-tax effect of interest. The choice is largely a matter of personal preference.

Graham Company had ROA of about 10.3% in 19X6, calculated as follows:

$$\frac{\$103,200 + \$48,000}{(\$1,380,000 + \$1,550,000)/2} = \frac{\$151,200}{\$1,465,000} = 10.3\%$$

Return on Common Equity (ROE)

Return on assets gives a measure of operating efficiency. Common stockholders are also concerned with the return on their investment, which is affected not only by operations but also by the amount of debt and preferred stock in the firm's capital structure. Graham Company has no preferred stock but it does have debt. We shall explore the effects of debt and preferred stock on ROE in the following section.

ROE is computed as follows:

$$\text{ROE} = \frac{\text{net income} - \text{preferred stock dividends (if any)}}{\text{average common stockholders' equity}}$$

Average common stockholders' equity, in the absence of preferred stock, is simply the sum of the beginning and ending amounts of stockholders' equity divided by two. If there is preferred stock, the amount of total stockholders' equity attributable to preferred stock is subtracted to obtain common stockholders' equity.[1]

ROE for Graham Company in 19X6 is a bit over 13%.

$$\frac{\$103,200}{(\$770,000 + \$800,000)/2} = \frac{\$103,200}{\$785,000} = 13\%$$

Notice that ROE is greater than ROA. If the firm has been financed solely with common stock (that is, no current liabilities and no long-term debt), the return on equity and return on assets would be exactly the same. Net income would equal net income plus interest expense because interest expense would be zero, and total assets would equal common equity.

When a firm has no debt it is in much safer financial condition than if it has a good deal of debt. But debtholders do not participate in the earnings of the firm; they receive a stipulated, constant amount of interest. Hence the firm can increase its ROE if it uses debt, provided that its ROA is greater than the interest rate it must pay to debtholders. This method of using debt (or preferred stock) to increase ROE is called **leverage** or **trading on the equity.** It involves risk as well as the potential for greater return.

The Effects of Leverage

We can illustrate the effects of leverage by considering the ROE that would be achieved under different financing arrangements. Suppose that a firm requires total assets of $1,000,000 to earn $180,000 per year before interest and income taxes. The tax rate is 40%. Three alternative financing plans are possible: (1) all common stock; (2) $400,000 common stock and $600,000 in 7% bonds (interest expense of $42,000); and (3) $400,000 in common

---

[1] There are several ways of determining the amount of total stockholder equity attributable to preferred stock. The best method, where possible, is to use the call value of preferred. Call value is the amount that the firm would have to pay to retire the preferred stock, and it is usually more than par value. In the case of preferred stocks that have no call value, par value could be used.

stock and $600,000 in 8% preferred stock (dividends of $48,000). We can prepare condensed income statements under the three methods as follows:

	(1) All Common Stock	(2) Debt and Common Stock	(3) Preferred Stock and Common Stock
Income before interest and taxes	$ 180,000	$ 180,000	$ 180,000
Interest expense at 7%	0	42,000	0
Income before taxes	180,000	138,000	180,000
Income taxes at 40%	72,000	55,200	72,000
Net income	$ 108,000	$ 82,800	$ 108,000
Less: preferred stock dividends	0	0	48,000
Earnings available for common stock divided by	$ 108,000	$ 82,800	$ 60,000
Common equity invested equals	$1,000,000	$ 400,000	$ 400,000
Return on common equity	10.8%	20.7%	15%

The plans that included debt or preferred stock both resulted in lower earnings available for common equity, but a higher ROE than would have been achieved if all equity had been used.

Before we go on, please do not get the impression that dividends on preferred stock are an expense. They are not, but they must be subtracted from net income to reach earnings available for common stockholders because the preferred shareholders have a prior claim on the earnings of the firm. They must receive their dividends before common stockholders can receive dividends, so the amount left for possible distribution to common stockholders is reduced.

Unfortunately, leverage works both ways. It is good for the common stockholder when earnings are high, bad when they are low. Suppose that the firm earns only $60,000 before interest and taxes. We would then have the following results:

	(1) All Common	(2) $600,000 Debt	(3) $600,000 Preferred
Income before interest and taxes	$60,000	$60,000	$60,000
Interest expense	0	42,000	0
Income before taxes	60,000	-18,000	60,000
Income taxes at 40% rate	24,000	7,200	24,000
Net income	36,000	10,800	36,000
Preferred stock dividends	0	0	42,000
Earnings available for common	$ 36,000	$10,800	($6,000)
Common equity	$1,000,000	$400,000	$400,000
ROE	3.6%	2.7%	negative

As you can see, ROE is highest if all common equity is used, but the return is very low. Leverage can be used by firms that have relatively stable revenues and expenses, like public utilities. It is risky for firms in cyclical businesses like automobiles, aircraft, and construction, where income fluctuates greatly from year to year. A couple of bad years in a row could bring a heavily leveraged firm into bankruptcy.

Earnings per Share (EPS)

An investor considering the purchase of 100 or so shares of stock in a firm is not as concerned with the total income of the firm so much as with his share of that income. His share is his proportional interest in the firm. In order to make such determination simple, firms present earnings per share data. Earnings per share, or EPS, is the most widely cited statistic in the financial press, business section of newspapers, and recommendations by brokerage firms and other investment advisers. EPS is calculated as follows:

$$\text{EPS} = \frac{\text{net income} - \text{dividends on preferred stock}}{\text{weighted average common shares outstanding}}$$

The weighted average common shares outstanding is used because it represents the best measure of the shares outstanding throughout the period, rather than just at the end of the period. If we assume that Graham Company had 22,000 shares outstanding all through 19X5 and 19X6, as well as at the ends of those years, its EPS figures would be:

19X5 $\quad \dfrac{\$94,800}{22,000} = \quad \$4.31$

19X6 $\quad \dfrac{\$103,200}{22,000} = \quad \$4.69$

EPS in 19X6 was $.38 higher than in 19X5. This is an 8.8% growth rate, which we can calculate as follows:

$$\text{Growth rate of EPS} = \frac{\text{EPS current year} - \text{EPS prior year}}{\text{EPS prior year}}$$

For Graham Company:

$$\frac{\$4.69 - \$4.31}{\$4.31} = \quad 8.8\%$$

The growth rate of EPS is an extremely useful piece of information to a financial analyst interested in the common stock of a firm. In general, the higher the growth rate the investing public as a whole expects from a firm, the more it will be willing to pay for the common stock. High growth rates (15% or more) are one reason for the high prices of stocks like IBM.

Growth rates should be calculated over a number of years, rather than for a single year as we have done here. A single large increase in EPS does not mean that the firm is growing. It might simply reflect a rebound from a particularly poor year.

Dilution of EPS. Recent years have seen the increasing use of *convertible securities,* bonds and preferred stock that can be converted into common stock at the option of the owner. The fact that these securities can be converted into common shares poses the problem of potential decreases, or dilution, of EPS. Earnings would have to be spread over a greater number of shares. The calculation of EPS when dilution is possible can be incredibly complex.[2] We shall show you a single illustration, which is necessarily quite simple. Assume that a firm has net income of $200,000, 80,000 common shares outstanding, and an issue of convertible preferred stock. The preferred stock has dividends of $20,000 per year and is convertible into 30,000 common shares. Using the basic formula, EPS would be as follows:

$$\text{EPS} \quad = \quad \frac{\$200,000 - \$20,000}{80,000} \quad = \quad \frac{\$180,000}{80,000} \quad = \quad \$2.25$$

In some cases the $2.25 would be presented on the income statement and called *primary earnings per share.* Then, another EPS calculation would also be made, called *fully diluted earnings per share.* Fully diluted EPS is calculated assuming that the convertible securities had been converted into common stock at the beginning of the year. Had this occurred, there would have been no preferred dividends, but there would have been an additional 30,000 common shares outstanding for the entire year. We would calculate fully diluted EPS by adding back the preferred dividends on the convertible stock to the $180,000 earnings available for common stock and adding 30,000 shares to the denominator.

$$\text{Fully diluted EPS} \quad = \quad \frac{\$180,000 + \$20,000}{80,000 + 30,000} \quad = \quad \frac{\$200,000}{110,000} \quad = \quad \$1.82$$

You have probably spotted the fact that the numerator of fully diluted EPS is net income. This is not always so. For example, some of the firm's preferred stock might be convertible, some not. You cannot count on the numerator being equal to net income and it is safer to add back the dividends on the convertible preferred stock to earnings available for common stock.

Price-Earnings Ratio (PE)

The price-earnings ratio is the ratio of the market price of a share of common stock to its earnings per share. The ratio indicates the amount an investor is paying to buy a dollar of

---

[2]The computation of EPS is governed by *Accounting Principles Board Opinion No. 15* (New York: American Institute of Certified Public Accountants, 1969) and *Unofficial Accounting Interpretations of APB Opinion No. 15* (New York: American Institute of Certified Public Accountants, 1970). Together, these two documents contain about 100 pages.

earnings. The PE ratios of high-growth companies will sometimes be very high, while those of low-growth or declining firms will be very low. Assume that Graham Company's common stock sold at $60 per share at the end of 19X5 and $70 at the end of 19X6. The PE ratios are:

19X5 $\dfrac{\$60.00}{\$\ 4.31}\ =\ 14$

19X6 $\dfrac{\$70.00}{\$\ 4.69}\ =\ 14.9$

The PE ratio increased from 19X5 to 19X6. This could have happened because the firm's EPS had been growing rather slowly until 19X6 and investors believed the rate would increase in the future. This would justify a higher PE ratio. It is also possible that PE ratios as a whole increased across the market because of good economic news and expectations of good business conditions.

Dividend Yield and Payout Ratio

We have been viewing earnings available for common stockholders as the major return that accrues to owners of common stock. However, investors do not "get" EPS. They get dividends and, they hope, increases in the market value of their shares. The dividend yield, calculated as the ratio of dividends per share to market price per share, is a measure of the current cash income that an investor can obtain from a share of stock. In 19X6 the Graham Company declared and paid $73,200 in dividends, which comes to $3.33 per share on 22,000 shares. At the market price of $70, the dividend yield is about 4.76%.

$\dfrac{\$3.33}{\$70.00}\ =\ 4.76\%$

The payout ratio is the ratio of dividends per share to earnings per share. For Graham Company the payout ratio in 19X6 is calculated as 71%, which is $3.33/$4.69. In general, companies with high growth rates show relatively low dividend yields and payout ratios. Such companies invest the cash that could be used for dividends. Investors who favor high-growth companies are not looking for dividends so much as increases in the market price of the common stock. Because such hoped-for increases may or may not come about, investing in high-growth companies is generally riskier than investing in companies that pay relatively high, stable dividends.

Companies will therefore tend to attract investors who have particular philosophies about risk and return. American Telephone and Telegraph (AT&T) has been said to be a favorite of "widows and orphans," investors who are looking for high, safe dividends. International Business Machines (IBM) has been favored by investors who prefer to seek increases in the price of the common stock rather than income from dividends.

Ratios and Evaluation

The profitability measures described and illustrated here are used primarily by current stockholders who are trying to decide whether to keep the stock, buy more, or sell it, and by nonstockholders who are considering buying the stock. They are also used to some extent by long-term creditors like bondholders, but are relatively less important to bondholders than are the measures of solvency, the topic of the next section.

Comparison is again the key to making use of the ratios computed. Comparisons would normally be made both with prior years' ratios for the same company and with currently computed ratios for other companies. Critical to such comparisons, of course, is an understanding of the differences that can result when the companies being compared do not use the same accounting methods. For example, a firm that uses the sum-of-the-years'-digits method of depreciation will show lower net book values for its fixed assets than a firm using the straight-line method, with corresponding differences in both total assets and net income. Differences in inventory methods also affect profitability measures because they affect both total assets and net income. Until 1977, profitability measures could be significantly affected by whether the firm acquired major fixed assets through the issuance of long-term debt or stock or through the use of long-term leasing arrangements. To a great extent, the effects of the difference in financing arrangements were eliminated by the issuance of *Financial Accounting Standards No. 13*,[3] but some differences may remain. A special problem arises in comparisons of firms in the petroleum industry, where for many years two significantly different methods of accounting for the costs of unsuccessful drilling efforts have been generally accepted.

When using profitability measures, one must remember that a single transaction can have a significant effect on the ratios. Net income was used in many of the ratios in this section. When an extraordinary item of some kind has affected the net income for the year, many analysts would use, for their calculations, income before the effect of the extraordinary item.

SOLVENCY

Solvency refers to long-term safety, to the likelihood that the firm will be able to pay its long-term liabilities. It is therefore somewhat like liquidity, but it has a much longer time horizon. Both long-term creditors and stockholders are interested in solvency: the long-term creditor, because of a concern about receiving interest payments and a return of principal; the stockholder, because he cannot hope to receive dividends and increased market prices unless the firm survives.

Debt Ratio

One common measure of solvency is the debt ratio, which is calculated as follows:

$$\text{Debt ratio} = \frac{\text{total liabilities}}{\text{total assets}}$$

This ratio measures the proportion of debt in the firm's capital structure. It is also called the debt-to-assets ratio. Like some other ratios, there are variations that provide much the same information. For example, some analysts will calculate a debt-to-equity ratio,

[3]Financial Accounting Standards Board, *Statement of Financial Accounting Standards No. 13, Accounting for Leases* (Stamford, Conn.: Financial Accounting Standards Board, 1976).

which is total liabilities divided by stockholder equity. This variation gives debt as a percentage of the amount invested by stockholders. Some analysts will calculate a ratio of long-term liabilities to total assets, or of long-term liabilities to fixed assets like property, plant, and equipment. The basic objective is the same with all of these ratios: to determine how debt-laden the firm is. The higher the proportion of debt in the capital structure, the riskier the firm. Of course, firms in different industries can handle different percentages of debt. Public utilities typically have very high percentages of debt, manufacturing firms somewhat less.

We can calculate the debt ratio for Graham Company for both 19X5 and 19X6. The results are:

19X5 $\quad \dfrac{\$610,000}{\$1,380,000} \ = \ 44.2\%$

19X6 $\quad \dfrac{\$750,000}{\$1,550,000} \ = \ 48.4\%$

Notice that if we subtract the debt ratio from 1, we get the proportion of stockholder equity in the capital structure. This is usually called the equity ratio. It is, like the debt ratio, a way of measuring solvency, but from a different standpoint.

The debt ratio increased from 19X5 to 19X6, but whether it is near a dangerous level we cannot tell without knowing a good deal more. We can obtain some additional information by calculating the burden that interest expense places on the firm. We do this by calculating the ratio *times interest earned*.

Times Interest Earned

Times interest earned is a measure of coverage of interest expense generated by operations. The higher the ratio, the more likely that the firm will be able to continue meeting the interest payments. The calculation is given below.

$$\text{Times interest earned} \ = \ \frac{\text{income before interest and taxes}}{\text{interest expense}}$$

We use income before interest and taxes because interest is a tax-deductible expense. If a firm had income before interest and taxes that was exactly equal to interest expense, it would pay no taxes and show a zero net income. Times interest earned would be 1, which is extremely low.

The Graham Company had interest coverage of 4.8 times in 19X5, but slipped to 4.6 times in 19X6 because of higher interest expense.

19X5 $\quad \dfrac{\$200,000}{\$\ 42,000} \ = \ 4.8 \text{ times}$

19X6 $\quad \dfrac{\$220,000}{\$\ 48,000} \ = \ 4.6 \text{ times}$

Some analysts prefer to use a variation of this ratio. They will add depreciation back to income before interest and taxes in the numerator. Reasoning that depreciation does not require cash payments, these analysts believe that their calculation approximates the total amount of cash available to pay interest.

Cash Flow to Total Debt

A major study involving ratios computed for actual companies showed that the single best ratio for predicting failure of a firm was the ratio of cash flow to total debt.[4] Cash flow was defined as net income plus depreciation plus amortization plus depletion, and total debt as total liabilities plus preferred stock. The ratio is therefore computed as

$$\text{Cash flow to total debt} \;=\; \frac{\text{net income} + \text{depreciation} + \text{amortization} + \text{depletion}}{\text{total liabilities} + \text{preferred stock}}$$

The Graham Company has no amortization or depletion that we can identify, and no preferred stock. The values of the ratio are therefore

$$19\text{X}5 \qquad \frac{\$94{,}800 + \$75{,}000}{\$610{,}000} \;=\; \frac{\$169{,}800}{\$610{,}000} \;=\; 27.8\%$$

$$19\text{X}6 \qquad \frac{\$103{,}200 + \$90{,}000}{\$750{,}000} \;=\; \frac{\$193{,}200}{\$750{,}000} \;=\; 25.8\%$$

The decline in the ratio does not seem serious, though comparison of the ratio with the industry average might indicate a potential problem.

SUMMARY

Ratio analysis is used in making investment decisions. Analysts are concerned with trends in ratios and with whether ratios of a particular firm are in line with those of other firms in the same industry. Ratio analysis can be classified into three major types: liquidity, profitability, and solvency.

Which ratios are used and the emphasis placed on each depend on the type of decision to be made. Short-term creditors are primarily concerned with liquidity. Long-term creditors are more concerned with solvency than with liquidity and profitability, but the latter aspects are still important. Common stockholders and people considering the purchase of common stock are most concerned with profitability, but liquidity and solvency are still significant.

Ratio analysis must be used with care. Ratios provide information only in the context of a comparison, and comparisons with other firms must be more than simple ratio comparisons. Different accounting methods like LIFO and FIFO, sum-of-the-years'-digits depreciation and straight-line depreciation can cause similar firms to show quite different ratios.

[4] See William H. Beaver, "Financial Ratios as Predictors of Failure," Empirical Research in Accounting, Selected Studies, 1966, *Journal of Accounting Research*, 1967, pp. 71–111.

KEY TERMS

convertible securities	quick assets
dilution (of earning per share)	leverage
leverage	solvency
liquidity	working capital

KEY FORMULAS

Liquidity Ratios

Current ratio = current assets/current liabilities

$$\text{Quick ratio (acid-test ratio)} = \frac{\text{cash} + \text{marketable securities} + \text{receivables}}{\text{current liabilities}}$$

$$\text{Accounts receivable turnover} = \frac{\text{credit sales}}{\text{average accounts receivable}}$$

$$\text{Days' sales in accounts receivable} = \frac{\text{ending accounts receivable}}{\text{average daily credit sales}}$$

$$\text{Inventory turnover} = \frac{\text{cost of goods sold}}{\text{average inventory}}$$

$$\text{Days' sales in inventory} = \frac{\text{ending inventory}}{\text{average daily cost of goods sold}}$$

Profitability Ratios

$$\text{Return on assets (ROA)} = \frac{\text{net income} + \text{interest expense}}{\text{average total assets}}$$

$$\text{Return on common equity (ROE)} = \frac{\text{net income} - \text{preferred stock dividends}}{\text{average common stockholders' equity}}$$

$$\text{Earnings per share (EPS)} = \frac{\text{net income} - \text{preferred stock dividends}}{\text{weighted average common shares}}$$

$$\text{Price-earnings ratio (PE)} = \frac{\text{market price per share}}{\text{earnings per share}}$$

$$\text{Dividend yield} = \frac{\text{dividend per share}}{\text{market price per share}}$$

$$\text{Gross profit ratio} = \frac{\text{gross profit}}{\text{sales}}$$

$$\text{Return on sales} = \frac{\text{net income}}{\text{sales}}$$

$$\text{Payout ratio} = \frac{\text{dividends per share}}{\text{earnings per share}}$$

Solvency Ratios

$$\text{Debt ratio} = \frac{\text{total liabilities}}{\text{total assets}}$$

$$\text{Times interest earned} = \frac{\text{income before interest and taxes}}{\text{interest expense}}$$

$$\text{Cash flow to debt} = \frac{\text{net income} + \text{depreciation} + \text{amortization} + \text{depletion}}{\text{total liabilities} + \text{preferred stock}}$$

REVIEW PROBLEM

Financial Statements for the Quinn Company are given below.

Quinn Company Balance Sheets as of December 31

	19X7	19X6
Cash	$180,000	$200,000
Accounts receivable	850,000	830,000
Inventory	620,000	560,000
Total current assets	1,650,000	1,590,000
Plant and equipment	7,540,000	6,650,000
Accumulated depreciation	(1,920,000)	(1,500,000)
Total assets	$7,270,000	$6,740,000
Accounts payable	$220,000	$190,000
Accrued expenses	450,000	440,000
Total current liabilities	670,000	630,000
Long-term debt	1,000,000	950,000
Total liabilities	1,670,000	1,580,000
Common stock, no par value	4,000,000	4,000,000
Retained earnings	1,600,000	1,160,000
Total equities	$7,270,000	$6,740,000

Quinn Company Income Statement for 19X7

Sales		$8,650,000
Cost of goods sold		4,825,000
Gross profit		3,825,000
Depreciation	$ 420,000	
Other operating expenses	2,135,000	2,555,000
Income before interest and taxes		1,270,000
Interest expense		70,000
Income before taxes		1,200,000
Income taxes at 30% rate		360,000
Net income		$ 840,000

During 19X7 the firm declared and paid cash dividends of $400,000. There were 200,000 shares of common stock outstanding throughout the year. The market price of the stock at year end was $65. All sales are on credit.

Required: Compute the following ratios as of the end of 19X7 or for the year ended December 31, 19X7, whichever is appropriate.

1. Current ratio
2. Quick ratio
3. Accounts receivable turnover
4. Days' credit sales in accounts receivable
5. Inventory turnover
6. Days' sales in inventory
7. Gross profit ratio
8. Return on sales
9. Return on assets (ROA)
10. Return on equity (ROE)
11. Earnings per share (EPS)
12. Price-earnings ratio (PE)
13. Dividend yield
14. Payout ratio
15. Debt ratio
16. Times interest earned
17. Cash flow to debt ratio

Answers to Review Problem

1. Current ratio

$$\frac{\$1,650,000}{\$670,000} = 2.46 \text{ to } 1$$

2. Quick ratio

$$\frac{\$180,000 + \$850,000}{\$670,000} = 1.54 \text{ to } 1$$

3. Accounts receivable turnover

$$\frac{\$8,650,000}{(\$850,000 + \$830,000)/2} = 10.3 \text{ times}$$

4. Days' sales in accounts receivable

$$\frac{\$850,000}{\$8,650,000/365} = \quad 36 \text{ days}$$

5. Inventory turnover

$$\frac{\$4,825,000}{(\$620,000 + \$560,000)/2} = \quad 8.2 \text{ times}$$

6. Days' sales in inventory

$$\frac{\$620,000}{\$4,825,000/365} = \quad 47 \text{ days}$$

7. Gross profit ratio

$$\frac{\$3,825,000}{\$8,650,000} = \quad 44.2\%$$

8. Return on sales

$$\frac{\$840,000}{\$8,650,000} = \quad 9.7\%$$

9. Return on assets

$$\frac{\$840,000 + \$70,000}{(\$7,270,000 + \$6,740,000)/2} = \quad 13.0\%$$

10. Return on equity

$$\frac{\$840,000}{(\$5,600,000 + \$5,160,000)/2} = \quad 15.6\%$$

11. Earnings per share

$$\frac{\$840,000}{200,000} = \quad \$4.20$$

12. Price-earnings ratio

$$\frac{\$65}{\$4.20} = 15.5 \text{ times}$$

13. Dividend yield

$$\frac{\$2}{\$65} = \quad 3.1\%$$

14. Payout ratio

$$\frac{\$2}{\$4.20} = \quad 47.6\%$$

15. Debt ratio

$$\frac{\$1,670,000}{\$7,270,000} = \quad 23.0\%$$

16. Times interest earned

$$\frac{\$1,270,000}{\$70,000} = \quad 18 \text{ times}$$

17. Cash flow to debt ratio

$$\frac{\$840,000 + \$420,000}{\$1,670,000} = 75.5\%$$

ASSIGNMENT MATERIAL

Questions for Discussion

17-1 Dividend yield   A friend of yours told you that he bought some stock in NMC Corporation five years ago for $20 per share. The firm is now paying a $5 dividend per share and the stock sells for $100. He says that the 25% dividend yield he is getting is an excellent return. How did he calculate the dividend yield? Is he correct? What would you say the dividend yield is?

17-2 Ratios and accounting methods   The LIFO Company uses the last-in-first-out method of inventory determination. The FIFO Company uses first-in-first-out. The firms have virtually the same operations, same physical quantities of inventory, same sales, same fixed assets. What differences would you expect to find in ratios of the two firms?

17-3 Ratios and operating decisions   The Bronson Company and the Corman Company are in the same industry and have virtually identical operations. The only difference between them is that Bronson rents 60% of its plant and equipment on short-term leases, while Corman owns all of its fixed assets. Corman has long-term debt of about 60% of the net book value of its fixed assets. Bronson has none. The two firms show about the same net income because Bronson's rent and depreciation are about the same as Corman's depreciation and interest. What difference would you expect to find in the ratios of the two firms?

17-4 Ratios and accounting methods   The SYD Company uses sum-of-the-years'-digits depreciation. The SL Company uses straight-line depreciation. Both firms have about the same original cost invested in fixed assets. Their operations are also about the same. They have both been growing rapidly, in sales, profits, and amounts invested in all assets. What differences would you expect to find between the two firms in their income statements, balance sheets, and ratios?

17-5 Liquidity   Suppose that you are the chief loan officer of a medium-sized bank. Two firms have applied for short-term loans, but you can only grant one because of limited funds available for lending. Both firms have the same working capital, same current ratio. The firms are in the same industry and their current ratios are well above the normal industry averages. What additional information about the firms' current positions would you seek in making your decision?

17-6 Seasonality and ratios   The following independent questions deal with the problems of seasonality that must be confronted when performing ratio analysis.

1. The inventory turnover of the Robertson Toy Store, which does about half of its business in November and December, was computed at 22 times. The computation was based on the average of the beginning and ending inventories. The firm has a fiscal year end of January 31. Does the turnover figure reflect the firm's actual activity?
2. The president of the Skimpy Bathing Suit Company was bragging that his current ratio was 5 to 1 and his acid-test ratio 4 to 1. The ratios were computed on October 31. Would you expect the firm to have such ratios throughout the year? Explain your answer.

3. The accounts receivable turnover for the Long Golf Ball Company, which sells golf balls only in the northeastern United States, was only 2 times. The computation was based on the receivables at June 30, 19X7 and June 30, 19X8. Does the firm seem to have problems collecting its accounts?

17-7 Price-earnings ratio A friend of yours tells you that his investment strategy is simple. He looks around for the stocks with the lowest price-earnings ratios and buys them. He reasons that he is getting the most for his money that way. Do you agree that this is a good strategy?

Exercises

17-8 Effects of transactions Indicate the effects of each transaction on (a) the current ratio, and (b) the quick ratio. Assume that both ratios are greater than 1 to 1 prior to the transactions. There are three possible answers: increase, decrease, and no effect.

1. Pay a current liability.
2. Borrow cash on a short-term loan.
3. Borrow cash on a long-term loan.
4. Buy inventory on account payable.
5. Sell, at a loss, marketable securities held as temporary investments.
6. Collect an account receivable.
7. Record accrued expenses payable.
8. Retire long-term debt by paying cash.
9. Sell a plant asset for cash at a loss.
10. Buy equipment on a long-term note payable.

17-9 Relationships Answer the questions for each of the following independent situations.

1. A firm has a current ratio of 2.5 to 1. Its current liabilities are $50,000. What are its current assets?
2. A firm has return on assets of 12%, return on equity of 15%. There is no preferred stock. Net income is $600,000, and average total assets are $6,000,000.
   (a) What is average stockholder equity?
   (b) What is interest expense?
3. A firm has a current ratio of 3 to 1, an acid-test ratio of 1.8 to 1, and its cash and receivables are $90,000. Its only current assets are cash, receivables, and inventory.
   (a) What are current liabilities?
   (b) What is inventory?
4. A firm has accounts receivable turnover of 6 times, inventory turnover of 4 times. Both accounts receivable and inventory have remained constant for several years. On January 1, 19X8 the firm bought inventory. All sales are on credit.
   (a) On the average, how long will it be before the new inventory is sold?
   (b) On the average, how long after the inventory is sold will cash be collected?
5. A firm had current assets of $200,000. It then paid a current liability of $40,000. After the payment, the current ratio was 2 to 1. What were current liabilities before the payment was made?
6. A firm normally has accounts receivable equal to 35 days' credit sales. During the coming year it expects credit sales of $730,000 spread evenly over the year. What should its accounts receivable be at the end of the year?

17-10 Leverage A firm is considering the retirement of $1,000,000 in 8% bonds payable. These bonds are the only interest-bearing debt the company has. The retirement plan calls for the firm to issue 20,000 shares of common stock at a total price of $1,000,000 and use the proceeds to buy back the bonds.

Stockholders' equity is now $1,200,000, with 25,000 shares of common stock outstanding (no preferred stock). The first expects to earn $400,000 before interest and taxes in the coming year. The tax rate is 40%.

Required

1. Determine net income, EPS, and ROE for the coming year, assuming that the bonds are retired before the beginning of the coming year. Assume no change in stockholders' equity except for the new stock issue.
2. Determine net income, EPS, and ROE for the coming year assuming that the bonds are not retired. Again, assume that year-end stockholders' equity will be the same as at the beginning of the year.

17-11 Return on assets and return on equity   The Travis Company has annual sales of $10,000,000 and return on sales of 8%. Interest expense is $400,000. Total assets are $8,000,000 and the debt ratio is 60%. The firm has no preferred stock.

Required

1. Determine net income, return on assets, and return on equity.
2. Suppose that the firm could increase its return on sales to 8.5% and keep the same level of sales. What would net income, return on assets, and return on equity be?
3. Suppose that the firm reduced its debt ratio to 50% by retiring debt. New common stock was issued to finance the retirement, keeping total assets at $8,000,000. Sales are $10,000,000 and return on sales is now 8.8% because of lower interest expense that now totals $320,000. What are net income, return on assets, and return on equity?

17-12 Financing alternatives   The Marmex Company has just been founded by three people. The founders are trying to decide how the firm should be financed. There are three choices:

1. Issue $2,000,000 in common stock.
2. Issue $1,200,000 in common stock, $800,000 in 8% bonds.
3. Issue $1,200,000 in common stock, $800,000 in 9% preferred stock.

Income before interest and taxes is expected to be $400,000 per year. The tax rate is 40%.

Required

1. Compute net income, earnings available for common stock, and return on equity for each financing choice.
2. Suppose that the tax rate increases to 60%. Redo part 1. Can you draw any conclusions about the effects of tax rates on the relative desirability of the three choices?

17-13 Return on assets and equity   The Randolph Company has average total assets of $2,000,000 and a debt ratio of 30%. Interest expense is $45,000 and return on average total assets is 10%. The firm has no preferred stock.

Required

1. Determine net income, average stockholder equity, and return on equity.
2. Suppose that sales have been $1,550,000 annually and are expected to continue at this level. If the firm could increase its return on sales by one percentage point, what would be its net income, return on assets, and return on equity?
3. Refer to the original data and your answers to part 1. Suppose that the firm retires $300,000 in debt and therefore saves interest expense of $27,000 annually. The firm would issue additional common stock in the amount of $300,000 to finance the retirement. Total assets would remain at $2,000,000. What would be the net income, return on assets, and return on equity? Ignore income taxes.

17-14 Ratios The following financial statements are available for the Massin Company.

Massin Company Income Statement
19X6 (In Thousands of Dollars)

Sales		$3,200
Cost of goods sold		1,400
Gross profit		1,800
Operating expenses:		
Depreciation	$240	
Other	860	1,100
Income before interest and taxes		500
Interest expense		60
Income before taxes		440
Income taxes at 40% rate		176
Net income		$ 264

Massin Company Balance Sheet as of
December 31, 19X6 (In Thousands of Dollars)

Assets			Equities	
Cash		$200	Accounts payable	$210
Accounts receivable		400	Accrued expenses	280
Inventory		350		
Total current assets		950	Total current liabilities	490
Plant and equipment	$3,200		Long-term debt	680
Accumulated			Common stock	920
depreciation	1,200	2,000	Retained earnings	860
Total assets		$2,950	Total equities	$2,950

The firm has 200,000 common shares outstanding. The price of the stock is $21. Dividends per share are $.80. The balance sheet at the end of 19X5 showed the same amounts as that at the end of 19X6.

Required

Calculate the following ratios.

1. Current ratio
2. Acid-test ratio
3. Accounts receivable turnover
4. Inventory turnover
5. Gross profit ratio
6. Return on sales
7. Return on assets
8. Return on equity
9. Earnings per share
10. Price-earnings ratio
11. Dividend yield
12. Payout ratio

13. Debt ratio
14. Times interest earned
15. Cash flow to debt

17-15 Current asset activity The treasurer of the Billingsgate Company has asked for your assistance in analyzing the firm's current liquidity. He provides the following data.

	19X6	19X5	19X4
Total credit sales	$480,000	$440,000	$395,000
Cost of goods sold—all sales	320,000	290,000	245,000
Accounts receivable at year end	64,000	48,000	31,000
Inventory at year end	50,000	44,000	38,000

Required

1. Compute accounts receivable turnover for 19X5 and 19X6.
2. Compute days' credit sales in accounts receivable at the ends of 19X5 and 19X6.
3. Compute inventory turnover for 19X5 and 19X6.
4. Compute days' sales in inventory at the end of 19X5 and 19X6.
5. Comment on the trends in the ratios. Do the trends seem to be favorable or unfavorable for each ratio?

Problems

17-16 Effects of transactions on ratios For each of the following transactions, indicate its effects on the firm's current ratio, acid-test ratio, and debt ratio. There are three possible answers: (1) increase, (2) decrease, and (3) no effect. Before each transaction takes place, the current ratio is greater than 1 to 1, the acid-test ratio less than 1 to 1.

	Effects		
	Current Ratio	Acid-Test Ratio	Debt Ratio
Example: An account payable is paid.	+	−	−
1. Inventory is bought for cash.	___	___	___
2. A sale is made on account, with cost of sales being less than the selling price.	___	___	___
3. Long-term bonds are issued for cash.	___	___	___
4. Land is sold for cash at its book value.	___	___	___
5. Marketable securities being held as temporary investments are sold at a gain.	___	___	___
6. Common stock is issued in exchange for plant assets.	___	___	___
7. An account receivable is collected.	___	___	___
8. Long-term debt is issued for plant assets.	___	___	___
9. A dividend payable in cash is declared, but not paid.	___	___	___
10. The dividend in 9 is paid.	___	___	___
11. A short-term bank loan is paid.	___	___	___
12. Depreciation expense is recorded.	___	___	___
13. Obsolete inventory is written off, with the debit to a loss account.	___	___	___

17-17 Comparison of firms Condensed financial statements for the Amex Company and the Corex Company are given below. Both firms are in the same industry and use the same accounting methods. Balance-sheet data for both firms were the same at the end of 19X4 as at the end of 19X5.

Balance Sheets End of 19X5
(In Thousands of Dollars)

	Amex Company	Corex Company
Cash	$ 185	$90
Accounts receivable	215	170
Inventory	340	220
Plant and equipment (net)	850	810
Total assets	$1,590	$1,290
Accounts payable	$150	$140
Other current liabilities	80	90
Long-term debt	300	500
Common stock	700	300
Retained earnings	360	260
Total equities	$1,590	$1,290

Income Statements for 19X5

	Amex Company		Corex Company	
Sales		$3,050		$2,800
Cost of goods sold		1,400		1,350
Gross profit		1,650		1,450
Operating expenses:				
Depreciation	$280		$240	
Other	1,040	1,320	900	1,140
Income before interest and taxes		330		310
Interest expense		30		55
Income before taxes		300		255
Income taxes at 40% rate		120		102
Net income		$ 180		$ 153
Earnings per share		$.90		$.77
Dividends per share		.40		.20
Market price of common stock		$12.00		$11.50

Required: On the basis of the data given determine the following:

1. Which firm seems to be more liquid?
2. Which firm seems to be more profitable?
3. Which firm seems to be more solvent?
4. Which stock seems to be a better buy?

Support your answers with whatever calculations you believe appropriate.

17-18 Construction of financial statements using ratios The following data are available for the Wasserman Pharmaceutical Company as of December 31, 19X4 and for the year then ended.

Current ratio	3 to 1
Days' sales in accounts receivable	60 days
Inventory turnover	3 times
Debt ratio	40%
Current liabilities	$300,000
Stockholder equity, all common stock	$1,200,000
Return on sales	8%
Return on common equity	15%
Gross profit ratio	40%

The firm has no preferred stock, no marketable securities, and no prepaid expenses. Assume that beginning-of-year balance-sheet figures are the same as end-of-year figures. All sales are on credit and the only noncurrent assets are plant and equipment.

Required: Prepare a balance sheet as of December 31, 19X4, and an income statement for 19X4 in as much detail as you can with the available information. Round the calculation of average daily credit sales to the nearest dollar.

17-19 Dilution of EPS The Boston Tarrier Company has been very successful in recent years, as evidenced by the income statement data given below. The treasurer of the firm is concerned because he expects the holders of the firm's convertible preferred stock to exchange their shares for common shares early in the coming year. All of the firm's preferred stock is convertible, and the number of common shares issuable on conversion is 280,000.

Boston Tarrier Company
Selected Income Statement Data

	19X6	19X5
Net income	$2,150,000	$1,800,000
Preferred stock dividends	600,000	600,000
Earnings available for common	$1,550,000	$1,200,000

Throughout 19X6 and 19X5 the firm had 420,000 shares of common stock outstanding.

Required

1. Compute primary EPS for 19X5 and 19X6. Round to nearest penny.
2. Compute fully diluted EPS for 19X5 and 19X6. Round to nearest penny.

17-20 Inventory turnover and return on equity The Timmons Company is presently earning net income of $300,000 per year, which gives a 10% return on equity. The president of the firm believes that inventory can be reduced through the use of tighter controls on buying. Any reduction of inventory would free cash, which would be used to pay a dividend to stockholders. Hence, stockholders' equity would be reduced by the same amount as inventory.

Inventory turnover is now 3 times per year. Cost of goods sold is running at $2,700,000 annually. The president hopes that the turnover can be increased to 5 times. He also believes that sales, cost of goods sold, and net income would remain at their current levels.

Required

1. Determine the average inventory that the firm currently holds.

2. Determine the average inventory that would be held if turnover could be increased to 5 times per year.

3. Determine the return on equity that would be earned if the firm could increase turnover and reduce stockholders' equity by the amount of the reduction in investment in inventory.

17-21 Ratios—industry averages The president of the Brewster Company has been concerned about the operating performance and financial strength of the firm. He has obtained data from an industry association that show the averages for all firms on certain ratios. He gives you these ratios and the most recent financial statements of the firm. The balance-sheet amounts were all about the same at the beginning of the year as they are now.

Brewster Company Balance Sheet
as of December 31, 19X6 (In Thousands of Dollars)

Assets		Equities	
Cash	$860	Accounts payable	$975
Accounts receivable	3,210	Accrued expenses	120
Inventory	2,840	Taxes payable	468
Total current assets	$6,910	Total current liabilities	$1,563
Plant and equipment (net)	7,090	Bonds payable, due 19X9	6,300
		Common stock, no par	4,287
		Retained earnings	1,850
Total assets	$14,000	Total equities	$14,000

Brewster Company Income Statement for 19X6

Sales	$11,800
Cost of goods sold	7,350
Gross profit	4,450
Operating expenses, including $650 depreciation	2,110
Operating profit	2,340
Interest expense	485
Income before taxes	1,855
Income taxes at 40% rate	742
Net income	$ 1,113

The firm has 95,000 shares of common stock outstanding, which gives earnings per share of $11.72 ($1,113,000/95,000). Dividends are $5 per share and the market price of the stock is $120. Average ratios for the industry are:

Current ratio	3.8 to 1	Return on equity	17.5%
Quick ratio	1.9 to 1	Price-earnings ratio	12.3
Accounts receivable turnover	4.8 times	Dividend yield	3.9%
Inventory turnover	3.6 times	Payout ratio	38.0%
Return on sales	7.6%	Debt ratio	50.0%
Return on assets	13.0%	Times interest earned	6 times
		Cash flow to debt	25.0%

Required

1. Compute the ratios shown above for Brewster Company.
2. Prepare comments to the president indicating areas of apparent strength and weakness of Brewster Company in relation to the industry.

17-22   Generation of cash flows   The Humbert Company must make a $600,000 payment on a bank loan at the end of March 19X9. Selected data for December 31, 19X8 are given below.

Cash	$110,000
Accounts receivable	380,000

Estimated cash payments required during the first three months of 19X9, exclusive of the payment to the bank, are $210,000. The firm expects sales to be $720,000 in the three-month period, all on credit. Accounts receivable are normally equal to 40 days' credit sales.

Required

1. Determine the expected balance in accounts receivable at the end of March 19X9. Assume that the three-month period has 90 days.
2. Determine whether the firm will have enough cash to pay the bank loan on March 31, 19X9.

17-23   Evaluation of trends and comparison with industry   Comparative balance sheets and income statements for the Marcus Manufacturing Company appear below. Your boss, who is the chief financial analyst for the Catch Hanmattan Bank, has asked you to analyze certain trends in the firm's operations and financing and to make some comparisons with the averages for firms in the same industry. The bank is considering the purchase of some shares of Marcus for one of its trust funds.

Marcus Manufacturing Company Balance Sheets
as of December 31 (In Thousands of Dollars)

	19X7	19X6
Cash	$ 170	$ 180
Accounts receivable	850	580
Inventory	900	760
Total current assets	1,920	1,520
Plant and equipment (net)	2,050	1,800
Total assets	$3,970	$3,320
Current liabilities	$ 812	$ 620
Long-term debt	1,640	1,300
Common stock	1,000	1,000
Retained earnings	518	400
Total equities	$3,970	$3,320

Selected data from 19X5 balance sheet:

Accounts receivable	$510
Inventory	620
Total assets	2,940
Stockholders' equity	1,320

Marcus Manufacturing Company Income Statements
(In Thousands of Dollars)

	19X7	19X6
Sales, all on credit	$4,700	$4,350
Cost of goods sold	2,670	2,460
Gross profit	2,030	1,890
Operating expenses	1,470	1,440
Income before interest and taxes	560	450
Interest expense	130	100
Income before taxes	430	350
Income taxes at 40% rate	172	140
Net income	$ 258	$ 210
Earnings per share	$2.58	$2.10
Market price of stock at year end	$32	$28
Dividends per share	$.96	$.80

The following ratios are averages for the industry in which Marcus operates.

Current ratio	2.7 to 1	Receivable turnover	8.5 times
Quick ratio	1.4 to 1	Inventory turnover	4.2 times
Debt ratio	52%	Return on assets	10%
Price-earnings ratio	11.5	Return on equity	13.5%
Dividend yield	4.5%	Return on sales	5.0%
Payout ratio	48.0%		

Required

Compute the ratios given above for the Marcus Company for 19X6 and 19X7 and comment on the trends in the ratios and on relationships to industry averages.

17-24 Trends in ratios As the chief investment officer of a large pension fund, you must make many investing decisions. One of your assistants has prepared the following ratios for MBI Corporation, a large multinational manufacturer.

	Industry Average All Years	Years 19X7	19X6	19X5
Current ratio	2.4	2.6	2.4	2.5
Quick ratio	1.6	1.55	1.6	1.65
Receivable turnover	8.1	7.5	7.9	8.3
Inventory turnover	4.0	4.3	4.2	4.0
Debt ratio	43.0%	38.0%	41.3%	44.6%
Return on assets	11.8%	13.1%	13.4%	13.5%
Return on equity	15.3%	15.1%	15.6%	15.9%
Price-earnings ratio	14.3	13.5	13.3	13.4
Times interest earned	8.3	9.7	9.5	8.9
Earnings per share growth rate	8.4%	7.1%	6.9%	7.0%

Required

What would your decision be in each of the following cases? Give your reasons.

1. Granting a short-term loan to MBI.
2. Buying long-term bonds of MBI on the open market. The bonds yield 7%, which is slightly less than the average for bonds in industry.
3. Buying the common stock of MBI.

17-25   Leverage   Mr. Harmon, the treasurer of the Stokes Company, has been considering two alternative plans for raising $2,000,000 that is needed for plant expansion and modernization. One choice is to issue long-term debt bearing 9% interest. The other is to issue 25,000 shares of common stock. The common stock is now selling at $80.

The modernization and expansion can be expected to increase the firm's operating profit, before interest and taxes, by $320,000 annually. Depreciation of $200,000 annually is included in the determination of the $320,000. The firm's condensed financial statements for 19X4 are given below.

Stokes Company Balance Sheet
as of December 31, 19X4

Current assets	$ 3,200,000	Current liabilities	$ 1,200,000
Plant and equipment (net)	7,420,000	Long-term debt, 7%	3,000,000
Other assets	870,000	Stockholders' equity	7,290,000
Total assets	$11,490,000	Total equities	$11,490,000

Stokes Company Condensed Income Statement for 19X4

Sales		$8,310,000
Cost of sales	$5,800,000	
Operating expenses	1,200,000	7,000,000
Operating profit		1,310,000
Interest expense		210,000
Income before taxes		1,100,000
Income taxes at 40% rate		440,000
Net income		$ 660,000
Earnings per share, based on 100,000 outstanding shares		$6.60
Dividends per share		$3.30

Mr. Harmon is concerned about the effect that issuing debt might have on the firm. The average debt ratio for firms in the industry is 42%. He believes that if this ratio is exceeded, the price-earnings ratio of the stock will fall to 11 because of the potentially greater risk. If the firm increases its common equity substantially by issuing new shares, he expects the price-earnings ratio to increase to 12.5. He also wonders what will happen to the dividend yield under each plan. The firm follows the practice of paying dividends equal to 50% of net income.

Required

1. For each financing plan, calculate the debt ratio that the firm would have after the securities (bonds or stock) are issued.
2. For each financing plan, determine the expected net income in 19X5, expected earnings per share, and the expected market price of the common stock.
3. Calculate, for each financing plan, the dividend per share that the firm would pay following its usual practice and the yield that would be obtained at the market prices from your answer to 2.
4. Suppose that you now own 100 shares of Stokes Company. Which alternative would you prefer the firm to use? Why?

TIME VALUE OF MONEY

What would you do if you had the choice between receiving a dollar from someone now and receiving a dollar from that person at some specified time in the future? Suppose that you could be absolutely sure that you would receive the dollar at the specified later time. Almost everyone would choose the first alternative as being the most desirable. We could say, generally, that a dollar now is worth more than a dollar to be received later. This statement sums up a principle: money has a time value.

The truth of this principle does not depend on the fact that prices are always going up, or that inflation would make the dollar received at a later time worth less in buying power. Nor is the statement true because of any *uncertainty* about receiving the dollar at a later date. (We assumed certainty.) The reason that a dollar now is worth more than the certainty of a dollar to be received in the future is that you could invest the dollar now and have more than a dollar at the specified later date.

Suppose that you could put the money into a savings account and earn 10% interest. If you did this with the dollar you received now, at the end of the year you would have $1.10, more than the dollar being offered to you at that later specified time. The advantage to taking the dollar now is that with this alternative you can have both the dollar and the earnings on it between now and the specified later date. The $.10 is what you would lose if you waited for the $1 until the end of the year. For the two alternatives to be equivalent, you would have to have a choice of $1 now or $1.10 one year hence.

The decision to take the dollar now can be viewed as the result of an analysis involving a comparison of the values of two alternatives. We compare the worth *now* of receiving a dollar now, and the worth *now* of receiving a dollar later. Our conclusion was that the present worth (called **present value**) of a dollar later is less than the present worth of a dollar now.

We shall compare the present values of the two alternatives: a dollar now or a dollar a year hence, given that the earnings rate is 10%.[1] The present value of the dollar now is $1. The present value of a dollar one year hence is the sum of money you would have to

---

[1]Although we are using years in the examples, the more general notion used in practice is that of a period, which could be any length of time. At the end of the appendix we illustrate the use of periods other than one year. For now, because it is simpler and because interest rates are usually stated as rates per year, we shall assume that a period is one year.

put into the bank now in order to have $1 at the end of the year. That sum is $.91 [$.91 + (10% × $.91) = $1]. Later in this appendix you will see how this can be readily determined. At this point you need only be convinced that the sum must be less than $1. The decision facing you is between an alternative with a present value of $1 and one with a present value of $.91. The intuitive choice of the first alternative is now supported by a mathematical analysis.

Many economic decisions involve investing money now in the hope of receiving more money later on. Any analysis of such decisions must consider the time value of money. Suppose that you have the chance to invest $10,000 today with a promise that you will receive $11,000 at the end of one year. Should you make the investment? To choose between receiving two equal sums at two different times is easy. The wisest choice is not always so obvious when, as in the present example, the alternatives are a given sum of money now and a larger sum at a specified later time. We can keep the $10,000 or invest it. We know that if we must wait for the money, the amount to be received should be larger than the amount available to us now, but how much larger? It depends on what else you could do with the cash you have or could borrow to make the investment.

Suppose that you could earn a rate of 12% per year by making some other investments. If you invest $10,000 at 12% per year, you have $11,200 at the end of one year [$10,000 + ($10,000 × 12%)]. Comparing the two alternatives, you could have $11,200 at the end of the year as a result of a $10,000 investment now; or you could have $11,000 at the end of the year for a $10,000 investmest now. All other things being equal, you would choose the first alternative. In this instance the comparison was between the two values at the *end* of the year.

What happens when the time horizon is extended beyond one period? Suppose you can invest $10,000 today in order to receive $12,000 at the end of two years. Should you make the investment if the prevailing, relevant interest rate is 10%? First determine how much you would have at the end of two years if you invested at a rate of 10%, as follows:

Now   You have $10,000
At the end of year 1   You have $11,000 [$10,000 + ($10,000 × 10%)]
At the end of year 2   You have $12,100 [$11,000 + ($11,000 × 10%)]

The interest paid in the second year is 10% on the total amount that you would have at the end of the first year, not 10% on the $10,000 you originally invested. This is the unique feature of **compound interest**: you earn the quoted interest rate on both the original amount invested and on the interest that you subsequently earn. Thus, if you put $10,000 into a bank account paying 10% interest, at the end of the first year you could withdraw $11,000 and then redeposit it to earn 10% on the entire amount for the second year.

When we compare the values of each available alternative at the end of the two years, we can see that it is not desirable to invest $10,000 now in order to receive $12,000 at the end of the two years. We could have $12,100 by investing elsewhere. Again, the comparison was between the two values at the end of the investment term.

Although it is possible to compare alternatives by focusing on some future date, it is more common in practice to compare alternatives in terms of their *present* values. In the usual situation, you will be confronted with alternatives that promise a specific amount or amounts of money at one or more specified times in the future. The usual analysis of such alternatives involves comparing the present values of the alternatives. In all instances it is necessary to consider an interest rate.

PRESENT VALUE OF A SINGLE AMOUNT

In evaluating an opportunity to receive a single payment at some time in the future at some interest rate, we must determine the present value of that choice. Instead of determining how much we would have at some future time if we invested $1 now, we want to know how much we would have to invest now to receive $1 at some future time. In an earlier example we saw that if the interest rate is 10%, an investment of $1 will accumulate to $1.21 at the end of two years ($12,100 on a $10,000 investment). The present value of $1.21 two years from now is thus $1. The procedure to determine present values is called **discounting,** and the interest rate used is called the **discount rate.**

Formulas can be used to determine the present value of a sum of money to be received in the future. Tables have been developed that allow you to determine present values without the formulas. Table A, for example, shows the present value of $1 to be received at various times in the future, at various interest rates.

Suppose we wanted to find in the table the present value of $1.21 to be received two years from now when we know that the interest rate is 10%. (We know already that the present value is $1, and that is the answer the table should give us.) We refer to the 10% column and the row for two periods, and we find the factor .826. This means that the present worth of $1 to be received two years from now is $.826 when the interest rate is 10%. We expect to get $1.21, not $1, so we must multiply the factor by $1.21. This multiplication produces a present value of $.99946. This is not significantly different from $1, the minor difference being due to rounding in preparing the table.

A few characteristics of Table A, page 646, are significant and should be understood. As you move down any column in Table A, the factors become smaller. You should expect this because the longer you must wait for a payment, the less it is worth now. If a dollar now is worth more than a dollar in one year, then surely a dollar one year hence is worth more than a dollar two years hence. The factors also become smaller as you move across the table in any row. As the interest rate increases, the present value of the amount to be received in the future decreases. This should also be expected. The higher interest rate you can expect to earn on the sum invested now, the less you need to invest now to accumulate a given amount at the end of some number of years.

In summary, the longer you have to wait for your money and the higher interest rate you can earn, the less it is worth to you now to receive some specified amount at a future date. The concept of present value must be understood to make decisions affecting more than a single period of time.

PRESENT VALUE OF A STREAM OF EQUAL PAYMENTS

Sometimes it is necessary to find the present value of a series of payments of equal amounts to be received at the ends of a series of years. This stream is called an **annuity**. Such a computation would be necessary to find the present value of, for example, bond interest received annually for a number of years. It would be possible to find the present value of an annuity by finding the present values of each component of the stream and adding them. For example, what is the present value of an annuity of $1 per year for four years at 10%?

Received at End of Year	Amount to Be Received	Present Value Factor (From Table A)	Present Value of Future Receipt
1	$1	.909	$0.909
2	$1	.826	.826
3	$1	.751	.751
4	$1	.683	.683
Present value of this annuity			$3.169

This procedure is cumbersome, especially if the annuity is to last for a large number of years. You are multiplying the same number ($1) by several different numbers (the present value factors). You know that the sum of these multiplications is equal to the product of the constant number ($1) and the sum of the different numbers. If you add up the present value factors (3.169) and multiply that sum by $1 you will get the same answer. (This can be verified at a glance because we are using an annuity of $1.)

There are many practical situations in which you would be dealing with a series of equal payments over several periods of time. These could be analyzed by using Table A and the lengthy procedure exemplified above. But the task is made simpler using Table B, which adds the present value factors for you. Look at Table B in the column for 10% and the row for four periods. The factor is 3.170. This is the present value of a series of four $1 receipts when the interest rate is 10%. (The factor, 3.170, is rounded up from the sum of the factors given in Table A.)

In general, the values shown in Table B are the cumulative sums of the factors from Table A. The factor for an annuity for one period is the same in Table B as the factor for a single payment in Table A, at the same interest rate. Try adding down Table A and checking each successive sum with the factor in Table B. Any differences are due to rounding.

All the factors in both tables relate to future receipts (or payments) of $1. When dealing with payments of amounts other than $1, the factor must be multiplied by the number of dollars involved to compute the present values. You can use Table B only when the payments in the stream are equal. When the payments in the series are not equal you must revert to Table A and discount each of the future amounts separately, although there are some shortcuts that can be used in certain situations.

STREAMS OF UNEQUAL PAYMENTS

What if a number of payments are to be received in the future, but they are not of equal amounts? The method to arrive at the present values of such a stream just described, using Table A, is cumbersome. In some cases it can be avoided.

If most of the payments are equal, you can find the present value of the equal portions of each payment using Table B, then discount separately the remainder. We shall illustrate this method by modifying the previous example. Instead of receiving $1 per year for four years, you will receive $1 at the end of each of the first three years and $2 at the end of the fourth year.

From Table B we know that $1 per year for four years has a present value of $3.170 at 10%. We can find the present value of the stream except for the extra $1 to be received at the end of year four. Looking in Table A for the present value of $1 to be received at the end of four years, we find that the extra $1 has a present value of $.683. Adding the

$.683 to the $3.17, we obtain $3.853. We can check this by discounting each payment separately.

Received at End of Year	Amount to Be Received	Present Value Factor (From Table A)	Present Value of Future Receipt
1	$1	.909	$ .909
2	$1	.826	.826
3	$1	.751	.751
4	$2	.683	1.366
Present value of this series of payments			$3.852

The difference of $.001 is due to rounding.

Suppose that only $.60 is to be received at the end of the fourth year. We now have a stream of equal payments of $1 for three years, then a $.60 payment at the end of the fourth year. Two shortcuts can be used: (1) use Table B to find the present value of a stream of $1 payments for three years, then add to it the present value of $.60 to be received at the end of four years (from Table A); or (2) find the present value of a stream of $1 payments for four years, and subtract the present value of $.40 at the end of four years. The $.40 is the difference between the $1 payment included in the annuity and the payment actually to be received. The two solutions are as follows:

1. Present value of $1 per year for three years at 10% $1 × 2.487 = $2.4870
   Present value of $.60 at end of year four at 10% $.60 × .683 =   .4098
   Present value of this series of payments $2.8968

2. Present value of $1 per year for four years at 10% $1 × 3.170 = $3.1700
   Present value of $.40 at end of year four at 10% $.40 × .683   (0.2732)
   Present value of this series of payments $2.8968

COMPUTATIONS FOR PERIODS OTHER THAN YEARS

In many instances where present values of some future payments are to be computed, the payments may be made more frequently than once a year. A savings bank may pay a 5% interest compounded quarterly or even daily. The interest on most bonds is paid semiannually, but it is common practice to quote an annual interest rate.

If interest is compounded more often than annually, the rate of interest actually being earned for the year is different from the quoted interest rate. Suppose a savings bank pays 6% interest compounded semiannually. How much will you have at the end of a year if you deposit $1,000 today? You will earn $30 for the first six months ($1,000 × .06 × ½). For the second six months, interest will be earned on the $1,030 ($1,000 + $30) and the interest earned will be $30.90 ($1,030 × .06 × ½). Hence, at the end of the year you will have $1,060.90. Based upon your original investment you could say that you earned at the rate of 6.09% per year, because the interest of $60.90 for one year is 6.09% of the $1,000 invested for that year. The 6.09% is called the **effective interest rate** and is to be distinguished from the quoted or **nominal rate** of 6%. We could say that the investment is earning 3% per period (6% divided by the two compoundings per year). Each period you are earning 3% on whatever sum is invested.

For any particular nominal interest rate, the effective interest rate will be greater the larger the number of compoundings per year. Turning the situation around, for a given nominal rate, it will take a smaller investment at the present time to obtain a fixed amount of money at a future date, the larger the number of compoundings per year. To prove this we shall return to our example of the savings bank. If you desired to receive $1,060.90 at the end of a year, you would have to put in $1,000 now if the interest rate is 6% compounded semiannually. If the interest were compounded annually, you would have to put in more than $1,000 now, because a $1,000 investment would only earn $60 in that year. The present value of $1,060.90 a year from now when the rate is 6% compounded semiannually ($1,000) is thus smaller than the present value of $1,060.90 a year from now when the rate is 6% compounded annually.

Compound interest tables are constructed on the basis of an interest rate *per period*. Hence, you must be careful to identify what interest rate you are dealing with in any given situation. If you are interested in the present value of an amount to be received 10 years from now using an effective rate of 10%, you would look in Table A in the 10% column and the row for 10 periods. (Remember that an effective rate is a rate per year.) If, on the other hand, you were interested in the present value of an amount to be received 10 years from now using an interest rate of 10% compounded semiannually, you would look in Table A in the 5% column (10% divided by the number of compoundings per year) and the row for 20 periods (10 years × the number of compoundings per year).

In most situations you will know the nominal interest rate. Hence, to complete the desired computation you must convert the nominal rate to a rate per compounding period and revise the number of periods to take into account the compoundings.

Suppose that you want to know the present value of a stream of receipts of $1,000, which will be collected every six months for the next five years. Assume that the discount rate is 10%. The annual rate is 10% and the receipts are to be collected semiannually, so we must divide the annual rate by two to get a rate of 5% per six-month period. You are now using a six-month period, so you find the factor for 5% for 10 periods, the number of actual receipts in the stream. The factor from Table B is 7.722, and the present value of the stream is therefore $7,722 ($1,000 × 7.722). If the discounting had been done incorrectly using 10% for five periods (to correspond with the five years) for $2,000 (the total of the receipts in each of the five years), the present value computed from the table would have been $7,582 ($2,000 × 3.791). It can be seen from the present values that it is advantageous to receive $1,000 twice a year rather than $2,000 once a year. This confirms the general notion introduced at the beginning of this appendix: the sooner cash is received, the better.

The number of periods to be used when consulting the tables for a given situation is the number of years times the number of compoundings per year. The interest rate to be used when consulting the tables is the nominal annual rate divided by the number of compoundings per year. In this manner you are stating the interest rate per compounding period.

A practical problem exists that involves applying almost every technique in this appendix. Suppose that you could buy a bond that will mature (be retired) in 10 years. The bond carries a nominal interest rate of 6%, and interest is paid semiannually. On your investments you desire to earn 10% compounded semiannually. How much would you be willing to pay for a bond with a face (maturity) value of $10,000?

First you must recognize that your investment is really two investments in one. If you buy the bond you will be contracting to receive (1) $10,000 10 years from now; and (2) regular payments of $300 ($10,000 × .06 × ½) every six months for 10 years. What is each of these investments worth to you now? The price you would be willing to pay for the bond is the sum of the present value of each of these investments.

To compute the price you would pay for the bond, you need the following:

1. The present value of $10,000 to be received 10 years from now. You desire to earn 10% compounded semiannually, so you will refer to Table A for the present value factor for 20 periods (10 years × 2 compoundings) at 5% (10% divided by 2 compoundings). The factor is .377, so the present value you are looking for is $3,770 ($10,000 × .377).
2. The present value of an annuity of $300 to be received each 6 months for 10 years. You desire to earn 10% compounded semiannually, so you will refer to Table B for the present value factor for 20 periods (10 years × 2 compoundings) at 5% (10% divided by 2 compoundings). The factor is 12.462, so the present value you are looking for is $3,739 ($300 × 12.462).

Thus, the price you would pay for this $10,000 6% bond is $7,509 ($3,770 + $3,739).

USES AND SIGNIFICANCE OF PRESENT VALUES

Should you invest a sum of money now in order to receive a larger amount later (the amount could be a single payment or a stream of payments)? This decision should be based on the amounts of the cash to be invested and received later, the length of time over which the inflows are received, and the interest rate.

Where the dollars to be received in the future are known, it is necessary only to refer to the tables for an appropriate factor, multiply by the number of dollars to be received in the future, and compare that amount with the dollars that must be invested now to receive the amount or amounts in the future. If the result of the multiplication is greater than the amount to be invested now, we say the present value of the future returns is greater than the investment and the investment is desirable. Such an investment is said to have a positive net present value. If the result of the multiplication is smaller than the required investment, the opportunity is not desirable and we say it has a negative net present value.

The most common use of present value tables is to find values of future payments. In some situations, however, you may wish to find the interest rate that will be earned if so many dollars are invested now and so many returned in the future. The procedures to follow when using the tables for that purpose are discussed in the next section.

The use of present values is not limited to accounting. You may apply your knowledge of present values in the study of economics, finance, and statistics. Some specific applications of present values in accounting are discussed in Chapters 8, 9, and 15.

DETERMINING INTEREST RATES

When you wish to know what interest rate is being earned on a given investment with known future receipts, you also use the present value tables. The interest rate so determined is called the discount rate, the time-adjusted rate of return, or the internal rate of return.

To find the present value of a stream of equal future receipts, you multiplied the amount of the regular receipt by a factor that incorporated both the length of the series of receipts and the interest rate being earned. This can be shown mathematically as follows:

$$\begin{array}{c} \text{Present value of} \\ \text{future receipts} \end{array} = \begin{array}{c} \text{amount of each} \\ \text{future receipt} \end{array} \times \begin{array}{c} \text{factor for interest} \\ \text{rate and waiting period} \end{array}$$

In prior examples, we were looking for the value to the left of the equal sign.

In trying to find the interest rate you would be earning on a given investment when you know the future receipts, you are looking for the interest rate that equates the present values of the future receipts with the investment required to produce those receipts. Using the mathematical representation above, you are stating that the value to the left of the equal sign is the investment required now. You know the amount of the future receipts and you know one element in determining the factor required—the waiting period. We shall illustrate the method of determining the missing element in our equation—the interest rate.

Suppose that you have an opportunity to invest $3,791 today and receive $1,000 per year for five years beginning one year from now, and you want to know the interest rate you would be earning. Substituting in the mathematical representation above:

$$\$3,791 = \$1,000 \times \text{(the factor for the interest rate for 5 periods)}$$

The solution is 3.791, which is obtained by rearranging the equation to show

$$\text{Present value factor for 5 periods} = \$3,791/\$1,000$$

Because the $1,000 payments are an annuity, we can look in Table B for the factor in the 5-period *row* that is closest to 3.791. That exact factor is found in the 10% column, so the investment yields a rate of return of 10%. We can check this by multiplying $1,000 by 3.791, giving $3,791 as the present value.

In general terms, the basic equation above can also be shown as

$$\text{Present value factor} = \frac{\text{present value of receipts}}{\text{periodic receipts}}$$

The formula can also be used in situations in which a single payment is involved. Suppose you could receive $1,450 at the end of four years if you invested $1,000 today. The factor to be found in Table A would be .690 (rounded), which is $1,000/$1,450. Looking across the 4-period row in Table A we come to .683 in the 10% column. The rate of return is therefore a bit less than 10%.

Notice that you can also use this modification of the basic equation if you know the amount of receipts, the amount of investment (which is the present value), and the interest rate, but want to know the length of time. Suppose that you could invest $1,000 now and receive $300 per year, but the number of years is uncertain. If you desire a 14% rate of return, you can compute the number of years over which you would have to receive the $300 payments.

$$\text{Present value factor} = \frac{\$1,000}{\$300} = 3.333$$

This factor is for 14% and an unknown number of years. Therefore we look down the 14% column in Table B and find that 3.433 is the factor for five years. If you received five $300 annual payments you would earn slightly more than the desired 14%.

DETERMINING REQUIRED RECEIPTS

In some kinds of decision-making situations you may wish to know the receipts, either single payment or annuity, that would give a particular rate of return, given the necessary investment and the life of the receipts. The basic formula can be rearranged as follows.

$$\text{Periodic receipt} = \frac{\text{present value}}{\text{present value factor}}$$

Suppose you can invest $10,000 now and hope to receive $3,000 per year for six years. You would like to earn a 12% return. If you do receive $3,000 per year your return would be about 20% ($10,000/$3,000 = 3.33 which is close to the factor for 20% and six years). However, you are uncertain whether you will actually receive $3,000 and want to know the minimum annual receipt for six years that will give a 12% return.

$$\text{Periodic receipts} = \frac{\$10,000}{4.111}, \text{ the factor for six years and } 12\% = \$2,432$$

Thus, if you receive at least $2,432 each year for the next six years you will earn at least a 12% return.

This method can also be applied to single payments, and the only difference is the table to be used. Suppose that you can invest $1,000 and will receive a single payment at the end of five years. If you wish to earn a 14% return, you would have to receive back $1,927 (rounded), which is $1,000/.519, the factor for a single payment at 14% at the end of 5 periods.

SUMMARY

Many situations or decisions arise that involve cash inflows and/or outflows at different points in time. Such situations require recognition of the fact that money has a time value. To compare or evaluate a situation that involves cash flows occurring at different points in time, it is necessary to use the values of those flows at the same point in time.

Almost all managerial accounting decisions involving cash flows at different times use, as the point of analysis, the *present* value of those flows. The present value of a single cash flow at some time in the future can be computed manually or determined with the help of published tables such as Table A. When a number of future cash flows are involved, it is usually easier to compute their present value by using published tables such as Table B. Although tables such as Table B are constructed using the assumption that the individual amounts in the series of cash flows are equal, it is possible to deal with uneven cash flows by using Tables A and B.

The present value of a future cash flow (or a series of future cash flows) depends on the amount of the flow(s), the interest rate, and the length of the waiting period. In some situations, the present value is known, but one of the other facts is not known. The tables can also be used to determine the value of the unknown factor.

Applications of the concept of present values include the computation of bond prices and the analyses of other long-term investment opportunities. Chapters 8, 9, and 15 of this book all include managerial problems that must be analyzed using present values.

KEY TERMS

annuity
compound interest
discounting
effective interest rate

nominal interest rate
present value
time value of money

KEY FORMULAS

$$\text{Present value of future receipt(s)} = \text{amount of each future receipt} \times \text{factor for interest rate and waiting period (present value factor)}$$

$$\text{Present value factor} = \frac{\text{present value of receipt(s)}}{\text{receipt (or periodic receipt)}}$$

$$\text{Periodic receipt} = \frac{\text{present value of receipts}}{\text{present value factor}}$$

REVIEW PROBLEMS

1. Find the present values of the following sets of payments if the discount rate is (a) 10%, (b) 16%, (c) 20%.

Received at End of Year	*i*	*ii*	*iii*	*iv*	*v*	*vi*
			Amounts			
1	$1,000	$1,000	$1,500	$2,000	$ 0	$1,000
2	1,000	1,000	2,000	2,000	3,000	3,000
3	1,000	1,000	2,000	2,000	3,000	3,000
4	1,000			2,000	3,000	0
5				5,000	4,000	5,000

2. Find the discount rates for the following situations:

	Investment Required Now	Periodic Receipts	Number of Years for Receipts
i	$ 3,605	$1,000	5
ii	$12,300	$2,000	10
iii	$20,860	$4,000	10
iv	$ 9,380	$3,000	5
v	$10,000	$3,050	5

3. Fill in the blanks for each of the following situations. All involve a single payment to be received at the end of the number of years given.

	Investment	Year in Which Payment to Be Received	Payment to Be Received	Interest Rate
i	$_____	4	$4,000	14%
ii	$1,000	5	$1,464	_____
iii	$3,000	___	$5,290	10%
iv	$5,000	7	_____	14%

4. Fill in the blanks for each of the following situations. All involve streams of equal annual payments. Round dollar calculations to the nearest $1.

	Investment	Annual Cash Payments	Number of Years Payments to Be Received	Interest Rate
i	_____	$1,000	10	14%
ii	$10,000	_____	8	10%
iii	$10,000	_____	8	14%
iv	$20,000	$5,000	___	8%
v	$10,000	$2,000	8	___

Answers to review problems

1. i. Stream of equal payments of $1,000 per year for four years.
    (a) At 10% — 3.170 × $1,000 = $3,170
    (b) At 16% — 2.798 × $1,000 = $2,798
    (c) At 20% — 2.589 × $1,000 = $2,589
  ii. Stream of equal payments of $1,000 per year for three years.
    (a) At 10% — 2.487 × $1,000 = $2,487
    (b) At 16% — 2.246 × $1,000 = $2,246
    (c) At 20% — 2.106 × $1,000 = $2,106
 iii. Stream of unequal payments for four years. The easiest method is to find the present value of a $2,000 stream of payments for four years and subtract the present value of $500 at the end of one year.

(a) At 10% — 3.170 × $2,000 = $6,340.00
   (Table A, one year, 10%) .909 × $500 =   (454.50)
                                                            $5,885.50

(b) At 16% — 2.798 × $2,000 = $5,596.00
   (Table A, one year, 16%) .862 × $500 =   (431.00)
                                                            $5,165.00

(c) At 20% — 2.589 × $2,000 = $5,178.00
   (Table A, one year, 20%) .833 × $500 =   (416.50)
                                                            $4,761.50

iv. Stream of four equal payments and larger amount at end of fifth year. Either method discussed can be used. We will discount the four equal payments and add the present value of the fifth one.

(a) At 10% — 3.170 × $2,000 = $6,340
   (Table A, 5 years, 10%) .621 × $5,000 =   3,105
                                                            $9,445

(b) At 16% — 2.798 × $2,000 = $5,596
   (Table A, 5 years, 16%) .476 × $5,000 =   2,380
                                                            $7,976

(c) At 20% — 2.589 × $2,000 = $5,178
   (Table A, 5 years, 20%) .402 × $5,000 =   2,010
                                                            $7,188

v. Stream of unequal payments beginning at the end of year two. Although there are shortcuts, it is probably simplest to discount separately.

(a) At 10%

Received at End of Year	Amount to Be Received	Present Value Factor (From Table A)	Present Value of Future Receipt
1	0		
2	$3,000	.826	$2,478
3	$3,000	.751	2,253
4	$3,000	.683	2,049
5	$4,000	.621	2,484
Present value of this series			$9,264

(b) At 16% the present value is $7,712.
   Computations are similar to those for (a), only using the factors for 16%.

(c) At 20% the present value is $6,873.

2.
$$\frac{\text{Investment required}}{\text{periodic receipt}} = \text{the factor}$$

i. $\dfrac{\$\ 3,605}{\$\ 1,000} = 3.605$ for five years, = 12% in Table B

ii. $\dfrac{\$12,300}{\$\ 2,000} = 6.15$ for ten years, 6.145 for 10% is the closest factor

    iii. $\dfrac{\$20,860}{\$\ 4,000} = 5.215$ for ten years, closest factor is 5.216 for 14%

    iv. $\dfrac{\$\ 9,380}{\$\ 3,000} = 3.126$ for five years, closest factor is 3.127 for 18%

    v. $\dfrac{\$10,000}{\$\ 3,050} = 3.278$ for five years, closest factor is 3.274 for 16%

3. All of these problems require the use of Table A.

    i. 2,368. $4,000 × .592 (the factor for 14% for four years)

    ii. About 8%. $1,000/$1464 = .683, which is very close to .681, the factor for a single payment in five years at 8%.

    iii. About 6 years. $3,000/$5,290 = .567, which is very close to the six-year factor at 10% (.564). In this case, you know the interest rate, so you are looking for the factor in that column which is closest to .567.

    iv. $12,500. $5,000/.400 (.400 is the factor for seven years at 14%)

4. All of these problems can be solved by using the equation:

$$\text{Present value} = \text{annual payment} \times \text{present value factor}$$

The present value, in each case, is the amount of the investment.

    i. $5,216. $1,000 × 5.216 (the factor for 10 periods at 14%)

    ii. $1,874. $10,000/5.335 (the factor for 8 periods at 10%)

    iii. $2,156. $10,000/4.639 (the factor for 8 periods at 14%) Notice that the cash payment is higher here than in ii because the interest rate is higher.

    iv. About 5 years. $20,000/$5,000 = 4.0, which is the factor for 8% and an unknown number of years. Moving down the 8% column in Table B we find 3.993, which is the closest factor to 4.0 under 8%.

    v. About 12%. $10,000/$2,000 = 5.0, which is the factor for eight years and an unknown interest rate. The closest factor in the 8-period row is 4.968, which is the factor for 12%. The true rate is slightly less than 12%.

ASSIGNMENT MATERIAL

1. **Computations—present values** Find the present value of the following sets of payments if the discount rate is as noted for each set.

Received at End of Year	Set A at 6%	Set B at 8%	Set C at 14%	Set D at 24%
1		$2,000	$1,500	$3,000
2		2,000	1,500	3,000
3		2,000	1,500	4,000
4		2,000	1,500	4,000
5		2,000	1,500	
8	$10,000		2,500	

2. Missing factors Fill in the blanks for each of the following independent investment opportunities.

	Investment Required Now	Periodic Receipt	Number of Years of Receipt	Interest (Discount) Rate
A	$16,950	$3,000	10	____
B	$16,775	_____	10	8%
C	$____	$5,000	13	18%
D	$10,000	$2,500	____	24%
E	$34,340	$8,500	7	____

3. Computation of bond prices You are considering investing in some corporate bonds. Each bond is different and because the companies are different you believe you should earn a different rate of interest (effective interest rate) on each investment. The relevant data for each bond are provided below.

	Bond of Company			
	A	B	C	D
Face value	$10,000	$5,000	$20,000	$20,000
Nominal (stated) interest rate	10%	8%	6%	12%
Years to maturity	7	8	7	7
Interest paid	Annually	Annually	Semiannually	Semiannually
Desired interest rate	12%	10%	10%	10%

Required: Compute the price you would pay for each bond.

4. Present values and rates of return The following information is available about two investment opportunities.

	A	B
Required investment now	$10,000	$20,000
Cash flows, annually for 7 years	$ 2,500	$ 4,700

Required

1. Compute the approximate rate of return that each investment yields.
2. Compute the present values of each investment if the desired rate of return is 10%.
3. Repeat requirement 2 assuming that the desired rate of return is 18%.
4. Suppose that the desired rate of return is 16%. Determine the annual cash flows that would have to be received for each year in the seven-year period to make each investment provide a 16% return.

5. Present values—unusual timing Although many situations involve cash flows occurring at or near the the end of a period, still others involve flows at or near the beginning of a period. It is possible to use Tables A and B to deal with such situations also. For each of the situations below, compute the present value of the cash flows described.
(a) A receipt of $5,000 exactly four years from today; the interest rate is 9%.
(b) A receipt of $1,000 per year at the beginning of each of five years beginning today; the interest rate is 8%.
(c) A receipt of $10,000 per year for seven years, the first receipt to arrive exactly six years from today; the interest rate is 12%.

Table A
Present Value of $1

Interest Rates

Periods	5%	6%	8%	9%	10%	12%	14%	16%	18%	20%	24%	25%
1	.952	.943	.926	.917	.909	.893	.877	.862	.847	.833	.806	.800
2	.907	.890	.857	.842	.826	.797	.769	.743	.718	.694	.650	.640
3	.864	.840	.794	.772	.751	.712	.675	.641	.609	.579	.524	.512
4	.823	.792	.735	.708	.683	.636	.592	.552	.516	.482	.423	.410
5	.784	.747	.681	.650	.621	.567	.519	.476	.437	.402	.341	.328
6	.746	.705	.630	.596	.564	.507	.456	.410	.370	.335	.275	.262
7	.711	.665	.583	.547	.513	.452	.400	.354	.314	.279	.222	.210
8	.677	.628	.541	.502	.467	.404	.351	.305	.266	.233	.179	.168
9	.645	.592	.500	.460	.424	.361	.308	.263	.225	.194	.144	.134
10	.614	.558	.463	.422	.386	.322	.270	.227	.191	.162	.116	.107
11	.585	.527	.429	.387	.350	.287	.237	.195	.162	.135	.094	.086
12	.557	.497	.397	.355	.319	.257	.208	.168	.137	.112	.076	.069
13	.530	.469	.368	.326	.290	.229	.183	.145	.116	.093	.061	.055
14	.505	.442	.340	.299	.263	.205	.160	.125	.099	.078	.049	.044
15	.481	.417	.315	.274	.239	.183	.140	.108	.084	.065	.040	.035
16	.458	.394	.292	.251	.218	.163	.123	.093	.071	.054	.032	.028
17	.436	.371	.270	.231	.198	.146	.108	.080	.060	.045	.026	.023
18	.416	.350	.250	.212	.180	.130	.095	.069	.051	.038	.021	.018
20	.377	.312	.215	.178	.149	.104	.073	.051	.037	.026	.014	.012
30	.231	.174	.099	.075	.057	.033	.020	.012	.007	.004	.002	.001

Table B
Present Value of $1 Annuity

Interest Rates

Periods	5%	6%	8%	9%	10%	12%	14%	16%	18%	20%	22%	24%	25%
1	.952	.943	.926	.917	.909	.893	.877	.862	.847	.833	.820	.806	.800
2	1.859	1.833	1.783	1.759	1.736	1.690	1.647	1.605	1.566	1.528	1.492	1.457	1.440
3	2.723	2.673	2.577	2.531	2.487	2.402	2.322	2.246	2.174	2.106	2.042	1.981	1.952
4	3.546	3.465	3.312	3.240	3.170	3.037	2.914	2.798	2.690	2.589	2.494	2.404	2.362
5	4.329	4.212	3.993	3.890	3.791	3.605	3.433	3.274	3.127	2.991	2.864	2.745	2.689
6	5.076	4.917	4.623	4.486	4.355	4.111	3.889	3.685	3.498	3.326	3.167	3.020	2.951
7	5.786	5.582	5.206	5.033	4.868	4.564	4.288	4.039	3.812	3.605	3.416	3.242	3.161
8	6.463	6.210	5.747	5.535	5.335	4.968	4.639	4.344	4.077	3.837	3.619	3.421	3.329
9	7.108	6.802	6.247	5.996	5.759	5.328	4.946	4.607	4.303	4.031	3.786	3.566	3.463
10	7.722	7.360	6.710	6.418	6.145	5.650	5.216	4.833	4.494	4.192	3.923	3.682	3.571
11	8.306	7.887	7.139	6.805	6.495	5.988	5.453	5.029	4.656	4.327	4.035	3.776	3.656
12	8.863	8.384	7.536	7.160	6.814	6.194	5.660	5.197	4.793	4.439	4.127	3.851	3.725
13	9.394	8.853	7.904	7.487	7.103	6.424	5.842	5.342	4.910	4.533	4.203	3.912	3.780
14	9.899	9.295	8.244	7.786	7.367	6.628	6.002	5.468	5.008	4.611	4.265	3.962	3.824
15	10.380	9.712	8.559	8.061	7.606	6.811	6.142	5.575	5.092	4.675	4.315	4.001	3.859
16	10.838	10.106	8.851	8.313	7.824	6.974	6.265	5.669	5.162	4.730	4.357	4.033	3.887
20	12.462	11.470	9.818	9.129	8.514	7.469	6.623	5.929	5.353	4.870	4.460	4.110	3.954
30	15.372	13.765	11.258	10.274	9.427	8.055	7.003	6.177	5.517	4.979	4.534	4.160	3.995

INDEX

A

Absorption costing
  applying overhead, 434–5
  compared to variable costing:
    basic illustration, 425–33
    evaluation, 442–4
    interpreting reports, 430–3
    summary, 430
  defined, 425
  income determination, 428–9
  inventory valuation, 426–7
  predetermined overhead rates, 439–42
  and standard fixed costs, 433–6
  summary of procedures, 442
  and volume-cost-profit analysis, 443
Account payable budgeted. *See* Budgets, cash disbursements
Accounts receivable budgeted. *See* Budgets, cash receipts
Accounts receivable turnover, 605
Acid-test ratio, 604
Actual costing, 426, 442, 473–6. *See also* Absorption costing; Process costing; Variable costing
Allocated costs, 204–5
  and absorption costing, 443
  and joint products, 215
  multiple allocations, 443
  in performance measurements, 321–7, 352, 397
  transfer prices and, 321–7
Analyzing financial statements, 600–16
  approach and purpose of the analyst, 600–2

  liquidity analysis, 603–8
  profitability analysis, 608–14
  ratios and evaluation, 607–8, 613–4
  solvency analysis, 614–6
Annuity, present value of, 634–5
Application of overhead, 434–5. *See also* Absorption costing; Variances
Artificial profit center, 314, 323
Asset disposal decisions, 276–8
Assets in performance measurement:
  allocations to segments, 351–2
  measurement of, 353–4
Avoidable costs, 57, 97–9, 204. *See also* Joint products; Separable costs; Transfer prices

B

Behavioral considerations. *See also* Goal congruence; Motivation; responsibility accounting
Behavior of costs. *See* Cost classification, behavior
  in budgeting, 126, 136–8
  and cost centers, 324–5
  and divisional performance evaluation, 355–61
  and standard costs, 392–6
  and transfer prices, 324–7, 358–61
Benefit-cost analysis, 100. *See also* Not-for-profit organizations
  benefits, 102
  revenues and costs, 102
Benefit-cost ratio. *See* Profitability index

Book rate of return, 253–4, 355–8
Book values:
  in capital budgeting, 273–4
  in divisional performance measurement, 353–4, 355–6
  in short-term decision making, 202
Break-even point, 22–5. *See also* Volume-cost-profit analysis
  effect of taxes on, 49
  formula, 24
  graph, 22–3
Budgeting:
  capital, 128, 242–56, 271–90, 529–30
  comprehensive, 124–181
  conflicts, 136
  financial, 125, 616–81
  and human behavior, 136–8
  long-term, 169–76
  multiple product firm, 92–6
  in not-for-profit entities, 176–81
  operational, 124–63
  program, 179–80
  revised pro forma financial statements, 165–7
  social consequences of decision making, 288–90
  statement of objectives, 125
  zero-based, 180
Budgets, *See also* Standard costs; Variances
  capital, 128, 174
  cash, 3, 125, 127, 128, 161–9, 567
    disbursements, 163–5
    receipts, 162–3
  as "check-up" devices, 137–8

comprehensive, 124–181
continuous, 128
and control, 126, 398–9
expense, 128, 133–6
as feedback devices, 138
financial, 125, 161–81
flexible, 133
imposed, 136–7
long-term, 169–76
for manufacturing firms, 141–3, 168–9
organization of, 126–8, 131
and planning, 125–6
production, 141–3, 168–9
project, 128
purchases, 128, 139–43
sales, 128. *See also* Sales forecasting
static, 133
time periods, 126–8
unwise adherence to, 138, 178–9, 399
Budget variance. *See* Variances

C

Capacity:
fixed facilities, 216–8
idle, 434
normal, 433
practical, 434
Capital budgeting, 245–59, 271–90
acceptance criteria and decision rules,
144, 244, 246, 251, 281
application of statistical decision theory,
529–30
cash flow and book income, 244–5
cost of capital, 243, 251
decision rules, 251, 281
effects of taxes and depreciation, 245,
248–9
income taxes in, 248–9, 273–4, 284–8
investment decisions vs. financing
decisions, 255–6
mutually exclusive alternatives, 278–82
ranking investments, 280–2
replacement decisions, 273–6
and resource allocation, 243
salvage values in, 250–1, 273–6
sensitivity analysis, 282–4
techniques, 244
book rate of return, 253–4
evaluation of, 255, 280–2
net present value, 244, 246
payback period, 252–3
profitability index, 280–2
time-adjusted rate of return, 249–50
types of situations, 246–7, 271
unequal lives in, 176–8
uneven cash flows in, 249–51
working capital investment, 272–3
Capital gains, 385–6
Cash. *See also* Statement of changes in
financial position
budget, 161–5

disbursements budget, 163–5
flows
in capital budgeting, 244–5
and income taxes, 245, 247–8
replacement decisions, 273–5
uneven, 249–51
minimum balance, 165
receipts budget, 162–3
"resources" as, 567–72
Cash-flow-to-total-debt ratio, 616
Centralization. *See* Decentralization
Certified Management Accountant, 9
C.M.A. examination, 9
Committed costs, 55, 56–7, 96–9. *See
also* Fixed costs
in performance reporting, 319
Common-size statements, 603
Complementary effects, 108–9
Complementary products, 92
Compound interest, nature of, 633
Comprehensive budgeting, 124–81. *See
also* Budgeting; Budgets
Conflicts in budgeting, 136
Continuous budgets, 128
Contribution margin, 17
in analyzing sales price and quantity
variances, 90–2
defined, 17
income statement compared to financial
accounting, 19
negative, 209
percentage, 24–7
per unit, 17, 24, 26
weighted average, 93–6
Control chart, 393–4
Control function, 2, 4–5. *See also*
Responsibility accounting;
Standard costs
Cost:
allocations, 204–5. *See also* Allocated
costs
analysis in not-for-profit organizations,
100–1
average per unit, 19–20
avoidable, 57–96–7, 204
behavior, 16–25, 51
misconceptions, 20–1
mixed costs, 50–5
classification, 7, 16
behavior, 7, 16–8
functional, 7, 18
object, 7, 18
by responsibility, 7–8
committed, 55, 56–7. *See also* Fixed
costs
controllable. *See* Responsibility
accounting
differential, 201, 202
discretionary, 65–6. *See also* Fixed
costs
engineered, 55
fixed, 18, 55–7
committed, 56–7

control of, 397–9, 436–9
discretionary, 55–6
on performance reports, 399
standard, 433–6
flows, 469–70
incremental, 203. *See also* Differential
costs
inventoriable, 430
joint, 97–8
mixed, 50–5
opportunity, 202–3
period, 430
product, 430
programmed, 55
replacement, 354
separable, 96–7, 319
standard, 383, 384
step-variable, 54–5
sunk, 202
total, 19–20
unavoidable, 57, 96–7
variable, 17
Cost-benefit analysis, 100
Cost center, 314. *See also* Responsibility
accounting
Cost flows in a manufacturing firm, 469
Cost of capital, 243, 251, 326
Cost structure and managerial attitudes,
60–1
Cost systems:
illustrated, 472–85
job order, 471, 483–5
process, 470–1, 473–83
standard, 471–2
types of, 469–72
Currently attainable performance, 395
Current ratio, 603–4
"Cut-off rate of return," 243

D

Days' sales in accounts receivable, 605–6
Days' sales in inventory, 606–7
Debt ratios, 614–5
Decentralization, 315, 318–20, 346–8.
See also Responsibility accounting
Decision making:
function, 2, 3–4
long-term, 242–56, 271–90
short-term, 200–19
under environmental constraints, 218–9
Decision rules:
in capital budgeting, 251, 281
dropping a segment, 207
make-or-buy, 211
sale of joint products, 214
in short-term decisions, 201
undertaking a joint process, 216
Decision tree, 528–9
Depreciation:
and cash flows, 245, 248–9
in divisional performance measurement,
353–4

and retention of funds, 577
and taxes, 248–9, 285–6
Differential costs and revenues, 201, 204
Dilution of earnings per share, 612
Direct costing. *See* Variable costing
Discounted cash flow techniques, 255. *See also* Capital budgeting
Discounting. *See* Capital budgeting; Present values
Discretionary fixed costs, 55–6, 96–9, 133, 319
Discriminatory pricing, 218
Dividend yield, 613
Divisional performance, 346–61
  assets
    allocated, 351–2
    measurement, 353–4
  behavioral problems, 355–61
  liabilities, 352–3
  measures
    net income, 348
    residual income, 349–50
    return on investment, 348–9, 355–8
  problems in evalution, 350–5
Divisional profit, 348, 350

E

Earnings per share, 611–2
Economic order quantity, 638–40
Effective interest rate, 243n, 636–7
Effectiveness, 382
Efficiency, 100, 382
Efficiency variances, 386
  labor, 388
  variable overhead, 389
Equivalent production, 474–5, 490–5
  for different cost elements, 490–5
  first-in-first-out, 481–2
  weighted average, 480–1
Evaluation criteria in responsibility accounting, 315. *See also* Divisional performance measurement; Responsibility accounting
Evaluation function, 2, 5. *See also* Budgeting; Divisional performance measurement; Investigation of cost variances
Expected values, 132. *See also* Statistical decision theory
Expense budgets, 128, 133–6

F

Federal Trade Commission, 218–9
Financial accounting:
  cost and expense, 16n
  income statement contrasted with contribution margin approach, 18–9
  and managerial accounting, 7–8

Financial budgeting, 161–81. *See also* Budgeting Financing decision vs. investment decision, 255–6
"Financing gap," 175
Financing requirements, 170–6
  debt vs. equity, 170, 175. *See also* Leverage
Fixed costs, 18
  avoidable, 57
  budgeting for. *See* Expense budgets
  Budget variances. *See* Variances
  committed, 55, 56–7
  control of, 397–9, 436–9
  discretionary, 55–6
  and managerial action, 55–7
  and multiple products, 97
  on performance reports, 319, 399
  standards for, 433–42
  unavoidable, 57
  volume variance, 437–9.
Fixed facilities, use of, 216–8, 541–7
Fixed manufacturing overhead. *See* Absorption costing
Flexible budget, 133, 396
  allowances, 133, 135, 136, 315, 384
Flow of costs, 469–70
Formulas:
  accounts receivable turnovers, 605
  book rate of return, 253
  break-even point, 240–5
  cash flow to total debt, 616
  contribution margin, 17
    as a percentage, 24
  current ratio, 603
  days' sales in inventory, 606
  days' sales in receivables, 605
  debt ratio, 614
  earnings per share, 611
    growth rate of, 611
  economic order quantity, 539n
  equivalent production, 474
    first-in-first-out, 481
    weighted average, 480
  fixed cost factor in mixed cost, 52
  flexible budget allowance, 134
  inventory reorder point, 537
  inventory turnover, 606
  labor variances, 388
  margin of safety, 61–2
  multiple regression, general form, 70
  normal equations of simple regression, 66
  payback period, 252
  payout ratio, 613
  present value of future flows, 247
  price-earnings ratio, 612
  profitability index, 281
  purchases, 140
  quick ratio, 604
  residual income, 350
  return on assets, 608
  return on equity, 609
  return on investment, 348

sales price variance, 92
sales volume variance, 91
standard fixed cost per unit, 433
target profit, 26, 27
times interest earned, 615
total cost, 19
unit cost for a process, 480–1
variable cost factor of mixed cost, 51
volume variance, 438
working capital, 562
Functional area, 1, 124
Funds flows. *See* Statement of changes in financial position

G

Generally accepted accounting principles, 8, 424
Goal congruence, 312–3. *See also* Behavioral considerations; Motivation; Responsibility accounting
Gross profit ratio, 603

H

High-low method of cost estimation, 51–2
  compared to scatter diagram method, 53, 60
  compared with regression analysis, 65
Historical costs:
  in divisional performance measurement, 353–4
  standards, 395
Horizontal organization structure, 318–20
House brands, 215

I

Ideal standards, 395–6
Idle capacity, 434
Imposed budgets, 136–7
Income determination and product costing approaches, 428–9
Income taxes:
  in capital budgeting, 248–9, 273–4, 284–8
  capital gains, 285–6
  depreciation and, 245, 248–50
  investment tax credit, 287–8
  operating loss carryovers, 286–7
  profit planning and, 48–9
  progressive tax rates, 284–5
Incremental costs and discriminatory pricing, 203, 204
Incremental profit or loss, 206, 207
Incremental tax rates, 284
Indicator methods of forecasting, 129–30
Intercompany transactions. *See* Make-or-buy decision; Transfer prices

Interim periods:
cash deficits, 165
sales forecasting, 132–3
Internal rate of return. *See* Time-adjusted
rate of return
Inventoriable costs, 430
Inventory:
carrying costs, 535–6
control models, 534–40
cost flows, 469–70
lead time, 536
order quantity, 538–40
policy, 128, 136, 139, 141, 165
reorder point, 536–7
safety stock, 536, 537–8
turnover, 606–7
valuation. *See* Absorption costing;
Variable costing
Investigation of cost variances, 313–4,
526–9
Investment centers, 314, 319, 346–61
Investment in working capital
in capital budgeting, 272–3
Investment tax credit, 287–8
Investment turnover, 349

J

Job order costing, 471, 483–5
Joint cost, 97–9, 316. *See also* Separable
costs
and absorption costing, 443
allocation of, 204–5
in joint products, 212–5
Joint process, 212
Joint products, 212–5
Journal entries:
flow of costs
actual process costing, 473–6
standard process costing, 476–80
job order costs, 484   5

L

Labor variances, 386–9
Law of demand, 99
Lead time, 536
Leverage, 609–11
Liabilities in divisional performance
measurement, 353–4
Linear programming, 541–7
Liquidity analysis, 603–8
Long-term budgets, 169–76
asset requirements, 169–70
financing requirements, 170–6
Long-term decision making. *See* Capital
budgeting
Losses and seasonality, 20
Loss leaders, 208–9

M

Make-or-buy decision, 209–11, 360–1
Management:
and accounting information, 1
by exception, 2
functions, 1–2, 3–5
by objectives, 2
Managerial accountants:
activities of, 9
as managers, 2–3
Managerial accounting and financial
accounting, 7–8
Managers. *See also* Organization structure
line and staff, 2
Manufacturing costs:
flows of, 469–70
purchases budget, 141–3
types of, 58–9
Margin of safety, 61–3
Materials variances, 390–2
Minimum rate of return, 245, 349, 350
Mixed costs, 50–6
high-low method, 51–2
regression analysis, 53–4, 65–71
scatter diagram, 52–3
step-variable costs, 54–5
Money, time value of. *See* Present values
Motivation. *See also* Transfer prices
behavioral problems of divisional
performance measures, 355–61
budgeting and human behavior, 136–8
goal congruence and, 312–3
Multiple products. *See also* Joint products
and absorption costing, 439–42
complementary products, 92
dropping a product, 206–9
fixed costs and, 97–9
joint and separable costs, 96–9
weighted average contribution margin,
93–5
Mutually exclusive alternatives, 278–82.
See also Capital budgeting

N

National Association of Accountants, 9
Natural profit center, 314
Net income as a divisional performance
measure, 348
Net present value, 245, 246. *See also*
Capital budgeting; Present values
Nominal interest rate, 637
Normal activity, 433
Not-for-profit organizations:
benefit measurement, 102, 289
budgeting in, 176–81
cost analysis, 100–1
fixed expenditures, 102–3
social benefits and costs, 289–90
volume-cost-profit analysis, 100–3

O

Operating loss carryovers, 286–7
Operational budgeting, 124–43. *See also*
Budgeting
Opportunity costs, 202–3
make-or-buy decisions, 211, 360–1
in segment analysis, 207
shadow prices, 546–7
Organization structure:
choice of structure, 321
decentralization, 315, 346–8
horizontal, 315, 318–20
vertical, 315–8
Overapplied overhead, 434–5

P

Payback period, 252–3
Payoff table, 531–4
Payout ratio, 613
Perfect information, value of, 527–8
Performance evaluation function, 2, 5. *See
also* Behavioral considerations;
Responsibility accounting
Performance reports, 317–20
and fixed costs, 319, 399
Period costs, 430
Planning. *See also* Budgeting; Decision
making; Profit planning
budgets and, 124–5
function, 1, 3
Practical capacity, 433
Predetermined overhead rates, 439–42
Present values, 632–40. *See also* Capital
budgeting
determining interest rates, 638–40
determining required receipts, 640
of single amounts, 634
of streams of receipts, 634–6
tables, 646
uses and significance of, 638
Price-earnings ratio, 612–3
Price variances, 386. *See also* Variances
labor, 388
material, 390–1
sales, 92
Price-volume relationships, 99–100
Pricing:
target, 27–8
transfer. *See* Transfer prices
variable costing and, 442–4
Process costing, 470–1
actual, illustration of, 473–6
equivalent production, 474–5, 480–2
multiple processes, 482–3
standard, illustration of, 476–80
Product cost, 430
Product costing. *See* Absorption costing;
Cost systems; Variable costing

Production budget, 127, 141–3
Product line, 96
Product margin, 98
Profitability index, 280–2
Profitability ratios and analysis, 608–14
Profit center, 314, 319, 323. *See also*
    Responsibility accounting
Profit graph, 22–3
Profit planning, 16–30
    income taxes and, 48–9
Pro forma statements, 3, 124
    in budgeting, 124–5, 128, 165–7
Program budgets, 178–9
Progressive tax rates, 284–5
Project budgets, 128
Purchases budget, 128, 139–43

Q

Quantity variances. *See also* Variances
    labor, 386–9
    materials, 390–2
Quick ratio, 604

R

Ranking of investment opportunities,
    280–2
Rate of return:
    book, 253–4
    internal, 246–7
    minimum acceptable, 245, 349, 350
    target, 243
    time-adjusted, 246–7
    true, 246–7
Rate variances. *See also* Variances
    labor, 388
    materials, 390–1
Ratios:
    evaluation of, 607–8, 613–4
    liquidity, 603–8
    in long-term budgets, 170–6
    profitability, 608–14
    solvency, 614–6
Regression analysis, 53–4, 65–71, 129
    multiple regression, 66, 69–71
    simple regression, 66–9
Relevant range, 21–2, 99–100
    price-volume interrelationships, 99–100
    and step-variable costs, 54
    time periods, 22
Reorder point, 536–7
Reorder quantity, 538–40
Replacement costs in divisional
    performance measurement, 354
Replacement decisions in capital
    budgeting, 273–6, 278
    incremental approach, 273–5
    total-project approach, 275–6
Residual income, 249–50

Resource flows. *See* Statement of changes
    in financial position.
Responsibility accounting, 312–28
    allocations, 321–6
    cost centers, 314
    evaluation criteria, 315
    investment centers, 314. *See also*
        Divisional performance
        measurement
    profit centers, 314
        artificial, 314, 323
    relationship to organization structure,
        315–21
Return:
    on assets, 608
    on equity, 609
    on investment, 346–9, 355–8
    on sales, 21, 27, 38–40, 348–9, 603
Risk and cost structure, 60–1
Robinson-Patman Act, 218–9

S

Safety stock, 536, 537–8
Sales budget, 128
Sales forecasting, 129–33
    expected values and, 132
    historical analysis, 131
    indicator methods, 129–30
    interim periods, 132–3
    judgmental methods, 131
    which methods to use, 131–2
Sales mix. *See* Multiple products
Sales price variance, 92
Sales volume variance, 91
Salvage values in capital budgeting,
    250–1, 273–6
Scatter diagram, 52–3, 59–60, 129
    compared to high-low method of cost
        estimation, 53
    contrasted with regression analysis, 65,
        67–8
Seasonality, 20, 58
    and budgets, 127–8
    losses, 20
    and ratios, 605, 606
    sales forecasting, 133
Segment analysis, 206–8. *See also* Joint
        costs; Multiple products
    complementary effects, 208–9
    dropping a segment, 206–9
Sensitivity analysis:
    in capital budgeting, 282–4
    in linear programming, 545–6
Separable costs, 97–9, 204. *See also*
        Avoidable costs; Joint costs;
        Multiple products; Segment
        analysis
Service departments, 321. *See also*
        Transfer prices

Shadow prices, 546–7
Short-term decision making, 200–19
Simulation, 96
Social benefits and costs in decision
        making, 288–90
Solvency analysis, 614–6
Special orders, 215–6
Spending variances, 386. *See also*
        Variances
Split-off point for joint products, 212
Standard costing, 471–2, 476–83
Standard costs:
    and budgets, 323n, 383–4
    and control, 436–9
    currently attainable, 395–6
    for fixed costs, 397–9, 425, 433–42
    ideal, 395
    in nonmanufacturing activities, 401–2
    and performance reports, 396–7
    predetermined overhead rates and,
        439–42
    revision of, 396
    setting of, 394–6
        engineering methods, 394
        managerial estimates, 395
    in transfer pricing, 323–4
    for variable costs, 384–5
    variances. *See* Variances
Standard error of the estimate, 69
Standard fixed cost, 433. *See also* Fixed
        cost
Standard process costing, 476–83
Statement of changes in financial position,
        561–86
    cash resources, 567–72
        formal statement, 569–70
    categories of resource flows, 563–5
    depreciation and funds retention, 577
    reconciliation of net income
        and cash from operations, 567–9
        and working capital from operations,
        572–3
    working capital resources, 572–5
        formal statement, 573–5
    working without a cash budget, 570–2
    worksheet approach, 583–7
Static budget, 133
Statistical decision theory, 525–34
    in capital budgeting, 529–30
    decision trees, 528–9
    developing probabilities, 534
    payoff tables, 531–4
    in sales forecasting, 132
    "utilities" in, 530
    in variance investigation, 526–9
Step-variable costs, 54–5
Stockout costs, 536
Sum-of-the-years' digits method, tax
        advantage of, **250**
Sunk cost, 202
    joint costs as, 212

T

Target profit, 25–30
    formula, 26
    and price determination, 27–8
    as return on sales, 28–30
    after taxes, 48–9
    volume, 26
Target rate of return, 248
Tax shield of depreciation, 248
Time-adjusted rate of return, 246–7. *See also* Capital budgeting; Present values
Times interest earned, 615–6
Total costs, 19
Traceable costs, *See* Separable costs
Trading on the equity. *See* Leverage
Transfer prices, 314, 321–8
    allocations and, 321–6
    individional performance measurement, 358–61
    effects of, 324–7
    effects on total income, 326–7, 358n
    methods of setting, 323–6, 358–61
    unavoidable costs and, 359–61
True rate of return. *See* Time-adjusted rate of return
Turnovers:
    inventory, 606–7
    investment, 349
    receivables, 605

U

Unavoidable costs, 57, 97–9. *See also* Joint products; Separable costs; Transfer prices
Underapplied overhead, 434–5
Unequal lives in capital budgeting, 278–80
Uneven cash flows:
    in capital budgeting, 249–51
    present values of, 635–6

salvage values as, 250–1
    working capital investment, return of, 272–3
Unit costs. *See also* Absorption costing; Variable costing
    average total, 19–20
    equivalent production and, 480–1
    standard fixed, 425, 433–42
    standard variable, 384–5
    total, 19–20

V

Variable costing:
    advantages of, 442–3
    compared to absorption costing
        basic illustration, 425–33
        evaluation, 442–4
        interpreting reports, 430–3
        summary, 430
    defined, 425
    disadvantages of, 443–4
    income determination, 427–8
    inventory valuation, 426
    and pricing, 442–4
    and volume-cost-profit analysis, 442–3
Variable costs, 16. *See also* Mixed costs; Standard costs; Step-variable costs; Variable costing
Variable overhead variances, 389–90
Variances, 135
    budget, 135, 386, 436–7
    control charts, 393–4
    efficiency, 386
    fixed overhead
        budget, 436–7
        volume, 437–9
    interaction effects, 392
    interpretation of, 392–3
    investigation of, 313–4, 526–9
    labor, 386–9
    material, 390–2
    rate, 386

sales
    price, 92
    volume, 91
    total, 386
    variable overhead, 389–90
Vertical organization structure, 315–8
Volume, measures of, 57–60
    manufacturer, 58–9
    normal activity, 433
    practical capacity, 434
    selling and administrative costs, 60
Volume-cost-profit analysis. *See also* Profit planning
    graph, 22–5
    income taxes, in, 48–9
    in multiple product firms, 94–6
    in not-for-profit organizations, 100–3
    price-volume relationships, 99-100
    relevant range, 22–2, 25
    and variable costing, 442–3
Volume variance:
    fixed manufacturing overhead, 437–9
    sales, 91

W

Weighted average contribution margin, 93–6
"Window dressing," 608
Working capital. *See also* Liquidity; Statement of changes in financial position
    composition of, 604
    and the current ratio, 603–4
    defined, 172, 562
    investment in
        capital budgeting, 272–3
    ratio, 603–4
    "resources" as, 572–5

Z

Zero-based budgeting, 180